Bauman

Bauman

A Biography

Izabela Wagner

polity

First published in 2020 by Polity Press

Polity Press
65 Bridge Street
Cambridge CB2 1UR, UK

Polity Press
101 Station Landing
Suite 300
Medford, MA 02155, USA

ISBN-13: 978-1-5095-2686-4

A catalogue record for this book is available from the British Library.

Library of Congress Cataloging-in-Publication Data
Names: Wagner, Izabela, author.
Title: Bauman : a biography / Izabela Wagner.
Description: Cambridge, UK ; Medford, MA, USA : Polity Press, 2020. |
   Includes bibliographical references and index. | Summary: "A
   comprehensive account of the life and work of one of the most
   influential social thinkers of our time"-- Provided by publisher.
Identifiers: LCCN 2019051800 (print) | LCCN 2019051801 (ebook) | ISBN
   9781509526864 (hardback) | ISBN 9781509526895 (epub)
Subjects: LCSH: Bauman, Zygmunt, 1925-2017 | Sociology.
Classification: LCC HM479.B39 W34 2020 (print) | LCC HM479.B39 (ebook) |
   DDC 301--dc23
LC record available at https://lccn.loc.gov/2019051800
LC ebook record available at https://lccn.loc.gov/2019051801

Typeset in 10.5 on 11.5 pt Times New Roman MT by
Servis Filmsetting Ltd, Stockport, Cheshire
Printed and bound by CPI Group (UK) Ltd, Croydon

For further information on Polity, visit our website: politybooks.com

People in a state of exaltation crave not knowledge but legends; not the comparative distance of history, but the affirmation of their *raison d'être*, their beliefs by tradition. They want unambiguous explanations and uniting symbols.

(Jerzy Jedlicki, 1993: 163)

In memory of Keith Tester

Contents

Acknowledgements

Contrary to popular belief, even single-author book projects aren't the product of a solitary worker (Becker, 1982), and many people formed links in the long chain of collaboration that led to this finished book.

I am deeply grateful to Arthur Allen, my friend of eight years and my closest collaborator, without whom I would not have been able to give English-speakers the pleasure of reading this book. Arthur is a successful writer, and author of *Vaccine: The Controversial Story of Medicine's Greatest Lifesaver*. As a writer and editor in the health and science section at Politico in Washington, DC, he is a very busy journalist, but found time for Bauman's biography because he is also an enthusiastic historian. Since the beginning of our friendship, we have helped complete each other's expertise, skills and knowledge. When we met in 2011, Arthur was working on his book *The Fantastic Laboratory of Dr. Weigl* (2014), and I became his research assistant for Polish documents and his consultant on parts of Polish history. Thanks to my contribution to Arthur's project, I learned a lot about World War II, postwar documents, the Institute of Remembrance (IPN) and other archives in Poland. This knowledge was critical to much of the documentation of the present book.

I am not an English native speaker, having taught myself the language after a formal Polish–French education. Arthur not only corrected my mistakes, detected false French cognates and polished my English, but also challenged my purposes and pushed me to be more accurate, sceptical and clear. He perfectly understood my jokes, personal style and emotional way of writing, which was crucial for maintaining my specific form of expression – the biggest challenge in 'cultural translation'. Through his corrections, Arthur obtained an expression of what I wanted to say, but did not know yet know how to say!

His contribution was not only editorial but also historical. Arthur's remarks, questions, advice and formal suggestions (such as separating chapters or reformulating titles) helped me shape my narration in clearer, yet scientifically pertinent, ways. I am deeply grateful for the hours, days and months Arthur devoted to correcting this manuscript (he also edited my previous book, *Producing Excellence*, Rutgers University Press, 2015), and for his enthusiastic feedback and tips. We worked on these three books together while exchanging only mutual trust and fascination in our work; if the latter is not rare, the former is exceptional. Our friendship and collaboration made the writing a less lonely and more pleasant activity.

I am grateful to the many people who trusted me and spent time recalling their experiences of Bauman as a teacher, colleague, friend or relation. This long list starts with Aleksandra Jasińska-Kania, who made possible my two interviews with Zygmunt Bauman; she prepared our meetings, which were extremely rich in new data. I am also grateful for our interviews and discussions that took place after Zygmunt Bauman passed away. Aleksandra Jasińska-Kania also introduced me to Bauman's daughters.

I am deeply grateful to Anna Sfard, Lydia Bauman and Irena Bauman for their trust, the enormous boost they gave my research, and the fascinating conversations we shared. They not only accorded me their time and responded to all the questions I asked, but also gave me free access to two unpublished manuscripts by their father. These unique texts (which I obtained in December 2017) confirmed my previous hypothesis and filled out the picture I drew from my interviews with Bauman. I wish also to thank the Bauman family for the rights to publish family pictures. I am particularly grateful to Lydia Bauman for her trust, and access to her private journal that described the family's travel to Israel in 1968. She also agreed to the use of the portrait of her father that she painted.

I am immensely grateful to the thirty-nine other people living in different parts of the world whom I interviewed for the book. In Warsaw (in chronological order of our interviews), I met Karol Modzelewski, Barbara and Jerzy Szacki, Andrzej Werblan, Józef Hen, Aleksandra Jasińska-Kania, Michał Komar, Stanisław Obirek, Marian Turski, Adam Michnik, Jerzy Wiatr, Tomasz Kitliński and his parents, and Adam Ostolski; in Pozna, Roman Kubicki and Tomasz Kowalski; in Geneva, Bronisław Baczko; in New York, Irena Grudzińska-Gross, Krystyna Fischer and Jan T. Gross; in Israel, Emmanuel Marx, Shalva Weil and Uri Ram; in the UK, Griselda Pollock, Tony Bryant, Janet Wolff, Keith Tester, John Thompson, Alan Warde and Monika Kostera. This last interview was conducted by Skype. I would also like to thank three individuals who did not want their names to be mentioned. I also spoke on the phone and/or exchanged letters with Adam Chmielewski, Leszek Kwiatkowski, Joanna Tokarska-Bakir, Włodek Goldkorn, Aleksander Perski, Elżbieta Kossewska, Barbara Toruńczyk and Peter Beilharz.

I wish to thank particularly Włodzimierz Holsztyński, for our correspondence and his lengthy and detailed account of the opposition activity at the University of Warsaw in the lead-up to March 1968. I am also deeply grateful to him for the permission to cite his poems. Holsztyński's talent completed my narrative in moments when academic language was inadequate in comparison to poetic aesthetics. I would like to thank Barbara Netrepko-Herbert for her translations of Holsztyński's pieces, as well as for the translation of Janina Bauman's poems. I am thankful to Łukasz Gos for his translation of the Antoni Słonimski poem.

This book benefitted also from the talents of other artists – photographers Agata Szczypińska, Michele Monasta, Łukasz Cynalewski and Tomasz Kowalski. I wish also to thank art historian Dariusz Konstantynow for our discussion, and for allowing me to publish one piece from his collection of anti-Semitic caricatures.

I thank the Bauman family for permission to reproduce Zygmunt Bauman's photographs and Janina Bauman's poems, which I found in secret-service files at the IPN. I wish to acknowledge Beata Kowalczyk and Mariusz Finkielsztein for their help in my data collection and their work in the archives of the IPN, the University of Warsaw, the Polish Academy of Science and the New Archives (Archiwum Akt Nowych). Jarosław Kilias helped me with the Polish Sociological Society archives and Wanda Lacrampe assisted in scouring the PZPR Party Archives in Milanówek. I would also like to thank the writer Anna Kłys, who spontaneously offered her help with research in the Poznań City Archives. I wish also to thank Patryk Pleskot from the IPN for his help in studying former secret-service archives. In the final stage of my work, Dariusz Brzeziński from the Polish Academy of Science introduced me to colleagues from the Bauman Institute – Marc Davis and Tony Campbell. They invited me to give a lecture at Leeds University, where Griselda Pollock enabled me to consult documents at the Archives and the Special Collection's Janina and Zygmunt Bauman Archive (hereafter the Bauman Archive). My research there would not have been successful (many documents were not yet catalogued) without the help of Jack Palmer, Timothy Procter and Carolyne Bolton. Jack also helped me with expert information about Leeds University and the British sociological milieu, and helped me access articles and books. Mariusz Finkielsztein, Andrzej Nowak, Pietro Ingalina and Katarzyna Kwiatkowska-Moskalewicz also did a great deal to help me find sources in Polish, English and French.

I drew constantly on the help and support of Beata Chmiel in several different ways. First, she helped me collect most of the press articles and Polish books cited in this volume, obtaining these materials quickly and efficiently. Moreover, for the last five years she has sent me everything she detected online about Zygmunt Bauman.

(My home has limited access to the internet.) Beata showed me overwhelming support and enthusiasm for my work and opened numerous doors for me – interviews, exchanges of letters and discussions. She was an excellent guide and adviser in the process of book delivery. Other people gave me strong support through inspiring talks and discussions. I am indebted to my friends Alicja Badowska-Wójcik and Ryszard Wójcik, as well as to Claire Bernard and Paul Gradvohl, who advised me wisely when I needed it. I warmly acknowledge Lucyna Gebert for her support, connections and precious information.

One of the last and most crucial phases of book production is obtaining comment on the manuscript. I wish to thank deeply everyone who read and commented on my drafts and gave me encouragement. My first reader, Mariusz Finkielsztein, never hesitated to indicate my mistakes, such as overly long passages or confusing explanations. As a specialist in academic boredom, he was particularly attentive to the rhythm and speed of the narration. I wish to thank also Jean-Michel Chapoulie, Stanisław Obirek, Michał Komar, Beata Kowalczyk, Anna Rosińska, Beata Chmiel, Maciej Gdula, Adam Ostolski, Natalia Aleksiun, Włodek Goldkorn, Andrzej Nowak, Agata Czarnacka and Monika Kostera for their comments and questions on the manuscript.

I am particularly grateful for the very careful and expert reading of the whole manuscript by Jan Tomasz Gross, Agnieszka Wiercholska and Aleksander Perski – the summer of 2019 was animated by our discussions, joined also by Danuta and Henryk Kowalski; we spent hours talking about Polish history, communist engagements and 1968, as well as our own experiences of emigration. This was a perfect frame for the final touches to the book.

I wish also to thank my reviewer for motivating advice and pertinent questions that made the book shorter and more precise. I am grateful to John Thompson from Polity Press, for his patience, help and deep understanding of my working conditions. He was always encouraging, supportive and stimulating. It was a pleasure to know that my work mattered and was expected, but without unnecessary pressure. I would also like to thank the copy-editor Leigh Mueller for her patience and perfect eye, which detected some remaining mistakes. And I wish to thank everyone from Polity for their work and involvement in this project.

A long process of data gathering (started in November 2013) went into this book, with many travels, physical absence and mental unavailability. My family supported it with understanding; thankfully, each of us is passionate about our own work. I am grateful to my children Filip Saffray and Anna Saffray-Borowski, as well as their families, for their tolerance and comprehension, with deep excuses for my absence at moments very important for them. Because of my strong involvement in this project, Bauman's life was frequently the first topic of discussion in our home for six years. I am deeply grateful to my husband, Philippe Saffray, for his infinite patience, incredible support and deep understanding of my work. He was my constant coach and the first partner for all discussions, helping me form all of my hypotheses and questions. Though his profession is different, Philippe shared my passion with enthusiasm and loyalty. When I had difficult moments of doubt and weariness, he made those moments shorter. Without his encouragement, support and fruitful discussions, this book would never have been finished.

A book project involving interviews conducted in different parts of the world requires financial support. I wish to thank Kościuszko Foundation for their support of my project focused on Polish scientists in America from the 1968 emigration. Thanks to this scholarship, I spent the spring semester of 2016 at the New School for Social Research in New York City and did several interviews with emigrants, including many who knew Bauman. I wish also to thank Griselda Pollock, Jack Palmer and the Bauman Institute for their invitations to Leeds, where I finished my process of data collection. I covered some limited travel expenses through research funds granted by the University of Warsaw, but most of these fees were covered by my family, including my parents. Without their encouragement, I would never have been able to finish my book.

Last but not least, I express my gratitude to Keith Tester, who provided great support in the preparation and writing of the second half of the book. He always provided me the best feedback, professionally stimulating discussions and inspiring exchanges. Our short but very intense intellectual relationship abruptly ended when he died, and this book is devoted to his memory.

Introduction

22 June 2013: Wrocław

The location is a 600-seat university lecture hall in Wrocław, a picturesque city built on twelve islands in the meandering Oder River that has fully recovered its glory after utter and almost complete destruction during World War II. The hall is packed beyond capacity with university students and faculty, with young people crowding the steps or standing along the walls next to TV cameras covering the lecture. The globally renowned intellectual Zygmunt Bauman is today's distinguished speaker. This tall, slim 88-year-old sits on the stage between the organizer and the Wrocław Mayor, Rafał Dudkiewicz, with two bodyguards hired by the university standing nearby. The tension is high. Two months earlier, the French-German leftist politician Daniel Cohn-Bendit had cancelled a lecture here due to death threats. Again, today, the organizers fear disruption by xenophobic nationalistic groups.

Bauman is an excellent speaker. Several of his books (of the more than fifty he has published) are bestsellers, written in a style accessible to a wide public. His vision of the world is an inspiration to engaged youth and social movements. Bauman is the rare intellectual who has become a celebrity, and his talks attract thousands of people when he's travelling, from Italy to Brazil and from Greece to Portugal. He also, of course, has a public in Poland. The topic of today's lecture is the ideals of the Left, old and new, and the challenges faced by leftist movements in the current configuration of capitalism.[1]

As the mayor takes the microphone to say a few words, he is drowned out by people at the back of the lecture hall who have entered at the last minute, as well as others planted in the crowd – about 100 in total. They yell abuse, wave their arms, making fists and threatening those onstage. 'Dudkiewicz, why did you invite him?', they shout. 'Communism out! Nuremberg for communists!'

'The communists will hang!' Some of the protesters 'raise their hands in the Nazi salute', event organizer Adam Chmielewski will recall later.[2] Bauman looks concerned – nervous, though not panicked. The astonished university public seems unable to believe what they see with their own eyes.

One of the slogans screamed by the protesters is 'NSZ – National Armed Forces!' They are referring to the radical nationalist military underground group that fought the Nazis and also the Polish Left during and after World War II.[3] As a young man, in the immediate aftermath of the war, Bauman had been an officer in the KBW, an intelligence unit of the Polish Army that chased down the remnants of the NSZ. That story is old – more than sixty-five years old – but these right-wing radicals act as if it happened yesterday. They have reclaimed the mantle of the NSZ and its radical nationalist, xenophobic anti-Semitism. Some wear T-shirts with the acronym of the NOP (National Rebirth of Poland),[4] the party that organized the protest with the ONR (National Radical Camp).[5] Both groups use the symbol of the *falanga* which anti-Semitic and fascist groups employed on their flags in the interwar periods (Cała, 2012). They carry banderoles – narrow banners of the type used by groups that organized anti-Semitic riots at Polish universities in the 1930s.

After several minutes, the police arrive, to applause from the university audience. The aggressive group leaves the hall, promising to return. They leave Bauman sitting alone, completely folded upon himself. He will give his talk, but no one will remember it. They will only remember the thugs, who show that fascism still has the power to seduce young people, and that there are those who refuse to accept the right of people like Zygmunt Bauman to identify themselves as Poles.

In the remaining years of his life, Bauman would not comment publicly on the incident. But the slogans and symbols employed by the protesters were familiar to him from his childhood in Poznań, where he suffered from anti-Semitic bullying and racial laws that forced him and other Jews to sit on the 'ghetto bench' at school (Tomaszewski, 2016: 206–19). Perhaps he felt that his life had made a complete circle, or that the old forces were coming back again. The twentieth-century utopia he had hoped for – an end to wars, the disappearance of racial and ethnic conflicts and the possibility of an equal society – all these seemed to be gone. The world was confronting an old ghost, the xenophobe's hate of the 'other'.

Why was Bauman such a target of hate? Why did these young people want to put him in jail? What had he done that made him such a scapegoat for part of Polish society? And how could the same person be acclaimed and admired by millions of people and hated by others?

Who was Zygmunt Bauman?

Bauman, who died in 2017, was a sociologist, philosopher and public intellectual. He became known to other sociologists in the 1960s, when, as a young Polish scholar, he gave presentations at international conferences, and became well known among a wider academic community with the publication of *Modernity and the Holocaust* (1989). This book won awards and was recognized as an important contribution to understanding the Shoah, and as an important critique of modernity. Bauman, a remarkably disciplined scholar and writer who learned about communication on the front lines as a messiah of socialism to illiterate Polish soldiers, went on to become a key figure in the development of post-modernist theory; his eclecticism and humanist approach inspired Bauman's colleagues to call him the 'modern Simmel' (after the eminent German sociologist Georg Simmel).

After his retirement, Bauman stepped out of the confines of academic writing and pursued a larger, younger audience. It was an unconventional step for a 75-year-old scholar, but a remarkably successful one. A retired British professor, a Polish Jew by birth, he was embraced by readers around the world following the publication of his groundbreaking book *Liquid Modernity* (2000), which became an almost overnight bestseller. The books that followed popularized Bauman's vision further, and his analysis of contemporary Western societies struck a chord with millions of readers, making him one of the most prolific, widely read and influential intellectuals in the twenty-first century. Bauman presented his vision of the world in a way that spoke to people. He was cited by journalists, writers, activists, artists and also scholars and public intellectuals. He captured the speed and permanent modifications of the world and was seen as an oracle, although Bauman never pretended to predict the future. He would say that the world filled him with pessimism, but the remarkable creativity of humans provided some reserve of optimism. This was the voice of an elderly intellectual whose experiences of war and escape, discrimination and persecution made him particularly attentive to the processes that led to war and dictatorship.

Bauman was discreet about his private life. In our interviews for this book, he would often say that his biography was typical for his generation and had not particularly influenced his work.[6] But, after learning the details of his life, I was convinced of the opposite – his work is deeply grounded in personal experience, especially the series of traumatic events that began in his childhood and lasted into his forties. In an unpublished manuscript (Bauman, 1986/7) addressed to his children and grandchildren, Bauman revealed the interstices of this life and, in the process, acknowledged as much.

Bauman sought to build a better world. In the different phases of his adult life, he was never a passive observer of society, but rather an activist who lived by his ideals. He was a witness to and a participant in many of the tragic events that fundamentally transformed our world – experiencing anti-Semitism as a youth in Poland, a flight from the Nazis, an exiled life in Soviet Russia, hunger, the soldier's life of combat, the life of a communist propagandist in the implementation of a pro-Soviet regime in Poland, the collapse of Stalinism, and the interplay between authoritarianism and partial democratization in postwar Poland. Bauman was twice a refugee, in 1939–44 and in 1968. He did not choose a nomadic life, but it was thrust upon him. For most of his life, Bauman tried his best to be a good Pole, but Poland did not accept him as one. His Polish identity was contested by anti-Semitic rules, laws and persecution – Bauman's perception of his identity was not accepted by those who controlled it from the outside.

The feeling of identity (Who am I?) and *master status* (How do others perceive me?) are two axes that cross in the book you are reading.

Here, I am thinking with Everett Hughes (Chicago's leading sociologist), who presented in 1945 the concept of master status. With this term, he defines the social identity imposed by others.[7] Contradiction of status occurs when someone tries to play a social role while lacking the necessary features expected by society. This situation occurs often when people from discriminated groups occupy prestigious positions, or try to.

Already, as a child, Bauman could not be accepted as first in his school class, despite his superior results, because he was a Jew, and the top spot was reserved for a non-Jewish Pole. Master status in this case was a major factor in determining and limiting his social roles. This continued through much of Bauman's life in Poland: the tension between his self-identity – Pole – and the master status imposed by those around him – Jew. His experience was a common one in Poland. Bauman had many other roles: student, soldier, officer, scholar, academic, father, emigrant and immigrant. But the status that dominated was his ethnic-cultural origin, which imposed perceptions and strongly influenced his interactions with others.

On a personal level, he learned how the tribal behaviour of societies divides people into 'us' and 'them' – the 'conflict', as Bauman wrote, 'about whose blood is redder'. Bauman wrote constantly about this issue, seeing it as the origin of humanity's problems. Certainly, his own life would never be entirely free of the torments of tribalism.

In the first part of Bauman's life, he was affected by extreme forces that stripped agency and the sense of empowerment from individuals. This dynamic probably shaped his conviction that life consists of hazardous situations, that a person's control over his or her life was severely limited, and that individual character may enable possibilities for adjustment to a given situation, but the situation is determined by history and politics. This vision of human beings entrapped by a powerful world outside their control is contrary to the ideology popular in the second part of the twentieth century, which presents the individual as the shaper of his or her fate. While the neoliberal world was claiming 'If you want you can get it', Bauman stated the opposite. He described a society whose ideology leads its citizens to believe their agency is confirmed by consumption – an omnipresent illusion of the power of the individual.

His books, addressed to readers in Western society, stated that, while capitalism promised that happiness could be achieved through purchases and consumption, instead it destabilized everything that civilizations had created: social relations, love, rules, morality, values – in Bauman's terms, it 'liquified' them. The once-solid processes and rules of the 'modern' era, with its sense of constant development and progress, were now liquid, characterized by a taste for the new, the next and best solutions, innovation for its own sake. The feeling of 'liquidity' – its temporality and lack of stability – characterized our times. The previous mode of life, perceived as solid, fixed and clear, was giving way to something new, not yet really established – a kind of work in progress. Our own times were an in-between period, during which each member of a developed society had to be flexible, because previous frameworks, rules and values were no longer available. Precarity was the consequence of our societies' modifications.

In the Liquid World, everything changes so quickly that it brings the feeling that life is provisional. Liquid Times are defined by uncertainty. If, in previous generations, large numbers of people spent their whole lives in the same workplace, with the same occupation, and frequently the same partner and family living in the same house, residents of the Liquid World were obliged to change their workplace and occupation, adapting themselves to the dynamic environment. This contextual instability is related to a high degree of geographic mobility. The liquidity dynamic modified social relationships, which became fragile. Social ties became brittle, increasing people's solitude. The persistent belief that buying the latest product in fashion would make us happy was a powerful illusion. This is the Baumanian deconstruction of our Western societies.

Bauman knew a lot about illusions, beliefs, belonging and engagement. He was a former missionary for socialism, who learned lessons from engagement in seeking to build a new society during the first part of his life, then spent the second part of his life telling people about the danger of inhuman engagements and beliefs. His transformation was different from that of colleagues who, criticizing their earlier belief systems, jumped headlong into new, opposing ones (from communism to capitalism). Bauman kept his values and dreams about social justice, but critically analysed the systems that were being produced, ostensibly to achieve noble goals.[8]

This book, the first extensive biography of Bauman, places his work in the context of his life, and hopefully will enable readers of his work to revisit his books with deeper insight into their messages, which emanate not only from Bauman's voluminous scholarship and thought, but also from his iconic life experiences.

1

A Happy Childhood 'Under Such Circumstances'

Poznań (1925–1932)

A significant birth place, a critical time . . .

Zygmunt Bauman was born on 19 November 1925 in Poznań in Poland. The morning edition of the most popular local newspaper, *Kurjer Poznański*, carried news that day direct from Rome. 'Enthusiastic ovations in honour of Mussolini', it reported. 'Fantastic speech by the Prime Minister at the opening session of Parliament. Today's session of the chamber of deputies began in an ambiance of extreme excitement, full of enthusiasm and cheerful guests in honor of Mussolini' (*Kurjer Poznański*, R. 20, 19 November 1925; evening edition, p. 2).

The evening edition of the *Kurjer* contained Part Seven in a series of articles entitled 'Society of Poznań District and Pomerania in Reconstructed Poland',[1] written by the well-known nationalist politician Roman Dmowski.[2] The first part of the text was published on 12 November, the day after the seventh anniversary of the independence of the new Polish state, following 123 years of partition by Russia, Prussia and the Austro-Hungarian Empire. Dmowski underlined the importance of the nationalistic awareness of the masses. There was a matter of great importance, that of uniformly closing ranks against the Jews, a task in which Poznań could be said to lead (R. 20, 19 November 1925; evening edition, p. 2). This was the world into which Zygmunt Bauman was born.

It was a less than auspicious day for those who belonged to this 'ethnic minority' – a term that was not in use at the time. Jews had lived on Polish soil for over 1,000 years, but the majority considered them 'outsiders', 'others' – less than full members of Polish society. The situation of Polish Jews differed from that of Jews in France or Germany, where from the late eighteenth century there was a greater degree of assimilation. In Poland, Jewishness was not only a religious status; Jews were portrayed as distinct in many categories – culture, nationality, ethnicity – to demonstrate that, although they had lived for centuries on the same ground as Catholic Poles, they were a distinct people.

In a private essay addressed to his daughters years later,[3] Bauman explained the situation of the Polish Jew in its historical context:

> I cannot avoid history. History decreed that the state of 'being Polish' has been through centuries a question of decision, choice and action. It has been something one had to fight for, defend, consciously cultivate, vigilantly preserve. 'Being Polish' did not mean guarding the already well formed and marked frontiers, but rather drawing the yet-not-existing boundaries – *making* realities rather than expressing them. There was in Polishness a constant streak of uncertainty, 'until-further-noticeness' – a kind of precarious provisionality that other, more secure nations know little about.
>
> Under such circumstances one could only expect that the besieged, incessantly threatened nation would obsessively test and re-test the loyalty of its ranks. It would develop an almost paranoiac fear of being swamped, diluted, overrun, disarmed. It would look askance and with suspicion at all newcomers with less-than-foolproof credentials. It would see itself surrounded by enemies, and it would fear more than anybody else the 'enemy within'.
>
> Under such circumstances one should also accept that the decision to be a Pole (particularly if it was not made for one by the ancestors so distant that the decision had time to petrify into rock-solid reality) was a decision to join in a struggle with no assured victory and no prospect that victory would ever be assured. For centuries, people did not define themselves as Poles for the want of easy life. Those who did define themselves as Poles could rarely be accused of opting for comfort and security. In most cases, they deserved unqualified moral praise and whole-hearted welcome.
>
> That the same circumstances should lead to consequences pointing in opposite directions, clashing with each other and ultimately coming into conflict – is illogical. Well, blame the circumstances. (Bauman, 1986/7: 21–2)

Defining oneself as a Pole was an individual decision, but one that had to be confirmed by the host society. To speak of the 'assimilation' of Jews, or an identity that fused Polish and Jewish culture, was not only a matter of personal identification but one that inevitably involved Polish society as a whole. In this case, 'the circumstances' Bauman spoke of were different from those that enabled the assimilation of Jews in France and Germany before the arrival of Nazism. There was a saying, popular in the twentieth century – and still today – that, while one could be a French Jew or an American Jew, there was no such thing as a Polish Jew. You had to choose – one or the other![4]

Bauman explained this specific case of the Polish identity from the *longue durée* perspective:[5] 'It is one of the mysteries of social psychology that groups that ground their identity in will and decision tend to deny the right of self-definition to others; by questioning and denigrating the validity of self-determination they wish perhaps to suppress and forget the frail foundation of their own existence. This is what happened in the inter-war Poland' (Bauman, 1986/7: 21–2).

Historian Paweł Brykczyński in *Ready for Violence: Murder, Anti-Semitism and Democracy in Interwar Poland*, argues that anti-Semitic nationalism was a major force in culture and politics to a greater extent than some Polish historians are ready to admit:[6] 'Certainly, it was not a hegemonic force. Anti-Semitic nationalism faced strong competition, led by gifted and charismatic political leaders such as Piłsudski,[7] created by strong socialist, radical, liberal and moderate conservative camps who gathered around him' (Brykczyński, 2017: 28–9). Brykczyński suggests that the essence of the conflict between Dmowski and Piłsudski's supporters – paraphrasing Benedict Anderson[8] – involved different ways of constructing imaginary communities (Brykczyński, 2017: 36–7). While for Piłsudski Polish society included all Polish citizens, without regard to religion or ethnicity, for Dmowski, Polish status was reserved for Catholics. Thus, the problem of anti-Semitism played a key role in the conflict between supporters of Dmowski and of Piłsudski.

In interwar Poland, relationships between the two neighbouring communities were dynamic, with strong distinctions from region to region, based on which of the tripartite powers had ruled in each. Under partition, the rules of housing and access to the professions and occupations were different under the tsars and kaisers, and the demography of the Jewish populations also differed. Poznań – the capital city of the Wielkopolska region – in 1921 had 169,422 inhabitants, of whom only 1.2% were Jews.[9] This demographical situation was exceptional for Poland's larger cities, where, after the rebirth of the independent state (1918), Jews made up around a third of the population (1921 data showed Warsaw was 33.13% Jewish; Łódź, 34.6%; Kraków, 25%). It is apparently why Dmowski was so enthusiastic about Poznań, with its modest proportion of Jews and 'patriotic attachment to the Polish nation'.[10] The language of the period included a word *zażydzenie* (Jew-infestation, or Jewification).[11] The *Warsawian Dictionary* from 1927 defines the term as 'polluting by Jews . . . filling a territory with Jews, to overcrowd with Jews'. As an example of usage, the authors of the dictionary cite the novel *Marzyciel* (Dreamer), by Władysław Reymont, the 1924 Nobel Prize-winner, whose hero states: 'I will die there and forget about this stinking, Jew-infested country.' It was frequently noted in newspapers and magazines that Poznań was one of Poland's less 'Jew-infested' cities.

In an earlier section of Dmowski's *Kurjer Poznański* series,

he refers to Poznań's advance in the 'process of civilization . . .
Wielkopolska, as the oldest and most occidental part of Poland, was
more civilized than the other parts. Before it had even more Germans
and fewer Jews [than today]' (R. 20, evening edition, 13 November
1925). Once again, the prevalence of Jews is associated directly with
the progress of civilization. 'Economic development' was the scientific camouflage for well-developed, widespread anti-Semitism.

Anti-semitism was strong in Poznań in 1925, although the presence
of Jews in the city was much lower than it had been only a decade
before. In the late nineteenth century through to 1918, Jews were
an important part of Poznań's economic and political life. In those
years, the Jewish population identified strongly with Germany and its
situation was similar to that of other Jewish communities in Prussia.
Three ethnic groups – Prussian Germans, Poles and Jews – co-existed
in a city whose business language was German. Polish was spoken
at home, but the Germanization policy imposed by Bismarck discriminated against the use of Polish in public places. Unsurprisingly,
National Democrats looked back on this period with disgust:

> In 1853, naturalized Jews were elected to the city council for the first
> time; their number exceeded the number of Polish delegates, worsen-
> ing the far-from-perfect relationship with the Polish population . . .
> For Poles striving to regain their lost independence, Germanized Jews
> who flaunted their Prussian loyalty and servility became in some cases
> a more hostile group than the Germans themselves. Jews of Poznań
> would experience this hostility particularly poignantly after WWI.
> (From the official site of the POLIN Museum of the History of Polish
> Jews)[12]

At the end of World War I, Germans and Poles struggled for control
of the territories around Poznań, culminating in the Wielkopolska
Uprising of 1918–19. The strongly Germanized Jewish population
of the region supported the Weimar Republic in this confrontation, believing that Poland's newly independent state would not last.
When Poland definitively took control of Wielkopolska, most Jewish
families left the city for German-controlled territories – these were
Jews who had 'betrayed' the Polish state by supporting Germans in
Poznań. At the same time, the 1917 October Revolution brought
'Eastern Jews' – often bourgeois families fleeing the Soviet Union
– to Poznań, where they supported the Polish state. Despite this,
anti-Semitism increased, an artefact of Polish nationalistic muscle-
flexing in the interwar years. Poznań's Polish-Catholic inhabitants
tended not to distinguish among different Jewish groups, whether
their traditions were linked to Germany or the Pale of Settlement.
For Polish Catholics, they were all just Jews.

Historian Rafał Witkowski notes that, in 1922, German was still the official language employed in synagogue councils and associations, but by 1931 only 15 per cent of Poznań's Jews were German Jews, in the sense of speaking German and identifying themselves as Germans (Witkowski, 2012). Clearly, the missing population had been 'replaced' by families coming from the East.[13]

The family

Zygmunt Bauman's parents were also new inhabitants of the city in the 1920s. In the Poznań administrative registry list, we can read that Zygmunt's father Maurycy had moved to 17 Prusa Street on 1 July 1923.[14] The same document notes Maurycy's date of birth as 20 February 1890, in the village of Słupca, about 50 kilometres east of Poznań. The Jewish community had settled in this town around 1870, and by 1900 Jews made up 20 per cent of the population – 25 per cent by the time Maurycy Bauman left for Poznań.[15] Bauman's mother, Zofia, was born on 10 February 1894 in Rypin, near Włocławek, which since 1620 had had a large Jewish community. Her maiden name is written in different ways in various documents – as Zofia Kon on the address registration and Zofia (Zywa) Cohn in other documents, mostly created after World War II. The third person mentioned on the Poznań registration card is Tauba, Zygmunt's older sister, whose date of birth, in Słupca, is given as 28 January 1919. Zygmunt Bauman, the family's second and last child, is also listed in the registration.

The biographical information in this document varies somewhat from that of official documents from later in the family's life. Zygmunt Bauman himself provides slightly differing accounts of his family members and their histories in documents such as the thirteen-page Special Questionnaire from 1950 drawn up by the Polish secret political police (Urząd Bezpieczeństwa). Many of the birthdates and spellings change from one document to another, a common situation for people who emerged from World War II:[16] they often emerged from the tragedies of war, deportation and escape with new forenames, surnames, birthdates and birth places. The Baumans had changed their name from Baumann – 'builder' in German – to the more 'Polish-looking' Bauman, probably after Poland became an independent state in 1918.

Sometimes the changes were unintentional, the result of shifts in official language from people schooled in a variety of tongues – Polish, German, Russian, Yiddish and Hebrew,[17] which entailed three alphabets: Cyrillic, Hebrew and Latin (in addition, Polish contains many letter–accent variations that are not present in other Latin-alphabet languages). Bauman's mother's name, for example, was of Yiddish /Hebrew origin, and could be transliterated either as

Kon, Kohn, Kahn, Con, Cehn or Cohn. In fact, several genealogy sources say that all those versions are variants of the name Cohen, a royal name in Jewish tradition – from Hebrew, it is translated as 'priest', referring to the priestly clan of biblical times who were keepers of the original Temple.

Surname changes could also be intentional, but surnames most often changed because the registrars used different languages or alphabets or came from different cultures. This was the case with Hebrew names written by Polish officials or Soviet soldiers schooled in the Cyrillic alphabet, who, during and after World War II, were charged with filling out official documents. Either the registrar or the person whose name was being changed might alter it with the purpose of asserting an identity, or the necessity of being perceived as a member of one group or another. Bauman's sister was born Tauba (as registered in the Jewish community), then became Teofila, to conform to the Polish 'version' of Tauba. After moving to Palestine, she took on the Hebrew name Tova. In postwar documents, her birth place also was modified: according to her Poznanian registration card, she was born in Słupca, but in postwar documents the birth place becomes Włocławek, where her mother's family lived. The two towns were 110 kilometres apart and belonged to different countries.

In January 1919, the month of Tauba's birth, Włocławek was not a quiet place. A conflict between Communist Party members and their opponents led to a series of pogroms against the Jewish district, although, in contrast to Poznań, Włocławek's Jewish community had supported the Polish Army and the new independent government. In the months that followed World War I, pogroms involving soldiers and civil populations were frequent in cities and towns with a Jewish population (Jastrząb, 2015). Włocławek's January 1919 pogrom could be not explained by motives other than hatred of an ethnic minority that was in a good economic position. Włocławek's Jews owned about 60 per cent of its businesses, and had been a mostly well-assimilated group for decades. The well-known Jewish landowners and personalities of the city included many Kohns. Zofia's family owned a construction business and belonged to the local bourgeoisie.

Changes in birth year were perhaps the most frequent types of document modification in this period. For example, Zofia, Zygmunt's mother, is listed in prewar documents as being born in 1894, but in postwar papers, in 1896. Many people took the opportunity of wartime and postwar bureaucratic chaos to rejuvenate themselves. In state-regulated societies with fixed retirement ages and negligible or symbolic retirement pensions, this was a good strategy for working longer.

Changes of occupation were often telling indicators of the shifting social pressures under which Bauman and his family lived in the twentieth century, and of the changing perceptions of what constituted 'social capital' or 'social class'. In prewar documents, Maurycy Bauman's occupation is listed as 'trader' (*kupiec*), while at the moment of Zygmunt's birth his father owned (or co-owned) textile stores (*sklep bławatny*). In the early 1930s, after bankruptcies, the Great Depression and the boycott of Jewish shops by the Polish community (which was particularly well organized in Poznań), Maurycy became an accountant or bookkeeper (*buchhalter*) for a local company, Sławiński & Toczkała. In response to several administrative postwar questionnaires, Zygmunt Bauman gave two prewar occupations for his father: first, as a merchant or store owner; second, as an accountant. For example, in the document 'Explanations of the CV', from 3 January 1950, we read: 'Up until 1939, after bankruptcy, my father worked as a bookkeeper and at the same time partially as a travelling salesman, first in the firm Toczkała, then in the Skowrońscy enterprise in Poznań.'[18]

These changes of information were aimed at characterizing Bauman's origins in a way that diminished his 'capitalistic' pedigree. In postwar Poland, having a father who had owned a business or sold goods – by consequence, a bourgeois and capitalist – was a huge obstacle to career advancement, especially in the Army, the Communist Party and other important institutions. Being a travelling salesman or accounting employee was much better than being a capitalist. This was one of the 'delicate' issues in the biography of Zygmunt, from the perspective of his Polish hierarchy after the war. In the late 1940s, it was not so much his Jewish origin that was a problem, since some Jews were members of the institutions in which he served. His social and professional family history – his bourgeois origin – was much more serious.

Maurycy Bauman originated from an educated family. As Zygmunt wrote in his private essay:

> My father's father was a village shopkeeper – a smaller chip of a family stem which on its other branches (so I heard) carried also some learned rabbis and renowned tsadiks. He started his business in a small village of Zagorov, moving later to a minor regional centre of Slupca. As far as I know, my grandfather had no education but the one provided by the religious school (kheder).[19] (Bauman, 1986/7: 3)

Zagórów was a small village near Słupca whose late-nineteenth-century population was less than 3,000, about one-fifth of them Jews. Zygmunt's grandfather had moved to Słupca before the birth of Maurycy. Two of his other children were also merchants, while a third male was an engineer. All three emigrated – the oldest,[20] before World War I, to Karlsruhe, Germany, and then Palestine; the second, Szymon, in 1905, to the United States where he 'probably was the owner of a factory' in Little Rock, Arkansas, as Zygmunt wrote in an 'explanatory CV annex' in 1950;[21] and the third, Beniamin, in 1923, emigrated directly to Palestine, where he settled in Tel Aviv. Maurycy also had a sister, Zofia Izbicka, who was married to a salesman or commercial agent and emigrated to Lucerne, Switzerland in 1908. Such emigration patterns were not exceptional for people who lived in this part of Europe at the time.[22] The industrialization of Western Europe and the USA attracted large numbers of youth, who left insecurity and poverty for promises of a better life. It is not clear whether any members of the family remained in Słupca in 1939.

In his private essay, Zygmunt sheds some light on the educational strategy in his father's family – one typical of the social changes that occurred in the first decades of the twentieth century in Eastern Europe:

> Grudgingly, the grandfather agreed to support only the secular education of his youngest son. My father was not the youngest, so like the rest of his brothers he had the village melamed for his only teacher. Yet all the sons, except for the eldest who stayed with the father in his shop, rebelled and left home one by one. . . . My father's rebellion took another form and did not include changing places. He learned perfect German, decent Russian, bearable Polish and a smattering of English and French, and set about devouring books.[23] (Bauman, 1986/7: pp. 4–5)

Maurycy was an 'autodidact', a book lover and a dreamer, ill-fit for his career as a clerk or businessman. The occupation that was designed for him by his father, and by society, was compatible with the rules governing life in the region in the early twentieth century: a Jew from a middle-sized city should work in commerce. In those times, too, the rule was that sons followed their father's occupation – this was the most common way to choose a professional trajectory. It was a choice that was not really a choice.

> As my father came from a respectable business family, he must have been assumed to be a good business prospect. My mother's dowry was to provide the take-off. The rest was to be up to him. No one, perhaps, took a close look. So it went unnoticed, I suppose, that my father combined a rich spiritual life with an appalling dearth of practical sense. That man dreamed of being a scholar; they wanted him to be a merchant. Brilliance was mistaken for business acumen. (Bauman, 1986/7: 7)

In his essay, Bauman describes his parents as an 'unmatched', or even 'ill-matched', couple. They came from different family backgrounds, different regions and lifestyles. Zygmunt's father wanted a modest, solitary life focused on reading and studying; his mother had lived the life of the daughter of a bourgeois family in a provincial town that had more than its share of cultural sparkle, as Bauman would write later:

> My mother's father was one of the 'pioneers of progress' whose confidence in the progressive character of their skills and deeds was reinforced and multiplied by their belief in the progressiveness of their newly acquired Polishness. My mother received a strictly Polish education, much like her four sisters and the only brother: she had only as much Yiddish as one could not help but imbibe from the clatter of Wloclawek streets – just enough to tell later to her husband the secrets she did not want her children to overhear. She was also brought up in an atmosphere of seemliness and decorum more akin to the pattern of Polish gentility than the shtetl tradition. She was introduced to romantic novels, intelligent conversation, music. (Bauman, 1986/7: 6)

However, the progressive Cohn family was run by a despotic father ('patriarchally strictly biblical', as Bauman defined him), and all the liberal ideas learned in the laic schools did not keep him from arranging the marriages of all his daughters, Zofia included: 'They all married moderately successful and relatively well-off businessmen. So did my mother. Or so, at least, it was hoped. . . . The ill-matched couple married, and moved to Poznań, at the . . . moment of the city's return to the Polish administration after more than [a] hundred years of unbroken Prussian-German rule' (Bauman, 1986/7: 7).

Maurycy, according to the registry, came to Poznań in 1921 and lived first on Masztalarska Street with the Szefer family, and some months later on Bukowska Street with the Probański family. These were probably rental agreements. The first address was located in the Jewish district, and the second in the Jeżyce quarter, where the family rented an apartment at 17 Prusa Street after 1923. The choice of this address reflected Zofia's strong belief in the assimilation process:

> My mother's life-long defiance of reality . . . manifested itself in renting a flat in a residential area which had avoided harbouring Jews though the centuries of the city's tormented history. It was a quiet, clean, bright, self-respecting and respectable district, with all the streets named after national or local luminaries of Polish culture, inhabited by professionals, civil servants, military men, gentlemen and gentlewomen, a few widows left by their illustrious husbands to glow with their past glory. (Bauman, 1986/7: 8)

The choice of the flat must have gone against Maurycy's wishes and was a source of suffering for him, as he would have preferred to stay in the Jewish district of the Old City. However, the major worry for Zygmunt's father was his inability to play the role of breadwinner for his family, mainly because of his lack of interest in commerce. 'The mercer [textile] shop opened in the trading area of the city was his hell and his prison. . . . Even before the start of the Great Depression my father was declared bankrupt' (Bauman, 1986/7: 9).

Maurycy Bauman tried to get out from under total defeat by going to Paris, where he looked for a new venture thanks to some new loans, promises and business propositions. This absence was noted in the municipal registry with an absence reported there from 22 September to 14 October 1931.

Zygmunt remembered it this way:

> During his absence we fed for several weeks on cabbage soup – courtesy of the janitor's wife, who kindly loaned us a barrel of pickled cabbage from her own supply. After a while a telegram arrived, and I heard my mother, thus far her normal, boisterous self, sobbing. I never read the telegram, but I know its content by heart. Cheated of all his money by the smart Parisian guys who pretended to rent him a shop while laughing up their sleeves at the sight of the unworldly, hapless sucker, my father asked my mother whether she still wanted him back. This is my first, fully my own, vivid, unfading recollection: loud knocking on the door . . . and my father – unshaven, in a coat soaking and dripping with dirty water, covered with weeds and slime.

He had been round to the offices of the better-off Jewish merchants, begging for a job, then walked to the beautiful bridge over the Warta River, and jumped: 'A squad of boy scouts who were passing by dived into the freezing water and fished my father out – against his will' (Bauman, 1986/7: 9).

His father's bankruptcy dominated Zygmunt's memories of his childhood. In an interview conducted by Tomasz Kwaśniewski,[24] Bauman said his father had jumped because he lost everything: 'I remember how the furniture was removed from our apartment. The bailiff often visited us. But when the information about this suicide attempt spread around Poznań, out of pity he was hired as a bookkeeper. He earned a poor salary, he was discriminated against and humiliated, but somehow he was able financially to support us.' Maurycy never explained his suicide attempt to the children, Bauman said, but:

> I can reconstruct it. There was an old-fashioned concept of 'family breadwinner'. He had a wife and two children, he had to feed and

clothe them and pay for their schooling. If he couldn't, he was a nothing, a villain unworthy of life. If he was unable to save his children and wife from starvation and humiliation, he was worthy of contempt. (*GW*, 10 February 2009)[25]

This story marked the family deeply. The press noted: 'A Jew attempted suicide. Saved by the Polish scouts' (Bauman, 1986/7: 9–10). Bauman asserts that it was his father's incompetence, rather than the boycott of Jewish shops in Poznań, that caused his bankruptcy. But the boycotts, which would reach a crescendo in the Depression era, had begun as early as 1920. On 19 November 1925, the day Zygmunt Bauman was born, the *Kurjer Poznański* contains an announcement for the 'Organizational Meeting of the Union for the Defence of Polish Industry'.[26] The idea of boycotting Jewish shops and firms was already popular[27] and became an important focus of Dmowski's right-wing anti-Semitic Endecja party.

Once the boycott was implemented, some Jewish businessmen tried to evade it strategically, as Fira Mełamedzon-Salańska recalled: 'We hired four salespeople. My father chose only Poles because he did not want our business associated with a Jewish owner' (Niziołek and Kosakowska, 2016: 67). Mełamedzon-Salańska's father was a good businessman who had the resources and savvy to dodge the boycott. Maurycy did not. Both families belonged to the middle class, but the Baumans had limited resources that were insufficient for a 'middle-class' lifestyle in this context. They were not the typical 'poor Jews', people who had lived for generations in poverty in the *shtetel* or in the cities, working in factories or modest shops and doing small handcraft jobs. They were stuck in the middle between bourgeois and working-class Jews.

'I was . . . poor. That is, my parents were', Bauman wrote in the letter to his daughters:

> We did not live in poverty. Not by comparison with the abject misery and squalor a few blocks down, where shoddy workshops waited in vain for a stray customer and the children of unemployed workers and rural migrants churned mud of unpaved roads with their bare feet. I do not remember being hungry – even during the memorable 'cabbage weeks'. And yet our life was a continuous struggle for survival with my mother fighting desperately to make ends meet, with cash always short in the second half of every month . . . I considered it natural that books and shoes and socks are things one gets as a birthday present. I do not remember having toys. (Bauman, 1986/7: 14–15)

Even with such limited resources, originating from middle-class families as they did, Maurycy and Zofia Bauman had cultural expectations that matched their social origins, such as the conviction that children should receive a musical education. When I asked Bauman in a 2015 interview about this subject, he said that his mother wanted him to play piano:[28] 'We had a small apartment and she wished me to play, and this is curious because typically that was an indispensable element of a daughter's upbringing . . . I had an older sister but nobody forced her to do anything and I was forced to play piano – I do not know why.'

Boys from middle-class Jewish families typically played violin in this part of Europe (Wagner, 2015: 15–19). But Zofia Bauman did not exactly follow fashion. As Bauman told Kwaśniewski, 'my mother was full of projects, ambition and energy. Educated, she devoured books and was prepared for an interesting life, but was condemned by fate to be a housewife who had to patch holes' (*GW*, 21 November 2010).

Zofia originated from a region whose Jewish community had a broad tradition of religious emancipation. The first secular school for Jewish children was opened in 1859 in Włocławek, and the process of secularization and Polonization of Jews was very important in that area. Zofia was an emancipated, atheist, educated woman, yet within her environment she was mainly perceived as a Jew . . . an 'assimilated' Jew, but what did that mean?

Melamedzon-Salańska's memoir provides an excellent description of what 'assimilated Jews' meant in this time and place:

> We were not religious Jews, we lived like Christians. We didn't keep a kosher house – I ate pork sausage and ham – and we didn't have a Sabbath dinner. We did not go to the synagogue, even though we lived next to it. On Saturday our shop was open, like almost all Jewish businesses in Poznań. Only on the big holidays – New Year or Yom Kippur – daddy closed the shop because it would be shameful to work on those days . . . But even on Pesach, while we would buy matzoh, we also ate plain sourdough bread – unthinkable for religious Jews. And we never celebrated Shavuot or Purim at all. (Niziołek and Kosakowska, 2016: 73)

Maurycy's relationship to religion was probably even more distant: 'My father was a practicing Jew but a non-believer. He always fasted on Yom Kippur and then spent the day in the synagogue – it was his practice.'[29]

In these Polish-Jewish families, grandparents were frequently the vehicles of religious tradition, and that was also the case with Bauman's paternal grandfather:

> I remember him as a tall man with a long beard which would be white if not for the yellowish stains of tobacco. He hardly spoke any Polish, or any other language for this matter, except Yiddish. Our

communication was therefore limited. He insisted on teaching me the Bible, of which I had the vaguest of ideas. As I could neither read nor understand Hebrew, and his knowledge of Polish was confined to the few words one needs in a life spent mostly at a shop counter, the Bible remained a total mystery to me long after Grandfather's religious instruction. (Bauman, 1986/7: 4)

This was the typical outlook of a nineteenth-century, small-town Polish Jew – so different from the following generation, to which Maurycy belonged, in which the Zionist ideal was growing.[30] 'He was a believer in the idea of Zionism', Bauman told me of his father; 'As long as I knew about it he was a Zionist, and what he was before I was born, I don't know, but I suppose he was a Zionist then, too.' Zionism before World War II was mostly a dream, rarely fulfilled. Bauman told me a Jewish joke circulating at the time: 'What's a Zionist? He's a Jew who uses a second Jew to send a third Jew to Palestine.'

In the essay Bauman wrote for his daughters, he states:

I think my Father's Zionism – heartfelt, life-long and central to his world-vision – was part of his rebellion; it *was* his rebellion. . . . Zion was something which had no room for the darkness and filth of the shtetl, for greed and callousness, for penny-pinching or people made into treadmill horses. Some sort of a brotherhood and universal goodness, . . . He did not find his Zion in Israel when he finally settled there. This was his ultimate defeat.[31] (Bauman, 1986/7: 4–5)

Maurycy would have liked to take *Aliyah*,[32] but Zofia refused. She wasn't enthusiastic about the idea of emigration, her son told me. However, Bauman's wife Janina, in her autobiography, gives a different account:

Zofia (Zygmunt's mother) paid me a surprise visit. . . . All agog, I listened to the sad story of her family. As long as she could remember, Zofia began, her husband had dreamed of emigrating to Palestine. In the late 1930s they had seriously considered settling there. Her daughter Tova wanted to go. Konrad [Zygmunt] was too young to be asked; Zofia, though hesitant, had never objected. They were about to leave when war broke out.[33] (J. Bauman, 1988: 50)

Zygmunt had been attending primary school before the war began. The experience contrasted highly with his family life: 'Through my childhood, I swam in warm parental love. It kept the cold outside. To think of it, there were all sorts of reasons to feel cold' (Bauman, 1986/7: 10).

2
A Pupil Like No Other
Poznań (1932–1939)

In your homeland necks are bent
To whoever's most powerful,
For the vanquished – disdain and spit,
As they are led to slaughter . . .

In your homeland, God does not lower himself to strangers of the
   faith.
My motherland takes the whole world
In the embrace of the cross.

. . . Though favored by the evening fog
And the starless night
How is it that you drive me from a homeland
That you don't even know?
              'Two homelands' by Antoni Słonimski (1938), translated by
                                    Łukasz Gos-Furmankiewicz

The world outside of the family – a solitary Jew

The Bauman family spoke Polish at home and lived much in the
same way as most of the other residents of Poznań. They weren't
Catholic, which meant everything. 'By Polish standards', Bauman
wrote in his private manuscript:

> Poznan was a truly exceptional city. It managed to combine a virtual
> absence of Jews with the most vituperative anti-Semitic sentiments.
> . . . Poznan became the brain center and the fortress of National
> Democracy – a party which sought to captivate the mind and the soul
> of the rest of the country with the enchanting vision of a Jew-free life.
> The sophistication of its theoretical blueprints benefitted enormously
> from the lack of opportunity to apply them in practice. (Bauman,
> 1986/7: 11–12)

'In order to become a Pole, you had to be a Catholic, or at least a Christian', writes Anna Landau-Czajka, an expert on the assimilation process (Landau-Czajka, 2006). Would it have made a difference if the Baumans had converted to Catholicism? Conversions always raised suspicion, and the ultra-nationalists did not accept them. In short, 'Assimilation was not a matter of personal belief nor of a perfect knowledge of Polish culture, language, customs and family traditions. It depended only on the goodwill of the Polish people' (Landau-Czajka, 2006: 65).

Because of Zofia's desire to live in a Polish-Catholic area of Poznań, the family had moved to Jeżyce, and they sent their son to a Polish primary school, which occupied a single building on Słowacki Street, and where Zygmunt was the only Jew. The school was still there when Bauman returned in 2000. 'Nothing has changed', he told me. 'I even walked in the courtyard – it seemed to me terribly tiny and when I was child it seemed to me tremendously large.' The courtyard was a place of intense childhood memories, Zygmunt recalled, without too much complaint or elaboration: 'I was discriminated against there.' He told Kwaśniewski: 'I did not play any sports, because I would not dare to go on the court. If I did, I could not kick the ball, but they would kick me instead of the ball. And not just because I was a fat boy, but because I was a Jew. . . . I was beaten and kicked, and scared to go out on the street.' How did he know he was the only Jew in Jeżyce? 'If there was another one, the hooligans would have pointed him out to me' (interview with Tomasz Kwaśniewski, *GW*, 21 November 2010).

Bauman suffered a very intimate persecution at the hands of his teenage persecutors:

They seemed to compete between themselves for the hunting privilege. I was too rare a prey to be shared with others. The gang that was on top at any particular time played a double role, that of my hunters and my protectors – against the poaching schemes of the rival gangs, . . . We greeted each other with something akin to joy: a foretaste of the all-too-familiar ritual, in which all the actors know their roles by heart and everything goes according to plan, in the end confirming once more that the world is an orderly and by and large secure place to be. (Bauman 1986/7: 12)

As a youth, from roughly 7 to 13 years of age, Bauman played this remarkable 'prey-friend' role. His existence allowed young boys organized in groups to perform the 'Jew persecution ritual', which enabled them to become 'patriotic Poles'. Since the leading feature of this nationalistic identity was anti-Semitism, the boys proved their commitment to the 'defence of Polishness' by hunting the Jew. This behaviour reflected the preoccupations of adult society.

In much of the local interwar media – including the earlier cited
Kurier Poznanski – the major subject was the 'Jewish problem',
and all the discriminatory events, university riots and pogroms that
occurred in different Polish territories were largely analysed from
the anti-Semitic perspective. This position reflected the opinions of
Endecja,[1] Dmowski's party. Jew 'hunting' was a typical activity for
youth gangs fighting over territory in an urban space.[2] Perhaps it
was training for later participation in pogroms.

According to family members' accounts, the trauma of these early
experiences was easily re-awoken in Bauman throughout his entire
life. In his late eighties, for example, he once lost his balance and fell
in a public space. When people around him tried to take his arms
to help him stand up, reflexes learned in his childhood on Poznań's
streets kicked in, and he pushed his helpers aside. The trauma, the
fear of being a prey, was doubly strong because it was connected
with extreme feelings of insecurity.

'The most traumatic of encounters with my appointed persecutors bore heavily on the rest of my childhood, tearing apart forever
the veil of false security', Bauman wrote to his daughters:

> One time my mother, having finished her shopping, came to collect
> me after school. The current holders of the hunting privilege – two
> unemployed teenagers . . . – were on their usual post, and the four of
> us took the road home. On this occasion, the two stayed a few steps
> behind, but otherwise their demeanour was unaffected by my mother's
> presence. They duly went through their by then traditional motions
> and produced in the predictable succession all their by then familiar
> sounds. I looked at my mother. She kept me close, but pulled her head
> between her shoulders, fixed her eyes on the cobblestones, and studi-
> ously avoided looking back on our escort. It suddenly dawned upon
> me: my mother, the all-powerful and all-knowing, had no power to
> defend me, did not know what to do! She was humiliated, she was
> afraid! From then on, and for many years to come, I lived in fear.
> (Bauman, 1986/7: 13)

Even home was only a place of relative security. One day (as
Bauman recalled in his private manuscript), Zofia called in a craftsman who created a supplementary security system for the entrance
door to their apartment: 'From that day on I also developed an
obsession. I could not go to bed without first opening the front door
and sneaking silently outside to make sure that no bandits lay in
wait on the staircase. Yet even this effort to allay my fears was not
enough to ward off nightmares' (Bauman, 1986/7: 14).

Many books tell the stories of Holocaust survivors and their
postwar trauma, their obsessions and feelings of insecurity. In
Bauman's case, the trauma of anti-Semitic treatment began many

years before World War II, in a country that was considered relatively democratic, during a time of peace and relative prosperity.[3]

Family and home were the antidote to constant discrimination. The Bauman home was a modest but warm place; both parents showered Zygmunt with love. His first wife, Janina Bauman *née* Lewinson, described Maurycy Bauman as a discreet person who 'never talked much, never complained, never wanted anything for himself' (J. Bauman, 1988: 130). He was the opposite of his wife, who, in the first meeting of the Bauman and Lewinson families, in 1947, was remembered by Janina in the following way:

> The exuberant person who greeted us at the door filled the heart with rapture and awe from the first sight. She was in her early fifties and very stout, wearing a full black dress adorned with a heavy amber necklace. Her long amber earrings framed a pale face of striking beauty. Her hair was slightly grey, her skin was fair and smooth and her wise bottle-green eyes stared at me searchingly. The way she moved and spoke contained a youthful vigor. (J. Bauman, 1988: 47)

Zofia Bauman was clearly the driving force of the family, and her son was her unique happiness, as is apparent from the letter to Zygmunt's daughters: 'For my mother I was her only companion for most of the day, and perhaps the only promise that life could be still more interesting and enjoyable in the future' (Bauman 1986/7: 16). From my own interview with Bauman, Zofia appears to have been an exemplary mother, well educated, open-minded, curious and full of life – and also an excellent cook.

> In the kitchen there was a stove with fireworks always hot, hot, my mother was cooking, and I was sitting at the kitchen table, doing homework, and at every stage of cooking she came to me: Taste this, 'honey'. 'Honey' tasted and grew fat. . . . As a boy, I was fat and suffered from it. I was ridiculed, it was easy to recognize. Obesity was not as prevalent as it is today. (Interview with Tomasz Kwaśniewski, *GW*, 21 November 2010)

In addition to the stigmatization caused by anti-Semitism, young Zygmunt's size subjected him to discrimination, though not to the same degree. Being 'fat' was nowhere near as stigmatizing as being a Jew: As he wrote to his daughters:

> Jewishness was to me almost a family matter – other members of the family were the only Jews I saw and knew about. This made my Jewishness a practical issue rather than a theoretical one. What made it more practical still was the world outside the family. Seldom did I hear other boys passing by in the street make comments on my

fatness; yet very few of them failed to notify me that they had duly noted my Jewishness. (Bauman 1986/7: 11)

For all that, as an exception in a Catholic school and city, his situation was 'secure and in a curious way pleasurable. To my schoolmates, I was "our own Jew" and "our own fatty" which gave them duties along with rights. . . . I did not feel victimized or even singled out for special treatment' (Bauman 1986/7: 18).

If Bauman didn't feel victimized in the primary school, this is because his teachers liked him and encouraged his good progress. Already in the first years of schooling, Bauman coached weaker pupils. However, due to his particular status (Jew), he was excluded from the after-school activities, because they were organized by the Catholic Church. Young Zygmunt sought the classical escape for lonely, persecuted children: books. As the future author of over eighty books wrote: 'Books, which for many years were my only friends, I borrowed from a library a few blocks away. The "Association for Popular Reading" was a non-profit organization aimed at making books accessible to people who could not afford to buy them' (Bauman 1986/7: 15).

The activity of intense reading was to characterize Bauman throughout his life. He started out reading 'books for boys':

> everything written by Fennimore Cooper, Jack London, Zane Grey, Karl May, Jules Verne, Robert Louis Stevenson, Aleksandre Dumas – from among Polish authors, Kornel Makuszyński. Later – all or almost Polish classics, prose and poetry (Mickiewicz, Prus, Sienkiewicz, Żeromski, Orzeszkowa, Słowacki etc.). Two or three years before the escape from Poznań I bid farewell to children's literature. Victor Hugo, Charles Dickens and Lev Tolstoy were my new meals for starters. (From letter to Keith Tester, 2015/16)

Whenever circumstances allowed, he read – intensively, perhaps even compulsively – in a way that his father had shown him by example: as an escape from a life that hurt too much. Love for books was a precious legacy from both parents, who, while poorly matched, were united in their love of literature. As a child, he watched his parents reading for long hours with great pleasure. Bauman's parents educated him in the value of books through their own love of them.

Books inspire dreams, and, like all children, Zygmunt had dreams about his future. Responding to Tomasz Kwaśniewski, Bauman said:

> I had very ambitious plans because I wanted to be a cosmologist or a cosmonaut.

T.K. – You wanted to fly?
Z.B. – To explore, to understand how it all came about, where it came from.[4]

Zygmunt dreamed to escape from the difficult reality of being a 'chosen person' – a stigmatized child whom the school would not reward for his abilities or results, almost all of whose childhood companions were the gangsters who accompanied him, and who was condemned to loneliness by his origins. He also dreamed about having a dog – a dream common to only children and those with much older siblings. His parents refused out of concern for his safety. If he had a dog, he would have a best friend, but daily walks, even close to their home, would expose him more frequently to anti-Semitic attacks, they reasoned, in refusing his request.[5]

As a Jew, Zygmunt was in an exceptional situation. The city's Jewish children mostly lived around Wielka Street, in the city centre. Spacial segregation was typical for most Polish cities as a consequence of earlier laws that limited where Jews could live, or traditional settlement patterns that enabled religious Jews to walk on the Sabbath to their synagogues, religious schools, shops and other institutions. In Poznań's Jewish district, children attended religious Cheder and Yeshivah schools – there were no secular Jewish schools like those that existed in cities such as Łódź or Warsaw, which had a network of CISZO schools[6] created and run by the Jewish socialist party, the BUND.[7] It supported the language and culture of Yiddish as the native language of the country's 3 million Jews. 'Mathematics, literature, history, life sciences and other classes in my school were taught in Yiddish', recalled Włodzimierz Szer,[8] born in 1924 in Warsaw: 'Every day there were also lessons in the Polish language' (Szer, 2013: 20–1).

Jewish children attending this kind of school, of course, studied in an atmosphere free of danger, discrimination and humiliation. This was the experience of Marian Turski,[9] a year younger than Bauman, who attended the best school in Łódź, a religious Jewish middle school that drew from an elite population. There was certainly anti-Semitism in Łódź and Warsaw, Turski recalled, but 'we never had such problems at school!' Most Polish students of Jewish origin lived and studied surrounded by other pupils, neighbours and teachers who belonged to their community.[10]

As for Bauman, he accepted the differential treatment as his reality, a kind of higher law structuring the life of a Jew. His teachers recognized his scholarly skills, to the point that they asked Zygmunt to coach weaker students. This was a positive aspect of that reality, an encouragement and positive recognition. And Bauman liked school, despite its dark sides. That situation would change after he finished primary school in June 1938. Over the following summer, the Bauman family experienced a significant change. Zygmunt took entrance exams for the gymnasium, and his sister Tosia (the diminutive for 'Tova') emigrated to Palestine.

Zygmunt's sister: Teofila – Tosia – Tova and her generation's destiny

'When I was born, both my parents seem to have been overwhelmed with joy, which filled my almost seven-years-older sister with despair', Bauman would write. 'She rightly sensed a dangerous competition in someone who was both male and younger (in all probability, the youngest) child. She did not relish sharing the heretofore undivided attention of the parents. As it turned out, her worst premonitions came true. Their attention remained undivided, only it now turned the other way' (Bauman, 1986/7: 10).

This was a typical story of a second child's arrival in a family organized around an only child. In many cultures, when the second child is a boy, and the first a girl, the girl enters a difficult situation, and so it was with Tosia: 'She [Bauman's mother] did not invest much hope in my sister; my sister was a girl, the only thing a girl could look forward to was a good marriage' (Bauman, 1986/7: 12–13).

Teofila, whom everyone in the family called Tosia, graduated in 1938 from gardening school, one of the trade schools organized to prepare young Jews for life in a kibbutz by Zionist community groups like ORT[11] (Gezelshaft tsu farshpraytn meloche un erf-arbeyt tsvishn yidn), Hechaluc[12] and Gordonia.[13] It was growing difficult to leave Poland at the time. Candidates for *Aliyah* were numerous, and the number of visas to Palestine was limited; emigration to the United States, Canada and France was also difficult without independent wealth or major support from a relative abroad. And, of course, after 1935 the massive exodus of German Jews had constituted a major element of immigration to those countries, making it difficult for others to find a foothold.

Young people like Teofila–Tova–Tosia, 19 at the time, lacked economic options in Poland. Bauman's sister finished her programme in gardening a year after the Polish Association of Gardeners in Warsaw concluded its May 1937 meeting with two resolutions: introducing a requirement[14] that accredited Polish gardeners be 'Aryan'; and requiring Polish gardeners to renounce the purchase or sale of products from or to Jews. In any case, there were no Jews enrolled in the gardeners' association (Kłodź, 2015: 803–4). Teofila Bauman could not hope for a place in the gardening profession, obviously; nor was there any place for her in Polish universities, had she desired to pursue her education there – not because she was a woman, but because she was a Jew. No Poznań high school would provide a diploma that enabled a Jewish student to attend university, and even those with such a diploma would not enter Poznań University, which strictly imposed a *numerus nullus* rule,[15] whereby not a single Jew was accepted for study.

While we generally think of the university world as a place of freedom and struggles for human rights, Polish universities, beginning in the 1920s, were arenas of repression. Prominent positions in their student organizations and faculty were held by extreme-right, fascist and anti-Semitic groups. Reaction to the anti-Semitic wave inside the Jewish community was multifaceted.[16] The limitation of Jewish presence in the universities was a cause of important political struggles at the Ministry of Higher Education, in Parliament, at the universities and inside various political groups.[17] Racist rules were progressively implemented throughout the late 1920s and the 1930s, with the situation becoming extremely tense after the death in 1935 of Piłsudski, the popular Polish leader who was strongly opposed to Dmowski's Endecja. Piłsudski's death cleared the way for the domination of Endecja and its affiliated Związek Akademicki Młodzież Wszechpolska (All-Polish Youth), which transformed Polish higher learning into a largely anti-Semitic environment. At this time, collaborations with German universities were strong, and Polish universities often hosted 'personalities', such as Hans Frank or Joseph Goebbels (both gave speeches at Warsaw University). The manifestations of fascism and anti-Semitism were both institutional and personal, with the hostility extending to other minorities such as Ukrainians (Hnatiuk, 2016). Allegiance to the anti-Semitic cause, among students, was signified by the wearing of a green ribbon (an action organized by the Green Ribbon League: Liga Zielonej Wstążki), which showed that the wearer was not a Jew and enforced the 'ghetto bench' – separate spaces for Jew and non-Jews, with Jews forced to stand while Christian students were sitting).[18]

The university administration, meanwhile, put a special stamp on the identity papers of Jews, and fraternities were ethnically exclusive (Aleksiun, 2014: 126). University rectors imposed the segregationist laws, and most professors were not opposed to their implementation. However, especially in the late 1930s, there were some examples of individual and collective acts of resistance to these racist regulations by non-Jewish students and faculty. Protest letters against the ghetto bench were signed by some faculty members (Markiewicz, 2004: 109–10),[19] while other professors,[20] and the rector of Lviv University, Stanisław Kulczyński, refused to sit while Jewish students were standing, or refused to begin their classes while the racist rules were imposed. Some non-Jewish students tried to protect their Jewish colleagues and 'pro-Jewish' professors,[21] both of whom – along with the students they sought to protect – were frequently the targets of beatings and other pressures from the majority of students. Riots broke out at several universities, forcing rectors to close these institutions in order to restore peace (Aleksiun, 2014). The price of maintaining the peace, however, was generally the enforcement of racist regulations. *Numerus clausus* limited access of Jews to the most popular faculties, with enrolment expected to reflect their proportion in the general population. Medical studies were particularly difficult to follow, even for those lucky enough to be enrolled, because of a rule requiring 'ethnical-religious' separation in anatomy–physiology courses (Jews weren't allowed to dissect 'Christian' bodies) (Maramorosch, 2015). Not surprisingly, the huge majority of Polish Jews studied abroad. France, Switzerland, Belgium and even Austria were major destinations before Nazi occupation.

In Poznań, after several student protests (November 1931, March 1933), *numerus nullus* was imposed and the university space was 'cleansed' of Jews. These events and troublesome times at the university strongly influenced the whole educational sector. The gymnasia, or high schools, also implemented pro-Aryan rules. Bauman recalled the climate of anti-Semitism fifty years later, in the following way:

> In the years immediately preceding the war, anti-Semitism grew more venomous and pervasive. . . . We read of mounting physical violence, of the beatings of Jewish students in the universities, of mini-pogroms in a rising number of rural areas and small provincial towns, of self-styled fascist troopers marching through the Jewish shtetls, watched over rather apathetically by police not particularly eager to be involved. (Bauman, 1986/7: 13–14)

This was the situation at the moment when Teofila Bauman emigrated. She had no dowry, as Zygmunt's parents' financial situation did not allow them to spare any money. According to accounts by her relatives, Teofila had no interest in further pursuing an education. Following the tradition of the time (all Zofia's sisters had been married off through arrangements), Zofia started to look for a husband,[22] and initially found a wealthy widower with two children who were older than Tosia. He was an old German Jew, fluent in German and Yiddish but speaking Polish poorly, who owned land in southern Poland. Tosia found the arrangement distasteful, and her mother agreed. The search for a husband resumed, this time with a happy ending – true love.

In the summer of 1938, the National Exposition took place in Poznań, and the Baumans rented their flat near the fairgrounds (today the location of the Poznań International Fair) to a young man who came from Palestine for business. Tosia and her future husband immediately fell in love, and she departed almost immediately to marry him in Palestine, returning with husband and baby girl (and pregnant with another child) in August 1939. Thanks to their British passports, Tosia and her family were able to flee Poland when the war began some weeks later.

Bauman recounts the story in his private manuscript; a slightly different version appears in some of his official postwar documents. In the CV Bauman provided in 1949 as part of his application to join the Communist Party, he states:

> my parents made her [Tosia] leave Poland for Palestine, making use of the chance visit by a Palestinian citizen, Barzilay Yedidya – Mizrachi.[23] She married him and today she is still in Palestine, where she works in the laboratory of the Givat Brenner fruit cannery. She divorced her first husband and is the wife of a tractor driver, Gabrieli. She became a Zionist-chauvinist, in the process stirring up nostalgic feelings about a Jewish state in my father.[24]

A year later, in an Army questionnaire, Bauman added: 'she was Zionist and probably joined the Mapai' (a socialist and peace-oriented group that was popular among Polish-Jewish emigrants in the late 1930s) (Zygmunt Bauman – Ankieta specjalna, 1950).[25]

Zygmunt, meanwhile, remained in Poznań to study for high school exams: 'The anxiety about the outcome of the entrance examinations came on the top of my sister's whirlwind romance, marriage, and abrupt departure. It was a long, hot, and consequential summer' (Bauman, 1986/7: 19).

Gymnasium on the ghetto bench

Public primary schools in Poland in the 1930s accepted minority children, but secondary schools, following the universities' example, applied selective rules. Prior to World War II, secondary schooling in Poland was intended to educate the middle classes for careers in the professions or business. The gymnasia were institutions for a select population. However, Jewish students in state gymnasia experienced many aspects of *numerus clausus*, as well as social ostracism and anti-Semitism expressed openly by teachers and classmates (Aleksiun, 2014: 111, note 3).

In Poznań, only two schools (in his manuscript, Zygmunt Bauman speaks of knowing only one) were open to Jewish pupils. Candidates had to pass very rigorous exams to get into them.

> My parents could hardly afford the high fees of a gymnasium . . . but there was not a moment of doubt that they would make any sacrifice to see me through. So the true problem was to get admitted. . . . The Berger State Gymnasium was the only secondary school which settled

for numerus clausus – confining the number of Jewish pupils so that it
would not exceed the percentage of Jews in the total population of the
area. In Poznan conditions, this meant less than one percent. I graduated from my primary school with excellent marks, but the chances of
admission were still very slim indeed. . . . First came written exams in
Polish literature and in mathematics. The candidates reaching the top
marks in both were to be admitted; the rest had to stand competitive
oral examinations. I attended both written examinations. A week later
my turn at the orals had arrived. (Bauman, 1986/7: 19–20)

Due to the enormous stress, Bauman responded poorly to the
teacher who conducted his interrogation, and was almost rejected,
when suddenly the director of the gymnasium announced that both
written exams were excellent and Zygmunt had already been admitted. The emotions caused by this situation remained alive even fifty
years later: 'The director's words, the examiner's suddenly sour and
disappointed face, the deafening pounding of my heart, the tears
of my mother who waited, half alive, outside – all melted into the
experience of an excruciating happiness; the happiest memory of my
childhood years. My first achievement – by my efforts alone, and
against overwhelming, indomitable odds' (Bauman 1986/7: 19–20).
   So Zygmunt Bauman passed through the 'eye of the needle' and
became one of the rare Jewish students enrolled in a state gymnasium in Poznań. According to the Berger Gymnasium's school
archives,[26] five of the forty-nine students in the 1938–9 class were
Jewish, or 10 per cent, the average proportion of 'Jews to Poles' in
the country (to use terminology from the interwar period). Three
of the five Jewish students flunked their final exams in the first class
and had to repeat the year, leaving only Zygmunt and one other
Jewish student in his class at the Berger Gymnasium.
   In the 1930s, Berger was considered the best secondary school for
boys in Poznań and the whole Wielkopolska region. According to
its originating document, written by founder Gotthilf Berger, the
school was supposed to accept students without regard to their ethnicity and religion. We can imagine how happy Zygmunt's parents
were that their son was part of this elite institution. He was happy,
too, but quickly learned that acceptance into the school hadn't
altered his place in the student body.

A few weeks later the great day came. Proudly donning my Berger
Gymnasium's cap, this visible and indisputable pass to the ranks of
the gloried Polish intelligentsia, I arrived at the door of the first form.
I had no time to cross it before I was submerged in an avalanche of
kicks and punches. Pushed and pulled from all sides, I lost control
over my legs and found myself moving – moved, rather – toward the
distant left rear corner of the room. Someone's arms thrust me finally

on the last bench. 'Here is your place, Jew! And don't you dare look elsewhere.'

It took a few minutes to come round – all the more so, as the din in the classroom continued unabated. Only when I recovered my senses did I notice that I was not to be alone in the ghetto to which I had been assigned. . . . Four pairs of eyes filled with tears of shame, trying not to look in the other eyes, who witnessed their humiliation. . . . I belonged now to a group, to a category, which could be classified and branded and summarily treated. (Bauman, 1986/7: 20–1)

Bauman was no longer alone in his situation; now he was joined by other young dreamers. The first day's reception, and what followed, was meant to cut them down to size, to subdue and shame them:

As far as I am aware, not one of our teachers objected to our forceful confinement to a ghetto. Some took care to manifest their approval by selecting the residents of the ghetto for special treatment. . . . The teacher of geography made it publicly known that knowledge possessed by the Jews must have been obtained in a not entirely honest way and thus took care to mark it lower than similar knowledge revealed by non-Jewish pupils. . . . Some other teachers, however, studiously disavowed the invisible ghetto walls. One or two – the teacher of history in particular – seemed to be ashamed to teach in a classroom so divided. The gradation of teachers' attitudes was roughly replicated among the pupils. No one however, either among the teachers or among our non-Jewish classmates, tried to defy the 'facts of life'. The division was solid and permanent, as those who wished it to remain so acted, while those who did not like it – watched. (Bauman 1986/7: 24–5)

The solid and permanent division was reflected in the grading in this select institution, in which being promoted to the next year was a challenge. Eight of the forty-nine students in Bauman's class did not finish the first year (one because of bad health, another for financial reasons), and five dropped out the following year. The average grade, on a scale of 1 to 5, was 3 – only six students received a 4, or 'good' grade, and only one obtained a 5. Zygmunt Bauman's score was the second-highest in his class. And yet, he believed, his teachers discriminated against him. One explained to Zygmunt that he would have liked to give him the best grade, since he deserved it, but 'you understand very well that with your origin it is impossible. You cannot be the best in the class. This place is reserved for a Polish kid.'[27]

Grade by grade and subject by subject, comparing Bauman's results with those of his top competitor bears out this statement.

The first in the class, Kazimierz Skrzypczak, obtained an average grade of 4.4, while Zygmunt received a 4.0. Skrzypczak led the class at the end of the year in all subjects except gym, drawing and manual work. Bauman was unable to get the best grade in religion (which focused on Catholicism), and in geography and drawing he received a 4.0. It is clear that his geography teacher believed that Jewish students did not acquire their knowledge in a 'totally honest way' – he evaluated Zygmunt's progress suspiciously, although Zygmunt's grade in 'behavior' belied such an accusation: he received the maximum grade of 5. He received perfect marks also in Polish language and history, and in Latin, biology and mathematics. At age 14, Bauman started to study English, and got the best grade during two semesters in the language that would become his third fluent tongue several years later. In manual works and gymnastics, he received a 3 – confirming his status as a nerdy child. Everyone seemed to know quite well that, however well you did your work, if you were a Jew you would never be first in the class.

This was a 'natural fact of life' (as Bauman cynically described this permanent discrimination), part of the negative picture of the Jewish community transmitted by Polish schools. As the historian Kamil Kijak wrote, 'In the textbooks for the youngest public school pupils, national minorities did not appear at all. In the textbooks for the older classes, the Jews were presented in an unequivocally nega-tive way . . . The Jew was unequivocally a stranger. These texts did not include Jews as ordinary citizens or full members of a common fatherland' (Kijak, 2010: 176).

In secondary school, Bauman's situation simultaneously improved and worsened. It worsened because the environment inside the school was much more aggressive. It improved because a few other teenagers shared his identity – a small group of 'others' with whom to share stigmatization, isolation and discriminatory treatment. Bauman recalled fifty years later: 'Being now a member of [a] group, of a category, sharing my predicament with others in a "preordained" way that neither they nor I could challenge, changed my life in a most radical fashion. Suddenly, I stopped being a soli-tary case, a person left to my own devices and able to rely on none but myself' (Bauman, 1986/7: 25).

At 13 years old, after passing with excellence a very competitive entrance exam to the elite school, Zygmunt needed to learn how to feel less human. Both the victims and aggressors learned from this destructive process, which prepared victims to receive the attacks, and taught the youths belonging to the dominant group that the people in the ghetto bench were less than human. It was a wide-spread practice – 'obvious', 'natural'. Racism followed the Jews at each step of their lives – from birth, through school, university, companies and institutions, in professional life – everywhere. Thus, it is not surprising that, during the years of German occupation, Jews suffered from the hostility or simple indifference of their neighbours. The process of transforming them into less-than-humans had started years before World War II and contributed to the Holocaust. Institutional racism spread daily, step by step[28] – bringing ever-tightening new restrictions.

This all-pervading and deadly illness did not poison only Polish society – several countries in Europe were under the charm of fascist and nationalist ideologies. Each of them – Germany, Italy, Spain, Poland, Rumania, Hungary – dreamed of a great Homeland composed of a 'pure' race of a single ethnicity. This was the silly dream that resulted in World War II. In Poznań, acts of protest against this inhuman treatment were rare and weak. And in the autumn of 1938, especially after Kristallnacht,[29] the treatment grew worse. As thousands of German Jews fled the country, the German government expelled several thousand Polish Jews across the German–Polish border, where most of them stayed in prison-like refugee camps in Zbąszynek. For several months, beginning in October 1938, the Polish government put up obstacles against receiving this population, arguing that they were not genuine Polish citizens because of their Jewishness.[30] The anti-Semitic press regurgitated the anti-Semitic climate in Polish towns and cities: there was a steady flow of stories about the camps at Zbąszynek, which were described as the start of a fearful, massive wave of Polish-German-Jewish refugees, in the context of high unemployment and tax increases. In Poznań, the closest Polish city to Zbąszynek, the ambience was particularly unfriendly for non-Catholic Poles. The atmosphere at the Berger Gymnasium reflected the environment around it – anti-Semitic, racist treatments were 'obvious'; a great majority of the people (both persecutors and persecuted) saw them as normal.

This was a hard life lesson that Zygmunt Bauman learned early – one's fellow students and teachers could be racist and discriminatory. Włodzimierz Szer, enrolled in a secular Jewish school in Warsaw, and Marian Turski, enrolled in religious school in Łódź, were spared this feeling early in their lives, as were many young Polish Jews. Zygmunt Bauman, however, felt his minority origins practically from birth. However, in the final months of his life in Poznań, he had at least met his reference group and could share similar experiences with friends who also felt 'less human' at school – people with whom he could share dreams of a future without racial discrimination.

Belonging – a *szomer* in Hashomer Hatzair

The Hashomer Hatzair (Hebrew: Young Guard) was one of the most influential Zionist organizations in the interwar period, although it did not aspire to become a mass movement. Its members, *szomer*, were obliged to work for the implementation of the Zionist program by promoting Jewish national funds, mastering the Hebrew language and finally making alija, followed by work on collective farms (kibbutzim) in Palestine. Hashomer Hatzair saw itself as raising the national vanguard of Jews by creating close friendships and a sense of brotherhood and family ties among its members. (Aleksiun, 2002: 33)

Bauman had no need to replace his family, but he was certainly seeking friendship and, like most teenagers – especially those who were outcasts in school – a peer group.[31] And so it was that Zygmunt enrolled in the Zionist youth organization that met in a large hall in an unused synagogue at the corner of Dominikańska and Szewska streets. It was a

shoddy room in one of the buildings quietly living out their old age in the few streets left of the old Jewish quarter.[32] Inside that room, I found several boys and girls of more or less my age. Together, they constituted the Poznan branch of Hashomer Hatzair. The rest was a maelstrom. I was now in a group that accepted me for no reason other than its inability to get rid of me. The other boys and girls were not 'special cases' . . . I was not a special case anymore. We talked, we quarreled, we danced, we fought, we behaved in a way I thought was reserved only for normal people, of which I evidently was not one. Inside these flaking walls I was all I could not be outside. I ate the forbidden fruit of the tree of freedom, and it dawned upon me that life could be different than it was – not just on two afternoons every week.
Suddenly, the world did not look unshakeable and preordained. Neither did the choice seem, as it had before, 'take it or leave it'. I felt I would not take it anymore. And I did not intend to leave it. (Bauman, 1986/7: 25)

The group gave Bauman power, restored dignity, agency and dreams. It filtered into his entire attitude towards the future, and the life around him. From now on, racist treatment would no longer be 'natural' – it would be something to change, to fix, to abolish. And the changes would be made by the members of a young and dynamic organization. This feeling was shared by other *szomers* who felt liberated by these meetings from the weight of tremendous discrimination. Being a part of a Jewish religious community was a different experience. Bauman got his bar mitzvah,[33] but that was considered a basic ritual – nothing specific. Hashomer Hatzair was what shaped his feelings of belonging.

'We held meetings, delivered presentations and had a stream of visitors who came to lecture or speak with us from szomer friend groups from Włocławek, Warsaw or Kalisz', recalled another *szomer* from Bauman's group, the daughter of a successful Poznanian businessman:

> There were about a hundred people, all young people. We danced the hora, girls and boys, singing and holding each other's arms, circling and stomping. . . . And here we were told about the situation of Jews in Palestine! There were lectures about our history and culture. Kibbutz letters came from those who had already gone there . . . it awoke a pride in me to be a Jew! . . . Up until now I had some connections to Jews whom I liked, but I had more friends among Polish women. Among *szomers*, I began to identify myself as a Jew as such. I found myself among my peers and felt that I was one of them. I belonged somewhere. (Fira, in Niziołek and Kosakowska, 2016: 36)

'The world I wished to put in place of the existing one was conceived after the pattern of the <u>Hashomer Hatzair </u>branch', Bauman wrote:

> Looking back, I think it was the life we practiced, rather than the life we fantasized about, which sedimented in the lasting image of [a] just world, which from then on, and up to this day, I was to dream of, run after, mislead myself that I could find.
> This alluring world was given the name of Zion, yet I do not believe that the name referred to any particular geographically defined place. As far as I was concerned, Zion was located in Winiary woods, where for the first time in my life I had my own share of May Day delights in the secure company of my new friends. Zion was the curious world without bullies. A world in which people were liked or disliked for what they did rather than for what they were. In Zion people were equal unless they made themselves otherwise. There were no Jews and Gentiles, no rich and poor, no haves and have nots. Everyone had the right to be respected. (Bauman 1986/7: 25–6)

Hashomer Hatzair was a preparation for their future lives, a training ground for becoming active and creating a life instead of suffering through one, and it provided a lesson the *szomers* gained for ever, at least in Bauman's case. This was a turning point, a life, a durable transformation,[34] that gave Bauman a passion for changing the world to a better place, with a socialist orientation. The Hashomer Hatzair period also corresponded with a period of physical change for Bauman: he became a rangy young man, and was to remain so the rest of his life. Happiness, however, was short-lived. In September 1939, the war began.

'From my brief, barely half-a-year long Hashomer Hatzair experience, I emerged determined to change the world. And a socialist. And slim. Indeed during these fateful six months I lost all my fat. Soon after, I lost my home – forever. And my homeland – for the first time' (Bauman, 1986/7: 26).

3

The Fate of a War Refugee (1939–1944)

Poznań–Molodeczna

we had our Pal in the desert
we prayed to Him
we were scolding him
we were not His
chosen people
we were His only one

you had your own Gods
and you and you and you
but you liked ours
and He liked you such a tease

once He got promoted
you
in His name
persecute us

(Włodzimierz Holsztyński, 'Pal', 3 June 2008)

The outbreak of war

Polish Radio, Friday, 1 September 1939, 6.30 a.m.:

This is Warsaw, broadcasting to all Polish radio stations. This morning at 5:30 a.m., German troops crossed the Polish border, breaking the non-aggression pact. Several cities were bombed. In a moment you will hear a special message from the President of the Republic of Poland [Ignacy Mościcki]:[1] 'So, we are at war! Today, all other matters and issues become secondary. All of our public and private lives are switched onto a special track. We have entered a period of war. The nation's entire efforts must go in one direction. We are all soldiers. We must think about one thing only: fight until victory.'

Like all Polish families, the Baumans, enjoying a visit by Tosia and her husband and newborn daughter on a summer break from

Palestine, presumably listened to this message several times on that disastrous Friday morning. Like all of Poland, they had followed closely the news of tension along the Warsaw–Berlin line. At 8.30 a.m., they would have heard the air-raid sirens warning the city of Poznań that German planes were approaching.

The general mobilization, ordered on 30 August, sent the entire country into a frenzy of movement. Veterans tried to join their regiments, while some families fled the cities for the countryside, looking for a safe place to pass the 'war days'. Others tried desperately to return from their summer holidays in order to rejoin family members at home. Everywhere, mobs of people filled train stations, while cars and trucks and horse-drawn carts clogged the roads. Most Poles had been at least dimly aware that war was coming in the last days of August, and they tried to prepare for it, but most were foolishly overconfident. The war wouldn't last long, they thought. Poland would repel and drive out the German Army in a matter of days – perhaps weeks, certainly not months. Even the worst-case scenario predicted peace by Christmas. Why the great optimism? Because powerful allied countries – the United Kingdom and France – had promised to come to Poland's rescue if Hitler dared to violate its territory. The German Army would confront stiff resistance not only from the Polish Army, but from the West, with a massive attack by the British and French armies. The belief in this scenario was widespread and very strong. It explains why the civilian population only began its massive exodus eastward after bombs began falling on 1 September. Everyone was stunned by the aggressiveness of the German Army, by its efficiency, by the speed of its victorious advance and the power of the military on the battlefield – and its murderous attacks on unarmed civilians.

Poznań came under heavy bombardment that first day. At noon, thirty-one Heinkel He-111s, flying under cover from a Bf-109 fighter squadron, attacked the airport, the central train station, military barracks in Jeżyce, and bridges on the Warta River. The second raid occurred in the afternoon, and the third around dusk. The Bauman home was at the centre of this cyclone of violence. About 100 bombs fell on the railway station and on a factory producing military uniforms just two blocks from the Bauman home.

The next day, Marshal Edward Rydz-Śmigły, the military commander-in-chief, ordered a retreat to the east during a break from the bombing; soldiers, government officials and civilians, using a variety of transportation, fled Warsaw that day and the next. On 3 September, the UK and France declared war on Hitler over the attack, awakening hopes in many Poles. Yet the whole country was falling apart under the German *Blitzkrieg*. The last day when Polish trains ran with any regularity was 3 September, and the next day most bridges on the Warta were destroyed, rendering rail transport impossible.

The Baumans' experience of the first days of the invasion was the same as that of thousands of other Polish families. Maurycy Bauman was at home, but, at age 49, he was not concerned with the general mobilization. Among the Polish-Jewish population, only professional soldiers and officers (who were usually physicians) were mobilized. Jews were not considered Poles and were not expected to join the call-up.[2] Bauman had been preparing to enter his second year at the Berger Gymnasium on Monday, 4 September. The family escaped the day before.

He would describe this escape to his daughters:

> we left Poznan in . . . the night of September 2. We made our way to the station stealthily, in complete darkness, hiding in the doorways when a successive wave of enemy planes approached. We took only as much as we could carry in our hands. My sister lost the few belongings she had brought from Palestine; she had her daughter to carry.[3] (Bauman, 1986/7: 26)

'We did not pack. We fled!' Bauman would recall.[4] 'It was not far from our apartment to the train station. But what could we take with us?' Maurycy was in poor health and had a severe leg injury that made it difficult to walk. 'My mother and I – a very boyish boy – were responsible for carrying everything', Bauman recalled:

> We grabbed what was at hand and took the very last train that left Poznan. . . . My father was raised in such a Puritan spirit that he at first refused to take the train, because it was impossible to buy tickets. All the cashier windows were closed and we could not pay for our ride. He couldn't accept that. . . . his conscience would not allow him to travel without tickets. That is why we ended up on the last train. . . . We went by train only as far as Inowroclaw, because the tracks ahead were already destroyed. German planes were targeting the train stations and trains all the time. Very quickly, the trains stopped circulating. We might have lost our lives during this escape . . . because in Inowroclaw, my father did not want to leave the station until he found someone to pay for our journey up to then. So our escape was very dramatic.

'The bombers pursued our train all along the way', Bauman wrote in his manuscript:

> We stopped several times to scatter and hide beneath the tracks. Finally in Inowroclaw, a hundred miles away from Poznan, the train ground to its final halt. The tracks further east had been pulverized

and the railway network did not operate any more. The Inowroclaw station building lay in ruins. Emboldened by the total lack of resistance, German planes strafed the stuck trains with bullets. German pilots clearly enjoyed the chance to display their flying skills. They flew just a few yards above the ground, then drew whimsical loops and circles in the sky, only to dive again. Time and again they flew over so close that I'll wager I could see the malicious grin on the face of the pilot. (Bauman, 1986/7: 26–7)

'It was a nightmare', Bauman told me. 'Bands of German soldiers would pass us on the road and throw us into the ditches. This happened several times. There was no Auschwitz or Treblinka yet . . . but the mood was already quite unpleasant.'[5]

This last sentence was pronounced with tightened lips. The expression 'the mood was . . . quite unpleasant'[6] sounds ironic, but it was a way for Bauman to overcome a difficult, painful emotion from a traumatic event that occurred when he was a 14-year-old boy. He was forced to reconstruct a dramatic flight by masses of people: children, the elderly, women as well as men (most Polish men were still in the Army, trying to stop the German invasion),[7] the lame and the sick, some already injured, many in a state of shock because of the tremendous noise, with bombs falling all around and dying people crying and screaming.

Luftwaffe planes bombed in several waves, killing and injuring thousands. Panicked and defenceless, civilians tried to escape or hide in trenches or in forests. When they left their hiding places, Messerschmitts – German fighter planes – came in groups and, flying very close to the ground, strafed the fleeing people with machine guns. These were the pilots whose faces Zygmunt Bauman observed. This happened on many Polish roads in September 1939. The deadly performance of the Luftwaffe airmen caused incredible fear and panic. It was a unique, unforgettable experience, to be preyed upon by a merciless, powerful hunter. Time ran slowly for everyone who took part in this exodus. Any second could be the last. As a teenager, like all those escaping, Bauman witnessed death on a daily basis. 'Hundreds of thousands of people had experiences like this', Bauman told me, underlining a point he made many times in our discussion: 'There was nothing unusual about my case.'

From Inowroclaw, the family travelled in a peasant's horse cart to Włocławek, a distance of 65 kilometres. There:

my aunts seemed to have expected our arrival, though I cannot remember their joy at the news of our lucky escape. We were put in a flat vacated by a family who escaped further east, and left to our own care. Not that we were in control of our fate. The hard-pressed remnants of the defeated army rushed eastward – on horseback, on horse carriages, on foot. Soon the streets were empty of soldiers and an uncanny, frightening silence followed. And then the Germans came. On motorcycles, on trucks, in tanks. (Bauman, 1986/7: 27)

The first days of the war brought immediate and radical changes. The German Army advanced very fast and imposed new rules on the occupied territories with implacable power and terror – especially when it came to the Jewish population. Polish Catholics were not required to wear a cross or other stigmatizing signs on their clothes, as Polish Jews were. Włocławek was one of the first cities that imposed the 'yellow patch':

A few days later, my mother cut my yellow pajamas into pieces in order to sew triangles on the backs of our coats – the signs of our Jewish distinction now officially recognized by our new rulers. Sporting these signs, we now walked on the roadways – a few inches below the level of ordinary people, who walked, as before, on the sidewalks. (Bauman, 1986/7: 27)

After the years of invisible distinctions – being seated in restricted 'ghetto benches', having 'Jew' stamped in one's ID cards and student documents, having few or no options to study – it was time for Zygmunt Bauman to receive a proper label of discrimination that made persecution official and easy. The criminal treatment the German authorities imposed on Włocławek and its Jews ranged from physical harm to psychological degradation.[8] This was experienced first-hand by Bauman when his father was publicly humiliated by a German soldier.

The German invaders' sadistic activities frequently included cutting off the beards of Orthodox Jews. But one did not have to be an Orthodox Jew to be singled out for ill-treatment. Bauman began his account to me of his father's humiliation with a general psychological statement, a remark that distanced the experience from himself:

It has been described a thousand times, how the child regards his father as an omnipotent god and suddenly sees him humiliated, collapsing his entire worldview. This happened to me when the Germans ordered my father to pick up dirt from the street – with bare hands. They didn't give him a . . . shovel or spade . . . As I saw it, I said that I could not stay there. And this was lucky . . . because everything could have been completely different.

This last part of the sentence is heavy with significance, because almost everyone who belonged to the Jewish community in Włocławek in September 1939 perished in the Holocaust.

Bauman's sister Tosia, her husband and her baby daughter were among the lucky ones. Their escape, which began when they boarded a train for Berlin from Włocławek, coincided with the bitter experience of his father's humiliation, which may partly explain why Bauman gave such a brief description of it in our interview. Bauman seemed truly to struggle with this memory, more than perhaps any of the other dramatic events of his life. He delivered the last sentence with a sardonic curl of a smile, as if suppressing a bitter joke, which he then masked with the ritual gesture of preparing his pipe. Bauman preferred to wave off this burning memory with a dismissive gesture and words to the effect that such were the wartime experiences of Poles. But, of course, not all Poles experienced this particular variety of suffering.

'And so, three Jews with yellow triangles on their backs saw off at the Wloclawek station three Jews without badges', Bauman wrote in the letter to his daughters:

> Well, they did not exactly see the train departing. Just before my sister, with her daughter in her arms and her husband at her side, was showed (with a lot of bowing and saluting) into the carriage reserved for German officers, a German patrolman pointed his finger at my father: You, Jew, come here and sweep this filthy platform clean! With his back to the train taking his daughter away, tears in his eyes, his hands loaded with soggy papers and moldy leftovers of soldiers' snacks, kept on the move by the prodding of the rifle butt – this was the image of my father which my sister took with her on her journey to what was now her only home. (Bauman, 1986/7: 28)

The family was split into two parts: Tosia with her husband and daughter left Poland and returned to their home in Palestine, while Zygmunt and his parents returned to their relative's home in Włocławek – for the moment. 'I remember returning to our flat shattered, but desperate: I would not stay here anymore', wrote Bauman in his manuscript. His father wished to wait for the end of the war in the small Jewish town like Izbica – his birthplace – but Zygmunt strongly opposed this idea:

> I remember everything in me militating against this idea. A child's instinct? A premonition? The neck suddenly hardened during the evenings spent in the Hashomer Hatzair room? A new conviction that the world could be better, and that one ought to help it to be such? I do not remember any thought – just the feelings. The feelings were strong, however. So strong, as a matter of fact, that they did prevail in the end over my father's nostalgic solution. And thus my parents survived the war. And I am writing these words, forty-odd years after Hitler's death. (Bauman, 1986/7: 28–9)

The last sentence is reminiscent of many accounts of survivors of Nazi persecution. They are words of grace, a retrospective grace – they were condemned, yet by some miracle here they are, still alive many years later, while the personification of their misfortune has been dead for decades. Such facts help the survivors believe in a kind of final justice . . . a happy ending to an impossible story. Yet at the time, casting about for an improvement of their situation in Włocławek, there was no such thing as a 'good' strategy. No one could know what would happen.

The Baumans organized their escape. Zofia's family lent them money for hiring a peasant driver, a pair of horses, a horse cart. Everything was ready by mid-October. The Baumans went toward the eastern border.

The trip did not really follow the initial plan, but the urgency of departure was clear as the Nazis occupied Włocławek: 'the first days of their [the Nazis'] stay there were so terrible that I threw a fit with my parents, saying that I did not want to stay'.[9] And so the family left Włocławek, in a wagon at first, but the horses were already near death[10] and they died during the trip, near Mława, already under German control, and the Baumans continued on foot. 'I did a lot of walking in my youth', Bauman said.

They were part of a large group that slowly walked from cottage to cottage, using secondary roads to avoid the attention of German soldiers. They were on their own. No Red Cross or any other group brought them medicine or clothing or anything to eat. Each family found shelter and food on its own:

We bought food from the peasants. That was my mother's job. We didn't have food stamps yet (later, and in the postwar period, the Polish government introduced food stamps). Peasants would sell you food, but they preferred to barter for goods. But that was actually a positive thing – the longer we walked, the fewer the possessions we had to carry![11]

After reaching the area near the border with Soviet-occupied Poland, Bauman's family waited for the opportunity to cross clandestinely. This was some weeks after the Soviet invasion of Poland's eastern territories, which began on 17 September and caused plans for the reorganization of Polish defences to be aborted. Under the Molotov–Ribbentrop pact, the Soviets annexed the eastern territories, creating a new geopolitical situation with a Soviet–German border (or demarcation line). The Polish state never signed an agreement of capitulation, though the mayors of some cities did (Warsaw capitulated on 25 September). With no puppet government, and most Polish leaders fleeing to London, the Soviets and Germans simply enlarged their territories, making Poland disappear from the map of Europe.

To reach the closest point on the new border with the Soviet
Union, Bauman's family had to cross about 300 kilometres, from
Włocławek to Wojciechowice – a journey that took two weeks.

> By the end of October we finally arrived at Wojciechowice – a tiny
> village a few hundred yards from the frontier, which now ran between
> Ostrołęka (on the German side) and Łomża (on the Russian side). We
> rented a room in a peasant farmhouse. We were lucky to find one, as
> all the buildings in the village were filled to the brim with other refu-
> gees like us, hoping to cross the border. (Bauman, 1986/7: 29)

Amid the confusion and uncertainty, and some continued fighting
with Polish forces, the weather grew cooler and it became more and
more difficult to cross the new border secretly.

The family's odyssey crossing into the Soviet sector was as dramatic as the earlier part of their journey:

> By the time we reached the border, the Russians had stopped rou-
> tinely allowing people to enter. Before then, they had let anyone in.
> ... My father was self-educated, but well educated, and he spoke
> German very well.[12] At that moment there was a Wehrmacht gar-
> rison in Wojciechowice. My father met a German captain – a very
> educated guy – and they spoke several times in a really friendly way.[13]
> This captain was uncomfortable because he couldn't help us, he said.
> The Russians weren't accepting refugees because too many people
> had gathered in Wojciechowice trying to cross. But he promised to
> find a solution by meeting 'the commandant of the other side of
> the river'. This was exactly how he put it! 'Perhaps', he said, 'we
> can reach an agreement and the Russian will let you in'. It was very
> interesting – the three of us sat on the German side of the river
> and watched 'our' captain drive his very elegantly furnished car to
> the exact middle of the bridge, where he stopped. I believe it was
> a real bridge, not a pontoon. And on the other side he met the
> *Krasnarmiejcy* [Red Army soldiers]. Their rifles hung from strings
> and of course they came on foot. They met halfway. I have of course
> no idea what they said to one another, but the captain returned and
> told my father, 'Unfortunately they have orders to not to let people
> in, and we can do nothing.'[14]

Although the crossing attempt failed, Bauman was impressed by
the Red Army soldiers he saw for the first time in his life: 'They
started on a leisurely walk in our direction; the closer they came,
the better we saw their ill-fitted uniforms, loosely hanging buttons,
unpolished and well-worn shoes. They looked like angels to me. Or
messengers of Zion' (Bauman, 1986/7: 30). However angelic they
looked, the soldiers would not let the family enter Soviet territory.

That was bad news, but it did not discourage Zofia. 'As opposed to my father, my mother was a very feisty person', Bauman recalled:

> She said: 'No, I won't accept that so easily! I will go to the German commander in Ostrołęka!' You should understand that my mother looked like a local peasant woman – she was dressed the same as all these women from small villages, and she joined with a real local peasant woman who was headed to the market at Ostrołęka.
>
> That very same day, after my mother had left to try to see the commandant in Ostrołęka to ask him to enable our passage – which by the way, was an effort of terrible naïveté, completely idiotic in fact – the Wehrmacht captain came to my father and said: 'Sir, I have nothing to do with this decision, but I came to tell you that we are being withdrawn (the Wehrmacht was being liberated from its border control duty) and will be replaced today by Grenzschutz – so it may get very bad for you.'[15]

Bauman continued:

> My father and I were there but my mother was gone. It was a terrible situation because we didn't know when she would be back. ... We only later learned that exactly the same time she entered that city – Ostrołęka – the refugees from there and from the surroundings, everyone who was waiting to cross the border, were rounded up by Grenzschutz and driven to Ostrów Mazowiecka, where the first mass execution in Poland occurred.

If the family had remained together, as it turned out, they probably would all have died. A thread of unlikely coincidences saved all of their lives.

Bauman's mother would miraculously escape death – or perhaps not so miraculously:

> My mother's beauty was always Slavic rather than Jewish. Now, roughly dressed and with an enormous shawl around her head, she was virtually indistinguishable from the peasant women. She removed the only trace of her Jewishness – the yellow triangle – and coaxed our landlady, whom she befriended from the first day, to harness a horse and drive her to Ostroleka, where she hoped to use her power of persuasion to enlist the cooperation of the German district commandant.

Looks were perhaps the decisive element in being caught or escaping, because the predators were looking for a certain type. Luckily for Zofia Bauman, she did not have the type of beauty that corresponded to that of stereotypical Jewish women: the black hair and dark almond-shaped eyes. Her features were more typically 'Aryan', and she blended in with the peasant wives come to Ostrołęka to exchange goods at the weekly market.

Father and son also survived, thanks to a certain stubbornness. As the captain had warned, the Grenzschutz, or border control, took over the German side of the frontier and

> shortly afterwards we heard a loud command reverberating through the village: 'Alle Juden raus!' From houses, barns and stables, men, women and children emerged, pushed and kicked by soldiers in strange uniforms towards the building of the village chief. When we joined the crowd, we heard the Grenzschutz officer announcing that we were to be transported to Ostrow Mazowiecka, where all Jews wishing to pass to the Russian side were gathering. . . . We could not go to Ostrów. We could not go anywhere, as long as mother was away. We had to wait for her return. I did not discuss this with my father, yet I knew he thought the same. We understood each other without words as we sneaked behind the nearest building and ran towards the woods that stretched over both sides of the border. Soon we saw a solitary Russian border guard, sitting on a wooden log, watching birds and humming, rifle lying on the ground at his feet. Gasping for breath, my father declared: 'I am here to wait for my wife. I am not going anywhere until she comes.' I think this was the longest day of my life. (Bauman 1986/7: 31)

The soldiers who did the killing in Ostrów Mazowiecka, which was 30 kilometres south of Ostrołęka, already had extensive experience of persecuting civilians. But, on 11 November, they killed about 600 Jews (Bartniczak, 1972: 63), a mass execution of local people and refugees who were waiting, like the Baumans, for an opportunity to cross the border.

Bauman and his father were separated from the border by a small river and a 'floating meadow',[16] and Bauman got the idea that they should go to sit in the meadow and wait for his mother to return. There was no one there at all, but

> after a while, a healthy-looking chubby man appeared, a *kolkhoznik* (Soviet farmer), with a rifle on a rope, and he started to babble. My father spoke a little Russian, but . . . he was fluent in German and not Russian. I didn't speak a word of it. So it was difficult conversation, but he was so good-natured. And he said he must take us to his village, where a warm bed and some food were waiting for us. I was terribly opposed to the idea, but he had the rifle on the rope, and we followed him.[17]

It was after 2 p.m. in the afternoon, already starting to turn dark at this time of year. They followed the farmer to his country house

and sat down outside until the man offered to take them to his commander's office to find them a place to stay.

> We followed him, walking in complete darkness – me, my father, and
> this soldier . . . just the three of us. And suddenly . . . I didn't know
> the local geography, but somehow I felt that he was taking us back
> to the German side. In the spur of the moment I made an immediate
> decision: I lay down on the ground, and I began to cry out in what I
> imagined was Russian. Even now I remember what I said: 'Maja mat
> tut – maja mat tut' ['My mother is here!']. I lay on the ground and
> refused to go any further. And this good man really did not know
> what to do with us. He couldn't take us on his back. He shot up a
> flare but nothing happened. So he joined us, sitting on some sort of
> rubble pile in the middle of the field. We waited. . . . Then suddenly,
> a Soviet officer rode up on a foamy horse and exchanged some words
> with the farmer, then spurred his horse forward, trying to scare us. I
> was screaming. My father was shaking. But the officer realized that it
> was all for naught.[18]

Though terrified, Zygmunt and his father stayed rooted to the
spot. They did not run towards the German side. The officer said
something to the farmer, Bauman continued, 'and went back,
galloping away very quickly and disappearing in the darkness'.
The farmer shooed at them with his hands, indicating that he
intended to turn his back and that, when he turned around again,
'we should be gone. That was it. And because it was a moonless,
very dark night, it was very easy to disappear. A few steps and we
weren't there anymore. And then by night we continued our walk
to Łomża.'

Journey through Soviet lands: November 1939 – June 1941, Mołodeczno

Łomża was in the Soviet-occupied zone, the first city past the new
border. It was a small Polish town that suddenly, in September 1939,
became the first 'freedom' city – or, at least, one free of German
occupation. East of Łomża, ethnicity was no longer particularly relevant; in the Soviet Union, the Baumans were simply 'refugees from
territories incorporated by the Third Reich'.[19]
   'The city already was teeming with refugees, and we could not
find a place to spend the night', Bauman recalled: 'My father asked
in several places and finally someone told him, there is a woman
who will take you in for a night for money. We went there and who
did we see inside?' His mother! 'The capstone of a day full of mira-
cles.' The family was together again, an exceptional fate in those

deadly times. Once together, they decided to get out of Łomża. 'You couldn't reach out your hand without slapping someone, it was so crowded, that city', Bauman recalled: 'There were three times more refugees than residents.'

'[W]e took the train to Bialystok, the biggest town in this part of the Russian-occupied Poland', Bauman wrote: 'We found Bialystok not very different, though; the same homeless crowds, sky-high rents, thousands of uprooted people searching for lost relatives and the means to survive another day. We had spent all the money brought from Włocławek and father desperately tried to earn some more.' One more time, Maurycy failed to earn the money and Zofia took the situation in hand – a decision was taken:

> We had to move elsewhere – away from the buying and selling crowds. But where? Here my love of geography came in handy. Molodeczno seemed like just the right place to go. Small yet not a village, far enough from the German border to not be easily reached by other refugees, and located in what promised to be quite picturesque countryside. The last pennies left we spent on the rail tickets to Molodeczno. (Bauman, 1986/7: 33)

Mołodeczno was typical for a Belorussian town in late 1939 – packed with refugees,[20] or 'Bieżency', the Russian-derived name for all refugees from German-occupied Poland in the territories under Soviet control. The train for Mołodeczno was not overcrowded – in fact, there were no other refugees on the train, since flight east was not a popular strategy among the refugees, who were unenthusiastic about going alone to a place where they had no friends or connections.[21] The Baumans lacked any such support, yet they managed to find a good situation in their new temporary home. As Bauman recalled, 'We were lucky, because my father got a job and my mother got a job. And I went to school.' In a 1951 manuscript containing his curriculum vitae (the document signed by *Major* Bauman), Bauman wrote, 'We settled in Mołodeczno, where my father worked as a bookkeeper at *Wojentorg Zach Okręg Wojskowy* [a national company that furnished the Soviet Army], and my mother cooked in the officers' canteen'.[22]

'It was a garrison town, and not much more than that', Bauman wrote, twenty years later:

> Rambling barracks, scattered over a vast fenced-off flat terrain, occupied most of the space. .... Rooms for rent were aplenty when we arrived and we found one in no time in one of the peasant households. Jobs were also plentiful ... [The] next day after our arrival my father was offered the first position he asked for: he became – who else? – an accountant in a big trade warehouse serving the local garrison.

His first impression was one of horror and dismay: 'Everybody steals! They ask me to enter in the books goods which evaporated before being put on shelves; or they delete [from the list] as faulty, things of perfectly usable quality. How can a state be made of theft?' (Bauman, 1986/7: 34).

Maurycy, who, during a heavy bombing, wished to buy a train ticket, was not able to learn how to do the 'creative accounting':[23] 'He never made peace with either the idea or the practice of "thieving democracy". . . . He continued to suffer – but, as was his habit, he now suffered in silence' (Bauman, 1986/7: 33–4).

From their earliest days in the Soviet Union, Bauman's family was made aware of the particularities of the new system implemented after the 1917 Revolution, which had changed Russia at each level of human activity. Stealing was a widespread practice and 'thieving democracy' presented new ground rules that Zygmunt and his parents needed to learn quickly. That is not to say that Maurycy started to act like others. Zygmunt assessed his father's approach to the new system in the following words: 'My father was once again a bookkeeper, even if the books he now kept were fantasy books rather than exercises in realism, socialist or otherwise' (Bauman, 1986/7: 34).

Maurycy could not easily change, but Mołodeczna offered opportunities – 'a veritable revolution' – for Zofia, Bauman recalled. After a short test, Zygmunt's mother was hired by the garrison mess as a cook: 'Her conjurer talents fit the thieving democracy very well. . . . Her art was acclaimed, praised, cherished. My mother was happy. She loved her new life, the sleepy town, the army whose officers looked at her with the eyes of loving dogs, the country, which kept an army of men such as these' (Bauman, 1986/7: 34–5).

Zofia's gift would save their lives and improve their living conditions several times during the war. She had a talent essential during a war or crisis period – she knew how to make do with little. Zofia was not a professional cook, but 'she had a lot of energy', Bauman recalled. 'And she had the following rule: in order to make good food, you either needed very good ingredients or you spent the whole day in the kitchen. We couldn't afford high-quality products, but she knew how to make real delicacies from nothing. It was incredible!'[24]

There is a Polish nickname for such dishes – *zupa na gwoździu* (the English equivalent is 'stone soup') – popularized by the writer and journalist Melchior Wańkowicz. During the war, the creation of a tasty soup based on nothing was a strategy for survival. 'In the Soviet Union', Bauman recalled, 'this skill was golden. She engaged herself as a regular cook in a garrison cafeteria and was quickly promoted to chef. This was a great relief for my father, who could get out of the burdensome feeling that he had to earn enough to take care of the family, because it was the man's duty.' Actually, in the Soviet Union, wives were professionally active. Moreover, during the war, and even during the pinched years afterward, the talent for cooking was a golden key to a decent life. Sometimes, as in the case of the Bauman family, it could be a lifesaver:

> The Soviet government declared all the inhabitants of the occupied Polish territory Soviet citizens. As we were refugees, however, from the part of Poland over which the Russians did not proclaim yet their jurisdiction – a special paragraph had been inserted in our passports forbidding us to stay at a distance less than 60 miles from the state border. Mołodeczno was a mere 40 miles from then-independent Lithuania. We were threatened with deportation. . . . The fatal paragraph was never deleted from our passports, yet the deportation order did not arrive either.[25] (Bauman, 1986/7: 35–6)

Zofia's cooking talents thus kept at bay a threat that would create misery and even death for thousands of Poles. Soviet authorities did not send the family to Siberia in 1940, or even after the 22 June 1941 Nazi invasion. Thousands of other refugees who had fled into Soviet-occupied territories to escape Nazi occupation, and others who were already living in the areas when Stalin occupied them, were 'sent to Siberia'.[26] Stalin had innumerable justifications for such actions, all part of his policy of managing ethnic or other groups he perceived as hostile through spatial isolation. The Soviet territories were huge, the climate was harsh, the distances vast, and there was much work to be done in the forests and isolated industrial outposts. It wasn't necessary to jail people to make them obedient and docile. The Baumans, in this sense, were lucky. And, thanks to his parents' jobs, their only son could attend school in Mołodeczno – without having to put up with *numerus clausus* or a 'ghetto bench'.

Mołodeczno – one student among many

In the first school year after the start of the war, students in Belorussian schools had quite a different experience from in the past. Mołodeczno was a Polish town before World War II, but its population was multi-ethnic and multilingual.[27] During the initial war years, school directors played quite a powerful role. They were instructing waves of immigrant children who came to the school throughout the year with classes already under way. Their parents frequently lacked documents: no IDs, passports, no school certificates or other evidence of the child's previous education. Flexibility was an important value in those days, and transgressions were the rule. Bauman recalled his enrollment: 'They asked me what kind of education I had had. That was when I told the first lie in my life. I said I had finished the 2nd year of gymnasium. In reality, I had only been through the first! But they started me in the 3rd year and I managed well.'

Bauman gave a different version in 1950 when filling out his CV for the Army, his employer. There he wrote, 'I studied in Russian secondary school – in 6th and 8th grade (I took 7th grade during vacation and passed the exams).'[28] In the Poland of 1950, when life histories had to be free of all moral blemish, it would have been unacceptable for Zygmunt Bauman to write 'this was when I told the first lie in my life'. In reality, of course, his grade-skipping was not unusual in those years. In Polish territory controlled by the German Army, Polish children returned to school following the German occupation, although later in the fall the Germans closed all schools except for primary schools and occupational training – as *Untermenschen*, Poles did not deserve or require the education and culture that German children merited.

There were no such restrictions on the education of Polish children in Soviet-controlled territory, but the new regime progressively brought communist ideology into the curriculum of all schools, universities and workplaces. This highly complex transition of the territory – from Polish state domination, through a brief phase of Belorussian 'liberation', and finally into a Soviet republic – took a matter of weeks. It is fascinating to examine this process as it occurred in a secondary school, from an individual student's perspective.

More than forty years later, Bauman recalled the experience in the following way:

No one, it seemed, questioned my credentials. For my new colleagues, I was the most Polish person of them all. Here, at the far outskirts of the interwar Republic, Polishness as such was continually in doubt. The vernacular was a curious mixture of Russian, Polish, Yiddish and this uncodified peasant dialect which some intellectuals dreamt to elevate into the literary Belorussian. There were Poles, Russians, Jews, Belorussians, among my new class-mates, but this did not seem to matter. The category to which one belonged seemed to some a matter of accident, for some others a question of self-definition and choice. No one around spoke Polish as pure and refined as mine. No one moved with equal ease through Polish literature and history. In the new context I looked so frightfully Polish that I aroused suspicion and the hatred of the deputy headmaster – a militant Belorussian national-ist and Pole-baiter. A few days after I joined the school he called me to his office and told me in no uncertain words that the rule of the Polish invaders was over, and that I and my ilk had better take note, and that this was a Belorussian school with no room for Polish speakers, and

that either I learn Belorussian before Christmas or forget about my
education. I was shattered, but continued to give my answers in the
classroom in Polish. I had enough trouble with mastering the basics
of Russian; there were no 'teach yourself' books of any kind and I
learned Russian the most harrowing way – reading through the articles of Pravda, dictionary in my hand. The encounter with the deputy
headmaster did have, however, an effect – though not the one he
hoped for. Setting off the Belorussian language as the enemy of Polish
made me to hate the former. I never managed to force myself to learn
it. At the first opportunity I moved to a newly opened gymnasium
with Russian as the language of teaching. (Bauman 1986/7: 35)

This long excerpt encapsulates a complex transition in Zygmunt
Bauman's young life as a Polish Jew. After suffering for long years
from Polish nationalism and anti-Semitic exclusion in the Polish
education system, young Zygmunt was perceived, in a Belorussian
school under Soviet control, as a privileged Polish student whose
Belorussian principal suspected him as an agent of Polish dom-
inance. This is how it was in the complex world a Jewish child
entered in these chaotic times within an ephemeral school system
created by adults. This lesson was certainly invaluable for the future
sociologist and philosopher – a perfect case study, *in vivo*, an ideal
piece of fieldwork and participant observation in nationalistic education. What situation could have been better for understanding
the complexity of systems, power groups, negotiating skills and the
dynamics of social interaction? These experiences offered a powerful
grounding for his future work.

On a personal level, things progressed well for young Zygmunt:
'I remember Mołodeczno as a very nice time – it was a teenager[29]
period and I felt very comfortable there.' It must have been radical
and shocking for a boy schooled in an all-male high school to suddenly be thrust, at 14, into a coeducational school:[30] 'There were
girls there. First love . . . that's a very interesting story. Compared
to Poznań, I felt so much a part of the school. No one threatened to send me to Palestine, like they used to do in Poznań.' His
Mołodeczno schoolmates did not wield anti-Semitism against him.
'Not at all! There we were all kinds: Russians, Belorussians, Poles,
Lithuanians, Jews – all together. Miłosz described it all very well . . .
a complete mixture.'[31]

Czesław Miłosz, the late Polish Nobelist in Literature, who
was born and raised in Lithuania, describes this environment of
mixed ethnicities, languages, religions and traditions in the memoir
Wyprawa w dwudziestolecie / *An Excursion through the Twenties
and Thirties*. It was a culturally rich environment and an enormous
change for Bauman. For the first time, he was a student like any
other. For the first time, his grades were not altered to reflect his

cultural or ethnic origin. Graduating from the eighth grade in June 1941, he received a letter of congratulations for his performance, and during those two school years, Bauman recalled, he was a precious cultural resource for his Polish colleagues – not because of his Jewishness, but because he came from 'the real Poland'. After being a member of a persecuted minority group, suddenly becoming a recognized expert on the national culture must have been pleasant. When Bauman says he originated from 'real' Poland, he was referring to the fact that Poznań lay in a region of interwar Poland that was demographically dominated by Catholic Poles, while other territories nominally part of Poland, such as Belarus, were more mixed. Bauman carried Polish literature and poetry in his head. Everything he had learned, as a very good student in an excellent school, was a resource for his Polish friends. The teachers were excellent there. '*Chapeau bas!* [hats off]', Bauman said of his experience in Mołodeczno: 'I learned so much there!'

Bauman also witnessed how the Soviets were approaching the issue of religion in school. His gymnasium was a 'terrible mixture of denominations and nationalities' where it was 'a little difficult to manage religion'. One day, the students prepared a piece of theatre in which a girl knelt and prayed before a holy image. The school director intervened: ' "We can't have that picture." So the poor girl prayed to an empty space on the wall! With religions there were a few difficulties, but ethnicity meant little.'

It was a dynamic and happy period for the family, according to Bauman's depiction:

> The eighteen months in Molodeczno write themselves into my memory as an experience of constant bliss. With both parents at work, we were for the first time truly well-off – by the standards set by my childhood, at least. I was surrounded by friends and generally liked. Apparently I was also growing handsome. Girls became restless in my company. Some were downright aggressive. It was frightening, but pleasant. I felt free and needed. I found my Zion in Molodeczno. I joined the local equivalent of *Hashomer Hatzair* – *the Komsomol*. (Bauman 1986/7: 36)

In his curriculum vitae from 1951, Bauman notes that in 1940 he had 'joined the ranks of the WLKZM'.[32] This powerful and legendary acronym, which today belongs to history, signifies Всесоюзный Ленинский Коммунистический Союз Молодёжи, or All-Union Leninist Communist Youth League. It was commonly known as 'Komsomol', and it was an antechamber of the Communist Party. This was a crucial moment in Zygmunt's life. Finally liberated from ethnic discrimination, he notes in a 1955 CV, 'I was elected leader of the school section.'[33] The election marked the emerging evidence of a personal charisma that never again left Bauman. His schoolmates had chosen him as leader although he was a member of an ethnic minority and did not yet speak perfect Russian. He volunteered for the organization – an important distinction, because enrollment in Komsomol would not have been compulsory at that point. Bauman's quick rise to a leadership position in Komsomol shows his enthusiasm about the new system being implemented in former Polish territory.

It should not be surprising, considering Bauman's life experiences and age, that he was attracted to communist ideology. He perceived the new system, to some extent, as a prolongation of the socialist Hashomer Hatzair organization. The difference, in addition to the ideology (communist in the first, socialist in the second) lay in the general character of the Komsomol. Instead of holding twice-weekly secret meetings, this was an official, institutionally welcomed doorway to power, the 'daughter' of the Communist Party, and a stable place for young leaders. Was it odd to choose and support a system that promised hope and equality among ethnic groups, when the previous order supported massive discrimination and racial persecution? Was it incorrect to support an ideology that had abolished not only *numerus nullus*, but *numerus clausus*?

Wacław Szybalski, the Polish-American geneticist born in Lwow (now Lviv) in 1920, recalled that, in September 1939, during his first year at Politechnika Lwowska (the Lwow Polytechnic University), only a few Jews were accepted into the Chemistry Department because of racist policies.[34] After the Red Army took control of the region, however, Soviet authorities organized new enrollments to the polytechnic, as well as to Lwow University. The new system, which was based solely on the scholarly level of the candidates, increased the percentage of Jews in Szybalski's class to 90 per cent. At this time, at least, the communist slogans proclaiming ethnic equality were backed up in practice. This was a very powerful and attractive message to Jews and other minority members. It seduced many people – with the exception of those who had had negative experiences with the communists before World War II. Many remained suspicious, particularly those with political experience who were close to the parties that were hostile to communism. Among the many political strains of the Jewish community, the BUND stood out for its scepticism, and as a result the Soviets viewed its activists as opponents.

Many young people were highly engaged in politics in this period (according to historian Włodzimierz Kijak, the Jewish community was especially active politically, with gymnasia (high schools) serving as places of intense recruitment for the parties (Kijak, 2010)). Bauman was one of these young *engagés*. He was a pioneer in his family, since his father appears not to have been involved in

any political activity and does not appear to have discussed politics much with his son. After the war, Bauman's mother joined the
Polish Workers Party and supported the new political system in
Poland. Young Bauman's relative political naivety may explain why
the enthusiastic implementation of communism at his Mołodeczno
school attracted him so strongly. The new power imposed a system
that was more socially just and, above all, not racist.[35]

School's out – war's back in

In the spring of 1941, Bauman's Mołodeczno idyll came to a sudden
end:

> On the morning of 22 June 1941 I lay on the beach on the banks of the
> local river, surrounded by friends, basking in the sun and mulling over
> some topics I wished to crack during the summer holiday. Suddenly, I
> saw my mother running towards me. Come home immediately! War
> has broken out! . . . I saw the war first in the eyes of our landlady's
> nephew. Born on the Soviet side of the old border and brought up
> in a kolkhoz, he moved after the Soviet invasion to Molodeczno and
> settled into his aunt's household. . . . On June 22, his eyes filled with
> joy and hope. And with hatred, when turned in our direction. 'The
> Germans will not harm honest people, but some people they do not
> like – Jews above all, and with reason', he announced, his eyes resting
> thoughtfully and firmly on my father's face. Swarms of ants ran over
> my back. The quietly forgotten reality was coming back to claim its
> rights. (Bauman, 1986/7: 36–7)

The 'forgotten reality' was the anti-Semitism that had organized
prewar society. The final day in Mołodeczno for the Bauman family
was 23 June. The landlord's nephew's expression was confirmed by
a small incident:

> We lived far from the station, and our landlady's nephew refused to
> drive us there. So we took as much as we could squeeze in three bags
> and started on our next exodus. I remember returning for something
> I forgot to take; I found the nephew in our room, ransacking what we
> had left behind. He refused to let me in and kept hurling curses at me
> as I ran back to join my parents. (Bauman, 1986/7: 37)

The attitude of Bauman's landlady and her nephew was not rare
among people living in those territories. Many were happy to see the
Soviet Army running away, and welcomed the Germans, whom they
believed would bring order and a good economy. Anti-Semitism
was rife in Eastern Poland (after Poznań, Lwów was the leading

centre of the Endecja, with frequent pogroms), and the anti-Semites looked forward to taking over the goods and businesses of fleeing Jews. Not all Jews could escape, and their fate was tragic. In many of the territories occupied by the Soviets between September 1939 and the Nazi invasion, Jews were hunted as they had been in territories controlled by Third Reich soldiers. In the wake of the Soviet retreat in these villages and towns, the Jewish community attracted the hatred of neighbours who claimed that Jews had supported the Soviet occupation. The German invasion offered opportunities for revenge. Many assigned blame to the Jews for the Soviet occupation, and some would criminally aid the Germans in catching hidden Jews, or killed them with their own hands (Gross, 2001; Engelking and Grabowski, 2018). Individual or group actions were spontaneously organized, marshalling the hatred of ordinary people.[36] There were acts of 'intimate violence' (Aleksiun, 2017) among people who had peacefully cohabited for decades. Historians have traced many tragic individual or group murders[37] to the start of the German 'Operation Barbarossa'.[38] While for the Jewish community native to the eastern territories the threat of Nazi occupation was new, its meaning still unpredictable, for the Baumans, the traumatic experiences in Włocławek in the first weeks of the war left no room for doubt about the necessity of immediate departure.

> The next day my mother returned from her work early [Bauman wrote in his manuscript] . . . to tell us that the families of the army personnel would be evacuated from the town and that she was offered a place in the special train. There was little time to lose. . . . Unlike the Poznan train, this one was not full. Apart from the wives and children of the officers, only a few local people decided to move. The Soviets, apparently, did not make many friends. (Bauman, 1986/7: 37)

The German–Soviet war started on 22 June. By the 25th, Mołodeczno was already under Nazi control.

Zygmunt and his parents boarded the evacuation train on 23 June. Once again, Bauman's family had been forced to flee. This time, they tried to get as far east as possible.

4

Russian Exodus, 1941–1943

Gorki and the Forest

Escape into the Russian interior

It was a long, long way – first through the Westernmost territories, already ravaged by German bombers, then through the deep interior of Russia, far from the frontline, yet already in a state of war. The war in its very first weeks already showed itself in the haggard, tired look of men in uniform, in the absence of men in civilian clothes, in the bewildered faces of women suddenly left to their own care. Trains full of men in uniforms ran West; our train uncertainly, haltingly, crawled East. Garrison families disappeared one by one as they reached their home towns. The train slowly shrank until a few carriages were left filled with the homeless. People like us, with nowhere to go. (Bauman, 1986/7: 37)

Once again the Baumans were on the train, this time travelling towards the Far East, and without NKVD supervision – almost 'free' – an unusual circumstance for a Polish-Jewish family. They were once again in the last train and once again under bombing, and once again 'it was an ordinary thing for those times', Bauman said, in 2015.[1] Long train journeys were indeed the fate of thousands who fled war and terror at the hands of the Nazis. The 'last train' leaving Mołodeczno was neither part of a military convoy nor a regular passenger train. The refugees were in freight cars, rolling and stopping and continuously being shunted onto the side tracks to make space for military transports going in one direction or another. 'No one knew how long we would be travelling. We ended up spending about a month heading into the depths of Russia. But we were fortunate that our trip lasted a month, because we reached a place where the Germans did not come. So, the result was very good!' With this last sentence, Bauman smiled and again took up his pipe.

In movies, historical works, memoirs and novels, depictions of the use of freight cars to evacuate Jews forcibly – to and from ghettos,

to concentration and death camps – epitomizes the dehumanization
of Nazi Germany. But spending days, weeks and months in freight
passage was a common experience for refugees and others in somewhat less dire circumstances in Eastern Europe and the Soviet
Union. Travellers had to manage their lives amid the chaos of the
transports, amid bombings, delays and false starts, with little or no
food or water, non-existent hygiene facilities and a state of perpetual
ignorance about the ultimate destination of the trains. Inhabitants
of the villages around the train stations sometimes sold bread,
simple meals and boiled water, which probably saved many lives.
The cold, hunger and thirst, sleeplessness and lack of basic privacy
were exhausting. Still, those who had family members with them felt
lucky. They knew that at some point, perhaps in a matter of days or
weeks, they might rebuild a modest life and survive the war. These
refugees from Poland and other parts of Europe (with the exception
of those 'condemned to Siberia')[2] knew that eventually the authorities would order them to stop and settle down, and they would stay
somewhere for a while. Would it be permanent? No one knew.

Kolkhoznik life: modest stability in a country at war

Finally, somewhere halfway between Moscow and Ural, the family
was told to disembark. Someone had decided they should be settled
in a local *kolkhoz* (collective farm) that, having lost its men, badly
needed extra labour. The family stayed for a short time in the *kolkhoz*
at the village of Krasnyje Baki; then they moved to Shakhunia, a
district capital in the Gorki (now Nizhny Novgorod) district. It was
a town of 5,000–7,000 people, with an important switching station
on the train-track from Moscow through Gorki to Archangelsk.

'They put us up near some kibbutz', Bauman told me, then realized his mistake and said with a smile, 'No, not yet kibbutz – *kolkhoz*.
They left us there, and since my father had already learned how to
do accounting (in Russian), he decided to find a job. At that time, it
was relatively easy because most of the men disappeared suddenly
. . . they went to the Army. They needed people to replace those who
left, and my father was already too old to be conscripted.' Bauman
gave further description of the *kolkhoz*, which was called Udarnik,[3]
in his manuscript:

> Horsecars took us to a village still further north. As an advance against
> our future labour, we were offered some flour, potatoes and oil.
>   The next morning my Mother and I joined a long column of women
> and children taking to the fields. Only the two of us wore shoes. The
> rest walked in bast-shoes [fibre shoes], or strange moccasins made
> of straw. We walked for several miles before we reached the plot

were the harvesting was scheduled for the day: a vast field covered with overripe rye that had already started seeding. Some women worked with scythes; one rode a tractor, which moved a few yards with ear-shattering noise, only to grind to an abrupt halt and emit [an] enormous cloud of acrid smoke. From that point on, only scythes set apart the badly needed bread from hectares of rotten rye. Tall for my age, I was offered a scythe, but the woman in charge soon concluded that this would be a waste of the precious tool. I was assigned to a large group of women and children who raked and tied cut stalks. We worked in grim determination, in complete silence, disturbed only by the constant buzz of gnats hungry for animal blood. I remember them sitting tight on every bare inch of my skin. Having sunk their darts deep in my body they were too busy sucking my blood to notice my desperate attempts to shake them off. There was no way of getting rid of them; the few I managed to destroy were immediately replaced with new and hungry ones. The swarm evidently was getting regular reinforcements. Apart from my Mother and myself, nobody seemed to mind them. Gnats were clearly part of life, like the broken tractor, like the rotting rye, like the job obviously beyond human capacity, like the work from sunrise to sunset rewarded in the evening by a few boiled potatoes and hot water sprinkled with flour and salt.

    After several days I fell ill and had to stay home. My body was swollen, covered with blisters, boils and festering sores. The innumerable bites and bruises were infected. I was in pain, unable to move, to sit, to lie down. My Mother proved stronger; she stayed in the field one day longer. (Bauman, 1986/7: 38–9)

The combination of climate, insects and physical effort exhausted and finally sickened mother and son, although the working conditions did not seem to disturb the local population, who were accustomed to them. This was the Baumans' initiation to the harsh conditions, aggravated by a permanent lack of food, that were to characterize life in the Soviet interior.

Many war accounts are devoted to describing the penury of food and the daily struggle to cover the minimum needs that each family required for survival. Bauman was a teenager, in the middle of a growth period. In prosperous circumstances, adolescent boys who gobble up large portions of food remain hungry without double or triple rations. In the Soviet Union at war, food was a missing element, and many goods were restricted. Food was rationed and there were few possibilities of buying it on the black market, which was expensive and dangerous. The Baumans lacked connections or money to fill in the gaps in their nutrition. The effect of this situation was permanent undernutrition.

'I was hungry. I was to be hungry for the next two and a half years – till my army life started. Not occasionally hungry, but hungry

twenty-four hours a day, seven days a week. I imagined the bliss-
ful life after the end of the war as one huge baker's shop opened all
hours' (Bauman, 1986/7: 39).

The feeling of long-term hunger remains forever inscribed in the
memory of anyone who experiences it. Such hunger is a rare phenomenon in developed countries in the twenty-first century. Hunger
produces an enveloping feeling of privation, as much physical as
psychological, a sensation that one's life is in danger. It is a liminal
experience, menacing the healthy development of a child or teenager,
and it changes everything forever. The feeling is too strong ever to
be forgotten; it is deeply inscribed in the body and psyche, it creates
a specific sensibility and modifies the perception of life. Bauman's
case was not one of individual misfortune. This was a large group
deprivation, a massive fate that struck an entire society, a powerful
feeling that was shared by everyone in the USSR except for soldiers,
who were given special rations: 'The country was hungry. . . . Shared
hunger pained less. But it was painful all the same. And the pain
remained long after hunger ended' (Bauman 1986/7: 39–40).

After a month, Maurycy found a job as an accountant in the
prodkombinat, but the family's situation did not improve. Luckily,
however, Zofia found a job some weeks later that gave them new
access to food. She was hired as a cook in Canteen No. 1 of the
rajpotrebsojuz (district food cooperative).[4] Not even this could permanently resolve the problem of hunger, but it was an improvement
over the first weeks of their life during the Soviet–German war. In
Shakhunia, Bauman wrote, 'my Mother was put in charge of the
survival of that small particle of the vast country at war. And my
Father became, for many years to come, his wife's husband, hidden
and invisible in her giant shadow. I think my Father was relieved,
and happy' (Bauman, 1986/7: 40).

The family's refugee life did not correspond to the image of the
twentieth-century family, which runs on male work and is driven
by the father. In fact, across the USSR, the role of women had
changed significantly since the October Revolution, and, during the
war, women replaced missing men in the factories, collectives and
offices. In the case of the Baumans, the role division conformed with
both parents' characters; it was not so much an adaptation to social
conditions as a good matching of their personalities with the new
environment. Bauman's father was discreet; his mother dynamic
and full of energy. Her attitude towards life and her entrepreneurial
personality made their everyday lives easier.

Bauman pursued his education during the 1941–2 school year at
High School No. 14, founded in 1927. Bauman's background was
completely different from that of his classmates. They had been
educated according to the new manuals created in the Soviet way
– a particular brainwashing tool that prepared new generations for

life in a communist country. Russia had changed its political orientation from powerful monarchy to the communist system in 1917.
The new rules and distribution of power were implemented in a
country whose industrialization lagged behind countries such as
Great Britain or Germany. Soviet manuals were politically oriented
texts, largely dedicated to glorifying the new system and its leaders.
Stalin was a kind of czar in the new communist context. Soviet art
and culture should shape the new society and contribute to the
formation of a 'New Human' – a 'Soviet human'. Any focus on classical pieces of art, perceived as bourgeois expressions of an enemy
culture, was unwelcome.

But the war made significant modifications in the educational
corps. After June 1941, all healthy conscriptable Russians were on
the front line, and missing teachers were replaced by former professors (retired, or freshly liberated from jails and the Gulag for their
opposition to the new regime: Bauman, 1986/7: 40). Many of these
teachers were educated in the previous system and very attached to
the classics. They appreciated the knowledge of classical writers and
poets Bauman brought to his new school in Shakhunia.

A certificate dated 7 June 1942, written in Cyrillic, states that
Bauman Zygmunt Moisiejewicz (son of Moishe), Бауман Сигизмунд
Моисеевич, finished a full education programme at High School
No. 14[5] with the highest grade possible – отлично/excellent. Despite
the challenge of learning a new language, a new alphabet and much
new material in these turbulent times, in an atmosphere free from
ethnic discrimination he had done extremely well. Bauman received
a certificate with a golden frame.[6] All his grades were the same
– excellent: in Russian language, literature, arithmetic, algebra,
geometry, trigonometry, natural sciences, history, the USSR constitution, geography, physics, chemistry, astronomy, foreign language
(German), drawing and sports.

The evaluation of school work in different domains is a subjective[7]
activity (see Lamont, 2010), and teachers were more likely to give a
good grade to a charismatic student who expressed the right political
views. Yet, aside from any such considerations, Bauman clearly had
a broad capacity for study and analysis, and was extremely adept at
presenting his opinions, convincing his audience and, finally, being
a leader and guide at a very young age, as Principal Asafonov duly
noted in his final evaluation in June 1942:

> Comrade Bauman Sygmundovich Moyseyevich, has graduated from
> secondary school J.D. No. 14 ... with excellent honours. He has
> outstanding intellectual skills. He is a social activist: chairman of the
> school committee, chairman of the Komsomol committee, and editor
> of the school newspaper, disciplined but politically moderate. ... In
> his work he manifests initiative, accuracy and responsibility. He is

stubborn with a strong will. A good comrade. He enjoys outstanding
authority and respect among students and teachers.[8]

This opinion was important in Bauman's political career, although
it contained a couple of asterisks. First, Asafonov's assessment of
the student as 'politically moderate' in 1942 would have meant 'not
communist enough' – not enough of a committed Stalinist. The
second negative point is related to a personal characteristic that is
unwelcome in any hierarchical organization – Bauman's stubbornness. This could signify a dangerous independence or resistance to
the hierarchy, a person who was difficult to manage or subdue.[9]
However, his political activity showed he had the attitudes and
other skills typical of future political leaders. In a CV he prepared in
the 1950s,[10] Bauman described the experience positively: 'In 1942 I
graduated from 10th grade of the high school in Shakhunia (where
I was elected leader of the student council) with the grade of "otlic-
zno" (excellent) and a letter of praise.'[11]

But we learn from Bauman's 1987 manuscript that, despite the
opportunities suggested by his excellent school results, not all doors
were immediately opened to him:

> I finished school with a gold medal. This gave me the right of admis-
> sion to any faculty of any university of my choice. I was sixteen
> – the youngest among the graduates. On graduation day, I went with
> the other boys to the local military office and handed an application
> to an army school. Shortly all the other boys were called, but my
> application remained without reply. Perhaps I was under age. More
> probably, the army school had no room for an untrustworthy for-
> eigner (Bauman, 1986/7: 41)

There is nothing in the official files indicating that Bauman's failure
to be selected for the Army school was due to his status as a foreigner
– or his ethnic origins. The archives that contain documents from
the postwar period do not make it possible to reconstruct Bauman's
story step by step. Many points of data are missing or remain hidden,
and some of the information is simply erroneous.

A 27 December 1949 document in Bauman's military file, written
by a certain Pasakiewicz, reports that Bauman was educated 'at
Shakhunia Railroad Secondary School',[12] which suggests a technical
school. None of Bauman's other documents indicate he received any
technical type of schooling. However, between high school and the
start of university, he did spend a summer in the Shakhunia railway
workshops doing a volunteer welding apprenticeship. Here he got
basic knowledge about factory life – the hard physical work, craftsmen's knowledge – and he developed friendships with co-workers.
The works were a large plant dedicated to keeping the locomotives

of the region on the tracks – a serious and difficult task since the rolling stock was old and needed a lot of servicing.

At the time of Bauman's apprenticeship, there were only two categories of workers in many such Soviet installations – the very experienced, who were old, sick or both – and the beginners, too young or sick to join the Army. 'Things at the frontline (at those lucky moments when there was a definite frontline) went from bad to worse', Bauman writes:

> The Germans seemed to be set to cross the Volga. Almost everywhere, the Red Army was in retreat, losing many of its men and its arms. Nowhere else was the might of Germany being resisted. Russia fought alone the united industrial might of Europe. In our workshops the few old men and keen, but inept adolescents of my and still younger age took upon themselves to the job, on non-existing factories, of dozens of other specialised plants now bombed out of existence or hastily refurbished to serve the immediate needs of the army. The old craftsmen made miracles without complaint yet with a lot of intense, obstinate passion. If an important part or ingredient were missing, they would conjure up a substitute. We worked in buildings which themselves badly needed repair. The ventilators [had] long ceased to work, and the shops were filled with corrosive smoke and poisonous fumes. No one seemed to mind – least of all the old craftsmen, who knew all too well what this meant to their lungs. For me, awe and admiration are the feelings I remember best. I felt overwhelmed by the spectacle of human solidarity and dedication. I heard no grumbling and I did not grumble myself. We were all hungry and tired. We all spoke in hoarse voices and coughed up phlegm. We strained our eyes, bloodied and itching. Our hands were covered with burns and scars. Yet there was meaning in everything we did, and we had our share of joy and happiness when the impossible job was done and a dead locomotive was restored to life. After three months, I left the workshops with an injection of romantic utopia. . . . Not all inhuman conditions de-humanize. Some disclose humanity in man. (Bauman 1986/7: 41–2)

The experience left Bauman with a deep sense of admiration for the old workers who transmitted their knowledge with passion and patience to youths who gathered it in with great enthusiasm. Working conditions were difficult but the satisfaction of performing the tasks was enormous. Each restored train car was a needed victory at a time when the Red Army was on the defensive across the front. All of this went into the construction of an idyllic and utopian image of the universe of factory and workers, where men worked without competitive pressures, career struggles or rat race. The middle-aged men were gone, the war was everywhere, the country needed a huge effort, and they made it. Bauman saw something deeply human in the relationships among workers in that environment. This experience could be seen as a kind of fieldwork – a practice that completed the theoretical basis of his communism, acquired in the Komsomol. It was an important life lesson.

Becoming a university student – an outsider once again

When the summer of 1942 ended, Bauman left the rail workshop to attend university in Gorki, the district's main city. Just before Bauman boarded the train on his journey, his father, to his surprise, placed a letter in his pocket. It was the kind of letter that many parents give their children on occasions such as this – an important and powerful message from a father to his only son on his departure from home.

From Bauman's manuscript, we learn:

> This was a love letter. I was leaving my parents now, starting my own and different life – and Father hastened to let me know all he had felt over the years, the role I played in his life and what sort of man he dreamed I'd be.
>
> There was also fatherly advice. Life wisdom father wished to share with his son. The only capital he could bequeath. His only gift. Remember – he wrote: your people, your people only, can appreciate you and your work. Remember – he wrote; you are a Jew, and you belong to the Jewish people. . . .
>
> My people? Who were my people? And why were they mine? Simply because 'I belong to them?' Must I belong? And do I really want to belong? And if I did want to belong, why it ought to be a nation – something I have been cast into without my participation, by other people's selection? And why must there be a selection? Selection means rejection, division, antagonism – precisely the things I suffered from and found most repelling. I could not know whether the Jews were in this respect different from other 'peoples'. . . . Perhaps all the suffering comes from the need to compare whose blood is redder. Perhaps the evil is in the comparing itself. Perhaps the real issue is to stop comparing altogether, once for all. I guess the evil sits in the very compulsion to select and in the curse of being selected. Once one wants to belong, one cannot help setting off others whom one refuses to admit as one's kin. Belonging cannot but mean dividing, and setting double standards. Where standards divide, morality ends. Drawing the line between us and them, we efface the line between good and evil. (Bauman, 1986/7: 42–4)

These were Bauman's reflections some forty-four years later, not necessarily what he was thinking on the road to Gorki. Yet it was indeed so that, at this point in his life, Bauman chose to turn away from his father's advice of strong belonging to 'his people' and to make a life with a different philosophy. 'Above all, it shows how little I knew and understand at the time', he writes:

> I seemed to believe that moral will would overpower the dead weight of tribalism. And I seemed to be unaware that in the fight against the overwhelming odds, the moral will may well lose its only source of strength and only title to respect: its ethical purity. If that happens, there is little to choose between inhumanity of the will and inhumanity of the tribe. . ... All this I was still to learn, and learn the hard and unenviable way. (Bauman, 1986/7: 42–4)

We know from scientists who work on memory processes that people select the information they wish to keep, while discarding the rest. We are not like computers that save all data – emotions play a major role in this activity and remembering occurs through a selection process. What Bauman recalled best about this episode were the emotions provoked by reading his father's words. Yet the extract of the letter cited above offers a precious basis for analysing the process of Bauman's identity construction, the constant tension between the two aspects of his self-identification: as a Jew and a Pole. Bauman's was a continuing process of accepting their co-existence – a kind of 'impossible challenge' that he took on during his entire life. He disagreed with his father, and intentionally disobeyed – filial opposition that could be seen as a typical attitude of adolescent rebellion, or an example of the awaking agency that enables young adults to become independent.

Of course, it was not merely a rebellion against his father. Bauman was also taking a particular stand within a defined politico-historical context. The difficulty of the challenge was imposed by Bauman's situation. Being at once a Pole and a Jew was not a problem for him, but it was for the people in his environment. Yet he had made a decision. Not that it had come to him suddenly in the train. His stance undoubtedly resulted from a long process nourished by his previous experiences: rejection by Polish society, belonging to Hashomer Hatzair, acceptance by schools in exile, Komsomol activity. At this moment, Bauman was one of a not small number of young Polish Jews who believed that any return to the prewar situation would mean returning to the status of a second-class citizen. The belief in a better future defined Bauman's response to his father's careful advice. The advice was rejected.

This was to be one of several important turning points in Bauman's life. It occurred at a moment of departure and the beginning of adult life – a symbolic passage between childhood and manhood. Meditating upon Maurycy's letter on the train from Shakhunia to

Gorki, a distance of some 200 miles, Bauman was a young man in transition.

In autumn 1942, Bauman enrolled in the University of Gorki in physics, but his time there was short-lived. He might have remained for several years if he were a Russian citizen, but the infamous 'Paragraph 11' forbade foreigners from settling in Russian cities such as Gorki. The authorities discovered their mistake during the second month of his fall semester. As soon as they did, Bauman had to leave immediately, and study through correspondence.

The few short months in Gorki were no holiday. 'In the north of Russia winter starts early, and in the middle of October Gorki was a frozen city', Bauman wrote in his manuscript:

> There was no fuel, and central heating was set at a level barely sufficient to prevent bursting of water-pipes. We stayed in our coats all day long and did not take them off when we went to bed. I remember the difficulty of turning the pages of the book with hands never taken out of thick gloves without fingers. . . . [W]ith nineteen other students, I was allocated a bed in a room meant to accommodate four; most of the student halls had been converted into military hospitals. We did not mind the overcrowding; on the contrary this added a degree or two to the temperature of the room. The focal point of the room was an electric kettle, always kept boiling unless the electricity was cut off (as it was for at least eight hours every day). When writing essays or doing our equations, we warmed our hands pressing them to the kettle or to a cupful of hot water (Bauman, 1986/7: 44–5)

Life conditions were hard, but only a very small elite could enter the university, after a very strict selection process. Once accepted, students did not pay for their university studies, so what amenities they obtained in these harsh conditions were free, at least, under the system established by the October Revolution. Everything was free, but there wasn't much of anything. Power restrictions cut electricity for several hours a day. Conditions were crude. Long-time inhabitants of the region were used to them, but this was only Bauman's second winter in the area.[13] Not only the living conditions were hard – so was the social environment.

> Among the students, I was again the youngest. All others were either war veterans with wounds which disqualified them from further military service, or physically unfit who could not be enlisted. I was the only fit and healthy person; a circumstance which would have made me feel guilty, if not for the hope that my share of the war effort was still in front of me. I was not to be given time to contemplate my position, however. After two months of studying and freezing, the house administrator called me to her office to tell me that I had no right

to live in a big and important city like Gorki and I must return to Shakhunia immediately. (Bauman, 1986/7: 45)

Those who didn't respect Paragraph 11 ran the risk of immediate deportation, usually to territories more frozen even than Gorki. Zygmunt took the train back to his parents' domicile, which in the meantime also had changed. The Baumans had moved to Vakhtan, where Zofia was offered the supervision of feeding hundreds of lumberjacks. Vakhtan was a small settlement lost amid woods and marshes, 15 miles farther north than Shakhunia. In this forest village, everything was made of wood: houses, roads, even sidewalks.

Bauman's new life involved studying university-level courses while working in the forest city. 'My love for physics ended very quickly', he recalled: 'I would spend no more than 10 days or two weeks on campus, and return only to take exams. I never attended courses again, there was no possibility of it. . . . I had textbooks, I was supposed to learn the material, then return to pass the exams, which were given orally at the time.'[14] In a biographical note written for the University of Warsaw, his then employer, in 1955,[15] Bauman blamed health reasons – rather than Paragraph 11 – for his departure from Gorki. He probably omitted the true cause to avoid giving any appearance of criticizing this rigid and unjust aspect of the Soviet regime. There was, however, some truth in his official declaration: suffering under the wartime regime of poor nutrition, Bauman contracted scurvy.

Archival sources provide a variety of accounts of Bauman's activities during this university-by-correspondence period. According to a military document found in the IPN files, from summer 1943 to January 1944, Bauman 'worked as a teacher at the Vakhtan Middle School'.[16] In our interview, Bauman said he was not a regular teacher but worked in the local library. A CV written for the Party, however, states that he was hired as a librarian in Vakhtan 'with the objective of becoming a teacher'.[17] Finally, in his extensive CV from 27 March 1947, there is again a reference to teaching: 'I started work in Lesprodtorg [national timber-production firm] . . ., after a few months I took the post of teacher at the Vakhtan school where I lectured mathematics in grades 6–8'.[18]

In his private manuscript Bauman focused on another important activity that took all his free time:

Just how far Vakhtan was from everywhere else I learned the moment I entered the local library. To my utter amazement, I found there a full, unexpurgated chronicle of Soviet literary life since the early twenties. The successive waves of purges and auto-da-fes which maimed and truncated all public libraries I visited before, clearly bypassed this one. Nobody seemed to have cared about the danger of poisoning the minds of the forest people who communicated with the rest of the country only through trainloads of timber. The few months I spent in Vakhtan remained in my memory above all as the time of constant excitement and elation. At no other period of my life did I devour so many books. I swallowed full editions of Russian classics, printed in the times of scarcity and high hopes on newsprint, now yellow and crumbling. I devoured the Soviet literature of the twenties and the early thirties. I pored through long forgotten philosophical and historical debates of the country still free enough to disagree and debate. I read the authors whose very names had acquired the awesome power of sucking the person who pronounced them in public into the same non-existence into which they themselves had been cast. (Bauman, 1986/7: 45–6)

In the Stalinist USSR, all intellectual resources were constantly 'cleansed'. Freedom of speech did not exist and the authorities imposed the topics for discussion. Isolated as it was, Vakhtan's small library had escaped waves of 'purification', and Bauman was lucky to have access to these forbidden works without restriction. They would add to the large and diverse body of knowledge that young Bauman had accumulated despite the war and Soviet controls. This kind of activity – intensive reading of banned authors and forbidden literature – is one of the most important components of an independent education, and a basis for developing the capacity for critical thinking. It was a rare, almost impossible activity in this place and time: 'the nights belonged to books. I just imbibed them without digesting; I guess they needed time to incubate. But incubate they did. Slowly yet inexorably I began to see around me things I did not see before, even when looking them straight in the face' (Bauman, 1986/7: 46).

His reading would have a liberating power, opening his eyes to new worlds and perhaps offering a counterpoint to the powerful Stalinist propaganda. The books would help Bauman think differently, and provide a more nuanced observation of reality. Between the books and his prewar and refugee experiences, Bauman certainly would have perceived things differently from most inhabitants of Vakhtan. The Baumans lived in a village of forest people, whose job had great significance in the Soviet Union at that time. Timber was one of the country's major resources, and the war industries needed it desperately. Many villages existed solely to provide these wood products. They were often isolated, tiny communities – sometimes very cold places during the long winters. The work was dangerous and difficult. Bauman's father had become an accountant for the state forest company, and his mother became the manager of public catering at Lesprodtorg. Zygmunt managed to land a position with the same company, as an organizational manager. With a 10th-grade certificate, he qualified as an 'intellectual employee', in the terminology of Eastern Europe – which enabled him to get a job less painful than those performed by physical workers:[19] 'This was severe winter, with temperatures never rising above minus 30C for several months. During the day I worked in an office or walked long forest paths to reach distant lumberjack outposts and collect reports on the number of trees felled and the volume of logs cut' (Bauman, 1986/7: 46).

At the Institute of Sociology in Warsaw in the 1960s, Bauman sometimes surprised his students by using examples from the forest industry in his lessons; he knew a lot about lumbermen, their tools and the different species of tree. His Sociology students were unaware that this knowledge came not through reading but, rather, life experience.[20] Many years after the forest job, it continued to influence Bauman's writing about social development and the lives of people working in difficult conditions.

He spent his final months in Vakhtan working in the forest office by day, while reading intensively at night. He did his best to get the latest news from the front and politics. During the war, the newspapers, especially *Pravda* (Truth), and radio were the two principal sources of information. It was from the radio that Bauman learned about a group of Polish communists, as he recalled in his manuscript:

I heard on the radio (there were loudspeakers in every house, connected by cable to the only wireless set, kept in the local library) that in Moscow an Association of Polish Patriots was formed, and that the first action it undertook was to publish a newspaper *Free Poland* and a journal *New Horizons*. Immediately, I sent an application for membership and my subscription for both publications. The first copies soon arrived. I vividly remember the shock. The intoxication. The wild explosion of feverish fantasy. I read what I received from the first page to the last and back again. The titles of both publications merged in my mind [and] became one: Poland free, horizons new. Free Poland became my new horizon. With bated breath I read about the future dignity of my country. I read about things I knew before yet poorly understood: about community strife and hatred arising from poverty and injustice; about life without prospects and dreariness without end that rebounded in mutual suspicion and jealousy; about the nation tearing itself apart instead of coming to grips with its true problems, like lack of freedom and democratic rights. I read about things I did not think about before – about Poland of the future, a loving mother for her suffering children, a country of liberty and justice. I read about a dream country with room for everybody, however weak and wan. A country without hunger, misery and unemployment. A country in which one man's success will not mean another man's defeat. A new

Poland, yet at the same time a Poland which for the first time will be true to herself. In an equal and confident society, Polish culture, Polish letters, Polish language would finally blossom and reach the heights never dreamt of before. A free Poland of new horizons would be the pride of the free world.

I had my share of glasshouses. (Bauman, 1986/7: 46–7)

While this expression is unclear in English, in Polish it refers to the 1924 bestseller by Polish writer Władysław Żeromski (*Przedwiośnie* (The Spring to Come)), in which the protagonist, Cezary Baryka, a Russian-born Polish noble, obtains a patriotic education from books and stories. 'Glass houses' are the symbol of utopia, the idealized country, which shatters as Cezary comes to Poland for the first time and sees the huge disparity between reality and what he has learned from his father. In Żeromski's book, utopia could be built by revolution or through progressive hard work and social change. This, in effect, meant communism or socialism.

'I had my share of glasshouses', Bauman wrote. In other words, he bought into the dream of the believers, and clung to the ideal of a Poland of peace and justice. This 'intoxication', as Bauman described it, worked very efficiently upon the susceptible, and who could be more susceptible than a Jewish refugee, shivering in the temple-pounding frost of the Russian forest in winter, with little food and ever-present war? The ideas of the Union of Polish Patriots (Związek Patriotów Polskich – ZPP) conveyed by *New Horizons* and *Free Poland* presented an attractive mirage of a liberated Poland, a fantastic promise of a happy ending to a horrible war and prewar injustices. Bauman resonated deeply with the great diapason that sounded from the pages of *Nowe Widnokręgi* (*New Horizons*). I do not think this is surprising. In fact, it would be really incredible if this dream had failed to seduce young Bauman. Many older, more experienced people were taken in. The dream was beautiful, powerful, supremely alluring.

New Horizons was a socio-literary journal, published fortnightly,[21] edited by the Polish communist and writer Wanda Wasilewska (who also led the ZPP). With *Free Poland* (*Wolna Polska*), launched on 1 March 1943, it was, according to writer Stefan Jędrychowski,[22] one of two voices of the ZPP. Of course, the ZPP and its publications supported Stalin and, after the eruption of his conflict with the London-based government-in-exile, the ZPP became the Polish political partner of the Soviet government and the Red Army.[23]

In the middle of February 1943, the Polish communists Wasilewska, Hilary Minc and Wiktor Grosz were received by Stalin 'to discuss matters related to the further activity of the Polish left-in-exile'.[24] One of the results of this meeting was the publication of journals 'to increase the possibilities for Communists and left-wing Polish activists to influence Poles in the USSR both from a propaganda and ideological view point' (Nussbaum, 1991: 184).[25] The first Moscow[26] issue of *New Horizons* (no. 6, 20 March 1943) covered the news about the 25 April breaking of diplomatic ties between the government-in-exile and Stalin. Number 9, which Bauman probably read in the forest of Vakhtan,[27] contained a speech by Wasilewska.[28] The following excerpt helps to explain how Bauman's thoughts were shaped in the context of his 'intoxication':

> [Polish Prime Minister Wladyslaw] Sikorski's government-in-exile does not represent the Polish nation. ... We believe that in the near future we will be able to march shoulder to shoulder with the Red Army, demonstrating our love of Poland, our right to Poland, with weapons in hand under the Polish banner of Polish troops. ... Remember that you represent Poland and the Polish nation – you represent it in the way that our nation's greatness and heroism, and the greatness and importance of the moment, require of us.[29]

During the summer and autumn of 1943, Bauman read enthusiastically about Poland's past, future and current events. He read articles in the two publications that were critical of the prewar government's policies and political system, on the conflict between the government-in-exile and Soviet authorities over the Katyń massacre,[30] on the Anders Army's departure to the Middle East – which Soviet media presented as a betrayal – and other issues related to the war, not excluding the campaigns of terror and extermination against Poland's Jewish population. He also read articles dealing with Poland's future, with its negotiated border on the Curzon Line,[31] and the creation of a Soviet-influenced political system organized around leftist values.

The Polish papers also carried daily news about Polish military units being prepared to fight alongside the Red Army. The Polish communists, on 8 May 1943, had officially compacted with Stalin to organize a Polish division. A communiqué stated, 'The Soviet Government has decided to comply with the request of the Union of Polish Patriots in the USSR to create a Polish division named after Tadeusz Kościuszko on the territory of the USSR, which is to fight jointly with the Red Army against the German invader. The formation of the Polish division has already been started' (Nussbaum, 1991: 185).[32]

This military unit became a kind of surrogate for the missing Anders Army, which merged with the British Military Forces. After travelling through Asia and the Middle East, the Anders Army took part in operations in North Africa and Southern Europe as part of the Allied Forces. To keep up the new Soviet–Polish unit's morale, both Polish newspapers published inspirational speeches addressed to the soldiers. Bauman, who was nearly 18 years old, was influenced by the following words from Wasilewska:

> Beloved, dearest ones! We're going to the front. In a few days, we will start to march towards where all our dreams lead us – we will go to Poland. Our path leads straight to the country. . . . Soldiers! . . . I believe that the First Division will enter free Polish soil, will be the first to give our brothers the slogan: 'Grab your weapons!' I can hear these shouts already, I can see the tears of happiness and joy with which they will greet you there – at home. You will start the construction of a new Poland, Mother Poland, not a stepmother, a Poland in which men will be respected, a Poland that we dream about and are ready to die for. Today, your relatives and families that would say goodbye to you are not here with us. Therefore, take from me everything that your dearest could wish you. Receive from me the words of Poland's love for a Polish soldier who goes to win.[33]

It is no wonder that a speech like this would have inspired the young Bauman. Its tone was purely anti-fascist and nationalistic, and free of Stalinist cant. As Klemens Nussbaum noted: 'The paper avoided any kind of remarks that might betray its Communist profile. Its style was characterized by a very patriotic tone. National accord and unity were urged regardless of political opinions' (Nussbaum, 1991: 184). The trend to downplay communist language was perceptible at this time in most of the Soviet media. Włodzimierz Szer, Bauman's compatriot in exile, noted of the war context:

> It was obvious to the naked eye that as the Germans advanced, the primitive party propaganda changed in its definition of the nature of the war, which was no longer about the defense of Soviet power, communism and the Bolshevik party – these terms were rarely heard. Instead the deadly danger threatened Russia, our mother and country; and that was true. The sublime songs broadcast all over the radio talked about the holy nation's war.[34] (Szer, 2013: 126)

The battle of Stalingrad lasted five and a half months, and nearly all fresh recruits were sent into the fight. In early February 1943, the Soviets finally won, taking tens of thousands of German prisoners of war. The victory, psychological as well as military, was celebrated throughout the Soviet Union – the first major victory against the German Army. 'All Russia breathed a sigh of relief', Szer recalled:

> Hitler proclaimed national mourning and Stalin did something really clever in his own terms (not quite like him): he ordered a parade of prisoners of war on Red Square in Moscow near the Kremlin wall.

They marched with their *Feldmarschall* [army chief] and generals, and threw the banners of their regiments, brigades and divisions . . . under Stalin's feet, who received the parade. All the newspapers carried photographs of this incredible military parade. (Szer, 2013: 128)

Zygmunt Bauman, home-schooling university student and tree counter in a small forest town, and a passionate reader of *New Horizons* and *Free Poland*, certainly must have celebrated this victory as well. It created a huge change in the lives of even ordinary people, as Szer recalled over fifty years later:

After the Stalingrad victory, every daily message from the front in the newspapers ended with the words 'For Stalin, for Homeland'; it sounded just like 'For Tzar. For Russia'. Suddenly, in many places, churches were opened, under the principle of 'When in fear, God is there.' To Czykowka, where a small orthodox church had served for years as a warehouse for artificial fertilizers and other material, came an order from the regional [communist] party committee in Baranów to throw out fertilizers and clean up the building . . . church paraphernalia was brought in so people could celebrate their religion. I do not know where the objects of worship came from . . . people joked – or maybe it was not a joke – that they were brought from the Museum of Atheism. (Szer, 2013: 127)

In the Soviet Union in 1943, people experienced more freedom than previously, as all the regime's efforts were directed at the front – a popular front, moreover, with the Western powers – towards victory over Germany. All men over 18 were called up for the Red Army. In Europe, this threshold usually signifies the start of adult life, and during wartime, for innumerable families, it was a very sad celebration. Zygmunt's eighteenth birthday occurred on 19 November 1943. Even as a non-USSR citizen, he was required immediately to join up. Failure to fulfil this obligation was considered desertion. And, during the Great Patriotic War, desertion was punished by death. But no such idea entered Bauman's head. He'd been trying to become a soldier for months, and at age 18 he was all too ready to join the military. His initial assignment, however, was not to serve as a soldier in the Polish Patriot division, but rather as a militiaman in Moscow.

5

'Holy War'

1943–1945

Courage is not a lack of fear. Courage is a fear that has been over-come. Heroes feel fear, but they manage to strangle it before it controls them. That's why they are heroes.

(Julian Żurowicz[1] [Zygmunt Bauman], 1953a: 29))

Enrolment

On 19 November 1943, *Pravda* carried the following front-page story:

> After fierce fighting, troops on the Belarusian front liberated the city of Rechitsa, a major node of communications and an important stronghold of German defence on the right bank of the middle branch of the River Dnieper. Troops on the 1st Ukrainian front broke the resistance of the enemy and wrested control of the important railway junction at Korosten, a major stronghold of German defence. The Soviet people glorify the heroic soldiers of the Red Army!

Every page of *Pravda* was devoted to the war – there was no other news, nothing about any aspect of civilian life. This was the context for Zygmunt Bauman's eighteenth birthday.

A few weeks earlier, 'I was shaken out of a state of half dream, half fever by a call-up summons', Bauman wrote in his manu-script: 'Much to my amazement and dismay, I had been mobilized to the Moscow police' (Bauman, 1986/7: 47). Bauman probably hoped to be sent to the new 'Kosciuszko' division, but it was not to be. At the time, the commissioners were operating at a breakneck speed, sending off the candidates without physically examining them or even inspecting their files with any attention. The commission gave the recruit a *komandirovka*[2] – a letter telling the holder to get to the destination listed on it as quickly as pos-sible. That was it.

Bauman wrote in his manuscript that the call-up order came some weeks before his birthday, but one archival source says he was mobilized to the 7th Traffic Management Department in January 1944 by the Shakhunia commission,[3] while yet another document[4] says his military activity started in December 1943. In his manuscript, Bauman wrote that he had several weeks of training, but he told me there was no such thing: 'They just gave us the clothes; second-hand uniforms, actually. Then they put us out on the street and that was it! It is no big deal to learn how to wave your hands.'[5] He probably did receive some general military training in the November–December 1943 period, however, and it's possible an illness could have delayed his trip to Moscow.

No official document explains why Bauman was taken into the Moscow militia. It could be read as a favour, an effort to protect an active member of Komsomol who had finished Soviet high school with honours, was enrolled in the second year of university training and on track to becoming a member of the intelligentsia. Many educated candidates such as Bauman were not sent directly to the front, but rather tracked as NCOs (non-commissioned officers), and first spent some weeks in an officer training school. After some weeks of preparation, they, too, were sent to the front. But there were also reasons why a young Polish Jew would end up directing traffic in Moscow rather than fighting at the front. Military commissions applied various criteria when considering the recruitment of Jews to the 1st Division, according to historian Klemens Nussbaum. Some sent all Jews to the division, while others gave separate treatment to Jews who came from Central or Eastern Poland, mobilizing only the former. 'Most frequently, however', he writes, 'there was a total refusal to call up Jews' (Nussbaum, 1991: 190).

Alternately, the assignment could have been related to Stalin's paranoia and all-encompassing fear of conspiracies. 'At some point he decided to replace the Moscow militia and got the idea to recruit foreigners, such as Latvians, Lithuanians and Poles', Bauman told me; 'These groups didn't like Muscovites, so they would be unlikely to conspire with them. In my case this wasn't exactly the case – I really liked those Muscovites – but that was the premise.' Bauman spent three months 'regulating traffic', of which 'there was hardly any'. The only cars on the streets carried 'very important persons. Our job was to stand on the middle line, and we were not even allowed to look at them! We turned our heads when such cars passed by.'[6]

Service in the militia was a lifesaving option for Bauman, but he was unhappy about it. Like most young people who lived in the Soviet Union at that time, he wanted to take an active part in the war. 'I hated my new job', Zygmunt wrote in his manuscript, and after a few weeks there he applied to join the Polish Army:

Permission was granted, and together at the rank-stripping ceremony
I was dressed in a motley assortment of antique and threadbare
parts of uniforms worn by past generation of Moscow policemen,
given an ounce of caviar (to replace the pound of sausage due, but
'temporarily unavailable'), and sent on a 500-mile-long journey to
Sumy in Ukraine, where the new Polish Army was being put together.
(Bauman, 1986/7: 48)

The military document from a Lieutenant Pasakiewicz dated 27
December 1949 confirms Bauman's voluntary enrolment: '[Bauman]
retired at his own request from the militia and joined the Polish 1st
Army in the USSR. He was sent to the Polish Army officer's school
in Sumy, where he completed training on 16 June 1944.'[7] To effectu-
ate this transfer, Bauman had taken advantage of the fact that his
militia post was a few hundred metres from a Polish–Soviet friendship institute, the Union of Polish Patriots,[8] located at a place called
the Big Stone Bridge. Bauman went there one day and met Marian
Naszkowski, who got him out of the militia and into the Polish 4th
Division.[9]

Why the 'Red' and not the Anders Army?

Some of Bauman's anti-communist critics in Poland have attacked
him for having joined the Polish units of the Red Army during
the war, and not the so-called Anders Army. This is a completely
unreasonable criticism, first because Bauman was too young to have
joined the latter, which in any case did not normally accept Jews.

The Anders Army was created in Soviet territories in August
1941 on the basis of the Sikorski–Majski pact. This agreement
between the Polish government-in-exile in London and the Soviet
government allowed Polish citizens remaining in the USSR to join
the newly created military unit and fight under British command.
There were two categories of Poles in Russia at the time: those who
had been deported, jailed, put in the Gulag,[10] etc.; and those living
without specific restrictions other than the Paragraph 11 prohibition on foreigners living in big cities or within 100 kilometres of the
border. The 1941 agreement set a limit of 30,000 soldiers, but eventually 77,000 recruits and more than 43,000 civilians left the Soviet
Union.[11] They were named after General Władysław Anders, the
unit's commander.

Why did Bauman not join the Anders Army? First, he did not
turn 18 until late 1943, by which time it was too late – Soviet authorities forbade enrolment after April 1942. Bauman could have lied,[12]
but, even if he had wanted to join it, his family name would probably have disqualified him. All Poles knew it as a Jewish name, and

most of the commissions (composed of Polish officers) that selected soldiers for the unit would not accept Jews. In some places, commissioners would say that Stalin had taken Jewish refugees from Eastern, Soviet-occupied Polish territories 'under protection'. They had become Soviet citizens; in consequence, under Polish law they were no longer citizens, and could not be incorporated into a Polish Army.[13]

This wasn't exactly true, as historian Yisrael Gutman,[14] notes but 'it is true that during these later stages, the Soviets forbade the recruiting of some of the minorities, including Jews. This prohibition was not strictly enforced, but since it was open to varying interpretations it served the Poles as a pretext for closing the door to Jews.'[15] One of Gutman's informers added: 'During the examination, most of the Jews were marked grade "D" for physical fitness and were released from the service. . . . The Polish Army remained free of Jews – *judenrein* as the Germans put it. From then on, Jews were not accepted into the Polish Army; only Poles were accepted.'[16] Jan Tomasz Gross, citing Simon Redlich, estimated that, of 130,000 Polish citizens who left the USSR under the Sikorski–Majski agreement, 8,000 were Jews. Some 30 per cent of the Polish emigrants in the Soviet Union were Jews at this time, but only 6 per cent of the Anders Army recruits were Jewish (Redlich, 1971, in Gross, 1998).

Had Bauman wanted to join the Anders Army, his Komsomol engagement would have been a further red mark. The British Army and its Polish ally were generally anti-left, and Anders soldiers often blamed Jewish candidates for supporting the Red Army in September 1939, when the Soviets annexed eastern Polish territories. In fact, Jews did not generally support the Soviet occupation, and those who did sometimes had good reason, since the new regime promised to abolish the ethnic discrimination from which they suffered. In any case, young Jews with communist convictions who wanted to fight the Nazis had only one serious option, which was to join the new Polish Army under control of the Soviet authorities.[17]

4th Infantry Division

Bauman wrote little about his experience with the Polish Army under Red Army control, perhaps because of the lack of agency he felt at that time: he was a cog in a war machine and, like hundreds of thousands of other soldiers, had no impact on orders, decisions or events. At the April 1943 meeting of the Polish communist leadership and NKVD General Yury Zhukov that gave birth to the Polish force, Colonel Zygmunt Berling was designated commander of a division named after the Polish national hero Tadeusz Kościuszko. It was also agreed the unit would keep Polish traditions for its uniforms and distinctions, its anthems and state emblems (Nussbaum, 1991: 184–5). The Kościuszko Division would eventually become the First Polish Army, after it expanded and supplementary divisions were created: 'By March 1944, the Polish force included three infantry divisions, along with tank units, artillery and auxiliary units, in total 40,000 people' (Nussbaum, 1991: 186). The 4th Division (that included 6th PAL-infantry, Bauman's unit) was later called 'the Pomeranian' after the battles along the so-called 'Pomeranian Wall' of Nazi fortifications. At the end of the war, it was rechristened the Colonel Kilinski Division, after a hero of the Kościuszko insurrection.

Nussbaum, a former Kościuszko Division soldier and, later, Israeli historian, describes the unit's complex ethnicity and national identity:

> At the time there were 690,000 to 750,000 Poles in the Soviet Union, of whom 40–50 per cent were Jews. The reserves of young Poles capable of performing military service had been severely reduced as a result of about 70,000 being called into General Anders' army. The overwhelming majority of the Polish intelligentsia had evacuated together with this army. The Poles [Catholics] in the USSR were almost exclusively people who had been forcibly deported and were hostile to the Soviet authorities and their initiatives. . . . The Jewish community admittedly also was made up, to a large degree, of oppressed people, but many of them had come to the Soviet Union on their own accord, escaping from the Germans. These refugees did not labour under the same complexes *vis-à-vis* the Soviet Union as those who had been forcibly evacuated there. (Nussbaum, 1991: 187)

Or, as Bauman described the situation:

> This was a strange army, if ever there was one. The Red Army had recently recaptured a few patches of the pre-war Polish territory and eager to have a Polish ally at his side as soon as possible, Stalin took a somewhat illogical step and ordered to enlist local peasants, whom he a few years ago converted into Soviet citizens [and created] a Polish Army. And so the enclosure of the former Cadet School swarmed with fresh recruits of non-descript identity – themselves unsure where they truly belonged, speaking a sort of Polish heavily infused with Ukrainian words in the tuneful, meditative Ukrainian fashion. On the top of this crowd, only superficially sprinkled with a few 'true Poles' like myself, there were some NCOs of the old Polish Army, painstakingly gathered from the nooks and crannies of Siberia or Central Asia, where they scattered after release from POW camps. Higher up still only Russian was spoken. Polish commissioned officers had been murdered en masse in Katyń. Those who were lucky to escape that

fate had left Russia with Anders' Army after Stalin's brief but uncon-
summated romance with the Polish Government in exile. (Bauman,
1986/7: 49)

A similar opinion was shared by military historian Jerzy
Nafalski, also a former soldier in the 4th Division, and the author
of the book devoted to the history of this unit,[18] which he qualified as 'atypical'. The average age of the soldiers was 34, Nafalski
wrote, and men up to 42 years of age were recruited – almost
every fifth soldier was over 50. At the other extreme were many
very young juveniles who 'to some extent lowered the age of the
"statistical" soldier' (Nafalski, 1978: 25–6). Zygmunt Bauman was
one of those young people who joined the 4th Division. He even
committed an act of forgery (very popular in those days), changing his birth year from 1925 to 1924. As he explained in an annex
to his handwritten Army CV on 3 January 1950,[19] he was afraid
that otherwise he would have been considered too young to join
the officer school.

The training camp was organized in Sumy (Nafalski, 1978: 7), a
small Ukrainian city about 200 miles east of Kiev. Bauman arrived
in April 1944. 'When we entered, marching in the military column
into the barracks gate, we were welcomed by a military orches-
tra', Nafalski wrote; 'Sounds of the Polish march that we heard
caused an unforgettable emotion. Tears ran down our faces. We
experienced a great and beautiful thing' (Nafalski, 1978: 10). These
recruits had arrived after long and arduous journeys, travelling over
long distances across the Soviet Union, frequently after experiencing
horrible privations, imprisonment and/or forced labour. For Polish
Jews, there was an additional motivation to muster, as many
witnesses have testified – here they were accepted as Poles, were
considered just as Polish as their Christian compatriots. According
to Nussbaum:

> Acceptance into the army itself and the attainment of soldier status
> was viewed as beneficial by the Jews. Their social position was
> changed. Hitherto, they had belonged to a disintegrated group of
> people dispersed over the enormous area of the Soviet Union, con-
> demned to hunger and misery, regarded as a suspicious and foreign
> element. Their acceptance into the army enabled them to make a
> break with that existence. They entered a community. Admittedly they
> were subject to military rigor, but they lived under human conditions
> and were guided by humane principles of co-existence. (Nussbaum,
> 1991: 204)

For some there was a feeling of release, a sense they had entered an
antechamber of home. As Bauman wrote later:

At the gates of the pre-revolutionary Cadet School in Sumy, I arrived on my last legs and barefoot; most of my officially allocated clothes fell apart together with their long-past glory. The first thing I heard at the gate was the Polish language. The first thing I saw was the Polish Eagle adorning the gate and on the cap of the sentry. I felt I had reached the end of my wanderings. I was home. (Bauman, 1986/7: 48–9)

The mustering-in camp was mobbed, with waves of candidates arriving every day: 'Approximately 500 people arrived daily at the recruitment centre in Sumy. The barracks were quite roomy, but not sufficient to accommodate all the new 4th Infantry Division soldiers. Nearby villages were designated for organizing the individual units' (Nafalski, 1978: 18). According to the memories of former soldier Wacław Zakrzewski, Sumy had been heavily damaged in the war, and the barracks were located about a kilometre outside the city (Czapigo and Białas, 2015: 158). Most of the training took place in Sumy and another Ukrainian town, Zhitomir. Between May and June 1944, 135 units were created, with 73,544 new soldiers, according to historian Marcin Białas (in Czapigo and Białas, 2015: 164). Zygmunt Bauman was one of them.

Officers' cadet school

Bauman spent three or four weeks[20] training at the cadet school and became an NCO (non-commissioned officer). Even in wartime, this was a remarkably accelerated course, but, as Bauman explained:

There was a saying, 'no bachelor certificate but a sincere desire will make you an officer'. But during the war, a bachelor's degree meant something. Very few of us had it. This is why they accepted me to officer school. . . . We were a very small group, fewer than twenty, and we lived in barracks that previously were part of a czarist cadet school. . . . Only a few of us had a diploma, only a few spoke Polish. The majority of officers spoke Russian and poor Polish.[21]

This shortage of suitable officer candidates was not unique to the Sumy school. It was also observed at the much larger, and somewhat older, Polish officer candidate school in Sielce on the Oka River. 'At the school, almost all were Russian officers, who were called "pop" – which meant, "in charge of the duties of the Poles".[22] These were mostly officers of Polish origin who, during the Second Republic of Poland, lived in Russia or in Soviet Ukraine or Belarus. Some spoke Polish quite well, with the so-called "Lviv" accent, but there were also those who murdered the language' (Szer, 2013: 129).

The lack of a fluent Polish-speaking command was a source of conflict. The Russian-speaking officers with their bumbling Polish were
sometimes perceived as an alien power (see several testimonies in
Czapigo and Białas, 2015).

Bauman also mentioned this problem: 'To command the new
Polish troops the Red Army lent its own officers', he wrote:

> Some of them could trace Polish ancestors and still bore Polish-
> sounding names; many Poles settled in Russia after their term of
> Siberian exile, or having involved themselves in Russian revolutionary
> struggles. Most of the 'borrowed' officers did not aspire to any Polish
> connection whatsoever. Virtually none of them, Pole or non-Pole,
> spoke any Polish language or was willing to admit that he now served
> in an army which differed from the Red one in anything but the design
> of the uniforms. (Bauman, 1986/7: 49)

Of course, there were hardly any Polish officers to be had in the
wake of Katyń and the Anders Army's departure. 'The small group
of about 200 Polish communists, and a reserve officer group of
about the same size – mostly Jewish – could not fill all the staff posts
in the army', as Klemens Nussbaum noted; 'The training of new
staff, even at an accelerated war pace, required time, and moreover
the selection of trusted officer candidates was made more difficult
due to the attitude of the Poles'[23] (Nussbaum, 1991: 188). The newly
created army lacked trusted candidates with Polish roots to handle
senior positions. Bauman, however, had many qualifications (skills
in Polish and Russian, a cultured and educated background, communist political involvement and a clean past), and was thus a
perfect officer candidate. Moreover, his role as a Komsomol leader
showed political trustworthiness (Bauman concealed all traces of his
activity in Hashomer Hatzair). He had the perfect background for
becoming a 'political officer':

'The founders of the Association of Polish Patriots, old Polish
Communists and Socialists or veterans of the Spanish Civil War,
now dressed in generals' and colonels' uniforms, faced the mind-
boggling task of making that awesome concoction into a Polish
Army', Bauman wrote:

> The Army was in Russia, commanded by all-too-Soviet officers and
> about to fight alongside the Red Army on the Russian front. What
> was far from being clear was the Polish identity of that Army. And so
> the generals and the colonels fished for anybody who could help to
> inject the Army with the Polish spirit. Everyone with a good ground-
> ing in Polish culture and some higher education was set aside for
> this task. With my first year of physics completed and the second
> well advanced, and with my experience of solid Polish education, I

was fished out almost immediately after crossing the gate. (Bauman, 1986/7: 49–50)

The desire to inculcate a sense of 'Polishness' was a common theme for everyone concerned with building this Polish Army, whose political leadership was given to the ZPP, Nussbaum notes. There was a need to break down the recruits' distrust of the Army, which they saw as a Bolshevik creation, and to win them over to the ZPP programme:

> The organizers took care to ensure that soldiers came into contact with and felt an atmosphere of Polishness in their unit. . . . All the Catholic holidays were celebrated as well as the prewar military and state holidays. All means of influencing soldiers were employed, above all through their patriotic feelings and their yearning for the Homeland. The slightest ideas of any political changes of a socialist character in Poland were kept from them. In fact quite the opposite; an effort was made to assure the soldiers that there would not be a similar system in Poland to that of the Soviet Union. An independent, democratic and just Poland for everyone was talked of. National solidarity and the unity of the whole nation in the fight against the Germans was proclaimed (Nussbaum, 1991: 188).

This crucial camouflage was to be applied by the political officers. Bauman was selected to become one of them.

A political officer in Berling's Army

> I found myself among [a] bizarre group of people – of all ages, all types of biographies, all religious and political denominations, all shades of ideological spectrum. The only thing which united them was the unswerving loyalty to their Polish identity and perfect command of Polish. No one had a military training worth speaking about, not unlike most of the generals and colonels who selected them. Yet in the span of three weeks we were to be trained into the officers of the Polish Army. We were to serve as 'deputy commanders for political affairs' – a Polish antidote against the Russian allegiance of the commanders. (Bauman, 1986/7: 50)

The education of political officers was supervised by Major Józef Urbanowicz (deputy defence minister in the 1970s). Urbanowicz was very popular and close to the young cadets. The training started in the third week of May 1944 (Nafalski, 1978: 25), and Bauman was in the first group at Sumy. The process of training was described by a former soldier, Bolesław Dańko:

The educators wore the officer's uniform, which consisted of chrome boots (leather tanned with chromium salts, resistant to moisture and mould), *Galife* blue trousers, jacket, main belt with crossbar, field bag, pistol and cap. At first they had no distinction on the shoulder straps. Later, they were given military degrees, mostly warrant officer. Such a military rank in the prewar Polish army existed, but not as an officer's grade. In the division such a soldier was considered a first officer, equivalent to a junior lieutenant in the Red Army. (Dańko, in Czapigo and Białas, 2015: 58–9)

Bauman, after complaining about the poor condition of his militia uniform, received a new outfit that corresponded to his significant new role (Dańko, in Czapigo and Białas, 2015: 58). As one of the few political officers, Bauman was to become deputy commander of a small unit. He took a three-week training course to prepare. It 'consisted almost entirely of lectures about Polish history and literature – something I enjoyed enormously. What I enjoyed less was the "military" part of our training, conducted exclusively by a pre-war sergeant who of all mysteries of the military arts remembered only the marching drill.' The sergeant's efforts to infuse the 'overly intellectual riff-raff' under his command failed to instil a spirit of military discipline, Bauman added (Bauman, 1986/7: 50).

Bauman's job was to give talks to the soldiers, and the repertoire of themes was not broad, according to what has been written by other former political officers. The topics included the September 1939 defeat, the future democratic Poland, and the London government, one wrote. The listeners generally didn't ask questions; that could lead to accusations of being unreliable, and, besides, none of their real questions would be answered. The majority accepted the Russian proverb: *тише едешь дальше будешь* (The quieter you go, the further you'll get). 'If there were sincere discussions, they occurred within a very narrow circle of colleagues' (Dańko, in Czapigo and Białas, 2015: 59). Another former soldier spoke about their preparation for talks, which included lectures from Lieutenant Jerzy Putrament, the company's deputy commander for cultural and educational affairs:

He discussed the situation on the international scene, commented on current events on the fronts, with particular emphasis on the eastern front, explained the dangers of the future Poland without specifying its system or territorial shape. It was to be a democratic Poland in which social justice was in force. There was no mention of socialism, of Marxist–Leninist ideology, of any leading political party. We had to fight as allies of the Soviet Army for [a democratic] homeland. However, the activities of Marshal Piłsudski, and Poland's capitalist past, were heavily criticized, and notably absent were topics such as

the Ribbentrop–Molotov Pact and the invasion of the Red Army on
the eastern territories of the Commonwealth.[24]

Putrament, a left-wing graduate of the Stefan Batory University in
Vilnius, with a literary past, provided lively and interesting lectures,
spiced with anecdotes from his prewar life. 'He impressed me with
his knowledge and erudition', wrote soldier Roman Marchwicki: 'I
liked his sharp and rude statements, spoken with a Vilnius accent.
His often controversial attitudes, different from the official views,
enabled him to inspire confidence' (Marchwicki, in Czapigo and
Białas, 2015: 68–9).

Putrament was perhaps the model educational officer described
in accounts of the era. The goal of the officers was to bring their
audience to acceptance – and hopefully to active support – of the
new regime that would be implanted in Poland once it was liberated
from German occupation. The political officer was the 'soul' and
'brain' of the Army. He was to be the spine of the future political
system in Poland.

Indoctrination had to be performed smoothly; one couldn't jar
people with the prospect of enormous social and economic change.
At the Sielce officer school, Putrament talked about a future democratic Poland, about social justice.[25] 'Words such as socialism and
communism were not used at all' (Szer, 2013: 130). The Army was
composed of a population diverse in age, social class and ethnicity,
and responses varied from person to person. Jewish soldiers, as
Nussbaum noted, who had suffered ethnic discrimination in prewar
Poland, were more open to the organizers' aims. 'The mirage of
a democratic Poland diffused by ZPP propaganda worked more
quickly and more strongly on them' (Nussbaum, 1991: 199).

The political officers' work was more difficult with older Catholic
soldiers, former workers and peasants. As one former officer wrote,
this period 'was not easy in terms of political work . . . I talked in the
train about agricultural reform',[26] but 'my listeners were either completely passive sick or elderly soldiers in their fifties, Silesians and
Łódź inhabitants from the Wehrmacht or prewar-NCOs – military
settlers in the Eastern Polish territories. To exaggerate . . . I added a
few facts on the pitiful lives of the workers, the lack of a future for
the intellectuals. . . . I exaggerated!'[27] (Daniel Rudnicki, in Czapigo
and Białas, 2015: 177–8).

No 20-year-old, even one dressed in the beautiful uniform of the
political officer, was particularly credible to a group of exhausted,
sick 50-year-olds. They were eager to return home, but a change of
the political system was perhaps not among their goals in the middle
of the war.

Bauman was thrust into a theatre that required mixtures of
subtlety and bombast. The talks and discussions were performed

during military transport, during pauses in camp, between the battles. They were frequently given in hospitals, but also in freshly liberated cities, towns and villages – everywhere, in short. The political officers gave their half-prepared, half-spontaneous speeches from the backs of trucks and train wagons, from classical podiums or ordinary furniture, to groups of people thirsty for news from the battle and about the political future. The future they presented was the abolition of social class divisions. While the soldiers were mostly peasants and workers, many of the political officers were Polish Jews, who had earned the trust of the Soviet commanders. 'There were more representatives of the intelligentsia amongst the Jewish soldiers, particularly amongst the refugees from central and western Poland', Nussbaum writes: 'The Jews also earned greater trust due to their uncompromising attitude to the Germans. It should be assumed that these were the main and decisive reasons for there being so many Jews in the officer corps' (Nussbaum, 1991: 199).

Nussbaum's research showed that more than a third of the 1,360 political officers in all units were Polish Jews – exactly 34 per cent in the 4th Division (Nussbaum, 1991: 196–7). Apart from their propagandizing function, they were also liaisons between the Soviet line officers and the rank and file. They sought to neutralize the soldiers' feeling of alienation from the predominantly Russified officer corps (Nussbaum, 1991: 190). They enabled the communication that, over time, transformed this diverse group into a united army. And they believed in what they were saying: in a future Poland without discrimination or social injustice. Yet the fact that most of the rank-and-file soldiers expressed anti-Semitic opinions and were suspicious of communist ideas and the Soviet political system posed a huge challenge. Only one value unified everyone: Poland.

When Polish soul needs a Polish name

Troop morale is a crucial element of any army. Strange as the Polish Army was as a military formation, it required Polishness to unify and homogenize the diverse group serving in its ranks. This was a crucial part of daily educational activities, but also in the special events for recruits. At concerts and theatre presentations, patriotic songs and dance performances should inspire courage, faith and a sense of power in the struggle for liberation of the home country. Artistic expressions packed an emotional punch that sometimes lodged in the memories of soldiers even more powerfully than battle experiences. 'The day I remember best was a visit of the army theatre', Bauman wrote in his manuscript:

and of the visit, I recall most vividly one song. The huge ballroom of the old Cadet School was tightly packed with hundreds of soldiers; for many of them, this was perhaps the first experience of a live performer on stage. A brittle dark-haired girl climbed the scene and began to sing – in a thin, almost childish, yet soft and velvety voice. The song was dedicated to Warsaw. The lyrics spoke of the beauty of Warsaw streets, the joy of walking them again, of breathing the air of that most loved of all cities. I had never been to Warsaw, I had never heard about Warsaw streets. In my part of the country, Warsaw was not held in high esteem: a dirty, disorderly Oriental place, unlike the neat, tidy, civilized and Western Poznan. And yet I wept. I could not stop myself although I did try . . . hard – I was, after all, in that under-defined age when one has to prove one's still uncertain manhood. Apparently, one can feel nostalgia for the future. I felt it, anyway. (Bauman, 1986/7: 50–1)

This was a powerful dream based on nationalistic feelings with a new twist. Polishness before World War II had been reserved for Catholic Poles. Here, in the middle of Russia, it was being claimed by Poles with Jewish roots. The director of the theatre that performed for the Polish soldiers – Leon Pasternak – and the majority of his actors were Jews. So were many of those working in other institutions charged with cultivating Polishness in the Army, such as documentary filmmakers and journalists from *New Horizons, Free Poland* or *Soldier of Freedom*. Moreover, the political leadership of the Army was largely Jewish. (Among the seven principal members of the ZPP, only the communist journalist Wanda Wasilewska was not born into a Jewish family.)[28]

The communist authorities, aware of the widespread anti-Semitism among Catholic Polish soldiers, made huge efforts to hide the contribution of Polish Jews. For authors of news articles, the solution was to employ fake, typically Polish names. At *New Horizons* and *Free Poland*, the journalists H. Minc, W. Grosz, A. Lampe, P. Hofman, S. Wierbłowski, J. Stryjkowski and R. Juryś each used a pen name 'to cover up their Jewish origins and to give readers the impression that a larger number of Poles worked with the paper', Nussbaum writes (Nussbaum, 1991: 184). For officers, the concealment required more than just a pen name. Jewish officers were instructed to change their first names and surnames, not to admit to their Jewishness and to give their nationality as Polish, Nussbaum writes. Some followed those rules and others refused: 'Of those who changed their names, some had been persuaded to do so by the arguments used, and some did so out of opportunism, believing it would open the path to a military career. . . . [However,] [p]eople whose names had been changed had their records shamefully marked by the letter "Ż" so that those in authority would know' (Nussbaum, 1991: 195).[29]

This policy of name-changing followed the Soviet model of dealing with Jewishness. Jan Gross has written that there were two models of anti-Semitism: the classical form, practised in pre- and post-war Poland; and inculturation, which was implemented in the Soviet Union:

[T]he ghetto was tolerated in the classic model of anti-Semitism, manifested first of all in the contact between the Jewish and dominant ethnic communities in the state. . ... In the Soviet Union, it was *vice versa*. The insularity and self-separation of the Jewish community were unacceptable to the Communists. Jews could stay Soviet citizens and have all rights due to them, but they were not allowed to keep autonomy and cultural separateness. So the eternal dilemma: how to be a Jew and a citizen of a given state at the same time? – remained unresolved. In the classic discrimination model Jews were not allowed to become actual citizens, in the Soviet model – Jews were deprived of their Jewishness. However, in practice this last model meant opening access to jobs, colleges, schools, professions that were previously unattainable for Jews. (Gross, 2010: 607)

In the first period of Soviet administration, 'Jews – especially the young, who perceived the closed world of their own community as weighing on them – got the chance of social advancement and recovered, so to speak, a sense of personal dignity. It was for them a stunning and unforgettable experience', Gross writes. The Soviet system offered them a chance to break away from traditional connections, because Sovietization broke the traditional social controls of the Jewish community. 'In other words', writes Gross, 'it was the prospect of emancipation, detachment from Jewishness that attracted young Jews to cooperate with the new system, not an affirmation of some common Jewish–Soviet relations or interests' (Gross, 2010: 607).

Bauman was invited to change his name:

A day or two after the concert I was called to one of the staff offices. I was met there by a woman in a captain's uniform. She asked about my past, my present thoughts, my intentions. It was a long leisurely pleasant conversation. When I thought we had finished and prepared to leave, she said something which made me freeze in my chair; I thought I misunderstood and asked her to repeat. There was no mistake, though. I was asked to change my name. You know, your name does not sound hundred-percent Polish. It is not an awful name, of course, there are other names much worse, much more foreign-sounding and ridiculous. But still . . . We are a Polish Army, you see. And you yourself have said that you feel Polish. So what about a nice Polish name? I do not remember my answer. I was too discomposed and agitated to control my words and to record them in my memory. But I flatly refused the offer. I was not ashamed of my name. And I did not feel my Polishness was something like a badge, or a name. It was inside me, where it was safe, and it did not need a certificate. (Bauman, 1986/7: 51)

Bauman was sure of his Polish identity and his Polishness. As a Polish soldier, fully enjoying his rights and without the discrimination that was common in the prewar period or in Anders' Army, he lived on an equal basis with Catholic Poles. For Bauman, this was not about politics, changing one's identity or creating a military career: he merely wanted as a soldier to bring freedom to his homeland.

A soldier's life

According to one document, Bauman was appointed platoon leader on 16 April 1944, and promoted to warrant officer on 26 August.[30] A 27 December 1947 document signed by Lieutenant Paszkiowicz says Bauman finished his military training on 6 June 1944, and was assigned to the 6th Artillery Regiment of the 4th Division. The modest differences in detail are typical of the small errors and omissions in Bauman's record. Between spring 1944 and Liberation in May 1945, Bauman's life was 'entirely part of the history of the 4th Division', he recalled. After the training camp, 'we were transported in very comfortable conditions by freight train (other units usually moved on foot) from Kharkov to Ołyka. We built a camp in the forest near Kowel, and then we went to the front', Bauman told me in our interview:[31]

> It was the time of the Warsaw Uprising . . . we were standing on the other side [of the Vistula River] on the right side of Warsaw in Saska Kepa. . . .. [long silence] . . . We watched how the 3rd Division was almost destroyed after a failed raid, and we stood there until January . . . and in January began the real war. In the beginning we were a little bit behind the front line but afterwards came Kołobrzeg. Starting with the Pomeranian Wall it was all different – we were in the first line of the front.

The artillery unit was organized around the village of Syrowatka, near Sumy, and was under the command of Major Edward Kumpicki (Nafalski, 1978: 19–20). Bauman joined the regiment in Ołyka, near Kowel in Volhynia, a region now in western Ukraine. Gaining technical military knowledge was crucial for fighting, but also for building authority, since Bauman was so much younger than most of the soldiers whom he outranked. He took a brief artillery course, on the final day of which he was summoned to a briefing where he was told he would be appointed a deputy company commander, with full powers but no commission:

> To deserve a commission, we had to pass the practical test. Some of us were nonplussed – this was not what we expected. One person asked the question which I guess was on everybody else's lips: Without rank, how can we gain the authority we need to command? The colonel in charge of the briefing, a veteran of the Spanish War, old communist and a high-calibre intellectual, responded: 'If you do not gain authority without rank, rank wouldn't help anyway.' . . . Looking back, I believe this last and curt lesson was more important than all the lectures and exercises the course had to offer. And perhaps not just that one course. (Bauman, 1986/7: 51–2)

Bauman learned the lesson well, as evidenced in various military documents and interviews with people who worked with him. They described a 'natural authority' as one of his most characteristic attributes.

Asked about the experience of 'being an artilleryman', Zygmunt responded with a smile:

> It would be a selfish statement to say I was an artilleryman. I was the deputy commander of the fifth[32] artillery battery . . . Do you think that everyone in an artillery regiment is an artilleryman? You need to know something in this area and I was a debutant . . . Fortunately I served under a great battery commander. His name was Lange; he was a descendant of Polish Siberians [people condemned to live several years in Siberia]. He felt himself a Pole. He was very nice and very capable, very smart, and this is why the battery was always in top form . . . We had four seventy-six [76 mm cannons] and one howitzer. . . . good old-fashioned cannons that are no longer in use, . . . but we had Studebakers from US supplies . . . so-called war help – these were American trucks.[33]

Bauman, recognizing that his senior position at this young age did not result from military knowledge or soldiering skills, shied away from playing the hero. He was 'only' the deputy, with an excellent, experienced boss who knew how to 'handle cannons'.

The following citation is an important one, because Bauman analyses his peculiar situation at that moment, and interrogates his identity – his *master status*.[34] How did subordinates perceive him at that moment? 'I was an 18-year-old with no commission, but already in charge of fifty-odd souls, most of them seated in bodies twice my age', Bauman wrote to his daughters:

The only commander trying to impress it upon those souls that the language through which they made themselves audible was Polish rather than Russian, Ukrainian, or 'local'. The only person trying to achieve this with at best a condescending disdain or ironic indifference from platoon commanders, nominally my subordinates, but in fact by far my superiors: truly trained and experienced military men. How did they see me, my soldiers? As an alien, I presume. Yet, alien as a Jew? Or as a Pole? Or as a man in power – something they learned not to expect anything good from and were thoroughly fed up with – whether it came in Polish, Russian or German disguise? I did not know then and I would never know. The thing I knew was that – rank or no rank – I was a Polish officer, fighting for the Polish cause. In the artillery battery to which I was assigned, I was Poland. (Bauman, 1986/7: 52)

Bauman – a Polish officer – also shared regular tasks with his soldiers. The 4th Division moved to Ołyka on 17 June. Until the end of July 1944, they stayed there, digging in to protect themselves from German raids. As they did each time they were in a single place for a few days, the company built dugouts, using shovels, saws and axes, and set up guard, as Szer recalls:

During the day the officers conducted exercises so that the army was not bored and went to sleep tired . . . When we could we built . . . furnaces and chimneys from American smoked-meat cans. Such canned, swallowed stew (stewed or smoked pork) were then the only visible sign of US aid in the infantry; the weapons and ammunition were exclusively Soviet. These square cans, about a metre or more in length, could be connected and made a chimney. (Szer, 2013: 134)

Especially in the first months, when the division was not directly engaged in frontline battles, the soldiers had more time for cooking and enjoying meals. The canned meat, for the time, was:

great: greasy, tasty and nutritious. The best portion in our menu, which consisted mostly of dense bread and coffee. Every day a platoon received a few loaves of bread and shared the bread as soon as the conditions allowed, according to the established ritual: people sat in a compact group on the ground, and in front of each other, face to face, one boy sat – often, though, not always – it was 'zaśpiewajło' [the singer, in a dialect].[35] Behind him, one of the team leaders cut the bread into equal parts, showed the freshly cut piece of bread over his head so that everyone could see and called: ready! Then the zaśpiewajło sang out the names of members of the group, in no particular order, until everyone got their allotment. In my platoon, there was an absolutely fair distribution of the important material goods – no possibility of

fraud or 'exploitation of man by man'; in the other military divisions
the rules were the same. (Szer, 2013: 135)

Keeping a busy schedule, organizing each activity while leaving
only modest amounts of private time, was a way of maintaining
control of the troops. Former soldier Roman Marchwicki recalled:

> The schedule of the day included only a little free time after dinner.
> In practice, however, even then we studied the rules and manuals,
> and sometimes we had to do the cleaning work for the unit. It was
> rare that I could sit down and read some scrap of press to learn what
> was going on in the world or what was happening in big politics. I
> could read the two pages of the newspaper *Soldier of Freedom* cover
> to cover, but I had problems with *Free Poland*, published by the
> Association of Polish Patriots – because of its size it took too long to
> read. (Czapigo and Białas, 2015: 68)

Obviously, the sources of information were severely restricted – only
the communist press was available.

Bauman realized at this moment how little a human being
could control his time when he belonged to an organization such
as a military division. 'I came very quickly to the conclusion',
Bauman told me, 'that the true privilege was not to sleep later,
but rather that the sergeant give you permission to get up half
an hour or one hour before the general wake-up, because then
you could take an unrushed shower, with no crowd. At that time
I realized that getting up early is a greater privilege than getting
up later.' Getting up earlier meant a 'private' hour, stolen from a
day that belonged to the organization. Bauman maintained this
habit during the rest of his life, usually spending the early hours in
writing and reading.

Letter writing was another private realm for the soldiers. It was
strictly controlled by censors, of course, but Bauman and other
soldiers found ways to inform their friends and relatives – Bauman
wrote frequently to his parents – about advances and defeats.
Bauman would write, 'Uncle is already in Poland', instead of 'we
are already in Poland'. It was not difficult to get past the censor's
pen. But the 'Poland' that 'uncle' had re-entered was destined not to
be the same country after the war.

New borders, new political order

Jan Karski, the famous hero of World War II, was known for his
bravery in entering and escaping from Nazi concentration and
death camps to report on the extermination of European Jewry. He

was also a member of the Polish government-in-exile in London. In a 1997 interview with historian Andrzej Friszke, Karski said that:

> after [the tripartite meeting of Churchill, Roosevelt and Stalin in 1943 at] Tehran, I realized that territorial concessions would be a necessity for Poland. The problem was only, in what form this would occur, in order not to complicate the political situation of the London government. I believed that independence would somehow be maintained in Poland. At the same time, there was no doubt for me that cooperation with [Soviet] Russia would be necessary for our country. . . . It is necessary to realize – and then, now and for the future – that the fate of Poland is not solely in the hands of Poles. It also depends on the nature of the rule of the great powers and on international political constellations. . . . [As] early as 1943, England and the United States entered into a secret agreement, of which they did not inform the Poles, that the Soviet government would be responsible for military operations east of the Elbe River, and the USA, England and France to the west.[36]

This distribution of European territories put Poland under Soviet control. Stalin's wish to move his borders west was achieved by a winning army that progressively liberated Polish territories from German occupation. By the end of July 1944, the 4th Division was ordered to regroup in the area of Lublin, an important city within the newly traced borders. Early on 29 July, the division units transited through Łuck, Kowel and Luboml; crossed the Bug River near Drohuski; and entered Chełm, outside Lublin. In his 1978 book, Nafalski described the deep emotions of the troops as they crossed Poland's eastern border, but it was a new border. Most of the soldiers in the campaign viewed the towns and cities they previously had liberated as part of Poland, not as Ukraine or Belarus, their future identity. While emotions were undoubtedly high, there is some doubt as to when the troops felt they were really 'entering Poland'. It was probably not felt the same by everyone, considering Poles' doubts about the Tehran Conference – a post-Nazi iteration of the Molotov–Ribbentrop pact – that transformed the old Curzon Line into the new Soviet border with Poland.[37]

But in 1978 Poland, no book would be permitted to describe this ambiguity and tension. Nafalski presents the official version:

> The solemn, and at the same time joyful, mood appeared at the moment of entering the road leading to the Bug. Here was something that cannot be expressed in words. The soldiers' eyes shone with joy and emotion, and tears fell from some faces, which no one was ashamed of. The soldiers squeezed and kissed, blessing themselves for a happy arrival in the country and the possibility of fighting for its complete liberation. Then General Kiniewicz gave a passion-

ate speech to the soldiers, who spontaneously swore allegiance to the Polish soil and assured they would defend it against the enemy. (Nafalski, 1978: 32)

The 4th Division entered Chełm on 7 August, just two weeks after the Kościuszko Infantry Division.

Bauman recalled crossing the Bug, which the authorities proclaimed as a highly symbolic moment. 'A military train took us to the other end of already fully re-conquered Ukraine', he wrote to his daughters:

We disembarked at Olyka woods, not far from Kowel, a Polish property before the war, now annexed to the Soviet Ukraine. For a few days we stayed in the woods and went through the final preparation for joining the war action. Late in the evening I sat in the tent with my battery commander and the commander of the first platoon . . . We had our order for the next day: to cross the river Bug into the undisputed Polish territory. I think all three of us, though perhaps each for different reasons, were excited and restless. My battery commander turned to me. Tomorrow, we will be in Poland. I wonder what you think. Did you like it in Russia? You are a member of the *Komsomol* like me, I bet you would like to return to Russia when the war is over . . .

'No, I answered. I am a Pole, and I am about to return to my country.

'But would not Poland be much like Soviet Russia? What is the difference' – my commander pressed on. (Bauman, 1986/7: 51)

On 21 July, Soviet armies, followed by the main forces of the Polish Army, entered Chełm and Lublin. The Polish Army then consisted of six infantry divisions, five artillery brigades, one tank corps and a tank brigade, an anti-aircraft artillery division, a mortar regiment, fifteen sapper battalions and other auxiliary units (Nussbaum, 1991: 186).

Bauman's group – 6th PAL (Light Artillery Regiment) – remained in Chełm handling garrison service (Nafalski, 1978: 32). After Chełm, Bauman and his unit went to Lublin. 'My first sight when my battery entered Lublin was Majdanek . . . – one of the most horrible extermination camps the Nazis built in occupied Poland. The corpses were still lying around in heaps, their recycling begun yet unfinished', wrote Bauman in 2016 in a letter to his friend Keith Tester.[38] It was a crucial moment for Bauman, a personal experience of concentration camp atrocities that contributed to the powerful message of *Modernity and the Holocaust* decades later.

Chełm and Lublin were important Polish cities in July 1944, because it was there that the victorious army began implementing its

new political power to represent the Polish state. A manifesto communicating the new political orientation was published on 22 July
in Chełm, signed by Polish Communists and printed in Moscow.[39]
The document was signed by members of the Polish Committee of
National Liberation (President Edward Osóbka-Morawski, Vice-
presidents Wanda Wasilewska and Andrzej Witos). It specified that
power belonged to the Krajowa Rada Narodowa (KRN – State
National Council), and stripped the London government-in-exile
of all legitimacy. The document invalidated the last version of the
Polish Constitution (from 1935) and said the basis of law was the
former, 1921 constitution. The new shape of Poland (losing some
eastern territories while gaining western counterparts) was mentioned, as well as the agricultural reform, which promised peasants
access to their own fields. It also promised free access to education,
health care and housing, and state support of small private businesses and co-operatives. Lublin was to be Poland's provisional
new capital, housing a provisory state government, signifying a new
political order for the country. The provisional government promised free elections once the war ended, transforming Poland in a
direction compatible with the new geopolitical order.

Opposition to these changes was huge from the outset, with the
conflict pitting the London-based government and its underground
military unit, the Home Army or AK,[40] against the new power,
backed by the might of the Soviet Union. The provisional government increased its power progressively, viewed by local units of the
AK as an invader and enemy. The situation inside the liberated
territories at times veered towards civil war, as local underground
groups refused to recognize the new power and remained mobilized, fighting for the return of the London government. The new
powers hoped to secure their position in the long run, and legit-
imize it through postwar elections. To expand popular support
for socialist reforms, an education campaign was mobilized by the
same people who had been in charge of indoctrinating Polish Army
soldiers – political officers like Bauman.

Bringing the new ideology to everyone

The Soviets had enabled the creation of the Polish Army, according
to official accounts, 'to enable the Poles to participate in the war
against the Germans', Nussbaum writes:

> Events connected with its creation as well as its later activity testify,
> however, to the fact that the fight with fascism was not its primary
> concern nor an aim in itself but a means for realizing definite *political*
> aims. The Soviet Union created, armed and equipped the army, which

was to safeguard politically and militarily the operation of imposing a communist government on Poland. (Nussbaum, 1991: 183)

The political discussions, talks and debates conducted by political officers took place everywhere and with all kinds of people. There were two categories of listeners: first, the soldiers – they needed to know what kind of Poland they were fighting for. Second was the liberated civilian population. Daniel Rudnicki described how such talks were organized: 'Immediately after arriving in the city [Włoclawek], in a nice large theatre hall I organized a meeting, where I spoke a little about the origin, character and combat trail of our army and the current situation on the fronts. Characteristically – you would not see the same thing in Lublin – every word in Pomerania [here] was believed without reservation' (Rudnicki, in Czapigo and Białas, 2015: 272). According to this testimony, propaganda work was much easier in recovered central and western territories than it was in the east. The main goal was to encourage the civilian public to vote for the new political system – one that was no longer capitalistic but 'on the way to communism'. These public talks were crucial, given the permanent lack of information and the widespread feelings of insecurity in the newly liberated Polish territories. Another political officer, Józef Hen, who later became a popular writer, recalled the hunger for information and the sympathy he received in Kraków after entering the city in late January 1945, and in smaller towns along the way. 'I spoke everywhere . . . people surrounded our truck . . . they all came together around this truck very slowly and they said, "Please, lieutenant, say something – talk to us." After one performance of the troop's propaganda theatre, 'a guy shouted from the gallery: "Mister Lieutenant! You are a nice guy!"'

The propaganda officers, for the most part, insist that they ardently believed in the better future they were peddling to liberated Poles. 'At that time, our (and my) political orientation (we were freshly baked officers from the plough – exiles, convicts, forest workers, and *kolkhozniks*– suddenly returned to life and handed with news from one source) was too small and naive to properly assess and understand the true intentions of our military authorities',[41] wrote Jan Prorok:

Their actions seemed right and obvious to us, and the overriding goal: making a free and independent Poland – deserved the highest sacrifice. . . . From people with the rank of cadet or freshly baked lieutenant, we heard: 'We are going to Poland by the shortest route', 'Our army is and will remain apolitical', 'We will build a free and independent Poland' . . . 'Land for the peasants' . . . I, however, and not only me, believed in all this . . . All the deviations from the originally proclaimed clichés were explained by the needs of the moment. After

all, it was war and tactics were the most important thing; tactically
thought-out actions on the front and in the rear. (Prorok, in Czapigo
and Białas, 2015: 161)

The political officers – out of strategic conformism or strong
engagement – believed in the indoctrination work they were carrying
out. Bauman was in this last category. This is not to say that he
wanted to implement the full Stalinian regime, but he supported
a programme of soft socialism *à la polonaise* – as did many on the
Polish Left. That was the long-term project. But in the summer of
1944, the most important objective was to push back the German
Army, defeat fascism and liberate the whole country as quickly as
possible.

The advance of the troops – Warsaw's time of waiting

The 4th Division was created only a few months before the deadly
uprising of August–October 1944, which left Warsaw almost completely destroyed.[42] As the Polish and Soviet Army fought into the
eastern districts of Warsaw, General Berling held the 4th Division
in reserve because of its lack of combat experience. The advance
stopped on the east bank of the Vistula River. The armies merely
looked on while as many as 200,000 Polish fighters and civilians
were crushed by the Germans on the other side of the river.

According to Karski, Churchill, British Foreign Secretary
Anthony Eden and US Secretary of State Cordell Hull had warned
the Poles not to start any military operations in Warsaw without an
agreement with Moscow. 'The Poles believed that they were wiser
and that they knew Russia better. They did not listen to warnings',
Karski wrote:

The tragedy was that Churchill and Roosevelt should have clearly
said: we have a secret agreement, we agreed that Poland will be in the
Soviet zone, so we will not help you – not because of a lack of friendship, but because of our commitments. . . . Under this agreement,
Stalin would not interfere in the activities of the Allies in Africa, Italy
or in France. But Moscow was responsible for all military operations
in Poland, and nothing could be done without Stalin's consent. . . . In
this state of affairs [the uprising] was the greatest tragedy in the history
of Poland. (Karski in Friszke and Karski, 1997: 16)

Indeed. Improvised military units led by AK soldiers with the
support of civilians (even Boy Scout troops) fought in deadly street
combat against huge German Army units employing new technol-
ogies such as unmanned explosive tanks (Leichter Ladungsträger

Goliath), flamethrowers and self-propelled howitzers. Polish soldiers, immobilized by Stalin's decision, passively watched the
massacre of the Warsaw population. Except for some military
reconnaissance and the spontaneous action of Polish soldiers (from
Berling's Army), who crossed the river to rescue survivors, all divisions were frozen.

In the many books written about this tragic event, authors have
described Stalin's waiting tactic as part of a strategy to destroy
an urban population likely to oppose the new regime. According
to Karski, the London government and its supporters aimed to
liberate Warsaw and seize power before the Red Army-supported
provisional government could do so. Their failure and the subsequent destruction of the AK in Warsaw meant that Stalin faced less
opposition to establishing his will in Poland.

On 12 September 1944, parts of the 4th Infantry Division set
off towards Praga, on the right bank of the Vistula, and reached
the river's banks later in the month (Nafalski, 1978: 45), although
Bauman's unit did not advance towards Warsaw until 28 September.
Nafalski describes the situation from the perspective of the soldiers
waiting at the capital's gate at that moment:

> While . . . Praga [district in Warsaw] returned to life with great hap-
> piness due to the expulsion of the invader, the main part of the city,
> located on the left side of the Vistula, was burning. Hitler's cruelty
> was enacted by mindless subordinates, who once again repeated his
> barbaric triumph: burning works of art, destroying historic archi-
> tecture and anything that testified to the culture and the past of the
> nation, murdering hundreds of people. Probably never before has
> there been such a strong will to fight and avenge the Nazi crimes as at
> that time. The soldiers clutched their weapons and waited impatiently
> for the order to cross the Vistula. (Nafalski, 1978: 45)

The Army's passive attitude was very difficult for soldiers. The
chief of the Polish forces, General Berling, would be christened with
the nickname 'the tragic general'. On 30 September, in fact, Stalin
fired him. The reason for this decision is a source of controversy;
some historians support the explanation given by Berling himself –
that it was due to his disobedient attitude towards Stalin's order not
to help the insurgents.

From the end of September into January, for over three months,
Bauman and his fellows watched the tragic, slow death of their
capital with a feeling of powerlessness and injustice.[43] During those
months, there were several cases of spontaneous crossings, some
severely punished by Russian supervisors, who treated such cases
as desertion and punished them accordingly – with the death sentence.[44] Those who crossed knew that seeking to help the Uprising

was an almost suicidal action. The majority, like Bauman, simply waited.

The communist offensive began on 12 January, with Army units finally crossing the river after a wait of up to six months. The Soviet–Polish Army, which liberated Warsaw after five days of fighting, had never seen an equivalent level of destruction. Warsaw had been burned to the ground, its citizens imprisoned in camps, with some fleeing into the countryside. It was certainly not a joyful victory.

From Warsaw through the Pomeranian Fortification Wall to Kołobrzeg

The 4th Infantry Division crossed the Vistula on the night of 16 January in the Ostrówek – Góra Kalwaria district and, after marching through Jeziorna, headed towards Warsaw, which was already free. Branches of the 4th Division continued past Warsaw in pursuit of the enemy, moving to Pruszków and then Bydgoszcz following the 47th Soviet Army. By 28 January, troops were already in Bydgoszcz, although heavy equipment arrived late and a lack of petrol caused difficulties in positioning the forces (Nafalski, 1978: 107–9).

Contact was made at a German strategic defence known as the Pomeranian Wall, which Hitler's forces had furnished for defence. Infantry and artillery were crucial in overcoming the German forces, with many killed and wounded on both sides. There was no time for Bauman and his fellow educators to give political talks – only for military action and the pursuit of fleeing German soldiers. Polish divisions fought alongside Soviet units on the frontline. The battle of Kołobrzeg was the first battle that took place in Polish territories in which the Polish Army alone was engaged. It began with Soviet Marshall Zhukhov's order on 6 March, and concluded on 18 March.

'The march, broken by small skirmishes, lasted until 9 March and in the morning we approached Kołobrzeg', recalled soldier Józef Dubiński in an oral history: 'It was still winter: snow reached above the knee on the fields and roads, with weak frosts at night and thawing during the day. . . . Almost always, we moved on the front under the cover of the night. We rested during the day and marched that evening toward Kołobrzeg' (Czapigo and Białas, 2015: 263). Nafalski, the military historian and 4th Division soldier, recalled Kołobrzeg as 'an arsenal of all the weapons the Germans produced'; Kołobrzeg garrison had about 6,000 soldiers – swollen, on the eve of the struggle for the city, to a force of 10–12,000 with some of the 50,000 Wehrmacht soldiers who had fled Soviet guns after previous battles in early March. 'Hitler was interested personally in the defence of Kołobrzeg and gave the order to defend the city "to the last soldier". Every soldier or civilian able to handle arms, regardless of age, was subordinated to the commander of the defence', writes Nafalski. Himmler sent a large number of SS men to Kołobrzeg to use terror to discipline the Army and civilian populations (Nafalski, 1978: 213–14).

While a huge number of Red Army units laid siege to the city, only Polish Army soldiers fought directly against the Germans to break their resistance. The Polish leadership from the 1st Army was not informed of the reinforcement of German units, and its troops were initially stunned by the heavy defence of the city. The 3rd and 6th Infantry Divisions were joined by the 11th Regiment, the 9th Regiment of howitzer artillery, and a squadron from Bauman's artillery regiment, which sought to clear a path for the infantry (Nafalski, 1978: 219). Bauman participated in the combat from the start until almost the end. Some echo of his experience can be found in the novel *Na Kołobrzeg!* (To Kołobrzeg!), which Bauman wrote under the pen name Julian Żurowicz, released in 1953 by the Ministry of Defence publishing house:

> Who among you, fellow front men, has not experienced this feeling? Around you it is burning, roaring, flying deadly bullets, this is the battle. The enemy is right in front of you – in a moment you will fight him in a deadly duel. You know the way forward leads only through the death of the enemy. And you know you will go this way, because this is the way indicated by your Homeland – the Homeland you defend, the Homeland you love. But your throat is closing up, as if you had a wad of cotton in your chest, the beating of your heart exerts an unbearable pressure. You don't know the cause. Is it excitement? Anticipation? . . . In any case, it interferes with the fight. So you check whether you have dug in properly, whether the ammunition is dry and clean, you check and adjust the viewfinder. You think about the enemy and how to destroy him. And the intrusive feeling disappears. (Żurowicz [Bauman], 1953a: 27)

Kołobrzeg was one of the most intense urban battles on the Eastern front and one of the deadliest battles in the history of the Polish Army. '[T]he frequency of battery fire during the intense infantry operations was as big as in any battle so far', recalled Master Sergeant Zbigniew Mossakowski; 'Gun positions were constantly changing because we were following the infantry units, supporting their operations. We were constantly under enemy artillery and mortar fire. There was no time for food or even the shortest rest' (Nafalski, 1978: 237). Casualties were numerous and transporting the wounded to safety was extremely dangerous. 'The enemy soldiers, led by the SS men, did not recognize international military laws or any humanitarianism – despite the fact that our health teams provided medical care not only to wounded Polish soldiers but also to German ones', Nafalski wrote: 'Enemy snipers shot at the wounded, paramedics and sanitary wagons' (Nafalski, 1978: 233).

On 17 March, the second-to-last day of the battle, Bauman was shot in the right shoulder blade. Two weeks of fighting would leave 1,266 soldiers dead and 3,138 injured (Czapigo and Białas, 2015: 239). Bauman's division lost a fifth of its strength. Of the 5,780 members registered on 20 March 1945, 257 died at Kołobrzeg, including 21 officers and 70 non-commissioned officers. Another 62 troops disappeared, and 716 were wounded, including 60 officers and 185 non-commissioned officers (Nafalski, 1978: 269).

Bauman was one of many soldiers whose military campaign ended at Kołobrzeg. The gunshot left him unable to move his right hand. But he was among the lucky casualties, because he was successfully transported to the military hospital in nearly Stargard Szczeciński. There, Bauman underwent surgery – without anaesthesia – in a Soviet-run hospital assigned to Polish soldiers. 'It was very painful', he recalled in our interview:

> They took off a piece of my shoulder. The doctor refused to give me a sling and even medical plaster was forbidden. He said that my shoulder should not be immobilized. Each movement was terribly painful. Not only that, he ordered me to move my arm. . . . There was a lake near the hospital at Stargard, and he told me to get into a boat and row, with this fresh wound.

Apparently the Soviet clinician knew what he was doing. 'Thanks to him, I regained normal function in my arm, as if nothing had happened', Bauman said: 'The pill was bitter but it cured. I healed quickly, and with no side effects. I was still very young – a stripling who healed as quickly as a dog.'[45] After five weeks of recovery, Bauman left the hospital,[46] eager to catch up with his division. 'It was difficult because nobody would tell me where my unit was', he recalled. He kept asking, and walking, and eventually got a lift from some soldiers in a car, and found his unit in the Koepenick district of Berlin, 200 kilometres from Stargard.

He arrived in Berlin probably on 7 May, with part of his division in the city but most still on the outskirts.[47] 'Berlin was engulfed in flames', Bauman said, 'there were gunshots all around me, but I didn't get to conquer Hitler's Chancellery or the Reichstag'. Bauman's division observed the war's end from a distance. 'On May 8, around 9.00 p.m., as division troops marched towards their designated stopping places, the dark sky suddenly lit up with colorful rockets and a cascade of light shells', Nafalski writes; 'The Soviet troops nearby proclaimed the joyous news that the war was over and the Wehrmacht command had capitulated' (Nafalski, 1978: 391).

The joy of finding his military family and celebrating the end of Nazi terror in Berlin, the heart of the German state, was diminished somewhat by the loss of Bauman's immediate commander. On the very day of the war's end, Colonel Kumpicki died, an emotional Bauman recounted in 2015. He was riding alone when a bomb, perhaps launched by mistake from a Polish or Russian plane, dropped on his jeep.

The war was over.

6

Officer of the Internal Security Corps

1945–1953

Give the toilers ownership, the fruit
Of their labor in villages and
Cities. Chase away the bankers, Lord,
Stop the growth of money from money
Let the vain be armed with humbleness,
To the humble give an angry pride.
Teach us that under Your sunny sky
'There is no more Greek and no more Jew.'
Knock the stupid crown from the heads of
Puffed-up men and the supercilious.
And set up the skull of a dead man
On the desk of a growling ruler.
Strike with your bolt when in glory's name
A haughty man seizes his weapon,
Do not permit an unjust sword to
Have for a handle the cross of Your
Agony. Let good-will be done, of
Noble hearts which grew up in defeat.
Give us back the bread of Polish fields,
Return the coffins of Polish pine,
But above all give our words, altered
Craftily by wheelers and dealers,
Their uniqueness and their truthfulness:
Let the law always denote law, and
Let justice mean nothing but justice.

(Julian Tuwim, 'Modlitwa – Kwiaty Polskie' (Prayer for a
Polish Spring), I/II/VII I fr., from Polish Flowers – Prayer 2,
trans. Adam Gillon (1968))

Was the war over?

The war officially ended with the capitulation of the Third Reich. It was time for soldiers to put on their civilian clothes and return to their prewar life. Bauman, however, was at this moment a soldier in the 4th Infantry Division of the Polish Army. His unit remained in the Eastern Occupational Zone of Germany until the end of May 1945. In early June, the entire division staff, excluding the artillery units, became part of the Internal Security Corps (KBW – Korpus Bezpieczeństwa Wewnętrznego), established by the new government on 24 May.

The KBW was created to secure the implementation of the new political regime, combatting all opposition to the pro-Soviet provisional government. Its immediate task was to secure the preparation and execution of a referendum, a kind of test of support for the new political regime, followed by elections a year later. If it encountered opposition to the new government, the KBW was instructed to collaborate with the Soviet secret police (NKVD).[1] Soldiers of the KBW were also instructed to protect state-owned locales, roads and rail tracks, factories containing machinery abandoned by the fleeing Germans – anything considered property of the state or of 'state interest'. The 4th Division's transformation into a KBW force was seen as important because the unit was viewed as the military elite of a poorly equipped and insufficiently trained Polish Army. The 4th Division's commander – General Bolesław Kiniewicz – had a sterling reputation for minimizing losses among his soldiers; he was considered a stable, robust commander, and ideal for the delicate mission of internal security. Bauman's incorporation into the security forces was not automatic, because he was an artilleryman, though his status as a political officer provided a profile highly attractive to KBW recruiters.

Bauman's military files contain the story of his KBW 'hiring procedure': 'After the end of the war in May 1945, Lt. Col. Fejgin[2] from the GZPW WP (General Quarter of the Political-Educational Unit of the Polish Army) arrived at 6 PAL and chose 2 political officers, among others me, for the KBW, which was a newly formed unit at the time. I came to Włochy near Warsaw, and I was directed to the KBW as a battalion deputy chief.'[3] From the perspective of the KBW commanders, Bauman was an almost perfect candidate.[4] He was a young military officer with heroic experience at the front, decorated for his courage (and injury) at Kołobrzeg with the War Cross and other distinctions. Bauman was also a solid political bet: very young and with no 'negative past'. Moreover, he had been educated in the Soviet Union and was a member of the Communist Youth Organization. The small defect in this almost perfect picture was his origin. Maurycy Bauman – Zygmunt's father – introduced two negative elements: he was a bourgeois and a Zionist. Not by accident, this information was window-dressed in Bauman's postwar CVs. For example, Maurycy's ownership of the shop before 1930 was omitted in the description of his prewar employment, which was limited to the period after his bankruptcy when he was a simple accountant. By the same logic, Bauman listed his class origin in these documents as 'intelligentsia' or 'working intelligentsia', incorporating the new vocabulary imported from the Soviet Union. In this way, he powdered out any 'bourgeois' origins. Maurycy's Zionist sympathies were left out of most documents, but these 'minor defects' would not have been a real obstacle to an upward career trajectory in the first months of KBW activity. The organization was growing very fast and political reliability was key.

KBW

In the middle of 1945, Poland was torn by a struggle for power between two opposing groups: supporters of the Underground State (Państwo Podziemne)[5] and the less numerous partisans of the Polish Committee of National Liberation (Polski Komitet Wyzwolenia Narodowego: PKWN).[6] Although the Provisional Government of National Unity (Tymczasowy Rząd Jedności Narodowej: TRJN)[7] nominally joined both struggling camps' leaders (Stanisław Mikołajczyk came to Poland from London, where he had been part of the government-in-exile, to become vice president in the national unity government), it remained under the strong influence of the incontestable Joseph Stalin. Military success in World War II had reinforced Stalin's international position and, thanks to the Yalta agreements, Stalin had won Western acquiescence in claiming Soviet influence over the eastern part of Europe, which the Red Army had liberated from Nazi occupation. Poland immediately became the leading 'must-become-communist' country in the region – a necessary 'friend' of the powerful Soviet Empire. To achieve this goal in the face of absent popular support and even outright opposition required the creation of a large network of security institutions. Together, they enabled power to pass into the Communist Party's hands. The security units were organized on a Soviet military model, incorporated into a highly complex network of institutions and political initiatives, mostly dependent upon Stalin's vision of a future Poland. The strategy that Stalin chose for keeping Poland under his influence was similar to the one employed in other Eastern European countries – running countries according to Soviet policy through efficient, all-powerful secret services – a supra-State institution.

While part of the state repressive apparatus, the KBW was far from the most bloody and criminal organization within the system. Its activities were minor in scale compared to the infamous Department X of military intelligence, or the Bezpieka[8] (Interior Public Security) (Chęciński, 1982: 62). When Bauman was incorporated into the KBW in May 1945, it seems to have been confined to military duties, for protecting the peace in the liberated territories. Like other recruits, after deciding to join the KBW, Bauman went to the headquarters of its political-educational unit at Włochy, a town outside Warsaw where recruitment and selections were proceeding at a feverish pace in May and June 1945. This was certainly one of the moments in Bauman's life that could be called a 'turning point' (Strauss, 1959). His life at the front was finished, and a new phase was starting, with more unknown than familiar elements.

At 20 years old, Bauman, a Pole with a Jewish family background, had become a Polish Army officer. It was an extraordinary promotion – impossible to achieve in the prewar Polish Army because of anti-Semitism – and it certainly must have made him feel that he had been recognized as a 'real' Pole. A Polish Army officer was a quintessence of Polishness, the value he so highly cherished. Now he was truly a citizen of Poland, like any other.

Some weeks after the war's end, Bauman came to Bydgoszcz to assist in the training of newly recruited KBW soldiers. The KBW saw itself as an elite formation, and Bauman was in charge of the political education of these troops. He probably hoped to teach Marxist–Leninist ideology in a nice classroom in front of motivated youths who were curious about the socialist revolution. But even simple goals were hard to achieve amid the desperate conditions of the place. Almost 20,000 people had been mobilized to the KBW by mid-April, but within two weeks there was a wave of desertions due to terrible food and housing, feeble political and educational work, and opposition from the underground forces. Several entire units defected. Some joined the underground, some returned home, some loitered about, while others eventually returned to the barracks. The commander of the 6th Regiment (Kraków) reported on 10 May 1945: 'food supply – very bad. Soldiers are starving, hunger is causing mass defections. Soldiers go home for bread, fat, then return to the unit' (Jaworski, 1984: 38). Even the officers' situation was not really comfortable. Bauman received a modest payment for his services, like most other KBW officers. '[T]he Army gave me a roof over my head and put food in my mouth', wrote Włodzimierz Szer, also a political officer:

I received a so-called custody order for renting a room from a family . . . and a canteen dinner (disgusting) or a packed lunch. The allowance issued every ten days consisted of two kilograms of *rąbanka* (pork meat – more bones and fat than meat), some canned fish, dry cookies and 200 cigarettes, or tobacco and rolling papers for cigarettes. I also got some money but it was ridiculously little. (Szer, 2013: 188)

One might imagine that Bauman had doubts about his position, but one idea strongly motivated him to continue to pursue a career in the KBW. Even then, Bauman was torn between the ideas of more idealistic Polish communists, and the Soviet Stalinist model, which relied on the efficiency of terror, general suspicion and perennial struggle with the 'interior enemy'. Yet he wanted to build socialism. In an unpublished manuscript (written in the 1990s), Bauman recalled:

I did not intend to stay in the army, wanting to return to university as soon as possible, but one way or another it was a contribution to 'building socialism' and that was high on the list of my plans; the assignment I have been assigned was the extension of military service and a signal that I should wait for a civilian life and pursuit of my private preferences. (Bauman, 199?: 10)

Bauman also saw his KBW career as his best hope for bringing his parents back from the Soviet Union. He was lucky; only the rare Polish Jew had parents who survived the Holocaust. Zofia and Maurycy were safe and in reasonably good shape in Russia. Once the war ended, the main goal of most Polish Jews was to reunite their families, and those familiar with the Soviet system knew this was impossible. Under these circumstances, it is difficult to imagine that Bauman could have refused the KBW. In the context of Poland in June 1945, it was only a theoretical possibility.

Another, less obvious element of his decision was related to the emotional aspect of his identity construction. Like other young soldiers, Bauman had received an offer he felt he could not refuse. It went like this: his Homeland needed him. In this army, created with the support of the Soviet Union, Poland needed Bauman, despite his Jewish origin. In his Polish uniform, nobody could order him to leave the country or to sit in a row reserved for citizens of second rank. A big Army family supported his right to call Poland his home. Bolstered by his status and this new situation, he went home to Poznań for a visit.

Not so sweet home

Bauman's visit to his prewar Poznań home is recorded in an odd place: a long, 'top secret' 1951 internal security report about Bauman's father, Maurycy, which I found in the archives of the

Institute of National Remembrance (IPN). An investigating agent writes:

> The new tenant of 17/5 Prusa Street, named Przyworski, informed the services of security that 'in 1945, after the liberation, the son of the mentioned[9] – Zygmunt – came to Poznań and from above-mentioned address, took with him the furniture of his parents – furniture left by them during their escape [in 1939]. Zygmunt Bauman was in the uniform of a captain of the Polish Army and used a military car. The tenants of this house do not know more about their [Bauman's family's] activity.[10]

IPN files are full of such reports, most of them based on gossip and denunciations. Some of the information is right, some wrong, most of it imprecise, all of it of questionable value.[11] However, there's little doubt that the individual who recovered the furniture at Prusa Street was Zygmunt Bauman. He was not a captain yet (his promotion came on 20 December 1946), but the person who transmitted the information could have misread the coded epaulettes. He would not have been recognized as a KBW officer, because the latter had no specific uniform markings at the time – only later[12] receiving a special band on the edge of the military cap. On the face of it, there appeared to be little exceptional in an officer coming home to reclaim family possessions. But in this case it was quite unusual.

First, Bauman was lucky even to find his building. Compared to Warsaw and several other Polish cities, Poznań was in relatively good shape. Prusa Street seemed unchanged, as did the rest of the Jeżyce district containing Bauman's primary school and other buildings from his childhood. Second, the huge majority of Polish Jews who tried to reclaim homes, properties or even modest belongings faced a difficult task – one that was nearly impossible but also extremely dangerous.[13] Being a Polish officer protected Bauman in this situation.

Bauman came to Poznań accompanied by a driver, and probably others who helped him move the furniture out. If he had come alone, the situation might not have been so easy, even if he was in uniform. Many Polish Jews who tried to recover properties paid with their lives. The new owners, as well as anti-Semitic criminals, killed an unknown number of people.[14] The end of the war saw a wave of criminal acts in the liberated territories. Assaults upon and murders of Jewish survivors were numerous in the anti-Semitic environment that was spread largely across the whole country (Cała, 2014; Tokarska-Bakir, 2018). Bauman was no doubt aware of the dangers of trying to recover his family's property, and that probably explains why he came in uniform, with company and in daylight hours.

Civil war or uprising?

The lives of ordinary Poles were dominated by precariousness, insecurity, fear and violence that historians have struggled to characterize. Some have called it civil war (PRL[15] historians and some newer scholars), a 'period of time with elements of civil war' (Kersten, 1991), or the period of 'big fear'[16] (Zaremba, 2012). Others say it was uncategorizable – a period of revolution, or even two revolutions (Łepkowski, 1983).[17] Right-wing historians of today describe it as a period of 'anti-communist uprising'. Most interesting, however, is to appreciate the perceptions of people during those times, which is why Joanna Tokarska-Bakir's approach is helpful in avoiding anachronistic and theory-dominated scholarly visions. A specialist on Polish anti-Semitism and author of an impressive analysis of the Kielce Pogrom (Tokarska-Bakir, 2018 [2020]),[18] she describes the essence of the period in the words of Henryk Pawelec, commander of an underground group in Kielce in 1945: 'The Soviets came, but there was continuity in the air. On the streets of Kielce, in queues, in offices, I constantly ran into my friends. It was said that soon there would be another war. But because this war did not take place, it *became clear that the previous one was not over*' (Tokarska-Bakir, 2018: 207).[19]

Unlike other East European states under Soviet domination, wrote Chęciński, 'armed resistance to the new regime indeed brought the country to the brink of civil war, but there are still no reliable data on the casualties inflicted by both sides' (Chęciński, 1982: 64). According to Chęciński, 8,000 supporters of the new power were killed (many of whom, perhaps even 20 per cent, were *innocent* Jews), while somewhere from 80,000 to 200,000 regime opponents were killed. The underground groups hunted the representatives of the new power,[20] and also Polish Jews (Cała, 2014: 17; Tokarska-Bakir, 2018: 128–33). Bauman belonged to both categories, creating a double hazard. This too justified Bauman's enrolment in the KBW and his engagement in building a political system he thought would bring social justice and an end to ethnic discrimination.

The swell (*martwa fala*)[21]

It was common to view the 'Jewish problem' – as the Jewish presence in Poland had been described since the beginning of the twentieth century – as requiring an apocalyptical 'solution' like the one brought about by the Nazis. 'It was not unusual to say that: "Hitler deserves a monument"', writes Alina Cała (2014: 19). During the six years of German occupation, 90 per cent of the prewar population of Polish Jews died. Several studies show the participation (active or passive) of a part of Polish society in this process.[22] After the German capitulation, the unwelcome attitude towards Jews did not change. Alina Skibińska underlines the '[c]omplete indifference of Polish society towards people returning from the camps, regardless of their nationality' (Skibińska, 2014: 48).

The danger was not only 'complete indifference', and a lack of support – or even of empathy (with a few exceptions)[23] – but downright resistance or aggression towards returnees and survivors.[24] Rare were exclamations of joy at the return of a prewar neighbour: 'returning Jews were greeted in their native towns on arrival with an incredulous: "So" – followed by their first name, as they usually were on a first-name basis with their Polish neighbours – "you are still alive?"' (Gross, 2006: 36). There are few references to returning survivors in postwar administrative documents. The 'problem' of recovering one's old home or belongings was treated individually, among neighbours in small communities. Militias did not systematically get involved (Gross, 2006; Gross and Grudzińska–Gross, 2012; Cała, 2014; Sznajderman, 2016; Krzyżowski, 2017; Tokarska-Bakir, 2018). Usually the new owners refused to restore prewar goods to their Jewish owners, using threats to enforce their decisions (Gross, 2006: 39–47). There was (and still is) a term for these confiscated goods: *pożydowskie mienie* – 'post-Jewish goods'.[25] The seizure of Jewish goods enabled a growing post-World War II Polish bourgeoisie to benefit from modest properties and goods left by the 'missing' Jews (Tokarska-Bakir, 2018: 286–7). In some cases, people trying to recover prewar property were killed – some because they demanded the return of their goods, some simply because they were Jews. The strategy of many Poles was to chase away the demanding Jews, which most often meant pushing them to emigrate.

The exodus of the Jews began immediately after the German capitulation. It is estimated that about 50,000 Jews survived the war in Poland (Cała, 2014: 17); about 200,000 (Cała, 2014: 17) Jews returned from the Soviet Union, out of the 1 million Polish citizens who had fled there.[26] Of those 200,000, perhaps 120,000 had left Poland by 1947 (Cała, 2014: 17). There were several important waves of emigration. It was not an entirely legal process (Israel did not yet exist), but was tolerated and silently supported by the provisional government. Many Jews undertook *Aliyah* and went to Palestine, while others settled in other corners of the world. 'Consciously or not, an ethnic cleansing took place in the Polish provinces, initiated by deportations carried out by the Nazis, and ending with the expulsion of Jews from Poland in 1968', writes Cała (2014: 27). A small minority remained in Poland, some waiting for relatives to return from the USSR, others to build a new society, despite the hostility, dreaming that both communities could co-exist rather than remaining 'separated in the common space regulated by the social order', in Bauman's words (Bauman, cited in Sznajderman, 2016: 114).

'The swell' – as Polish intellectuals referred to the silent but efficient anti-Semitism of the non-Jewish citizens – and the massive emigration of the Jews concerned Bauman. He might consider himself a Pole, but the people around him considered him a Jew, and he needed to take this into account in his decisions. The KBW gave him security, a kind of substitute family and the power of agency. He was among those who thought they would change the country with a new system that supported a society not divided into religious or ethnic groups.

'Comrade Bauman Zygmunt'[27]

In June 1945,[28] Bauman became a deputy chief of the 5th Independent Protection Battalion,[29] based in Bydgoszcz. On 11 July, he was promoted to second lieutenant. Bauman was one of the 552 officers of the KBW in the autumn of 1945; there were 1,551 NCOs and 21,290 troops (Depo, 2012: 125, note 3). He was a political officer in charge of freshmen's education, which in the KBW was directed from the Communist Party Central Committee, according to historian Jerzy Depo (2012: 129, note 25).[30] Most of Bauman's days would have been spent on political training and political proselytism,[31] introducing a new generation of KBW soldiers to Marxist–Leninist doctrine.[32]

Bauman joined the Party early in 1946, a year before it officially established units within the KBW. Maurycy's bourgeois past and Zionistic sympathies were no obstacle to joining the Party, because Bauman neglected to mention them in his application and other questionnaires. Instead, for 'social origin', he wrote: 'son of clerk'.[33] This explanation was acceptable. The rest of his CV was quite strong: Soviet school training, Komsomol participation since his teenage years. There was really no choice of where Bauman would pursue his political activity in 1945. The party supporting the Soviet Union was the PPR, which in the immediate postwar was struggling for domination with the socialist PPS and the PSL (Mikołajczyk's Peasant Party).

In his 2013 interview with Tomasz Kwaśniewski, Bauman said:

I went to the KBW because I was a faithful Party member. The Party sent me there, I was there. It did not occur to me that I could do it differently. It was not by choice. It has never been a choice. I mean, I chose only when, in the Moscow militia, I went to the Union of Polish Patriots and asked them to arrange for me to be transferred to the

First Army. And then, they made the KBW from the 4th Division – it was like a continuation. When the war ended, I was expecting demobilization, I dreamed about going back to university, but it [demobilization] did not come, and it did not come to my mind to ask to leave the army. Besides, I wanted to build socialism, and this was a form of building socialism.[34]

So there is nothing surprising in Bauman's official enrolment request, dated 22 January 1946. In this short manuscript, he seeks admission to the Party by stating, 'I wish to struggle for popular democracy among the ranks of the party of Polish working masses. I promise to respect the statutes and to implement the programme of the PPR.'[35]

There is some confusion over the time of his enrolment in the PPR, because, while the Party archives[36] say 'January 1946', Army Security documents describe him as a member since 1945, suggesting he may have been unofficially 'inscribed' in the Party before his official request.[37] The procedure required letters of recommendation, which Bauman received from Major Kazimierz Faryna and Colonel Jan Szachoćko. According to the letter, which remains in Bauman's Party file, Faryna met Bauman in 1944 in the 4th Division, where he was a high-ranking member of the politico-educational department. By the war's end, Faryna was deputy chief of a motorized division. He wrote that:

> Comrade Bauman . . . has devoted all of his young life to the cause of working people. Politically aware.[38] Fought well in battles at front. Educated soldiers in the spirit of popular democracy and by his own example fighting on the frontline, inspired soldiers who followed him into the fight with the fascists. Now he educates soldiers in the spirit of popular democracy and hate for the reactionaries. I recommend him to PPR.[39]

The recommendation from Szachoćko, Bauman's boss at that moment, describes him as 'an outstanding politico-educational officer. He has a large political horizon. He is seriously respected by subordinates and his superiors.'[40]

It's worth noting that Faryna and Szachoćko do not appear to be 'Jewish' names. If Bauman asked them for the recommendations (if he had a choice), he may have been consciously seeking an introduction through 'Polish' sponsors rather than a 'Jewish network'. Historian Andrzej Werblan, the former senior adviser to Władysław Gomułka (leader of postwar Poland until 1948, and again from 1956 to 1970),[41] states that Polish communists were always troubled by the image of a 'Jewish' party, even before World War II. 'In the KPP the term "Comrade Jew" was coined', Werblan said in an interview; 'The [party leaders] divided people into "Comrade

Pole" and "Comrade Jew". They were not prejudiced – they were internationalists! But they were always counting up the numbers of each, not because of themselves and their opinions but because of the people around them. They were constantly worried about being described as a *Żydokomuna* [Judaeo-communists].'

As early as 1935 or 1936, in correspondence between the Central Committee in Moscow and Warsaw communists, a Russian official complains that the Polish Party's Warsaw committee is composed only of Jews. (A respondent points out that only five of the seventeen members are Jewish.) A similar discussion concerned the Łódź committee. Werblan checked the names in the Soviet document titled 'Regulation of the National Composition of Cadres' and found that:

> the criteria used by [the Soviets] for establishing their Jewishness were more strict than the Nuremberg Laws.[42] At least half of the committee members have nothing to do with Jewishness. They were completely Polonized – already their parents were . . . However, in the KPP they were categorized as Jews. Moreover, the people who maintained this correspondence [about calculating the proportion of Jews in the Party] were themselves in the same category – Poles with Jewish roots.[43]

From these comments, it is clear that communist leaders feared that Poles would turn away from the Party because its leaders were of Jewish origin. This fact strongly influenced strategies and career tracks. And it could explain why Bauman chose 'genuine' Poles for his political godfathers.

'Comrade Semion'

In a 2007 interview, Bauman acknowledged that he had cooperated with Polish intelligence agencies for three years as a counterespionage agent. 'Every good citizen should participate in counter-espionage', he said; 'That was one thing that I kept secret, because I signed an obligation that it would be kept secret' (interview with Aida Edemariam,[44] *Guardian*, 2007). Around 1990, Bauman wrote in his private manuscript:

> I perceived the proposal to cooperate with military information as befits a greenhorn; I knew about those things only from the novel and I believed that helping military counterintelligence was an obvious patriotic duty . . . It was probably the only point in my life story about which I have not spoken; signing this document included the obligation to keep it secret. I was not allowed to break this duty. And I did not break it. (Bauman, 199?: 10)

The IPN archives contain an internal military service personnel file titled 'Semion'. File ZA-21808 contains the inscription 'secret special signification', with an indication that it was opened to public access on 4 April 2008. 'Semion' is handwritten, followed with another inscription: 'inf.' (informant).[45] 'Semion' was Bauman's pseudonym in the military secret service. There is no such name in Polish. The secret behind this pseudonym is only visible when viewed through the lens of ethnicity. Семён (pronounced Siemion) is a Russian Jewish name, equivalent to Solomon.[46] Solomon was a Jewish king, the son of David, the sage of the sages, the most knowledgeable rabbi and biblical source of wisdom. Solomon is an important figure not only in the Old Testament, but also in the Koran. For Muslims, Sulayman is the Prophet and king; Solomon's seal is a symbol of magic power in the form of a pentagram (which is also the emblem of the Soviet Union). The choice of this pseudonym raises questions. Did Bauman choose it? Was it a school nickname? He was certainly perceived as a smart Jew, so could that be the moniker his friends used – Solomon – a school nickname, perhaps in a Soviet school, or already in Polish primary or secondary gymnasium? Or it may have been his name in Hashomer, whose members sometimes took a Hebrew name, especially if they hoped to emigrate soon to Palestine.[47] Or perhaps Bauman's Zionist father preferred to refer to him as Solomon. 'Zygmunt' is of German origin, signifying victory and protection. In Poland, the use of nicknames was very common within families or at school. It's unclear who chose Bauman's secret-service pseudonym – his handlers, or Bauman himself.

The documents in the IPN archives give only a partial story of the career of 'Semion',[48] yet the very revelation of Bauman's role as a spy of some sort generated much negative feeling towards him after the file was found at the IPN, where Poland housed the archives of its secret services after 1999. The opening of these archives initiated a witch-hunt, and Bauman was one of the witches. After returning to Poland in 1988, he became well known across the world, but some fanatically anti-communist historians began to draw a bead on him. Some isolated documents from the 'Semion' file, released in prejudicial ways without taking context into account, contributed to the construction of an erroneous picture of Bauman's complicity in the construction of communism in Poland, leading to smears in the Polish press.

The available documents give a puzzling picture of the situation from 1945 to 1948: missing pieces and a complex labyrinth of facts and lacunae to explore, beginning with the question of Bauman's official status in the secret service. 'Inf.', the abbreviation in the Semion file, means 'informant' (in Polish: *Informator*) – one of the three categories of secret collaborators (*tajny współpracownik*) recruited by the services. The other, higher categories were agent and resident. While references to informers are mentioned in documents as early as 1945, the exact definition of the three terms appears in official documents only in 1953. The informant, or informer, is described as:

> a secret collaborator of security organs who is or has connections with an environment under scrutiny by the security organs; the secret collaborator reveals persons conducting hostile activities. The informant can also be a secret collaborator recruited for a special task – observation of suspects, protection of objects of special significance ... Unlike the agent, the informant does not have direct access to the host organization, intelligence network, conspiracy, or group, but is in the environment of potentially hostile and suspicious people. The informant observes systematically the manifestations of hostile activity, reveals the persons conducting hostile activities and can help in reaching organizations or hostile groups.

The document says informants' tasks include mainly observation and informing the secret police about the activities of specific persons and communities, 'disclosing persons conducting hostile activities', and preventing 'espionage, sabotage and subversion'. The informer is 'the lowest position in the hierarchy of cooperation categories'.[49] Chęciński describes these spying networks as mainly operating through the *Bezpieka*, but similar structures existed in other security units.[50]

There was nothing exceptional about Bauman being recruited within his military unit. Everyone in such a unit was subject to this kind of proposition, which would have been nearly impossible to refuse.

The enrolment of Bauman in the military secret service working inside of the KBW took place on 3 November 1945 in Bydgoszcz. In this first reference to his activity as an informant, he is described as a 'resident'. According to the IPN website, a resident is:

> [a] secret collaborator, politically tested, who, by order of the security apparatus, manages a number of informers assigned to him. Due to the function performed, the resident must be a highly trusted person ... the most trusted UB/SB employees were chosen, preferably former UB/SB functionaries. ... Residents gave the UB/SB informants orders from the leading officers, gave them remuneration and received reports from them.[51]

This would mean Bauman had other informants under his control, and played a higher role in the network than as a simple tattler.

Another handwritten document, addressed to Captain

Szuchmostow, the Pomeranian regional information chief of Army internal security, describes an effort to recruit Bauman as a resident: 'During our discussion, he expressed the wish to collaborate. Politically well developed, modest; welcomed among soldiers and colleagues. The discussions with him will take place in the office or in other places depending on the situation.' It seeks Szuchmostow's permission to complete the recruitment. In the centre of the document, someone has written in Cyrillic with an indelible, violet-coloured copying pencil:[52] 'санкционирую'. This is a term usually employed in the documents to signify: 'I give legal sanction.' This simple term carries high significance here, placed in the middle of the document, with a specially coloured pencil using Russian for a precise effect (as it probably was in the previous, Czarist military system). A graphologist would recognize the handwriting as probably that of an older person.[53] It signifies that ultimate power lay in the hands of the Russians – Polish secret-service documents were validated by a Russian-writing superior.

How well did Bauman carry out his spy work? There is some information in the documents in which superiors characterize Bauman's work and 'attitude'. On 29 April 1946, we read: 'A good collaborator in his work, is working on himself (*pracuje nad sobą*). He has an important sense of responsibility, brings a lot of political material. Politically aware.'

A year later, on 8 May 1947, he is characterized as an informant in a document concerning his work in Szczytno (a town near Bydgoszcz):

> To get material from him during the informant's period of work as informant in the KBW training regiment and as education instructor, it was necessary to pressure him constantly. The tasks which we ordered him to do, he did. The material he gave us had a political character but, because of his position, he did not give us any valuable material. In his work as officer – serious. In his private life – without vices.

The document is signed by an information officer, with a short inscription, probably from Bauman's sponsor Faryna: 'I agree with the characterization.'[54]

Exactly two years after Bauman's enrolment, on 4 November 1947, another element enters into the story. Semion is categorized again as informant, no longer as resident: 'He is well trained. His materials are valuable and give detailed analysis of work about the politico-educational apparatus (*analiza pracy aparatu polityczno-wychowawczego*). *Because of his Semitic origin he cannot be employed for investigations.* He comes to meetings on time and respects the rules of cover. In his private life, without vices.'[55]

The language suggests that Bauman has been demoted, but there's no evidence of this in other documents, which simply trace his workplace changes – his moves from Bydgoszcz to Szczytno, and Szczytno to Warsaw; his departure for the KBW department of personal affairs. On 27 May 1947, Bauman is still described as a resident and not an informant.

There would appear to be a crucial distinction between inform- ant and resident: between someone who took orders and one who gave orders. Perhaps 'resident' did not mean the same thing in this context? Bauman was performing a kind of double spying service for twin institutions – the *Bezpieka* and Military Information. Yet any political officer in his position would have been required to give all information to superiors. The assessments of Bauman's work vary, but the hierarchy appears to have been disappointed by the weak yield from his snooping. They appear to have gradually lost faith in Bauman, whatever his spying or spymaster role. Under pressure, he provided ho-hum material – no scoops, no real secrets. Over two years, the documents show a steadily declining estimation of Bauman's spying value by senior KBW levels.[56] Moreover, taking into account the historical developments of Poland at this time, we can also decipher in those progressively less positive opinions the general attitude towards people with 'Semitic origins'. The file note of November 1947 makes it quite explicit: his role as a secret agent will probably end . . . simply . . . because he is a Jew. The last docu- ment marked 'Top secret' notes the following: 'The commitment of Captain Bauman Zygmunt alias Semion, was destroyed in his pres- ence on Aug. 6 1948 in accordance with the commission's decision'. This was signed by the deputy head of the 1st Branch of the KBW information board – Captain Sławiński.[57]

It is difficult to say what exactly was meant by the 'commitment' that was destroyed. Usually, Party activists were automatically informants, and could be asked to collaborate without a formal process. Why, given his political commitment and military role, was Bauman officially enrolled in 1945? Was it a factor of the postwar chaos and the debutant character of the services? Or did it have to do with his 'Semitic origin', which kept him from being employed for investigations (*rozpracowanie*). The suggestion is that Jews were not trusted, which restricted Bauman's implication in such activities – that he did not provide valuable material is the crucial information about the quality of Bauman's services as a spy.

Could Bauman have refused to collaborate with the secret police?[58] Writer Michał Komar, whose father Wacław Komar was head of military intelligence until 1949, then in 1952 imprisoned and tor- tured, told me in an interview, 'every soldier of Kościuszko's Army was most certainly pushed to collaborate with secret services. That goes without saying. Moreover, as a KBW officer, Bauman was undoubtedly "invited" on a regular basis to report about what he saw and heard and from whom. It was a routine practice, well known in all armies of the world.'[59] Bauman's past in the Komsomol and the Moscow militia were also settings for 'seduction'[60] by the Soviet secret services. To say 'no' there would have been an invitation to the Gulag, deportation or imprisonment. In a book titled *It Was Not Necessary to Teach Them Flogging: The Trials of Humer and Investigation of UB Officers*,[61] the former Polish communist leader Adam Humer explains to author Piotr Lipiński: 'it was not necessary [to recruit for the NKVD] . . . party members and *Komsomol* people were not recruited at all. They were automatically loyal and would collaborate' (Lipiński, 2016: 33). The logic was obvious: all members of communist organizations belonged to the system and, in consequence, collaborated with its extensive secret networks in order to do battle with the opposition and the 'internal enemy'.

In 2007, the *Guardian* journalist Aida Edemariam asked Bauman: 'Did counter-espionage mean informing on people who were fighting against the Communist project?' He responded: 'That's what would be expected from me, but I don't remember doing [anything like that]. I had nothing to do – I was sitting in my office and writing – it was hardly a field in which you could collect interesting information.' Edemariam pursued: 'Did you do anything at all that might have had adverse consequences?' 'I can't answer that question,' Bauman responded: 'I don't believe there was any. At the same time, I was a part of a wider scene, and of course everything you do has consequences.'[62] In the years that followed the installation of the pro-Soviet government in Poland, everyone hired to a 'sensitive' post (government, offices, factories, etc.) was asked (with more or less pressure) to collaborate with the secret services, and their career depended upon their activity as a 'TW' (*Tajny Współpracownik* (secret collaborator)). So it was in Eastern Europe, where the rules were exported from the USSR. 'A highly developed and efficient system of a parallel state', said Andrzej Werblan, who was at the centre of communist leadership in the 1950s and 1960s, '– in which everyone is spying on everyone – will survive longer than the state system itself'. Political regimes may change; the network of secret police remains.

Bauman was part of this system and not exceptional – a member of the state power structure with a biography befitting his position. How would a Solomon practise 'Solomonic judgement' in this setting? Perhaps by collaborating with the powerful hierarchy without giving one's superiors material with any real value, and this seems to be what Bauman did. The important question was not Bauman's category in the secret papers (informant or resident) but how he used his position – what information he transmitted to his military security superiors. The hierarchy was not impressed by this material; they found nothing interesting in his secret reports. Their opinions suggest they were not really surprised: the mediocre work could be explained by his 'Semitic origins'.

KBW mission – tracing an 'internal enemy'

The KBW, an internal security unit, in collaboration with other security services (MO – militia; UB – secret police) and Army units, was in charge of pacifying postwar Poland. In 1946, in the internal KBW journal *On Guard*, Brigadier General Konrad Świetlik wrote: 'The most haunted defender of Polish democracy, the most beloved, the most aware of her soldiers is and must be – the soldier of the Security Service. He defends democracy from the most dangerous enemy – the internal enemy.'[63]

Who was this 'internal enemy'? It was anyone opposed to the revolutionary changes. Throughout those years and the rest of the communist period, the term 'internal enemy' was frequently invoked to describe those who menaced the 'progress of the revolution'. The term was used strategically, sometimes against a scapegoat, or as a smokescreen for other problems. The internal enemy was more dangerous than the external enemy, because he could be anywhere. The internal enemy was an average person – he looked like you and me! To preserve the changes it imposed, the new power needed to eliminate this obstacle. In 1945–7, this took the form of mortal fraternal combat.

Partisans and supporters of the London government-in-exile did not give up after their perceived betrayal by world leaders at Yalta and Potsdam: 'Those ill-disposed to the authorities viscerally opposed the delusions of those who joined the new order', wrote Krystyna Kersten in her book *The Establishment of Communist Rule in Poland, 1943–1948*:

They saw this as threatening to everything Polish and to the most precious values they held. They felt that this would lead to the Sovietization of Poland. Resistance was nothing less than a patriotic obligation. So is it possible to say that one patriotism was true and another false? . . . Can it be said of the young people who fell on both sides, and were often buried next to each other, that only one was a 'good Pole'? Can it be said that the ideological motivation of those who established themselves in power in the name of the ethos of the left was better than that of those who fought it, often inspired by ideology traditionally labeled as right? Or vice-versa? . . . This is not tantamount to justifying torturers from the Office of Security and members of the National Armed Forces (NSZ)[*] who murdered unarmed Jews and 'reds' (the word was already in circulation at that time). Where was the boundary of permissible methods 'in the struggle for the consolidation of people's power' or 'in the struggle with the red peril' in Poland in the mid-1940s? (Kersten, 1991: xxvii–xxviii; note '*' reads 'Cited in Gmyr (2012: 167); journal no. 34, 1946, p. 1')

These questions can still be difficult to resolve theoretically, morally and historically. However, taking into account the perspective of some participants, the story is less symmetrical than Kersten's excerpt suggests. The 'moment when war became peace' was not as clearly defined – at least in the eyes of people like Bauman – as Kersten suggests. The Hughesian concept of *master status*, which I mentioned in the Introduction, helps us to understand Bauman's situation at war's end, and allows the reconstruction of his perspective at that moment. For minority-community members, murders of Jews by the new government's opponents provided an important motivation. Like other Polish Jews, Bauman could never wish for the return of prewar Poland – that would have been illogical. Moreover, the regime's promises of equal treatment and social justice were attractive enough to justify his involvement in postwar activities to retain control over freshly liberated regions. This was the perspective of all Left-oriented people, as well as ethnic minorities. For Polish Army soldiers with battle experiences, joining the KBW at that moment was not perceived as servitude towards the Soviet Union and Stalin (the common perception nowadays), but as a necessary step in the construction of the new Poland.

Despite its long period of collaboration with the Soviet Red Army, the Polish military retained some measure of independence. Among the most remarkable differences was the presence of Catholic priests in the military corps, who celebrated Christian festivals as well as regular rites of religious practice. In the first years of the KBW, a Catholic Church military structure was officially incorporated to perform religious services.

Another element which is frequently forgotten is political diversity. At the end of World War II, there was an array of political parties. As was mentioned earlier, Stanisław Mikołajczyk, a prewar politician and a key leader of the government-in-exile, returned to Poland after the war as leader of PSL (the Polish Peasant Party) and Deputy Prime Minister, though he fled to England and the United States in 1947 after being unsuccessful in a fraudulent presidential election.

Not all of Poland's parties of the Left saw eye to eye with the Stalinists either, since Stalin had jailed and killed Polish communist leaders. On the Left, the predominant view was that a plurality of voices would lead to implementation of a 'Polish way to socialism'. Bauman shared this opinion:

The night before crossing the Bug River [1944] I took into confidence two of my colleagues: chief of battalion Lange and the platoon chief, whose name was Bormotow. I told them – obviously stupid on my part – that we would build socialism differently. 'How?' they asked me. I was so callow and naïve that I responded: 'Here everyone is screaming: Stalin, Stalin! We will decide what to do [on our own].'[64]

The first priority was keeping the peace, which was at risk within months of the German capitulation in a nation awash in poverty, chaos, armed skirmishing and insecurity. IPN's historians write that, in the eastern and central provinces of Poland, nearly 20,000 'pro-independence' combatants[65] operated in several dozen partisan units. Their activity could be referred to as an 'anti-communist uprising': 'In the eastern provinces, the local communist authorities and their forces were simply "swept away from the face of the earth"'.[66]

With underground activities menacing the country, the provisional government reorganized its security services, including the KBW, in December 1945. Bauman became senior instructor, then deputy chief of the politico-educational department in the Pomeranian Region for the WBW (Wojska Bezpieczeństwa Wewnętrznego (the Army of Internal Security)) – a new section of the KBW after the reorganization. Bauman remained in that position until July 1946; that February he was promoted to lieutenant.[67]

'For me the army was not an authority', Bauman told Kwaśniewski;

The authority was only one man, my boss: Colonel Zdzisław Bibrowski. He taught me and he was at the same time very critical toward the world he had helped create. He was also convinced that, with all the defects of that world, it was necessary to achieve its declared goals, which meant equality, liberty, fraternity. Bibrowski impressed me. He was much older, with an excellent education. . . . He knew what he was talking about. He was politically aware, well-read, he knew how to think. In KBW there were not a lot of people like him.[68]

During this period, KBW units in Bauman's group took part in combat against underground forces that were at the peak of their activity. In February–March 1946, Bauman fought in battles around Ostrołęka (north of Warsaw) as chief of an operational group. In a personal questionnaire on 25 October 1948,[69] he described the fighting as an 'operation against "Młot"'[70] – a regional leader of the forces whom the Polish government described as 'bandits', and which the anti-communists called heroes, or żołnierz wyklęty ('cursed soldiers').[71]

'Młot', or 'Hammer', was the pseudonym of Zbigniew Kulesza, son of Mikołaj and Rozalia, born 11 July 1919 in Długosiodło –

a village 70 kilometres northeast of Warsaw.[72] Kulesza was also known as 'Oleśnicki' and 'Grabicz' – both typical Polish family names. The copious documentation produced by the security services on Kulesza[73] provides a fascinating picture of the underground activity of this 'hero'[74] – whom Bauman tried to capture – and of the events in the years after liberation from the Nazis.

Kulesza attended secondary school, and his occupation is listed as 'wood industry technician' in a document produced by Department 'C' of the Citizen's Militia (MO) in Olsztyn, dated 9 September 1982. Six years older than Bauman, 'Młot' might have been working with the latter at Vakhtan's wood factory in Russia if he had fled Poland during the war. But he stayed in occupied Poland, and by 1946 he and Bauman were on opposite sides of the barricade. According to MO documents, Kulesza was active in the Home Army (AK) and its military organization during the Occupation – in 1941, joining military security under the command of General Władysław Sikorski, chief of Polish forces in the Allied Army.

At the end of the war, Kulesza became part of the NSZ (National Armed Forces), making a brilliant career in the underground. Beginning in 1945, he led the reorganization and unification of various anti-communist groups in central Poland. As commandant of the Orawa District, 'Młot' was highly rated by his national superiors, and he was eventually ordered to expand into three other districts in the Masovia area (Krajewski and Łabuszewski, 2008: 34). Kulesza 'took part in assaults[,] in murders' and, during the amnesty of 1947, forbade subordinates to reveal themselves, according to the MO documents.[75] In April 1947, he ceded leadership of the district to his deputy, Kozłowski Józef, alias 'Las' (Forest). On 22 April 1947, he revealed his identity and underground role to a security officer in southwest Poland; he was arrested on 30 November 1947. Kulesza was sentenced in May 1949 to life imprisonment,[76] but released in December 1956 by an amnesty.[77] As of 1974, Kulesza was working in a small privately owned factory near Olsztyn.

Since 1989, the perception of postwar underground figures has changed, of course. 'Reactionaries' such as Kulesza were rehabilitated and became heroes; he was decorated with a national medal for his military activities. But the heroism of his exploits remains in doubt, if one lends credence to the records of the security services. One of the most detailed descriptions came in testimony from Czesław Kania, a close collaborator of Kulesza. Kania, alias 'Nałęcz' and 'Witold', joined the 'Młot' organization in 1944, and in June 1945 began working directly under Kulesza's supervision. His testimony is of high quality, probably because his responsibilities included writing accounts of the group's activities and editing notes from the underground court martials conducted by Młot. Testimony from Kania after he was captured in a military action in June 1948,[78] confirmed by several other documents in the 'Młot' files at the IPN, indicate that Kulesza's underground activity included attacks on the communist authorities, such as the 5 October 1945 action that resulted in the disarming of the military outpost in Rozogi, in the county of Szczytno (Krajewski and Łabuszewski, 2008: 29). But there were also murders of civilians.

Historian Jerzy Kijowski suggests that the IPN historians have sometimes tended to whitewash the activities of the underground fighters, and takes as an example the question of terror tactics used against civilians in acts assigning collective responsibility. Analysing an IPN publication by Krzysztof Kacprzak, Kijowski notes that Kacprzak had written that 'in District XVI[79] NZW never applied . . . collective responsibility to guilty people, but only punished them for specific crimes'. Yet this was contradicted, Kijowski points out, by an earlier statement in the same publication regarding the shooting of Wacław and Józefa Cudny and their two young daughters, Krystyna and Stanisława. The underground fighters 'spared the two youngest kids', Kacprzak wrote – but this was a 'curious interpretation of familial murder and collective familial responsibility' (Kijowski, 2010: 190).[80]

The Kania documents – which, of course, must be read critically – indicate that in the summer of 1945, 'Młot' ordered him to recruit young people and expand the underground network in the area under his command. He also ordered the fighters to collect weapons, uniforms and all kinds of military equipment, in order to begin building strong combat units that would help the organization take power. 'For the same purpose I also received a command to conduct intelligence activities in my area', Kania told his interrogators:

> I was asked to detect and eliminate people cooperating with the existing regime. This was compatible with the orders received from the district command at that time, signed by the chief of staff, Captain 'Łużyca'. This order gave me the right to apply all kinds of penalties against people having democratic points of view, including the death penalty. Acting as the deputy of the second battalion, I carried out the orders sent to me by 'Młot' and based on the reports from the intelligence network, I ordered to punish by whipping some people from the settlement of Myszyniec in Ostrołęka district, for allegations that they were leftists and cooperated with the security authorities.[81]

Whipping was one of the lighter punishments practised by the 'forest people'. We read in the same document that 'Młot' and his colleagues also condemned people to death. The underground network performed secret interviews and created a list of people who worked or collaborated with the UB and MO. After trial, they were executed by commandos. 'Młot' also condemned non-communists

– such as robbers and ordinary criminals – to death, Kania said.[82] Death was dealt out daily by the underground organizations. Many Polish civilians were condemned for their political opinions, as were Red Army soldiers. 'In November 1946', according to one document in the 'Młot' file:

> a group of NZW members under the direction of Roman Gawczyński ('Dzierżynski')[83] – head of the [special action commando] brought two trucks to the village of Zdunek near Myszyniec [in the] Ostrołęka district . . . robbed from soldiers of the Soviet Army in Myszyniec. These cars were placed at the disposal of the NZW staff. Following the order of 'Młot', the two Soviet Army drivers were shot and buried in a forest near the village of Zdunek, near Myszyniec, Ostrołęka district. The names of the murderers of the soldiers are unknown.[84]

The report from Kania's interrogation states that 'Młot's' people terrorized not only communists and their supporters, but also anyone whom they were suspicious of, sometimes using blackmailing techniques reminiscent of the Sicilian Mafia.[85] '[I]n August 1946, by order of "Młot"', Kamian testified, 'I sent a warning to the mother of a UB officer from Ostrołęka. Her name was Olszewska Bronisława and she lived in the village of Lipniki, near Łyse. I told her she should make her son Henryk stop pursuing our members. If not, we would kill her and her son.'[86]

Such pressure tactics – while not unknown to other underground forces in conflicts around the world – were a far cry from the nobly proclaimed ethos of the Polish soldier. The Geneva Convention prohibits such treatment of relatives and others not engaged in direct conflict. In this conflict, however, civilian victims were numerous. While both sides killed civilians and people not involved directly in the conflict, the ethnic character of some of the murders committed by some underground groups shatters this idea of symmetrical cruelty.

Statistics compiled by the security services from the Białystok district showed fifty deaths caused by the NZW during the postwar conflict; seven in 1945, twenty-four in 1946, fourteen in 1947 and five in 1948. They included nine functionaries of the military and internal security police, including a unit chief; one member of the Polish Communist Party (KPP); four members of the PPR (including two local secretaries); four Polish Army soldiers; one citizen of the USSR; two office employees and '29 others'.[87] This last category is the most interesting one. We know from documents provided by Jewish committees and recent historical studies that Jews comprised the largest group of civilian victims (in all Polish territories in the postwar years). However, the security service reports contained no reference to religious or ethnic affiliation, notes Andrzej Żbikowski

(Żbikowski, 2014: 85). The anti-Semitic character of crimes and cruelty perpetrated against Holocaust survivors was simply withheld. The following incident, from Kania's confession, describes a probable example of these crimes against 'anonymous victims' in 1946.

In a forest hideout in the Soborki district, 'Młot', Kania and a third rebel leader interrogated a trader from Ostrołęka. According to Kania's account, 'in the course of the interrogation, this trader admitted that he had collaborated with the UB services of Ostrołęka. Based on that revelation, he was sentenced to death by "Młot" and "Burza" and executed by men under the command of "Las"'. Kania did not recall who specifically did the killing, or whether he was involved in the decision to kill the trader, according to his testimony. 'We took some products the murdered trader had with him – about three dozen spools of sewing thread, a few men's combs, 10 mirrors, 10 women's combs.'[88] The document does not say how the trader was led to admit his collaboration with the government forces, or what specific acts he confessed to – and, in any case, such confessions lack validity since both the new regime and the underground frequently used torture to extract them. Nor can we readily understand why the fighters would have captured a nameless street peddler carrying nothing more than some thread, mirrors and combs – but he might well have been arrested because he was a Jew. Before 1939, Ostrołęka's population was largely Jewish, and street peddling was a leading Jewish occupation.[89] It may well be that the underground soldiers captured the peddler because they assumed that, as a Jew, he was a collaborator with the new communist regime. This fitted into the stereotypical conviction that remains common in Poland to this day – the notion of *Żydokomuna*: 'Judaeo-communism'.

'Judaeo-communism', wrote historian Andrzej Żbikowski, is:

a stereotype exploited in political engagement, but also a well-worn phrase suggesting that virtually all Jews were advocates of Communism. It was widespread in the thought and language of many Poles from at least the mid-1930s. It provided for certain strata of society a moral alibi, aside from 'ordinary anti-Semitism', justifying their passivity toward the murder by the Germans of almost three million Polish Jews. It motivated more than 10,000 others to take an active part in the murder. (Żbikowski, 2014: 67)

How many of the 'other' category were people whom 'Młot' and his band executed? Anti-Semitism was part of the culture of the Polish resistance units,[90] which 'as a rule', wrote Skibińska, 'did not admit Jewish partisans. As a matter of fact, some units of the Home Army (Armia Krajowa – AK) or National Armed Forces (Narodowe Siły Zbrojne – NSZ) would even go as far as murdering

Jews hiding in forests and on farms' (Skibińska, 2014: 53).[91] This was the approach during the German occupation, and it did not change after the war: 'Radical nationalist underground formations, such as the NSZ, are known to have been hostile towards Jews who were in hiding throughout the Nazi occupation. During this period the NSZ murdered scores of Jews, motivated by anti-Semitism' (Żbikowski, 2014: 63).

There were several cases in which groups of Jews died during partisan assaults on trains and buses, and others where Jews were murdered on the assumption they were politically suspect, writes Żbikowski. An October 1945 report from the Białystok headquarters of the underground WiN organization states: 'All the Jews are collaborators with the UB and the NKVD as agents, confidants, and informers. Almost all managerial positions in the UB are held by Jews' (quoted in Żbikowski, 2014: 83).[92] This false affirmation, frequently repeated and still employed in historical, political and public discourse, was perfectly deconstructed by Joanna Tokarska-Bakir in her book *Cursed: A Social Portrait of the Kielce Pogrom* (2018), which showed how strong and widespread popular convictions were regarding the level of Jewish participation in communist leadership. Such convictions made it impossible to distinguish whether victims were ethnic or political targets. Many died simply because, like the anonymous peddler condemned by 'Młot', they were victims of deeply ingrained stereotypes in Polish society.

In any case, many hundreds of people died in the postwar period because they were suspected of belonging to the 'enemy' camp. In 1945 and 1946, in the area of Ostrołęka, 'NZW Units liquidated several dozen informants, agents and functionaries of UB' (Krajewski and Łabuszewski, 2008: 39). The new regime had to respond to these attacks, and the KBW was part of the military response. In February 1946, at the peak of activity for 'Młot', Bauman left Bydgoszcz with his unit and came to Ostrołęka as the chief of an operational group. There are no open-access documents about the security activities of KBW, so we have no way of knowing the daily activities of Bauman and his soldiers in the forest. We know only that they tried to catch 'Młot' and failed – 'Młot' gave himself up to the authorities more than a year later.

Bauman himself wrote about the episode in his second private manuscript from 1990. He described:

armed forces scattered around Bialystok, sometimes coming from underground organizations, but mostly ordinary criminal gangs . . . they attacked militia posts, stopped trains, pulled out passengers, took their money and often executed them on the spot. The task of our expedition was to arrest the attackers: the soldiers were equipped for this purpose with a list of addresses where the perpetrators of the assaults supposedly lived. . . . We were commanded by a 'specialist in tracking terrorists' sent from Russia, but his expertise turned out to be of little use in Polish conditions.

Only rarely did they ever turn up a 'rebel' at the addresses they were given, on the basis of local denunciations:

> I have no idea what this 'expert' wrote in the expedition report (hardly anything remains in my memory from this expedition beyond the memory of cruel frost and a great experience: the premiere of 'Forbidden Songs'[93] in Białystok cinema), but they did not send me anymore into the 'action'. I was kept away from any 'responsible' tasks requiring people with harder nerves and smaller scruples . . . My function with the 'expert' was, by the way, a replica of what I was doing together with other political and educational officers in the 4th Division. (Bauman, 199?: 12)

One more time, Bauman provided cover for Russian commanders. The information about Bauman's role accompanying the Soviet 'expert' points to the greater struggle that faced the authorities: the Soviet Union controlled the country, which was supposed to be 'independent'. But Bauman does not provide much specific information about what actually happened in the field. Perhaps he was still feeling the obligation to keep military secrets? However, there is a text – a fictional one, to be sure – that suggests these two months 'in the terrain' were not only about freezing temperatures and good cinema. Bauman published this piece under the pseudonym 'Julian Żurowicz'.

KBW in action, by Julian Żurowicz

The story is titled *W Krzeczuchach znów spokój* (Peace Returns to Krzeczuchy) – with Krzeczuchy being an imaginary village with a very Polish-sounding name. The book was published by the Ministry of National Defence in 1953, when Bauman was in the process of leaving the KBW, in a series called 'The Library of the Soldier – Popular Literary Pieces'. This was educational propaganda in the spirit of social-realist conventions,[94] in which military actions were described as a patriotic service by good soldiers to bring social peace. In this literature, soldiers were not an element of state repression (as in the post-1989 literature) but groups of workers ensuring the security of the ordinary people.[95] Our heroes are close to the protected population (in *Krzeczuchy*, the peasants), sharing their social origins and culture. The story contains many detailed descriptions of events that strongly suggest Bauman was putting to use his personal experience of military action.

In the first sentence, we are vividly introduced to a conflict erupting inside the small KBW team. One of the soldiers has expressed doubts about his commitment. It is harvest-time and, as a peasant's son, he wishes to rejoin his family to help his father, and also because he has learned via a letter that a band of reactionaries are menacing peasants in his home who have accepted land distributed by the new government (the agrarian reform broke up the largest pre-1939 properties; the plots were turned into collectives or distributed to poor peasants).[96] This soldier complains of waiting and 'doing nothing' at a time his family needs him to work and protect the land. The discussion among fictional KBW colleagues depicts a real problem Bauman faced as a leader of the group: his soldiers wanted to return home but had to remain in service. They felt the 'call of their fields' and missed their families. Bauman, as a political officer, had to persuade them to stay in their KBW ranks and serve the new Poland.

Despite its propagandistic message, the Bauman–Żurowicz piece is well written and the reader is quickly immersed in the story, trapped by a narrative typical of detective fiction or action literature. A group of soldiers is in pursuit of the leader of a reactionary 'bandit group' in a village where a few powerful and prosperous families live and everyone else suffers from hunger and poverty. The description of the relationships shows the author's sensitivity to social inequality, and in particular to the difficulties of women. Bauman–Żurowicz presents the tragic situation of women from poor peasant families who are forced into marriages with wealthy older neighbours. 'Wrona[97] bought her [his young wife] in the same way one buys equipment', writes Żurowicz–Bauman: 'He, an old man standing above the grave, who had already sent two wives to the other world, in his later days allowed his greed to reach Krystyna – a young flourishing girl sought after by young boys in the village' (Żurowicz, 1953b: 20). Krystyna is sold to cover the debts of her poor widowed father who has many children to support; Wrona buys her for 20 metres (2,000 kg) of rye (Żurowicz, 1953b: 21). Another old and powerful peasant abuses a young woman who works as his servant, having been adopted by him as a child. These mistreated, powerless people will play a crucial role at the moment of justice.

A theme of the book is that women can emancipate themselves by moving to the city, escaping the traditional role of peasant spouse. In the city, they can work in the factories or study. Moreover, they can choose their life partners. In the novel, access to factory work and education are powerful factors of change. The poor can also improve their living conditions by joining in the agrarian reform and accepting parcels of land distributed by the new regime. The former leaders of the village, rich peasants, oppose the reform or any changes; Wrona's son is a rebel in the forest. The village also has positive characters, supporters of the new regime. Dworowski,[98] a reserve second lieutenant in the Kościuszko Army, has become a local PPR activist after returning home after the war. He supervises the implementation of the agrarian reform and works on political changes in his village. His father, an enthusiast of the new system, is one of the poorest peasants to get new land. Wrona and the shop owner have decided the young PPR activist must die to sustain the old order. They make a plan for an underground group to execute him. But a new element hinders the crime – the arrival of the KBW soldiers, on a mission to find guerrilla arms hidden on a farm.

Meanwhile, Wrona has launched his plan and Dworowski's death seems fated. . . . The new powers are weak, the old connections and power relationships in the village seem to leave the poor with no agency. Except – and this is the twist – the abused women, having been beaten nearly senseless by their partners, intervene. One of the women tells the KBW soldiers that underground fighters have entered the village to murder Dworowski and his family. The KBW group jumps into action, liberating Dworowski as he is being tortured by two men. They arrive too late to save Dworowski's father, who is beheaded with an axe after refusing to buckle under to blackmail.

Graphic as it is, Bauman's story reflects the postwar times, when torture, collective family punishment and cruel murder were practised on a daily basis. The novel ends with a quasi-Hollywoodian happy ending. The underground band's arms cache is discovered, the bandits are captured and imprisoned – but without torture. And Wrona escapes . . . only to die in a swamp: 'He lived in the swamp and croaked in the swamp', the novel concludes (Żurowicz, 1953b: 89). The sceptical soldier from the first chapter, missing his family and its rural life, recognizes the value of serving the people as a KBW soldier. Everything ends well: injustices undone, fighting ended, criminals punished – except for one element: a secret agent connected to foreign intelligence services, who pays for information with US dollars,[99] tells his allies to move into the cities to prepare strikes to liberate Poland from Soviet occupation.

This final plot twist might have been inspired by the biography of 'Młot', who escaped KBW custody and hid in Wałbrzych (Waldenburg), a Lower Silesian mining city, where he was suspected of continuing underground activity. This novelistic transposition raises another question about this fiction and the reality it reflects: who among the KBW soldiers, in the novel, could represent Bauman?

Is Bauman Słucki?

Authors can hide real personalities behind fictional characters – including themselves. Via an alter ego, they may express feelings arising from circumstances they lived through, as a way of healing trauma,[100] or to reveal forbidden secrets. Like a lot of soldiers, Bauman kept silent about the details of his actions in the secret service.[101] Yet he did smuggle some elements of his experience onto the pages of his novel, and there are hints that the chief of the KBW group in the novel – Second Lieutenant Słucki – might have in some sense stood in for Bauman. Like Bauman in real life, the Słucki character is an early riser: 'The commander has the right to lie down later and get up earlier than his soldiers', he jokes at one point (Żurowicz, 1953b: 94). Słucki's charisma and his authority over subordinates also reflect accounts of Bauman from his superiors. Słucki is not a romantic hero, but rather a human being, exhausted by military service: 'He was very tired now, so he drove away the dream, closing his eyelids, smoking one cigarette after the other' (Żurowicz, 1953b: 94).

Unlike many of the other figures in the novel, Słucki is a three-dimensional character, a kind of anti-hero who refuses to put on airs over his leading role in the mission: 'Słucki was confused by the signs of gratitude. He gave an order that all the soldiers be thanked [instead of just him]' (Żurowicz, 1953b: 97). This was the communist ideal of a KBW leader – charismatic, yet collaborative: the hero of the novel is the KBW rather than an individual. The novel fits well into the 'educational soldier novel' genre, with the characteristic social realism of the times, but it contains a significant absence: Jews. There are no Jews among the soldiers, the village inhabitants, nor in anyone's thoughts. This is another characteristic trait of postwar literature emanating from PPR/PZPR propaganda shops. Even in passages describing the Nazi occupation and its tragedies, there is no mention of any Jew. And Słucki, the name of the protagonist most clearly identified with the author, is a very Polish name – a feature that distances him from Bauman.

Szczytno – mission 'to fix everything'

Though 'Młot' remained free and active for some months, the operation against him was ending when Bauman, freshly promoted to lieutenant (*porucznik*), returned to his old job as an instructor in Bydgoszcz. In May 1946, he was decorated with the Silver Cross of Merit. As in all armies, such decorations were important for promotions and career construction in postwar Poland. Yet it was only a

weak form of promotion. Had he truly been considered an efficient
fighter, Bauman would have been sent back into combat, the best
way to advance in the military. Instead, he was returned to military
intelligence – as a teacher. The brevity of his field experience probably indicates the value the military attributed to his martial skills.
This was not Bauman's strength. His assets lay in teaching and
politically preparing a young generation of soldiers. And, in June,
the hierarchy decided to transfer him again.

'In July 1946', wrote Bauman in his official CV from 1947,
'I was moved to the post of lecturer in politics at the Military
Intelligence School in Szczytno.'[102] A document written on 10 July
1946 reflects the view of his KBW superiors. Noting his various
honours (the Polish Silver Cross of Merit; the Baltic, Oder and
Nysa, and Freedom and Victory medals; Russian honours for the
liberation of Warsaw and Berlin, and victory over Germany; and
the Grunwald Badge),[103] it gives a glowing account of his performance and character:

> In his period of work as a senior politico-educational specialist in
> WBW [a unit of the KBW] in Pomerania, Bauman Zygmunt showed
> himself to be a talented, well-trained and disciplined officer. He worked
> considerably to increase his knowledge. He showed great concern for
> his soldiers. He was one of the best lecturers and organizers. Thanks
> to his honest and healthy initiative, he contributed greatly to the
> improvement of the state of work in the domain of political education
> in our units. Lieutenant Bauman has a large amount of information,
> is ideologically sure, and stands firmly in the ranks of active fighters
> for People's Poland. His morality is at a high level. He is a good candi-
> date to become vice-commander of WBW for the politico-educational
> sector or a battalion commander.[104]

The document is signed by Major Faryna,[105] the deputy leader of
the local WBW school.

A report from a commission visiting Szczytno at this time indicates
the gravity of the problems Bauman and the KBW/WBW hierarchy
faced there in mid-1946. 'The economic condition of the regiment
is bad', it states; 'There is chaos and disorder in the whole logistics
area.' The regiment had no potatoes and was undernourished. The
flour provided by a mill in nearby Olsztyn was unusable, producing
bread that 'resembles clay and causes frequent gastric distress. Due
to the lack of stoves, some companies receive uncooked food and
must prepare it themselves.' The report continues:

> Rooms in the barracks are not suitable, with an almost complete
> lack of beds, tables, benches and other equipment. About 50% of the
> windows are broken. Toilets and sinks are unused due to a lack of

water. The municipal water system supplies water for only 2 hours
a day. . . . electrical installations are destroyed, there is a complete
absence of bulbs.

Thanks to the lousy infrastructure, soldiers went unwashed, failed
to change their clothes for days on end, and carried lice, and the
hospital was overrun with scabies. Soldiers mostly slept on the floor
and there were no medicines. The document accuses a 'Colonel
Sawicki' of having thrown away '50 kilograms of precious DDT
insect powder' to make room in a vehicle for officers.[106]
This document leaves no doubt that conditions of life and military
service in Szczytno were dreadful. Another part of the document
reports on the steps Bauman took after his arrival:

> As far as political work is concerned, it only began with the arrival of
> Lieutenant Bauman – the lecturer of doctrine and discipline. Until his
> arrival, Lieutenant Kujszczyk did absolutely nothing; he showed no
> initiative and gave not a single briefing or talk. Lieutenant Bauman,
> meanwhile, on the very same day of his arrival called a briefing of
> politico-educational officers, ordered them to make outlines for talks
> and continued the normal political work the next day. Later, Bauman
> arranged and provisionally organized the political department and
> lectures.[107]

Bauman stayed in Szczytno two semesters. The report said that
his work increased discipline and organization in the camp, and
improved its relationship with local inhabitants, a problem in
various KBW bases, Joanna Tokarska-Bakir found. In 1946, a
KBW report said that 'despite rallies, meetings, the "wall newspaper" and "other types of agitation work", the population still had
poor connections with the KBW'. The author of the report hoped
to repair relations by organizing a free concert and a dance party.
In another report, Lieutenant Minkiewicz of the KBW Political
and Educational Board notes that 300 people were arrested in
Białystok on suspicion of contact with underground groups. Some
200 of them were released, but in terrible condition. The KBW
officers were apparently good at beating, and, as a result, the population began to fear the Army and, 'as soon as a car engine noise is
heard, all the men flee into the forest', Minkiewicz wrote.[108] There
were also accusations that KBW soldiers were 'raping German
women and murdering Jewish families on the coast' (Tokarska-
Bakir, 2018: 387).
In short, the population was not enthusiastic about the KBW and
feared the agency. Bauman tried to improve things; as an educational instructor, he probably tried to persuade and teach soldiers
to protect the local population rather than preying upon it. There

is certainly no evidence that Bauman, unlike some members of the KBW, was responsible for any negative conduct with civilian populations.

In short, there is nothing in the available documents that indicates Zygmunt Bauman was a communist criminal. He was an activist, supported the communist ideology during his KBW period, and was a party ideologist working on indoctrination of young recruits. Such a profile in young Polish-Jewish members of the intelligentsia with his life experiences was very common. He was a political officer like many other educated people.

On 20 December 1946, Bauman was promoted to captain,[109] presumably due to the quality of his performance as a political agitator and educator of soldiers. But Szczytno and its officer school were certainly not a good locale in which to construct a brilliant career. Nor was it a place where a young officer could have a pleasant and inspiring cultural life. In May 1947, Bauman finished his teaching duty and was transferred to Warsaw, a place with considerable professional possibilities. In June 1947, Bauman became deputy chief of the ZPW KBW (Zarząd Polityczno-Wojskowy KBW (Politico-Military Board of the KBW)) propaganda section. It was a new stage in his life – moving to the capital city, to a position of intellectual importance, and certainly the start of a 'normal' postwar life, where one might pursue a family as well as higher education. A new life reborn from the ruins – this was the fate of the city of Warsaw. It was also the destiny of Bauman.

7

'A Man in a Socialist Society'

Warsaw 1947–1953

Every human action has two aspects. One aspect is the world of values, . . . allowing people to classify, define, order their experiences derived from contacts with the situation and with other people, to choose among various goals that could be realized, to refuse one measure and take a second, etc. The other side of the issue is the external situation, which is essentially some kind of pressure system, a necessity that cannot be escaped, an arrangement of necessities that set the limits on our freedom to choose or take action. The objective shape of a situation means that some ideological proposals, certain goals, certain values turn out to be dreams, unreal dreams whose acceptance could only cause great internal suffering while others, otherwise less valuable, simply impose themselves under the principle of biotechnics, the art of living, of what is possible – the art of doing what is real, which may lead to the achievement of less lofty, but more certain goals.
(Zygmunt Bauman, '. . . Man in a Socialist Society' (1967: 3–4))[1]

Warsaw in the late 1940s

'Poland was a very backward country before the war, which was exacerbated by the occupation', Bauman said in a 2007 interview with Aida Edemariam (in the *Guardian*):

In an impoverished country you expect deprivation, humiliation, human indignity and so on, a whole complex of social and cultural problems to be dealt with. If you looked at the political spectrum in Poland at that time, the Communist Party promised the best solution. Its political programme was the most fitting for the issues which Poland faced. And I was completely dedicated. Communist ideas were just a continuation of the Enlightenment.[2]

Warsaw was a vibrant place in the summer of 1947, a city under reconstruction. Since the winter of 1945, when Stalin and Bierut decided to retain Warsaw as Poland's capital, the Office for the Reconstruction of the Capital (Biuro Odbudowy Stolicy) had focused on rebuilding the 90 per cent of the Old City destroyed by the Nazis, as well as other parts of Warsaw that lay in ruins.[3] 'Our favourite Sunday walks were to the Old City, to watch how they rebuilt it', Bauman said in a 2013 interview: 'It was impressive to see how Poland rose from the rubble . . . In 1945, when I returned from the front, it was rubble. [Reconstruction] consisted of moving bricks from one place to another. And then suddenly, something like these [new buildings] grew into the sky. It was a shocking and very pleasant experience.'[4]

What Bauman described was not an urbanist miracle. People came from every part of Poland to participate in this giant and politically important project, which aimed to return the city to life as quickly as possible, and at the same time to erase signs of the war. Massive gangs of volunteers helped to reanimate Warsaw, and the whole country followed the progress of reconstruction. 'I remember how the East–West route was built and opened. What a joy it was, how we danced', Bauman said: 'And then, there was the house where "'Empik"[5] is now. You know, on the corner of Jerozolimskie and Nowy Świat streets. A huge inscription hung there: "We built this house in fourteen days!"'[6] The reconstruction of Warsaw progressed fast enough for institutions that had operated in other cities (mainly Łódź) since liberation to be reinstated – for example, Warsaw University. Its professors gradually moved back to Warsaw, where, one by one, its departments opened their doors.

Bauman had come to Warsaw to meet his parents returning from the USSR around June 1946, the peak of a repatriation process that saw 1 million Poles leave the USSR.[7] While no documentation has surfaced of Bauman's reunion with his parents after two and a half years of separation, one can imagine the joy they must have felt. The Baumans were lucky to be a family again after the war and Holocaust. But the family was no longer a large group. Maurycy's relatives had emigrated years before the war, and, from Zofia's family, a brother and three sisters had been killed and only one sister survived. The two women inherited some goods as the last survivors of the large Cohn family, but this inheritance seems to have led to problems in their relationship.

'In spring 1946 my parents returned to Poland', Bauman wrote on 24 October 1949, in his Party CV:

My mother's only surviving sister, Leokadia Szymańska from Włocławek, who owned a sawmill and tenement houses, persuaded my mother to accept the inheritance of the murdered sisters – half of a house in Włocławek and one quarter of a house in Siemianowice. In 1948, my mother sold her parts of both houses, and broke up with her sister. The sum she received for the Włocławek house – PLN 75,000 – she donated to the Common House.

The Common House of the Party (Wspólny Dom) was the building that symbolized the merger of the PPR and PPS, a long winnowing process that resulted in the removal of 110,000 'dubious' members of the two leftist parties. After this 'cleansing', the final reunification took place in December 1948, with most power remaining in the hands of the PPR under the leadership of Gomułka.[8] Donating to the Common House signified a strong commitment to communist ideology; donation of a family inheritance left no doubt about one's political engagement. Zofia Bauman's donation was substantial and meaningful in the postwar period, when people had nothing and any resources went to rebuilding and purchasing houses, furniture and other goods. In another document, Bauman described Leokadia as 'a bourgeois' – a heavy charge in this era. The sisters stood on opposite sides of the political map. Moreover, their war experiences were different. Leokadia spent the war under German occupation using a false name (Szymańska), while Zofia with her husband and son escaped to the USSR. Selling off the family's inheritance would have been a sensitive topic in any case, but committing the proceeds to the Common House of the Party was probably, for Leokadia (if she learned about it), a betrayal. For Zofia, it signified deep political engagement, which Bauman underlined in several of his CVs – perhaps to balance his father's Zionist background. Bauman, like everyone else with a job in postwar Poland, was required to describe their parents' political orientation as part of standardized questionnaires (ten to twelve pages or more, depending on the year and the purpose) that required detailed information on the life of the person and their close relatives, including those living abroad. Employers – mainly state organizations – sought to know everything about their Polish citizens.

'My parents live with me in Warsaw', wrote Bauman in the 1949 questionnaire: 'My father works as a bookkeeper in "Solidarity" [a co-operative firm]. Mother is an inspector of WSS cafeterias [a national chain of modest restaurants]. From September 1947 she was a member of the PPR. After the unification, she became a member of PZPR.'[9] Sharing a house with their son enabled Bauman's parents to stay in Warsaw, where housing was scarce and residence laws were very strict. The state frequently requisitioned rooms from multi-room apartments, and it was not unusual for an entire family to be allocated only a single room. Bauman was an officer working at the board of the KBW in Warsaw, and as such had a functionary's apartment. His parents, whose professions were not as socially powerful, probably would not have had access to a flat on their own. Their address, Flat 19, 14 Sandomierska Street, was near Rakowiecka Street, an area of army and state buildings which had a separate entrance under military guard.[10]

'The flat consisted of two little rooms, a kitchen and a bathroom', Zygmunt's wife, Janina Bauman, wrote decades later:[11] 'It was full of sunshine, perfectly tidy and clean, decorated with potted plants and replicas of great Russian paintings of the 19th century. It was such a sharp contrast to our own squalid room [where she lived with her mother after 1945] that I felt as though I had entered a world of luxury to which I didn't belong' (J. Bauman, 1988: 47–8). Zygmunt Bauman was certainly privileged to have his apartment at Mokotów, a pleasant, leafy district in the centre of Warsaw. His job brought him a good place to live and a good salary, in exchange for political fidelity and strong involvement in the 'politico-educational' KBW mission.

An ordinary life in a specific workplace: Bauman's career at the KBW

Poland in 1947 was not yet at peace, and the KBW Political and Educational Board, where Bauman worked, was an active place. The first postwar parliamentary elections occurred on 19 January, as required by the 1945 Potsdam Agreement of Stalin, Churchill and Truman. The elections were supposed to ensure democratic management of Poland and to stabilize the country by permitting an adequate representation of society in its power structures. Bierut and his faction (PPR) were surprised by the negative results of the referendum they organized in 1946,[12] and falsified the results to keep power in their hands. The parliamentary elections took place under similar circumstances. Vote falsification ensured the victory of the PPR, but the Party leadership still viewed the situation as unstable. Indoctrination and propaganda activity were key to improving public opinion regarding the new regime, in the Party's view. Bauman was an active and creative element of the system. One of his most important tasks, which he performed frequently, was writing political texts with the objective of communist indoctrination. Producing such literature required good historical knowledge and a background in the Marxist literature, with mastery of 'classics' such as Lenin's work. Long office hours were devoted to the preparation of all kind of speeches, some presented later by himself, some by others. Decades later, Bauman would describe this work as boring and not really important. 'My job there was very dull, in fact', he told the journalist Edemariam, who added: 'He wrote political pamphlets for soldiers.'[13]

Bauman was also in charge of organizing training and political education aimed at promoting the 'enlargement of the socialist/communist[14] conscience'. A KBW archive document illustrates part of Bauman's day-to-day activities as an organizer of training for political officers. It concerns an 'Agitator Course Programme for the regiment', signed and probably written by Bauman, who, at the time, was in charge of organizing the KBW's educational section under Colonel Bibrowski (mentioned by Bauman as his chief and a trusted man in the KBW).[15] The detailed schedule from the programme, dated 16 February 1950, is certainly dull, but explains the topics that future agitators were expected to master.[16] The day began at 8:30 a.m. with a press review, followed by a 15-minute introduction by Captain Komorowski and then a one-hour lecture, also by Komorowski, entitled 'Agitators of the Soviet Army – Our Pattern'. From 10 to 11 a.m., Captain Trzaska presented 'The Tasks of an Agitator', followed by a three-hour 'practicum' involving 'an exchange of experiences'. An hour of lunch was followed by another one-hour lecture, entitled 'The Fight for Vigilance'. At 3 p.m., Lieutenant Kulczyk presented 'The Tasks of the Agitator in the Fight for Vigilance and Keeping Military Secrets'. The final hours of the workday were spent on 'Educational Games and Practical Classes'. Dinner was at 7 p.m., followed by a movie.

The following day's schedule was equally full, beginning with a 7:45 a.m. press review and a one-hour demonstration of weapon use. Then Captain Trzaska gave a one-hour presentation on 'setting a personal example as the basis for an agitator's work'. Then Bauman gave a three-hour presentation, 'The Press in the Work of the Agitator'. After lunch, a one-hour demonstration-lecture, 'How to Read a Book', by Lieutenant Kalisiewicz, was followed by a lecture, 'The Role of the Agitator in Publishing a Wall Newspaper' (Captain Trzaska). The day concluded from 4 p.m. to 5 p.m. with a Bauman lecture, 'The Role of the Agitator in the Political and Militant Training of Soldiers and the Fight for a High Level of Discipline'. The evening included a theatre piece (no title indicated). The final day again started with a 15-minute press review, followed by two hours of lectures on production co-operatives. Then Second Lieutenant Cabaj taught ten soldiers military songs, while others trained at the shooting range with Kulczyk. After lunch, Bauman lectured on agitators in the internal struggle – probably a reference to political conflict with the 'internal enemy', a hot topic at all political and military meetings at the time. The final lecture dealt with the Six Year Plan – Poland's economic development plan – and the ways to achieve its goals. At 6 p.m., the conference ended. The programme was signed, 'KBW Capt. Bauman, head of the 2nd Branch'.

The training session was typical for military organizations at the time and a good example of Bauman's work. He thought, wrote, spoke, organized and managed ideology, and discussed it with others. This was not the strategic game of an opportunist or a conformist. As he underlined several times in interviews later, Bauman believed in 'the cause'.

Believing in a better future

'I had to think [early in my life] about social relations', Bauman said in his 2013 interview with Kwaśniewski:

> About . . . fathers jumping in the Warta River or schoolmates kicking and strangling you. When I entered the Army I started to have serious talks about it. And not on my own initiative. . . . [but from] wiser, more experienced people who were already involved before the war. And not only in communism. The 1st Army was, in a sense, built more on a nationalist [than a communist] basis. So I listened to both: the right and the left. They made me aware of the political and social map of Poland. They did not teach this at school, so I had no idea that there was any left wing, right wing, nationalism, chauvinism, Sanacja or Endecja. Or that before the war in Poland there were 8 million hidden jobless people in the country. . . . Well, imagine now that you are 18 years old again. Of course, you think about girls, undoubtedly, but in your free time, what else do you think about? Exactly: about what the world is like, and what you could do to make it different. So I listened to all this and associated my own childhood experiences with it, and I came to the conclusion, as did many young people at that time, that when you compared all of Poland's political options, the communists had the best one. Well, please, see how I felt. They came to us and said, 'We will give land to the peasants.' And I knew that the peasants suffered because they did not have land. Factories for workers. Wonderful, my father will not have to bow. Everyone will be equal. Education will be free. Great! Education was a very important matter for me. There were also various slogans against discrimination and humiliation. The latter especially became a very important concept in my life and it continues to be.[17]

No more discrimination. No more humiliation. These were powerful promises and there were elements of the postwar system that helped to maintain the illusion of their possible implementation. Bauman was 'unflinching in his faith', Janina Bauman wrote in the *roman à clef* she based on her life with Bauman:

> yet sound and clear in his reasoning, Konrad [Janina refers to Zygmunt as 'Konrad' in the English edition of her book] explained that there would be no room for anti-Semitism, or any other racial hatred, under Communism – this fairest of social systems, which would guarantee full equality between human beings regardless of language, race or

creed. We were particularly lucky, he stressed, to have been born at the right time and in the right place to become active fighters for this noblest cause. The greatest of historical changes was happening before our eyes, here and now. To stand by as idle witnesses would be to miss a unique opportunity. Running away would be betrayal. I listened enthralled. Here was the voice of an honest Communist; his arguments seemed sound and he truly believed in what he was saying. (J. Bauman, 1988: 49)

Many younger Poles, especially those from groups that suffered discrimination before the war, believed in the change. 'In luring the Jews with equal rights, the Polish version of Communism from the beginning did not have a clear attitude toward them', wrote Joanna Tokarska-Bakir. On the one hand:

Anti-Semitism was considered a declining product of the class struggle, levelling off as the revolution progressed. Those who felt it was not being eradicated fast enough, including Jews, usually were accused of Zionism, which was understood as an 'improper' nationalism. With no way out, they really became Zionists. [On the other hand], at the same time, communist authorities from the start paid obeisance to 'proper' nationalism – a nationalism that could be co-opted to legitimate communism, as articulated in the words of Jakub Berman at a 10 Oct. 1947 meeting of the Central Committee of the PPR: 'It is our great achievement as communists that we can create a national party deeply rooted in Polish society, in different layers of the nation, in the working class, in the peasantry, in part in the intelligentsia. This is our greatest treasure, which we must guard. To again enter the enchanted circle of the KPP [the pre-war Polish communists, who propagated an internationalist ideal] would be the greatest disaster. (Tokarska-Bakir, 2018: 210)

The promises formulated by the communists in the postwar years look like a utopian project today. It is difficult to embrace the perspective of these people, deeply immersed in the construction of a new system. 'Utopians, when they are building their utopia, imagine everything, including such details as streets, houses, and the schedule of the day', Kwaśniewski stated in his interview with Bauman: 'Do you remember details that you particularly cared about?' Bauman responded: 'I did not interpret what I was doing as a utopia. It was a reality.'[18]

For Bauman, reality meant belonging to, and being active in, the Party. A PPR activist since 1945, Bauman, on 12 December 1948, was accepted into the PZPR with ID no. 0660454, his documents issued by the Committee of Military Unit 1719.[19] On 28 December, he passed a verification process. According to the report by the commission dated 15 January 1948, 'a jury composed of Major Jan Fuks, Major Władysław Minkiewicz and Major Kazimierz Sitarek found the following':

> [Bauman] led party work in the school in Szczytno, where he increased the size of the unit from 12 to 60 members, including 30 members he personally recruited. However, he gave insufficient political vigilance to the recruitment, accepting members who were [later] removed from the Party [in late 1947]. He is a devoted and diligent person. A good speaker. Without addictions. Moral conduct without a flaw. His work is beneficial to the Party.

This document was important for Bauman's trajectory in the overlapping of Party and professional careers that constituted the *nomenklatura*: 'one of the basic tools that guarantee that only people who are ideologically reliable, who are highly qualified and who act in the social, political and cultural interests of the country, will be called upon to fill management positions' (Smolar, 1983: 43, in Hardy, 2009: 30).

This mutual interdependence was a feature of the postwar Polish military, especially in the case of political officers like Bauman. His brilliant career progress suggests that propaganda and political education were domains he mastered with brio. In July 1947, Bauman began his new job as a trainer on the board of the politico-educational section of the KBW Department of Political Training. Only a few months later, he became chief of the first department, and, ten months later, on 20 December, took over leadership of two departments (first and second) of the politico-educational board. On 10 July 1949, he was promoted again, to chief of the Department of Propaganda and Agitation, and in May 1952 was promoted to major, and became the chief of Department II of the political board. Bauman held this position for less than a year before the military discharged him on 16 March 1953.[20]

Student in the Academy of Political Science – 1947–1950

In parallel with his intense KBW activity, Bauman in 1947 began studies at the Academy of Political Science (ANP: Akademia Nauk Politycznych) in Warsaw. The ANP, which had opened as a private school in 1939, did not function until 1945, and in November 1946 was nationalized. The academy had four faculties: administration, diplomacy, journalism, and social sciences, where Bauman was enrolled. The social sciences department included the following domains: sociology, political economy, social doctrines, statistics and demography, modern history, socio-economic history, social policy and social legislation. The rector of the ANP was an internationally known statistician-demographer, Edward Szturm de Sztrem. Szturm had been educated in Czarist Russia and France, and from his youth was a socialist activist. Though he could easily have settled in the West, Szturm was animated by the idea of building a socialist state and decided to return home after the war. On 3 June 1947, he asked the Education Ministry for permission to create a chair in sociology (which Soviet scholars suspiciously regarded as a 'bourgeois' science), with the following rationale:

> Sociology as a theory of society and social science that constitutes a basic discipline for the study of various social issues. The necessity of lecturing and conducting research in this field is motivated by the fact that this science is a basic one, and students must learn its methods to engage with the most difficult problems in the study of society. The absence of sociology at the Faculty of Social Sciences would create a critical vacuum in our studies.[21]

Thanks to this urgent request, Bauman was able to study sociology at the ANP. Its course offerings (most of which were compulsory) were extensive, and the faculty included renowned personalities in the Polish intellectual and political world.[22] In his first year, according to the programme, Bauman studied 'Selected Problems in Philosophy', 'Dialectical Materialism' and 'Historical Materialism' (the last two form the basis of Marxist theory) with Professor Adam Schaff. Schaff was a Marxist philosopher educated in Paris and Moscow, and the official ideologist of the reunified party (PZPR). This orthodox Marxist, who was to become Bauman's first scholarly mentor, was well known in Poland. Another important figure was Professor Manfred Lachs, a famous jurist and specialist in international law who in 1966 was elected as a judge for the World Court – the International Court of Justice at The Hague – and was the Court's president from 1973 to 1976.[23] Under Lachs, Bauman took a class entitled 'The Encyclopedia of the Law', and also studied legal courses under Professor Biskupski entitled 'Knowledge of the State and Law' – and 'Polish State Law'. Bauman's courses also included 'General Economic Geography' (under Maria Kiełczewska) and history – 'The Economy of Pre-Capitalistic Formations' and 'The History of the Nineteenth and Twentieth Centuries' (taught by Juliusz Bardach). Żanna Kormanowa taught 'The History of Doctrines and Social Movements'. Kormanowa was a fanatical supporter of Stalinism and was greatly feared among Polish historians.

As can be seen, the major topics of study were bound tightly to the new political orientation. However, there were also less politically sensitive subjects, such as research methodology classes on statistics, logic and the 'techniques of intellectual work'.[24] The second year was devoted mainly to the economy, with courses on public finance, history and social policy, as well as 'Capitalist Economy' and 'Economic Law', which prepared students for the new economic system and, in particular, socialist central planning. The third year required students to choose a speciality: the choices were organization and management, public administration or extra-scholarly activities (it is not stated whether this is nature, sport, music or art). Bauman chose the first option, and took courses that included statistics, 'Economy of Popular Democracy and Socialism', 'Techniques and Organization of Labour' and, finally, 'Sociology', taught by Professor Eugeniusz Modliński (a labour law instructor who specialized in social benefits).

In the late 1940s, sociology was not widely institutionalized as a discipline, and it was hard to find sociology professors even in Warsaw, and even for a rector with an extensive network, such as Szturm de Sztrem. Yet the ANP faculty were well chosen. Some were internationally recognized stars, and others would become well known. Others were well-known professionals, active politicians or Party leaders. Many had studied and worked abroad and were familiar with work cultures other than Polish. This tacit knowledge, discreetly diffused, created among some students a deep thirst for mastery and a desire to include an international dimension in their career.

The ANP was a place that breathed internationalization, as Lachs wrote in 1985:

When nearly 40 years ago . . . I started lecturing at Wawelska Street [ANP] . . . I did not realize what difficulties lay ahead in the days, weeks and years. All generations were witnesses to and participants in our turbulent history, yet many people had lost their bearings so often . . . It seemed to us in 1945 that our problems could be solved without difficulty. That was not to be.

He continued:

Once on the periphery of the great world, a province pushed into the shadows, Poland finally began to win its rightful place in Europe. It is rare to find a nation where interest in international issues was greater than in Poland, whether among students or journalists or poets. . . . This bond with international issues . . . results from the experience of history, because our lives more than in many other nations are connected with events in the international arena. (Lachs, 1985, in Sobiecka and Ślężak)[25]

From the start of his higher education, Bauman acquired an ability to see the broad international context, to analyse historical processes and social changes across the borders of a single state or continent. At this stage of his life, education also engaged him deeply in social change.

All of the instructors at the ANP were close to the leftist party (socialist and communist), more so than at the university, where a modest pluralism was still preserved. The ANP was preparing the future socialist elite: political leaders, diplomats, journalists and high-ranking state administrators. Some of the professors, including the rector, might have enjoyed comfortable lives in Western Europe but instead had chosen to return home to rebuild Poland. They were animated by the idea (perhaps utopian, from today's perspective) of creating a new society without discrimination. They thought they were making history.

'Through forty years I found myself close to the greatest historical events', Lachs said at his seventieth birthday celebration: 'History did not bypass my life. On the contrary, history enriched my life, which was made possible by the Polish People's Republic. It was the Polish People's Republic that made me noticeable in the crowd, noticeable both within and outside my country' (Lachs, 1985, in Sobiecka and Ślężak).[26]

This enthusiastic and engaged approach must certainly have attracted young people. For students, Bauman included, the faculty were not only teachers but moral and political authorities to follow. The ANP differed from the university not only in its faculty profile, but also in the organization of its student population. 'All lectures and seminars started late in the afternoon because most students had to work during the day to earn their living', wrote Janina Bauman: 'Thousands of people attended the three faculties, most of them trying to make up for the wasted years of war. Many were still in the army and wore military uniforms. The vast lecture theatres and spacious seminar rooms were always full' (J. Bauman, 1988: 37).

Zygmunt's first idea was to pursue physics and mathematics, his subjects in Gorki before his military engagement. But when he appeared with the Soviet documentation at the University of Warsaw, the administration declared that he would have to pass an entrance exam again. For a busy military officer, it was more manageable to study sociology than physics and mathematics. These academic domains required full-time attention, which was incompatible with Bauman's arduous duties at the KBW. Evening and weekend courses were the only possible option for Bauman. Moreover, as his wife Janina mentioned, he started the academic year late, and was not an assiduous lecture-goer: 'Some time passed before I saw him again. He seemed to miss lectures quite often, perhaps too busy to go to them all' (J. Bauman, 1988: 40). (The Polish text[27] of Janina Bauman's book contains more precise wording: 'he seemed to be busy with his army job' (J. Bauman, 2011: 31).)

Despite the organizational difficulties, Bauman made himself known as an excellent student. 'The seminar began. The tutor bustled about his desk, rustled his sheets and gave a fascinating talk about a remarkable new novel. He then called upon the audience to discuss the book', Janina Bauman wrote. The book under discussion was *Samson* by Kazimierz Brandys. 'Soon I saw him [Bauman] raise his hand. He stood up and stepped forward to the rostrum. Facing the audience, he began to speak. I listened fascinated. His account of the novel was thoughtful, original and striking, sparkling with witty remarks. The students listened engrossed, now and then bursting into laugher. Obviously pleased, the tutor nodded his approval' (J. Bauman, 1988: 39).

Bauman impressed others besides his future wife. His oratorical abilities were a major asset throughout his life and in different careers, as agitator, teacher, military officer, university professor and public intellectual. This exceptional ability was visible even in Bauman's student years. At 22 years of age, his war experiences and military career gave him different perspectives from other students. The war had prevented most of the younger generation from studying in the domain of their choice,[28] but there were not many so well trained to speak passionately about Poland's future, to display a vision of social justice built on the country's discriminatory past. Brandys' book *Samson* is the life story of a Jew persecuted in prewar Poland who fights and dies in the struggle against the Nazis – a topic that Bauman certainly had mastered. Given his youth and charisma, it is not surprising that in this institution for future Polish elites, he met the love of his life.

Janina Lewinson

Janina was born on 18 August 1926 in Warsaw – nine months after Bauman, and in a social environment that was quite different from his. The Lewinson family in interwar Poland included a number of distinguished medical doctors.[29] Janina was the first child of Alina Fryszman and Szymon Lewinson, and 'grew up in a happy family', she would write:[30]

My father was a doctor and surgeon dealing with people's kidneys and bladders. My mother's father, Grandad Aleksander, was a doctor too, his fame well established in Warsaw before I was born. My paternal grandfather, whose name was Maks, ran a music shop in the most elegant part of the city, until he went bankrupt. I remember him as a modest old man with plenty of time and warm feelings for myself. Somehow I knew that he and Grandma Viera were poor and dependent on my father, while the other grandparents, who lived on Border Street, were rich. They were rich not only because Grandad Aleksander was a gifted doctor and surgeon but also because Grannie Eva's family was well off. Grannie Eva's family was the *crème de la crème* of society; great-grandfather served for years as both head of the Jewish Council and counsellor of the City of Warsaw. There were lots of uncles, aunts and cousins on both sides of the family, most of them doctors; others lawyers, engineers or suchlike. Except for my great-grandfather, who died before I was born, no one in my large family spoke Yiddish, wore beards, skullcaps or traditional Jewish gaberdines. Nobody was religious. We were all Polish, born on Polish soil, brought up in the Polish tradition, permeated with the spirit of Polish history and literature. Yet Jewish at the same time, conscious of being Jewish every minute of our lives.[31] (J. Bauman, 1988: 1–2)

As a child, Janina lacked for nothing: 'In our vast flat in Sienna Street,[32] which included father's private surgery, I lived with my parents, Sophie [a younger sister] and a maid and a cook. There was always a nanny, or a governess and later a French teacher too' (J. Bauman, 1988: 2). Janina's mother spoke four languages (perfect command of German saved their lives several times during World War II), and Janina from early childhood learned French – the language of Polish elites. In her early years, she was homeschooled by private teachers and governesses. Then:

In September 1937, being 11, I was finally sent to school. I went into the sixth form, the last years of primary education in a private school. 'Our School' as it was called, was run by a Jewish headmistress, all of the teachers were Jewish and so were the pupils. Yet, it could hardly have been called a Jewish school, since apart from the Jewish history lessons, everything was strictly Polish, even Christian holidays were observed. (J. Bauman, 1988: 6)

This was a school specifically for wealthy Jewish children; an institution that, in addition to good education, gave the children and their parents precious protection from the anti-Semitic treatment that was widespread outside. Janina did not suffer from the same discrimination and maltreatment that Zygmunt experienced in primary school. She was privileged because her parents had money and lived in Warsaw (where 368,392 people, 29.1 per cent of the inhabitants, were Jews),[33] where there was a good secular Jewish school. However, this protective cover would eventually fall apart:

It had been decided since I was born that I would follow in my father's and grandfather's footsteps and become a doctor. . . . There was, however, a major obstacle to this family daydream. At that time, it was hard for anyone to get into medical studies at Warsaw University – for a Jewish boy or girl it was almost impossible. . . . Practically, the only way a Jew could get in was to gain a good certificate from a state high school. But there the same obstacle lurked

again: there were severe restrictions on the number of Jewish children
admitted to state secondary schools. One had to be truly brilliant and
pass the qualifying exams with top marks to be accepted. My father,
obsessed with the idea of my becoming a doctor, decided to give
me this chance. So, in June 1938, I sat the state-controlled exams,
perhaps the most difficult exams of my life, wishing I could fail and
thus escape the ordeal I anticipated. Strangely enough, I passed with
the highest marks and was admitted to a state high school for girls in
the city. . . . September came, . . . and there I was in the new school,
which I had already feared and hated in advance. It was even worse
than I had anticipated. I was the only Jewish girl – not just in my
form but in the whole gymnasium (the first four years of secondary
school). (J. Bauman, 1988: 8)

Zygmunt and Janina passed their entrance exams to public
gymnasia in the same year, 1938, and, thanks to their excellent
marks, were enrolled in those select institutions. She was admitted
to Hoffmanowa in Warsaw, he to Berger in Poznań. Bauman was
luckier than Janina – he was not the only Jew in his class. As a consequence, he had friends, while she was alone. Both, however, were
in a similar situation in regard to grades – teachers typically gave
them lower marks than they deserved simply because they were not
Catholic Poles. Despite being best in her class in Polish literature,
Janina got 4 out of 5. 'I could not and I still cannot explain this
strange incident', she wrote half a century later:

> other than my being Jewish, I think it went against nationalist feelings
> to admit that the Polish language and Polish literature could have
> been mastered by a Jewish child better than by forty-three children
> with pure Polish blood in their veins. . . . For the first time in my life,
> I felt myself a victim of real injustice from a person I particularly
> respected (J. Bauman, 1988: 10)

Teachers, who in principle should have been moral authorities for
young students, mirrored the social and ethnic injustices practised
outside of school.[34] Anti-Semitism came also from peers, sometimes
more painfully than injustices suffered at the hands of adults. In
the school for girls, the forms of aggression were not the same as
those practised by boys. Janina was not beaten, as Zygmunt was;
she suffered another type of hostility. Shunning, mockery and verbal
attacks were the tools of persecution employed by female schoolmates. Lewinson was set apart as an outsider, although the ghetto
bench rule probably was not applied at Hoffmanowa Gymnasium
(due to the almost complete absence of Jewish students). The isolation treatment she suffered was also motivated by social class
differences, Janina Bauman realized later:

I can see now that being Jewish was only one reason for my estrangement. I belonged to a well-off professional family while most of my forty-three classmates were workers' or craftsmen's children, some of them very poor. The state high school with its low fees was meant for them not for me. So I was a double stranger in this school, and feel in my heart I still bear some resentment towards my parents for having sent me there. (J. Bauman 1988: 11)

The Lewinsons, like the Bauman parents, decided that, despite the racist segregationist laws, their child would get the best public Polish education possible. Their strategies were similar despite the social class differences. Janina lived in luxury in the middle of Warsaw (Sienna Street, then Graniczna Street), spent summer holidays at the family villa in Konstancin (a bourgeois suburban town) and had maids, while the Baumans rented a modest three-room apartment in Poznań.

They did share some experiences. The first was the early meeting with the phenomenon of bankruptcy and its consequences. This was a more acute issue for the Baumans, leading to the father's suicide attempt and subsequent unemployment, while the Lewinson grandparents, following their financial trouble, got financial support from their son. In addition, they both were forced to leave warm and happy homes to be exposed as strangers to anti-Semitism in school. Their experiences would truly diverge, however, during World War II, when they trod the two different pathways available for Jewish Poles. While the Baumans escaped to the Soviet Union, the Lewinsons were exposed to, and survived, the full horrors of the Holocaust. The experience of Janina's family was crucial inspiration for Bauman's major work *Modernity and the Holocaust* (1989),[35] as he has acknowledged in interviews. Janina did not describe her war experience to Zygmunt immediately after they met, but recounted it many decades later in her first autobiographical book, an exceptional account of daily life in Warsaw for a family condemned to die in the Holocaust.

From the first day of the war, the Lewinson family was separated. Janina's father, Szymon, was mobilized to the Polish Army as a physician and reserve officer, and sent off to Poland's eastern border. He was permitted to bring his family, but Janina's mother declined because her mother was terminally ill. With the 17 September 1939 Molotov–Ribbentrop Pact, the Red Army annexed eastern Polish territories. Janina's father, her uncle and thousands of other Polish officers were interned and later killed in the Katyń massacre.[36] The family would have no news of him for years, during this time holding out the hope he was alive somewhere in the Soviet Union.

Janina, her mother and younger sister Zofia spent the Occupation in Warsaw, surviving thanks to a series of fortunate events. They survived the Warsaw bombing of 1939 in the house of Janina's grandparents – their own house was completely destroyed and the family apartment on Graniczna Street was requisitioned by Janina's grandfather's driver. Thanks to his *Volksdeutsche* status,[37] this man, who had long served them, had the right to take over their dwelling. The family, including Janina's dying grandmother, were cast out on the pavement in the autumn of 1940 and moved to the Ghetto, where they stayed for two years. During their early months there, Janina and Zofia were enrolled in underground schools and the family survived thanks to the sale of their goods by 'Auntie Mania' (Maria Bułat),[38] who had been Alina's nannie and became a member of the Lewinson family. As a Christian, Maria was forbidden from living under the same roof as the Lewinsons, but her residence outside the Ghetto[39] provided an opportunity to help Alina and her daughters. Maria became their guardian angel and an indispensable factor in their survival. Her actions saved their lives many times; after selling off the family's jewellery, porcelain and paintings, she sold her own property to provide them with sustenance. The Lewinson uncles also played a key role in protecting Alina and her daughters from deadly Ghetto liquidation actions, and in finding them a hideout on the Aryan side.[40]

It was rare for any size of family to survive intact in the Warsaw Ghetto. Usually, parents who were lucky enough to do so placed their children in Catholic families.[41] Yet, except for short periods, Alina and her daughters stayed together during the war. The separations were mainly due to Janina's bad health. She contracted tuberculosis in the Ghetto, and several times during the war (and after) suffered heavy crises with high fever and loss of consciousness. Despite having good hiding places, they were obliged to change shelters several times. Such changes were extremely dangerous, although the family possessed an excellent fake ID with a very Polish name, Lubowicka.[42]

Unlike many who survived on the Aryan side,[43] Alina and her daughters unfortunately bore 'the visible signs of Mediterranean origin'. When they left their hiding place, they needed constantly to cover their 'Jewish look' – the black curly hair, dark eyes and healthy-sized noses that were all too characteristic of the 'Jewish type'. Alina would don a dark widow's hat, while Zofia would pretend to be injured, with a bandage on her head. Janina, however, would go as she was, with the idea that at least one should appear normal so as not to attract undue attention. Despite the lack of a good 'look', they passed through a thousand miraculous situations and somehow emerged with their lives.

Their life in hiding ended on 1 August 1944, when the Underground Army (AK), in accord with the London government-in-exile, initiated the Warsaw Uprising to liberate the city from German occupation before the Red Army arrived. While Bauman waited on the opposite shore of the Vistula River, waiting for orders from Stalin to join the battle, which never came, his wife-to-be, with her mother and sister, was hiding in caves converted into underground shelters. They lived for days and nights without water, food, light or fresh air, terrible conditions for a tuberculosis patient. Janina suffered a dramatic fever crisis, and only the heroic efforts of her mother enabled her to survive.

The Lewinsons might have died in innumerable ways between 1939 and the war's end – bullets and bombs, tuberculosis, typhoid and typhus, murder at the hands of the Gestapo or the Catholic Poles who sometimes betrayed Jews.[44] The Lewinsons were black-mailed more than once, but escaped by paying and fleeing before the Nazis caught up with them.[45] However, they survived also thanks to the support of non-Jewish Poles who risked their lives to help them. After the capitulation that followed the failed Warsaw Uprising, the family was led to Pruszków, where they underwent the final German selection (the Nazis sent more than 150,000 people to concentration camps or forced-labour camps). The Lewinsons were selected for Germany, but thanks to Janina's mother's cunning they escaped the deportation. They were sent to the countryside and stopped in Zielonki, a small village near Kraków in southern Poland, where they were hosted by friendly peasants from October 1944 to April 1945. After bouts of tuberculosis and undernourishment, Janina returned to Warsaw with her mother and sister following the war's end.

Their survival was a miracle. However, their situation was very difficult in a devastated city only slowly returning to life. The Lewinsons awaited the return of Szymon with decreasing hope, since there was every indication that he had died. Already a year before the Liberation, Janina happened to see a German newspaper spread over a freshly cleaned floor and read the name of her father on a supposed list of victims of the Katyń massacre. For years, political lies surrounded this tragedy, a massacre of thousands of prisoners of war in violation of all international conventions. Who had given the order – Hitler or Stalin? For Janina and her family, there was no question – the Red Army, which had saved them and freed the Jews, could not be the wanton killer of their father and husband. In postwar documents, in the spaces for answers to questions about his wife's father, Zygmunt Bauman would write: 'killed by Nazis', or 'died in Holocaust'. This was compatible with the official version of the postwar Polish authorities. In fact, Szymon Lewinson was one of 25,000 officers killed by the Soviets in the spring of 1940. Szymon and his brother Józef, also killed at Katyń, were Polish war heroes.

While waiting for her husband's improbable return, Alina Lewinson worked as a translator. She obtained a tiny room at

Poznańska St. 38, in the centre of Warsaw. It was too tiny for three women,[46] and after sticking together for so many years during the worst of times, the family had to split up. Zofia, 15, entered a Jewish orphanage in Śródborów (a western Warsaw suburb), where she attended a good gymnasium and had decent living conditions. Janina enrolled in evening school – Wyspiański High School – to complete her high-school studies and prepare for her baccalaureate (*matura*) exam. Like the majority of Holocaust survivors, she developed a strong Jewish identity.

'I belong to the Jews', she noted in her journal under the date of December 1944:

> Not because I was born one or because I share their faith – I never have. I belong to the Jews because I have suffered as one of them. It's suffering that has made me Jewish. I belong to people who have been murdered or who are still struggling to escape death. If some of them do survive the war, and if I survive myself, I'll join them. Our shared experience of this ordeal will bring us together. We'll build a home of our own, a place of our own, a place for all homeless Jews where we can live in peace and dignity, respected by other nations and respecting their rights in turn. That's what I believe and where I belong.
> (J. Bauman, 1988: 181–2)

Unsurprisingly, in spring 1946, Janina joined a group organized by the Zionist Ihud Party that focused on preparing young Jews to emigrate. Janina was very enthusiastic about the idea of starting a new life in Palestine and decided to leave Poland as soon as possible – without passing her Polish baccalaureate exam. Her mother was not surprised by this news, nor was her sister, who as a teenager had joined a clandestine Zionist group and prepared herself to *berihah* (escape).[47] The majority of Jewish survivors decided to leave Poland, and many chose to join a kibbutz before emigrating. Janina's preparation consisted of intensive Hebrew courses and some occupational training – emigrés were expected to be ready to do hard physical work. Shortly before the departure of her group, however, Janina became ill and spent several weeks at home. She recovered just in time to pass her baccalaureate exams. There was no time to celebrate, however, because of her serious health problems, and she spent several months in a Jewish sanatorium near Warsaw.

While she was there, on 4 July 1946, the inhabitants of the city of Kielce, with the support of some people belonging to the local militia, Polish Army and KBW units, attacked the building of the Jewish organization. The place housed almost 100 people, mostly Holocaust survivors, many of whom had been liberated from concentration or death camps, others who had returned from the Soviet Union. The survivors were in transit – mainly preparing their emigration. A lynch mob filled with blind hatred towards Jews set upon the building,[48] killing and wounding people of all ages – men and women, even pregnant women and children. The Pogrom left about forty dead, and more than forty injured. In other Polish towns, there were similar anti-Semitic occurrences, though none as deadly. The pogroms and the Polish population's support for the perpetrators showed the ruling party that anti-Semitism remained widespread in Poland. The pogrom and the reactions to it shocked Jewish survivors, (Cała, 2014: 23) leading some who had been undecided about their future to decide to leave. Historians estimate that, between July and September 1946, in the wake of the Kielce Pogrom, about 95,000 Jews fled Poland, 'at a rate that reached an average of 700 per day'.[49]

In the Jewish sanatorium where Janina was progressively recovering, everyone spoke about departure. Baccalaureate diploma in hand, Janina started to plan her future, but the options were limited by her health. Physicians advised her to avoid the big city, so she decided to accept the job as a children's tutor in the Jewish orphanage where Zofia lived, and worked there from November 1946 to April 1947. In addition to the work experience, the job gave Janina a political education, in that her bosses opportunistically supported the new government. Moreover, she personally witnessed numerous falsifications after the parliamentary elections of January 1947. The deceptive political activity of her bosses, the pressure to conform with the new power, which she saw as corrupt, and the conflict over Zionism among some employees led Janina to quit. In the spring, she moved back in with her mother in Warsaw and found a job as a typist at the Central Committee of Polish Jews. The job was not really satisfying, and Janina decided to study journalism and was admitted to the Academy of Social and Political Sciences – the ANP. She also joined Gordonia, another Jewish movement that prepared young people for life in Palestine. Unlike the Ihud-linked group, the socialist Gordonia told its members to finish their studies before emigrating, since the new country needed specialists and professionals. Janina postponed her plans for departure until after graduation.

Madame Janina Bauman

In the spring of 1947, as a first-year journalism student, Janina Lewinson met her future husband on the college bench. For both of them, it was love at first sight, a real *coup de foudre*. In her autobiography, Janina recalls the moment when she met 'a tall handsome officer bearing the rank of Polish Army captain . . . Never before had I seen eyes like those – a pair of brilliant, ripe plums brimming with the joy of life' (J. Bauman, 1988: 39).[50] The romantic beginning of their sixty-one years of life together was delayed by Janina suffering another health crisis, but, despite it, the couple decided to be married only nine days after their first date. 'Although we were very impatient we had to wait five months before we could get married', Janina Bauman wrote:

Konrad [Zygmunt] applied to his military authorities for permission to marry me. In reply he was ordered to submit several documents proving that I was a suitable person to be an officer's wife. They wanted to know all about my social background and political beliefs. I had to prove my health was sound, namely that I had never suffered from a venereal disease. They needed a certificate from the local council stating in black and white that I was 'morally flawless' – not a thief or a prostitute. . . . The health certificate was easily obtained. No one was interested in my TB, so Uncle Jerzy, a doctor, needed no tests to confirm that I was healthy, not a VD ['Venereal disease' added in note] carrier. Another relative of mine, Uncle Leo, an old Communist highly respected by the establishment for his past work, provided me with [a] certificate from two high-ranking officials who happened to be close friends of his. They both declared that despite my wealthy origins I was a loyal citizen of the Polish People's Republic and fully trustworthy. My political involvements were fortunately overlooked in both statements: it did not occur to Uncle Leo that I had any political views whatsoever.[51] (J. Bauman, 1988: 179)

Though Janina's political sympathies were overlooked in these statements, her husband was bound to inform his hierarchy about them: 'in 1947, my wife was in a Zionist environment and sympathized with the organization "Gordonia" / she was not a member /. It seems that now she has been freed from Zionist influences, / actually, probably superficial /',[52] he wrote in a 1950 questionnaire. Bauman did not mention her previous engagement with Ihud, or her emigration projects, information that could have hurt his marriage plans if seen by powerful people. Leon Plocker,[53] Janina's uncle – a prewar communist and director of the central clinic of the Ministry of Public Security – asked his friends for a 'moral appreciation' of Janina, and these attestations of good citizenship were provided by Henryk Toruńczyk[54] and Leon Rubinsztejn,[55] senior security officials who had been communist participants in the Spanish Civil War.[56]

Toruńczyk's claim to 'know personally' Janina Lewinson was probably false, since she wrote in her book that she did not know 'Uncle Leo's friends'. Yet even the signatures of these two senior security officials were not enough to seal the marriage. A local council had to provide a certificate of the candidate's 'moral respectability'. Such procedures had also been required of Polish Army officers' wives before the war; the only difference was the bureaucratic form, typical of the Soviet system, while in prewar Poland this process of collecting information was informal and more discreet.[57] The official goal was in both cases the same: to determine whether the woman was worthy of being an officer's spouse – which in this context also meant that she would not collaborate with enemy secret services, since her husband-officer would provide access to secret military information, putting 'state security' at risk. Janina Lewinson's Zionist sympathies created a certain vulnerability – for the institution, in theory, but mainly for Janina and Zygmunt.

'A dream of belonging'

Both Baumans had a dream, but their dreams were not the same. Since their first date, the problem of Zionist sympathies had been an important personal issue. Her position was typical for the majority of the Polish Jews: 'How can I be part of a nation that does not want me?' (J. Bauman, 2011: 39). This was a core problem for the Jews – they could be 'integrated', 'assimilated', but did the local population want them?

Bauman was optimistic about the future of Poland. His dream of belonging was different. He was in tune with Jewish communists who, along with BUND members, were deeply opposed to emigration from Poland (Aleksiun, 2002: 254). '[Zygmunt] not only had never considered living in Palestine – he actually strongly disapproved of my involvement', Janina Bauman wrote in *A Dream of Belonging*:

> Zionism, he claimed, like any other nationalism, was incompatible with his strong communist beliefs. We all knew only too well what horrors nationalism could lead to and there was no reason to believe either that the Jews were the chosen nation or that their nationalism was any more justified or less dangerous than that of other peoples. ... The Jews are not a nation. They live all over the world, speak a thousand languages, are an organic part of the countries where they were born and brought up (J. Bauman, 1988: 49)

As it happens, while Bauman never spoke of an affiliation with Jewish organizations, this was not strictly so. From the Polish version of Janina Bauman's book, we learn that Bauman's family was registered with the Jewish Committee in Warsaw (J. Bauman, 2011: 34). This small detail arose as part of the story of their first missed date. Janina, who was too sick to attend the theatre with Zygmunt, wished to inform Bauman, and sent her mother to him with a note. But she was ignorant not only of Bauman's address but also of his first name (she called him 'My Captain')! Janina's mother, happily, was able to find his name and address on the list of Warsaw inhabitants in the Jewish Committee's record book. How did it happen that Zygmunt, apparently distant from any Jewish community, was on that list? Perhaps he had inscribed the family, or his father Maurycy or mother Zofia had. The list was fundamental to locating Holocaust survivors or learning of the fate of those who perished, so the Baumans may have put their names on the list for that reason. Or, perhaps, the family felt some kinship with the Warsaw Jewish community.

Whatever the case, Zygmunt's perspective on the Jewish state and emigration project led her to sever her relationship with the Gordonia group. Since it was Zygmunt's dream to build a new Poland free from all discrimination, Janina adapted herself to this dream. They would help build a new Poland together. Emigration was no longer Janina's plan. They both focused on their studies and marriage.

Life under Stalinism

The young couple passed the final exams of their first year with flying colours. Zygmunt received the highest grades possible in all fourteen subjects, according to Janina Bauman, while she obtained marks of 'good' and 'very good'.[58] They set 18 August 1948 as their wedding day – Janina's twenty-second birthday. During the holiday months, Janina met frequently with Zofia to learn 'the arts of cooking and keeping house'. While preparing dishes, she listened to family stories, mainly about Zygmunt's childhood. This was a good departure for creating communication with the in-laws, which was particularly important in their case, since the Baumans shared Zygmunt's tiny flat with his parents after their marriage. The room occupied by Janina and Zygmunt was in the passage between his parents' bedroom and the bathroom, which restricted intimacy but was typical of living conditions in Warsaw three years after the war. Varsovians considered themselves lucky to find even such a pinched *pied-à-terre* (this penury of flats was to continue for decades).

The Baumans planned to celebrate their honeymoon in Szklarska Poręba – a tourist city in the mountains of southwest Poland – and arranged a room in a KBW-owned villa. Yet history intervened in their private life. In May 1948, Stalin had declared Yugoslavia's Marshal Tito a traitor. During the summer, Czechoslovakia came under attack over its leadership's lack of 'fidelity' to the Soviets. Israel's creation and official recognition spurred anti-Semitic phobia in Stalin, who suspected all Soviet and communist Jews of supporting the new Jewish state. The USSR began a campaign

against 'cosmopolitism and Western influences', and all these tensions were perceptible in the satellite states. In Poland, conflict
broke out in the Plenum of the PPR's Central Committee, where
Władysław Gomułka was accused of 'right-wing-nationalist deviations'. Massive purges began and the situation became unstable.
Bauman, as a KBW officer and Party member, was called for service
and his vacation was cancelled. Janina took the train to the mountains alone. Bauman arrived in the middle of their honeymoon, but
once again he was called back to his unit. Janina was not informed
about the reasons for his absence, presumably because Bauman was
required to keep things secret. Political officers of his generation did
not share much of their professional lives with family members.[59]

The first period of their life together was clouded by politics.
First, there was the nearly ruined honeymoon. Then Bolesław Bierut
became the first secretary of the Central Committee of the Party
(PPR), which fused in December 1948 with the much weaker Polish
Socialist Party to create the PZPR (Polish Unified Workers Party).[60]
It became evident at this point that the Polish way to communism
would employ a Soviet style of government. The changes occurred
step by step. Bauman was busily enrolled in this process, since the
KBW was one of the core state security institutions. His activity as
political education chief was appreciated by the hierarchy and he
progressed fast.[61] According to his wife, Bauman worked long hours
and came home very late (in Poland, office days typically finished
around 3 or 4 p.m.). In addition, he pursued his studies at the ANP
and was active in the Party.

Janina decided not to stay home waiting for her busy husband.
She took a job at the headquarters of Polish Film. Despite political
changes and several waves of purges in the institution (film was a
propaganda tool whose production was strictly controlled), Janina
managed to continue working there until 1968, rising by the end
to senior adviser in the Supreme Board of Cinematography at the
Ministry of Culture and Art. She began as a secretary in the programme department with a salary grade of 11 – with 13 being the
lowest. It paid very little money, but within three days of starting
Janina was promoted to junior programme officer with grade 9
(J. Bauman, 1988: 63). Janina was passionate about movies, never
missing new films, and wrote very well, so the institution seemed a
perfect place for her.

Her job was to provide reports on Western movies that, after a
selection process, Polish Film would buy. She would watch up to
four films a day – Italian neo-realism, French comedies and drama,
British productions. 'I was very happy at this early stage of my film
career', she wrote: 'My only sadness was that Konrad [Zygmunt], an
even greater film enthusiast than myself, could not sit next to me in
the sweet darkness of the projection room and share my pleasure'

(J. Bauman, 1988: 65). At the height of Poland's Stalinist period, she had daily contact with the newest pieces of Western cinema, without censorship. The Iron Curtain did not cover Janina Bauman's eyes. She was a privileged person. This access reflects the trust that her superiors must have had in her work and her 'moral attitude'. It probably helped to have a KBW political officer for a husband, and an Uncle Leo caring for big shots in the Ministry of Public Security. This network made up for her lack of experience and the absence of previous communist engagement. Unfortunately, from her perspective, she would have to exchange this job for a publicity manager's position (bigger salary, less satisfaction). In the early 1950s, Janina changed again, after her maternity leave, becoming a translator of French and Russian press articles about recent films. Janina combined her job and ANP studies efficiently thanks to an arrangement that allowed her to leave work earlier than others, so she could catch evening lectures. Janina Bauman was probably as busy as her husband.

'It is hard for me now to see', she wrote later:

> how, with such a full and busy life Konrad and I were still able to find time to enjoy ourselves together. But the truth is we did. We had lots of friends, mainly Konrad's fellow officers and their wives, who were always ready to go out, to throw a party or attend one. We loved dancing; we rushed to see every new play in the Warsaw theatres – new theatres opened all the time – and we adored concerts. Konrad was a great football fan, so we rarely missed any international match. But more than anything else we were fond of films, and I was quite happy to spend all evening in the cinema after having seen three or four films during the day. . . . As we worked, studied and danced, the iron hand of Stalin was tightening around our necks, helped by our own hard work and youthful enthusiasm.[62] (J. Bauman, 1988: 67)

Youthful enthusiasm and the desire to belong led Janina to join a communist organization, the academic branch of the ZMP (Związek Młodzieży Polskiej (Union of Polish Youth)). Her activist task was related to her professional skills – she reviewed new films for the ZMP press, mainly Soviet productions. Because of this activity, Janina started to focus on the political messages in the films she reviewed and watched, leaving aside the artistic meaning. This switch in perception was an adaptation to the Stalinist regime, which grew more and more intrusive.

Meanwhile, Zofia found a job as manager of the Warsaw Food Co-operative (Warszawska Spółdzielnia Spożywców), and the family hired a maid, who slept on a cot in the kitchen. Zofia's position was particularly precious to the family because it allowed them to eat healthily while avoiding waiting in long lines in the food shops like most other Poles. To have good food was key to

Janina's recovery from tuberculosis. Her fragile health was a source of worry, especially for her doctor relatives, and especially when she declared that she was pregnant. Interestingly, the English version of the book contains more details on this subject than the Polish translation. It delves into the lack of family planning policy in Poland in the postwar era, but also Zygmunt's happy response, including a romantic anecdote describing him dancing in the street (in Poland, a huge transgression) after they left a Sunday concert of the Warsaw Philharmonic (J. Bauman, 2011: 54).

The couple's first daughter, Anna, was born on 16 November 1949, in the military hospital in Warsaw. The birth would have at least temporarily distracted the Baumans from the spectacle enveloping Polish society at the time – the celebration of Stalin's seventieth birthday.

How Polish society loved Stalin

The writer Michał Komar, in his book *Soon It Will Explode* (2015), aptly characterizes the cult of Stalin in Poland in this account of the rolling celebrations to mark the Soviet tyrant's birthday. 'Joseph Stalin was born on December 21, 1879, and thus 1949 was his seventieth birthday. Following in the footsteps of other communist and workers' parties, with the Universal Communist Party (Bolsheviks) at the head, the Central Committee of the PZPR set up a Seventieth Year Celebration Committee for Joseph Stalin's Birthday', Komar writes. The scope and effects of this celebration, and the enthusiasm accompanying them, and the gifts created for Stalin, 'outgrew the imagination of the organizers'. Astonished by their success, the committee decided to hold an 'Exhibition of Gifts from the Polish Society for Generalissimo Stalin' in the National Museum. This included generous gifts from the government, from ministers, from metallurgists and miners, from peasants on co-operatives and individual peasants, and from highlanders. The gifts came from Kurpie and Silesia; from youth schools around the country; from students, lawyers and doctors: 'There were two hundred chests eleven wagons, and more . . . Not only the quantity is puzzling, but also the variety of ways the human soul uses in its always incomplete, always crippled attempts to express love' (Komar, 2015: 22). There were strangely kitsch and incredible objects, some even consumable, such as the Wedel factory's[63] chocolate cake 'made by the best professional in the factory, 1 metre in diameter and 25 cm high', reported *Życie Warszawy* (Warsaw Life – a newspaper):

The cake is decorated with red iced roses and topped by a chocolate figure depicting a female worker. . . . She holds in her hand a small cake with the inscription 'Gift of the crew of the Wedel factory in Warsaw', below this another inscription: 'To Genius Comrade Joseph Stalin'. 'I made this cake so cleverly – said its creator – that in half a year it will be as tasty as today.' (Komar, 2015: 23)

There were also other astonishing and politically significant gifts such as a blue globe with – according to *Trybuna Ludu* – '24 red lights, which set the limits of two worlds: the world of socialism, democracy and peace and the world of capitalistic slavery, unemployment and war hysteria'. There were cards from the rectors of Polish universities and non-affiliated scientists ('I can clearly see the way a scientist must walk. This is the path illuminated by the rays of Your [Stalin's] genius – the way to socialism', and 'instead of the current bourgeois science, proclaiming an apolitical approach and objectivism and essentially hostile to people and progress, a new science arises'). As for the fur hat 2 metres tall – 'there was not a word in the newspapers about it, although it was difficult not to notice' (Komar, 2015: 24). This giant fur hat was created at a co-operative in Legnica co-founded by Chaim Fogelman.[64] A BUND member, he did not particularly like Stalin but, having been accused by envious workers of taking fur remnants from his workplace, Fogelman decided to compensate by sewing the largest fur hat in the world for Stalin: 'The hat was unusual, unparalleled in size, shocking in its enormity, not made to measure for a human being, but for a giant' (Komar, 2015: 26).

The gift-giving was motivated by conformism, opportunism and fear, but also by a desire to escape in fantasy from a difficult situation – and, perhaps, by humour. The ridiculous effect of the totality of objects trotted out for Stalin reflected the Kafkaesque feeling of the period. A manifestation of support for Stalin could save someone's life (as in Chaim Fogelman's case). Sometimes reality exceeded even Kafka's stories.[65]

However, the regime was not really funny. People were accused easily, and ever-present suspicion created a climate of fear for everyone. The authorities jailed suspects or political opponents without investigation. This was the case with Gomułka, arrested in 1951 and freed three years later without trial. Hundreds of ordinary citizens were captured, falsely accused and tortured.[66] To keep control of the population, a dictatorial system needs victims. When they view it as fruitless to try to modify politics, many people follow their leadership without conviction, a protective or opportunist strategy that the historian and politician Andrzej Werblan, a contemporary of Bauman, described as *realpolitik* logic: you do what you think is possible in a given geopolitical context. Others believed and naively served the system – or not so naively.

'We were often high-minded to others because we had a sense of ourselves as missionaries', said Marian Turski, the Auschwitz survivor, journalist and postwar communist.[67]

The missionary thinks, 'I'm the bearer of truth', and there is a sense of superiority in relation to those who lack it, and the relationship with other truth-bearers is that of a crony . . . maybe it's a superficial impression but as I sum up my impression from those years. . . . 'We are a minority, we are individuals. But we know the truth. We spread the truth. We are the bearers of the truth and want to convert [the majority who does not believe] according to the logic: it is not dangerous to expose myself [as a communist, marginal] since, because of my minority status, I am already exposed [to anti-Semitism]. I will convince other people that it is in their own interest, they are ignorant people and they need to be convinced. I act for them, for their wellbeing.'

At the same time . . . I saw arrogance, careerism . . . From the Party that first had 10,000 and 50,000 members, suddenly, 3 million – evidence that it was rubbish. We did not realize at the time, that the most important motherfuckers [people in leadership positions] were corrupted first, because they knew how to blackmail you. They were creating careers, but you didn't see this until later. Nevertheless, at the beginning, I would say there was an evangelistic spirit . . . we were a product of the nineteenth century. We had this attitude composed from three elements: a bit of nationalism, a bit of connection with the peasantry, and a bit of sacrifice of our private lives. . . . We need to make the sacrifices and do the missionary work while others [in the same organization] make careers and get better cars and nice apartments. With time, you adapt to this and become more or less corrupt.[68]

Corruption had various incarnations. One of them was reporting on one's colleagues, friends and even family (parents feared that their children, encouraged to speak about their parents at school, would say something leading to their punishment). The training and encouragement to denounce were widespread.[69] Janina Bauman described how her boss convinced her to report on her co-workers using the template of an 'Agitator Journal'. This was a kind of political diary, which was presented to Janina as a 'reporter's notebook' but was really just a way of denouncing people. Janina was lured into writing it by her own self-image as a writer, and by seeing an opportunity to join the Party by showing proof of her engagement in the 'cause'. And she did it. As the result of her 'reporting', her closest colleague, Jacqueline, lost her membership in the Polish communist youth group, and her job (J. Bauman, 1988: 74–7; 2011: 58–63). Zygmunt Bauman's reaction to this event gives us insight into how people could support a system so obviously mistaken and abusive:

I was left on my own with an unbearable burden of guilt and shame. Konrad [Zygmunt] was the only person I could turn to. He was deeply shaken when he heard the story. He sank deep into uneasy thoughts. He was devastated for Jacqueline, but obviously for me too. He said it was a deplorable mistake to have told Barski [the person who asked Janina to write the report] what I knew about my colleagues. He was clearly not a man to be trusted. Unfortunately, . . . [Zygmunt] explained, the Party ranks were still full of untrustworthy individuals, ruthlessly ambitious climbers and ideologically immature members. Yet, despite this transitory weakness, despite the grave mistakes often committed in its name, the Party was the most powerful agent of social justice and had to be implicitly trusted. You cannot make an omelette, he said, without breaking eggs. You cannot make a revolution without accidentally hurting some of the innocent. The Soviet Revolution had created many victims and there had been many mistakes. Casualties could occur in our far less bloody Polish revolution too. . . . It was heartbreaking but we had to put up with such things if we wanted to fight for a better world. (J. Bauman, 1988: 77)

The Polish edition of her book includes another interesting remark from Bauman: 'this is a sickness of the transitory stage' (J. Bauman, 2011: 62).

This approach was typical for many postwar communists. In our interview, Turski said his milieu was affected by the 'great myth' that the Spanish Republic had lost the Civil War because of a

Fifth Column. . ..[70] This is the very simple difference between people who supported the communist regime [dictatorship] and those who were against it. Those who supported it believed it was better to put nine innocents in jail to catch one culprit, a traitor, a criminal. The opponents believed (and in the first part of World War II, I was part of this group) that it was better to let the guilty one go free rather than jailing nine innocents.

Walking through the Łódź ghetto in 1943 after a Soviet victory over Hitler's forces, Turski's mentor told him:

'You see now why Moscow did not give up? Because they did not have the fifth column. Because there were purges. This is why they escaped the fate of Madrid.' . . . People ask, How it is possible that people believed in Communism? Well . . . this is something I was able to condemn in the missionaries in Peru, in Mexico, when they forced people to convert. I did exactly the same as those missionaries did.

The Baumans were like Turski and many others – idealists, and, like missionaries, they believed they could bring 'truth and happiness' to ignorant people. Eventually, political dynamics generated doubts and weakened their convictions about the 'truth'. But this came later.

The calm before the storm . . .

Despite political tensions due to the Korean War, after the summer of 1950 some positive changes occurred in Bauman's family. They moved to a larger flat in the same building (with three rooms, meaning the couple no longer had to live between the parents and the bathroom). This was probably a result of their baby's birth and also Bauman's promotion, which at 25 made him one of the youngest majors in the Polish Army. Having a better financial situation, the Baumans decided to hire a nanny for their daughter – Ms Waczkowska was in charge of domestic tasks and childcare. This arrangement enabled Anna's parents to work and to be active in the Party as well. Zygmunt finished his first level of study, getting a bachelor's degree with Good and Very Good grades, and Janina, who took more time because of Anna's birth, graduated a year later.

Bauman decided to continue his studies and enrolled for two years in the Party School (Szkoła Partyjna PZPR), which specifically trained future Party elites. Janina Bauman engaged herself in political work, and in 1951 became a Party member. Her job and her intense political activity, which involved collecting money or doing political indoctrination in the countryside, were sources of satisfaction. She felt herself to be an active participant in the construction of a 'new Poland', especially after being promoted in October 1950 to the Department of Documentary Film Chronicles, one of the most important areas for propaganda. The chronicles were short films, produced once or twice weekly, that were played before each feature movie in Polish theatres. Given the popularity of cinema in this pre-television era, these films had an enormous impact on the population. Janina Bauman was in charge of translating news texts from French and Russian, a job she loved, while hoping to progress to an assistant director's position.

But at the end of the summer of 1951, at a time when the Baumans were doing well (although Poland's economic situation was dire, with the shops starting to empty of goods and food), a small translation nearly cost Janina her job and Party membership. While they were helping a friend translate a speech by Stalin from a documentary film,[71] a typist working with Janina translated Stalin saying to his East German colleague Wilhelm Pieck, 'I wish you many successes on the *shameful* path you have been following for a year.'[72] Instead of writing 'chwalebny' – a Polish word for 'glorious' – she wrote 'haniebny' (shameful). While they appear quite different in writing, when spoken quickly the two words could easily be confused. Both women were tired, under pressure, and failed to double-check the text. Then it was sent to a higher editorial level, where the mistake was also missed, apparently because of deadline pressures. It was only after the film had been publicly shown that a Russian producer discovered the terrible sentence. Janina and her assistant were accused of political sabotage. The director of Polish Film – Stanisław Albrecht – was immediately summoned to the Office of Public Security (UB). On 27 September 1951, after his discussion with UB agents, Albrecht wrote an official letter to Rita Radkiewicz (Janina's direct supervisor):

> In relation to the errors committed in the dialogue of the film 'Democratic Germany' I order that Citizen Janina Bauman, Editor WFD (Production of Documentary Films) be immediately dismissed and put at the disposition of the HR [Department of Human Resources] of the Polish Film Direction ... The execution of this action should be reported to me within 24 hours of the reception of this document.[73]

Janina Bauman was lucky; she was essentially demoted, an exceptionally indulgent punishment given the circumstances. Radkiewicz had undoubtedly been informed by phone about what happened and convinced Albrecht that it was a simple typing mistake, not an instance of political disloyalty by Janina. Rita Radkiewicz was very powerful; her husband Stanisław Radkiewicz was none other than the minister of public security. It was Janina's fortune that Radkiewicz, who had been her boss for a few years, liked and trusted her. The secretary who worked with Janina was not so lucky: she was simply fired, as were staff members in overall charge of the dialogues.

Bauman was placed in the educational film service, which represented a kind of punishment. In Stalinist times, a harmless-appearing mistake of this kind could result in a charge of sabotage and lead to jail. For Janina, the only trace of the incident in her record was a note from her hierarchy to secret services. After some months of uninteresting work, Janina replaced a departing colleague as an editor in the script office:

> The people responsible for the development of the new Polish cinema still strained their minds – if not always their hearts – to follow the commandments of social realism. Working in the Script Bureau on the lowest rung of the ideological ladder, I became one of them. I didn't realize in 1952 that we, the editors, were working more or less as censors. We did our work with a lot of good will and with deep conviction. We often strongly disapproved of decisions made by the professional censors who looked at films as though they were news-

paper editorials and cut them as they wished, refusing to accept that they were also works of art. Yet, to some extent, we were players in the same game. (J. Bauman, 1988: 101–2)

Authors and directors had no choice but to play the censorship game. Sometimes their films were simply rejected outright, as in the case of Wajda's famous movie *Man of Marble*, which was only produced twenty years later.[74] In the best of times, negotiations between author and censor resulted in a movie that was both artistically good and politically correct. Józef Hen, one of the most popular Polish novelists and screenwriters in the second half of the twentieth century, recalled Janina Bauman as friendly, professional, helpful and supportive of authors.[75] Despite the miscue, her career was well launched. Zygmunt, however, started to have problems in his job.

In the spring of 1952, Bauman's Jewish background began to exercise a drag upon his military career, even as it officially was moving forward. On 1 May, Bauman became chief of the Political Board of KBW Section II. But six weeks earlier, on 22 March, his direct superior, Colonel Bibrowski, and Colonel Muś, the KBW chief, signed off on the following assessment:

Evaluation of political attitude:
Absolutely devoted to the idea of socialism. He has very extensive political knowledge and extensive theoretical preparation. Despite his petty-bourgeois origin, he experiences no ideological fluctuations and puts political issues sharply and decisively, even in personal and family matters.
Assessment of occupational skills:
In performing his duties, he exhibits exceptionally high qualifications. Very intelligent, perfect organizer, full of initiatives both in designing and performing superiors' instructions. Fast, punctual and observant at work. He has a wide mental horizon, the ability to observe, analyse and infer; however, sometimes he exaggerates in drawing conclusions (which is undoubtedly a kind of self-defence against awareness of his origins). A passion for military service; disciplined and demanding.
Moral and personal values:
Honest in his personal life. A firm defender of his positions, but willingly accepts criticism. . . . Character a bit soft.
CONCLUSION
In spite of exceptionally high ideological and mental qualifications, his origins and his father – who lives with him and demonstrates a desire to go to Palestine – limit his perspective in the KBW. His origins, when combined with his high level of education and quick promotions, have resulted in some reserve among certain officers (including old Party members). Therefore, in the longer term it would be necessary to enable him to enter a scientific path.

Signed: Chief of the Political Board Colonel Z. Bibrowski [and] Chief
of KBW Col. W. Muś.

In the top right-hand corner of the document, someone has written
in pencil: 'candidate IKKN, document in the file, candidate MBP –
2 years school ZW'.[76]
    The pencillings probably represent the practical solution that had
been chosen for Bauman – IKKN was a school where Party elites
obtained doctoral degrees. ZW was a school within the Ministry
of Public Security where Bauman could teach. The surprising
incoherence between the glowing opinions about Bauman and the
disappointing conclusion makes sense only through the lens of ethnicity. We should remember that the events of 1952 in the Soviet
bloc occurred in the shadow of the Slansky affair, the show trial of
thirteen Czechoslovak communist officials, eleven of whom, including Rudolf Slansky, were Jews. Bauman's colleagues, older Party
members, were possibly jealous of his quick career rise and distrust-
ful because of his Jewish origins.
    Once again, anti-Semitism was playing a determining role in
Bauman's life. Though he was a major in the Polish Army, and
a charismatic teacher and leader, he was perceived first as a Jew
rather than as a Polish officer. Despite belonging to the inside of an
elite military formation, his 'master status' – how those around him
perceived him – was, simply, 'Jew'. Despite all the Party talk about
freedom and non-discrimination against ethnic or racial groups, the
doors of further promotion had been closed.[77]
    Bauman's career in the Polish Army was finished, but that did not
mean an immediate departure. People were not simply fired in the
People's Republic of Poland. There was a kind of agreement, especially for those with high positions, that everyone was entitled to a
salary and a roof over their head. In the spring of 1952, the decision
was to put him 'smoothly' on the 'scientific' track.

Between the Army and the university

The transition from one social world to another was conducted
through the Party, which was the common element of both uni-
verses. Following the guidelines set out in the document cited
above, Bauman applied to the IKKN (Instytut Kształcenia Kadr
Naukowych (Institute for the Education of Scientific Cadres)).
The institute had been created by Adam Schaff[78] – who already
knew Bauman from the Academy of Political Sciences (ANP) – and
opened its doors in 1950. The school was organized on the 'tutor-
ship' model of the Institute of Red Professors in Moscow, which
was based on the structures of Cambridge and Oxford Universities.

Each student had his or her own tutor with whom he met weekly (Schaff, in Czarny, 2015: 28). On 15 April 1952, Bauman wrote a letter seeking enrolment as an *aspirantura* (equivalent to a doctoral student): 'I have had a passion for scientific work for a long time. I have never been able to fulfil my desire to devote myself to this work because of my professional military service. Currently, I have assurance from my Army chain of command that they look favourably on my interest in joining the IKKN and will release me from the Army.'[79]

As we've seen, the Army indeed supported the plan. After finishing his courses at the ANP in 1950, Bauman had continued to study in the Party School, which was not a true university but a training institute focused on Marxist–Leninist theory. There are few traces after his passage through that school, other than one enthusiastic sentence from Colonel Bibrowski in a 1950 file.[80] The IKKN was a good next move for a party functionary. Adam Schaff wanted to create an elite school and provided very strict entrance procedures. Competition was stiff, including laureates from full-time universities and students with publications and prestigious diplomas under their belts; the IKKN was a school for doctoral rather than master's candidates. Bauman had never studied full-time in the postwar era. The ANP and Party School were not real universities, they were institutions that reproduced the *nomenklatura*. This fact resonates in a document produced by an author, apparently a professor, following an oral examination of Bauman that did not leave him overly impressed:

> From the conversation with Comrade Bauman I inferred that he had mastered the history of the Polish and International Workers' Movements in quite a wide range. He also has basic knowledge in the field of dialectical and historical materialism. Regarding the specialization he chose (Theory of State and Law), he has weaker orientation. Graduating from the Academy of Political Sciences (ANP) does not guarantee detailed knowledge of any field of law. I believe, however, that we should be interested in the candidacy of Comrade Bauman for the Department of Theory of State and Law. [Signature illegible]. Dated May 20, 1952.[81]

While there is no trace of acceptance or rejection in Bauman's files, he did not end up attending the IKKN and instead ended up at Warsaw University, pursuing extramural studies. Different elements may have contributed to this situation. It would have been impossible for Bauman to study at the IKKN while working at the same time. Lectures occurred throughout the working week from morning to evening in one building, and lunch was served in a local canteen. Students were given good stipends but were required to focus exclusively on their studies. Bauman had been promoted in May, and would not have been able to take the new position while engaged full-time in studies.

At the same time, Bauman's wife reported, he was growing disenchanted with the Army due to the departure of a respected colleague, a colonel who was moved to a lower position because of his Jewish origin (J. Bauman, 1988; 104). His direct supervisor, Bibrowski, left in June 1952, spending two years in Korea as a part of the Polish Team in the Neutral Nations Supervisory Commission.[82] Perhaps it was the lack of protection from superiors that kept Bauman from studying at the IKKN? Perhaps his only possibility of studying was the university extramural (evening) study?

The first indication that the Ministry of Public Security had sent Bauman down to Warsaw University is an express-mail letter from the director of the university department at the Ministry of Higher Education to the dean of the Department of Philosophy and Social Sciences, dated 10 October 1952. It states that the ministry had agreed to accept Bauman to study for a master's in philosophy.[83] A day before, Bauman had received a somewhat hostile letter from the dean of the Department of Philosophy and Social Sciences noting that it was a week since classes had started, and asking whether Bauman 'would like to inform the department immediately if [he] has abandoned his studies? If not – you are asked to come to the university immediately.'[84] Bauman apparently complied, because, on 18 October 1952, he signed a student oath.[85]

For a few months, Bauman worked at the KBW during the day and studied in the afternoon. But his double life didn't last long. In December 1952, the Doctors' Plot broke in Moscow (Rapoport, 1991), and a campaign of anti-Semitism enveloped the Soviet Union and its allied states. The trumped-up charges against a group of mostly Jewish doctors facilitated an ethnic purge of Jews across Eastern Europe. It did not spare Poland or the KBW, where Bauman was one of many targets.

'One day in January 1953', wrote Bauman's wife:

[Zygmunt] and I spent an exhilarating night at a showy officers' ball in the barracks. . . . Twenty-four hours later, . . . [Zygmunt] was summoned to his new boss and dismissed from the army on the spot. This was a terrible shock, a bolt from the blue. . . . The reason given for this sudden dismissal was that his father had maintained some suspicious contacts with the West: he had, they said, been a regular visitor to the Israeli embassy. In agony, . . . [Zygmunt] went straight to his father. The old man did not deny it: he had been to the Israeli embassy twice to ask their advice about emigration. In a state of frantic despair, . . . [Zygmunt] accused him of being secretive and plotting behind his back. (J. Bauman, 1988: 105)

The Bauman flat, we should remember, was in the middle of the military zone, a risky place to have a possible spy – or, at least, this was how the authorities presented the situation.

Suddenly, the Baumans were in a terrible situation. Bauman lost his job and fell out with his parents, who left the flat without a word several days after Bauman lashed out at his father. Maurycy and Zofia moved to an apartment over the restaurant that she managed (Bazyliszek on the Old City Market). Bauman spent the next week at home, plunging into reading and studies. He dyed all his military clothing a dark colour and stripped off the decorations and epaulettes. In doing so, he transformed his military uniform into a civilian one (not an uncommon practice at the time, cloth and new clothing being scarce). Other consequences followed. Bauman's sunny, three-room apartment was partially taken over by a young officer and his family. The Army ordered the Baumans into a small, dark apartment without a bathroom, in an annex on the barracks terrain. The situation was clear: Bauman had been ejected by the system. He was no longer a 100 per cent Pole. Bauman still had the Party, although the incident with his father could also have damaged that relationship. This is probably why, at the end of January 1953, Bauman took what must have been an agonizing decision, and wrote out the following declaration, which was added to his Party file:

For the following reasons:
– Zionism, which has always been a bourgeois spy network, transformed into an ordinary band of American spies and saboteurs;
– My long-term efforts to change the Zionist sympathies of my father, Maurycy Bauman, did not yield results;
– Attachment to Poland cannot be reconciled with an opportunistic attitude towards Zionism, even if this view is shared by my own father,
– I solemnly declare to the party that I am breaking off all contact with my father.
– signature: Bauman – 30.01.1953[86]

A way of life had ended, and the future was not at all secure. Bauman was just beginning his university study, and the family's material conditions were poor. Bauman received his last payment from the Army in March 1953, and Janina's salary covered only the basic needs. But, in another sense, he was now free: a missionary removed from his church, spat out by the system that he had helped to create.

8

A Young Scholar

1953–1957

As a student, Bauman would come to the university wearing his KBW
uniform, including jackboots and a gun. Once during a lecture the
gun slipped off his belt and dropped on the floor in front of Professor
Kotarbinski. 'We don't play with those here', Kotarbinski responded.
'Please take this away.'
(Anecdote circulating in the Faculty of Philosophy and
Social Sciences, Warsaw University)[1]

Warsaw University – Faculty of Philosophy and
Social Sciences

The Department of Philosophy was a vibrant place in January
1953.[2] It had separated from the Department of Humanities in 1952;
since the war, philosophy had become an intensely political field,
because the new system needed to develop an intellectual discipline,
and practitioners of it, to frame its movements.[3] Marxism progressively became the dominant 'scientific discipline' – in fact, the only
accepted doctrine – for practising social sciences. The university,
perhaps even more than other institutions, saw a rapid changeover
to the Marxian perspective as a result of the struggle between the
seriously diminished prewar establishment and the new elites, who
were proponents of Marxist ideology.

Sociology was particularly exposed to these changes because of
its political potential. As a social science, the field had been institutionalized earlier in Poland than in other Eastern European
countries. The first Chair of Sociology was created in 1919 for Leon
Petrażycki[4] at Warsaw University's Department of Law and Political
Sciences. The second was opened in 1921 for Ludwik Krzywicki;[5]
other chair-holders inside the Department of Humanities included
Stefan Czarnowski[6] in cultural history (after 1930), and, in sociology, Stanisław Bystroń[7] (1934). Interest in the new discipline was
not restricted to Warsaw; departments were created in Poznań, in

1921, by Florian Znaniecki[8] after his return from Chicago, and in Kraków, by Stanisław Bystroń, in 1930. All the professors who pioneered the discipline in Poland had studied sociology abroad, and they brought diverse backgrounds representing various intellectual and methodological approaches. This diversity was a particularity of the Polish academic milieu, where different schools were represented, reproduced and mixed: French, German and Austrian, as well as American. Polish sociology was not a peripheral milieu that looked to the centre and copied it. All the scholars mentioned above developed their own approaches and original concepts. However, the institutionalization of the discipline was not as advanced as it had been in the United States, where the first department of sociology and history was created in 1889 at Kansas University.[9] At Warsaw University, only a few individuals got degrees in philosophy with a speciality in social sciences or sociology in the prewar era. During the war, there was no regular or official teaching of the subject, although some clandestine courses took place in Warsaw.[10]

In 1947, the Department of Sociology[11] opened with two cohorts of students, taught by Stanisław Ossowski and Maria Ossowska,[12] Nina Assorodobraj,[13] Stefan Bystroń and Stefan Nowakowski. 'The future of sociology promised to be very successful. The demand for sociology classes was very large' (Kraśko, 1996: 126). However, the new regime considered sociology a 'bourgeois' science that could not exist as a separate discipline, and it continued as part of the curriculum of the new Department of Humanistic Studies, later splintering off as the Department of Philosophy and Social Sciences. In the late 1940s, the faculty included various intellectual and political perspectives. The disciples of the so-called Lwów–Warsaw School of Philosophy[14] (led by Maria and Stanisław Ossowski) constituted one camp, and the Marxists (Nina Assorodobraj) another. For a short period, as in other university environments, co-existence was tolerated, with different students adhering to each current. But the power dynamics came to depend on the political winds of Party and government.

In 1951, the Ossowskis, though known for their socialist engagement, were deemed representatives of bourgeois science and banned from teaching. Such a destiny was not particular to sociology – philosophy professor Tadeusz Kotarbiński,[15] who had moved back to Warsaw from Łódź, and Władysław Tatarkiewicz[16] suffered the same experience. A group of professors were paid not to teach (they were officially delegated to research). Tatarkiewicz's demotion occurred in the wake of the publication of the 'Letter of 7' (signed by the sociologist and journalist Henryk Holland, Leszek Kołakowski and Bronisław Baczko – both engaged communists and later 'revisionists' – Henryk Jarosz, Arnold Słucki, Anna Śladkowska and Irena Rybczyńska). The letter accused Tatarkiewicz of

privileging 'objective-bourgeois' science instead of Marxist engagement (Kołakowski read the letter in front of Tatarkiewicz during a
seminar). This event, among others, showed the power of students
politically engaged in the construction of communism – they could
get eminent, well-established professors fired. Conflict in the seminars reflected a general Polish struggle between prewar and postwar
systems and old and new intellectual approaches. The Education
Ministry's policy was gradually to push aside professors who did
not support the Party, while placing Marxist scholars and activists in high places. By the early 1950s, there was no more room
at the university for political and academic diversity. Instead of
teaching at the university, the banned professors were hired by the
new research institution, the Polish Academy of Sciences (Polska
Akademia Nauk), or PAN.

The PAN was created on 30 October 1951. Bauman was hired
there after his graduation, remained until his ouster in 1968, and
returned punctually after the postwar system collapsed in 1989. It
was intended to be a core institution for research work and was
strictly controlled by Party authorities. Some professors from
Warsaw University joined it as their exclusive workplace; others
continued to teach while conducting research there. Affiliation
improved their social status, since PAN enjoyed prestige, and
increased their modest incomes.[17]

The map of the university world was strictly determined by politics. Leaders were chosen through political channels, and complete
obedience to the Party was imposed. The institutional framework
for higher education and careers within it was modified in 1951 by
reforms that literally copied the Soviet system. The Ph.D. student
became a 'Candidate of Sciences', and a 'doctorate' title replaced
what formerly had been *habilitation*. The role of the Minister of
higher education was strengthened: he chose administrative leaders
and faculty as well as distributing positions in the hierarchy
(Rutkowski, 2016: 421–2). The earlier autonomy of the university
and its departments was severely limited.

The changes were felt particularly strongly in the University of
Warsaw's Department of Humanities. The authorities replaced
the previously dissolved sociological chairs in 1952 with chairs in
the history of philosophy and social thought (Nina Assorodobraj)
and historical materialism (Julian Hochfeld).[18] The Institute of
Philosophy was entrusted to Adam Schaff,[19] with whom Bauman
had attended lectures at ANP. The shift was under way as Bauman
started his master's degree: 'prewar' professors were becoming the
weaker camp.[20]

Master's study under Stalinism

Bauman and his colleagues mostly attended lectures by Marxist scholars, such as Czesław Nowiński (dialectical materialism), Julian Hochfeld (historical materialism), Adam Schaff (methodology of the history of Marxism) and Nina Assorodobraj (history of philosophy). Bauman also attended lectures in psychology with Tadeusz Tomaszewski and natural science and biology with Włodzimierz Michajłow. He studied languages as well: Russian (only one semester – he was already completely fluent) and English. Tadeusz Kotarbiński, a member of the Lwów–Warsaw School of Philosophy, may have been the only lecturer Bauman studied under who was not a Marxist. Bauman did not have classes with Stanisław or Maria Ossowski, who only returned to their lecturing positions in 1956, when Bauman was already an associate professor.[21] Bauman later described Hochfeld and Ossowski as his mentors (see Tester, 2001); Hochfeld was a direct mentor, through the classic master–student relationship; the link to Ossowski was indirect, via readings, lectures and discussions. In fact, colleagues refuted Bauman's claim of a lineage to Ossowski.

Bauman's claim to be a student of Ossowski was 'an absurd and complete fabrication, but he repeated it several times and surely remembers it like this', said Professor Jerzy Szacki: 'This was certainly not a twisting of the truth, but rather the selectivity of memory.' But the explanation was not entirely unfounded, as Professor Barbara Szacka, Szacki's wife, explains. Bauman was in the same faculty as Ossowski, attended his lectures and felt strongly influenced by him. Yet it is easy to understand why Bauman's identification with Ossowski irritated people. Szacki notes: 'To be a disciple of Ossowski was to belong to a special group . . . closed . . . a special relationship. . .. it was a seminar . . . to which we did not belong'.[22]

The students in Ossowski's seminar – his disciples in the classical sense of the term – were an elite group that kept its distance from others. Affiliation with a master carries with it the symbolic power of belonging to a school, with traditions, and the full weight of an intellectual inheritance – an authentic place of origin, something like having a famous ancestor. This privileged master–disciple relationship is a key element in intellectual careers and plays an important role in the selection and nurturing of support networks, providing a framework for the transfer of knowledge and the creation of appropriate conditions for knowledge creation.[23] This is a safe place where various ideas can be discussed and argued about, where new ideas are forged, where people are considered at a high level of performance while gaining access to that master. 'A seminar . . . to which we did not belong' means that Bauman and Szacki were not part of the elite.[24] Not yet, in Bauman's case.[25]

Being older than his colleagues posed a challenge for Bauman in this phase of his student life. His soon-to-be friend, the sociologist Jerzy Wiatr,[26] and other younger students were fresh from the college of social sciences when they began studying philosophy in the 1952–3 academic year. 'Bauman was in uniform, because he was still in active service when he joined the lectures', Wiatr recalled in a 2017 interview:

> At first ours were loose relationships, as you would expect among a large group of student colleagues – that year there were about a hundred of us, organized in different groups. . . . Wesołowski [a leading sociologist] was in the same group as Bauman, I was in a different group. But . . . we soon became very close – it will sound funny, but in a sense that was thanks to Stalin's death.

Bauman and Wiatr were asked in the spring of 1953 to write a plenary paper for a giant university session devoted to Stalin's last achievements. The paper, their first work together, appeared as a supplement to the journal *Po Prostu* (Simply),[27] and Bauman got Wiatr to read it. 'His relationship to me was a little bit that of an older brother. The six years of difference in our age was huge', Wiatr said: 'Zygmunt was already a fully grown-up man with a position, etc., and when we met I was just a stripling. But we soon became very close.'[28]

Wiatr touches on important points here. The first is the transitory character of those first months that Bauman spent at Warsaw University. His transition from officer to student was quick, probably due to his brutal eviction from the Army. The second aspect is the particularity of Bauman as a student. He was an outsider to the majority because of his age and experiences, his position and level of engagement. It was probably Adam Schaff who proposed Bauman and Wiatr to write the paper and deliver it publicly at the ceremony commemorating Stalin. This would have been a major distinction for a first-year master's student, but Schaff was aware of Bauman's engagement with Stalinism from the ANP and the KBW. Schaff, who led the Institute of Philosophy at the time, could be confident that Bauman would meet political expectations. After all, writing propaganda texts had been his speciality,[29] and having the younger Wiatr read it added another very 'authentic' voice of Polish youth expressing admiration for Stalin (Wiatr was of Warsaw intelligentsia origins).

Another important element that Wiatr mentions was his perception of the ethnic element in their friendship:

> I will say it right away – one thread may be significant, which is that I have no Jewish roots. Zygmunt, when he appeared in this circle,

mainly – or perhaps only – had colleagues from the Army, also of Jewish origin. In a sense, I was the first non-Jew to be so closely linked to him. To be sure, this is a reflection that comes to mind only now, because at the time we were a very special generation – the left-wing intelligentsia immediately after the war was in a sense blind to ethnic diversity.[30]

It was true that Wiatr was one of Bauman's first non-Jewish friends. Whether the leftist intelligentsia was blind to ethnic differences is less clear. In our interview, Wiatr challenged the thesis of the relentless anti-Semitism of Poles. Yet he also recounted realizing just before their marriage that his first wife had changed her name to hide her Jewish origins during the Occupation. 'Origin was not at all important for people', Wiatr said. Yet if this was so, why did his wife – and so many other Jews – not return to their family names once Poland was liberated?[31] If Wiatr was correct, it would mean that the postwar university had been a cosmopolitan community where everyone was free to emphasize his or her origin. But perhaps Wiatr employed a different meaning for the word 'blind'. He may have meant that people didn't want to see ethnicities and wished to escape the old problem in Polish society – the Polish–Jewish relationship. This problem existed before, during and after the war, but in the postwar era Jews had become 'invisible'.

This blindness and invisibility correspond with Bauman's presentation of himself. He was very discreet about his familial origin: 'Zygmunt never showed his Jewishness', said Wiatr: 'It's not that he was hiding – he did not change his name – but he never showed off his Jewishness.' As an example, Wiatr notes that, during the Suez Crisis of 1956,[32] 'Zygmunt showed not a shadow of pro-Israeli sympathy. At the time there was no climate of anti-Semitism here.' Whether by tacit agreement or unspoken deal, no one spoke about either Jewishness or anti-Semitism. It was an invisible issue. Bauman lost his job and was kicked out of the military because his father visited the Israeli Embassy. He knew that being a Jew could be 'an issue' – a risky one. Yet, somehow, it was assumed not to be an issue for Bauman, although his military career had been blocked because of the supposition that, as a Jew, he was not to be trusted.

Despite the difficulties in his professional and personal life – the blow from the Army, the decline in income and housing, separation from his parents – Bauman did well in his first years at the institute. According to the student *carnet* (index) listing his courses, professors and grades, he obtained only the highest grades on his final exams in both the first year (in Biology, Logic, Dialectical Materialism, Historical Materialism, Psychology, and History of Philosophy) and the second (History of Polish Philosophy and History of Marxist

Philosophy). The latter two subjects were taught by his master's adviser, Schaff, the most prominent Marxist ideologue in Poland at the time. Educated in Moscow, Schaff returned to Poland in 1946 as a devout Stalinist. He created the IKKN (see chapter 7) and in 1953 led the Institute of Philosophy at the university. A combination of academic influence and strong political engagement made Schaff a powerful person. He was surrounded by dedicated communists, including his brilliant assistant Leszek Kołakowski.

Leszek Kołakowski – younger by age, older by status

Three years younger than Bauman, Kołakowski was higher on the academic ladder and more visible in the postwar university world. An *enfant terrible* of Polish communism, Kołakowski was to become one of the most famous Polish intellectuals of the twentieth century. He met Bauman at the university in 1953, at a time when both were Stalin supporters. Both would become revisionists and friends, banned from Poland in 1968 – to be precise, they left Poland, though with different statuses. Kołakowski was invited as a visiting professor to McGill University in Canada, while Bauman and his family were banished in an anti-Semitic purge. He was evicted from the university, his wife fired, and the state withdrew his Polish citizenship, forcing him to abandon his country and become stateless.

Once abroad, the two intellectuals maintained a complex relationship over the following decades as their political visions evolved differently. Kołakowski, like the great majority of Polish intellectuals (including those who had been Stalinists), became an anti-communist liberal, immersed in Catholicism, strongly focused on Poland's liberation and on the conservative values seen as the most promising for that end: identity, traditionalism, national conservatism. Bauman, by contrast, was an exceptional case because he remained a socialist, developing universalist reflections on society. Kołakowski settled in UK as an Oxford professor (and a part-time professor at the University of Chicago) and specialist in Marxism; later, he focused on the philosophy of religion. The institution in which he taught was one of the most prestigious in the UK. Bauman, who also settled in Britain, accepted a position at Leeds University but declined offers to specialize in Marxism or Eastern Europe. He developed his own theoretical reflections, which went beyond the circles of academia. In terms of reputation outside the academy, Kołakowski was mainly celebrated in post-Soviet countries. His writings (mainly journalistic essays) were used as the ideological basis for political changes in Poland – in particular, its exit from the socialist system. Kołakowski was cherished by post-1989 leaders and politicians for his 180-degree conversion from communism to

Catholicism, a transformation that Bauman never underwent. Yet Bauman's long-term influence, especially outside academia, considerably exceeds that of Kołakowski. The father of *Liquid Modernity* received worldwide attention with his reflections on social dynamics, becoming the ideological inspiration for global movements such as Occupy.

In the 1950s and 1960s, however, their paths often crossed at Warsaw University, but they entered the institution by different routes. Bauman came through the 'kitchen door' (ordered in by the Ministry of Higher Education as part of his dismissal from the Army) while Kołakowski came in by the main entrance. Kołakowski's academic trajectory was exemplary for sons of the Polish intelligentsia.[33] After getting a baccalaureate degree, he went straight to the university. Immediately after the war, living in Łódź, Kołakowski enrolled with great enthusiasm and energy in two activities. He was politically active in the radical ZWM-Życie (Union of Independent Socialist Youth – Life) – the academic section of the PPR.[34] At the same time, he was a star student. The philosopher Marian Przełęcki recalled, 'I met him at the first course with Ossowska. He was the youngest of us, just 18 years old, but immediately stood out.'[35] In 1946, Kołakowski met Schaff (freshly graduated from Moscow), who had received the chair in contemporary social doctrines at Łódź University. The young student frequented Schaff's seminar and they worked together politically as part of the 'intelligentsia executive' that dominated PPR-Łódź (Merda, 2017: 138). By then, Kołakowski already had what Bourdieu would call the *habitus* of the intellectual elite member: 'Well spoken, knowing literature, speaking some foreign languages.'[36] Journalist Tomasz Potkaj remarked that 'discussions took place in the smoky premises of ZWM *Życie*, at 48 Piotrkowska Street, in the seminar of Stefan Żółkiewski (a leading Marxist ideologue and editor-in-chief of *Kuźnica*), also in the apartments of Ossowski and Kotarbinski, during all-night philosophical boozing'.[37] 'The discussions were extremely sharp, but Marxists were not at all dominant, though certainly more visible', according to Przełęcki (interviewed by Potkaj). Kołakowski was the leading orator and ideologist of the communizing youth, 'full of wit, ironic, literary', as Woroszylski described him. 'Like other members of ZWM-Życie, he had a gun pinned at his belt.'[38]

Warsaw University, including its Department of Philosophy, was reactivated in Łódź immediately after the war, when the capital was still utterly in ruins. There, as in most of Poland, the environment was anything but peaceful, especially for communists. Members of political organizations such as ZWM-Życie had to protect themselves. Combining political activity with studies, Kołakowski devoted his time to reading, writing and discussing philosophical and political opinions. His academic career was brilliant and his rise rapid.

In 1949, Kołakowski followed Schaff[39] to Warsaw and took the position of junior assistant to the Chair of Dialectical and Historical Materialism. He wrote his master's thesis on conventionalism in 1949 under the supervision of Janina Kotarbińska (Merda, 2017: 139). The following year, Kołakowski assisted Schaff in the creation of the IKKN, known as 'the Janissaries School'[40] – a breeding ground for the new Marxist scientific cadre. Kołakowski began work on his Ph.D. thesis under Tadeusz Kroński,[41] but after complaining about his teaching (according to Schaff) moved under the latter's supervision (Merda, 2017: 139). In both the IKKN and the university's Department of Philosophy, Kołakowski was Schaff's assistant. For a busy professor like Schaff, this job included supervision and advising of master's students, and even teaching. Bauman was enrolled in the master's seminar with Schaff when he prepared his thesis, and almost certainly met Kołakowski during this period. While Bauman was academically behind Kołakowski, he soon reduced the distance. However, Bauman never equalled Kołakowski's professional status in Poland; only the latter became an 'ordinary professor'. After being evicted from the KBW, Bauman jumped into the academic career path with both feet. He had no other option.

Rapid take-off of an academic career

Bauman's release from the Army became official on 27 March 1953.[42] Since it was a principle of socialist Poland that no healthy adult could be without a job, that situation was quickly fixed. The Ministry of Higher Education imposed Bauman on the university – a procedure that Poles describe as 'bringing in a briefcase' (*przyniesiony w teczce*). Bauman's written request for an assistant position in Dialectical and Historical Materialism[43] contains a handwritten annex that clarifies the situation. Someone has written: 'The candidature of citizen Bauman has already been approved by the Commission for Qualification. According to the declaration of the Institute of Philosophy the full-time position [*etat*] shall be allocated to extramural courses in the Law Faculty, by the decision of the ministry.' In another unsigned manual annotation, someone has written: 'The director of the Institute [of Philosophy] strongly supports this request . . . [Bauman] will be under scientific supervision of prof. Fritzhand Marek'.[44]

The Army took care of its former soldiers, especially officers in sensitive corps such as the KBW, and it had arranged with the Ministry of Higher Education to find a landing place for Bauman. Since 1948, the ministry had reinforced the presence of PZPR members inside university structures (Rutkowski, 2016: 404), and Bauman was a good candidate to reinforce the Party's presence in politically relevant university circles. A year before, a new Soviet-influenced reform law (Schaff was a key proponent) imposed Marxist–Leninist doctrine on all departments and scientific tracks. Yet there weren't enough qualified lecturers to meet the need for such courses.[45] Bauman, as a former KBW instructor, was a perfect candidate for this job. As a lecturer of Marxism–Leninism and active Party member, he was well placed for an academic career. In addition to his strong profile, Bauman's candidature was supported by Schaff, without whose support he could never have been hired. The unit he joined, directed by Hochfeld, came under the chairmanship of Schaff himself, who thanks to his powerful status could 'organize a position' for someone who needed it, even a 'suspect' individual like Bauman.

He was hired on 15 February 1953,[46] at the start of the second semester. Bauman had been 'liberated from his functions' at a high level of the KBW. Such a designation enabled Schaff to ensure that Bauman was not a *persona non grata* and could be hired. In the CV he wrote out in anticipation of his hiring, Bauman stated: 'I was not punished, I was released without any explanation regarding my work and political attitude.'[47] Schaff was able to guess the reasons for Bauman's eviction. The anti-Semitic climate in the Party and intelligence services was certainly familiar to Schaff, himself a Jew.[48] In 1953, however, the ethnic discrimination campaign had not yet reached Warsaw University.

Bauman's early academic career was on a very fast track, making up for time lost serving in the Army. In January 1954, six months before getting his master's, Bauman was promoted to adjunct professor in Hochfeld's department.[49] (On 29 December, Bauman would probably have attended Kołakowski's public Ph.D. defence, which drew most of the Philosophy Department.[50]) Six months later, on 25 June 1954, Bauman defended his master's thesis, entitled 'Methodological and Historical Approach of the Baden School and Its Influence on Polish Historiography'.[51] The jury included Jan Legowicz,[52] Julian Hochfeld and Adam Schaff, and he was asked two questions. The first: Why was the Baden School judged to be idealistic? The second concerned the practical meaning of the critique of idiographism (the study of specific scientific facts and processes). His responses received the highest grade: Very Good (5/5).[53] In several documents that followed the exam (such as opinions by Schaff or Hochfeld), we find, likewise, high marks: 'MA thesis excellent, much above the expectations this level of work requires. He [Bauman] proved that he is made for an academic work [career].'[54] These excellent opinions were the result of Bauman's hard work and the enthusiasm with which he plunged into his new university environment. The only thing that hadn't changed in his life was his Party commitment.

While studying, Bauman obtained a position as secretary of the university Party committee, where he led the recruitment process and was charged with interrogating new candidates at the university.[55] This was a powerful role and Bauman awakened fears in many around him. 'Zygmunt was such a tough Party member', recalled Barbara Szacka. Her chief, Nina Assorodobraj, had suggested Szacka join the Party but 'I know that was impossible. . . . I can say that Bauman "saved me" from joining the Party because of what I saw at his interrogation of a candidate.' Bauman's questioning of the candidate, a member of the English Department, was brutal:

> 'What did your father do? Why?' . . . I was sitting in the audience and I could not imagine how I would go through the same procedure! Condemning my father's views and renouncing him?! My father died in Katyń; he was a Legionnaire [an officer under Piłsudski] and had prewar views that I never concealed. But I could not imagine undergoing this torture. . . . Zygmunt was really terrible. . . . Then he changed.[56]

While he may have been a Stalinist in his Party work, the radical changes in Bauman's professional and personal life affected him deeply, according to Janina Bauman. He 'buried himself in work, spending all days and nights on it. He was no longer the same person. The radiant zestful boy became a weary man. His grudge against his father was turning into deep sorrow and bitter anxiety about his parents' fate' (J. Bauman, 1988: 106). Gradually, Bauman made peace with his parents, a process that was easier in 1954 after he completed his master's thesis. 'By then he had changed a great deal', wrote Janina:

> Since he had left the army he seemed to see things more clearly. Though still a sincere socialist – which deep in his heart he has remained to this day – he now began to see that all was not right in this world of his. He became more and more aware of contradictions between words and deeds. . . . He was no longer a blind worshipper of the Party line (J. Bauman, 1988: 115)

Doubts began to erode Bauman's faith. They were fostered as a result of the intimacy of the Historical Materialism section and the intellectual honesty of its leader, Julian Hochfeld. As Bauman has repeatedly underlined, Hochfeld played a crucial role in his intellectual formation as well as his professional socialization within the university world in the 1950s. Hochfeld was a mentor and a friend who protected his disciple to the end (Hochfeld died suddenly in 1966). In 1964, Bauman would state that his theoretical views were formed under Hochfeld, 'to whose inspiration and criticism, broad intellectual horizons, and eternal creative unrest in large measure I owe their present form'.[57] Their relationship was more than the usual professor–student one. Hochfeld created helpful conditions to protect the fragile development of critical and independent thinking in Bauman. (Schaff, by contrast, was only briefly Bauman's intellectual overseer, and not a friend: they never developed a true master–disciple relationship.) Hochfeld was devoted to his students, an open-minded intellectual who, during the worse years of Stalinism, freely expressed doubts and criticism about the communist regime within his small circle of trust. 'I was interested in Bauman, because I was very curious about anyone who belonged to Hochfeld's circle', said Andrzej Werblan, a communist *apparatchik* in those years.

Julian Hochfeld – a man in a trap

Before creating his 'circle' at Warsaw University, Hochfeld led a fascinating life.[58] He was born in 1911 in Rzeszów (at the time, part of the Austrian Empire) to a Polish-Jewish family. His father was a lawyer and vice mayor of the city. Hochfeld studied law and administration at the Jagiellonian University in Kraków, where, at the age of 18, he was already involved in politics – first in Związek Niezależnej Młodzieży Socjalistycznej Życie (The Union of Independent Socialist Youth – Life), the academic youth branch of the Communist Party, and then in the Polish Socialist Party. He was the co-editor of *Płomienie* (Flames), the young socialists' journal, and after graduation spent a year in Paris at the École Libre des Sciences Politiques,[59] where he observed the success of the Front Populaire (Popular Front), which convinced him that socialists and communists must co-operate (Gdula, 2017: 201). Back in Poland, he became an editor of *Dziennik popularny* (Popular Journal), which was read by leftists critical of Poland's right-wing anti-Semitic government.[60] In 1937, Hochfeld received his Ph.D. in political economy and statistics in Kraków.[61] With academia closed to him because of his Jewish background, Hochfeld joined the movement to implement co-operative housing projects in Warsaw. In the first days of World War II, he volunteered and was captured, spending two months in a German military jail as a Polish soldier, then escaped to western Ukraine. When Hitler attacked the Soviet Union in 1941, Hochfeld fled east and joined the Anders' Army. For about six months, he was a delegate of the London government-in-exile in Dushanbe, Tajikistan. When the Polish exiles cut off their official relationship with the USSR in 1943, the Soviets jailed him for several weeks and then he left with the Anders' Army, travelling through the Middle East until he reached London in September 1944 (Chałubiński, 2017: 31).

Hochfeld was a socialist in the government-in-exile (and well integrated into British socialist circles). Though he could have easily and comfortably established himself in the UK (Wiatr, 2017b: 15), Hochfeld returned to Poland in August 1945 and was appointed to the State National Council for two consecutive terms, and also was a Member of Parliament. At the same time, he was a member of the Central Executive Committee of the Socialist Party, and strongly supported the idea of socialist realism (in this context, a political, rather than artistic, current). At a meeting with socialist students, Hochfeld 'said openly that Poland had "lost the war"',[62] Wiatr wrote.[63] He had no illusions about the Stalinist system, which he knew through his own experience in the Soviet Union and one of its prisons. Yet he returned home, bypassing an easier existence:

> He chose another, risk-filled path, because he saw this as his duty to Poland. He probably counted on the fact that the 'Polish Road to socialism', of which he was one of the most important theorists, could be implemented despite Soviet domination. Its implementation meant the creation of a non-Soviet, more democratic and humanistic variant of the socialist system. (Wiatr, 2017a: 15)

This humanist variant was presented in a manifesto published in 1946 by Jan Strzelecki, who edited *Płomienie* some years after Hochfeld. He argued that humanistic socialism took into account the individual aspects of sociological processes, not only class determination, but Schaff interpreted the text as revisionist and attacked Strzelecki. Hochfeld defended Strzelecki, but the latter's vision was not accepted by supporters of Stalinism (Grochowska, 2014: 178–82).

Another important discussion about Marxism took place on the pages of the journal *Myśl Współczesna* (Contemporary Thought) in 1947–8, where Ossowski and Schaff presented different visions of the theory.[64] Ossowski, a socialist, represented the non-communist, typically Western appreciation of Marx, while Schaff subscribed to the orthodox communist vision. Hochfeld's contribution to this exchange was original; for Hochfeld, said the sociologist Maciej Gdula:

> Marxism belonged to the fabric of modern science, which meant accepting the material nature of the world and exploration of the interdependence between phenomena and causalities. Marxists focus on investigating the transformations of productive forces and the material side of social processes. . . . based on empirical research, [this approach] critically complements the findings of the other perspective of a more 'idealistic' character. (Gdula, 2017: 202)

Defining Marxism this way created a space for dialogue with other, non-Marxist approaches. Hochfeld practised and popularized 'Open Marxism',[65] originally an idea from Kamierz Kelles-Krauz[66] that stood in opposition to Marxist dogma. 'Hochfeld understood Marxism as a mental creation containing theories of various degrees of generality', wrote his biographer, Mirosław Chałubiński. By its very nature, Hochfeld believed, Marxism had to be open to analyses of a changing world and non-Marxist social theories.[67] This idea inescapably favours a democratic and pluralistic culture, since 'ideological unification, typical of monocratic systems, is practically without exception the negation of democracy and pluralism' (Chałubiński, 2017: 35).

That vision was unacceptable to Schaff and other Stalinist scholars. The rigid attitude of the communists reinforced the doubts of socialists about plans to reunify the two parties. Hochfeld opposed the socialist party's fusion with the PPR, arguing that pluralism reinforced democracy. He supported the hegemony of the communists 'but pluralism was important to him', wrote Andrzej Werblan (Werblan, in Modzelewski and Werblan, 2017: 42). Bauman's mentor was a sociologist of rare provenance. As a lawyer and active politician, he had insider knowledge that he could link to an academic theoretical framework of the state, governance and political parties in national and international contexts. In the immediate postwar years, he believed the system would be authoritarian but soft; he knew that democracy under Soviet dependence was impossible (Modzelewski and Werblan, 2017: 42). This approach, representing a kind of Third Way, was an important but frequently ignored position in a political environment generally presented as a black-and-white picture of Stalinists versus London-supported partisans. Hochfeld's position influenced Bauman's work and his thoughts about how to survive as an honest scholar at a time of all-pervading propaganda and censure. Hochfeld taught him to navigate carefully in a stormy environment. 'Hochfeld, to do something sensible, even small, was ready to compromise', Bauman wrote to writer Magdalena Grochowska (Grochowska, 2014: 329).

Eventually, *realpolitik* led Hochfeld to join, unenthusiastically, the PZPR, but his previous polemics with Schaff had cost Hochfeld his political position in the newly unified Party and relegated him to a scientific career, as would happen to Bauman a few years later. He had been diverted to the academic track after a personal interview with none other than Jakub Berman, the 'right hand of Stalin' and prominent communist leader, in early September 1948 (Chałubiński, 2017: 32). Convinced that he needed to keep up his political activity despite the increasingly Stalinist atmosphere, Hochfeld joined Schaff's aggressive camp and, at the plenary meeting of the PZPR Central Committee in November 1949, 'submitted a humiliating self-criticism and – indirectly at least – joined the condemnation of Władysław Gomułka's line', writes Wiatr. In an article published in *Myśl Filozoficzna* (Philosophical Thought), where he was deputy editor-in-chief, Hochfeld 'severely and unjustly' attacked works by Józef Chałasiński and Stanisław Ossowski. To assess this action in hindsight, one must remember the scale of pressure exerted at that time, which included physical threats (Wiatr, 2017a: 16). Mirosław Chałubiński compared Hochfeld's creed with similar actions, such as Kołakowski's attacks on the Lwów–Warsaw school (Kołakowski and Baczko attacking their professor, Tatarkiewicz), or Chałasiński's vendetta against his teacher, F. Znaniecki (Chałubiński, 2017: 33–4). This was the intellectual practice of the times: to attack one's intellectual parent and then be attacked by other students. Chałasiński himself, in November 1947, turned coat and began to praise Stalin. He was promoted and became rector of Łódź University, replacing the expelled Kotarbiński. In 1949, Chałasiński sat near Stalin in his theatre box, celebrating the dictator's seventieth birthday (Grochowska, 2014: 194).

Such was the intellectual climate of Stalinism, in which people lived in fear of losing their jobs and careers, and even their lives. The next step in Hochfeld's Sovietization took place in 1951 during the First Congress of Polish Science, where he declared that 'sociology and Marxism were two separate lines of development in scholarship, and only the latter was progressive' (Kraśko, 1966: 136, in Gdula, 2017: 2002).

In his non-fiction essay *The Captive Mind* (1953), Czesław Miłosz presents a menagerie of intellectual types seduced by the 'new church'. For them, faith in a better future under communism excused all negative aspects of the system they supported. In possession of the ultimate Truth, they blinded themselves to its anomalies and crimes. Turski compares this type of intellectual to a missionary figure.[68] Maria Hirszowicz, in her book devoted to intellectuals trapped by Stalinism, describes two main types who supported the system: true believers (Miłosz's Captive Minds) and organization people. The former were attracted by, and defended, communist ideals; the latter were faithful to the institutions (Hirszowicz, 2001: 26–7). Hochfeld can't easily be pigeonholed into either of these categories. He was a sort of maverick,[69] seeking to maintain his socialist values in a very hostile environment – different from those at the edges of the system who did not really belong (like Strzelecki) and from permanent opponents (such as Jan Józef Lipski). He played a strategic game and a double role, as a party official and professor. In the first realm, he showed enthusiastic support for Marxism. Doing so gave him access to academia, where he could play a more questioning, critical role.

Schaff and the party rewarded Hochfeld for his open endorsement of Stalinism. He became a professor at Warsaw University in Dialectical Marxism in 1951, and a year later a Chair was created for him, replacing one of the liquidated sociology chairs orphaned by banned non-Marxist professors. Meanwhile, Hochfeld was building his own academic team, a new generation of students who would become independent thinkers and who, despite growing up inside the dictatorial system, were able to criticize it and try to change it. This process conformed with the principle of socialist humanism as Hochfeld understood it, thereby creating a new school of Marxism. He was a charismatic teacher surrounded by assistants and students, among them Zygmunt Bauman.

The 'circle of Hochfeld'

Hochfeld's first assistant was Jan Strzelecki, who, despite his very short period of work (he was fired at the end of 1952), significantly influenced the team. 'Formally [he] had no power, but in terms of the meritocracy, he was second after God', said Wiatr (in Grochowska, 2014: 325). At a time when many people followed the communist dictatorship, either opportunistically or out of fear, Strzelecki remained loyal to his values. His attitude was a kind of moral compass for the rest of Hochfeld's team – a life emblematic of the socialist humanism he defended.

Six years older than Bauman, Strzelecki had enrolled at Warsaw University's law school in 1937. In parallel, he started his political activity, mainly publishing anti-fascist texts in social democracy journals. During World War II, he became close to the leaders of the future Polish Socialist Party, and from 1942 he and Lipiński were co-editors of *Płomienie*. Strzelecki was also active in underground Left groups, supporting activists from the BUND (the Jewish socialist party) and helping Jews escape from the Ghetto.[70] Moreover, he pursued his education at the underground university, studying with Kotarbiński, Suchodolski and the Ossowskis. When the Warsaw Uprising began, Strzelecki took part in the street battles and was injured, managing to hide in southern Poland until the end of the war. In 1945, he re-entered the re-activated Warsaw University in Łódź, deciding to study sociology. Strzelecki became the assistant of Stanisław Ossowski, his mentor, and a year later followed Ossowski to Warsaw, where in 1949 he defended his master's on the sociology of knowledge, based on the works of Karl Mannheim.[71] In 1946, Strzelecki spent a few weeks in jail, accused of membership in the anti-communist organization Liberty and Independence (Wolność i Niezawisłość). Despite his later discharge, the authorities viewed Strzelecki with suspicion. When Ossowski's chairmanship was ended, Strzelecki lost his job as assistant, and Hochfeld offered him financial support – apparently out of his own pocket, pretending that it was a scholarship. This allowed Strzelecki's family to survive (Grochowska, 2014: 197). Hochfeld and Strzelecki had been close political colleagues since 1946, when as young students they joined the Socialist Party's Supreme Council. Like most Party members at the time, Hochfeld and Strzelecki expressed their distance from Stalinism and communism. Strzelecki, supported by Hochfeld, popularized the idea of socialist humanism.[72] Schaff sharply criticized their 'revisionist attitudes' in the press.

Both Hochfeld and Strzelecki believed it was useless to oppose the communists firmly, seeing Poland's difficult situation as partly due to its history, geography and social reality (see Grochowska, 2014: 178–80). But, while Hochfeld moved closer to the PPR out of a principle of realism, Strzelecki remained loyal to his humanist creed.[73] From the beginning, the ambiance established by the two men enabled studies, projects and discussions that went beyond official topics and frameworks. The members of Hochfeld's team, including Bauman and Wiatr, who obtained assistant positions while still students, benefitted from these privileged conditions. The protected environment extended to Schaff's master's students as well – a peculiar circumstance because Schaff was an orthodox Marxist, the leader of the Stalinization process at the university, and strictly opposed socialist humanism. Unlike Schaff's orthodox seminar, Hochfeld's was a space of relative freedom. But not all of the students studying in his department could attend it. Only Wiatr and Wesołowski were enrolled; Bauman, Aleksandra Jasińska[74] and Albin Kania were mentored officially by Schaff, and attended his seminars – Bauman as a Warsaw University student; Jasińska and Kania, her future husband, as IKKN students. Another important part of the team was Maria Hirszowicz. After their graduation from different institutions, they became the active members of Hochfeld's circle.

All of the master's students working in Hochfeld's unit graduated in 1954.[75] They were divided into two groups: Bauman and Jasińska did their work on sociological classics, while Wiatr and Wesołowski used traditional sociological methodologies in their study on 'workers' memories' from the interwar period. The only thesis in the group that showed a strict Marxist approach was that of Albin Kania.[76]

While their thesis topics were diverse, the 'school' shared 'common research issues, a common system of values and a similar type of political commitment, and – to a very significant degree – a master who was not only a guide in our scientific work, but also a great authority and a friend', as Wiatr would recall (Wiatr, 2017a: 17). The relationship orchestrated by Hochfeld, based on trust and the maintenance of close master–disciple ties, enabled the transfer of

'forbidden' sociological works. Hochfeld's students used qualitative methods and a Polish prewar speciality – biographical research
using personal diaries – to examine workers' memories. This was
unusual in a period when any prewar scholarship was tainted and
unwelcome. Hochfeld also retained another 'bourgeois' element –
direct contact with research participants (workers in the Żerań car
plant). This enabled the Hochfeld group to conduct field investigations into the transformation of the 'consciousness of the working
class' (Grochowska, 2014: 325).

'These were bad times for science', Wiatr recalled:

> but even in these difficult years Hochfeld was able to give his teach-
> ing a far-from-orthodox template. I remember a lecture from his
> seminar based on the book by Franz Borkenau,[77] which he lent me
> from his library. It was probably the only university seminar east of
> the Elbe where the work of leading Western socialists was discussed in
> a factual way and devoid of ideological anger. (Wiatr, 2017a: 16; see
> Grochowska 2014: 32)

Hochfeld performed, and taught, the art of 'barking in a muzzle':[78]
'Hochfeld's scholarly language was largely free of ideological jargon,
while his articles were stuffed with political aggression and Stalinist–
Leninist orthodoxy' (Grochowska, 2014: 328). His disciples learned
how to navigate in a hostile environment while sharing a stimulating
intellectual entourage. Members of the team exchanged and read
one another's drafts and collaborated on papers[79] in an unusually
free space at the university.

'It was unique', said Bauman in an interview: 'It never happened
again in my life . . . just a team of people discussing with each other,
every work the object of interest to the whole team. Nobody was
lonely there, no one worked in isolation. I have not seen this again
anywhere else.'[80] Indeed, such organization of work based on open
sharing of knowledge occurs more frequently in life science research
groups than in social science or the humanities. The unusual environment stimulated hard work, and probably also helped soothe the
ever-present fears of the time.[81] By the standards of the time and
place, Hochfeld's circle did spectacular work: they read Western
publications, discussed non-Marxist theories and used 'old-style'
(non-Marxist) research methodologies. The students learned how
to accomplish decent sociological work under the worst political
regime imaginable, long before the 'thaw' began in October 1956.[82]

When Strzelecki was fired from Warsaw University (for the second
time, at the end of 1953), Bauman took his place as the second
member of the team after Hochfeld. This was due to his age and
social status: he was slightly older than the others, with the exception of Maria Bielińska-Hirszowicz, and was a family man and

former officer. He was viewed as one of the grown-ups in the group, with duties to match. In July 1953, Bauman spent a month in Sopot (a Baltic resort town near Gdańsk) as an organizational 'chief' of a summer camp Schaff created for students in the humanities and social sciences. The idea was to teach students about ideology and classics of philosophy in a summery environment (such camps were traditionally organized by Warsaw University in attractive holiday destinations). It was not a 'stupid indoctrination', Barbara Szacka recalled: 'The lectures were at a good level . . . it was not cheesy. Obviously, it was ideological, since dialectical philosophy and historical materialism were dominant.' Bauman was there as an 'organizational guardian', she said. Though associated with Hochfeld, he was by no means considered an outsider, and he was associated with the 'harsh power' of the university's party structures (Barbara Szacka, interview, 2016). He may have appeared harsh or haughty in the summer of 1953, but the summer camp was mostly for single students, looking for fun. Bauman was far from his wife Janina and daughter Anna, and troubled by financial difficulties (which is probably why he accepted the camp position in the first place).

Hochfeld also made Bauman responsible for some accounting and organizational tasks in the department. Wiatr recalled one day when Hochfeld became unhappy over the way Bauman had managed some financial matter and said, '"I had enough of this behaviour in the shops in Nalewki" [the Jewish commercial street in prewar Warsaw known for its 'stingy shopkeepers']. Zygmunt was upset! Hochfeld looked at him and said: "Zygmunt – so you think I'm an anti-Semite?" And we all started laughing – that's how it was in our group. We were so inoculated against anti-Semitism that Hochfeld could make the crack about the shop in Nalewki.'

This story illustrates several important points. The use of humour and ethnic stereotyping, which could be abusive, was not so when it came from Hochfeld's mouth. Rather, it reflected a kind of Jewish-Polish style, self-satirical and acid, which Hochfeld used to resolve an organizational tension. The reaction of other members (laughter) probably indicates a relaxed ambiance and the non-hierarchical style of the relationship, which at that time and at the university was rare. Feudal relationships between masters and disciples were the domi-nant model in Poland. The collegial style in Hochfeld's group was also probably related to the conviction among his students that they were doing interesting and perhaps dangerous work. At the height of Stalinism, Hochfeld was standing the imposed intellectual model on its head, Wiatr notes. He held a seminar devoted to the critics of social democracy, but the criticism was not of an annihilating type. He told his students to read Western books in their original version, as written by 'revisionist' authors ('revisionist' means challenging orthodox Marxism). In the 1952/3 academic year, this was simply unthinkable in the Soviet Union, or elsewhere in Poland (Wiatr, in Grochowska, 2014: 335). By requiring his students and collaborators to read 'revisionists', Hochfeld was preparing the ground for a revisionist movement. 'Daily arguments with his university friends and colleagues helped to clarify his [Bauman's] mind', Janina wrote later: 'His first critical essays followed. He was no longer a blind worshipper of the party line' (J. Bauman, 1988: 115).[83]

Bauman finished his master's under Schaff's supervision, then was passed on to Hochfeld officially, and began his Ph.D. research on the Labour Party's conception of socialism. The topic was close to Hochfeld's interests and far from Marxist orthodoxy. It was a space of relative freedom.[84] Bauman's academic career was well launched. 'Hochfeld was the head of the cathedral', Wiatr says, but Bauman, his protégé, was 'the real boss, because Hochfeld never had time' (Grochowska, 2014: 335). Bauman had the ability and energy to perform several tasks in parallel.

The life of a young scholar

The salary of an assistant professor could not replace the pension of a KBW major in socialist Poland. Scholars were 'state workers' with low incomes,[85] Warsaw was expensive and had a housing shortage, and academics were encouraged to take several jobs in order to piece together a living wage. Beginning in January 1953, and throughout the rest of his life in Poland, Bauman usually had several jobs.

According to documents in the archives of Warsaw University, the rector had nominated 'citizen Bauman Zygmunt' to the position of 'assistant scientific worker', with Level 7 pay, from 15 February 1953 to 15 February 1955.[86] Another document described his obligations: 36 hours a week, including 18 hours of teaching, 6 hours to organize and programme studies, and 12 hours of research and teaching preparation.[87] The position was confirmed after a two-month trial and he was hired finally for an indefinite period.[88] The same file contains a letter concerning Bauman's pay, along with a family allowance for his daughter, Anna. Another document from the spring of 1953 mentions that Bauman has no other jobs. In November 1953, however, Bauman became an editor of the philosophical journal *Myśl Filozoficzna* edited in the Department of Philosophy. Both jobs provided a modest salary, though grade and seniority were rewards at the university.

This was a difficult period for the family. 'I remember days when there was nothing to eat in the evening', wrote Janina Bauman: 'Sometimes because of lack of money, sometimes because the queues in the shops were so long; sometimes because there was simply no food to be bought. ... [Zygmunt] did everything he could to help but he was studying full time now and his heart was set on completing his degree as soon as possible' (J. Bauman, 1988: 111). Bauman 'devoted most of his time to the studies. At night, at the kitchen table pushed between the couch and the wardrobe, he wrote his master's thesis at a rapid pace' (J. Bauman, 2011: 92). Their apartment was very small and unhealthy; Janina had to remain home with Anna during her daughter's frequent illnesses. The couple had no money to pay someone to take care of their child. The Polish version of Janina Bauman's book contains an account of extra jobs Bauman did to try to improve their financial situation: 'He wrote a short story for a radio contest and won the second prize. Then he "produced" a criminal short story, which I quite liked, but unfortunately he did not find a publisher' (J. Bauman, 2011: 92). I found no unpublished crime novel from this period, but there were two military novels that Bauman signed as Julian Żurowicz, both published in 1953 by a military publisher.[89] However, Janina's account is silent about those novels, perhaps because such socialist realist products were jeered at, or even considered criminal, in the Poland of the early twenty-first century. Or perhaps Bauman was no longer proud of them?

The death of Stalin on 9 March 1953 brought some hope for future change. Gradually and faintly, the ever-present fear began to weaken in the society. In Bauman's house, there was also a need for the construction of a 'normal life'. In June 1954, he defended his master's thesis, and on 14 July he was nominated to the Commission of Qualification, the body that made career decisions about researchers in the Department of Philosophy.[90] In October 1954, Bauman was hired to a second, parallel full-time post as an associate researcher in the section of Dialectical and Historical Materialism at the Polish Academy of Sciences (PAN).[91] This job was a big help to the family budget. On 21 December 1954, the Commission of Qualification granted Bauman the title of assistant research professor (*adiunkt naukowy*), to begin on 1 January. That increased his salary at the university from 920 to 1,300 złotys a month. In 1955, Bauman's new salary was about 30 per cent more than the average in Poland. Moreover, in addition to the university and Polish Academy positions, Bauman got a third, very interesting offer, six months later. The Directorate of the Party Central Committee School appointed Bauman, with the clearance of the PZPR leadership, to chair the school's Department of Dialectical and Historical Materialism.[92] His three salaries now probably totalled around 3,000 złoty.

From this accumulation of jobs, we can deduce that Hochfeld was a very powerful protector and promoter for Bauman, helping him to obtain attractive positions and decent money. '[E]verything went smoothly' (J. Bauman, 1988: 116), wrote Janina about that period. The year 1955 was a good one for the Bauman family, which managed finally to leave the Army lodging in Mokotów. In September, the Baumans moved to Bielany, in the northern part of Warsaw. Hochfeld probably helped Bauman find the apartment, located in a new block at 1/222 Aleja Zjednoczenia Street that already was showing the signs of its shoddy postwar construction. The apartment was composed of two small rooms on the ground floor with the windows facing north, and a small kitchen (without windows). The apartment was cold and dark, disagreeable characteristics in a country of long dark autumn and winter months, where access to light and sun is very important. It was also far from the city centre, meaning hour-long commutes for both Zygmunt and Janina on malfunctioning public transport. However, for the first time in years, they had a 'civilian' house with no military guards at the entrance gate and without a high protective fence.

The move to Bielany was probably facilitated by the administration[93] because Janina was now pregnant. She was expecting twins, which meant a considerable change in their familial situation. Having three children was unusual; most intelligentsia couples had only one child in this era because of the women's professional careers and the small apartments. One breadwinner was insufficient, and large families had ceased to be common in Poland. Three children in a household with two working parents posed a huge logistical challenge. The Baumans accepted it, however.

The end of 1955 was a very intense period. Zygmunt, at 30,[94] was preparing his Ph.D. thesis, and was now the father of three children in a city that lacked many basic goods. In this period, most women would spend several hours a week in long queues waiting for products. Bauman shared this duty with his wife; he was not a 'traditional father'. Half a century before the cultural shift towards paternal participation in housework and childcare duties, Bauman took over tasks that were the traditional domain of women. Housework was not an entirely new activity for him, because he had also been very involved in the care of Anna. However, after the birth of the twins and Janina's subsequent illness, he was for a time obliged to perform all the traditional maternal duties. Bauman managed the house cleaning, cooking and his university occupations.

This difficult period revealed a generally well-concealed aspect of Bauman's personality. In an emergency, his sense of responsibility and his strong physical endurance enabled him to deal with sleeplessness, disorganization and irregular, poor-quality meals. Another important character trait appeared following the birth of his new children, which took place at a luxurious private clinic. The expensive clinic, which had a very high reputation, was owned by an old obstetrician. The Baumans could not have afforded the care there, but the owner was a longtime friend of Janina's grandfather and so they did not have to pay. The girls, Irena and Lydia, were born on 16 December 1955. The newborns were healthy, but Janina was very sick. Her physicians tried to cure her with antibiotics, which were still very new and expensive, and accessible only with a special authorization that Bauman spent hours in line at the Ministry of Health to obtain. Then he spent additional long hours in line at the pharmacy, where he paid an extremely high price for the drugs. Those expenses ruined their budget, and the antibiotics were totally ineffectual in addressing Janina's health problem,[95] which worsened steadily. After she had spent six weeks in the hospital, Zygmunt decided to take Janina and the twins home. Bauman 'now took charge of our whole life', Janina would write: 'Already breadwinner, cook, nanny, cleaner and washerman, he now became my doctor' (J. Bauman, 1988: 122). Under the supervision of a local physician, Bauman followed the prescribed orders with the 'toughness of a former soldier' (J. Bauman, 1988: 122). Slowly, Janina recovered, but for months Bauman was nearly exclusively in charge of their family. 'It was . . . [Zygmunt] who stayed up at night to feed our two babies', wrote Janina:

> Bending over their cot, he held a bottle of milk in either hand, waiting patiently till they were empty. Later, he would often wake to change their nappies, while I stayed in bed, sleepless but unable to move. The girls were hard work. . . . The winter was fierce, the days very short. In the cold dark mornings . . . [Zygmunt] would bend over the bath and wash dozens of nappies. There was no means of drying them in our small, freezing flat, so they had to be hung out in the courtyard. . . . Then he took . . . [their older daughter, Anna] to her nursery school and collected her eight hours later. In the meantime, he lectured, supervised his students, worked on his doctorate and argued at political meetings. He also did all the shopping, waiting in endless queues. (J. Bauman, 1988: 123)

It is difficult to imagine how Bauman managed all those tasks. He was a full-time lecturer and a Ph.D. student finishing his thesis. In addition to his personal duties, he had to respond to a feverish, agitated environment at the university. Polish society was progressively waking up.[96] Yet no one could have predicted that the winter's end would bring about such enormous changes.

The 'thaw'

Despite a common perception that the thaw began with Khrushchev's 1956 speech to the twentieth Communist Party Congress, and the Poznań riots in June 1956, the signs of de-Stalinization were visible in Poland well before then.[97] Historian Andrzej Werblan, a participant observer of the political dynamic, believes the thaw process arose originally out of tensions within the Party. There were two groups, later called the 'Puławians' and the 'Natolinians' (from their meeting places in Warsaw: Puławska Street and the Natolin district). The Natolinians supported the politics of Bierut and were loyal to Soviet leaders, while the Puławians sought more independence from Moscow and less Party control over individual and professional life. The Puławians were mainly older communists sceptical of Stalinist and Soviet politics. Some had fought in the Spanish Civil War and knew types of communism outside the Stalinian model; they were not true believers and were not surprised by the so-called 'revelation of Światło'.

Lieutenant Colonel Józef Światło defected to West Berlin and to the United States at the end of 1953, and the following autumn he publicly revealed hidden sides of the communist system: police terror, torture of political prisoners, the 'bourgeois lifestyle' of the communist elite, the Moscovian influence and the widespread networks of informers. Before his escape, he had been deputy chief of Department X in the secret police and was himself known as an overseer of the torture of political prisoners. Światło's revelations were broadcast in Polish by Radio Free Europe beginning in September 1954. While listening to this radio was forbidden, everyone at high levels in Warsaw heard and talked about the allegations. Hochfeld's team, informed via Party sources, discussed the news, which was impossible to ignore, even if some dismissed it as Western propaganda. The events that followed the broadcasts showed that the power structure was beginning to crack (Kemp-Welch, 1996: 181). The Ministry of Public Security was dismantled in December 1954, and some of the leaders of the institution were imprisoned and put on trial (including Colonel Fejgin, one of Bauman's superiors at the KBW), revealing criminal practices performed in the name of the state. Władysław Gomułka, who had been Poland's de facto leader until 1948, when he was removed from power and later imprisoned, was freed on 13 December 1954. There was more open discussion of these actions around Poland, but the 'loosening of the reins' was slowed by Bierut, who remained faithful to Stalinian legend until Khrushchev's speech definitively killed it. That was the turning-point event, one that could no longer be explained away by attributing counterrevolutionary or 'imperialist' attributes to the reformers.

Bauman most certainly did not get much sleep in 1956, and not only because of his arduous parenting duties.[98] On a frigid February night, Khrushchev gave his ostensibly secret, four-hour speech condemning Stalin's crimes: the purges, the Gulag, the use of torture and other acts of terror. Supporting his argument with the classical

texts of Marx, Engels and, foremost, Lenin, Khrushchev showed
how Stalin had distorted a system that in principle was not characterized by dictatorship and totalitarianism. In short, Khrushchev
maintained that communism was still the best policy, but Stalin was
a devil who had abused power, creating and nourishing a condem-
nation-worthy cult of personality. Pandora's Box was wide open.

While 1,436 Party delegates were invited to hear the speech, efforts
were made to restrict knowledge of it (the text was not published
in the USSR until 1989!). Translations were sent to Soviet-bloc
countries via diplomatic cables coded 'top secret'. Khrushchev was
worried about the reaction of active supporters of his predecessor,[99]
for the speech and its revelation of de-Stalinization measures[100]
created an earthquake that threatened to shatter decades of
Stalinism practically overnight. De-Stalinization measures and the
speech were discussed by everyone who had heard the speech or seen
the translations, however, and by those who heard snippets or the
general outline through the grapevine. The intensity of the discussions about the speech was feverish.

Bierut remained in Moscow after the speech, though historians
still disagree on whether this was because of his poor health or his
loyalty to Stalin (Kemp-Welch, 1996). In Poland, where the hard
line had already been punctured by Światło's revelations, agitation
increased day by day as incomplete and unofficial news leaked out.
Bierut kept in touch with Poland by phone with growing concern,
and the situation worsened with an unofficial plenum of the Central
Committee on 3–4 March 1956, at which Member of Parliament and
secretary of the Party Central Committee Jerzy Morawski reported
back on Khrushchev's speech. 'He cited Khrushchev's statement, at
a reception for foreign delegates, that the struggle with the "cult of
the individual" was by no means over but would continue until all
remnants had been eradicated from social life, including science and
education, art and literature', according to one account: 'Professor
Schaff then reported on ideological responses' (Kemp-Welch, 1996:
183).

At the PZPR's Institute of Social Science, where Bauman was the
director of the social research section, as well as at other academic
sites, Schaff organized discussion to try to keep events from spinning
out of control. Hochfeld's team members were part of these passionate discussions. The notion of freedom for science and education,
the abolishment of the Stalinist cult of personality, were beautiful
promises. The Party, and Warsaw intellectual circles, buzzed with
intense discussion.

On 12 March, sixteen days after Khrushchev's famous speech,
Bierut 'suddenly' died in Moscow.[101] In Poland, gossip and sour
anecdotes attributed his death to poisoning, or suicide, though no
evidence of foul play ever surfaced. He was buried in Warsaw on 16

March. Khrushchev himself was in the honour guard. 'The return of their late leader in an open coffin was a shock to many Poles' (Kemp-Welch, 1996: 185). Bierut had not been popular in Poland, but had ruled with Stalin's backing for eight years. 'Despite the public face of solemnity and sadness, the secret police reported many instances of "hooligan" and anti-state activity', according to one account (Kemp-Welch, 1996: 187). Hochfeld's group had mixed feelings, for while Bierut represented the harshest side of Stalinism, he was also the father of their good friend Aleksandra Jasińska-Kania.[102]

There are various accounts of how Polish readers obtained the 'secret report', which shortly leaked out. The different accounts help us to understand the particular social processes of this era. According to historian Anthony Kemp-Welch, an original copy of the Khrushchev Report was given to Bierut at the twentieth Congress and transported to Warsaw by returning delegation members. Bierut's copy was made available to select readers at the top of the Central Committee; Schaff certainly would have had access to it. Bauman probably did not get hold of it immediately – perhaps, given his fluent Russian, he might have, had he finagled his way into Schaff's deepest confidence on a Party career path in the previous year. But he had not, and was not in the inner circle of the regime.

Bauman probably read a Polish version that came to be available very quickly. Designated 'exclusively for intra-Party use' and planned as a restricted edition of 3,000, 15,000 copies of the Polish text were immediately printed, and it was through Poland that it was distributed around the world. Stefan Staszewski, the Warsaw Party secretary, gave copies to correspondents from *Le Monde*, the *Herald Tribune* and the *New York Times*. Like any rare good with a skyrocketing demand, the speech appeared on the black market at a high price – 500 złotys,[103] 40 per cent of Bauman's monthly university salary. However, Bauman, like other well-advanced Party members at the university, obtained it for free. The objective of the relatively large distribution was to engage the Party in struggle over the document, since various members were claiming it was a fake and part of a counter-revolutionary plot (Kemp-Welch, 1996).

Werblan indicates that Khrushchev brought his speech to Warsaw when he arrived for the funeral, and that it was quickly translated and published in Polish.[104] It was titled: 'On the Cult of Personality and Its Consequences' ('O kulcie jednostki j jego następstwach'). Bauman would have obtained it in early March. Interestingly, when interviewed on the subject, he said, 'when I listened . . . ', suggesting he may have heard about it on the forbidden Radio Free Europe. Or he may simply have misspoken. In either case, what he learned was profoundly disturbing.

'The breakthrough for me, really, was 1956, and listening to

Khrushchev's paper', Bauman said in a 2013 interview with the
journalist Tomasz Kwaśniewski:

> Then the vivisection of my own guts began. I started scratching, ana-
> lysing, whether I really had helped start the construction of a new man
> or had participated in building a murderous system. . . . [T]he disap-
> pointment came from the fact that I learned about the things that were
> behind the curtain. I will not say that it was hidden, but covered up,
> because a lot of people knew what was going on.
> – That there were murders? [asked the journalist.]
> – That this was a murderous system. That hundreds of thousands, and
> even millions, had been destroyed in the course of the revolution.
> – So you knew?
> – I knew about the Moscow trials, but I did not realize that this plague
> in Ukraine was consciously organized.[105] I did not really believe in
> the crimes of the defendants in the Moscow trial, and especially
> when similar processes took place in Rumania, Czechoslovakia or
> Hungary. Because they were completely fantastical things. Putting
> Gomułka in a 'glass house' [w mamrze, slang for jail] was also
> suspect. What is really strange and what I cannot myself believe . . .
> is the fact that I knew least of all about what the secret police had
> done in Poland. But, in the Army, such practices were impossible.
> It was not a taboo to discuss such things – nobody had anything to
> talk about. It was unthinkable. Maybe because we were not part of
> such an environment. . . . Nobody around me was scared because
> their family member was missing.

It is important to remember that KBW units were autonomous
from the Ministry of Internal Security. The news about what had
gone on there came out after Światło's escape, which was followed
by the dissolution of Department X and then the whole ministry, in
1954. By then, Bauman had been out of the Army for over a year.
Like many Poles who believed in the new system, Bauman had difficulties accepting the contents of the Secret Speech: 'Even after
Khrushchev's talk, even though I knew that there were murderers
in the Kremlin, I did not know that they had also practised much
closer to home', he told Kwaśniewski.

'That a Party member – I was still a faithful Party member – could
admit that murders had been carried out. That was a great thing.
If it had come from the Voice of America,[106] I probably would not
have paid attention to it. I'm telling you honestly how it was',[107] he
said.

For others, the Krushchev speech was not a total revelation. 'For
me, it was the shedding of a dreaded burden', Wiatr recalled. He
had lived in Poland during the Occupation and read about Katyń
in underground newspapers.[108] His father-in-law had been a com-

munist activist in the prewar period and told him about Stalin's slaughter of the Party's Polish leadership. 'I did not have to wait for Khrushchev to tell me. Maybe I did not know the scale of it. To learn that the victims could be counted in the millions – that would have surprised me. Because I saw this top of the mountain – not what it was under water. But . . . Zygmunt was unaware and it was all new, and such a blow to his faith', Wiatr said. 'For Zygmunt, this communist ideology was . . . a new faith. This is perfectly understandable' given their different backgrounds, said Wiatr; 'We talked for a long time but there was a big difference between us: I was euphoric and Zygmunt was ruined. Well, maybe he was not broken, but he took it very hard. . . . but he quickly got to his feet' (my interview with Wiatr, 2017).

This excerpt illustrates the different reactions to the Khrushchev speech among the 'believers' and the 'political realists'. Active Party members were in both categories and both remained in the Party after the Khrushchev speech. In his interview with Kwaśniewski, Bauman said:

My first reaction was: damn, the villains got into the managerial positions, we must remove them and replace them with others. A normal human reaction. When October came and Gomułka spoke to the rally, there was national excitement that something new was beginning. There were queues lined up along the entire train path when Gomułka was going to Moscow to talk about mutual relations. I was convinced, like many, many others, that they would just put an end to the mistakes and distortions. That the murderers were removed, and normal, honest people would come in and everything would be OK. And then, Gomułka began to behave in such a way that it was no longer possible to doubt that he, too, was not going to stop the mistakes or distortions. . . . And that dragged out my process of leaving the Party. . . . I sat there and hoped that it would be possible to exert some influence. From outside the Party, I knew, it was impossible, because the Party is deaf to such a[n exterior] voice.

This period was intense, politically and intellectually, within the Party ranks and at the universities and in intellectual circles, where, after the end of 1955, critiques of the political situation intensified. In late 1955, a group of young intellectuals created the Crooked Circle Club,[109] which historian Krystyna Kersten describes as an enclave of the free-thinking. The group included philosophers, historians, sociologists and artists, and in 1956 they decided to open a section for studying public opinion. It was a discussion club – critical of the regime – in which many sociology students were engaged. They frequently invited the 'revisionists' to present their recent studies (see next chapter).

Radical voices were published in *Po Prostu*[110] – subtitled, at the time, *The Journal of the Students and Young Intelligentsia*. Bauman published there, as did other 'revisionists': Bronisław Baczko, Marek Fritzhand (chair of Bauman's department), Leszek Kołakowski and others (see in Rutkowski, 2016: 426). At the beginning of 1956, the whole university discussed the Five Year Plan, especially the part on higher education. On 22 April 1956, *Po Prostu* published a 'Letter to the Members of Parliament and Scholars' requesting fundamental changes in study programmes, loosening of formal disciplines and updates to required Marxist–Leninist teaching. Two days later, Professor Julian Hochfeld, speaking as a member of the Polish Parliament, issued a critique of higher education in Poland. Three days later, a new minister of higher education was appointed in a reshuffle. The government announced some reforms to improve the quality of teaching and working conditions of scholars at the university, with community elections of the rectors and deans.

A long story of the attribution of the doctorate

Amidst all this agitation, Bauman passed smoothly through his Ph.D. process. In Poland, the final stages of a Ph.D. consisted of a long trek composed of an opening defence (*otwarcie przewodu*), several exams and a public dissertation defence. Next, a special commission, named by the ministry, decided whether to confirm the candidate and grant him or her the title.[111] Bauman opened the process with a 15 March 1955 letter to the Department Council, accompanied by a Hochfeld document stating that his mentee's dissertation would be ready for consideration in mid-1956. Bauman's 'social activity, his work – teaching and research', Hochfeld wrote, 'are too well known in the department for me to be required to mention anything more here'.[112]

In November 1955, Bauman got foreign-language certificates in English and Russian, each with the highest possible grades. The following month, on the day before his twins were born, he passed an obligatory exam in dialectics and historical materialism. The head of the jury was Professor Jan Legowicz, and its members included Fritzhand and Hochfeld. Bauman was required to discuss two precise questions. The first concerned Engels and his statement: 'The more ruthlessly the science advances, the more it finds itself in harmony with the interests and aspirations of the worker' (Engels, 1888: 376). The second was: 'Contemporary difficulties in building the economy, politics and culture in the People's Republic of Poland in view of the basic controversies between Leninism and opportunism regarding the construction of socialism and the path towards socialism.'[113] Bauman scored the maximum on the first section, with a slightly lower mark on the second, possibly because his political interpretation of the current situation did not meet the expectations of the whole jury. The next stage of the process involved an examination in the history of philosophy on 8 May, with a jury composed of Tadeusz Kroński and Leszek Kołakowski. Bauman was asked about receptions of philosophy in the Middle Ages, and positivist sociology in the second half of the nineteenth century. He received a 'Very Good', the highest score.

The final test was the public defence of his doctoral thesis, 'The Political Doctrine of the British Labour Party' ('Doktryna polityczna brytyjskiej Partii Pracy').[114] The 500-page dissertation was a sociological analysis of the 'sources of opportunism inside the British workers' movement, the dissection of philosophical views of British socialism and discussion about the political views of the Labour Party' (Fritzhand – cited from the original manuscript 'Opinion' from the Ph.D. thesis process dossier).[115]

The reviewers for the 16 May defence were Adam Schaff and Karol Lapter. The latter had an interesting biography. A historian and a communist activist, Lapter put his university training on hold during World War II, during which he was a worker in the UK and wrote some articles for British communist journals. He probably met Hochfeld at this time, and both decided to return to Warsaw after the war. In 1956, Lapter was a scholar at the PZPR's Institute of Social Sciences; later, he was Chair in Contemporary History in the College of Social Science at the KC PZPR (Wyższa Szkoła Nauk Społecznych KC PZPR (Higher School of Social Sciences – Central Committee PZPR)) created by Schaff. Lapter was very positive about Bauman's work. In his 4½-page handwritten report, he judged Bauman's dissertation to be of much higher quality than Dvorkin's study devoted to the same topic (Dvorkin was a well-known Soviet author).

Schaff, the other reviewer, provided a 6-page opinion expressing doubt about whether the dissertation was really a piece of philosophy. However, he underlined the quality of Bauman's work in terms of originality, mastery of the literature, independent thinking and 'pushing the science ahead'. Bauman's public defence took place on 20 June at noon in the Philosophy Department lecture hall in Potocki Palace. The council voted unanimously (11–0) for attribution of the Ph.D. title to Bauman. The report was signed by, among others, Kotarbiński, Assorodobraj, Nowakowski, Legowicz, Schaff, Fritzhand, Hochfeld and Kołakowski.[116]

The Baumans organized a party to celebrate his achievement. But the general ambiance of the time was not propitious for celebration. Six days after Bauman's defence, on 28 June, the first postwar riots on Polish soil erupted in Poznań. Workers from the prestigious Cegielski factory (train production) took to the streets, and many

Poznań inhabitants joined them. The militia and Army troops were called in to stifle the protest, resulting in more than fifty deaths. It was a shocking event, and a feeling of insecurity dominated the country as negotiations for the new leadership pitted the Puławian revisionists against the Natolinian hardliners. Both sought to seduce the popular Gomułka. He and his small group curried favour with the Puławians, old communists who were not obviously closely connected to Moscow and wanted more individual freedom, less secret-police control, but no plurality of political parties. In 1956, the country was not in a position to consider a pluralist system.

Meanwhile, the final stage of Bauman's Ph.D. process – approval by the Ministry of Higher Education – dragged on for several months. His department dispatched a dossier containing all the documentation on 14 July. But the degree was not validated by the university commission until 24 June 1957,[117] in part due to a prolonged external evaluation by historian Bronisław Krauze. He was asked for his review in July, and again three months later, and again on 5 November,[118] and finally, on 21 November, Krauze signed his 5½-page review, which was generally positive. Fritzhand's final sign-off[119] confirmed the earlier opinions. Such delays in reviewing were frequent in Polish academia, but politics may have played a role as the ministry struggled to carry out its promised reforms. There wasn't much Bauman could do about it, but the lack of the qualification had a major impact on his salary, significant for a father of three. For Bauman, as a Ph.D. student, it was a long year of multiple exams. For Bauman the Party man, it was a year of shock and awakening. For Bauman as a citizen, it was a long year of struggle and hope.

October 1956 was a hot month as the universities began their academic year. The ambiance of revolution and change was perceptible. Bauman 'no longer spent much time at home: he became passionately involved in political struggle, which was growing daily more intense', wrote Janina (J. Bauman, 1988: 126). On 16 October, the Party met and, without seeking Moscow's permission, removed Marshall Konstantin Rokossovsky, a Soviet citizen, as defence minister. In response, Khrushchev flew to Warsaw three days later to reinstate Soviet control, but, against his wishes, Gomułka was elected Party leader on 21 October. Two divisions of the Soviet Army, with tanks, were sent towards Warsaw, and the Polish Army – including Bauman's unit, the KBW – was called up to take position for an eventual military conflict *against* the USSR. On 24 October, Gomułka gave a famous, defiant speech on the parade ground near the Palace of Science and Culture (Stalin's enormous 'present' to the Polish nation). 'Lost in the many hundreds and thousands, I shared the enthusiasm of the crowd', Janina recalled: 'Half of Warsaw's population seemed to have come out of their own free will to hail their returning leader, back after eight years of persecution and imprisonment, It seemed that – for once – the nation was united; communists, non-communists and anti-communists alike; workers, farmers, intellectuals and all' (J. Bauman, 1988: 127).

While support for Gomułka's leadership and opposition to the Soviets was clearly strong, the threat of a Soviet military intervention was palpable. Revisionist activists – Bauman among them – slept away from home to avoid possible sweeps.[120] In the end, in exchange for Poland's agreement to remain in the Soviet military alliance, Khrushchev accepted the choice of Gomułka and called back the Red Army.[121] Warsaw remained intact, unlike Hungary, where Soviet intervention triggered a massive combat. At the end of October 1956, Poland's future seemed brighter, including in academia. Newly elected rectors and deans took up their positions on 1 December; of eleven elected functionaries, only three were Party members (Rutkowski, 2016: 437).

It had been, despite its difficulties, a happy year for the Bauman family. On Sundays, the grandparents visited the flat in Bielany, bringing whatever they could get their hands on to support the young family. Towards the middle of the year, Towa, Zygmunt's older sister, was permitted to visit Poland for the first time in seventeen years – part of a thaw in the regime's attitude towards 'foreign' visitors. She spent three weeks in Warsaw that summer, a reunion that helped everyone put aside the unstable political situation and the difficulties of daily life, with their continued shortages, low-quality food and the housing pinch.

These moments of familial happiness ended in December, when Zygmunt's mother, Zofia, died after a protracted sickness. After her funeral, Maurycy immediately went to the Israeli Embassy and sought an emigration visa. He left Poland in February 1957, realizing his Zionist dream by joining his daughter Towa at Guivat-Brener, one of the large Israeli kibbutzes. Maurycy's departure was one of the first in the so-called 'Gomułka *Aliyah*' – the second wave of Jewish postwar emigration,[122] which saw 50,000 Jews leave Poland. Various elements fed into these events. A general loosening of state control included some opening of borders, and at the same time criticism of Stalinism quickly morphed, in some mouths, into expressions of anti-Semitism. The fact that some of the Stalinist leaders (a minority) had Jewish origins fed into the old stereotype about the bond between communism and Jews – the *Żydokomuna* (Cała, 2012: 482).

Janina's sister and brother-in-law, with their daughter, left in the same year for Israel. Yet Zygmunt and Janina, despite their close family ties, felt they were Poles and believed in their work in Poland. And they were successful. 'Having a chance to be in a good moment in a good place' is a saying popular among scientists engaged in prestigious careers. Zygmunt had obtained his Ph.D. at a moment when not only his team,[123] but the entire milieu of Polish sociology, was experiencing an effervescence.

The rehabilitation of sociology at Warsaw University

Sociology in Poland post-1956[124] benefitted from Gomułka's decision to allow relative freedom of ideas in academia.[125] The previously shuttered *Sociological Review* (*Przegląd Socjologiczny*) was reopened, and other journals, including *Culture and Society* (*Kultura i Społeczeństwo*) and Hochfeld's *Socio-Political Studies* (*Studia Polityczno-Socjologiczne*) were launched. Moreover, two new academic sociological institutions were created in the Polish Academy of Sciences: the Institute of Philosophy and Sociology, and the Section of Sociology and the History of Culture. Warsaw University rehired previously banned professors and offered them new positions. In 1957, five sociology chairs were created in the Department of Philosophy at the University of Warsaw: the returning Stanisław Ossowski took over the Chair of Sociology; Stefan Nowakowski, Sociography; Maria Ossowska, History and Morality; Nina Assorodobraj, Social Demography. Julian Hochfeld transformed his own Chair from Dialectical and Historical Materialism to Sociology of Political Relations.[126] Perhaps not surprisingly, not a single chair was directly connected to Marxist theory.

'The second half of the 1950s and the 1960s at the University of Warsaw', Bauman said in 2013:

> saw transformation on a global scale. Ours was the only university where you could learn about absolutely all sociological trends. They were presented in lectures, and this poor student was exposed to this internally contradictory sociological world, which was neither east nor west of Warsaw. The pertinent fact was a complete tolerance for everything. . . . Of course there were theories, one was called right, the other called wrong, but the rule was that we had to know everything. . . . In Warsaw, we learned about trends in Paris before the Parisians did, because the Parisians were divided into cliques. For Professor Stefan Żółkiewski, everything Parisian was great – when a book came out in France he immediately held a presentation in Warsaw to convey its content.[127]

This openness to the world was one of the most important elements of the Warsaw intellectual milieu – an opening not just to French sociology but also to American, German and, obviously, Soviet schools, in sociology but also other disciplines. Books were rare and sometimes nearly inaccessible, but if students and academics couldn't read the books, at least they read the reviews of the books. Bauman had privileged access to publications due to his various roles as a member of Hochfeld's department, a Ph.D. and PAN researcher, and as chief of the Section of Social Studies at the Party Higher School. The most secret library of 'Western' books was accessible to Bauman as a member of the Science Committee of the Central Committee of the PZPR. The Party and academic libraries enabled Bauman to learn the latest news from the intellectual world abroad. Some of these books and articles were rare, some forbidden – which, of course, greatly increased their attraction. Schaff is said to have had access to all the forbidden books in Poland – those he ordered to know what was being published, and those sent to Ossowski (and later Kołakowski) and confiscated by the censor. These books were sources of independent thinking and 'revisionist' ideas.

Publishing 'revisionist' articles

The new publications became less controlled and some journals were created – such as *Polish Science*, which contained articles devoted to sociological studies conducted in France, the USA and the UK (*Nauka Polska*, 1, 1956, pp. 130–7 and 138–43). The thaw also included Polish 'bourgeois' scholarship. In spring 1956, an ensemble of work by Stefan Czarnowski – a well-known prewar Polish sociologist – was published. Schaff noticed this as a signal of change, and, for the first time since World War II, a large Polish delegation attended the (3rd) Congress of the International Association of Sociology, in Amsterdam in August. In his speech there, Adam Schaff remarked that Polish sociology, though mainly Marxist, had not abandoned bourgeois scholarship.[128]

The chain of positive events was not uninterrupted, however. On 15 October, Schaff published a brochure retracting the revisionist attitude he had shown in Amsterdam, and demanded fidelity to orthodox Marxism: 'Does the creation of the section of sociology signify the revision of interwar sociology and the departure of the period of "coexistence" of sociology with Marxism?', he asked.[129] He raised questions about the aims of empirical sociological research, and the meaning of active Polish presence in the international sociology community (two Polish sociologists, Ossowski and Szczepański, had joined International Sociological Association (ISA) committees). Two days later, the government named Schaff as head of a new Institute of Philosophy and Sociology inside the Polish Academy of Sciences. Some of the seven sections of the institute were led by 'bourgeois' sociologists. Yet, at the same time, Schaff had come out with a conservative text maintaining that

Marxism was the only scientific approach, including in the social sciences.

Critical responses to Schaff came quickly – from Bauman and his colleagues. This was an act of courage, considering that Schaff was not only the leading social scientist in Poland, but Bauman's first mentor, a man upon whom his career to an extent depended. Bauman and his colleagues from Hochfeld's circle – Maria Hirszowicz, Włodzimierz Wesołowski and Jerzy Wiatr – published the first critical response to the brochure on 11 November in *The New Culture* (a non-academic journal).[130] Marxism must coexist, the authors maintained, with other sociological methods and theories indispensable to the empirical study of society. The tone of this criticism was strong: 'The [Schaff's] publication leaves a feeling of deep regret, disappointment and desolation. . . . Until we clearly say that during the Stalinist period we were practising not science, but an ideology whose main function was to suppress the social sciences – we will fail to arrive at a starting position for a reliable and not partial repair.'[131] Wiatr described this text as 'formally a polemic with Schaff's book, but in fact a programme for releasing sociology from these sociological bonds' (my interview with Wiatr, 2017).

Two weeks later, Bauman alone wrote another critical text with the strong title 'Against the Monopolist Approach in the Sciences'. It clearly showed Bauman's opposition to Schaff and orthodox Marxist positions.

'Let all flowers bloom', wrote Bauman:

the optimal conditions for the development of scientific philosophy and sociology can only arise when in the centers educating philosophers and sociologists and at universities there are various kinds of philosophy and various types of sociology representing various scientific schools. . . . Let scientific disputes be settled by scientific methods. Let administrative privileges disappear in science. We want the philosophy of the Communist movement to become a scientific philosophy. Liberate her from her own, extra-scientific privileges, which are actually millstones tied to her feet.[132]

With the publication of this position, Bauman firmly pitched his tent as a revisionist,[133] a position he would never again abandon. He observed and analysed, using sociological tools elaborated not exclusively by Soviet intellectuals. In the following years, he would become one of the Polish intellectuals who introduced Western works into Eastern European sociology. This was his 'speciality' and, in the eyes of the secret services that constantly evaluated and criticized his work, his 'main default' (see next chapter).

While Kołakowski is the best-known revisionist writer of mid-twentieth-century Poland, Bauman's contributions to this literature are under-acknowledged.[134] In January 1957, Wiatr and Bauman published an article in *Myśl Filozoficzna* on the spirit of October 1956, titled 'Marxism and Contemporary Sociology'. The authors invited their readers to examine non-Marxist approaches in sociology, stating that discussion and controversy were essential to academic activity and could not be approached only as political struggles (Łabędź, 1959). This paper had an important impact in the sociological milieu of Eastern Europe. The Soviet journal *Philosophical Questions* (*Voprosy Filosofii*) harshly condemned the authors for their revisionist attitude. The official Bulgarian party journal, *New Times* (*Nowe Wreme*), also criticized Bauman and Wiatr. Wiatr defended their argument as 'a programme for the release of sociology not from Marxism but from dogmatism', as he said in 2013. It was an argument that Hochfeld called 'Open Marxism. A Bulgarian sociologist in *Nowe Wreme* wrote a review in which he used the term "Wiatrists and Baumanists". We signed it Wiatr/Bauman because Zygmunt insisted that if we respected only alphabetical order, I would always be behind him', Wiatr joked. The Bulgarian sociologist included Kołakowski in the Wiatrist/ Baumanist camp, although he already had a more prominent position in revisionist circles (my interview with Wiatr, 2017). Shortly after Wiatr published the paper with Bauman, he changed his mind and joined the anti-revisionist camp. But the 1957 paper remained a revisionist manifesto on a par with texts by Kołakowski, Lukacs, Djilas and Lefebvre (Łabędź, 1959).

Bauman wrote other papers that could only have been published in this short period of 'freedom', including: '"On the need for party sociology" [O potrzebie socjologii partii] printed in "Philosophical Studies" and "Treatise on Bureaucracy" and "Thoughts beyond time" printed in a brochure entitled "Creativity", "On intra-party democracy", publications in "Simply" – all of this was published in the form of less or more truncated by censorship, and a few months after publication, considered again completely uncensored' (Bauman, 1986/7: 21).

Bauman published these articles at a time when most intellectuals continued to censor themselves out of a well-seasoned sense of caution. But Bauman had decided to ignore the advice of Edward Lipiński: 'First of all, do not think', Bauman quotes his friend as saying; 'If you cannot stop thinking,[135] then don't talk! And if you can't stop talking, don't write. If you cannot stop writing, never, ever publish! Under any circumstances.' Lipiński, a great scholar and a supreme tongue-biter, did not publish a single word in Stalinist times.[136]

Still, the freedom to do empirical research progressed significantly after October 1956. Previously, socialist planning had no need to check reality, under the logic that the Party knew everything and planned everything, and society just followed the plan (for five or six years). With the thaw, a critical approach became possible. In addition, scholars were no longer restricted to reading and writing about Western sociological literature – now, for the first time, they could go to the source, including by attending conferences and even obtaining fellowships abroad, in the USA, France, the UK and Canada, with support from organizations like the Ford Foundation and the British Council. Bauman, with his fresh Ph.D. thesis on the British Labour Party and his excellent CV, won a scholarship at the prestigious London School of Economics (LSE) for a year, opening a window to a new phase of his life.

9

Years of Hope

1957–1967

Opening doors to the West

Bauman was fortunate to graduate in 1956, a year that witnessed a spectacular increase in the ability of Polish scholars to travel abroad. Polish Academy of Sciences, records show 39 visits outside the country by its members in 1955, a number that increased to 349 in 1956, and 549 in 1959 (Pleskot, 2010: 293). From 1956 to 1967, Bauman frequently made scholarly visits of varying length. In 1956, he travelled to Moscow for a few days to observe the Soviet higher education system. He then left for a post-doctoral scholarship ('post-doc')[1] for nearly a year, and over the following decade frequently travelled abroad for invited lectures, conferences and congresses, with longer stays as a visiting professor. He became a scholar with international mobility.

The 'democratization' process of 1957 opened the door for foreign foundations to finance scholarly and artistic activity. The foundations responded enthusiastically, as reflected in the report of the Ford Foundation from 1957:[2]

> [A]nother event in Europe bearing on the aims of the Foundation's program – particularly that of furthering democratic relations between East Europe and the West – was the change in Poland that opened new opportunities to strengthen free contact. The Foundation appropriated $500,000 for an exchange of professors, students, and professional specialists between Poland and the United States and Western Europe.

Bauman's 1957 'post-doc' contract in the UK was one of the first awarded by the Ford Foundation in Poland after the war, and one of only three it awarded in sociology that year.[3]

It was no simple thing for a scholar to travel abroad from Poland, even in this period of looser restrictions. The authorities set up complicated, time-consuming hurdles to exercise control on prospective travellers (Pleskot, 2010). Preparation for such travels involved a multiple-stage trek through various institutions, starting with the scholar's university or research institute, with stops in the ministries of education and foreign affairs and the passport bureau of the Internal Affairs Ministry. The bureaucratic steeplechase involved the collection of scholarly papers (certificates, invitations, language-skill confirmations, letters of recommendation), letters of engagement from the university and financing institution, and a permit to leave with a certificate indicating that one's teaching load would be picked up in one's absence. Male scholars had to procure a military certificate of completed service (in Poland, males were enlisted in the military for two years, except graduates who were enlisted for two to six months). Finally, Party approval was required prior to departure. It was also necessary to obtain a certificate attesting to one's political reliability, written by superiors. The first stage in this long process of document collection was the letter of invitation and promise from the hosting institution. When, at the level of the university, all those documents were accepted, the entire folder was sent to the Ministry of Higher Education for acceptance. Clearance by Party committees at the university and central level was required; the Party's Committee for Science maintained a list of people authorized for professional travel. Once this thick folder was assembled, it was sent to the Ministry of Internal Affairs' First Department (intelligence) for approval. In those years, the passport was a precious document, and one that Polish citizens did not keep at home. Scientists could travel with one of two categories of passport: professional (*służbowy* – which belonged to the academic institution) or private passports, used for tourism and sometimes for shorter academic stays – the procedure to get these was much simpler. Passports were deposited in specific offices and only released to the individual when justified by an invitation to travel or work abroad. Upon return to Poland, the passport was returned to the appropriate authority. Interior officials took advantage of contacts with the scholar on departure and return to seek a pledge of co-operation with the intelligence services (Pleskot, 2010). They asked scholars to take notes during their stay abroad and to prepare and submit a final report once home.[4] At each level of this bureaucratic journey, the candidate was checked and re-checked. The process usually took months, and many people missed their conferences or other invitations due to the lengthy procedure. It was almost impossible to meet all the requirements of the university and authorities, historian Patryk Pleskot recalled, and it was not unusual for scholars to cut corners.

Of the three sociologists who won Ford Foundation scholarships in 1957, Bauman went to the UK, Witold Zakrzewski and Stefan Nowakowski to the United States (Kilias, 2017: 82–3). Zakrzewski and Nowakowski were older than Bauman, and both had been habilitated. Interestingly, all three of the awardees had connections to Hochfeld. Zakrzewski had reviewed the Ph.D. dissertation of Hirszowicz (who was mentored by Hochfeld), and Nowakowski belonged to Hochfeld's department. Those relationships indicate Hochfeld's powerful position in the sociological milieu at that moment. He was leading the way towards an acceptance of American 'bourgeois' sociology within Polish scholarship through his positive review of American methodology, as it was presented in Lazarsfeld's book *The Language of Social Research* (see Sułek, 2011: 124). The administration probably viewed him as a progressive, but trusted, Marxist – an embodiment of the October 1956 changes in sociology. It is not surprising that Bauman was among the pioneer candidates, considering the international stature of his mentor. Hochfeld had contacts with many scholars abroad, especially in London where he had been active during World War II, and in Paris, where he studied in the late 1930s. Hochfeld had had an international career and his disciples moved in a similar direction. Bauman's field was the Labour Party and he spoke English,[5] so his choice of the UK was not difficult.

As Poland opened its scholarship to Western influences, it also invited in some Western visiting scholars. In 1957, as the newly appointed director of the Polish Institute for Foreign Affairs, Hochfeld hosted several foreign scholars. One of the first was C. Wright Mills (Columbia University), a section (ninety pages) of whose book *The Power Elite* Hochfeld arranged to have published through the institute (Wincławski, 2006: 228). This publication made Mills' work accessible to a Polish audience and was the starting point of intellectual collaboration. Hochfeld also wrote prefaces to Mills' books when they were translated into Polish, although unfortunately they were not published, because Hochfeld was censored after 1957.

Mills and Hochfeld developed a strong friendship based on shared political attitudes (as critical and engaged socialists) but also on their 'outsider' situation within their respective academic milieus (Wiatr, in Hochfeld, 1982: 391). Bauman probably attended Mills' July 1957 lectures in Warsaw, and later they maintained a correspondence suggestive of an intense intellectual exchange and, despite rare face-to-face meetings, a friendship.[6] Ralph Miliband of the LSE came to Warsaw with Mills, and later became a close friend of Bauman (Kilias 2017: 56).

These visitors from the West – socialists, sociologists and engaged scholars – were curious about the state's implementation of socialist ideas, and without exaggeration we can say that this visit and their contact with Polish intellectuals were inspiring for their political activity. Mills and Miliband were key members of the nascent 'New Left'

in their respective countries. The movement was rooted in disappointment with Soviet communism following Khrushchev's Secret Speech
and the crushing of the Hungarian Revolution.[7] The old Western
Left had split between those who continued to support Moscow and
others who hoped to create a new Left that was free of bureaucratic
and authoritarian traps. The close friendship between Miliband and
Mills started around this time, and the Polish visit was very important to them, as Miliband mentioned in his obituary of Mills (1962).
'Adam Schaff', wrote Miliband, 'as the philosopher of official Poland,
and Leszek Kołakowski, as the most acute of the young Polish "revisionists", showed us two parts of an equation to which neither had
the complete answer, nor could have.'[8] In Miliband's continuum of
Polish intellectual Marxism – bound by the charismatic revisionist
Kołakowski at one extreme and by Schaff, whose Soviet *apparatchik*
style corresponded with the exotic image of the Eastern communist, at
the other – Hochfeld was somewhere in the middle.

Mills and Miliband, who were deep in the construction of the
New Left movement, wanted to learn from the mistakes of Poland
as a socialist state project in action. Certainly, scholars from the two
sides would have discussed 'Open Marxism' with Hochfeld and the
members of his circle. Kazimierz Kelles-Krause, the Polish socialist and philosopher, had created the term 'Open Marxism' and,
after World War II, Hochfeld had popularized it. This school of
thought proposed an unorthodox, non-Stalinist type of Marxism;
its 'openness' consisted of the implementation of an anti-positivist
(dialectical) method, and inclusion of praxis and history within the
original Marxist concepts. In Poland, this non-deterministic current
was called 'Marxism with a human face' or 'humanistic Marxism'.
The New Left fathers visiting Poland were very interested in this
vision of Marxism. They must also have spoken about the October
1956 thaw and the changes that followed, and others which were
expected (or hoped for). Members of Hochfeld's circle, such as Mills
and Miliband, were critical of Polish socialism and passionate about
improving their world. While belonging to two different worlds, the
participants in these intellectual exchanges had much in common as
engaged intellectuals.

Charles Wright Mills was a colourful figure,[9] an unconventional
critic and analyst of capitalism without belonging to any Marxist
church. A radical who supported socialist ideas, he practised public
sociology and was present in the media, seeking through his scholarly work and intellectual engagement to improve the existing
system. His dream was to make society better. A year before visiting
Poland, Mills was promoted to full professor, then spent the following year on sabbatical in Denmark on a Fulbright scholarship,
which enabled him to travel around Europe. A talk in April 1957
introduced him to Miliband, a member of the LSE student union.

Miliband was a year older than Bauman, born in 1924, and they shared certain biographical elements. '[H]e belonged to a generation of socialists formed by the Russian revolution and the second world war, a generation that dominated leftwing politics for almost a century',[10] Tariq Ali wrote of Miliband in 2015. Like Bauman, Miliband was for the first part of his life a Polish citizen. He was born in Brussels to Polish-Jewish parents who had emigrated to Belgium.[11] His father was a BUND[12] member, so socialist ideas were in his family background. His home language was Yiddish, and like Bauman he joined Hashomer Hatzair a year before World War II. Miliband escaped Nazi occupation with his father by emigrating to the UK. While studying there, he suffered from anti-Semitism, but was enrolled in the LSE, where he worked closely with his mentor, the historian and socialist Harold Laski (educated partially in Vienna and Berlin). Like Bauman, Miliband served during World War II in the Army, fighting Nazis as a chief petty officer in the Belgian section of the Royal Navy, working in intelligence and supporting the Allied landings at Normandy and Toulon. In 1946, Miliband returned to the university, and a year later enrolled in a doctorate programme, writing a thesis about the French Revolution. In parallel with his research, he lectured in Roosevelt College in Chicago, then at the LSE, completing his degree the same year Bauman did – in 1956. All those common points set the stage for the long-lasting friendship they developed years later, when Bauman joined the faculty at Leeds.

Bauman's research topic for his fellowship, the British Labour Party, made the LSE an excellent host, and the mentor who agreed to supervise Bauman, Robert Trelford McKenzie, was the leading subject expert. The Canadian McKenzie, born in 1917, in 1955 had published *British Political Parties: The Distribution of Power Within the Conservative and Labour Parties.*

The prospect of spending a year abroad was complicated by Bauman's family situation; the twins were only a year and a half old. But Bauman and his wife recognized the fellowship as a rare opportunity. '[T]o say no would be sheer madness', Janina recalled:

> But to accept seemed sheer madness too: it meant a year away from home. Neither he nor I could imagine how we could survive for such a long time without each other and how I could possibly cope on my own with what was already a heavy burden for both of us. There was little time for debate. Within a week the decision was made: [Zygmunt] would go to London. (J. Bauman, 1988: 131–2)

And so began the bureaucratic obstacle course, but he managed it with no major hold-ups. Bauman was still an active Army reserve member, and his service in Polish intelligence would have created concerns about him being posted abroad for a long period of exposure to Western services. He was undoubtedly instructed on how to behave and, presumably, to collect information while overseas. The regime was most interested in spying on its own citizens living abroad, as Igor Czernecki noted in his paper about Polish Ford Foundation award recipients (Czernecki, 2013: 298). After World War II, London was the centre of political opposition to the Polish communist regime, continuing to host a Polish government-in-exile. Yet, while Bauman was in an ideal situation for creating contacts with the Polish diaspora in the UK, I found no evidence that he reported anything to the intelligence services from his London stay. In Janina's writing, Bauman's time in London is portrayed as a solitary period of intense scholarly activity.

Visiting scholar at the London School of Economics

Bauman departed for London in October 1957. Janina's mother, who was preparing to join her daughter Zofia in Israel, postponed her departure and moved into the Baumans' small apartment to help Janina. The Baumans recalled enduring their separation for a year,[13] but Ford Foundation documents describe it as lasting nine months (Kilias, 2016: 83). Bauman's stipend, managed by the British Council,[14] was a frugal one – amounting to about £30 a month, he recalled later.[15] 'I had to save a lot', said Bauman; 'Of course, the pound was worth more than today, but it was difficult to live on that sum.'[16] The life of a post-doc on a scholarship contract is rarely easy. The lack of money, loneliness and pressure of expectations from advisers, colleagues and, foremost, from himself – the wealth of the opportunities to learn and improve, complete and enrich one's knowledge – would have made this a unique experience.[17]

Bauman's first reaction upon arriving in London was disappointment with his level of mastery of the native language. 'His English, which had been thought good in Poland, in London caused him no end of trouble', Janina reported (J. Bauman, 1988: 132). This was a common enough complaint and one that in all cases requires a period of adaptation. Separation from his family, and the tough living conditions, were less easy. 'The first few letters from . . . [Zygmunt] were sombre', wrote Janina: 'He was terribly lonely. He found a place to live – a basement room, cold, dark and damp. It cost £11 per month out of his £38.50 allowance. He lived on cheese and rough dumplings that he cooked for himself, trying to save money' (J. Bauman, 1988: 132).

'I was as poor as a church mouse', Bauman told Kwaśniewski in 2010 in *Gazeta Wyborcza*. He couldn't afford normal bacon, but discovered that British butchers used scraps of bacon as dog food, and was able to buy them for a quarter of the price; 'It was the same bacon as any other, it tasted the same, just as nutritious, so I lived for ten months buying that. And ate it with pasta.'[18] In such a situation, the work provides the energy that drives young scholars. They feel lucky to be part of a prestigious university; Bauman spent most of that year at the library.

The LSE library bore no resemblance to any library in Warsaw, where World War II had caused enormous damage and the poor economic situation after 1945 did not allow for the recovery of lost books. Due to the political situation, an enormous volume of works judged 'bourgeois' or counterrevolutionary were absent there. The LSE's library was enormous, and its archives contained volumes on the history of the labour movement. Equally as important and irreplaceable as the books, however, were the professors and colleagues who, via 'scientific talks', helped to direct his work. Bauman started his friendship with Ralph Miliband, and followed the lectures of Oakeshotte, Glass, Titmuss and Ginsberg (Tester, 2001), making incredible progress. Bauman was truly 'in the right place at the right time'.

His life was compatible with the contemporary saying, popular among post-docs: 'eat/sleep/post-doc'. All of his time was focused on work, with no children to care for, no meals to prepare, and no cleaning, no teaching hours, preparation of lectures or corrections of exams, no Party meetings or administrative work. Bauman always got by on little sleep, and in his London year he was able to devote eighteen hours a day to research. His class schedule was light. According to a 14 July 1958 LSE graduate school document, Bauman studied Social Class, Social Movements and the Social Elite, and 'attempted a sociological analysis of the history of the British labour movement'.[19] Such an academic schedule would be the dream of any scholar engaged in a big research project, where working conditions constitute an important factor of success.[20] So it is no surprise that he reported back that his research was 'going fast and extremely well' (J. Bauman, 1988: 132).[21]

After a month, Bauman was able to obtain a cheaper, nicer room, renting an attic from a worker's family. '[B]right, flowery wallpaper; a sloping ceiling hanging low over an antique bed', as Janina described it; 'A tiny window overlooking a little back garden; two well-worn armchairs facing a gas heater framed by a wooden mantelpiece ... The only snag is it's freezing cold unless we turn on the heater' (J. Bauman, 1988: 135–6). At the end of November, Bauman wrote that he had saved enough money to pay for her to visit. Her arrival in March provided the opportunity for a romantic replacement for the honeymoon that was broken up by Zygmunt's military obligations eleven years earlier. Janina was very happy but a little shocked by his appearance when they met: 'He was dressed in a new plastic anorak and held a bunch of tulips. I burst into tears, he looked so thin and frail: he had been starving himself all that time to pay for my trip' (J. Bauman, 1988: 135). Over half of a century later, Bauman recalled this visit:

> So Jasia [the diminutive of Janina] got off at Liverpool [Street] Station and after the grey Warsaw of those days, she was bewildered by the world's colour. She had to buy stockings, but it turned out she was completely incapable of that. In Warsaw, when she was looking for stockings, she asked: do you have this size? If they did, she'd ask for two pair. She didn't think about color, or patterns. Yet here there was a vast counter, with dozens or even hundreds of varieties of stockings. How to choose?[22]

So it was for visitors arriving for the first time in the West from 'behind the Iron Curtain': 'Everything around seemed bustling, colourful and abundant' (J. Bauman, 1988: 135).

The couple filled their time with activities: visiting museums, watching movies and concerts, visiting pubs and clubs, travelling around London on the bus, by foot or tube (Janina compared the London Underground to 'Orpheus in hell': J. Bauman, 2011: 111). They also attended an all-night party at the house of an LSE colleague. All these experiences were entirely different from the life they knew in Warsaw. Evidently, the month passed very fast. As Janina returned home in mid-April, she wrote that she could have brought back to Poland not only Zygmunt but 'a few other things: a washing machine, a self-service shop, the National Gallery, freedom of speech, trust . . . yes, trust – in this country they don't see you as a thief or a crook unless you behave as one. It will be hard without this back home' (J. Bauman, 1988: 140–1).

This was a very succinct description of the missing elements of Polish life: freedom of speech, and trust. The next ten years of Polish life for the Baumans played out along this double axis of mistrust and censorship. Their lives were in constant flux over what it was possible to say or publish without dire consequences. And there was permanent questioning: who could you trust?

Habilitation and docent

Bauman left London in the summer of 1958 after completing his scholarship. McKenzie, his mentor, wrote in his letter to the British Council that working with Bauman had been 'one of the most rewarding academic experiences . . . despite his rigid Marxist background'.[23] While London scholars saw him as a rigid Marxist, in Poland Bauman was already perceived as a member of the 'revisionists club'. After his November 1956 publication criticizing Schaff's vision of the Marxist intellectual, no one doubted that Bauman was much more flexible and open to other sociological currents and approaches than most of his colleagues. Bauman's work in England would become the basis for his habilitation, which came only three years after he received a Ph.D. – an exceptionally rapid ascent through academia, especially if we consider Bauman's other activities as a scholar, teacher and journal editor.

Under Polish law, habilitation involved several stages of verification of the scholar's capacity as an independent scholar – that is, as an academic capable of carrying out original research while mentoring Ph.D.s. In humanities and the social sciences, a published book[24] constituted the basis for examination of the candidate's achievement. There are some similarities with the Ph.D. defence as carried out in much of Western Europe, the United Kingdom and the United States, such as a Department Council's selection of a jury for the defence and other administrative procedures. A habilitation exam in the 1960s consisted of three parts: defence of the book's content, a public lecture, and questions following the lecture. After the vote of the Department Council, the final decision was handled by a council working for the Ministry of Higher Education (a Polish particularity). This long procedure was the topic of much complaint in the academic community,[25] and the rules changed quite often. When Bauman was close to taking his habilitation exam, he was forced to take a break while new regulations were launched. On 15 March 1959, Hochfeld announced in a letter his intention to start Bauman's habilitation process.[26] Playing a double role as Bauman's mentor and department chair (*katedra*), Hochfeld noted that his protégé had finished his book on the Labour Party less than a year after returning from London. In another document, he urged that Bauman be named a 'docent' with 'the position of docent' in the 1959–60 academic year. The title of docent was not the same as assuming the position, though both required habilitation.

Klasa-ruch-elita was published in 1960 by PWN (Polskie Wydawnictwo Naukowe (Polish Scholarly Editions)). The Department Council chose three rapporteurs to evaluate the work's scientific merit: Hochfeld and Edward Lipiński of Warsaw University, and Konstanty Grzybowski from the Jagiellonian University. On 31 May 1960, twenty-three members of the council heard the opinions of the rapporteurs. Despite a few criticisms, all three judged the work to be creative, methodologically sound, scientifically significant, and based on a large quantity of documentation. Nineteen of the Council members voted, and all accepted the book as worthy of habilitation, enabling Bauman to pass to his next stage. Moreover, eighteen of the nineteen voters waived the need for the traditional lecture. In its report to the minister of higher education, the Council noted that Bauman had published forty-seven titles:

ten dissertations, twenty-one reviews and sixteen important articles and brochures. That was an impressive tally, especially within the brief period it covered. The group concluded, 'the candidate has the entire right to acquire the level of docent'.[27]

The next step in this procedure was the minister's sign-off, which Bauman got in August, and the Superior Council (Rada Główna Szkolnictwa Wyższego) also confirmed the Council's decision. Professor Jan Szczepański, one of Bauman's reviewers, who was on leave abroad, sent a letter to ministry authorities confirming that Bauman was certainly an independent and mature 'scientific employee' ('pracownik naukowy').[28]

Four days before his thirty-fifth birthday, on 15 November 1960, Bauman obtained confirmation of his scientific title, and a ministry document signed nine days later put a positive seal on this lengthy procedure. But it wasn't quite over. To actually become a docent, Bauman had a few more hoops to jump through, including presenting a list of his publications,[29] which showed the remarkable tempo of his intellectual activity. In 1960 alone, in addition to his book, Bauman published three articles in *Philosophical Studies* (*Studia Filozoficzne*): 'Worker: A History of the Stereotype', 'Valuation in the Social Sciences' and 'Sociological Imagination and Sociological Reality' (a positive review of Mills' *The Sociological Imagination*).[30] His non-academic titles included a short book, *Careers: Four Sociological Sketches*;[31] a paper, 'Science and Ideology'; '10 Sketches about Everyday Sociology'; and twelve entries for the *Popular Dictionary*. The list includes thirty-three book reviews and a list of the courses he had taught, on dialectical and historical materialism (1953–5), Marxist philosophy (1956–7) and sociology of political parties (1959–60), as well as lectures on sociological methodology, the sociology of political relations, and sociology of the workers' movement.[32] On 25 February 1961, Bauman was appointed Chair of Sociology and Political Relations in Hochfeld's department.

Becoming an 'extraordinary professor'

The next step in a Polish academic career in the 1960s was to obtain two more scientific degrees: an 'extraordinary professorship' and an 'ordinary professorship'. Access to these levels required great scientific achievements, but Bauman had an impressive record; he performed the work of three academics simultaneously. To be sure, he did this while working in three different institutions. The University of Warsaw gave him the strong institutional basis; it was the leading university in Poland in many areas, with a strong Philosophy Department whose famed history (the Lwów–Warsaw school) made it the perfect environment for didactics and research activity. Bauman was also editor of the sociological journal (*Studia Socjologiczne* (Sociological Studies)) and a member of the research unit at the Polish Academy of Science. His third institution was the Higher School for Social Research, a Party institution. Though politicized, the position gave him insight into some of the research projects conducted within the Party, and provided a convenient framework for mentoring Ph.D. students. Bauman managed to juggle these three jobs, demonstrating remarkable skill in time management and work discipline.

In 1958, after he returned from London, the Party school appointed Bauman director of its social research section. Bauman wrote in a CV[33] that he conducted studies on various problems of Party life at the school. He clearly hoped the position would enable him to do research investigating PZPR elites and Party youth. But Party leaders did not tolerate this Hochfeldian emphasis on empirical studies for long. Under socialism, social processes were planned and pre-organized. There was no need to study the social engine because it was built with a Marxist blueprint. While the thaw of 1956 had awakened hope of a changing approach to scholarship, in time this was shown to be ephemeral. At the Third Party Congress in March 1959, leader Władysław Gomułka, celebrated as a symbol of change three years earlier, declared that the triumph of Marxism–Leninism was the objective of cultural policies. Lectures in philosophy, sociology and economy for all students should be conducted only in the spirit of Marxism. The message was clear: no bourgeois sociology, no empirical research, no critical analysis. Despite the speech, however, there was disagreement in the Party ranks on the development of the social sciences, and Bauman was among those who tried to keep alive the direction of 1956, through his writing and Party engagement.

'Bauman was one of our leading sociologists', Andrzej Werblan said in our interview, and by 'our' he was referring to the Party, where Werblan led the Science Section in the Central Committee and regularly met Bauman, who led a group of sociologists advising the Central Committee after 1960. Having a strong expert's position in the Party gave Bauman the hope, or illusion, of helping to repair the system. Like Hochfeld, he tried to make Polish socialism more 'human' and open to other currents of thought. As a trusted Party intellectual, he also enjoyed privileges, including access to 'forbidden bourgeois books' and the ability to travel abroad.

In late 1958, however, it became clear the Party would not allow him to publish his sociological studies of the Party, whose principal finding was that people joined it mainly for opportunistic reasons. Marxist ideology, he found, was the superficial cover for practical goals such as improved access to leadership positions, better

salaries and other material benefits. After struggling unsuccessfully
to publish his results, Bauman left the Party school in 1964.[34]

Teaching and mentoring students

Bauman's activities as a teacher and mentor are largely opaque
today. He taught in Warsaw more than fifty years ago, and, after
he was driven out, in the manner of socialist states, his name was
deleted from the record and people stopped talking about him.
While the institutional memory of Bauman is modest,[35] some of
his students provide testimony. Barbara Toruńczyk, a well-known
opposition activist, historian of literature and creator of *Literary
Notebooks* (*Zeszyty Literackie*), recalled: 'Bauman was a great, brilliant lecturer. He would sit at the podium in Ossowski Hall, dressed
in black, elegant and slim, seeming a little demoniacal against the
background of scarlet velvet curtains, which were always closed. He
had nice gestures – full of life and elegant at the same time.'[36]

Another student asserted that Bauman spoke so fast, and used
such difficult expressions, that his pupils were unable to follow him.
After a couple of minutes of rapid speech, with growing panic in
the classroom, Bauman would stop and ask if they understood. A
few courageous students would venture 'not a lot', at which point
he would laugh and begin again in a clear, accessible way. The
sociological language Bauman used was difficult to follow. One
student told his handler in the secret services that Bauman: 'has
important knowledge and is familiar with world literature, which
perhaps is why he gives very incomprehensible lectures (complicated terminology, tendency to theorize everywhere and at each
occasion) which makes students complain' (report 13 May 1964,
by 'Henryk').[37]

The eminent Princeton University historian Jan Tomasz Gross[38]
had less favourable recollections: 'I had one exam with Bauman
and I got a "three plus".[39] . . . At that time Bauman was a Marxist
sociologist – very Marxist-Theory-of-Society oriented, mortal
boredom and it was necessary to pass his exam.' Perhaps it was a
matter of the subject being taught, but there are other, more positive opinions. Several reports by the secret police[40] indicate that,
as a teacher, Bauman was 'in fashion' in the mid-1960s – not only
very popular among sociology and philosophy students, but also
drawing students from other faculties. One of those non-sociology
students was Irena Gruzinska-Gross, a historian of literature at
Columbia University, who, before being expelled from Poland in
1968 (in the ethnic purge that also drove out Bauman), was studying French philology. But that field had lost its fascination for her,
and she sometimes attended lectures by Kołakowski or Bauman. Of

the two, Kołakowski was the more charismatic lecturer, she said: 'people massively attended Kołakowski's lectures; Bauman was popular but not to the same extent'.

In addition to lecturing, Bauman mentored many young students, according to colleagues Barbara and Jerzy Szacki. They remember him as frequently surrounded by master's and Ph.D. students who wished to be part of his circle. On 30 June 1965, the list of Ph.D. candidates under his supervision at the University of Warsaw and the Higher School for Social Research[41] included twelve students, eight of whom defended their theses, while three were in process and one had finished his reviews. This is an impressive roster, since Bauman was only permitted to supervise Ph.D.s after getting his habilitation (in 1960). The topics of these theses are also impressive in their range and diversity, from studies of peasant activities, interest groups, governance and public opinion, to broader phenomena such as the ideology of free time, the social aspects of industrialization, German fascism, the Marxist theory of alienation and American contemporary sociology.[42] The last topic was presented by Aleksandra Jasińska-Kania, a colleague and friend from Hochfeld's circle. The document listing Bauman's students[43] includes pencilled-in notes on the status of those who graduated. Most of the eight held positions at universities.

Empirical research and publications

Empirical studies in the social sciences were not conducted by most Eastern European academics outside Poland, and Hochfeld's circle was one of the few spaces where empirical study could be carried out without strictures. Bauman's research was focused on the ideal of a successful life among Polish youth, as well as the 'evolution of career types'. On 30 June 1965, Bauman wrote out a scientific resumé in preparation for his promotion to extraordinary professor:

> Between 1959 and 1963, I conducted studies on the sociological determinants of social knowledge and the structure of sociological theories, which resulted in the academic manual 'Outline of Sociology'. It was later enlarged and published under the title: 'Outline of the Marxist Theory of Society'. Another result of my studies was a collection of dissertations, from the field of meta-sociology, published under the title 'The Visions of the Human World'. Since 1963 I have focused on the theory and sociology of culture. The first result of this new direction will be the book under preparation for printing, 'Culture and Society', which includes theoretical introductions, studies on the debut of differentiation of social structures and studies on the sociological problems of passage into industrial civilization.[44]

Bauman mentioned only his major completed works in this document, but many other projects drew his attention, notes former colleague Jerzy Szacki: 'Zygmunt was attracted to novelty, you could say he threw himself into every new thing . . . whatever was coming into fashion . . . Lange[45] wrote a treatise on cybernetics[46] – Bauman wrote on cybernetics. Then French structuralism – Levi-Strauss wrote a book, then, after two years, Bauman wrote a structuralist book. And post-modernism, of course. That was what he was looking for.'[47]

Before he delved into post-modernism, Bauman's primary interests were: (1) the sociology of political relations; (2) methodological issues and the sociology of sociology; (3) the sociology of culture.[48] This list appears in a February 1966 document forwarding Bauman's request to be promoted to extraordinary professor at Warsaw University. Signed by rector Stanisław Turski,[49] the paper states that, since 1961, Bauman had published thirty-two works, consisting of sixteen book reviews and sixteen longer articles or books. They included the monographs *Questions of Modern American Sociology* (1961), *The Party System in Contemporary Capitalism* (1962) (co-authored with Szymon Chodak, Juliusz Strojnowski and Jakub Banaszkiewicz) and *Visions of a Human World: Studies on the Genesis of Society and the Function of Sociology* (1964). The last book was quickly translated into Italian, Hungarian, Czech and Russian. Another collected work was *Workers: Problems of Disalienation of Work* (Bauman was the editor and wrote the introduction), and *Culture and Society: Introduction* (in print at that time). In addition, he had written twenty articles, two manuals (translated into Czech, Italian, Serbian and Hungarian), five large texts popularizing sociology, and sixteen pieces of journalism. 'The large and diversified achievement of Bauman testifies to his excellent methodological qualifications, wide interests, high scientific culture and deep sense of contemporary problems', Turski wrote: 'Zygmunt Bauman occupies one of the leading positions in contemporary Polish sociology.'[50]

Bauman had also taken a leading position in his professional group, the Polish Sociological Association (Polskie Towarzystwo Socjologiczne), which was created in December 1957 while Bauman was in London. Bauman had been a founding member a year earlier of the sociological section of the Polish Philosophical Association, which morphed into the Sociological Association, legitimizing the field as an independent discipline. From 1959, he was a member of the board, and in 1965 organized the Third Congress of Polish Sociologists.

As for Bauman's role in professional journals, he was an editor of *Myśl Filozoficzna* from 1953 until its dissolution in 1957, then became engaged in *Studia Socjologiczno-Polityczne* (Politico-sociological Studies). This journal, created by Hochfeld in 1957,

continued publishing until 1968. But Bauman's most important editorial role was at *Studia Socjologiczne* (created in 1961), where he
became editor-in-chief in March 1962.[51] This was a paid position,
since the journal belonged to the Polish Academy of Sciences, to
which he was affiliated.

International travels

It is possible to reconstruct Bauman's international travels year by
year, through records at his academic institutions – and especially
through the Passport Bureau and intelligence services, who considered his travels somewhat suspect.[52] It was not easy to leave Poland
at this time, and all travel was closely monitored. Visits to 'friendly
countries', of course, were much easier than trips to the West, even
for high-level scholars. Bauman's numerous travels are all the more
impressive in this context.

After his first short visit to the USSR in 1956, Bauman went to
the UK twice in 1957, first to participate in a UNESCO seminar in
London and then for the Ford Foundation scholarship. Bauman
took part in the World Congress of Sociology in Stresa in September
1959, and in 1961 went abroad four times: to the German Democratic
Republic for a meeting of Soviet-bloc philosophical journal editors
(in May), to Czechoslovakia (in August) for a sociological conference, to the USSR (October) with the mission of 'building
co-operation on studies of social processes',[53] and finally (also
October 1961) to West Germany for a UNESCO conference on youth
and technology. His speech there, 'Tools for Analysis: Orientations,
Values, Dreams', suggests his non-conformism and creativity. While
most scholars stuck to their professional vocabulary, Bauman
used common words to elucidate sociological concepts. 'Dreams'
are a driving force for many individual and collective actions and
processes – but difficult to study.

In 1962, the National Academy sent Bauman to another meeting
of philosophical journal editors in East Germany, and he attended
a seminar on contemporary Polish culture in Italy – with Janina,
according to a note in the secret police archives.[54] In 1962, Bauman
and others protested against the state's decision to withdraw permission for two sociologists – Andrzej Malewski and Stefan Nowak
– to participate in the World Congress of Sociology in the United
States.[55] Bauman declined to attend the conference himself –
officially to protest against the Vietnam War. The unofficial reason
was that Bauman had acted in solidarity with other members of the
Polish delegation, who did not agree with their government's decision. The services were not blind to this double-language; notes from
the secret service clearly state Bauman's true motivation. However,

by providing a cover story, Bauman kept his nose clean and was not prohibited from further travels. For the time being . . .

In 1963, Bauman attended a UNESCO conference gathering experts on the social aspects of industrialization in Cyprus. The following year, Bauman – with Janina – went to Czechoslovakia for a scientific conference through his affiliation with the university, on a grant supported by the Ministry of Higher Education. Later, in July 1964, Bauman was sent to the USA for an international seminar devoted to the sociological aspects of planning, and he took part in the Sixth International Congress of the Association for Political Science in Switzerland. The philosophical-journal editors met again in 1965 in Bulgaria, and later Prague University invited Bauman for a visit.

But Bauman's free-and-easy travel was drawing to a close. The first sign of this came in 1965, when he received an invitation to Manchester University as a visiting professor. Janina would write later that Bauman was suspended from international travel at this time (J. Bauman 1988: 164), but there was no official ban. In effect, the suspension of his travel rights occurred gradually, mainly through delays in procedure: 'Permission to go and a passport often arrived only on the very last day before he was due to travel', she wrote (J. Bauman 1988: 164). The IPN files mention only one formal refusal for a professional trip.[56] This was apparently in 1965, when Bauman was scheduled to attend a round table on problems of European administration, in West Germany. According to official documents, the Ministry of Higher Education approved the trip, but a Foreign Ministry commission that handled international travel refused the request and would not issue an official passport.

This signalled that Bauman was no longer in the category of 'trusted person', and coincided with a slowdown in the processing of his admission into the highest ranks of academia. Although official documents mention only one refusal, other travel projects were also affected, according to Janina's recollection, and it was only after a year of delays that Bauman was permitted to leave for Manchester to conduct a visiting professorship (J. Bauman 1988: 164), although British Labour Office delays might also have played a role.[57]

He left for Manchester early in 1966 and, after four months there and visits to the anthropology departments at Oxford and the LSE, went to Paris, where he met Janina. Together, they spent some days travelling around Europe, merging tourism with professional engagements in Yugoslavia and Czechoslovakia. After their return to Poland in the middle of the summer 1966, Bauman gave a month of summer lectures at the University of Syracuse, in New York state.[58] In early September he attended the Sixth International Congress of Sociology in Evian, and in November he participated in a conference of Czechoslovak sociologists. All told, Bauman spent over half the year outside Poland.

Janina also travelled abroad professionally – however, less than Zygmunt. Her most important travel took place in 1961, when the Ministry of Culture appointed her to the Polish delegation to the Locarno Film Festival, a recognition of her work and her language skills. Janina's fluent French and German, joined with Zygmunt's command of English, added considerable depth to their touristic travels.

After the peak of Bauman's absence from Poland in 1966, the following year was most 'quiet'. In 1967,[59] he joined – for the last time – his journal editors, in Yugoslavia, and attended a sociological conference in Czechoslovakia.

Correspondence with colleagues abroad

Bauman quickly was becoming a recognizable figure abroad. His oratory skills were so strong that few cared that English – his third major foreign language – was not his native tongue. Bauman was invited to take part in round tables, working groups and expert committees, and as a specialist in his areas of expertise. He was one of the scholars from Eastern Europe most frequently invited abroad, a fact reflected in his correspondence.[60] The volume of these letters is impressive considering that they were exchanged in a period of Cold War in which personal contacts with the West were under close supervision. When Bauman was expelled from Poland in 1968, censors reviewed them before they were sent to Israel with the other goods the Bauman family was allowed to take away.

Many of the letters were written in a tiny hand on almost transparent paper – difficult to read for censors who made an effort to leave no obvious trace of their clandestine inspections. Physical examination of the surviving letters indicates they were opened in a hurry. Each envelope was torn from one side or another impatiently, as if the recipient couldn't wait one minute more to read its content. This reflects Bauman's character: curious, impatient and always in a hurry. Some envelopes are without stamps, presumably because Anna, Bauman's daughter, collected them. This was a popular hobby in a country where stamps from other countries were a tiny window to the wider world, inaccessible for the majority. Bauman exchanged the letters with scholars writing in English, Polish, French and German (probably also in Russian). Most concern conferences and meetings, some publications, books and translations; some mix professional and personal content. Many include salutations to Janina, respectful and warm words and not just polite phrases. Those who met her knew how important Janina was for Bauman.

There are letters from famous and well-known scholars:[61] C. Wright Mills (Columbia University), Robert McKenzie (LSE),

Robert Merton (Columbia), Alvin W. Gouldner (Washington University), Amitai Etzioni (Columbia), Andrew Pearse (British sociologist working in Chile), Peter A. Savage (Indiana), Roger Giraud (ISA – Geneva), Norman Birnbaum (Strasbourg – Georgetown University), Rudolf Schlesinger (Glasgow University), Reinhard Bendix (Berkeley), Rey C. Maeridia (Brandeis), Seymur M. Lipset (Harvard), S. Friedman (UNESCO Paris), Roberto Bonchio (editor in Italy), Shlomo Avineri (Hebrew University), Peter M. Worsley (Manchester University), Max Gluckman (Manchester University), Maurice Godelier (EHESS / School for Advanced Studies in the Social Sciences – Paris), George Lavau (University of Paris and Sciences PO), Neil Joseph Smelser (Berkeley) and many others.[62]

The higher reaches of academia and sociology in particular were male wards in the 1960s, but there is one letter from a woman. In 1968, Bauman received enthusiastic confirmation of the publication of his article 'Semiotics and the Function of Culture' from the French journal *Recherches sémiotiques*, signed by the editorial assistant – Julia Kristeva.[63]

The correspondence[64] reveals Bauman as a charismatic colleague active in the international life of his professional milieu – a nice friend with a gift for inspiring interesting and funny discussions. His ironic sense of humour appears in a drawing preserved on a menu distributed at the Minnowbrook Conference,[65] which took place in July 1964. Bauman's picture gives an idea of his sense of humour and word-skills (see Plate section).

The correspondence reveals that Bauman was sceptical of the value of massive conferences. A letter from one friend states: 'I know that you consider the conferences as "vanity fairs".' Yet his travels provided a tremendous and rare opportunity for the Polish scholar to meet and speak with his colleagues, and helped to establish his international reputation. During the last decade Bauman lived in Poland, he travelled so often that, finally, early in 1968, the National Academy asked that he be given a professional passport valid for use in Europe and outside of it. This was not only a matter of convenience (this passport was kept by the owner at home, which enabled the avoidance of many bureaucratic steps), but a sign of huge support for Bauman in those troubled times. However, the request was formulated too late to be of use. Before any decision about whether to grant it was made, Bauman had become *persona non grata*.

Familial travels abroad (1959–1967)

In addition to his professional travels, Bauman was permitted to tour with his wife and family repeatedly during his last decade in

Poland. In 1959, he travelled with his wife and first-born daughter Anna to Israel, on a visa expedited because of the serious illness of his father, Maurycy. Bauman's employer at the Party Central Committee supported the trip with a letter expressing their trust in Bauman. Lydia and Irena – the 3-year-old Bauman twins – stayed in Poland: a strategic decision since a request for the whole family to travel would probably have been refused on the grounds that it was a ploy for defecting.

This first visit to Israel was probably difficult for Bauman, for a number of reasons. There would have been some mixed feelings of belonging and not belonging, which many Polish Jews felt when setting foot in the Holy Land, especially when close family members had settled there. Maurycy had left Poland in early 1957 and lived in a kibbutz close to his daughter Tova and her family. Janina's mother and her sister and family also had settled down in their new homeland. Despite their political differences, the joy of the meeting was intense, though tempered by worry over Maurycy's declining health. Both knew it would be their last time together – Maurycy would die the following year. 'I suppose my father lived his hopes again, vicariously, in me', Bauman wrote, many years later: 'I was to become all that he dreamed to be but was not. Thirty years later he would die in a distant kibbutz serenely, at peace with his life at last: under his pillow my first book was found – a gift he would have received two days earlier' (Bauman, 1986/7: 16).

The book, *Socjalizm brytyjski. Źródła. Filozofia. Doktryna politzczna* (British Socialism. Sources. Philosophy. Political Doctrine) had been published by the best Polish scholarly house – National Scholarly Editions. That was the legacy of his father's passion for books, the fruit of his respect for knowledge and love of learning that was transmitted from father to son despite war and exile. Bauman personified his father's dreams, though the Zionist engagement part was missing, and he had turned away from even the 'modern' Judaism practised by Maurycy.[66] Yet the nature of Bauman's intellectual engagement was not so alien to Judaism, which imposes on its members *Tikkun Olam* – the mission of repairing the world.

Janina[67] and Zygmunt returned in later years to visit family in Israel, and Zygmunt had his books published in Hebrew translation. They made other travels as a couple or with the family in Europe – never all together (the authorities rarely allowed an entire family to travel). The longest and most romantic trip (without children) was their 1966 re-encounter – following Bauman's Manchester sojourn – in Paris, to which Janina had been officially invited by Anna Hochfeld,[68] wife of Julian Hochfeld. The couple had lived since 1962 in Paris, where he was deputy director of the UNESCO Social Sciences Department. This would be the last time Bauman saw Hochfeld, for the latter died suddenly of a heart attack six weeks later. Bauman felt great affection and appreciation for Hochfeld, thanking him in a posthumous dedication for providing his theoretical training in Marxist sociology and for his 'broad intellectual horizons and constant creative anxiety'.[69]

The final letters between the two, dating to Bauman's stay in Manchester, depict an almost familial relationship, with Hochfeld informing his former Ph.D. student about his serious health problems, which kept him from work. In a final letter, Hochfeld appears set on resolving some kind of professional conflict (apparently related to people and not ideas), with a reference to a 'mistake' provoked by 'emotions that clashed over reason', which Hochfeld attributed to his poor physical condition. From the classical master–disciple relation, Hochfeld and Bauman had moved to a non-hierarchical friendship. The letter also discussed a loan of inexact quantity, the type of financial arrangement that a Pole living abroad would freely extend to a friend still inhabiting their native land (we should remember that all possession of and transaction in foreign currency were strictly controlled and partially forbidden in Poland).

Hochfeld notes that he was excited about the Baumans' visit and had reserved a room for them in the Mars Hotel, 117 Avenue de la Bourdonnais, a quiet establishment in the 7th arrondissement, near UNESCO. The letter contains a detailed description of the place: a tiny room with bathroom and 'double French bed in a small, clean and cheap hotel (36–40 Francs per night)'.[70] Bauman's mentor mentioned the necessity of leaving tips of at least 10 per cent for the 'servants' (służbie).[71] Hochfeld came to pick Zygmunt up at Le Bourget Airport on 25 May, and Zygmunt picked Janina up there when she arrived from Warsaw. They stayed a week in Paris, spending time with the Hochfelds, celebrating friendship, Paris and freedom.

'Those spring days in Paris shine in my memory like a dazzling light that casts into shade all the miseries of earlier and later times', wrote Janina: 'We were young again, we were free, we were together. Paris offered up its beauty like a huge table spread with delicacies for the starving. A thrilling day imperceptibly grew into an intoxicating night and then there was a day again' (J. Bauman, 1988: 165).

After the Parisian week, Janina and Zygmunt toured Europe in their new car, a Ford Cortina that Bauman had bought with his savings and his visiting-professor salary. They crossed France along the Loire and French Riviera. In Italy, they visited beautiful Renaissance cities as well as romantic places such as Verona (Romeo and Juliet's city) and Venice. Their travels continued through Yugoslavia, Austria and Czechoslovakia. In the following year (1967), they were back in Austria, where they managed to meet their family from Israel in Vienna, which was organized in secret. The family corresponded in code to avoid refusal from the passport authorities, and relatives of both Janina and Zygmunt met joyfully in the Austrian capital. However, a daughter had to stay in Poland as always, a hostage of the powerful state that wanted guarantees the parents would return.[72] If they wanted to be together, the family took its holidays within Poland. The children, who had more vacations, were also sent to summer camps at Śródborów, a small town near Warsaw where the TSKŻ (Towarzystwo Społeczno Kulturowe Żydów (Association of Jewish Culture)) organized various activities for the Jewish community. It was a way to get the children – who, unlike many Catholic Poles, did not have rural grandparents – out into the countryside. It was also a way to spare the youngest daughters the anti-Semitic bullying that Anna, sadly, experienced when she went to the camp with other Polish non-Jewish children.

Some sunshine before the storm

In the early 1960s, Bauman's family situation improved significantly. He was a habilitated and appointed docent, which increased his university salary, with additional income from the Party school and the National Academy. In 1962, when his boss at the University of Warsaw, Hochfeld, left for Paris, Bauman officially took over his administrative duties. He became acting chair of General Sociology and full chair in April 1964, an additional source of funds. Moreover, in those times, publishing (even sociological texts and books) was a good way of earning money. Bauman 'was well thought of as an author and publishers were only too keen to commission new works for him', wrote his wife: 'As authors were paid by the line, and paid handsomely, his salary was soon only a small part of his income' (J. Bauman, 1988: 148). Those resources were complemented by Janina's salary as she climbed in the hierarchy of the film institute, gaining increasing power as the accepter of scripts. Although she never had the last word, her decision could kill a manuscript, and without her agreement it was impossible to make a movie.[73]

The Baumans moved to a bigger apartment, on the third floor of 21b Nowotki Street in Żoliborz, a pleasant district in central Warsaw, close to the university and Janina's workplace, with good schools and a reputation as the 'intelligentsia quarter'. Their sunny apartment had three small bedrooms and one slightly bigger room, and two larger balconies. When they moved from the distant Bielany district, they lost their childcare, and after an unfruitful search for a new housekeeper, decided to organize their life without external support. Zygmunt, reported Janina, 'was still in charge of the household, shopping and cooking whenever he could, but we all tried to help out' (J. Bauman, 1988: 148). Zygmunt had flexible hours and, between teaching, could do some shopping, while Janina had a stricter work schedule (J. Bauman, 2011: 121). The sharing of duties was common for young Polish intelligentsia families – a factor of social progress related to political change and the poor economic situation (two salaries were necessary to survive – or at least had been at the start of Bauman's career). The socialist system allowed them to hold down full-time jobs despite having three children: the kindergartens were popular and accessible institutions, and Bauman's daughters were among the many Polish kids who grew up in them. But Bauman went beyond the norm for men in some of his household activities – such as sewing the kids' collars, and shields on their school uniforms. He was a very busy professional but, at the same time, a dad ready to do what was necessary to make family life run smoothly.

Unlike typical Polish families in the early 1960s, they bought a TV, an important sign of prosperity. Before buying the Ford Cortina in 1966, Bauman had owned a second-hand Polish-made car, a Syrena. The car showed where Bauman stood in the ranks of privileged Party members: the truly powerful got large new cars, like the Warszawa or the Russian Wołga. Bauman's Syrena was a Polish product, famous for its fallibility. Using it on trips outside of town on a Sunday, the Baumans were never sure how far they'd get. The car was capricious, its breakdowns frequent.

The Baumans also found time for their friends in the Warsaw intelligentsia, frequently hosting them in parties at home, called *domówka*. Their families were in Israel; friends were very important. There were tensions related to politics, and to the specifics of Bauman's professional engagement – tensions that led to some health troubles. These are not mentioned in the English version of Janina's book, but in the Polish edition she writes:

I do not remember exactly when Zygmunt's health problems began. They were to haunt him and intensify until the end of his stay in Poland. Sometimes he had pains in his heart, sometimes in his stomach, or in his teeth or spine. None of these ailments was a real disease, and when viewed from the perspective of time, it becomes clear that their cause was permanent nervous tension. He had too many responsibilities and had many problems with party authorities.

The Party expected its Marxist sociologists to justify every move they made. Bauman's team neglected to do this, and Bauman found himself acting as a mediator with the Party, often defending sociologists from criticism by the authorities: 'More and more, these functions brought Zygmunt into wrestling matches and conflicts with the party, causing his neurosis – and my panic' (J. Bauman 2011: 127).

Still, the Baumans were happy. '[W]e never thought it would all end like this: with betrayals and partings', Janina recalled: 'We lived a full, happy life and had a strong sense of belonging' (J. Bauman, 1988: 150). Interestingly, in the Polish version of her book, the first sentence is more detailed: 'In the early sixties, we never thought that soon we would have to break with everything that constituted our home, country, language, friends' (J. Bauman, 2011: 123) – the short list of what is most important in a person's life. The Baumans did not realize the fragility of their prosperity and happiness. A machinery had been thrown into action that followed their every step, documenting the extent to which they were 'strangers' from what the system expected of its citizens. They were spied upon as bad actors, as enemies who had to be controlled and put aside so as not to stir up trouble for the political system. Gradually, they were put in the category of 'public enemies'. This was for two reasons: Bauman's political and scholarly activities, and their ethnic origin.

10

Bad Romance with the Security Police

The Faculty of Philosophy of the University of Warsaw . . . was a real
nest of revisionism and general disobedience; the mere practice of sociology as a source of knowledge about the state of society (for which
the government demanded a monopoly) was potentially an anti-state
act and those guilty of practising sociology were by nature suspects.
. . . We were all the object of constant, official as well as 'unofficial'
scrutiny by the power structure and its organs. The archives of the UB
had large volumes that constantly grew and today have become . . . a
treasury of national memory.

(Bauman, 199?: 22)

'Anty-romans z Bezpieką', a phrase that Bauman used to title a
section of his journal on the postwar years, could be translated as
'bad romance with the security police'. In postwar Poland, the secret
police were tools of terror used for controlling the population. With
the support of various other state organizations, they encouraged
people in every social group to spy on and denounce each other.
The *Bezpieka*'s means of obtaining co-operation were many: financial retribution, blackmail, smearing of reputation, outright threats.
The specific techniques of collecting data through the employment
of 'informants', and the ubiquity of the services, made the *Bezpieka*
a state within the state. In 1945, Bauman was a tool in the hands
of the all-powerful organization of military counterintelligence (all
KBW officers were automatically obliged to collaborate with secret
services – see chapter 6). As a scholar, he was on the other side of the
barricade – spied upon, 'hunted prey', as Bauman describes himself
in his manuscript. And, of course, he was not alone.

The Department of Philosophy, which was tasked with ingrain-
ing Marxist ideology, was at the same time a nest of revisionism
because of its members' education, which nourished critical thinking. Bauman's group were Marxist idealists who sought to improve
a system they saw as distorted by the existing power structures. With
other intellectuals, and especially other sociologists and philoso-

phers, Bauman came under the microscope of the security organs. The activities of the academics were fertile ground for espionage, and the services collected enormous volumes of documents. Perversely, this rich archive, collected as a tool of repression, with its reams of tainted information subsuming real, half-real and entirely invented information, became after 1989 the source of 'national memory'[1] – and not always to good or accurate effect.

Bauman in the funhouse mirror

The metaphor of a distorting mirror seems apt for interpreting the documents created by the Polish secret services in the 1960s. Various categories of data were created: secret notes, service annotations, denunciations (spontaneous and ordered), expert sociological works and collections of gossip, lecture notes, essays and testimonies, ranging in size from two sentences on a scrap of paper to lengthy reports. The texts were general or detailed, original or rewritten, and were usually signed with a code-name – but sometimes with the real name and position of the security officer who had reported on or spoken with the informant. Rarely, they contained annotations referring to the office or individual who ordered the spying mission, or its goal ('rozpracowanie Pana X' (operational vigilance on Mr X)). The analysis of these documents constitutes a challenge.[2] While they are of uneven quality, the archives of the security services are an incredibly rich source of data, and crucial for understanding how a scholar and academic teacher could become an enemy of the state. They are vital for understanding how the *Bezpieka* turned Bauman into a revisionist, a 'pro-American, pro-Western sociologist' – and finally, a 'Zionist' accused of inspiring younger followers to counterrevolution.

This chapter is mainly based on documents produced by people who worked in various departments and sections of the Ministry of Interior Security.[3] However, the starting point for telling the story of the 'bad romance with the *Bezpieka*' belongs to Bauman himself.

> Considering the enormous authority of Leszek Kołakowski or Krzysztof Pomian's inestimable energy, my personal contribution to fomenting the rebel spirit at the faculty was, to put it mildly, secondary: it was limited to preaching heretical views in lectures and classes, refusing to participate in international delegations when one or more colleagues were refused a passport, and advocacy of a student accused by the rector of 'anti-state activity'

he wrote later (199?: 22).

The *Bezpieka* was concerned with anti-state activity that involved Bauman's students, but especially Bauman himself, and it worked hard to justify its conviction that Bauman was guilty of it. One document, a card dated 17 December 1968, indicates that Bauman had been under surveillance since 1959. In the category 'the nature of the case', written by hand in capital letters, there is: 'SYJONIZM [Zionism]'. The subject is a 'former Polish citizen of Jewish nationality, (former) prof. UW. Department Philosophy – leading anti-socialist activist from revisionist position'.[4] Many years before the anti-Semitic campaign that started in 1967, Bauman was already in the viewfinder. The document contains information about the intelligence section D III W IV (Department III, Section IV). According to the IPN archives inventory, this department of the Interior Ministry dealt with the fight against 'anti-state' and 'anti-socialist' activities. Created by Ministry Order No. 00238/56 of 29 November 1956, it existed under that name until 1989. Another department investigating Bauman's life was Department IV, which specialized in the scholar's milieu: 'Department IV [was charged with] combatting revisionist and liberal elements and protection of scientific, creative, cultural and youth environments against diversion and penetration.'[5]

The available documents suggest that authorities spied on Bauman intensively by late 1962. An introductory annotation, dated 5 October,[6] gives his basic demographic information, and a 'secret'-stamped 23 October document contains the names, professions and workplaces of his parents and wife, along with information about Maurycy's emigration in 1957, his sister Tova's address in Israel and the statement 'Bauman very often travels abroad', followed by the names of the countries he visited and the lengths of stay there, with the institution that sent him. These are the opening pages of his *Bezpieka* story. Later entries trace Bauman's 'actions against the state', corroborating his value as a subject of interest.

The first specific transgression concerns the boycott of the International Sociological Association Congress that took place in Washington, DC, in 1962. A note dated 19 November summarizes an article published in *Kultura*, a Parisian[7] monthly for Polish immigrants and intellectuals critical of the communist government. The article, and commentary by the *Bezpieka* officer who reviews it, deals with the repercussions of the authorities' refusal to issue passports for sociologists Andrzej Malewski and Stefan Nowak to attend the conference, which provoked Stanisław Ossowski, vice president of the International Sociological Association, to decline to go. The others who joined Ossowski's boycott, according to the officer, were 'Zygmunt Bauman – leading young sociologist of Marxist orientation, who also was involved in the conflict with Party censorship'.[8]

The secret services read *Kultura* as carefully as the political opposition and the intelligentsia who could access it; distribution of

Kultura was forbidden, but its articles frequently were transmitted by Radio Free Europe and the Voice of America. Positive mentions in any of these sources were proof of disloyalty towards the regime, and Bauman's participation in the boycott confirmed suspicions about his revisionist sympathies. In some ways, the latter were in plain sight. Bauman's public and very popular lectures outside the university clearly criticized the system and took place in central Warsaw at a locale where authors frequently presented their books and ideas.[9] A note in the IPN archives by a T. Chlebicki asserts that Bauman gave a lecture at the book club on 23 November, entitled 'Sociology and Society', attended by about 100 people: 'The public was very diverse, some young people probably [university] students, a dozen older women, 2–3 officers in the rank of colonels [6–7 words unreadable – crossed out by author].' The well-written, four-page note goes on to report the lecture's content, including the introduction, structure, principal themes, concepts and developments, without personal remarks or comments. The discussion after the talk is characterized as 'anti-government/Party'. Responding to a question about the development of sociology in Poland, Bauman is quoted as saying that, before 1956, it had 'a lot of abnormalities, which are commonly known. He did not deny himself the pleasure and said that the conflict between the Popular Power (*Władza Ludowa*) and the masses in those years caused suspension of sociological researches.'[10] The last sentence is charged with the subjective opinions of the security agent, which indicates that Bauman was already labelled 'revisionist', which was probably evident because of his 1956–7 publications and adherence to Julian Hochfeld's circle.

Bauman's close ideological and institutional affiliation with his mentor, who continually worked to popularize Open Marxism, was enough to colour him revisionist. Hochfeld was also a member of the Crooked Circle Club (see previous chapter), the intellectual platform for the free exchange of ideas. In 1962, the state declared the club anti-state and revisionist and shut it down, but new clubs sprang up where younger Marxists could discuss their ideas about how to improve the system.

The discussion clubs and their charismatic leaders – DNA of the Polish opposition[11]

Two groups[12] played crucial roles in the development of critical positions towards the government, and Bauman was one of the most important invited speakers. These were the Klub Poszukiwaczy Sprzeczności (Seekers of Contradictions Club) and Klub Dyskusyjny (Discussion Club, or Political Discussion Club, of University Youth). The first Seekers of Contradictions Club was created in March 1962 by Adam Michnik and his friends Jan Tomasz Gross, Włodzimierz Kofman and Aleksander Perski (Friszke, 2010: 359).[13] The three were high-school students at the time.[14] Interestingly, their club was named by sociologist Stanisław Manturzewski, a member of the dissolved Crooked Circle Club who studied Warsaw's youth.[15] To win the support of the authorities (permission for meetings, allocation of a meeting place, some funds for a winter camp), the club was chaperoned by the Socialist Youth Union, and affiliated to the Warsaw University Department of Philosophy. Michnik, 16 years old at the time, asked the notoriously orthodox Marxist Adam Schaff for his support and protection. 'Schaff had no idea what he was doing', Michnik told me in an interview;[16] 'He thought, "Such committed Communists and Marxists, why not?" Well, he was right in a sense, because he didn't know where we would end up.' None of them knew. Schaff may also have hoped to maintain control over this effervescent group. Some of the members were the children of his friends and neighbours, the sons and daughters of communists, some of them high-level officers and party *apparatchiks*.[17] A few had parents who were prewar BUND and PPS activists, intellectuals and professionals. They were the generation of the children of the leftist intelligentsia. And their beliefs and culture were often compatible with that of their parents, who usually shared their convictions on social justice and freedom.[18]

For this generation, students born after World War II, October 1956 was an open window and they cherished its legend. They hoped to make their society better, always inside the framework of socialism, much like the Crooked Circle Club had done, as historian Andrzej Friszke notes. Leading Polish intellectuals (Kołakowski, Baczko, Brus, Minc, Walicki) were invited by the high-school students to give talks. Bauman was the first invited speaker and initiated the club's activity with a talk titled 'What Is Society?' Jan Józef Lipski[19] had recommended Bauman to Michnik who, not knowing Bauman, went to his university office to invite him to speak. 'He was a great lecturer', Michnik recalled: 'Even if it was for striplings, he gave such a great talk. It was clear and convincing. He answered questions yet at the same time it was so persuasive. He was more direct than most of the professors. He treated us as partners, which, considering that we were boys, was unique.' Bauman was invited for his reputation of unorthodox thinking. He did not say openly '"Communism is bad", but he answered questions like a sociologist', Michnik said: 'It seems to me his relationship with young people was important to him for the rest of his life. He was an excellent teacher, a great interlocutor, a great and insanely nice man.'[20]

In the ambiance of widespread torpor that characterized the early 1960s,[21] this group brought some ferment and hope for change. The most active club members and participants in the discussions were called later *Komandosi* (Commando Group) – a name probably given to them by an officer of the *Bezpieka*, who noticed small groups suddenly appearing at public talks and asking provocative questions in sometimes outspoken ways.[22] The *Komandosi* were 'professional' troublemakers, masters of political controversy, raising sensitive issues, difficult discussions and uncensored questions. However, the 'Commando' term suggests armed actions, which were absolutely not within this group's scope. The intellectually challenging attitudes of the *Komandosi* grew out of the cultural capital derived from their family backgrounds, an excellent education, serious study and extensive reading of the appropriate literature. They were fearless in public, accustomed to political discussions in which they freely expressed critical opinions and cultivated a questioning spirit. In many aspects, this Warsaw elite youth was similar to the younger generation in Western Europe – more precisely, to the Parisian 'jeunesse'.[23] They read Camus, the existentialists such as Sartre, Simone de Beauvoir and the anthropologist Lévi-Strauss – authors in fashion. French was a very popular language and some *Komandosi* members read French books in the original language. When they weren't discussing politics and literature, they listened to jazz and hung out in small circles of friends, as was popular in Western Europe. Some, as the children of privileged parents, visited Western countries. The Seekers of Contradictions Club had ties to Western European socialist or communist youth visiting Poland. They were familiar with dissident, Trotskyist ideas, read Milovan Djilas' *The New Class*. No surprise, then, that the security services took interest in their activities 'no later than March 1963' (Friszke, 2010: 367).

In July, Gomułka condemned the Seekers of Contradictions Club[24] from the podium at a meeting of the Central Committee. He called its members 'fledgling revisionists' ('raczkujący rewizjoniści'; Friszke (2010: 361, 370); Gross and Pawlicka (2018: 47)). The club was closed, and its members pursued their activities in smaller groups, in their houses. The official reasons[25] for the closure included its 'inadequate' choice of keynote speakers, and the 'bad origin' of some of its members, who came from the Walterowcy,[26] a branch of the Polish Scouting Association created by Jacek Kuroń (born in 1934 in Lwów). The name honored Karol Świerczewski – 'Walter' – a general of the Polish Army killed in battles with the Ukrainian underground in 1947.[27] Kuroń imposed a specific educational model in his scouting work, employing teamwork, with the goal of 'making the world better', 'taking care of weaker persons', 'working for the future of society' and 'improving the existing system'.

'The idea of communism was for Jacek [Kuroń] and for us the idea of struggle for helping poor and discriminated people', said historian Marta Petrusewicz, a member of his group (cited by Bikont and Łuczywo, 2018: 285). Kuroń was inspired by Anton

Makarenko,[28] a Soviet pedagogue and writer who worked with delinquent children in the early 1930s. His principles were revolutionary: freedom of expression, consideration of humanistic values, and respect for the individual, regardless of age. Another source of inspiration for Kuroń was Janusz Korczak[29] (his birth name was Henryk Goldszmit), the Polish paediatrician, children's rights activist and pioneer of modern pedagogy who died in the Treblinka death camp in 1942, together with the children he had protected at a Warsaw Ghetto orphanage.

Kuroń implemented the self-governing 'Children's Republic' model that Korczak set up in his orphanage. Young members participated in each decision and were treated as adults (despite being teenagers). Korczak's principles aligned with the approach of Hashomer Hatzair (Korczak had created a branch of this Jewish socialist organization in Vienna in 1899). Kuroń took Korczak's ideas and expanded them beyond the Jewish community.

Long discussions, negotiations and participation in decision-making transformed Kuroń's students into critical, politically aware young citizens. Kuroń was banned from his scouting activity just as his friend Karol Modzelewski (born 1937 in Moscow, and a fellow former member of the Crooked Circle Club) returned from a scholarship in Venice, where he had taken part in passionate student debates about educational reforms and other political issues that animated Italy. The experience gave Modzelewski his first taste of freedom,[30] and he and Kuroń in October 1962 launched the Political Discussion Club. Modzelewski was a typical intellectual, erudite and precise in his argumentation, while Kuroń was an emotional, powerfully energetic activist. The first was a thinker, the second a doer (Bikont and Łuczywo, 2018), but both were charismatic leaders.[31] Modzelewski was then a Ph.D. student at the Faculty of History, and Kuroń was a master's student in history. While both belonged to the Union of Socialist Youth (ZMS) and PZPR, Modzelewski had the idea of placing their political activity under the protection of the university Party authorities and the ZMS.[32]

The club had meetings where expert speakers were invited to present a theoretical and scientific background for critical discussion on chosen topics. The idea was for the scholars to stimulate and develop tools and arguments. 'In the club a radical critique of PRL reality – political and economic – was created', writes Friszke (2010: 89). The Political Discussion Club aimed to reanimate discussion of the promises made by Gomułka in 1956 but quickly abandoned: more freedom and democracy, improvement of workers' lives and limitation of state bureaucracy. The meetings took place on Thursdays once a month, as had been the case with the Crooked Circle Club. The first meeting took place on 25 October 1962, with Bohdan Jankowski[33] speaking about moral-political conflicts in contemporary Poland. On 22 November, Professor Włodzimierz Brus[34] gave a lecture titled 'The Problems of Our Economics'. At the third meeting, on 13 December,[35] the invited speaker was Zygmunt Bauman and the topic was socialist democracy and bureaucracy (Friszke, 2010: 83). 'He was a well-known sociologist and enjoyed the sympathy of young people', Modzelewski says:[36]

> It was my idea to organize a meeting dedicated to the political bureau-cracy in Poland. I was not yet a supporter of such an expressive Marxist classic concept, but I thought it would be necessary to take the bull by the horns and discuss it. Kuroń and I understood the club as a place to ferment intellectual and political thought at the university, hence the idea to ask Bauman, because we knew he'd attract young people. The club was open, there were no memberships, and [I thought that] his lecture would be a very good introduction to discussion.

The discussions that followed the talks were dynamic and very critical of the power structure. Kuroń and Michnik were suspect individuals, so security agents were always present. 'I do not know this for a fact, but I'm sure they [the *Bezpieka*] wrote badly about Bauman and the club', Modzelewski said: 'They believed, of course, that Bauman was a revisionist, and that the club was a dangerous centre of hostile work.'[37] Modzelewski was right. Thanks to the record of Bauman's talk in the IPN archives, we can reconstruct the event:

> Received by *Styś* [officer's name], Warsaw 14 December 62. Secret.
> On December 14, 1962, I attended a discussion of the Political Club (in the hall of the Student Club at U.W.). The topic of yesterday's discussion was bureaucracy in the socialist system. The lecture was given by docent Bauman from the Faculty of Sociology of the University of Warsaw. Also present were prof. Brus [who gave the lecture a month earlier] and Stefan Jędrychowski [member of the Politbureau of the PZPR, a former minister, economist and politician]. Neither of them spoke at all.
> In his lecture, docent Bauman began by discussing the issue of democracy by giving several definitions of the term; he indicated that in his opinion the best definition of democracy was given by Marx and then Engels and Lenin. Then he began to speak about the administrative apparatus itself and its connections with the theories that are the basis of the socialist system. Citing Lenin's words, docent Bauman said that the existence of such an apparatus is necessary not only in the initial period when the system is just implemented, but also later when there are no longer any contradictions. According to Bauman, the problem is not in the existence of the apparatus but something

else: [it is necessary] to make sure that the ruling party (because it represents the interests of the whole society) does not plunge into alienation; [in that case] they would become a social layer or even a class in a classless system. Then he discussed the issue of egalitarianism, that all members of society should get equal opportunities, the right to an equal start. He stressed that a truly good system can only be a system where everyone can satisfy their needs. Thus, the so-called 'Homo economicus' case arose. Docent Bauman strongly protested against the perception according to which all actions of people who have power are the result of their desire to satisfy their material needs. According to him, prestige and many other reasons are equally important. As for the bureaucratic apparatus itself – of course it is a necessary thing, he stressed strongly, taking into account the necessity of Party control and social control. He illustrated it with examples of the Soviet Union and Poland.

Then the participants took the floor.

1. One student raised the matter of the personal composition of the administrative apparatus. If someone does not follow the rules of the game it is clear his place will be taken by someone who fulfils the conditions.
2. Another student: [developed] the issue of centralization and decentralization of the administrative apparatus. According to him, decentralization is better because it does not allow the alienation of bureaucracy.
3. Mr Kuroń firmly opposed the apparatus, because it leads to the creation of a bureaucratic class.
4. Karol Modzelewski – [emphasized] the necessity of the existence of this apparatus but also controls to prevent distortions – a second 1956. In principle, however, he agreed with what Bauman said.
5. A student [raised the problem of the] employment of professionals in the administrative apparatus, but also of co-operation with ideologists, with the right of control of those who are professionals.
6. The problem of the cult of the individual [was evoked by] an elderly gentleman, who did not agree with docent Bauman, though he only really disagreed on the formal issue. He described himself as the biggest leftist in the room.
7. Kuczyński – third-year economics student – [asked] two questions: 1 / the administrative apparatus attitude towards the apparent contradictions (outlooks, etc.) in socialism. 2 / is bureaucratic alienation connected to centralization (he favours decentralization) or something specifically dangerous for the system.
8. A few more voices on whether there is already a class (or a layer) of bureaucracy in Poland. Is there a guarantee that Stalinism will not arise again (in Poland) and perhaps the Poles are remotely directed.

... Docent Bauman ... appealed to those gathered to try to speak more concretely, in order to facilitate reaching the right conclusions

From 'Kicki' [Kicki was a famous student house in Praga], besides me were: Kuczyński, Lucyna Cholewa, Jerzy Kwiecień – political economics, Bohdan Knichowiecki – Polish philology 3rd year (ZMS), Lesek 3rd year of Polish study (on behalf of ZMS), Julka Brun – Polish studies (philosophy), Halina Flis 3rd year Polish studies. The 'Kicki' people said it was extremely interesting, they laughed at the writer, applauded Bauman, second speaker, Kuron and Modzelewski, [but] the first voice – a fucking moron [*skończony kretyn*]. [signed] 'Amatorka'

Comments: [by the officer of the security service] In the information 'Amatorka' reports the course of discussions at the ZMS club. She added that the discussion itself was not very interesting. The participants often spoke outside the subject or they covered the issue rather shallowly without any broader argumentation. There was even a voice speaking before Karol Modzelewski and after Kuroń who caused laughter to break out in the hall with his statements. This person (student) limited his statement to the affirmation that the disadvantageous financial situation of a group may cause dissatisfaction with the political system and, as an example, he gave writers, who according to him in present-day Poland are the most badly paid. He also asked whether the Poles are not remotely directed by Moscow. ... T. W. [secret collaborator – 'Amatorka'] also stressed that Kuczynski, a student of political economy [he was supervised by Professor Brus], recorded the event on a magnetic tape similarly to the previous ones. She did not make any other comments. The meeting with T. W. [Amatorka] in connection with the decision to eliminate her from the network was the last one and I did not schedule any other appointment. [Signed by] Senior Operational Officer Division III of Civic Militia, Command of Warsaw, C. Styś, lieutenant.[38]

This document reveals the level of detail the security services collected in their pursuit of control. In Poland at this time, any questioning of government policy was an act of courage, since political opponents could be blackballed or jailed for any suspicious speech-act. Bauman and the students may have perceived Stefan Jędrychowski – the economist, a Party member, and a member of the political elite – as official monitor. The spirited discussion shows the environment of fearless opposition among the youth, a kind of litmus test for a group the regime couldn't entirely control. The *Bezpieka* was right to be suspicious of these gatherings, because such clubs were the cradle of the Polish dissident movement.[39]

The Political Discussion Club officially existed for a year until its dissolution, at which point the membership organized themselves in smaller groups and pursued their activity underground – always in the presence of the *Bezpieka* (Modzelewski, 2013: 101–2), for, once a suspect came to the attention of the security services, his or her activity was under constant scrutiny. This was the case with Kuroń and Modzelewski, and with Bauman. Their public performances were monitored, as were all of their academic activities – publications, conferences and teaching – as well as professional and personal relationships.

The professional reviews by . . . the *Bezpieka*

Zygmunt Bauman was a very productive author from the beginning of his university career. From 1960 to 1962, he published several articles, six monographs and a manual.[40] This last work attracted special attention from the security services; his file contains three separate reviews of the book's contents, presumably by three authors, all of them sociologists (two used pseudonyms) at advanced stages in their careers. The reviews reveal the reception of Bauman by Party-line sociologists, who characterized him as a revisionist. Their texts reveal the indoctrination and specific language that were the legacy of the Stalinist period.[41] The first review, dated 6 September 1963 and signed with the pseudonym Adam Piotrowski, is a kind of meta-review, including the opinions of other specialists:

> From the scientific side this book is said to be the first Polish textbook of sociology since 1945 that is organized by problems and not historically. . . . It is also said that this is a book written from a Marxist position. Such a definition is of course underlined by all those who try to present this book and its author as a faithful ideologist of Marxism, and it is important to add that Marxism is not uniform, that there are different directions and schools. . . . In conversations about this book, in circles that support its author, one hears, above all, that he [Bauman] represents so-called 'Open Marxism', [which is] unconstrained by any dogmatism, either in the choice of subject or in the way of solving problems, that he does not hesitate to use valuable scientific output, especially foreign, especially American. And here seems to be the essential feature of this book – the author, while sticking to certain principles of Marxism, furnishes them with American ideological content. This is admitted by all reviewers.
> . . . The author of the book comes from the circle of the academic staff of prof. Hochfeld [and reveals . . .] the lack of ideological commitment on the side of socialism. The book, which is said to have been written from a Marxist position, has only the external aspects of a Marxist, whereas its content is almost completely sterilized of Marxist

tendencies. . . . There is a huge amount of influence from Western literature, especially American literature, on which the author bases his
analysis.[42]

The second review is more detailed and better reasoned, relying
on a quantitative approach to show the near absence of Marxist
thinkers and scrutinizing the author's use of superlatives to describe
'bourgeois' authors. The ironic tone of the review focuses on 'Open
Marxism':

> Mostly . . . 'Americanization' can be seen in sociology. [This phenom-
> enon] is represented by Hochfeld's school (Julian Hochfeld, Zygmunt
> Bauman, Jerzy Wiatr, Maria Hirszowicz, Włodzimierz Wesołowski,
> Szymon Chodak). In recent years [that school] has monopolized the
> right to speak in the name of Marxist sociology. Let us consider this
> from the example of Z. Bauman's textbook, 'Outline of Sociology;
> Issues and Concepts' . . . This is a handbook elaborated from uni-
> versity lectures that were given in 1961–62 by the author; already this
> work is widely used as a textbook at other universities (and even in
> Party training networks). . . . A quick review of the book from the
> point of view of the authors cited by Bauman . . . raises serious doubts.
> The index of authors shows that W. Lenin is mentioned in the text 6
> times and S. Ossowski 10 times (not once critically). French bour-
> geois publicist-sociologist Maurice Duverger is mentioned 7 times, the
> American bourgeois-sociologist Talcott Parsons 13 times. In the rec-
> ommended books for each chapter there is not a single book by Lenin
> nor is there one item written by contemporary Marxists (with the
> exception of the 'Hochfeld school'). Among the books recommended
> for supplementary reading, those that predominate are American
> bourgeois literature, non-Marxist Polish bourgeois authors and
> liberal sociologists such as Chałasiński, Ossowski and Szczepański.
> A similar picture emerges from the several hundred items of quoted
> literature. Bauman does not invoke a single position from the Soviet
> philosophical and sociological literature, nor a single position of
> contemporary Marxists outside of Poland. To be precise, the Great
> Soviet Encyclopedia is quoted once. The Soviet historians Maszkin
> and Sergeyev are quoted, but in matters concerning antiquity. . . .
> [The a]uthor refers to the bourgeois sociologists. He describes them,
> for instance, as 'the outstanding Swedish sociologist', 'the famous
> American sociologist', 'the famous West German sociologist' . . .
> (these refer to the Swedish author Myrdal, and to Goser, Dahrendorf,
> Warner, von Wiese, Glaser, Lazarsfeld, Parsons) . . . Ossowski is pre-
> sented not only as a sociologist but also as an authority in the theory
> of science. In describing the 'splendour' of quite banal terms in the
> field of philosophy, Bauman relies on the authority of Włodzimierz
> Tatarkiewicz. . . . Marx, Engels and Lenin are not mentioned once.

On the other hand, Polish bourgeois methodologists and sociologists are quoted almost entirely: Ajdukiewicz, Kotarbiński, Ossowski,
Znaniecki, Goszkowski and representatives of bourgeois American
science. As a model for applying the historical-comparative method,
he refers to Professor Ossowksi's book about class structure. . . . The
remaining chapters have very little to do with Marxism. . . . Bauman
describes social groups as 'the collection of people who are connected
by a psychic bond' (p. 236). And because this chapter discusses the
sociology of the family, the nation, the revolutionary groups of fascist
militants, the spiritual bond becomes their foundation – in this way
we get a whole concert of subjective sociology. . . . the morality of the
working class is characterized by excessive criticism of the bourgeoisie. This is an example of how the author, from a supposed Marxist
position, gives 'full submission to reactionary theories'. . . .
    The character of Bauman's book is typical of theoretical considera-
tions in Polish sociology in recent years.[43]

The third reviewer focuses only on the 'Open Marxist' transgression: 'It can be said with all conscientiousness that Bauman's book
is a special expression of this "open" Marxism, seeking agreement
and common language with the West not only in the scientific field
but also in any other field, in other words creating a bridge between
communism and capitalism based on the basic principles of Marxist
methodology'[44] (dated 17 October 1963).

Yes, Bauman was building a bridge. Ironically, a 21st-century
Polish author has maintained a totally contrary opinion, arguing
that Bauman had opposed 'succumbing to American fashion'
because it 'hindered the construction of Marxist sociology in
Poland' (Sułek, 2002: 139). Sułek was referring here to Bauman's
1961 article 'On Issues of Contemporary American Sociology'. It's a
very shallow assessment that fails to clarify that Bauman was referring to American quantitative methods and surveying techniques,
not to all American sociology. This is also clear in Bauman's excellent essay 'Sociological Variations', also published in 1961.[45] Here,
Bauman criticized Polish sociologists for blindly copying American
methods[46] (Lazarsfeld) without taking into account the specific
context and methodological limits of their surveys. Moreover, this
supposed contradiction in Bauman's attitude towards American
sociology must take into account one major feature frequently
missed by contemporary scholars: censorship.

All the texts Bauman published in Poland before 1968 passed
through the control of the censor, and thus wording decisions were
not entirely his to make. Some sentences (this is very clear in his
article titled 'Sociological Variations') were probably added simply
to make a paper publishable. This era is rife with stories concerning the peculiar relations between authors and their censors – the

negotiations, the text-altering strategies, the use of double-entendre, methods for slipping 'politically incorrect' information to the reader, etc. This is crucial when examining publications from countries such as Poland before 1968 (and into 1989, when censorship was abolished). People acting in the public sphere were constantly juggling their words, determining what they could get away with. It was a dynamic game with high stakes.

The infiltrated milieu

While the Department of Philosophy was considered a revisionist snakepit, everyone knew that it was also crawling with the 'agents' of the *Bezpieka*, as well as others who reported either regularly or occasionally. Academics and students were aware that their opinions could be preserved in their personal files thanks to these informers. Knowing this, the statements they were quoted as giving could have double meanings. For example, one Bauman informant noted: 'I have talked about the detention of a group of young science workers to several people, including Bauman. Unfortunately, this conversation did not give much, because Bauman referred to this matter disrespectfully and moved the conversation onto another track.'[47] The suggestion here is that Bauman knew the informant was reporting on him, and moved to avoid saying anything that could be used against him. People knew they were being watched.

The secret testimonies present a sometimes contradictory picture of Bauman. This may have been intentional, since various opinions gave the services material to draw upon later when they were formulating accusations. This extract, from a 25 October 1963 memo from source 'K', depicts Bauman as clever and manipulative: '"K" considers [Bauman] to be a talented and intelligent player. . . . As a specialist of social groups, Bauman likes to participate in personal games, he can turn certain situations in his favour. According to "K", Bauman is a conformist type, his position is adjusted "to the crowd".'[48]

Other reports on Bauman made him out as anything but flexible, conformist and strategic, such as this 'secret' report received by 'Rapało' in Warsaw on 13 May 1964:

I know him very little, I did not meet him at the university. I have had a very positive impression from a dozen or so social gatherings – a man who is absolutely 'non-posing', modest and funny. At the same time, he has great personal courage and does not hesitate to appear with new or unpopular positions. His personality is certainly something. He is probably (after Kłoskowska) the most talented sociologist of the middle generation, and invariably diligent. . . . He

is rather popular, although some people, among others Comrade
Schaff, have reservations about him (e.g., once, Schaff jokingly said:
'Comrade Bauman, you always have to criticize and disagree with
something'). But nobody denies that he is honest. . . . He has a very
wide circle of friends, he is liked by students. I know from my friends
that he maintains close relations with Janusz Kuczyński, Ryszard
Turski and K. Pomian (all former members of the *Po Prostu* group[49])
. . . He has a group of friends and he does not despise a glass [of
vodka] from time to time. Undoubtedly, a large individual and indi-
vidualist. I would like to emphasize, however, that I know him very
little . . . 'Henryk'

On 26 October 1964, Henryk reported on a long visit by Polish sociologists Hirszowicz, Bauman and Gostkowski to Czechoslovakia:

Docent Otahar Nahodil . . . spoke twice with B. and it seemed that
Bauman in assessing Polish sociology is guided by his own likes and
dislikes. In addition to this he represents revisionist tendencies in the
sense of separating historical materialism from sociology. Docent
Pomajźlik . . . disagreed with Bauman on his view about Soviet sociology and his opinions on the relationship between theory and practice
(the role of sociologists in social life). Finally, Docent Kadlecowa . . .
got the impression that Bauman sees the existence of only Western
[European and] American sociology, with the task of sociology in
socialist countries limited to the 'translation' of bourgeois sociology
into the language of socialist notions. In other words, he to some
extent restricts Marxist sociology to concepts developed elsewhere. Of
course, these are the impressions of the conversations, the interviewees were very cautious and 'fair' [towards Bauman] except Nahodil,
who has some grudges against Bauman. Why? [signed:] Henryk[50]

Informant Henryk honestly stressed the limitations of his data
collection: the interviewees were reserved, and politically correct. It
was late 1964, the regime in Czechoslovakia was strong, and speech
was tempered.

Probably the most interesting reports are those written by witnesses of small group interactions, when the discussion is passionate
and participants lose their self-control and say what they are really
thinking. One of the most important topics of discussion in Polish
politics was rising prices. In the state-controlled market, this was a
highly political decision, and one the regime feared because higher
prices hurt lower-income families and created the risk of spurring
workers' riots. Bauman's files contain denunciations of his reaction
to rising prices. A memo from Captain 'Lesław' from 25 November
1967 states, 'After the party meeting at the University of Warsaw
devoted to the decision to raise prices for groceries, Bauman, in a

group of three people, said "such price increases will deepen the existing division of society into those who eat ham and those who eat blood sausage".[51]

Bauman's sour sense of humour, noted frequently by friends, gave a concise illustration of the illusion of a classless society and the abyss between ideology and practice. In the academic world, the hiatus lay between so-called academic freedom and political censure. That provoked passionate discussions, debates and even conflicts at the university.

The crackdown

In July 1963, the authorities gave an order to dissolve all discussion clubs at the university, and the 'fledgling revisionists' went underground. Open discussions were forbidden, but the loss of freedom of speech created strong feelings within and outside of the university. One of the first responses was the 'Letter of 34', initiated by Antoni Słonimski. The document dated 14 March 1964, addressed to Prime Minister Józef Cyrankiewicz, was signed by thirty-four intellectuals (mostly writers, but also philosophy professors). In the two-sentence letter, the signatories protested against censorship and the lack of freedom of expression. Modzelewski organized an immediate rally of support on campus, leading to a sharp response from the Party's university unit and its youth branch. Modzelewski was kicked out of the Party and, from that moment on, his activities and those of his friends became illegal (Modzelewski, 2013: 102–3). While the '34' got important support from British and Italian writers, as well as some professors from Harvard University, Polish authorities tried to crush the movement by arresting and taking legal action against one of them to set an example.[52] But, as a warning to the Warsaw intelligentsia, this failed.

Beginning in March 1964, a group of young students led by Modzelewski and Kuroń worked on a much longer letter, a 124-page missive later known as 'The Open Letter to the Party'[53] (Friszke, 2010: 179), which laid out an independent political platform (Modzelewski, 2013: 105). The letter defined the Party-state elite as a political bureaucracy (Friszke, 2010: 912). While ostensibly designed for discussion in an underground group of ten people,[54] some parts of the 'work in progress' fell into *Bezpieka* hands. Kuroń was warned about the leak and he suspected the infiltration of their group, so he and Modzelewski decided to limit the manifesto to the parts they had written,[55] and publish it under their names. But before they could prepare copies, they were arrested, on 14 November, and the only two manuscripts were confiscated (Modzelewski had one on him (Bikont and Łuczywo, 2018: 433);

another was found in Kuroń's house (Friszke, 2010: 179)). Kuroń and Modzelewski refused to share the responsibility for the text with other group members. They were accused by authorities of 'anti-State' activity, but after some days of investigation and questioning, the Interior Ministry decided to drop the case. Probably, the authorities wished to avoid bad publicity, but their official motive was the fact that the manifesto had never been distributed. Instead, Kuroń and Modzelewski were ejected definitively from both the Party and the university,[56] in order to 'purify' both institutions of revisionist (and Trotskyist) 'elements'.

An official 'educational action' took place at the university to explain why this 'Open Letter' – which no one had read – was dangerous, and why its authors should be punished. The official propaganda was not very effective; the authors were presented in a positive light at the Department of Mathematics and Physics, while at Brus' Department of Political Economy, the whole affair was minimized. Maria Ossowska praised the authors and stated that discussions about the letter were nothing more than 'an attempt to intimidate the scientific community' (cited by Friszke, 2010: 194). Zygmunt Bauman focused on defending his vulnerable assistant Bernard Tejkowski, saying there was no direct proof of Tejkowski's direct contribution to the manifesto. Moreover, Bauman and his colleagues believed the *Bezpieka* had overreacted to the Kuroń and Modzelewski pronouncement.

'The idea of writing this letter was not smart', Bauman said in 2013: 'It wasn't a good idea to expose themselves in that way. However, I was totally opposed to the sanctions; I found that the Party's reaction showed weakness.' When I cited Bauman's words to Modzelewski, he laughed: 'He is absolutely right. It was stupid. But we were young and naive and wanted to change the world.'

They were idealists and they did not give up. Modzelewski, who has a photographic memory, reconstructed the manifesto line by line, and he and Kuroń added a short response to the Party's propaganda actions. They delivered fourteen typed copies to Party and ZMS leadership at the university on 17 March 1965. Another copy was destined for 'the West' (Radio Free Europe and other international news sources) (Friszke, 2010: 203). The letter immediately arrived in the hands of Gomułka, the Party First Secretary, and other leaders, and on 19 March, Kuroń and Modzelewski were arrested and charged with 'distribution of false information damaging the interests of the Polish state' (Friszke, 2010: 204). Their arrests awoke a wave of protests at the university that involved students and professors, including Bauman. He was in a quite delicate situation since he was suspected of having inspired parts of the letter. A 21 April secret memo found in the IPN archives says of Bauman:

In connection with the case of Modzelewski and others, Bauman got involved in the defence of his assistant Bernard Tejkowski. Tejkowski wrote a master's thesis about bureaucracy under the direction of Bauman. The work contains thoughts that can be found in the Modzelewski group's writings. He [Bauman] tried to prove, contrary to the facts, that Tejkowski had nothing to do with the document prepared by Modzelewski's groups, that he did not know about its existence until after it was revealed. . . . [Bauman is] strongly opposed to the proposal to move Tejkowski to another scientific area and to deprive him of the possibility of influencing students. He totally ignored the nature of Tejkowski's involvement in the affair. In connection with the dismissal of Tejkowski from the scientific function of PAN, Bauman privately supported the Modzelewski group, giving a negative assessment of the security authorities' actions in this affair.[57]

A disciplinary commission fired Tejkowski on 5 June.[58] Bauman was unable to protect his assistant,[59] who, according to *Bezpieka* notes, had denied Bauman's influence in the manifesto. In a 15 June extract from a source identified as 'Marcin', Tejkowski was quoted as telling a colleague that it wasn't true he had harmed Bauman. The note states:

He [Tejkowski] was being removed from the university because of his own views, not his association with the professor, he said. Furthermore, he was quoted as saying, Bauman endangers his own position at the university with his views of the authorities. Moreover Tejkowski . . . adds that Bauman is false/deceitful . . . through informal contacts he receives behind-the-scenes information including from high-ranking employees of the Polish Academy of Sciences.[60]

These are serious accusations, but Tejkowski's statement is contradictory, possibly reflecting his complex personality. Bernard (Bolesław) Tejkowski was invited to join the 'Open Letter' group because of his leadership role in the October 1956 events in Kraków, according to Modzelewski, who states that, in 1964, Tejkowski followed the line of the Confederation of Independent Poland, a nationalist anti-communist movement, which brought him into conflict with Kuroń: 'It was only later that Tejkowski fell into an anti-Semitic obsession that brought him (politically rather than by a real collaboration with security services) closer to Moczar's *Bezpieka*, and finally, in free Poland [post-1989], under the name of Bolesław, he became the leader of the nationalist skinheads' (Modzelewski, 2013: 104).[61]

Bauman himself believed that Tejkowski worked for the *Bezpieka*, and that, in fact, Tejkowski may have become his assistant as part of a *Bezpieka* plan to investigate him – a Trojan horse:

One day Benek Tejkowski appeared in my cathedral, decorated with the halo of ... former spiritual leader of the Cracovian student revolt of October 56, and prisoner of UB. It should have caught our attention that this provincial rebel persecuted by the services had been assigned a flat in the centre of Warsaw, on Hoża Street. There with impunity he opened a salon attracting the cream of independent-thinking Warsaw humanities students. ... We accepted the hero with open arms. I arranged for him the assistantship position, and agreed on his master's thesis about the theory and practice of bureaucracy. Tejkowski turned out to be hellishly (I use this term with deliberation!) smart, intelligent and an exemplarily hard-working man; the dissertation was created at an unbelievably fast pace and proved to be outstanding in every word. However, just before I got a copy for inspection, the original landed ... at the 'Party Control Committee', initiating a series of criminal trials conducted by Ms Gomułkowa [wife of the Polish Party leader]. All ended with a reprimand, with a warning. (Bauman, 199?, part 2, pp. 22–3)

Tejkowski was not the only source of Bauman's problems with the *Bezpieka*. According to the IPN sources, other informants reported that Bauman had a role in the 'Open Letter' elaboration. When Kuroń and Modzelewski were in jail, shut in separate cells, the security services sent a secret collaborator – *tajny współpracownik celny* – who reported that, on 5 June, 'J. Kuroń, speaking about the "Open Letter", said among other things that while working on this material he consulted several times with a docent of the Sociology Department UW, his good acquaintance Zygmunt Bauman, who was to help elaborate data about the labour market and the difficulties he expected in the implementation of the five-year-plan.'[62]

A Bauman speech to young sociologists was also reported on:

Bauman is the supervisor of the sociology students' circle and ... manages the writing of papers by young sociologists. Speaking at the National Conference of Young Sociologists in February this year, Bauman said ... the basic problem for consideration is how the economic model deforms and distorts consciousness. Because the discussion concerned the Polish economic model and Bauman's thesis was formulated in a negative way, its overtones were quite ambiguous.[63]

The emerging portrait of Bauman was clear enough: he opposed the authorities, while supporting and influencing young trouble-makers. Bauman had helped Modzelewski and Kuroń in another way while they were in prison, according to the informant 'Winter', who was Janina Bauman's mentor and MA supervisor (her thesis related to children's films), as well as the head of the research project. Janina trusted her former boss, as noted in this 11 April 1968 denunciation:

> On 23 March, on Saturday, I invited to my home Janina Bauman, the wife of Zygmunt B. . . . I asked her about the case of Kuroń and Modzelewski. Asked why her husband was the target of grievances from the highest persons in the state, she replied that it was probably about returning his Party ID. Also, when Kuroń and Modzelewski were arrested, the wife of one of them found herself in a difficult financial situation. When the university authorities learned that a student was raising money to support the families of the two arrested men, they moved to expel the student. But Bauman intervened to defend the student, saying there was some human honesty in supporting prisoners and their families.[64]

This was 1965, and Bauman was not yet a full professor, so it took some courage to take this kind of a stand. The majority of those who defended the rebellious students were full professors. In the hierarchical institution of the university, individuals with weaker positions had trouble effectively confronting official power. Bauman was not in a powerful position – in fact, his situation was already delicate. He knew he was being spied on, and his foreign professional travel had become problematic (delays in receiving his passport forced Bauman to cancel trips to Italy, France and even Czechoslovakia).[65] By the mid-1960s, dreams of reforming the Party from within were fading. In 1964, Bauman stopped working at the Party's Institute of Social Sciences (WSNS) due to his inability to pursue research freely, according to Jerzy Szacki. His studies of Party youth, engagement of new members, and Party elites found no acceptance in the leadership.

Warsaw University archives contain a document dated 22 October 1964, confirming that Bauman had only one job[66] – at Warsaw University – although he continued to be editor-in-chief of *Studia Socjologiczne*, published by the Polish Academy of Sciences. His list of troubles was long, his career in a slowdown, undoubtedly because of his unruly nature and 'reactionary' label.

Promotion under unfortunate circumstances

Bauman began the process of becoming an 'extraordinary' professor with brio on 29 June 1965. His achievements were impressive, his publication list very long. He had published five books since his last promotion in 1961: *Outline of Sociology: Questions and Concepts* (*Zarys socjologii. Zagadnienia i pojęcia*) and *Everyday Sociology* (*Socjologia na co dzień*) in 1962; *Ideas, Ideals, Ideologies*

(*Idee, ideały, ideologie*, 1963); *An Outline of the Marxist Theory of Society* (*Zarys marksistowskiej teorii społeczeństwa*, 1964); and, finally, a book that had a strong impact on many readers,[67] *Visions of a Human World: Studies on the Genesis of Society and the Function of Sociology* (*Wizje ludzkiego świata. Studia nad społeczną genezą i funkcją socjologii*, 1964). Bauman was also a very efficient mentor, with a large list of Ph.D. students.[68]

The reviewers for his promotion were nearly all enthusiastic. Jan Szczepański wrote that his achievements were unbelievable, calling him the most outstanding sociologist of his generation. Julian Hochfeld described Bauman's scientific input as impressive, qualitatively and quantitatively, as did Paweł Rybicki. Nina Assorodobraj, Stefan Nowakowski and Adam Schaff added very positive, though less engaged, reviews. Only one opinion was laconic and short. Maria Ossowska wrote that his nomination was 'plenty merited . . . He is characterized by a rare diligence and devotion to [social] sciences.'[69] The hardworking attitude she describes might suggest a lack of 'talent' or 'scholarly imagination', but amid the constellation of reviews, Ossowska's somewhat chilly evaluation[70] did not carry much weight.

The next step was the vote of the Department Council on Bauman's eligibility for the professorship. The council met on 5 October and approved his professorship by a unanimous vote (17/17). A month later, Bauman declared that he would limit his workplace to Warsaw University (he had already left WSNS). However, according to his colleague Szacki, Bauman's resignation from the Party school was not really a strategic decision. There was a fight, or at least an avid discussion, Szacki recalled, about the research Bauman planned to conduct on Party elites. The research was in the spirit of Hochfeld's studies, but it was viewed critically: 'It was supposed to be some kind of questionnaire survey, but at some point they stopped it. I do not know at what stage: while reviewing the questionnaire or even later, but it seems to me it was not considered a good idea [i.e., it was a dangerous topic].'

While much success was expected of Bauman, his political star had dimmed. He was no longer the young Marxist scholar with huge potential and amazing productivity, teaching talent and involvement, but, rather, a disobedient, uncontrollable, independent academic. His support of Kuroń, Modzelewski and their 'Open Letter' had moved Bauman into the untrustworthy category. To bolster his fragile situation, Bauman wrote a letter to Andrzej Werblan, director of the Department of Science in the Central Committee. They knew each other from Party expert meetings, Werblan recalled.[71] In the letter of 24 December 1965,[72] Bauman proposed the creation of a 'reference milieu' composed of Party sociologists, and a new sociological journal that, instead of obtaining its examples and theoretical models from American journals, would be a high-level Polish product derived from home-grown professionals. There would also be conferences and other events. Bauman tried to draw Werblan's attention to Marxist sociologists (without citing names), saying that, surprisingly, the authorities were more indulgent of non-Marxist than Marxist sociologists. He was speaking indirectly about himself and Hochfeld's group, which had lost official support. He emphasized the need for critical and meritocratic opinions. Bauman also tried directly to convince Werblan of his fidelity to the Party and willingness to be its leading voice in the sociological milieu. Clearly, Bauman was struggling to recover his place, while arguing that reforms were necessary, sociological studies indispensable, and that insider criticism should be taken into consideration. He was rather hopefully suggesting that the Party accept the 'Open Marxism' current.

To participate in the scholarly game, he needed a promotion. On 12 January 1966, the university senate (in a document signed by Professor Stefan Morawski) presented a proposal supported by professors Assorodobraj, Leśnodorski and Kołakowski calling for his promotion. Nineteen senators voted in favour, with one opposed and one abstention. A month later, the proposal was sent to the Minister of Higher Education, and there the sledding got rough. A note from the ministry dated 1 March, addressed to 'friend Tomaszewski' (historian Jerzy Tomaszewski), requested an opinion about Bauman's *Outline of the Marxist Theory of Society*, one of the books presented as a basis for his promotion, suggesting that the text was 'too similar to Hochfeld's work'.[73] Tomaszewski responded drily: 'Bauman absolutely deserves to be promoted. I know his book *The Visions of the Human World*, and this work alone is sufficient for his promotion to extraordinary professor.'[74]

There was clearly great tension between the university community and the Party and state authorities over Bauman's promotion. The ministry was seeking more control at the university, and for this purpose carried out a series of reorganizations that met strong opposition in the faculties (see next section). Since obtaining a professorship involved both institutions, any conflict between them slowed everything down. Moreover, Bauman's candidature was problematic beyond his link to 'Open Marxism' and its nourishment of revisionism. And so, his promotion got stuck in the ministry in 1966. A long period without any response was explained by an unrelated problem – the 'creation of a new chair'. Bauman had been acting chief of the general Sociology Chair[75] since 1964, when Hochfeld left for Paris to serve in UNESCO, a position that was scheduled to end in September 1966. The university expected him to take over a newly created Chair in the Sociology of Culture once his full professorship was cleared. In this period,

Bauman published *Culture and Society: Preliminaries* (*Kultura i społeczeństwo. Preliminaria*).

This plan was broken up by Hochfeld's sudden death in July 1966, only a few weeks after the Baumans had visited him in Paris. His death shocked the sociology community, some of whom suspected the security services of having poisoned Hochfeld (his disciple Szymon Chodak raised this issue in a letter to Bauman).[76] However, Hochfeld's letters to Bauman (in Manchester, at the time) indicate he was already very sick and complained about his health problems.

Bauman lost not only a mentor and friend in Hochfeld, but also a protector. Even if the latter's position had weakened in Poland because of the 'revisionist' accusations the authorities stamped on his Open Marxism, Hochfeld maintained relationships near the top and could have pushed Bauman's promotion through. Now, Bauman had no protection, and unhappy results followed.

On 3 October, the minister of higher education wrote to the university rector announcing that the Chair in the Sociology of Culture would go to Professor Józef Chałasiński instead of Bauman, who would remain as acting Chair of General Sociology. The ministry's decision may be explained by the political circumstances. The Department of Philosophy had become a source of political sourness in 1966 as the university became a centre of dissent. In a period of growing revolt, Bauman was no longer perceived as a trustworthy candidate.

The struggle for autonomy and academic liberty

Since the distribution of the 'Open Letter' from Kuroń and Modzelewski, the situation at the university had become explosive; their trial mobilized dissenting voices and the support of the university community, which in turn provoked a reaction from the authorities. As chief of the Department of Science and Education in the Central Committee, Werblan was in charge of keeping order at the university – a difficult position. The Party wanted to punish political troublemakers and their supporters; faculty and some students who were Party members cherished the idea of academic autonomy and the freedom of internal dissent and open discussion. The Interior Ministry and security services used central and regional units of the Party to pressure university Party members and the university hierarchy to suspend Adam Michnik, along with students who supported Kuroń and Michnik during their trial. Michnik was also punished for distributing the 'Open Letter', considered an 'anti-state text' (Rutkowski, 2016: 474–5). Temporary suspension was not enough, the authorities felt, because troublemaking (debates, letters, petitions, protests) continued. The state ordered a new wave of changes that limited the university's professional and institutional autonomy (1965). Key positions were filled with individuals who followed the Party line (Rutkowski, 2016: 477). Yet, although the reforms led to more departmental rigidity, individual disciplinary measures such as suspensions of student rights, and expulsions from student organizations and the Party, were not really effective. Tensions grew, and large numbers of students and faculty continued to meet to discuss sensitive issues.

The tenth anniversary of the 'October Thaw' offered an opportunity for negative assessments of the present. Gomułka, who had taken power in 1956 promising more freedom, had not kept to his agreement, and intellectuals were again struggling with censorship, curtailed freedoms and decreasing autonomy. An important event took place on 21 October at the Department of History. Michnik, with the support of the Socialist Youth Union, invited Leszek Kołakowski to give a lecture titled 'The Development of Polish Culture in the Last Decade'. Another key participant was the historian and philosopher Krzysztof Pomian (an assistant to Brus). For the first time, Kołakowski publicly criticized the regime with great power and clarity. Pomian spoke up for the autonomy of youth organizations and the engagement of youth in decision-making. The lecture hall was crowded with more than 100 people, who responded passionately to the remarks. Michnik and Jan Józef Lipski prepared a resolution calling for the liberation of Kuroń and Modzelewski. The discussion was stormy, because Party supporters were of course also present, and the consequences of this 'revolutionary ambiance' were immediate. A week later, Kołakowski was expelled from the Party, though he was not fired from the university. The same sanction was levied on Pomian a month later. Michnik was already being expelled from the university. The authorities wanted to show they would no longer tolerate anti-government, anti-Party, anti-system activities. But the disciplinary measures provoked a large backlash.[77] Michnik's expulsion sparked three signature-collection campaigns in support of the reversal of the action. Włodzimierz Holsztyński, a young Ph.D. mathematics lecturer, began circulating a petition among faculty in his department.[78] Holsztyński would say later that he had acted alone, without support from any political group, and even his colleague Jan Lityński,[79] mathematician and *Komandosi* member, was not aware of the action.[80] At the time, mathematicians and physicists who signed the petition were acting more out of conviction in supporting university autonomy and wronged students, than in the spirit of political commitment against the regime that engaged students and faculty in the humanities.

'The situation of the humanities at the university was fundamentally different from that of other scholars', Holsztyński said: 'They lived in daily contradiction with the communist system; the others weren't dealing with political and moral questions every day.'[81] By the same token, the scientists were less afraid to sign such a petition because most of them were less aware of the possible consequences of such support. Holsztyński and his friends got 128 signatures, mostly from 'hard scientists' on the faculty. Everyone who signed the documents knew the risk of being fired, prohibited from foreign travel (for some, the *sine qua non* for progressing in their research careers), or having their promotions delayed. For those who had families, like Holsztyński, it meant, as a breadwinner, exposing one's household to potentially serious consequences.

Students, meanwhile, risked being ejected from youth organizations, suspended or expelled from the university. For male students, the consequences were brutal, since two years of compulsory military service menaced them as soon as they left the university rolls. Despite that risk, a second petition was signed by 1,037 students. A third letter, defending Michnik's actions during the Kołakowski lecture, was signed by another 137 people. Considering the consequences of such acts, the proportion of active supporters (about 11 per cent of the 12,000 University of Warsaw students at the time) was quite high. The response of the authorities, unsurprisingly, was to step up control over the university community via spying, threatening procedures and disciplinary punitive actions organized by the Party and the part of the university hierarchy that followed its orders. The university became a difficult workplace for anyone who was labelled 'revisionist'. Bauman was in this category, even if he was not in the first ranks of the opposition. He was careful, waiting for a promotion that he expected would give him more independence and security. He was frequently abroad, yet still took part in campus discussions, actions and disputes. At the Philosophy Department, some turned in their Party ID cards in protest. Bauman did not. Not yet.

There were many subjects to discuss, however. Gomułka was struggling to keep control of the Party against Mieczysław Moczar, whose faction had lost out in 1956 but progressively recovered, and in 1967 menaced Gomułka's camp. Moczar and his supporters had gradually taken over positions of power in the Interior Ministry, employing a successful strategy based on playing the anti-Semitism card (Eisler, 2006: ch. 3). The Interior Ministry was an extremely powerful institution, a state within a state (*państwo w państwie*) that put Moczar's cabal in a strategic position. As Werblan told me, the most important role in the Polish state was played not by the government but by the secret services. Regimes and ideologies changed; this organization survived it all. The events that took place in the late 1960s seem to confirm this theory. In the spring of 1967, a major government-ordered increase in basic prices created displeasure across the country. The general situation was unstable and even a small event could set off a conflagration. The spark that provoked change was a military conflict that awakened fears of a third World War. This was not a war in Europe, but in the Middle East.

Becoming a Jew . . . again

In 1967, the war known as the Six-Day, or June, War inflamed Polish society. The whole country listened in on the radio (including the forbidden Radio Free Europe and Voice of America broadcasts) to the news of the Israeli–Arab military conflict.[82] Most of the public supported Israel, but the authorities followed the Moscow line and backed Egypt. We can imagine the impact of the conflict on Poles who had family and friends living in Israel, such as the Baumans. Some days before the outbreak of fighting, Janina's mother returned to Warsaw to visit her daughter and her children for the first time since she had emigrated. 'It was a happy time for all of us', wrote Janina:

> until news of a serious crisis in the Middle East suddenly shattered our peace of mind. All her joy gone, Mother stopped seeing people and stayed glued to the radio listening for news . . . The day after the Polish government broke off diplomatic relations with Israel, mother begged us to take her to the Israeli embassy. She felt lost and wanted to ask whether she should leave Poland at once or could stay a little longer until her visa expired. So, feeling very anxious and upset, [Zygmunt] and I drove her to the embassy that Sunday morning. Although Sunday was a working day at the embassy, the building seemed deserted. We wandered for a while from one empty room to another until in a messy office we finally came across some clerks busily packing. (J. Bauman, 1988: 167–8)

This event recalled by Janina would become the masterpiece in the construction of a Zionist case against Bauman. His contact with the Israeli Embassy in Warsaw was interpreted as a betrayal of the Polish state, as was the case for all Poles who visited the Embassy at the time. A note in Bauman's *Bezpieka* file from 14 June reports: 'According to information transmitted by Department II MSW, Dr Zygmunt Bauman, chief of the Chair of General Sociology at the Department of Philosophy UW, . . . visited the Israeli Embassy on 11 June this year.'[83]

A month later, this event was described in an 'information note' the following way:

> Secret – Dr Bauman Zygmunt is known at Warsaw University for his negative attitude towards the Party and government of Poland. His

revisionist opinions are well known, as well as his defence of Kuroń and Modzelewski. During the conflict in the Middle East, he showed a pro-Israel attitude in discussions with students. He participated in a party organized at the Embassy of Israel celebrating its victory. On 12 June 1967, he was seen exiting the Embassy of Israel with his wife. The information about his pro-Israeli attitudes came from an unofficial source – lack of witnesses. Bauman Zygmunt did not seek permission to travel to Israel.[84]

It's unclear whether the inaccurate change in the date of Bauman's visit – from 11 June to 12 June, was accidental or an effort to imply that Bauman attended a 'victory party' at the embassy on the 12th. The documents do not mention Janina's mother, who, obviously, as an Israeli citizen, needed to visit her Embassy, particularly at a time of military crisis. In addition to the recycled mention of Bauman's links to critical circles on campus, there is significant new information in the second document, which is dated 17 July 1967. In the right-hand corner, it states, 'Bauman Zygmunt, son of Maurycy and Zofia Cohn, born Nov. 19, 1925 in Poznań, member of PZPR, *nationality Jewish*.'[85] The message is clear: in June 1967, Bauman had become a Jew again, as he was before 1939 during the Second Polish Republic.[86] The return of nationalist and anti-Semitic policies was a huge step backward, all the more remarkable for a system ostensibly based on equality and the end of racist policies. This relabelling was a crucial element in building the image of Bauman as an enemy of the state.

To be sure, Moczar's camp had already started deploying anti-Semitism before the Israel–Arab war. Andrzej Friszke notes that, in the documents prepared by MSW (Ministry of Interior Affairs), individuals were identified as 'Polish nationality and citizenship' in the case of those with Aryan origins, while Jews were listed as 'gives nationality as Polish', or even 'nationality given as Polish, in fact Jewish'. Even in May 1967, 'the terminology that would become common in March 1968 was already deployed' (Friszke, 2010: 444).

In the late 1960s, Moczar and his coterie seduced the population with an explosive ideological mixture, joining the totalitarian state structure with a nationalistic and anti-Semitic ideology, promising to oust Jews from leading positions and replace them with a younger generation of 'real Poles'. This was an attractive promise for those nakedly seeking promotions, and it touched all layers of society. After the Six-Day War, 'The atmosphere of mistrust and prejudice rapidly thickened around us', Janina Bauman wrote: 'On 19 June, speaking at the Trades Union Congress, Gomułka made his own attitude clear, calling Polish Jews "citizens of two fatherlands" and comparing them to Nazi agents in prewar Poland. 'We felt suddenly unable to breathe freely. Outwardly, however, nothing much changed in our daily life' (J. Bauman, 1988: 169).

Moczar was not alone in employing the 'us and them' rhetoric. The 'Fifth Column' comparison was still blunt enough when Gomułka's speech appeared in the newspaper for the term to be removed (Friszke, 2010: 478). But those who heard the speech live on the radio were shocked and passed the information around. It was also read and analysed by Western radio stations. All of Poland got wind of it.

Gomułka was the organ grinder for an anti-Semitic diapason that brought on a new process of discrimination. The Baumans were not obliged to sign a statement condemning the State of Israel for aggression against Egypt, and after their trip to Austria in summer 1967 they went back to work as usual – except that the spying intensified. As a 'Zionist', Bauman was integrated by the authorities into the *kwestionariusz ewidencyjny*, a category for state enemies.[87] One day, when the Baumans were at work, their young daughter allowed agents posing as plumbers into the house, and they bugged the phone. When the girls described to their parents the unusual behaviour of the repairmen, who were mostly working on a balcony rather than under the sink – and another specialist came to repair a phone that worked perfectly – the family had no doubts about what was going on (J. Bauman, 1988: 171).

The academic year 1967/8 began under high tension. Although the university community was not strong enough to oppose the administration,[88] the Party and administration could not exercise complete control over Warsaw University. Kuroń and Modzelewski were free (Kuroń in May, Modzelewski in August 1967), and both continued their political activity, with strong support from younger people, for whom they were legends and heroes, willing to spend months in jail for their beliefs. Two important groups were under permanent investigation: those from an elite background, who originated from the Warsaw *Komandosi* and were led by Michnik; and a more middle-class cohort – provincial youth who lived in university housing, directed by Józef Dajczgewand. Meetings with stormy debates were more in fashion than ever. They took place at private homes, which people called salons,[89] and, as in previous years, there were also big events organized at the university. There were more than 100 informal circles of self-education, where young people discussed and analysed the burning issues of the day. The *Bezpieka* had to work hard to keep up with all the anti-state activity. Any time and place was a potential site for critical discussions – including birthday parties.

Bauman's daughter Anna, a freshman in the Physics Department, celebrated her eighteenth birthday at their apartment on Saturday, 18 November. Around eleven in the evening, as the party ended, militia officers outside the street door arrested a dozen guests on the pretext of hooliganism. Anna, observing from the balcony the action of the police, called Zygmunt, who jumped in his Ford Cortina and followed the police car. The young people were taken to Warsaw police headquarters for interrogation. Bauman called some of their parents, who came immediately and, due to their high Party positions, were able to free their children (J. Bauman, 1988: 171.) Some months later, those family positions would not have been enough.

A turning point occurred a few days later, on 22 November, at Warsaw University, where a large and provocative public meeting took place. Gomułka's personal secretary was invited to address the group and gave a boring, politically correct speech about the friendship between Poland and the Soviet Union. The discussion that exploded immediately after was the basis for several lawsuits and brought serious troubles to all the active participants. The speakers, or some of them, avoided the sophisticated intellectual double-talk of past events and openly attacked the USSR. This transgression was certainly inscribed in the spy-books under the category of anti-state activity. On 13 December, 200 people assembled for a stormy discussion following the lecture by docent Marian Dobrosielski titled 'Liberals and Marxists'. At this meeting, the *Komandosi* did not ask questions – they stood up and stated that they opposed the regime's principles and style of government, and they ridiculed its propaganda and ideology (Friszke, 2010: 499). Their radicalism signified open war and an approaching conflict with the Party.

The end-of-the-year festivities were not joyful that year. Janina realized that, after many years in which the Baumans had never noticed who among their friends was a Jew, suddenly this category had taken on significance. Unpleasant discussions with close friends helped them realize that, once again, a dividing line inside Polish society was rising to the surface. The Jewish community that in the prewar era had been divided into communists and Zionists suddenly, without taking into account the wishes of its individual members, was designated singularly as Zionist. At gatherings in their house, the Baumans' older friends began to say that, if they were only younger, they would leave Poland and start new lives elsewhere. One couple said they were fortunate not to have children, so, despite the bad situation, they would stay in Poland. The Baumans were different: younger, multilingual, with international professional positions and young children. Without a word, they understood each other (J. Bauman, 1988: 177–8). Janina's account is clear about this crucial issue, although no decision had been made yet. There was only a feeling . . . the feeling of being no longer welcome in their home.

As Janina wrote, in a poem found later in the files of the *Bezpieka*:

I know.
I know: you do not want me, so I will go.

I will not pretend in front of you.
I already understand and I know what I will do.
between you, I will not push my elbows.
....
I will go into my life and they will follow me like vipers
will crawl your low deeds
I will never wash from my forehead
A stigma of great unfulfilled guilt.[90]

11

The Year 1968

The Baumans spent New Year's Eve at a late dinner party with friends. Of the ten people there, four were Jews. The mood was subdued.

'Shortly before midnight our host switched on the television for a satirical programme', Bauman recalled in 1988:

> We had all been looking forward to it: programs on New Year's Eve were always particularly good, written and performed by the best satirists and comedians. They were irreverent, often daring as though the stiff, humorless face of the censor was looking the other way on that one special night. This time, however, the little screen breathed out sheer hatred. A hook-nosed puppet climbed up a huge globe, its arms widespread, its claws greedily clutching the surface. Small hook-nosed figures scattered around the globe pushed or pulled the big one up and up. At the same time an unfamiliar male voice sang out [Israeli Defence Secretary Moshe] Dayan's song thanking his 'brothers-in-law from all countries in the world' for their help and support. Our host stepped to the television and briskly switched it off. Too late. Four of us, Dayan's hook-nosed helpers, sat thunderstruck, profoundly shaken. (J. Bauman, 1988: 179)

This evening made a large imprint on the lives of many people. Descriptions of this satirical programme can be found everywhere: in interviews, biographies, memoirs and discussions with people who left Poland in 1968 and later. At this moment, the strength of anti-Semitism and its official support became clear. It was obvious that, now, people designated as Zionists had become undesirables in Poland, and that Zionist was simply a synonym for Jew – the stigma that was an original sin for Polish nationalists.

In early 1968, Janina and Zygmunt turned in their Party IDs, actions that very much interested the *Bezpieka*. From a note dated 5 January 1968:

1) On 01/04/1968 a party meeting devoted to the discussion of the attitudes of Party members was held at the Department of Philosophy. New Party identity cards were handed out, and Docent Henryk Jankowski informed those present that on Jan. 3 – Wednesday – Doc. Zygmunt Bauman had come to see him as a member of the executive leadership of the department and declared he had resigned the Party. As evidence, he returned his Party identity card. Jankowski told me that he asked Doc. Bauman to explain why, and Doc. Bauman said, according to Jankowski, that he refused to make a declaration that could be used by hostile sources such as Radio Free Europe. 2) The executive of the Department of Philosophy wished to speak with Bauman about his attitude, but Bauman said the case was over, and declined to give supplementary explanations. 3) Those present at the meeting received this information with great satisfaction. A smile was visible on the lips of the majority. Afterwards in corridor discussions, comrades openly expressed their satisfaction. [signature illegible].[1]

As the informer reports, some members of Bauman's department probably were happy with this news. Bauman was in the process of becoming a full professor. He was successful, popular among students, well known abroad, intellectually brilliant, an active revisionist with a strong personality – and, above all, independent. His success and career advancements awoke a lot of jealousy and he had enemies among his colleagues. Everyone had seen the satirical TV show on New Year's Eve (there was only one channel on television at the time), and they knew exactly why Bauman had quit the Party. They knew the system and correctly concluded that Bauman's career, if not finished, was crippled. He wouldn't become a full professor, they knew, and probably some were happy to think his difficulties would translate into their success.

The *Bezpieka* was not satisfied with Bauman's explanation. They asked 'Kazik' – presumably a faculty member – for more information.[2] Another document, 'extract from the denunciation of "M-55"', dated 15 March, shows how the case was handled. The 'Jewish' label is employed blatantly: 'During the current Party ID renewals, the scientific employees of Jewish nationality, Prof. Brus and Doc. Bauman returned their IDs without providing any specific explanation. Bauman even said, "I give no justification for this, because it could be used by reactionary circles."'[3]

Bezpieka files also contain Janina's account of the ID card return, from a conversation with her mentor – who unbeknownst to her was also the informer 'Winter':

Each of them [Janina and Zygmunt] did it for slightly different motives. She gave it back because they hadn't had a meeting for five years at the National Board of Cinematography, censorship was crazy and she saw people hurting. She was afraid that in the end people not enrolled in the Party would ask her what was happening and she wouldn't know how to defend what is going on now. She needed to choose – maintain her Party membership or be an honest human. She preferred to be an honest person and this is why she gave back her Party ID. Her husband gave back his ID in solidarity with Kołakowski, whose ID was taken away. That was not the only reason. At that moment, all the professors who saw themselves as honest persons gave back their Party IDs. Including Morawski, Baczko[4] and others.[5]

Returning one's Party card was perceived as an act of courage and strong disagreement with the Party – and, in consequence, with the state. This desperate act was so exceptional that it was kept secret. Party members did not speak about it. It was only two months later, at a meeting of the university's Party leadership, that Zbigniew Chrupek reported on the resignations of Włodzimierz Brus[6] and Zygmunt Bauman.

Bauman said in interviews that he decided definitively to resign from the Party at the end of 1967. '[O]n January 6,[7] 1968, I gave Dzidek Jankowski [Henryk] my Party membership card. . . . [he hesitates] . . . I had not yet decided to leave Poland [. . .] I did not expect. . . . Honestly, I was stupid [. . .] it was an important decision for me to drop out of the Party, but I did not expect what would happen next.'[8] After intervening at police headquarters after his daughter's birthday party, Bauman could still feel he belonged to the privileged circle. Any decision about emigration, whether forced or voluntary, is complicated, and it is difficult for individuals to characterize what motivates such a decision or when it is made. However, Anna Bauman recalled that, immediately after her return from a New Year's Party organized outside of Warsaw, her parents took her aside and solemnly declared that they had decided to leave Poland. Anna was shocked. This decision was kept secret inside of the family.

For Barbara and Jerzy Szacki, departmental colleagues, it was not evident before March 1968 that the Baumans would leave Poland. Perhaps Bauman tried to find a temporary solution, such as visiting professorship, that would allow him to leave until the storm passed. In any case, the Baumans lived from one day to the next in the beginning of 1968. The storm winds were building around them.

The revolutionary power of symbols

Dziady (*Forefathers' Eve*) is a play by Adam Mickiewicz, the nineteenth-century Romantic poet and author of many patriotic pieces that inspired Poles' hopes for the liberation of their country from foreign occupation. The National Theatre had scheduled to run

Bauman's parents, Zofia Kohn and Maurycy Bauman

An anti-Semitic caricature portraying a map of Poland with the proportion of Jewish minority, *c.*1938

(Opposite) Bauman's home in Poznań (photograph by Agata Szczypińska)

Zygmunt Bauman with his mother (and a dog), *c.*1938

ZMP (Union of Polish Youth),
with Bauman in the first row,
second from the right, crouched
with medals on his chest, late
1940s

Janina and Zygmunt Bauman
before their marriage, c.1948

Janina (Anna) Bauman, *c*.1946

;munt and Janina with friends, approx. 1948–9

(Overleaf) Bauman celebrating with colleagues in spring 1960,
likely for his habitation

Zygmunt and Janina with Zygmunt's father and sister in Givaat Brener, Israel, *c.*1959
(not long before Maurycy Bauman's death)

Bauman with colleagues, 1960s

A joke drawn by Bauman during a conference in New York in 1964

A graph and timeline of individuals whom Bauman met during March and April 1968, prepared by the Security Services

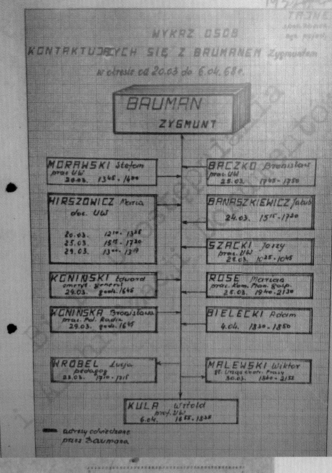

Zygmunt Bauman, as photographed by the Polish secret service

Awarded by the Russian Army
– For Victory over Berlin –
2 May 1945 no. 066894 – dated
11 June 1946

Polish Silver Cross of Merit
no. 12896/4252 – dated 24 May
1946 from the Presidium of
the KRN – the State National
Council

Awarded by the Russian Army
'For Liberation of Warsaw'.
17 January 1945 – dated 14
February 1946 no. 093927

Awarded by the Polish Army
– medal for Warsaw 1939–45
no. 001608 – dated 1 Februar
1951

Awarded by the Polish Army 'For Oder, Nysa and the Baltic' no. 25864 – For heroic acts and courageous behavior fighting the occupying forces – dated 2 June 1946

Ministry of Public Security 'Medal of Victory and Freedom' 9 May 1946 no. 3620

Received from the President of Poland – Bronze Medal – 'Armed forces in the service of the Homeland'

Cross of Valour (Krzyż Walecznych) – dated 19 May 1945 no. 5568. From chief of the Polish Military Forces 1st Army

Commemorative Medal for 10 Years of Popular Poland, no. 529022 – dated 22 July 1955 – received from the State Council

Warszawa, dnia 13.maja 1968

Bauman Zygmunt s.Maurycego
/nazwisko i imię, imię ojca/

Zofia Cohn
/ imię i nazwisko panieńskie matki/

Warszawa, ul.Nowotki 21b m.28
/ miejsce zamieszkania/

DO
RADY PAŃSTWA
POLSKIEJ RZECZPOSPOLITEJ LUDOWEJ
w miejscu

PODANIE

Proszę o zezwolenie na zmianę obywatelstwa dla
mnie i moich dzieci

/ nazwisko i imię, imię ojca, imię i nazwisko panieńskie matki/

Prośbę powyższą składam w związku z wyjazdem na stałe
do Izraela

A request for changing citizenship for Zygmunt Bauman and his children, completed by
Bauman himself (1968).

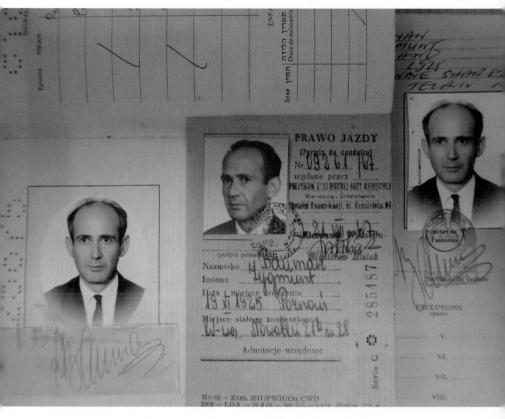

Bauman's passport, Polish driving licence and Israeli driving licence

Bauman in Israel, *c*.1968

(Opposite) Bauman at home in Leeds, with some of the books he wrote in several different languages, *c*.2010

(Overleaf) Bauman speaking in front of a large lecture hall in Florence, Italy, in October 201

Janina and Zygmunt Bauman, late 1990s/early 2000s

A portrait of Bauman, painted by his daughter Lydia Bauman

Bauman speaking at Collegium Civitas in Warsaw, *c.*2011-2012

Bauman, with Korolewicz and students at Collegium Civitas in Warsaw, *c*.2011–2012

Zygmunt Bauman and Aleksandra Jasińska-Kania, photographed in Italy

Professor Piotr C. Kowalski (Bauman's friend) carving an ice monument for his 93rd birthday in front of his childhood home, now a kindergarten

it as part of a celebration of the anniversary of the Soviet Revolution in November 1967. While ostensibly related to the struggle against the Russian czar, much of the public understood its performance as an act of resistance to Soviet colonization, which made it very popular among young people.[9] Under stage director Kazimierz Dejmek, well-known actor Gustaw Holoubek played Gustaw/Konrad,[10] giving a great performance that won the piece acclaim as perhaps the finest spectacle postwar Poland had ever seen. The authorities noticed that the play had become an act of political protest for students who attended it, and, on 18 January, they decided to curtail the run after only two more performances. The last performance took place on 30 January and attracted a large audience, including many artists and intellectuals. The National Theatre, which normally can seat 900 people, was crammed with youths, including scores (at least 115, according to the *Bezpieka*; Eisler, 2006: 178) who snuck in without tickets. The Baumans also attended this legendary final show (J. Bauman, 1988: 180–1) – they frequented theatres and concert halls thanks to Janina's position in the film industry[11] and their passion for dramatic arts and classical music. But attending *Forefathers* was above all a political demonstration. '[The] Theatre resounded with an immense clamor of applause and protest ... In the big square in front of the theater, a group of students with banners protesting the banning of the play was quietly waiting for the end of the per-formance. In the dark streets behind their backs, police lorries were waiting, too', recalled Janina Bauman (J. Bauman, 1988: 181).

This marked the beginning of a massive crackdown. Participants in the *Dziady* protests were punished, with thirty-five students arrested and others fined for anti-state activity. State propaganda blamed the uproar on an anti-socialist conspiracy prepared by the *Komandosi* group and its older mentors: Ph.D. students and revisionist faculty members such as Kołakowski and Bauman. A majority of those arrested were considered Jews, which helped the authorities build their theory of a Zionist conspiracy. The follow-ing day, Adam Michnik, who had organized the demonstration with his friend Henryk Szlajfer, contacted *Le Monde* correspondent Bernard Margueritte, who published an article about the student movement in Warsaw (Friszke, 2010: 524–6). Michnik and Szlajfer also told Margueritte that Bauman and Brus had returned their party ID cards (Eisler, 2006: 181). On 2 February, *Le Monde* pub-lished an article on the events, which mentioned the exclusion of Bauman and Brus[12] from the Party (Friszke, 2010: 526, n. 160). Brus and Bauman were both well-known scholars abroad. Michnik and Szlajfer knew that the illegal media would pass along the news to the Polish audience via Voice of America and Radio Free Europe. They had found a way around censorship and local propaganda to dis-tribute their position without distortion and manipulation. The *Le*

Monde article also reported on a petition to Parliament requesting the return of *Dziady* to the stage. The *Komandosi* group's petition stated 'We, Warsaw's youth, are protesting against the decision to ban the performance of "Forefathers' Eve" by Adam Mickiewicz, at the National Theatre. We are protesting against the policy of cutting off the progressive traditions of the Polish nation.' Within two weeks, the petition had been signed by 3,145 people in Warsaw (and 1,098 in Wrocław; Eisler, 2006: 181-2), including faculty and students from all departments. In response, the university began suspending and expelling students.

Kuroń and Modzelewski wrote and clandestinely distributed a text titled 'The Political Meaning of the Petition about "Forefathers' Eve"'. Its purpose was to provide an explanation of a protest that the authorities and pro-government organizations were trying to spin as a provocation manipulated by 'Zionists and imperialists' (Friszke, 2010: 541; Eisler, 2006: 224). In the meantime, the news media and some propaganda tracts distributed on campus employed anti-Semitic expressions, following the worst examples of the prewar Endecja movement.[13] One piece of anti-Semitic doggerel stated:

The national bard has become a clochard[14]
Do you know why?
Michniks and Szlajfers
Shout out to the world.
Someone remarked wisely
About a Fifth Column,[15] recently,
But Poles, blindly
are looking to Jews,
As usual – stupidly.

Come on brother, take a gun
Everyone has it in their hands.
Grab a Jew by the sidelocks
and kick him out of our land.
Excellent advice!
They spit on you, Poland,
But you still give them favours.
And you! Student! Drinking beer,
waiting for applause.
(Unknown author, cited in Eisler, 2006: 224–5)[16]

This sort of verse appeared on campus walls. The *Komandosi* group responded with texts: 'Strange Poets' by Karpiński (Friszke, 2010: 550) and 'Against Fascism' by Modzelewski (Eisler, 2006: 225). A 'war of tracts' enflamed the university community for the whole month of February (Friszke, 2010: 537–50). Through the distribution of illegal leaflets, students and faculty were informed about various actions and plans, and the wave of protests also brought in other 'creative intelligentsia' circles. On 29 February,[17] almost 400 authors came to a meeting of Warsaw's section of the Union of Polish Writers, where they requested the lifting of the ban on *Forefathers' Eve* and criticized the government's cultural policies.[18] The next day, a letter signed by 23 professors was sent to Prime Minister Cyrankiewicz, demanding respect for the Constitution and expressing concern about the growing curtailment of freedom of speech. Bauman did not sign this letter, while Kołakowski, Brus, Baczko and others did. Why? One explanation is that he wasn't told about it. The other is that, as the Baumans had decided to leave Poland, they needed to be careful. Any action against the authorities could be an obstacle to getting emigration documents. Still, the letter showed that part of the professorship had joined the students and writers in the circle of opposition.

There was no official response to the letters of protest. Instead, the Minister of Higher Education, Henryk Jabłoński, wrote a letter to the rector ordering the dismissal of Michnik and Szlajfer.[19] This order, clearly illegal since it violated university autonomy, was nonetheless carried out on 4 March, with Jabłoński ultimately responding to pressure from the Interior Ministry. Since mid-February, the *Komandosi* had tried to plan a large demonstration, although Kołakowski, Modzelewski and others felt it was misguided. The expulsions of Michnik and Szlajfer were the immediate pretext for the massive action on 8 March. The day before, the vice dean of the Philosophy Department, Jerzy Szacki, and other deans met with the rector requesting permission for the protest. At the same time, the Baumans hosted an informal meeting at their apartment.

'I remember [it] as a dramatic moment', recalled Barbara Szacka. She and the Baumans waited that evening with Kołakowski and others for her husband to come: 'When he arrived, finally, he said permission had not been granted . . . Leszek said sourly, "You will have blood on the streets."' Kołakowski lived on Bankowy Square, and on his way to the Bauman apartment on Nowotki he had passed the central police building and saw machine guns pointed at the streets.[20] Plans for the event were discreetly shared around the campus and at the polytechnical university, along with hundreds of leaflets demanding action with the slogan: 'Repression! The Autonomy of the University in Danger!' (Friszke 2010: 561).

The 8 March protest

In all Eastern-bloc countries, International Women's Day was celebrated on 8 March.[21] Flowers and sweets were brought to women that day, in offices, schools and other workplaces. It was usually a relaxed holiday, but that wasn't the case on the campus in 1968. Jerzy Eisler wrote in his book *Polish March 1968* that, for strategic reasons, the protest planners decided to give women the leading roles, figuring they were less likely to be arrested or attacked by the militia. Women were numerous in the *Komandosi* group, and from the beginning they had played important roles in the events. But the idea that their sex would protect the protest turned out to be wrong. What occurred was an unequal street fight between armed militia units and unarmed students, accompanied by some faculty members.

It was a bitterly cold day and snow covered the ground. That morning, watching out of the window of her office at the Ministry of Culture, near the university gate in front of the Presidential Palace, Janina Bauman saw trucks pulling up, as well as dozens of buses, with 'Excursion' written in their destination windows. 'Huge lorries covered with tarpaulins were making their way from the north to the south of the city', she wrote: 'The tarpaulins were slightly raised at the back to let in air and I could see they were tightly packed with men in civilian clothes. A sudden wave of wartime memories brought back times when lorries like these, full of armed Nazis, had rumbled along the streets of Warsaw hunting for victims' (J. Bauman, 1988: 184).

At noon, students and faculty swelled the central yard of the university in front of the Main Library. The several hundred people there, including secret-police agents and observers, listened to the declaration recited by Irena Lasota and Mirosław Sawicki (Friszke, 2010: 559). The meeting, as planned, was short, and those in attendance were preparing to leave when suddenly scores of middle-aged men dressed in hats and coats, carrying black sticks, got off the buses and marched onto the campus.[22] These were probably members of the ORMO (Ochotnicza Rezerwa Milicji Obywatelskiej (Voluntary Reserve of Citizens' Militia)), although some sources describe them as 'workers' or 'socio-political activists'[23] (Eisler, 2006: 237). Some were drunk. The students grew apprehensive.

The bussed-in 'excursioners' formed a cordon that kept anyone from leaving the square; their movements were remarkably similar to those of soldiers, and the association with World War II came immediately to mind. Someone started to scream 'Gestapo!', and other chants followed: 'Gestapo! Freedom! Democracy! No bread without liberty! No ban on Forefathers'! Destroy censorship! Agents out!' Some students were taken aboard the buses for ID checks, which enabled authorities to make a long list of participants. A few of the intruders began attacking students, and fighting began, but then suddenly an order came for everyone to sit down, and the students sat. Prorector Rybicki appeared on his balcony and addressed the crowd. He thanked the 'excursioners' for their intervention, and gave the students 15 minutes to disband. Instead, a delegation of students called on Rybicki to request that the security forces leave the campus, and that militia units waiting outside the side gate be dispersed. They also demanded freedom for a group of students who had already been arrested, and the reversal of the expulsion of Michnik and Szlajfer.

The tussles and fighting continued. The men in hats beat up two faculty members, but after the situation cooled for a while, some students left to go home and the men left the campus. Around 2 p.m., while a large crowd waited by the gate, Rybicki told the student delegation that the militia were leaving. But suddenly, around 400 members of the ORMO rushed onto the campus. As students sang the Polish national anthem and the Internationale (the communist anthem), the militia charged into the crowd, beating and seeking to arrest anyone who tried to escape. There were not many places to hide, because many campus buildings were closed and a wooden fence enclosed the plaza. It was an ideal hunting ground for the ORMO agents, armed with special leaden nightsticks. Groups of them snatched isolated students and faculty, threw them on the ground and beat them pitilessly. Then a new wave of militiamen rushed onto campus, cocooned in riot gear and armed with clubs, to reinforce the volunteer unit, and the men from the buses rushed back in. The militia started using their sticks and gas, and most of the protesters had no chance to escape. Some injured students, mostly women (Eisler, 2006: 243–4), waited inside the main building for the end of the violence. Even there they weren't safe, however, as militia entered the building and attempted to seize anyone they could find.

Bauman, with his students and some colleagues, fled the militia attack by seeking refuge in the Philosophy Department building (on the other side of the main entrance gate to the campus), on Krakowskie Przedmieście boulevard. When Bauman, with his students and some colleagues, was inside, another group composed of polytechnic students tried to push in to escape the militia. Barbara Szacka recalled:

It was a gruesome situation, because they [the militia] had thrown tear gas into the basement. We kept our students from leaving because it was dangerous outside. And then a big procession from the technical university entered the campus, and although the university was closed by the demonstration, a big group led by Professor Leśnodorski ... opened the door [of the Philosophy Department] to let in [the polytechnic students] and then closed the door [to keep out the militia].

The street was full of smoke.[24]

I remember that students asked if they were safe, and I could only say that we will be the first [to face the militia]. At that very moment these militia or security forces crashed through the door, and I remember the figure of Bauman, standing in front of them. They shouted 'Who are you?' and he answered . . .: 'I am a docent at the University of Warsaw!' . . . and they stepped back! It made a huge impression. I remember his figure; he was a very handsome man . . . tall, slim . . . I will never forget this horrible day.

If there was one thing Bauman had learned during his military life, it was how to impose authority. With his voice and body language, Bauman dominated the militia members, who, as if under a spell, left the building and went out to harass less fortunate students.

The battle enveloped the campus and its surroundings for about two hours. Screaming protesters sought refuge in shops and churches, which the ORMO and militia agents entered to grab and arrest them. The unequal combat spilled into the neighbouring streets, where hate-filled young men and regular militia attacked young women. 'Above all they beat the girls and above all the brunettes', one student recalled: 'Well, I thought, it's finally "Women's Day" after all! But . . . why brunettes? I understood it only later. I saw some militia soldiers drag a girl to the ground, and I remember that the crowd beat her' (in Eisler, 2006: 244). Dark hair corresponded to the physical stereotype of Jews in Poland. Polish women, according to the stereotype, had blue eyes and blond hair. The testimony points to the underlying racial populism that lay behind the state's response to the student protests.

The fighting spread to other parts of Warsaw as young people fleeing the university were chased towards the Polytechnic by militia forces. Beatings took place around campus housing; the violence went on until about 8 p.m. These were scenes reminiscent of the Occupation that Warsaw inhabitants hadn't experienced since the Liberation in January 1945. Now, the forces attacking university students were not foreigners.

There were no reports of deaths during the violence, but at least thirty injuries were reported (Eisler, 2006: 251). The victims were interrogated by police. But it was not the end of the rebellion.

A university divided

The events of 8 March provoked an important split in the university community, noted Professor Czesław Bobrowski, the dean of the Economics Department, who was beaten up during the disturbances. On one side were students and faculty, indignant over the violation of their 'sanctuary of freedom'; on the other, senior administrators, led by the rector, who utterly refused to engage with the matter that sparked the protest to begin with (in Eisler, 2006: 272). A group of seventeen professors, all Party members, sent a letter to the minister of higher education asking for a special commission to investigate the occurrences. (Bauman did not sign the letter – he was no longer a Party member.) Minister Henryk Jabłoński refused to accept the letter and declined any negotiations. The students, meanwhile, continued to press their demands and continued their actions, which spread eventually to other cities, including Kraków, Lublin, Katowice, Łódź, Wrocław, Gdańsk and Poznań. The government's response to the growing student movement was a 'divide and conquer' strategy. While sending out its security forces and allied hooligans to beat the students, Party cells launched propaganda actions in the factories and other workplaces to make sure students were blamed for the troubles. At all costs, the increasingly bold student movement had to be blocked from building coalitions with the workers.

On 11 March, Warsaw students gathered in the Auditorium Maximum, a neoclassicist university building from the 1930s. They put together a series of new demands, including changes in the press coverage of their movement and condemnation of the security forces' aggressive violation of university autonomy. That afternoon, the Philosophy Department faculty elaborated a similar statement, at a meeting that Bauman could have attended. While condemning the violence visited upon their school, the professors expressed indignation about a press that 'deliberately distorts events and misinforms society. Some of its organs are trying to spread anti-Semitic feelings and to differentiate the working class from the academic milieu' (Eisler, 2006: 285).

As students and faculty met inside the university buildings, security forces and government-organized rabble escalated the violence outside, with fights breaking out around the campus, and even near the Central Committee headquarters, during the afternoon and evening. The militia used tear gas and water cannons to break up a protest by 1,500 people (students from various Warsaw colleges and universities, as well as others – Eisler (2006: 292)). The protesters burned newspapers to protest against anti-Semitic expressions, and propaganda that vilified the students. The newspapers had published the names of protest leaders, along with their parents' professions, noting that they were not only children of privilege – but Jews. The articles mentioned some students' membership in the Babel Club, which organized discussions and dances for Warsaw's youth and was related to the TSKŻ – the Socio-Cultural Association of Jews. The tone of the newspapers was sneering and hateful. 'Those Jews'[25] were declared responsible for the 8 March riots (Eisler, 2006: 282–3). Contemporary historians have wondered why the government

decided to escalate its violence against the university. In all likeli-
hood, the impetus for the security force actions came from Moczar,
who wanted to show Party leader Gomułka that Moczar and his
Ministry of Interior Affairs controlled society and that Gomułka had
no place at the head of the state (Eisler, 2006: 287).

On 12 March, Professors Stefan Morawski and Jerzy Szacki of
the Philosophy Department prepared a resolution with the support
of the local Party unit. 'Today's most important task is to restore
peace at the universities', it said: 'However, this will be impossible
without taking into account the legitimate demands of the students.'
The massive faculty support for the students' demands included a
statement from Bauman's Polish Sociological Association, which
on 15 March declared:

> As sociologists, we know that the social movement of faculty and
> students on such a large scale could not arise solely as a result of
> the activities of troublemakers or even groups of political bankrupts
> behind them, but had a social basis and deep causes in the structural
> changes taking place in our society. Administrative coercive measures
> cannot permanently resolve the social and political problems related
> to the latest actions of academic youth. These are issues of socialist
> democracy and implementation of the principles of our Constitution.

The March crisis, in other words, resulted from the lack of democracy (Eisler, 2006: 355).

All this was in complete contrast to the official version of events
carried by the state propaganda tools, which focused on a select
group. 'The media repeated the same names over and over again',
wrote Janina, 'and it was not long before more were added to the
blacklist: prominent writers and professors who were responsible for
educating these young hooligans. On the fourth day . . . [Zygmunt's]
name along with those of many of his friends appeared in all the
daily papers, to be viciously spat on by the radio and television'
(J. Bauman, 1988: 187). 'Bauman' was a perfectly Jewish name,
unlike that of Kołakowski, who was not a Jew, and Morawski, who
had a Polish name. So Bauman was the perfect candidate to play
the role of global conspirator. His name confirmed the big theory.
Evidence was not required to confirm a belief, and, through belief,
to win a political point.

'The hate speech'

On Monday 18 March, a short warning strike ended at the university
and the rector closed the building of the Philosophy Department to
keep out mobs. The following day, Gomułka was scheduled to give

a speech to the Warsaw section of the Party, and all of Poland was preparing to watch. Students skipped lectures and left for home early to catch the speech. The Baumans gathered in front of their TV with their friend Basia.[26] The speech was given in the afternoon; as they got ready for it, they thought about Gomułka's speech from twelve years earlier, which had awakened so many hopes for a better future. This time, they didn't dare hope for much.

Unlike the October 1956 speech, Gomułka's March 1968 appearance seemed to go on for ever. It was held in the massive Congress Hall of the Palace of Science and Culture, the tallest building in Warsaw and a gift from Stalin to the Polish people that was not entirely appreciated. The 3,000 listeners included a large claque instructed to applaud or scream at strategic moments. The reactions of the carefully chosen crowd were orchestrated by propaganda specialists from the Interior Ministry – Moczar's people. Yet to say that the public response to his remarks was entirely scripted would be erroneous. The audience was only partially under control. The repeated applause and passionate calls of indignation were sincere. In some sense, this was the 'voice of the people', a people whose anti-Semitic feelings had been suppressed but now paved the way for the plan to evict 'Zionists' from Poland. For it was these Zionists who were responsible for the riots, and needed to be punished. That was the message of the speech.

'Dear and respected Comrades!' began Gomułka, 'in the last ten days, important events have taken place in the country. A large part of student youth in Warsaw, as well as in other academic centres in the country, has been cheated and brought on the wrong path by forces hostile to socialism. These forces have sown among the students the conflictual seed of anarchy.'[27]

The crowd reacted with enthusiasm, with people shouting 'Wiesław! Wiesław!' – Gomułka's code name from his years in the underground. He went on to give a detailed story about the anti-state activity of the intellectuals, giving examples, naming names – writers[28] and academics involved in a conspiracy led by Western, imperialist forces. Three-quarters of an hour into the speech, Gomułka moved on to the students, describing a meeting on 3 March in the flat of Jacek Kuroń – 'a group of a dozen or so people, mainly students of Jewish origin, known for their revisionist speeches and views' – where the 8 March demonstration was 'plotted'. Here it was, plain for the world to see – 'Jewish origin'. The audience listened in silence as Gomułka related the regime's version of events.

At one point, he hesitated while describing the resolution read by Irena Lasota. After stating that it was later read by two '*other* students', he added in a small and anxious voice: 'means . . . Polish . . . means Poles'.[29] These words are missing in the transcription of the more than 2-hour-long speech that appeared in *Trybuna Ludu*, the official Party newspaper. Why? Because the 'others' could not be blamed – as Poles, they couldn't have been part of the conspiracy. The student 'riots' could be explained very simply – any 'Pole' who engaged in the anti-state activity was manipulated, lost and naive. The 'Jews', on the other hand, were guilty, part of a conspiracy, and worthy of punishment. This was the point of the speech. This 'truth' emerged sentence by sentence, the pieces of the puzzle coming together to form a clear picture. Poland's history, its wars, struggles for independence and social justice, and its friendship with the USSR were all mentioned to highlight the party's historic role, while on the other side were the anti-Soviet forces, enemy-media and Polish emigration circles – and, of course, the 'Zionists'. All the elements of the conspiracy theory were evoked.

To careful readers of the official press such as the Baumans there was nothing new in the speech; Gomułka had merely maintained and reinforced the version presented in the media in recent weeks. But now that Gomułka had abandoned them, the Baumans and others like them had nothing more to hope for. The speech erased their modest hopes, but it was what the majority of Poles had expected. The attitude of the audience in Congress Hall was significant. As Gomułka's speech went on, and his tone became more and more aggressive, the crowd grew excited, their clapping longer and louder – at times he had to ask them to calm themselves. It was not just the reaction of a dutifully applauding claque – this was a real, spontaneous reaction: it was *vox populi*. When Gomułka promised to punish those 'guilty' of mob action, he received a sustained standing ovation.

'We know that some [people], in fact a small number, mainly employed in different humanities faculties at the University of Warsaw, a group of researchers, bear particular responsibility for recent events', he said, about three-quarters of the way into the speech. As the crowd's screams of indignation reached a crescendo, repeatedly interrupting the speech, he added:

> these academics such as professors Brus, Baczko, Morawski, Kołakowski, Bauman, and a number of others not yet mentioned by us, have fought for many years against our Party's policies from a revisionist position. Consciously and deliberately they poured hostile political views into the minds of the youth – they were the spiritual instigators of these troubling actions. Under the pressure of this group, the Council of the Faculty of Philosophy at the University of Warsaw, in their resolution of 12 March, did not hesitate to say, and I quote, 'the university youth movement, developed outside the framework of official organizations, has been a genuine mass movement for four days, uniting the overwhelming majority of UW students'. It is evident to us, it is obvious to us . . . Comrades calm down . . .

comrades . . . [screams of indignation] is obvious to us . . . that this group of politicians with academic titles has attempted to win the right to legalized anti-socialist activity in our country and puts their group interests above the good of Polish science and student youth. They are in fact a small group of research and teaching staff in higher-education institutions.[30]

At this point, the family stopped listening. Both younger girls 'looked with fear at their father. Basia [Bauman's friend] took both in her arms and with tears in her eyes said: "Don't listen to this, girls! This is all lies!"' (J. Bauman, 2011: 155).

'I could not imagine they would bring the Party's dirty laundry into public view like this', Bauman said in 2013: 'I could not have imagined that whenever I opened a newspaper, or turned on a television set, the subject would be "Bauman – the pig". This type of campaign was new.'[31] What's more, Bauman did not expect to be cited as the instigator of the 8 March protest, since he, like most of the faculty, opposed it. And, of course, the Philosophy Department resolution that Gomułka attacked was signed by all the council members, not just those whom he mentioned,[32] and other academic departments had issued similar statements. But, for all the incoherence in the speech, its message was clear: here are our enemies, a handful of agitators spreading revisionist ideas, who should be cleansed. Among the five, only Kołakowski was a 'Pole' according to the standards the authorities had begun to apply in 1967. The others were not Poles, they were 'Jews'. And the person who corresponded best to the stereotype was Bauman – his family name was the most Jewish-sounding, and he was young, popular, had international connections and more relatives in Israel than in Poland. He illustrated the ideal 'cosmopolitan', 'Zionist', 'Jewish' type. Nobody cared that cosmopolitan and Zionist were contradictory terms. Nobody was looking for a logical explanation – all they needed was the right scapegoat to focus the wrath of the frustrated people who listened to Gomułka's speech.

Towards the end of his speech, the crowd's anti-Semitism grew greater, at times making Gomułka appear uncomfortable, though he continued his smear campaign against the Jewish students and faculty.[33] When he attacked 'this group of politicians with academic titles . . . of Jewish origin or nationality' the crowd began to scream 'Go to Israel!' and 'Leave!'[34] 'Are there Jewish nationalists in Poland who adhere to the Zionist ideology?' he asked, and the crowd screamed 'Yes!!' Zionism alone was not a danger to Polish socialism, Gomułka said, but

this does not mean there is not a problem in Poland, which I would call the self-determination of some Jews – citizens of our country.

... Last June, during the Israeli aggression against the Arab states, a certain number of Jews in various forms showed their willingness to go to Israel to participate in the war with the Arabs. There is no doubt that this category of Jewish Polish citizens is emotionally and intellectually connected not with Poland, but with the state of Israel. They are definitely Jewish nationalists. Can you blame them for that? ... I suppose that this category of Jews sooner or later will leave our country.

With the crowd erupting in enthusiastic shouts of 'Out! Go to Israel! Leave!', Gomułka revealed what this had all been leading up to: 'At one time, we opened our borders for all who did not want to be citizens of our country and decided to go to Israel. Also today, for those who consider Israel their homeland, we are ready to issue emigration passports.'[35] Someone in the audience yelled 'At once! Today!'[36]

'The assembly turned into a raging mob', wrote Janina in her English version of her book (J. Bauman, 1988: 189). In the Polish version she says the Congress Hall 'smelled of pogrom' (J. Bauman, 2011: 156): 'In our cozy room, in our peaceful home, we suddenly felt ourselves in mortal danger. The enraged rabble would soon leave the Congress Hall and pour out onto the streets'[37] (J. Bauman, 1988: 189).

The fear of pogrom was once again real. Janina's dramatic wartime experiences came back to her immediately. Zygmunt, too, must have remembered how his mother in Poznań had reinforced their door to keep out the anti-Semitic criminals who struck on a daily basis. Parts of both families had fled after the Kielce Pogrom of 1946, others in response to anti-Semitic winds in 1956. The Baumans were not strangers to racial hatred and the deadly power of the crowd. As Zofia Bauman had done thirty years earlier on Prusa Street, Zygmunt, Janina and the girls locked themselves in their flat, blocking the front door with a heavy chest. They also 'looked for some sharp tools, just in case' (J. Bauman 1988: 190).

Fear was not restricted to those whom Gomułka had named. Barbara, Bauman's friend, immediately headed home, frightened for her husband, who was Zygmunt's colleague and could also be declared 'Zionist'. 'I hid him during the war, and again I had to hide him. After 25 years!' she cried (J. Bauman, 2011: 159). Many Holocaust survivors were afraid to leave their homes after the speech on 19 March. Some traumatized Jews spent days hidden in wardrobes, as they had done to escape raids by the Gestapo and their Polish accessories.[38] But there was no pogrom – or, more precisely, no traditional pogrom.

The state pogrom

Gomułka had taken the initiative in his own hands and was promising to deliver the same aim as every pogrom – to chase away the Jews. He used the term 'Zionist', but the effect was the same. Just as Hitler had defined who was or was not a Jew, Gomułka himself defined the 'Zionist' label, as writer January Grzędziński noted (in Eisler, 2006: 117). There were other similarities to the past. The *Bezpieka*, a state institution, defined Jews through ethnic profiling, taking a page from the Nazi anthropological manual.[39] Organizational practices implemented by the state to pave the way for the expulsions of 1968 were similar to the strategy implemented in Austria in 1938 by Adolf Eichmann, as the psychologist and 1968 activist Aleksander Perski (2013) has noted.[40] Finally, as the Endecja had done before World War II, Gomułka's regime stigmatized the 'Zionists' and 'Jews'. Both became antonyms of the Polish patriot (who was Catholic and not 'cosmopolitan').[41] This approach was shared by communists and some non-ideological bedfellows: Catholics, among others.[42] 'Without a doubt, thanks to March 1968, the Party cemented a bond with the nation. For a short time, but it worked', Bauman said in 2013: 'Above all that was because of the anti-Semitic slogans, dormant resources of folk anti-Semitism that could mobilize people to the Party's side.'[43]

It could be mobilized in part because the vision of the hurried departure of the 'Zionists' stirred dreams of the recovery of apartments, jobs, furniture and other objects and advantages left by the banished people. Gomułka's promise that 'those who are Zionists will leave' was in effect the declaration of a new kind of pogrom,[44] with the difference from earlier types being that in 1968 it did not start at the bottom,[45] but was launched from the top of the top. Those close to Gomułka would maintain later that he did not realize how 'productive' his hate speech would be. Gomułka wanted to reinforce his power, recovering it from the streets where Moczar's foot soldiers were in control. But once he had found and declared those 'guilty' in the 'Jewish plot', the logical next step was eviction. This is how pogroms work – developing out of a social process that channels a society's frustration and hatreds (see Tokarska-Bakir, 2018).

In historical pogroms, the Jews were beaten, robbed, persecuted, killed or chased from their homes and workplaces, schools and temples by groups animated by racial hatred. Gomułka's approach was to employ the state apparatus to elaborate the necessary laws, measures and rules for massive and ostensibly legal expropriations and expulsions. The state pogrom was much more efficient than the 'traditional' pogroms, performed by excited masses, whose actions were blind, destructive and out of control.[46] In the state pogrom, a highly sophisticated organization controlled not only who would be evicted (and who not) but also when and how the evictions would occur. There was a great deal of precision.

The state also decided who would fill the empty places and apartments and who got the goods left by the exiting Jews. Rare resources, suddenly available, were distributed in an organized way as unexpected gifts for those who most merited them. In this way, those who performed the state pogrom also benefitted from it. The state did not pay for this procedure, because its administrative costs were covered by the people being evicted.

This last element is symbolic and, we could say, post-modern because of its derisive character. The victims were 'initiating' the whole process themselves, by requesting departure and surrendering their citizenship. This was the first condition that enabled the launching of the process of departure, the procurement of travel documents and other necessary activities. The authorities made a very smart decision that matches with the Hughesian definition of 'dirty work'.[47] Through his speech, Gomułka launched a procedure to purge Polish society, meeting the wishes of a section of the Party. In doing so, he obviated the need for individual pogroms. The authorities did the dirty work institutionally – a white-glove pogrom implemented by the state and its servants, with the acclaim – or mute submissiveness, signifying permission – of the majority of the citizenry. In the Congress Hall, the public screamed: 'At once! Today!' – indicating their wish to see the immediate departure of the Jews. The Baumans got the message. However, it took three months before they could leave.

'At once!' in ninety-six days . . .

Starting on 11 March, Polish institutions received lists containing the names of their Jewish employees, and, in the final days of March, the 'liberation' of 'Zionist-occupied' workplaces began. The documents were so meticulously racialist that some people learned for the first time from the lists that they were actually 'Jews'.[48] Firings were fast and easy, supported by the Party and the state. Anti-Semitism became the official policy of Poland (Eisler, 2006: 116). Thousands lost their jobs.

Sometimes, as in Janina's case, the process began with a reassignment.[49] She was dismissed from her position as senior adviser in the National Board of Cinematography and moved to another office, where she was given tasks below her skill level and it quickly became clear that she had, in fact, nothing to do. She was asked to take free days immediately, but refused, saying she planned to go on vacation in August. This was a tactic in order not to make it any easier for her superiors to fire her, but, finally, on 1 April, Janina was sacked after eighteen years of work in the same institution.

On the day after the memorable evening of 19 March, Zygmunt went to work at the university as if nothing had happened. But the following day, on 21 March, campus employees went out on strike and Bauman stayed home, as the *Bezpieka*, which followed him without a break, noted.[50] Many intellectuals remained home that week. They were frightened. It was not safe to walk alone on the street. Janina managed to join Zygmunt on his walks home from work, and some of his students joined him, for further security.

By Saturday, however, the strike had ended; at a student committee meeting on Sunday attended by Leon Sfard, Anna Bauman's future husband, some expressed hope for further negotiations and a return to normality. That was not to be. On Monday 25 March, the newspapers and radio all communicated an order from Jabłoński, the minister of higher education. Five academics from the Department of Philosophy – Baczko, Kołakowski, Morawski, Bauman and Hirszowicz-Bielińska – as well as Professor Brus from the Economics Department, were sacked. Bauman was at home when the news came. 'From a radio broadcast I learned that I had been dismissed from my post and expelled from the university, and that it was me who had organized the anti-government student demonstrations', he told me.[51]

The news quickly spread around all of Warsaw.[52] Few had expected such strict measures, for, even in the era of Stalinist repression, Warsaw University professors had been banned from giving lectures but allowed to take other positions and pursue their research. Never before had a minister ordered the dismissal of a professor. Everyone was shocked by this abuse of power and disrespect of academic freedom. But that was only the beginning of the authoritarian decisions.

Students planned the next protest on 28 March to demand the return of their professors and colleagues. Despite the arrest of fifteen organizers, the meeting took place and students issued a statement: 'There is no Polish school of sociology without Bauman and Hirszowicz-Bielińska; there is no Polish school of philosophy without Baczko, Kołakowski and Morawski; there is no Marxist political economy without Brus' (in Eisler, 2006: 445). In response, Rector Turski expelled the next group of thirty-four students, while eleven others only lost their student rights. In the final days of March, information circulated that some departments would be closed – the faculties of economics, philosophy, psychology and education, and parts of the faculty of mathematics and physics. The campus was boiling. Now the authorities were truly at war, with students and faculty. As *Bezpieka* agent 'Janusz' reported:

Among the expelled academic staff of the University of Warsaw,
Z. Bauman and S. Morawski are still active. On 1 April, Z. Bauman
and a few other employees of his department met in the restaurant
'Crocodile', where they prepared a resolution. S. Morawski comes to
the faculty as if he was still its employee. The ambition of Bauman and
Morawski is to slow down the repression of the Faculty of Philosophy
and [prevent] its dissolution. Morawski and Bauman carry out many
discussions, during which they persuade interlocutors to solidarity.
A. Zabłudowski, E. Mokrzycki, and Skarbiński have already resigned.

Bauman and Morawski, on 2 April, convened a meeting of all
employees of the Faculty of Philosophy at which a number of
academics planned to sign publicly a resolution protesting at the
actions against the faculty. The rector did not give permission for
the meeting.[53]

The closure of the affected departments caused 1,166 students to
lose their places at the University of Warsaw (Eisler, 2006: 446). The
men were threatened with being incorporated into the Army (some
were immediately). That was the end of the 'Students March' – some
historians call it the Youth March, since other youth were involved
in the protests.[54] Socialist Poland had serious economic troubles:
rising prices, empty shops, shortages of basic goods and housing.
The students' requests for freedom of speech and autonomy were
among a long list of problems the authoritarian and bureaucratic
power decided to hush up. Blaming the students, especially those of
Jewish origins, was part of the smokescreen for these much broader
socio-economic issues.

Bauman's interpretation of the events of March 1968 in some
ways mirrors descriptions of Latin American politics in the post-
World War II era, during which coups d'état were for many decades
a common way of replacing the top layers of the military hierarchy
in some countries.[55] Bauman laid out his analysis several times,
including in a well-known 1968 article in *Kultura Paryska* titled 'On
Frustration and Jugglers'. During our discussion in 2013, Bauman
concluded with the same assessment he'd made forty-five years
earlier:

> 1968 among other things was an important event in that it allowed
> new people to get promotions. . . . The new system, created during the
> postwar reconstruction, had become obstructed. The age difference
> between the general and the lieutenant was ten to fifteen years. Well,
> [the people thought], God, should I wait eighty or sixty years before
> he will die or retire? It was a matter of crowded promotion channels.
> If one man is removed, twenty people can be promoted straight away
> – the freeing up of that one job opens the place of the one who moves
> up, and that in turn frees another space, and so on. It was, among

other things, a very large social mobility operation. Lots of people got places at the university because a lot of people left. What kind of impact did it have on society? ... How did it influence the culture? I do not know – this fitting a new crew for this so-called ship, the change of characters had to have some impact. The ambiance [must have changed] because normally you don't switch out an entire crew all at once. It's usually a slow process, so people have time to adapt and notice that something has changed. It was shocking.[56]

Historians estimate that over 13,000 people left Poland as a result of the 1968 events,[57] and many had occupied senior positions. As is common for this kind of social engineering, the purge focused on one specific group. In this part of Europe, the easiest target around which to mobilize popular hate was the Jew. The propaganda worked perfectly, joining old and new stereotypes.[58] Anti-Semitic texts flowed out of the press on a daily basis, and on the streets and in the institutions and workplaces, an ambiance of growing hostility made ordinary life very difficult for the stigmatized people. A growing group of people decided to leave their home country as it spat them out. The Baumans were in the first wave of departures.

In April, 'Jasia lost her job, I lost my job, and Anka was suspended'[59] from the Physics Department, Bauman recalled. The girls started to have problems at school: 'My twins came back from the school crying, because children are cruel, as you know.' The school near their home was very good: 'the teachers were impeccable, but the children were very cruel. Well, my daughters were coming back from school with tears in their eyes. ... It all coincided. I got three months' salary when I was released. So we had my salary for three months and then we were unemployed ... no savings... it was rather unpromising.'

Rather unpromising, and a very difficult situation, in which the parents could not protect their children. Schools reflect society at large, and the anti-Semitic ambiance that some children observed at their home infused the schools, or some of them. In fact, the schools reflected the binary reaction to the state's racist campaign. On the one hand, there were some where the ever-present aggressive environment was intensified with hate speeches and nasty behaviour, and on the other, ones where victims were protected. Janina Bauman reported both types of reactions to Gomułka's speech. At Stawki Street school – the state school attended by Irena and Lydia – there were aggressive children who repeated anti-Semitic slogans and even tried to beat up the girls, who were 13 years old; and another group that tried to protect them. As Bauman said, teachers were impeccable, which had not been his experience in prewar Poznań and was also not true of all schools in 1968.[60] Children labelled as Jews endured many painful situations. While Bauman has been highly restrained in his discussion of this topic, all of his friends recall the painful experiences of his daughters, and Bauman suffered for it, they said.

For those who emigrated in 1968, the racial abuse of their children was often the last straw that drove them out of Poland. Many, if not most, of the adults were Holocaust survivors, and while the transmission of trauma was not as well understood in 1968, the psychological effects were significant.[61] When parents saw no possibility of protecting their progeny, emigration became the only option, a survival strategy that was an essential part of the forced migration.

Anna, as noted above, learned about her parents' decision to leave on 1 January after returning from a New Year's party in Kazimierz with her friends. Her reaction was very emotional: 'She burst into tears', Janina wrote:

> She was eighteen and in her first year at university. She wouldn't listen and locked herself for hours in her room. Towards evening she calmed down a little and began to talk. She said she loved Poland and couldn't imagine living anywhere else. She insisted that the same was true for us: we would never be happy elsewhere. We knew she was right. But there was no other way and we told her so. (J. Bauman, 1988: 33).

The Baumans started the departure process on 23 April. The certificates they needed had a pyramidal structure, whereby, in order to get a document in one institution, several documents from other institutions were indispensable. The family issued their final request for a title of travel on 13 May, presenting five documents they had obtained by waiting in office lines for most of the previous three weeks. Unlike the majority of the emigrants, who left by train from the famous Gdański Station,[62] the Baumans decided to leave in Zygmunt's Ford Cortina. Since each stateless individual could take only US$5, it was necessary to request special permission to take more foreign currency. Bauman needed a document from the Polish Union of Vehicles (Polski Związek Motorowy) confirming that he could drive on international roads. He also had to show he had 1,100 Austrian schillings and car insurance. Bauman got a certification from the Polish National Bank showing he had obtained that quantity of schillings by selling the Polish state an equivalent amount of French francs and American dollars. The state itself established the exchange rate, which had nothing in common with the internationally established rate – a classic example of the power mechanisms practised by the state, a topic of some of Bauman's later work.

The next step was to get a visa. The Polish state would only accept departures for Israel, but it had severed diplomatic relations with Tel Aviv the year before, and the Dutch Embassy provided consular service for Israel. The visa with the number 3645/ne68 was issued on 29 April with no fee – a pleasant surprise. As a professional military officer, Bauman could expect to have trouble obtaining permission to emigrate, but on 8 May he received a certificate noting that the military did not require his services. As the process quickly advanced, Bauman, like the fathers in other soon-to-be-stateless families, called in a craftsman to build special chests for the family belongings. Packing and dispatching the goods of the evicted families was a booming business in the spring of 1968. There were rules against exporting certain types of furniture, and a weight and size limit on the volume of goods that could be taken. Bauman's specialist knew exactly how to prepare everything for a customs office revision. Each document accompanying the boxes required five copies and had to go into tremendous detail – including the title of every book that was packed away. The Baumans had many books, although they could not take them all because of the limitations on their baggage. Like many other members of the intelligentsia who were on their way out of Poland, a careful winnowing process was required. Many friends, students and relatives inherited valuable goods that couldn't be taken out of the country. It was a good time to be a trader, a buyer's market with many 'Jewish goods' suddenly available. There was a resonance to that term, in the vernacular as well as legal language, referring to the properties left by slain or departed Jews during the war. But in 1968 no one spoke openly about the sour way the term 'Jewish goods' hung over from the war – certainly it was no brake on the way those who benefitted from the situation trafficked in these properties.

Soon-to-become-stateless families packed up the material traces of their lives accumulated over the past twenty-three years. It wasn't possible to ship all their belongings, so Janina called a non-Jewish friend who had saved her family during the Nazi occupation by hiding them, and put him in charge of distributing what they would leave to people in need. The friend discretely disposed of their furniture and some books; a few objects were sold and some new things were bought – this was how a lot of the March '68 émigrés proceeded.

The craftsman contacted by Zygmunt actually had two jobs – as a business owner and as an informant for the *Bezpieka* codenamed 'Stolarski' ('Carpenter-ski' – it was not hard to figure out the identity of this informant), who was able to share the intimate details of many a departing Warsaw family. Among other information that concerned different families packing up their Warsaw life for ever, 'Carpenter-ski' reported:

On May 10, 1968 at 10 a.m., I arrived at the apartment of prof. Bauman at Nowotki 21b flat 28, tel 31-65-07, at his telephoned request. Professor Bauman told me that he had prepared documents for his departure to Israel, and that before depositing his entire document folder [to the passport office], he wanted to talk to me about making boxes for his things. He wanted to bring some furniture and a lot of books. He has a car and if he gets permission to leave, he will leave with his family in his car. He expects to get permission because he is not bound by any state secrets. He made an agreement with me already, because he worries that his date of departure could arrive quickly. He told me that there are fake stories circulating about him, including one saying that he had come to the university saying: 'Goys,[63] hands up!' And that in one lecture attended by only three non-Jews, he had to say 'the lecture will take place in the Jewish language', and added that he does not even know the Jewish language.[64]

This anecdote merits deconstruction. If 'Carpenter-ski' was telling the truth, perhaps Bauman, suspecting the craftsman was a *Bezpieka* agent, told him the story knowing that it would be reported to the services. That would be a kind of game played by Bauman with the omnipresent *Bezpieka*. Or perhaps Bauman was responding to a real piece of gossip, something that angered him since he would never have behaved this way with his students. But one element of the story was certainly true: Bauman lacked the 'Jewish-language' ability to handle a lecture in Yiddish, which was sporadically used in some families, usually by parents when they didn't want their children to listen.[65] That was the situation of Polish Jews in this era; those who had survived the Holocaust, and their postwar-born children, for the most part lacked even the rudiments of 'Jewish language'. At best it was a sort of 'argot', or dialect from the past.[66]

That linguistic circumstance created ironic situations, such as an interaction recalled by another 1968 emigrant, the Polish-American mathematician and poet Włodzimierz Holsztyński: 'I told [the eminent mathematician Karol] Borsuk about my decision to emigrate . . . He immediately reacted: "How is it possible? You are a Pole!" In the spirit of contradiction, but without conviction, I responded: "I am a Jew." "But you speak Polish?" asked Borsuk. "Yes", I responded. Borsuk then asked: "Do you know Jewish or Hebrew?" I said: "No."'

Speaking no Yiddish or Hebrew, the Baumans were like the majority of the 'soon-to-be-stateless' Poles. This was the core of the dramatic situation of the entire stigmatized group: they were pushed by the state – by their state – to request the resignation of their citizenship, as a result of which Poland – their home country, their linguistic and cultural home – stopped being their space of identity, their universe of cultural references, their security zone. They would become 'homeless' in the large and deep sense of identity, deprived of the right to be Polish citizens . . . of the right to any citizenship at all . . . state-less.

The procedure of becoming stateless was easy, fast – and expensive,[67] a cash cow for the struggling Polish state. Polish citizens had to petition the State Council for permission to change citizenship. Under international law, their situation was illegal. People generally renounce their citizenship only when they are applying for another (typically when marrying a foreigner, or emigrating) and the laws of one or both of the states in question forbid dual citizenship. In the case of the state pogrom of 1968, Poland forced its citizens to become stateless. There was no guarantee they would automatically become Israeli citizens; indeed, not all of them even went to Israel. The state blackmail consisted of the following: for wanting to leave, we take back your citizenship. And now go!

Bauman submitted his request on 13 May, with a one-page document carrying two sentences: 'I request permission for a change of citizenship for myself and my children. The following request is motivated by definitive departure to Israel.'[68] He added his name and Warsaw address, the word 'Israel', and his signature. This supposed 'formality' had heavy consequences, for by filing the request Bauman had his name inscribed on a blacklist of 'unwanted' people in Poland. For Bauman, so attached to his Polish identity, and permanently struggling to be perceived as a Pole, this document was proof of failure. Just as living in Jeżyce, the middle-class Polish area in Poznań, had not kept him off the ghetto bench before the war, being a Polish sociologist and university docent did not help prevent his fate as a Polish Jew in 1968.

Like most other Polish Jews, in 1968 he had no choice.[69] With this document, his battle to be a Pole among other Poles was lost. Bauman had to act on behalf of his two youngest daughters, deciding that becoming stateless was preferable for them in order to escape a new wave of discrimination, to keep his children from having to navigate the same path he had trodden.

The endgame of departure depended on further abusive, denigrating treatments at the hands of the state. Families were engaged in a suite of requests, collections of stamps, payments and administrative procedures. Every trace of their activity had to be sealed shut for ever. The state requested certificates from their workplace, from the libraries where they had borrowed books, and from any institution where they might have borrowed money (*zakładowa kasa pożyczkowa*). Zygmunt and Janina had to provide certificates of being debt-free at the tax office.

To add insult to injury, the families had to make advance payments for their utility and phone bills, and their rent – usually for six months, far longer than almost any of the Jewish families would end up remaining in Poland. And they had to pay to end these services, and file the documents at a housing office. Like most Poles, the Baumans did not own their apartment. They belonged to a co-operative that managed their rental fees and other administrative contracts. To get the document certifying that they were giving up the apartment, they had to advance several months in rental charges and utility payments to the co-operative. The co-operative managers, meanwhile, signed an agreement with future tenants, who would often visit the Bauman flat while they still lived there to have a look around, take measurements and plan their interior design. It was another act of symbolic violence against Bauman family intimacy – though understandable, in a way. Given the penury of housing in the capital, the Baumans' four-room, cozy home in central Warsaw was an attractive trophy. The state could take back anything that it had 'given'.

There was only one area where the Baumans managed not to be robbed by the state that was excluding them: payment for the children's studies. Many Jewish families at this time were forced to pay huge sums to 'pay back' the education their children had received from institutions of higher learning – sums that few families could afford,[70] and which the Baumans also would have been unable to cover. Luckily, Anna had been too young to graduate from the university with her physics degree.

As noted, those leaving Poland could only take $5 with them, and the authorities wanted documentation of any savings in their bank accounts. Those who had money spent it, though it wasn't easy to find worthwhile goods in the shops of Warsaw in 1968. Furthermore, all objects listed in departure documents for the customs office had to have evidence of use – no new objects! And it was illegal to use funds from abroad to pay for the vast admin-istrative documentation required for departure. The idea was that Jews should leave the country naked of economic resources.[71] There are several stories about people who bought Polish wool carpets and dirtied them intentionally. Others bought household appliances, unaware that the plugs abroad were different from in Poland. One attractive object was a samovar – it seemed like an easy product to sell, so almost every Jewish family leaving the country bought one.

The biggest obstacle was posed by the passport office. Zygmunt and Janina had filled out the typical travel document each time they travelled, but this time they needed a 'one-way travel document' – another document that did not meet international legal standards. On 17 May, the Baumans brought in a folder stuffed with docu-ments to begin collecting the stamps and franks and permissions required by the passport service. A final account by that office illus-trates how the Baumans' situation was presented in administrative language:

Application – May 17, 1968 – Citizen Bauman Zygmunt, 43 years, Lydia – 13 y.o, Irena 13, Anna 19, Janina 42; applying for documents for a trip to Israel, purpose: permanent residence. Justification: Jewish nationality, doc. doctor – currently is not working. Recently, he worked at the University of Warsaw as the head of general sociology chair. His wife, MA in philosophy – is not working. Recently she worked in Ministry of Culture and Arts . . . as an adviser. The daughter was a first-year student at the Faculty of Physics at the University of Warsaw – on May 7th she resigned from studies. In Poland they have no family. In Israel, his mother and sister are there from 1957. A promise of visa and travel fees in the joined file, they will take their own car to Austria. He travelled abroad in previous years, on business and tourism.

A later note, generated on 1 June, reports that Vice Minister Świtało had given permission for the Baumans' departure. A handwritten note in red pencil reads: 'Very urgent'. The passport fee was 5,000 zlotys.[72]

It must have been astonishing to see the notation of 'Jewish nationality' in these forms, since this category of nationality (*narodowość*) as a thing separate from citizenship (*obywatelstwo*) had disappeared twenty years earlier from official Polish documents. This was a return to the interwar administrative culture, when the minorities (Belorussian, Ukrainian, Jewish, etc.) were mentioned in official documents. None of the five members of the Bauman family had 'Jewish' citizenship, because such a thing did not exist.[73] Nor did they have Israeli citizenship; they were Poles – now, stateless Poles. The final documents seemed to corroborate the propaganda image of Zygmunt and Janina; they were 'unemployed' or 'did not work' – as though by their own wishes. Anna had 'resigned' from the university, as though she were lazy. 'No family in Poland and close relatives in Israel' supported the cover story that they were leaving to join family, rather than being expelled. Even in this short administrative document, propaganda has its impact. Surprisingly, considering the reams of documents collected by the services over the years, the description of the family situation had a major error: the mother and sister in Israel were Janina's, not Zygmunt's. The note at the bottom regarding Świtała's endorsement[74] shows the case had reached the highest levels, for Świtała was the deputy to Interior Minister Mieczysław Moczar, the dean of official Polish anti-Semitism. It is possible that Moczar himself, ultimately, signed off on the Bauman family's departure.[75]

This final signature was not to be taken lightly. Given the propaganda hate speech describing Zygmunt as a notorious public enemy, the Baumans feared they would be kept in Poland, or that Janina would be permitted to emigrate with the children while Zygmunt was obliged to stay in Poland, or even arrested. Not everyone who wished to emigrate was permitted to leave. As Agata Fijuth-Dudek has noted, the authorities were reluctant to allow the emigration of anyone with extensive knowledge of the state's functioning.[76] Evidently, the *Bezpieka* did not consider Bauman to be in that category.

The permit allowing them to leave reached Bauman's hands on 7 June. They were given twenty-three days to send off their belongings. Thanks to 'Carpenter-ski', they were already packed (about 2,000 books filled most of their allotted space), but had to pass customs control at the Gdański Station, and Bauman spent two weeks there watching employees go over each item in his crates – each book, folder and personal photograph – as they searched for supposedly anti-state manuscripts and notes. On Friday 21 June, Zygmunt shipped everything to a family address in Israel. Given the timing of the whole process, we can assume the authorities wanted Bauman to leave as soon as possible. 'It happened very fast', he said later: 'I was impressed that our documents were speedily prepared and waiting for us.'[77]

During those final weeks and months, the *Bezpieka* kept close watch on each member of the family. The Baumans tried to turn it into a sort of game, in which the goal was to lose the agents for a while and gain liberation from being shadowed. It really was not very pleasant, though. With the typical distance Bauman employed in telling personal stories, he recalled, 'I was spied on all the time and it was also very sad because . . . I do not know how much the Polish taxpayer paid for completely useless spying – useless because people knew that I did not have an underground organization. They knew it. This tracking was just teasing, and harassment to get me to leave.'

The Baumans were not an exception – most faculty members from the dissolved departments had their personal 'guardian angel'. At times, this led to absurd situations, as Bauman recalled in 2013: 'We were having a farewell meeting of friends, several dozen close friends, and from the window you could see the square by the entrance to our house on Nowotki Street – and all the benches were occupied by UB [*Bezpieka*] agents. Each of my guests had brought his agent.' A double farewell party, in a way – one group in Bauman's apartment; the other, silent group in the square outside. That was on Friday 21 June.

'That evening more people than ever came to see us. Even the empty flat could hardly hold such a crowd', recalled Janina in her book: 'In a dazzling heat, our visitors sat on the floor among jars of flowers, leaning against bare walls marked with the pale squares and rectangles where pictures once had hung. Though they knew they were being listened to, that each word was being recorded they talked for hours about their own and our precarious future.' They ate cherries and drank vodka. Among their closest friends were some who would follow the Baumans soon, and others who would never emigrate. There were people who came to embrace the Baumans openly, an expression of support to victims and disagreement with state policy and those who followed it blindly. Propaganda called these people – if they were not Jews – people in the 'Zone of Judaization [*Verjudung Zone*]'.[78]

Bauman had many visits from such people. One was Professor Ossowska, who was not a close colleague in the department, but wanted to show her sympathy and staunch opposition to anti-Semitic discrimination. There were also other unexpected shows of loyalty, such as a phone call from a wartime buddy. But there were insults, too, including racial epithets that ended one longtime friendship instantly. If the insults from anonymous or unknown people hurt, the impact was greater when they came from old friends. Some colleagues, and even friends, avoided the Baumans. The last month was an emotional roller-coaster. The farewell to life in Poland was progressing amid exhausting preparations for departure. The perfume of a new epoch was in the air . . .

For one final time, the Baumans played the game of cat-and-mouse with the *Bezpieka*, telling everyone they saw that they would be leaving Monday morning, then escaping early Sunday, just after their last visitor departed. The car had been packed the day before. Their manoeuvre appears to have tricked their 'guardian angels', who missed their unexpected departure. The first day they drove about 400 kilometres to the southwest, tired but focused on their new and unknown adventure. The twins were excited by the trip, but Anna had wanted to stay behind, to wait for her friend Leon. She cried about her 'Aborted life'[79] and the future boyfriend she worried she would never see again. Bauman convinced her to come along with the rest of the family. 'I knew [Leon] would be liberated soon', he would recall: 'They had nothing to charge him with. And I knew that when he got out he would have no choice but to follow us.'[80] It was of vital importance to Zygmunt and Janina for the family to stick together. They had learned that lesson during World War II.

On 23 June, a Sunday, at about 11 a.m., they reached the border, at a crossing point that had been assigned to them by the security services:

SECRET – To the director of the Board of Control of border circulation – Please make a detailed personal check, baggage and car, of citizen Bauman Zygmunt [personal data], who received a travel document for a permanent trip to Israel valid until 30VI 1968. Bauman goes definitively to Israel with his family, [list of persons], the aforementioned family leaves by car through GPK-Cieszyn. [Signed:] Deputy commander of the capital MO of the Security Service.[81]

The Baumans would spend several hours at the border while their car and luggage were meticulously searched. They were assigned to be strip-searched, too, even the children, before finally being allowed to go. Perhaps the *Bezpieka* were searching for Western currency or gold, or simply delivering a final traumatic souvenir from the home country. However, Anna and Lydia did not remember that this control was traumatic. Actually they remember nothing from that passage. Perhaps the officer in charge of the strip-search disregarded the order? The authorities in Warsaw received a final report by telegram from the border station at Cieszyn: 'In the implementation of telegram No. 2069 of 6.06. 1968, [added by hand: June 23, 1968 at 11h,] I report, that a detailed personal control was carried out on the persons listed in your telegram, and of their luggage and transport vehicle. . . . the controlled persons did not hide anything – the result of the revision was negative. [Signature – commander of inspection point.]'

What must Zygmunt Bauman have felt at this moment? Did he recall November 1939, the tumultuous escape with his parents? The negotiations with the Soviet border guard? Tobie Nathan, the psychiatrist and specialist in refugee trauma, states that childhood traumas are the worst (Nathan, 1994). But the suffering a refugee experienced in early life could be cured with time, in positive circumstances. It was worse when the victim was evicted a second time. The first trauma was awakened, to torment the victim in combination with the new trauma. The first time, Bauman had been a child. Now, he was the head of a family being evicted. For certain, there were no bombs falling, no dead bodies. But the origins of the escape remained the same. They were being punished for their Jewishness. They were leaving for ever.[82]

Now they belonged to nowhere.[83]

12
Holy Land
1968–1971

In dreams I've never met you, but now I understand
The sole place on this planet that has always been mine.
I can now answer, where is my homeland?
I had none until this moment, now I have Palestine.

(Janina Bauman, tr. Barbara Nykiel-Herbert)[1]

'The Family's Big Trip'

Lydia Bauman, 13-year-old daughter of Zygmunt and Janina, chose this title for the eighteen-page notebook she kept, describing the family's three-week trip from Warsaw to Haifa.[2] She wrote it in Polish with the perspicacity of a 'natural observer'. Through her untutored sociological eye, she describes the crucial elements of each day, providing the 'thick description' so prized by ethnographers (Geertz, 1973).[3] Lydia's journal-keeping was inspired by her mother, who since childhood had on a quasi-daily basis kept a diary that later became the foundation for her books.[4] Janina knew how important writing was, especially in the difficult periods of life. Writing allowed a person to reflect on feelings, to organize emotions to some extent, and to record what was important at a particular moment.

This particular moment marked the end of their life in one country with no hope of returning home – a familial uprooting. Lydia took notes each day of the journey, starting on Sunday 23 June at 2.15 a.m., when they crept out of their Warsaw apartment, escaping ever-present spies. While the Polish part of the journey is infused with sadness[5] and some anxiety (near the Czechoslovak border they met a Soviet military column headed into Poland), after leaving the homeland that had suddenly rejected them, the ambiance becomes more enthusiastic. Lydia wrote in her journal: 'Then, it was very nice. We travelled on beautiful and empty highways and we admired Czechoslovakia, sometimes stopping in small towns.' Zygmunt even said: 'It is a good thing to be a stateless person – we can finally travel together!' This was typical humour for Bauman: part of his strategy for living, to transform serious or sad situations into wide-eyed observations. After the 'unpleasant'[6] border crossing, they began the exciting part of the 'Big Family Trip'.

Zygmunt was the only driver in the family. At the end of the first long day and night of driving, they stopped at the Grand Hotel in Brno. Bauman felt at ease in Czechoslovakia, a country where he had given talks, where his books were translated, and where he was in general deeply respected, having helped to introduce Western sociology to academics who lacked the historical tradition of their colleagues in Poland. Moreover, when Bauman was ejected from the university in March, Charles University in Prague had immediately offered him a chair.[7] The Baumans all felt better in Czechoslovakia. While they were not yet in the 'Free West', the ambiance of freedom was everywhere in these halcyon days of the Prague Spring. The next day, Monday, the family spent the rest of their korunas (Czech currency) buying trousers for the teenage girls – a pleasant way to forget their circumstances. Although the Austrian border marked the Iron Curtain, their passage through it was short and pleasant. It took only five minutes to pass through customs, according to Lydia's diary, and an hour more to reach Vienna, where they went directly to the Jewish agency for immigration, the *Sochnut*.[8] This was a very important stage of the immigration procedure; at this point, the family had to decide where it would go.

Although their travel documents said they were going to Israel, most of the Jews leaving Poland in 1968 did not settle in the Jewish state;[9] the Baumans were among those who did, initially. In the Polish version of her book, Janina Bauman explained their choice:

> There were so many other possibilities. . . . We could have chosen England, Australia, Canada, or stayed in Vienna – invitations and job offers were coming from everywhere. However, we chose Israel. Not because of love for this country. Zygmunt had never favoured the Zionist idea, and my youthful longing has faded long before. It was probably a sense of duty that made the difference. The Jewish state had made it possible for us to travel and finance a trip, so it was necessary to go there, at least for a certain amount of time. We would work, pay back the debt. And above all, there – and only there – I had a little home: my mother and sister, Zygmunt's sister in a kibbutz, and thousands of people speaking Polish. (J. Bauman, 2011: 27)

Israel, then, was the only other possible home for the Baumans. Their sense of duty to repay the Israeli state's investment in them recalls the actions of Maurycy Bauman, who in September 1939 sought desperately to pay for the tickets that enabled the family's escape from Poznań.

From Vienna's *Sochnut* office, the Baumans travelled 35 kilometres to Schönau Castle, where there was a transit camp[10] in the middle of a beautiful old park, a kind of holiday hotel where Jews waiting to make *Aliyah* waited for their documents and the next charter plane to Israel. The Baumans spent two weeks there. According to their daughter's account, they had a busy schedule.

The troubles in Poland and Bauman's ouster from Warsaw University were widely reported overseas,[11] and his decision to emigrate did not surprise colleagues whom the Baumans encountered on their travels. On their very first day in Vienna, Bauman met Professor Ernst Florian Winter, the political scientist and diplomat, who invited him to give lectures and hold discussions with students and faculty – a very short visiting professorship. After meeting with students on Tuesday 25 June, Bauman gave a lecture that Friday. Lydia reported that her father was glad that his first lecture had gone well. For Bauman and other scholars of this exile, the invitations from foreign universities provided a sense of academic solidarity in a difficult time of statelessness and economic disruption.[12] Having participated in conferences, publications and visiting professorships abroad, Bauman had the advantage of being one of the best-known Polish social scientists in the Western world of academia. The offer to host his talks in Vienna was consistent with university practices when a well-regarded scholar colleague passed through town.

The Polish secret services were keeping tabs on the Baumans, of course. A report in the file states: 'Bauman is in Vienna where he gave some lectures and made a declaration whose main point is: I felt Polish, I feel Polish, and I will always feel that I am a Pole. I believe that when political conditions change in Poland, I will go back.'[13] At this juncture, Bauman's declaration seems premonitory, but in 1968 it was the purest fantasy.

Despite their complex situation, the family spent some time sightseeing in the city and enjoying the Prater, the oldest European theme park. Like a regular middle-class vacationing family, they ate sausages and ice cream, and went on rides – as Lydia assiduously recorded – at the Fun House, Fairy World, the Flying Saucer and the Barrel of Laughs. The parents went to the cinema and the girls spent their last shillings on Prater pancakes. For the first time in their lives, the family enjoyed a holiday together in the 'free world'.

From the pages of Lydia's diary, one could almost feel that it was a perfectly relaxing time, but Bauman was not really a tourist or an anonymous emigrant. No sooner had they arrived than Bauman was contacted by the Western media. As Lydia noted in her journal on Wednesday 26 June, 'my parents went with the editor of "Free Europe" [radio] to Vienna. We don't know why, because the parents are never eager to confide what exactly they are doing.'[14] But even their awareness of the fact was unusual – this kind of information was kept secret in the Soviet bloc. In Poland, Radio Free Europe was synonymous with the CIA: it was a subversive institution, 'Western propaganda', and by accepting an invitation to an interview the Baumans had definitively and officially placed themselves in the opposition camp. Bauman's participation in the broadcast was the prolongation of his struggle for more freedom in Poland. Many of those who left Poland did the same – officially, if they had decided to emigrate; attempting to hide their identities, if they intended to go back. In front of radio microphones, from the other side of the Iron Curtain, Bauman presented his analysis of the March 'revolt' and other political events.[15]

In Vienna, his life became split into two: Poland, and the 'new life' – a double presence.[16] If he had refused to give the interview to Radio Free Europe, Bauman would have been cutting himself off from the Polish past, a decision that several of the March 1968 émigrés made.[17] But Bauman lived his post-1968 life along two parallel paths: while becoming quite active in new places, he maintained strong ties with Poland.

The Baumans began preparing their Israeli future while in Vienna. They spent part of their time at Schönau Castle learning Hebrew and watching movies about Israel; Bauman had started intensive Hebrew study when the family was still in Warsaw in early 1968, Anna Sfard recalls: 'He had a small notebook with words in Hebrew and he took it with him everywhere. He learned the new words. Even waiting at red lights when driving his car, he made use of all of his time.'[18] The family also participated in cultural activities offered by the host organization. Anna remembered the Jewish music she heard in the building, including the very popular Noemi Shemer song, sung by Shuli Nathan, 'Yerushalayim shel Zahav' (Jerusalem of Gold).[19] This romantic and nostalgic tune prepared the new Israeli citizens emotionally for their meeting with the new homeland. *Shabbat* dinner on Friday evenings was a highpoint of the week, preparing the Polish emigrants for a life where traditional rituals were a significant part of life. Lydia humorously described the meal as 'fish, challah, bread without butter, soup made from a rooster corpse – broth with dumplings (*kluski*), boiled meat and rice in tomato sauce; sweet wine and compote'. The family's distance from the religious side of the Shabbat dinner is expressed in Lydia's sarcastic description of the soup ('rooster corpse') as well as her note on the 'artistic' part of the evening: 'The youth sang summer camp songs, and the rabbi was happy, because he thought they were religious hymns.' Bauman's daughters had gone to youth camps organized by Jewish organizations in Poland (Anna to a camp run by TSKŻ, the Association of Jewish Culture; the twins to

Śródborów, a camp with Jewish cultural activities). Moreover, Anna had visited her family in Israel in the late 1950s. But their encounters with Jewish traditions were entirely secular, which can be seen in the text written by 12-year-old Lydia. They were a typical Polish leftist intelligentsia family whose attachment to Jewish culture was of a distinctly lay nature.

The first Sunday of their stay at Schönau, the Israeli ambassador came and spoke with the Baumans, and whatever he said left them in a more positive mood. Moreover, during their stay near Vienna, Anna learned the good news that Leon Sfard had been let out of jail. Uncertainty remained, however, about whether he and his parents would be able to leave Poland.

As they waited for their documents, the family developed a daily routine. They were loyal customers in a nearby cafe-bar run by an elderly lady the girls called *babcia* (granny), who prepared drinks and snacks for them. The most interesting element of those daily visits to Babcia's bar was not the food, however, but the jukebox. Thanks to Lydia's detailed description, we know that Zygmunt and Janina listened to the music from the hit 1965 David Lean film *Doctor Zhivago*.[20] They were enjoying their stay at Schönau – it was almost a true holiday. In Poland, in the late 1950s and 1960s, the Baumans were hard-working, professionally active, socially busy people. They arrived home late and frequently had friends at the house. Zygmunt especially was often abroad travelling (in 1966, he spent less than half the year in Poland). They were not typical Polish parents who devoted time for the children. So the summer of 1968 was an exceptional situation. Everyone's busy life had abruptly ended, and now they all had time for each other. That had never happened before.

After two weeks in Austria, their documents were ready and the family packed the car and headed to Italy. They stayed at a small village on the Adriatic coast for four days, enjoying the place and relaxing on the beach. After the short passage to Venice (where, two years earlier, Janina and Zygmunt had enjoyed a romantic visit), they got on a ship that would take them to Israel.

On the two-day trip, which included a short stop in the Greek port of Piraeus, Zygmunt, Janina and Anna studied Hebrew intensively while the twins swam in the ship's pool and played games. They arrived in Haifa on 15 July, in the morning. Anna recalled it as a moving moment, with the beautiful panorama of Haifa – the promised land – and the Shuly Nathan song, which the captain of the ferry played as they landed: 'Yerushalayim shel Zahav Veshel nechoshet veshel or, Halo lechol shirayich ani kinor'.[21]

Tears flowed from the eyes of many of the immigrants.

Forced *Aliyah* – 'Strangers amongst Strangers'[22]

Aliyah, in Hebrew, means 'going up'. This is what diaspora Jews do
when they decide to live in the country where they will no longer
be members of a minority. The group of Polish Jews was called
the 'March *Aliyah*' after the events of March 1968 that motivated
their departure. The Baumans were among the first in the group,
and among its best-known members. Earlier Polish emigrants in
the postwar period had come in large waves or as singular arrivals,
of their own free will.[23] *Aliyah* was supposed to be a 'return', not
an escape. But the 1968 immigration was an escape,[24] and so its
members, at some point after their arrival, realized that even in
Israel they were in a separate category – 'Strangers amongst
Strangers', as Elżbieta Kossewska described them.[25] 'Those who
came to Israel, . . . with all the ambivalence of identity feelings, the
lack of unambiguous identification before the transformation from
Poles into Jews born in Poland, remained in a void, completely
suspended', Kossewska wrote: 'The problem of identity, national
affiliation, after removing the Polish identity, has become the fundamental problem of the March emigrants; that issue determined
first of all the process of their preparation and then their decisions
about whether to remain or leave the Jewish state' (Kossewska,
2015: 234–5).

The process of adaptation – or rather 'absorption', as the term
was used in Israel – was more difficult for the 1968 *Aliyah* due to
the stereotypes related to their geographic origin. The first *Aliyah*
of *chaluc* (pioneers) and their children no longer viewed Ashkenazi
Jews positively. Before the creation of Israel (1947), they had been
heroes building the new country. But World War II made them 'the
population that came from the territory of the Shoah'. Włodzimierz
Goldkorn[26] wrote about the shock he experienced arriving in 1968:
' "Lambs to the slaughter" – this is how Israelis often talked about
my grandmothers, uncles, my aunts and cousins. Some were even
more blunt: "soap" was how some of the Sabra[27] – the people born
in Israel – described those of us who came from areas where the
extermination camps functioned; it was the first thing I learned when
I came to Tel-Aviv' (Goldkorn, 2018: 133–4). The March 1968 emigrants would find many Israelis who shared a stereotypical view of
them as passive, Yiddish-speaking diaspora Jews,[28] bystanders and
victims of modernity, a perfect contrast with the New Israeli Citizen,
who spoke Hebrew and was courageous and worked hard in his (or
her) kibbutz to transform the desert into a nutrient-rich garden.
The Sabra's achievements had contributed to Israel's prosperity and
the fabulous victory over its Arab neighbours in the Six-Day War
of 1967. Diaspora Jews, especially those who 'came when it was

already done', were often viewed as second-rank citizens. 'Why only now?' people asked the newcomers.

The 1968 immigrants like the Baumans expected finally to be part of a majority. But they were not embraced as such. Even former Polish émigrés did not welcome them. One '68er recalled being asked: 'Where exactly are you coming from? There were no Jews left in Poland after we departed!' (Wiszniewicz, 2008: 589). There were other sources of alienation as well. Goldkorn remembers being shocked at the poverty of the annexed territories, which he visited in the first months after his arrival as part of the programme of integration. He agreed with his auntie, who immediately after his arrival told him, 'Forget about Europe, this is Asia' (Goldkorn, 2018: 135).[29]

The Baumans – *olim hadaszim*

'Forget about Europe' was good advice, but not easy to do, even despite the exceptionally good treatment they received – rare among most immigrants to new lands. They were called *olim* – in Hebrew, a person 'going up' – and the Israeli state offered all new *olim* (*olim hadaszim*) not only citizenship, but housing, medical care, free education including at the university, loans and good mortgages – everything to materially start a new life. The Baumans earned further privilege by belonging to the professional group most esteemed by the Israeli state – intellectuals and academics. Like most of the other March *Aliyah*, the Baumans were set up as well as an immigrant could hope for full adaptation to Israeli society.

Immediately after arrival they were offered an apartment near Tel Aviv airport, which they declined as too far from the university campus. Then they were off to the kibbutz Givat Brenner, where Tova, Bauman's sister, lived. The nights were spent in discussions with Tova, the days with Janina's mother and sister Zofia and her family in Tel Aviv. After the first night, the Baumans decided to let their younger daughters stay with their aunt Tova in the kibbutz. It seemed like a good way to encourage their immersion in Israeli society, and it worked. In the safe and welcoming environment of the kibbutz, Tova stopped speaking Polish with girls in less than two weeks, and after three months the twins were speaking adequate Hebrew, helped by intensive lessons with a Russian teacher who spoke no Polish. She enrolled Lydia and Irena in a kind of double linguistic training, in which they translated everything from Polish into Hebrew via Russian, which was less difficult than it sounds because the girls had studied Russian for two years while in Poland. Absorption into teenage society was equally quick for the girls, who thoroughly enjoyed the new environment.

Unfortunately, their parents did not accompany them in this rapid assimilation. After their stay on the kibbutz, the Bauman parents, leaving the twins there, continued on their way to the Holy City, where they were directed to the Jerusalem Adaptation Centre. In the modest buildings created for newcomers, each family had a small apartment with tiny rooms that was to be their home for some months. 'In this Adaptation Centre in Jerusalem was the flower of Polish intelligentsia', Goldkorn told me. The intellectual life in the centre was indeed effervescent, with new families constantly arriving. People helped each other and maintained quasi-familial relationships, since they were all experiencing the same thing.[30]

The biggest obstacle for the new arrivals was the need for a good command of Hebrew. The Baumans immediately pursued intensive language lessons – ulpan – in Jerusalem, 'starting . . . with scribbling from right to left the unfamiliar Hebrew characters' (J. Bauman, 1988: 34).[31] To learn the language fast required a specific approach, since those not enrolled in the intensive courses could spend most of their days speaking Polish, which was the lingua franca in the adaptation centre. Zygmunt, who liked to do everything at the fastest pace possible, dropped the group course after deciding his progress in Hebrew was too slow, and spent most of his time alone focusing on language acquisition. Since Bauman got a professorship at Tel Aviv University within a month of their arrival, the family got two apartment offers in Tel Aviv not far from the university. Bauman chose the cheaper place, and left Janina and Anna at the absorption centre, where they stayed until October.

Bauman spent September living alone in Tel Aviv, preparing his teaching job, which started in October. He planned to lecture in Hebrew, which was a huge challenge. His surroundings were quite a contrast after the Jerusalem centre, a place of passionate discussions about Poland and world politics, mainly in Polish. People were anxious about the world situation: the year 1968 was particularly rich for current events – with the Vietnam War, student revolts all over Europe, in the United States and on other continents. And then the Soviet Army invaded Czechoslovakia in August, ending the Prague Spring. Revolution was in the air, as were fears that World War III would break out. The Baumans organized their social life in this setting. They became friends with Samuel Sandler, an émigré Polish literature professor, and his wife, with whom the Baumans maintained frequent correspondence after the departure of the Sandlers for the USA.[32]

Despite Bauman's huge investment in the new working environment, he continued to focus on Poland privately, and also professionally. Towards the end of 1968, Bauman wrote a sociological analysis of the March events for the Parisian exile journal *Kultura*,[33] among other Polish writing.[34] Although his homeland had rejected him, Bauman maintained his interest in Polish affairs. That was not uncommon among the 1968 emigrants, who tended towards an extreme version of the double-life that many immigrants share in their reluctance to abandon ties and interest in the original homeland. As Bronka Karst, whose father Roman Karst was a literature professor who emigrated to the USA,[35] recalled, 'It was a paradox in my father's life that while he had suffered being thrown out of Poland, he could not function without Poland. He met every day with Jan Kott, they went for walks, visited each other to drink coffee – and talked every day. Daily! On the theory of literature and on Polish matters' (Wiszniewicz, 2008: 521).[36] Even younger people – former students and activists in the 1968 events – continued for years to be 'always busy with Polish affairs' and 'constantly discussing the Polish situation' (Wiszniewicz, 2008: 582)

Bauman's interests went beyond Poland, of course, to the more general area of how to create a more humane Marxism. Like other members of the March 1968 diaspora, Bauman continued to struggle for what they considered a 'better and just future'.[37] Some of the 1968 emigrants were politically active. The older ones had usually held white-collar positions in Poland as intellectuals, artists, professionals and administrators, or even military cadre.[38] They belonged to Polish society, and after the war had engaged in the implementation of the new social system. They perceived themselves as Poles, however they viewed their Jewish roots.[39] And many of them saw themselves as cosmopolitans, belonging to a European cultural universe without strong nationalistic self-identification.

Israel, in 1968, was just 20 years old, in a period of nation-building and political reinforcement of its national identity and power. The country lacked receptivity to the complex identity of the Polish '68ers. After the spectacular Six-Day War victory, leading Israeli politicians sought to consolidate national identity on the basis of a shared distinction from the Arab population. The conviction of superiority and support for a militarist government, without reservations, was the common glue that offered feelings of security while providing legitimacy to governmental policies. 'I think the general perception at this time was that Israeli and Jewish nationality were exclusive, and that it was not possible to split one's identification between two nationalities, two countries, two entities, two religions and so forth', the Israeli sociologist Uri Ram said in an interview in May 2017: 'There is a concept of Jewishness that does not cross boundaries – and public opinion wanted to keep the boundaries very closed. So anyone who played with a double identity was suspected of not being faithful to the nation.'[40]

Anyone who had a high-level position in Poland before emigrating was immediately suspect. 'If somebody worked with the regime [in Poland] there was some hostility, because the perspective was: this is a Jew, and the Soviet bloc is anti-Semitic', said Ram; 'Anyone who had something to do with the regime was suspected of being unfaithful to Judaism or Jewish interests.'[41] This might have included Bauman, with his past as a KBW political officer, Party member and former expert for a Party Central Committee. But any tendency for Israelis to view Bauman through this lens was to an extent disarmed by an interview with him that ran in *Maariv*. The interview had an important impact in Israel and in Poland (see next chapter), strongly influencing his image, while presenting a completely wrong picture. The interview was conducted in Polish and published in Hebrew. But according to Anna Sfard, he might as well have been speaking in Mayan: 'The journalist did not translate what was said – he invented it!' Sfard believes that Bauman sent a complaint to *Maariv* after he realized what had been published there by reading the Polish translation in *Kurier i Nowiny*, a Polish-language newspaper in Israel.[42]

But it was too late to correct the 'news'.[43] The message had already been sent – a message that would have been pleasing to Israeli readers of *Maariv*, but Bauman had actually sent only part of it; the article contained a mixture of made-up and truthful information. For example, it described Bauman in the March 1968 events as a 'Jewish professor and riot leader'. There was other information more compatible with Bauman's opinion that Judaism's gift to the world was primarily cultural, however. *Maariv* quoted him as saying:

> I believed that the Jews' historic task is not to build their own state. Every nation is capable of such a task. The task of the Jewish nation is to enrich the world's culture. It is a good role for groups in the position of national minority in all countries. From the psychological and sociological points of view, this is a positive phenomenon. For this reason, my first visit to Israel did not affect me at all . . . Then came the victory of Israel. I suddenly felt that I was happy with the victory.[44]

The first part of this quote aligns with what Bauman would write twenty years later to his daughters: that the Jews had a global cultural mission to fulfil. Bauman's enthusiasm about the 1967 victory was confirmed by his daughter Anna, and by secret reports of the *Bezpieka*. But this was nothing unique; many non-Jewish Warsaw inhabitants were gratified by tiny Israel's victory. What *Maariv*'s journalist did not mention was that, immediately after the 1967 war, Bauman became upset with Israel for failing to engage in more peacekeeping with its neighbours. Also, the article refers to Bauman's cosmopolitan identity, but not his Polish sense of identity. The latter could have gotten Bauman into trouble with the readers. As Ram notes, 'In Israel, once you are here, you are not considered a Polish Jew but an Israeli Jew. If you don't identify this way, it is a problem.' Bauman's statements as quoted by *Maariv* suggested that he occupied a halfway position, en route to conversion from cosmopolitanism to Zionism. Bauman was presented as a new convert into Zionism. Everything was changed to convince the *Maariv* public of Bauman's strong Israeli identity. In short, the newspaper had imposed a new *master status* upon him.

Israel had certain expectations of the émigrés, as 1968 immigrant Leon Rozenbaum said:

> This is finally your homeland. And you need to be Israeli and to accept everything as it is. . . . Our Polish habits were a source of scandals in the centers of absorption . . . they disliked our New Year's Eve parties, and at the same time they put in our heads various Jewish values, which, to many of us, were completely new. This country welcomed us with open arms and then started to strangle us with these same arms. It was a kind of Baptism, immersing us in the new world by cutting us off from Poland while pressuring us to transform into Israelis as quickly as possible. (Leon Rozenbaum, in Wiszniewicz, 2008: 588)

The *Maariv* article's author cut Bauman off from Poland by presenting him as a Jewish professor who embodied the Polish struggle for liberalization, a kind of superhero, overwhelmingly popular and well known:

> Polish students saw in him the symbol of their liberal strivings in the fight against the Polish communist regime. . . . His prestige increased among students and intellectuals. What could not be said on the street or written in the newspapers, Professor Bauman said in his sociology lectures. A true liberal and worldly man, Bauman was flooded with invitations from Eastern and Western countries . . . Students took their place in the lecture hall hours before each of his lectures. It was a great experience for them. The auditorium could not accommodate all listeners . . . The Jewish professor became for them a clear symbol of desires that could not be openly expressed.[45]

He was the hero who started a Polish revolution. Moreover, the Bauman presented in the article described an idealized and naive vision of Polish workers. The journalist presented his own view of events instead of citing Bauman's words.[46]

This article constituted a tricky introduction to the academic community. Bauman already was well known internationally as a specialist in political sociology and the sociology of culture, a fact that could arouse some jealousy among colleagues in the small young country that was Israel in the late 1960s. Moreover, Bauman's independent anti-governmental past suggested that he was not a conformist or career-oriented academic who respected hierarchy. He was an independent intellectual whose critical thinking shaped his work, and such characters are not easy to manage. Israeli academia was not yet open enough to welcome Bauman.

'Il n'y a qu'un soleil sur terre'
(There is only one sun on the earth)[47]

Israeli sociology emerged as an academic discipline in the early 1950s. It was formed at the peak of Labor's prolonged reign – during which statehood was attained – and complied unreservedly with the Labor movement's political agenda. Its functionalist nation-building orientation was congruent with the concerns of the dominant establishment of the new state: the consolidation of a unified and strong nation-state. This orientation was the dominant 'paradigm' in the field for more than two decades.

(Ram, 1995: 9)

This short introduction to the early decades of Israeli sociology sketches the frame of Bauman's new professional environment. Almost everything here was different from what he knew from Warsaw. Israeli sociology was a young discipline taught at new universities in a new state. The scholarship focused on a narrow functionalist approach, quite opposed to the plurality of methods and theories that characterized Warsaw sociology. Various European currents influenced Polish sociology through the curricula of professors who had studied in France, Germany, Austria and the UK, with a modest contribution from the United States. While some of Israel's sociologists had trained in Europe, their discipline was dominated by American functionalism.[48]

Another difference between Polish and Israeli sociology concerned links between the scholarly community and the political parties and government. Contrary to official Polish declarations, these ties were far from uniform and peaceful in Poland, where the Party line was only partially followed by academics. In fact, an important part of the opposition to governmental policies came from the university milieu. In Israel, sociologists strongly backed the Labour movement.

The relationship to Marxism was another important difference. In Poland, it had been one of the currents in academia even before World War II, and, postwar, it was imposed with varying degrees of success and methods. In Israel, Marxism had no real place at the university until the late 1970s, according to Ram.[49] Before then, a kind of conservative liberal spirit of thought dominated sociological thinking on campus: 'a sort of modernization theory, American modernization theory, structural functionalism and all that – under the leadership of Shmuel Eisenstadt', he said.

Eisenstadt's singular control over the sociological milieu at the Hebrew University would be significant in Bauman's career. In Poland, there were schools, traditions, coteries, networks and scholar-*apparatchiks* – genuine diversity without a single guru. Bauman had a collegial and friendly relationship with Hochfeld, his direct scientific and administrative supervisor over the years. And while, organizationally, Warsaw University was highly hierarchical, Bauman's boss was an independent and critical thinker, who controlled his own publications and teaching agenda while negotiating with the general political censorship of the state. Being obedient to another sociologist for strategic, career or hierarchic reasons was not at all in Bauman's repertoire. He paid the price for this, eventually, in that he failed to advance beyond docent (see chapter 10), but that was also because Hochfeld's death removed a powerful shield against the authorities, and his political activity and public criticism of the state led to the failure of his professorial career. (In December 1968, the Ministry of Higher Education officially informed the university that Bauman's promotion to professorship had ended because of his emigration to Israel.[50])

In Israel, the sociological milieu was small, and organized as a feudal system run by a 'Mandarin'[51] – Eisenstadt. Shmuel Eisenstadt shared some characteristics with Zygmunt Bauman. Two years older than Bauman, Eisenstadt had been born in Warsaw but emigrated at age 12 with his mother to Israel. Bauman attended Polish-language schools initially, then went on to learn Belorussian and Russian, including Cyrillic script, while Eisenstadt spoke Yiddish firstly, and after his emigration mastered Hebrew. Despite those challenges and geographical mobility, they both ended secondary school on time (Bauman at 17, Eisenstadt at 18). In 1940, after finishing his high-school education, Eisenstadt left Tel Aviv for Jerusalem, where he was enrolled at Hebrew University. From that moment, he studied under the mentoring of Martin Buber. This Lvov-born (in 1878) philosopher, a former honorary professor at the University of Frankfurt (on the Main), left Germany and emigrated to Israel in 1938 when the Hitlerian government forbade Jews from teaching. Buber had been a committed Zionist since his youth. In Israel, he taught anthropology and sociology at Hebrew University, where Eisenstadt was among his first Ph.D. students and an assistant in his department. Eisenstadt described his mentor as 'a very broad universalist, with a very strong emphasis on comparative things, and it was in this sense that he was very close [to], though different, from Max Weber', whom Eisenstadt named as the second major influence on his thought.[52]

Like Hochfeld, Buber was a socialist and politically engaged intellectual; he was one of the creators of the socialist BUND Party. From his youth, Buber had advocated cohabitation with the Arabic part of Israeli society in a binational state, and he was a leading member of the pacifist Jewish organization Brit-Shalom. Eisenstadt, his most brilliant student, did not share his mentor's vision of a binational state. Uri Ram noted: 'In his early works (cf. 1948, 1952) Eisenstadt managed to analyze the Israeli nation-building process almost without mention of the Arab issue, while in the 1967 book the issue appears only as a "minority" problem' (Ram, 1995: 32). Bauman, in contrast, was convinced of the necessity of peaceful Israeli and Arab cohabitation, based on equal rights.[53]

The two men's life experiences also affected their relationship. Unlike the majority of young men born in the 1920s in Europe, Eisenstadt spent World War II as a student, obtaining his Ph.D. in 1947 at the age of 25; however, he was also enrolled in the activities of the Israeli military units.[54] Bauman was six years older when he got his diploma because of the years spent in the war and the KBW.[55] Both men did postdoctoral work at the same institution, the LSE. Eisenstadt was there in 1947–8, with noted scholars such as the sociologists Edward Shils, Morris Ginsberg and Thomas Henry Marshall, and the anthropologists from Malinowski's seminar, Raymond Firth, Edward Evans-Pritchard, Meyer Fortes and Edmund Leach (Sztompka, 2004). Returning to Israel in 1948, Eisenstadt began his research and was hired by his alma mater. In 1959, he obtained a full professorship at the age of 36, which is extremely early in an academic career. Eisenstadt was a high-level performer and administrator (he was department chair for eighteen years, and a dean). Moreover, Israel's habilitation-less system made one's career path simpler and faster.

Eisenstadt's work was visible abroad;[56] he was the main Israeli sociologist of his time, and he was an author of most of the sociological studies of his country until late into the 1970s. He was active in international conferences, published in English and was invited to teach in the USA, where he became a close collaborator with Talcott Parsons. He wrote the first important book on Israeli immigration in the Chicago School tradition (he used Park's terminology, such as 'ecological settings', and employed Thomas' approach of studying 'attitudes'), and later implemented the Parsonian approach in most of his works.

This was vastly different from Bauman's sociological background. In 1961, Bauman published (in Polish) a sociological piece titled 'Sociological Variations' ('Wariacje socjologiczne'), in which he strongly criticized the 'fashion for the American mainstream sociology', especially Lazarsfeld. While the anti-American orientation was obligatory in the Cold War, and a response to the *apparatchik* sociologists' criticism of Bauman, the paper was not written to please the politicians (see chapters 9 and 10). Already in the early 1960s, Bauman's 'humanistic sociology' was incompatible with a strict structural functionalist approach. Bauman was never enthusiastic about Parsons, as Peter Beilharz noted in his recent book: 'This was a tradition that Bauman was allergic to, calling it Durksonianism. It is possible that Bauman's mashing of Durkheim and Parsons became a kind of roadblock for him. As he later put it to me, Parsons was truly the thinker and advocate of solid modernity. Marx and Weber, Freud and Simmel were all central for Bauman; not Durkheim' (Beilharz, 2020 MS: 98–9).

Bauman explained his incompatibility with Eisenstadt in the following way in a 2010 interview: 'I guess we differed in our understanding of what sociology is for, what is its purpose, what are the motives for our actions. Sociology was created 150 to 200 years ago to serve an administered society for managerial reasons. Have you heard of Talcott Parsons? Sociologists today often forget him.'[57]

The men had two very different understandings of sociology, and also different objectives. One aimed to formulate an independent and critical science; the other was devoted to creating a tool for the management of a society in which administration is a ruling institution. Bauman had already learned bitter lessons from his experience with Party *apparatchiks* who blocked the possibility for him to conduct research freely and critically. In contrast, Eisenstadt supported and, by his work, legitimized the Labour Party:

The success of Eisenstadt was due not so much to inter-academic circumstances as to the link he formed between academia and the governing establishment and to the affinity between the sociological perspective he promoted and the political agenda of that elite. Eisenstadt and his colleagues considered themselves more civil servants than independent intellectuals. Their vocation was not the pursuit of knowledge for its own sake, let alone the pursuit of a critical understanding of society, but rather the provision of professional support and counselling for various state and national agencies, with whose overall objectives and policies they fully identified (Ram, 1995: 25)

Bauman had had his fill of being a civil servant, counselling the Party and sharing ideas of social engineering.

Yet, while these philosophical and methodological differences are important, it seems the dominant 'incompatibility' factor was personality. An interviewee who knew both sociologists remarked:

I shouldn't say this, but Bauman is the complete opposite of Eisenstadt. Eisenstadt wanted to put everything in the shade, while Bauman wanted to open things up and had new ideas to develop and grow. Now, Eisenstadt was a world-renowned sociologist,[58] I cannot deny

that – I would even say that from one perspective he was a genius, his
mental equipment was fabulous, unbelievable, but . . . he was lazy. . . .
He liked to make others work for him. So he had an idea and he had
some people not to do fieldwork but to read for him, to write theses,
and he took the theses and put them together into a book. . . . It was a
very exploitative relationship and you couldn't finish your Ph.D. with
Eisenstadt in less than seven years.[59]

The students of academic 'Mandarins' often complain of their
'laziness', but it's a term that needs some contextual explanation.
Academics with many research projects involving large numbers
of collaborators divide the work according to the tasks performed.
These include gathering the data; doing analysis; writing reports,
papers and books; doing administrative work; and finally communicating the research within and outside the field. Management and
organization of the financial support for the research is a separate
category. Eisenstadt set up the financial and institutional support
for his research, designed the projects and set their theoretical
framework. Not surprisingly, he couldn't do all of the discrete tasks
himself.

Eisenstadt was an operator, a particular kind of research entrepre-
neur. He was a busy boss, with a lot of projects under his direction
involving students, former students, subordinate colleagues (he was
the department head) and other types of collaborators. Bauman, by
contrast, worked alone, and his final project was usually a book that
he wrote entirely by himself. This was a different style of sociology
from the large quantitative studies. Bauman always had students,
but according to the sources his style of mentoring was collaborative and not exploitative. This was quite different from the pattern
employed by the 'Mandarins', who had a kind of royal court.
Bauman was an independent and creative, hard-working scholar.
Some might describe him as 'workaholic' (he woke at 4.00–4.30
a.m.), and a compulsive writer, but that is not atypical in academic
settings. Exploitation of the labour of others was not in his repertoire, and he was not good at submitting his intellectual work to the
control of another person.

Inevitably, there were tensions that made their collaboration
impossible. Bauman's position was weaker than that of Eisenstadt,
Dean of Sociology in the most prestigious Israeli university. Bauman
was a professor in two new institutions, Tel Aviv University and
Haifa University, which were only beginning to forge their reputa-
tions. To accept a position at Hebrew University would have meant
submission to the 'big man' who dominated the department for
more than two decades, 'dominating the discipline and stifling the
development of autonomous critical or alternative trends in Israeli
sociology', as Ram wrote: 'No intellectual dissension was possible

while this small and closed group held the reins of academic sociology in Israel. As long as Eisenstadt and the department he created clutched the sole prism through which sociologists in Israel were accredited and sociological work was recognized, no alternative perspective could emerge, let alone thrive, in the Israeli sociological discourse' (Ram, 1995: 26).

By 1968, the Israeli social sciences were focused on the United States. 'The roots of Israeli scholarship were European and Eastern European, but after the war and the communist turn against Israel they shifted West', Ram says: 'There were people in Mapam, the workers' party, there were communist circles and radical anti-Zionists, but none of them intervened at the universities. The social scientists were completely Westernized.' Because Bauman came from the Eastern bloc, 'I think people did not take seriously his methodology, his theory, his approach, his perspective. I think they tended to relate it to something very anachronistic, a totalitarian background and Marxism.'[60] From the perspective of mainstream Israeli sociology in the late 1960s, Bauman was an outsider. He needed to find a place outside the mainstream institution, which was Hebrew University in Jerusalem. So he did.

An outsider in an outsider institution

In October 1968, Bauman was appointed Professor *Ordinarius* in the Department of Sociology and Social Anthropology at the University of Tel Aviv, and Guest Professor *Ordinarius* at Haifa University College. Haifa is about an hour's drive from Tel Aviv, but Bauman's apartment was close to the Tel Aviv campus on the northeast edge of the city, which was convenient for commuting. He travelled two or three times a week to Haifa, and liked the institution there very much. It was new, and its make-up of Israeli and Arab students corresponded with his belief in the peaceful cohabitation of different communities on an equal basis. In his 2010 interview with Israeli sociologist Shalva Weil, Bauman said:

> I don't think there was a sociological community in Israel. I worked both in Tel Aviv University and in Haifa University (not at Hebrew University in Jerusalem) . . . and there was no connection whatsoever. (Haifa, it is worth mentioning, had a pioneering, very young department of sociology, with people from kibbutzim, many Arab students and very cosmopolitan.) But there was little, if any, communication between sociologists at different universities.[61]

The thinness of the Israeli sociological milieu initially may have benefitted Bauman, giving him more freedom. Anthropologist

Emanuel Marx, Bauman's best friend from the Israeli period and his departmental colleague in Tel Aviv, said Bauman began teaching in Hebrew in only his second year there. 'It was just unbelievable', Marx recalled in our interview: 'The first year he started teaching in English; people did not understand him. When he started to teach in Hebrew people started to understand him. He even invented words in Hebrew, and he did it very well.'[62]

According to Anna Sfard, Bauman gave courses in Hebrew even during his first year (this seems to contradict Marx's version, but perhaps Bauman spoke in a mixture of the two languages at first). To prepare his lectures, Sfard says, Bauman wrote the Hebrew words out in the Latin alphabet so he wouldn't stumble over them.[63] This required a huge effort, and it was rare that a professor would attempt anything so linguistically bold. Hebrew is a difficult language to learn, even for those, like Bauman, who had been exposed to smidgeons of it as children. Bauman had learned a few rudiments as a Hashomer Hatzair activist and while preparing for his bar mitzvah,[64] in Poznań but this of course fell far short of preparing him to use modern Hebrew to teach sociology at a college level! And yet he spoke it well enough to bowl over his students, according to the anthropologist Chaim Hazan, a student in Bauman's Sociological Theory course at Tel Aviv University in the early 1970s:

> Having mastered enough Hebrew to deliver articulate and flawless lectures, Bauman captivated a select group of students not only as the classic scholar that he was, but mainly, and only for the ear of the cognizant, as a unique artist of ideas, 'a director of a play of thoughts', as he put it. In this sense he reshuffled the chapter and verse of conventional textbooks, and refreshed orthodox perspectives on the order of the social. . . . The brilliant aesthetics of his writing was only surpassed by the breadth and depth of his thinking. Bauman was indeed a mentor for life.[65]

Given the teaching mastery Bauman brought from Poland, it is perhaps not so surprising he could create a strong relationship with his Israeli students. However, this was not particularly the case with his colleagues, especially when compared to his relationships within Hochfeld's group. As Hazan notes, 'Unfortunately, his exchange with departmental colleagues was doomed to failure due to the blatant incompatibility in scholarship, originality and global approached to knowledge.'[66] Bauman was isolated, except for a few colleagues, among them Emanuel Marx. After learning that Bauman had been appointed at Tel Aviv University, Marx and his colleague Jonathan Sapiro read his book *Sociology of Everyday Life*, which had been translated into Hebrew. 'We decided that it is a beautiful book and very inspiring work', Marx said in an interview.[67]

Marx called Bauman a 'modern Simmel'.[68] They enjoyed each other's company, spending long hours talking about everything: 'Bedouins [Marx's research field], politics, and the Holocaust', said Marx. In the early 1970s, there was still much to be discussed about this latter topic. Marx had escaped the horrors of Nazi Germany at the last minute, and Bauman had escaped the worst of them by fleeing to the Soviet Union. Only Janina was a direct witness, and it seems that it was at this time that the Baumans began to discuss this tragic issue, which years later would become their common area of professional expression. Emmanuel Marx stayed a friend for life, a relationship that, in its levels of trust and intensity, was similar to the ties the Baumans had maintained in the final Warsaw years on Nowotki Street. During his Israeli period, Bauman was unable to create a large team of collaborators and friends. He missed having a sociological community where he could exchange and forge ideas, refine arguments, discuss the latest books and prepare challenging conferences. For all such activities, Bauman had to pursue discussions with colleagues abroad. He maintained an extensive correspondence with other sociologists, and his archive contains hundreds of letters, some several pages long, in which Bauman discusses and analyses sociological and philosophical issues. Bauman maintained his 'academic mobility' by attending scholarly events abroad during this period.

One imagines that Bauman no longer had to go through acres of red tape to attend conferences, now that he was free of Soviet-bloc hindrances. Yet his Israeli passport would not get him in everywhere. In 1970, the World Congress of the International Sociological Association took place in Varna, Bulgaria, and Bauman was invited by the section of political sociology as a panelist. This was an important acknowledgement of his work and his place in the network. However, Bulgarian authorities refused to provide him with a visa. Polish authorities had warned them about his 'anti-socialist' activities and his 'Zionist attitude', and that was enough. This extent of close collaboration between Eastern-bloc states was not common; many families separated by forced emigration met relatives in Bulgaria, Hungary and even East Germany without problems. But, as his secret police files reveal, Bauman remained a public enemy in the eyes of the *Bezpieka*, which kept close watch on his activities and those of his family – and not only when he left the country. The authorities had spies in Israel who kept an eye on Bauman, a measure of their belief that he was an important and dangerous character for the Polish regime. These files on Bauman (now he was a 'foreigner', no longer in the category of a Polish citizen) report on his meetings with other Poles in exile, his trips to Paris and 'attempts to organize an opposition', including an alleged proposal to create a group of emigrants active as a 'diversion commando'. From reading these documents, one would be inclined to think Bauman spent all of his time on 'Polish affairs'.

One of them, dated 27 August 1970, classified as 'secret – special significance' and entitled 'Extract from the information . . . sent by Department I of the Ministry of Interior Security' mentions: 'notes were made of attempts by RWE [Radio Free Europe] to organize a political diversion group composed from former members of the KPP [Polish Communist Party] and PZPR / Bauman, Jedlicki, Muszkat / Janusz Kowalewski / with A. Ciołkosz at the head; the goal of that group would be to inspire attacks on the country [Poland] and to analyse the situation in the PZPR and in the workers' movement.'[69]

Bauman did write some articles about the events of 1968, but he did not spend all of his time on Polish matters. He was active in his new environment, trying to organize a new life.

'It is not enough to leave, you have to arrive': the new life of the Bauman family

The sentence above, the motto of a major Polish-language Israeli newspaper, *Od Nowa* (Revival),[70] was addressed to left-oriented immigrants having trouble adapting to their new country.[71] It didn't always sit well with the émigrés. 'Israel was a real Soviet country at that time, such conformance to the rules', says Włodek Goldkorn: 'There wasn't a single newspaper that criticized the government.' For many of those who had escaped communist Poland, this was unacceptable. The Baumans belonged to that group – people who refused to replace Polish nationalism (the origin of their ejection from Poland) with Israeli nationalism (which expected them to shed their Polish background). Frequently, those who 'have not yet arrived in Israel' decided to leave the country for North America or Western Europe. The number of *Yeridim*[72] among the March *Aliyah* was very high, and the Israeli authorities worried about this 'lost' group's cost to their new state.[73] After three years in Israel, the Baumans left for the UK. There are some contradictory accounts of how this occurred. Janina wrote in her book that it was clear from the beginning that Israel was not to be their ultimate home. In our interview, however, Anna said her parents wished to stay with the rest of their family in Israel, and this desire for definitive settlement is certainly suggested by Bauman's decisions about the organization of the family's life in their first months spent in Israel. Having the 13-year-old twins remain for a year in a kibbutz certainly looks like a strategy to ease their immersion into Israeli society, considering that the Bauman family had always stuck together in Poland. For the first time, the Bauman family was spread among three cities: Tel Aviv, Jerusalem and Givat-Brenner

–though, to be sure, none was more than about an hour's drive from the others.

While the younger daughters remained in the kibbutz, near Tel Aviv, Anna started the 1968 autumn semester in Jerusalem at Hebrew University's Department of Mathematics. 'Ambitious like her father, like him always so keen to learn and to achieve perfection in whatever she did', as Janina wrote (1988: 34), Anna repeated her interrupted first year of studies, enrolling in physics and mathematics before concentrating on the latter. The teaching was in Hebrew, which she learned very fast. She lived in a small rented room, working very hard. In January 1969, Leon Sfard arrived in Israel with his family. For them, departure was a long and difficult process, since Leon, like all Polish males, needed special permission to leave the country without first serving in the military. In summer 1970, Anna and Leon married.[74]

For the first time in nineteen years, Janina and Zygmunt were alone without children. In October 1968, Janina joined Zygmunt in their apartment near the Tel Aviv campus. It was a *shikun* (public housing) – a sunny flat on Neve Shearet, 56/23, a housing project in Ramat Aviv known as 'Gomułkowo' from the name of the leader whose border-opening in 1956 had led to the departure of so many Polish Jews. Living conditions there were agreeable. 'It was a nice apartment', recalled Emanuel Marx – but not to be confused with the ambiance at Nowotki Street. In Poland, their home was an 'open house' – full of people coming and going, friends dropping by without calling first for long political discussions and passionate bridge parties, with young people coming by to see the twins and Anna. While some of their Polish furniture had been brought to Israel, the two apartments were alike only in that superficiality.

When their numerous packages arrived from Poland, the Baumans realized that some very important boxes were missing and one suitcase was exceptionally light . . . empty, in fact. These were the containers for the manuscript of Zygmunt's latest book in Poland, *Szkice z teorii kultury* (*Sketches in the Theory of Culture*). Just before it was to be published in Poland, the authorities had retracted the manuscript, and now they had confiscated it. Also missing were some handwritten notes, lecture preparations and reprints dedicated by their authors to Zygmunt with love, friendship and thanks. These latter losses were sentimental in nature, but the book manuscript was a major loss.[75] Yet all these losses paled in comparison to the confiscation of Janina's diaries.

Since her childhood, even in the most extreme conditions of war and ghetto life, Janina had maintained her journal. She wrote about the atrocities of the war and about her dreams and thoughts. Miraculously, through escapes and stays in hidden places, through bombings, fires and sudden displacement, she had successfully managed to preserve this secret journal, which she continued to keep after the war. As a journalism student, through married life, work and raising children, she continued to write about her life. She was unaware that after the war her mother, Alina, copied some pages of the journal. Thanks to those pages, Janina was able later to reconstruct their war story, while, in 1968, the original journal was requisitioned by security services that qualified these intimate and extremely precious pages as 'dangerous' disclosures. We can only imagine the feelings that both Janina and Zygmunt experienced when they became aware that the journals were missing. In 1972, Bauman wrote to Prime Minister Jabłoński (his former 'comrade') asking for missing pieces,[76] but did not receive a response. Years later, in the 1990s, Bauman repeated his request, hoping that perhaps the change in the political system would help him recover his private family belongings, but in vain. I found Janina Bauman's diaries while researching in the IPN archives in 2015. Immediately, I informed Zygmunt Bauman about this discovery. It was not until 2018 that the copies of Janina's journals, as well as other private documents, were recovered by Anna Sfard.[77]

The Polish authorities violated the privacy of the people it exiled by seizing their most precious belongings; the state-sponsored pogrom sought to control the memories of the banished individuals. These injustices were performed in the name of state security, and no one, after the collapse of the Polish communist state, was charged for this violence against the life histories of the abused families. The violence done to these individuals continues even after fifty years.[78]

As Bauman began lecturing in October 1968, he also started a research project entitled 'Cultural Focus and Semiotic Density',[79] which aimed to make Tel Aviv University one of the few cultural-semiotics centres in the world. Bauman also continued trying to get his earlier books translated, including a Serbo-Croatian version of *Zarys Marksistowskiej Teorii Społeczeństwa* (*An Outline of a Marxist Theory of Society*) and French translations of three books: *Essai d'une théorie marxiste de la société*; *Culture et société*; and *Visions du monde humain.*[80]

Bauman did not write much in his Israeli period, Anna Sfard notes. Presumably the slower and – for Bauman – less culturally inspiring rhythms of his Israeli life had an impact on his production. As Stanisław Obirek noted in an interview, Tel Aviv in the early 1970s was 'deeply provincial' when compared to Warsaw, which, while politically unfree, was an intensely active city intellectually. The 'cultural environment' and the university milieu in Tel Aviv were too small to offer inspiring conditions for new thought and the pursuit of an international career.[81] Bauman was not happy as an academic and was not accomplishing much as a sociologist.

For Janina, however, things were quite different. She enjoyed Israel

– first, because it reunited her with her family. She had a close relationship with Zofia, her sister, and with her mother Alina Lewinson, in part due to their tragic ghetto experience. Janina obtained a job as a documentarist at the major Israeli newspaper *Maariv*. The following academic year, the family was reunited, with the exception of Anna, who remained with Leon in Jerusalem. Lydia and Irena returned to their parents' home and were enrolled in middle school in Tel Aviv. Zygmunt and Janina felt the school's quality was inferior to the schools the girls had attended in Warsaw, where they obtained a strong European education. But the twins were happy and enjoyed life in the city with other youths. The following year, Lydia and Irena were moved to another school, run by the Alliance Française, where the educational level was higher. The school partially helped to resolve the parents' doubts about the girls' education in Israel, but other events interfered with their objective of making Israel a permanent home.

As soon as Bauman was able to communicate well in Hebrew, he found time for political activity. An interview conducted by the journalist Tomasz Kwaśniewski[82] suggests that Bauman's Party engagement in Poland had left him disillusioned with politics, but the picture is a bit more complex than the interview suggests. Bauman remained a socialist, if not a communist, and Israel, with its pluralist politics, offered him new options to join in the discussion. The ideas of the New Left had interested him since the Polish Thaw of 1956, when the visit of C. Wright Mills and Ralph Milliband to Warsaw, and Hochfeld's 'Open Marxism', sowed the seeds of a leftism distant from orthodox Marxism. Bauman's residence at the LSE in 1957 came at the time of the creation of the *New Reasoner* journal (later the *New Left Review*) by E. P. Thompson and John Saville, who declared their distance from the Soviet Union and condemned all imperial and dictatorial practices. As a post-doc at the time, Bauman could not openly sympathize with the New Left ideologists in their condemnation of the Soviet intervention in Hungary. However, he frequently met New Left people during his attendance at sociological conferences abroad, and he was very familiar with Mills and Milliband, as well as Theodor Adorno, Herbert Marcuse, Seymour Martin Lipset, E. P. Thompson and Peter Worsley.

The Six-Day War provoked tensions inside the New Left (in the USA and other countries) because of the strong criticism by some members of the Israeli state's Zionist ambitions.[83] The government's refusal to negotiate the return of annexed territories was a sensitive subject for Bauman, who became upset each time the topic arose. During the 1969 elections, according to the available sources,[84] Bauman supported Maki,[85] a small party that identified itself as communist and binational and believed militantly in the peaceful existence of Arabs and Jews, based on equal rights. This vision of the future was less and less popular among the citizens of the young state as they weathered a series of military conflicts with their Arab neighbours. The construction of Israeli nationalism was the powerful ideology that cemented culturally diverse newcomers in the country, helping them merge in a strong and unified society. There was not much political space for the vision of peaceful cohabitation of two groups that appeared so different, and even opposed to one another. In October 1969, two years after spectacular victory over their Arab neighbours, Israeli citizens voted for the new composition of the Knesset (Parliament). The coalition of leftist parties obtained almost 50 per cent of the seats, which, with 81 per cent of the population voting, was the coalition's best outing in Israelis' history. Maki, however, was a niche party, obtaining only 1 per cent of the vote, which was probably a huge disappointment for Bauman.

Thanks to his abilities as an agitator and political connoisseur, Bauman could inspire the New Israeli Left with talks explaining this political current. The unpopularity of the movement in Israel underlines the extent to which Bauman really believed in these ideas and did not express them opportunistically. Had he been more of an opportunist, he would have joined the Alignment Party, the most powerful group in Israel, born when Labour[86] merged with Mapam. Its leader was Golda Meir, the first female Israeli prime minister and one of the rare women heads of state in the world at the time.

Bauman was a utopian in his political activism as well as his writing. Supporting Maki at campaign meetings with Russian and Polish immigrants, he was probably perceived as a loser, blinded by a utopian vision. Yet Bauman consistently pushed an attitude of communist commitment, especially towards creating Arab–Israeli engagement. This attitude was not frequent among Poles living in Israel. 'He told us to vote for them [Maki]', one colleague recalled: 'I was shocked by his suggestion . . . I think that at the last moment Bauman changed his mind and gave his vote for another party.' It could be that, as an expert in political analysis, Bauman saw a vote for Maki as a wasted vote, and that the pragmatic sociologist won out over the utopian activist.

The main issue in the 1969 election for the Baumans and many who lived in Israel was how to maintain peace in this unstable part of the world. Nahum Goldmann, the founding president of the World Jewish Congress, was an important leader of Middle East peace efforts. He supported the idea of peaceful co-existence between Jews and Arabs as an indispensable condition of Israel's survival, and wanted to renew the communications between Israel and neighbour states that had been disrupted by the Six-Day War. In early 1970, Goldmann was invited by Egypt's leader, Gamal Abdel Nasser, to discuss future relations, but on 6 April, Golda Meier came out against negotiations, a blow to hopes for peace.[87] Bauman, at dinner with friends, commented: 'We should admit that Israel doesn't want peace.'[88] He did not keep this opinion private, expressing it in an interview with the newspaper *Haaretz* some months later. The article was entitled, 'Israel Must Prepare for Peace'.[89]

'My fears', Bauman said many years later:

> concerned the corrosive, poisoning properties of the occupation, its decentralized influence on the ethics and moral compunctions of the occupiers. I was afraid that the new generation at the time was growing in the belief that the state of war and military emergency was . . . a normal, natural and probably the only possible solution. My anxiety was aroused by the state, which learns to cover up its numerous and inevitably growing internal social problems and to wash its hands of them by inflating and exacerbating the sense of external threats, thus losing the ability to handle them. Inside the besieged stronghold, it is crime and betrayal to insist on differences . . . *Summa summarum* – I was afraid of the growing ignorance of Israel of how to live in a state of peace, the growing disbelief of the population in the possibility of living without war, and the fear of the political elite of a peace in which they would be unable to continue governing.[90]

'Picnic on the volcano'[91]

In mid-1970, the Baumans decided to leave Israel as soon as possible. The key element in this decision was the fact that, soon, their two teenaged daughters were leaving high school, which meant they would be incorporated into the Israeli Army. This was a problematic issue for many new Israeli citizens. There were other factors in their decision as well, notes Emmanuel Marx, who states: '[Bauman] was interested in staying but over time this changed. He wanted to leave, he wanted to be part of a big civilization. His wife had a job that was connected with her previous work; she was happy to have found a place to settle, but he had decided that they had to go.'[92] Marx underlined the professional side of the decision to leave Israel, saying that the country was too small for Bauman's professional ambitions. 'I think he didn't want to stay in Leeds, he wanted to go to really big places', said Marx.

'Oxford? Cambridge?', I asked.

'No', responded Marx:

> America! I'm not sure, but this is what I heard. If he had been lucky enough to go there he might have become a famous sociologist, but a very different one. I think he would have lacked depth. He would have written much less. And he would not have written about the Holocaust at all. The fact that he was sucked into Leeds was the luckiest thing that happened to him in his life I think.

The Baumans became *Yeridim* on 23 June 1971, three years to the day after leaving Poland. The whole process of moving to Leeds with the family took more than a year; the hiring process in academia is long. In the summer of 1970, the Baumans went to Canberra, Australia, for a three-month visiting professorship with an offer of a permanent position. That was tempting, but 'Janina refused, because it was too far away', Bauman said in several interviews. It was too far from Israel, where it was clear Anna would be staying at least for a while. The United States seemed to be closer – however, at that time, it could be difficult to move there permanently. Bauman's Polish colleagues from the pre-1968 years say there was some kind of option involving Chicago University. Many Polish scholars had escaped the Gomułka regime by going to the USA or Canada, even among those who had landed first in Israel. Bauman's friend Samuel Sandler, a professor of Polish literature, left Tel Aviv for Chicago University in 1969. Five years earlier, Bauman himself had applied for a long-term fellowship at Stanford's Center for Advanced Study in the Behavioral Sciences, but it had not come through. His past engagement with the KBW unit and involvement in the Communist Party would not have been evaluated positively by US authorities and might have blocked a longer-term US visa. Władek Poznański, who did his military service in KBW at a lower grade, described his own difficulties obtaining a US visa:

> interrogation on the American visa was difficult. They called me in for it three times! (and others only once). . . . The Americans asked me over and over again what I had been doing in the Internal Security Corps, what I did in the Army, whether I was on compulsory service, what they taught me. For them, the KBW represented subversion and spying – and there were indeed subversive units, but not in our regiment, from what I know. So I could tell the truth. The only thing I did not mention to them was that I had been told to join the Party in the Army. (Władek Poznański, in Wiszniewicz, 2008: 666)

Poznański was younger than Bauman and was only a simple soldier; the Americans knew that Bauman had been a KBW major and was engaged in Party activities as an expert for the Central Committee. One can presume that his only option would have been to agree to co-operate with the American services if asked to do so – or to change his political opinions completely, and his field of expertise. But he refused to play the anti-communist specialist in the political science milieu:

> After leaving Poland, I was inundated with offers to join all sorts of 'Sovietologist' establishments, with invitations to write for their journals. . . . I refused the offers. I had no intention of living the

second half of my life off the first (as things looked then, I could have lived quietly and happily ever after on my 'dissident past'). I wanted to remain what I was, a sociologist, and re-establishing myself in that role in new surroundings was to me a matter of personal honesty and self-respect. Most importantly, were I to have succumbed to the seductive offers and recycled myself as a 'Sovietologist', I certainly would have found myself out of place among the hosts (and very soon have been found to be out of place by them), as much as I found myself (and was found) to be out of place in 'real existing socialism'. Being 'anti-Communist' was certainly not enough to make us feel comfortable in each other's company. (Bauman, in Tester, Jacobsen and Bauman (2006: 273))

By declining such offers, Bauman found himself a fish out of water. No longer a part of Poland's 'real existing socialism' or Polish nationalism, he was also out of place in Israel, where 'the single fact of being a Jew was believed to be the highest value of its citizens' (J. Bauman, 2011: 28). Although Janina was strongly attached to her family, both Baumans were out of place there and looked for another home one more time.

'Our story was different', wrote Janina: 'We could not stay for ever. We were no longer young, our past was too full, our experience too bitter. It was too late to struggle again and we had no will to conform. So, after three years of a comfortable life, we decided to start from scratch again and settle in England' (J. Bauman, 1988: 36).

Anna remained in Israel, and both of the younger daughters came to England. Almost fifty years later, in a private discussion in Leeds about the migrant crisis in Europe, and British tolerance, which included allowing Muslim women into the university in the veil (contrary to the French prohibition against 'wearing visible religious symbols in public spaces'), Irena Bauman concluded: 'So Dad was right! The best place for an immigrant is the UK! He always told us this!'

13

A British Professor

Starting from scratch – 1 Lawnswood Gardens, Leeds

At the age of 46, Bauman again started making a new home from scratch. He and Janina didn't know at the time whether it would be their last move. They arrived in Leeds on 1 July 1971, after a week of travel – first by ferry, then in their old Ford Cortina, which broke down halfway. After getting the necessary repairs, they arrived at their first and last residence in the British Isles: 1 Lawnswood Gardens, Leeds.

They had purchased the house while still in Israel, choosing it because of its proximity to the school that Lydia and Irena would attend. It was located in an agreeable area on the newer, north side of Leeds, on a park across from a new section of the university campus. Nearby was another beautiful park with a cemetery, perfect for walking. Their cottage was one of several dozen houses built in the style of Yorkshire architecture – the houses were similar in size and style, but with some differences that gave the place a more picturesque air than many suburbs.

The Baumans had found the place after consulting with their good friend Leszek Kołakowski, who had just moved to the UK and wrote them a long letter in December 1970, responding to the question 'How to buy a house in England?'.[1] Kołakowski, the new owner of a house in Oxford, wrote:

> The house of the size you need (I think 3 bedrooms) with a supportable system of heating (whose importance I will not go into) costs from £6,000 to infinity. . . . How much the Building Society[2] will lend you depends on your income (the maximum is two years of the borrower's salary) and the age of the house (older houses cost less. If you would like to buy Westminster Abbey, I am afraid that you should pay cash; the same with Coventry Cathedral etc.). For new houses (all people complain about them – it seems they have the same number of

defects as Polish houses and you need to spend months negotiating to fix the windows that never close and other not-functioning apparatus, etc.) you can get as much as 95% of the mortgage. . . . To this amount you must add the following: municipal taxes, paid each half-year, and innumerable other fees accompanying the acquisition (lawyers, the city, the state, humanity etc. – in our case it was £200 because we are former millionaires). In sum, it is difficult to start without a minimum of £1,000. *C'est la vie.*[3]

The dry but humorous letter also expressed joy that the Baumans would be joining the British group of kicked-out-of-Warsaw academics. Friends were waiting in London, mostly, Kołakowski said, mentioning Maria Hirszowicz and her historian husband Łukasz. Barbara, part of the Hochfeld group, was Bauman's collaborator and a close friend of Janina. Kołakowski mentioned that his family had decided the Oxford house would be their last residence. In another letter from the same period, Kołakowski gave the exact amount of his house transaction, while asking that Bauman keep it a secret – a strong sign of the ties that bound the two men in that period. Following Kołakowski's advice, Bauman decided to buy an 'old' house – though not Westminster Abbey.

Their house had been built in the 1950s and the Baumans were the second family to live in it. It was a classical English house with a classical British interior and space typical for a middle-class family: a modest and functional home, cozy and warm – a perfect place for family life, with respect for privacy. The construction was like the other nearby houses: red brick partially covered with white roughcast. The door from the street opened directly into the living room; behind it was a small kitchen and a large dining room. On the first floor were four bedrooms and a small space where Zygmunt organized his first office. It was really a monk's cell, containing only what was strictly necessary. Janina's office was quite the opposite: the largest room in the house, with a beautiful desk and a lot of light. The whole house caught the daylight through charming stained-glass windows.[4] This 'very British ambiance' became the Bauman family's new place on earth.

'At first, I lived in a vacuum, rooted nowhere, bound to no anchor. It was a bad time for all four of us', wrote Janina about the early years (J. Bauman, 1988: 142). She was in charge of the housework, never a source of pleasure or satisfaction for her. Before 1968, she had led a life of responsibilities related to film production, a professionally accomplished woman with strong institutional support and validation. Being a housewife was difficult to accept, but she devoted herself to the family, trying her best to make their new house a warm place for her hard-working spouse and children. She made an effort to cook and, with time, became successful, though never surpassing

Zygmunt's probably inherited, but certainly well-honed, culinary skills. Although it was not her favourite kind of life, Janina decided to focus on her daughters, and found that the early period in the UK brought her closer to them.

The 16-year-old twins needed her support. They were not really happy about moving to follow their father: 'They were taken away from their Israeli school where they had only just settled down, put on a ship and brought to this foreign place – where they had to start over again' (J. Bauman, 1988: 142). These kinds of moves, especially when they occur multiple times, are difficult for children, particularly teenagers, who are starting to build strong emotional ties with peers.[5] Irena and Lydia again had to begin immersion in a new language (they had taken some English private lessons in Warsaw, at a rudimentary level), with new subjects, a different educational system, new work rules, and new styles of teaching, writing and evaluation. Everything was new.

The most difficult thing, probably, was the huge pressure on them related to the final exams that are obligatory for English 16-year-olds. When accommodating students suddenly thrust into a new language and culture, school directors generally try to get them to start a year behind to get up to speed. But Bauman, who had hopped around different school systems with no ill effect throughout his youth, thought holding the twins back a year would constitute punishment, so he negotiated with the Leeds school director and persuaded her to let them start without repeating a year. He promised they would succeed, and they did. Like their hard-working father, the girls toiled away at their exams and finished among the top of their class. But these efforts had a price, leaving both girls so exhausted that they had some health problems. Still, the pressure and strong focus on education paid off for the girls, as they were able to assimilate in time to have pleasant lives in college. They became entirely 'absorbed' in their English environment.[6] For their father, the transition took more time, although his relationship with Leeds University started before their move to England.

The welcome at Leeds University

In an interview with Simon Tabet, Bauman explained that his invitation to Leeds was 'miraculous'.

> To this very day I have no idea who recommended it: he or she never revealed him or herself. There is a British habit, when they advertise a chair or a professorship: they write to representatives of the profession within the country and ask for suggestions. Who could or should be approached? It is a competition for the chair, but I never

applied for the chair. One day, I just received a telegram on which was written: 'Are you interested in teaching at the University of Leeds?' So I replied by telegram: 'Yes I am'. And that's it. (Tabet, 2017: 134)

Bauman came to Leeds for meetings with faculty in the first week of January 1971. His sociology professorship position had been confirmed several months earlier. On 21 September 1970, the university published a notice in the local newspapers: 'The new professor of sociology at the University of Leeds is the distinguished Polish/ Israeli sociologist Zygmunt Bauman. His appointment will run from April 1971, when he will succeed Professor Eugene Grebenik, who has held the post since 1954.' The announcement noted Bauman's past at the University of Warsaw and his dismissal as a result of the 'rising wave of anti-Semitism in Poland'. It detailed Bauman's previous appointments, described his main research interests as the 'sociology of politics, the application of systems theory and the theory of information and semiotics to socio-cultural analysis', and noted his longstanding interest in England, beginning with his research thesis on British socialism.[7]

This short communiqué shows that the university was proud of its appointment of Bauman.[8] While displaying the international side of Bauman's career as an asset, it also anchored him in Leeds by mentioning his interest in the UK. His 'Britishness' appears throughout in the titles and subjects of his studies. That 'British institutional imprint' would serve to legitimate Bauman's appointment and reassure those who were sceptical about the choice of a 'foreigner' for the position. Of course, there was nothing new about UK universities hiring foreigners. Starting in the 1930s, many escapees from Nazi Germany had entered British academia, and the Leeds Social Studies Department had a very diverse past.

Leeds was not considered a prestigious university – rather, a place that prepared professionals for local industry and administration. But, during the 1960s, the school had become 'a major centre of sociological research and thinking' (Bagguley, Campbell and Palmer, 2018: 37). Its Social Studies Department had 'a strong theoretical grounding, historical and comparative and world-oriented (i.e. not methodologically nationalist in a concentration on Britain, or analogous to the "civil servant" role)', as Jack Palmer explained.[9] This cosmopolitan orientation was imported by Fernando Henriques (born in 1916 in Jamaica, a social anthropologist who became probably the first black dean in the UK) and continued by John Rex (born in 1925 in South Africa, an anti-apartheid activist and specialist in non-industrialized countries). By the 1970s, however, the department had started to lose some of its flair, and there was a desire to bring more diversity to the Social Studies Department: diversity in terms of focus on non-European cultures, but also political diversity. As a Marxist scholar from Eastern Europe, Bauman was a perfect candidate.

One of Bauman's students, Max Farrar, remembers:

> We revolting students had been rather pleased when, in 1970, Zygmunt's predecessor, a statistician, resigned. We set up a committee to appoint a professor of our own choice, and we wrote to Erich Fromm, Colin McCabe and Laurie Taylor asking them to apply for the vacancy. Unbeknown to us, Lord Boyle, the new Vice Chancellor of Leeds University, had expressed dismay at the complete absence of Marxists in his social science department. (Those were the days when Tories respected liberal education.) Ralph Miliband was head-hunted as Professor of Politics and Zygmunt Bauman became Professor of Sociology.[10]

In fact, Miliband was key to Bauman's 'importation' to Leeds;[11] he had left London for Leeds and wanted to build a strong leftist environment there. Another person who played a certain role in Bauman's Leeds installation was Peter Worsley,[12] an anthropologist at Manchester University. Worsley had invited Bauman for a visiting professorship there in 1966 after meeting him at the World Sociology Congress in Stresa, Italy, in 1959. As Worsley noted in his memoir:

> for the first time we met Russians and East Germans, but the delegation that made the greatest impact was the one from Poland, a country with a long tradition of outstanding social science, and where new shoots of independent thinking were emerging once more. I was particularly impressed by Zygmunt Bauman and was able later to play an intermediary part in getting him to the UK when he was thrown out, firstly, from Poland, during a phase of anti-semitism, but allowed to go to Israel. (Worsley, 2008: 136)

Bauman brought 'fresh continental blood' to animate a troubled social studies department, according to Max Farrar:

> In 1971, my third year as an undergraduate at Leeds University's moribund sociology department, he [Bauman] strode into the lecture and spoke rapidly in his Polish-inflected English. I thought 'At last we have a professor who is a real sociologist.' I was intrigued by his decision to come to England. Anti-Semitism had driven him out of Poland and into exile in Israel in 1964 [Farrar is mistaken – it was 1968], but he'd rejected Israel. He could be described as a migrant, and thus as an outsider.[13]

Bauman was familiar with British sociology when he arrived in Leeds. In Halsey's book on the history of sociology, Bauman reconstructed his perception of the British academic universe as follows:

Coming to Britain in the early 1970s, I was struck by the demographic composition of British sociology: a few old men (many fewer old women) who in most cases wandered into newly mushrooming sociology departments from outfits with different remits and names – separated by a huge gap from lecturers, recruited in most cases from the ranks of the recent alumni of the brand new, post-Robbins sociology courses, and all apparently born at almost the same time . . . It was probably the relative novelty of the discipline . . . that made the British public uneasy and suspicious – another oddity when gleaned from my continentally trained viewpoint. . . . [S]ociology had 'bad press', was the soap-operatic formula for a family black sheep, so it seemed natural for a perceptive mind like Bradbury's to assume that the cynical, trouble-making 'history man' must have been a sociologist. Once more, I was shocked: how remarkably prestigious the public position of sociology was by comparison in France, Germany, or indeed my native Poland, where it settled in the public worldview on the tide of the late nineteenth century rising optimism and self-confidence. Nothing much seemed to be expected by the British public from the newfangled discipline . . . Again, a sharp contrast with the esteem in which sociological know-how was held in continental Europe. There, sociology was by common consent a repository of important wisdom: a sort of non-governmental brain-trust whose practitioners were the obvious people from whom to seek clarification of the itinerary and advice about next steps to be taken at each successive junction. In Britain, I did not notice much interest in the sociologist's opinion. Hardly ever was it sought by the norm-setting media (except perhaps by a few off-mainstream periodicals, most notably *New Society* – but even there sociology was living out its original public administration and social policy incarnation) and in times of crises or 'moral panics' they were the 'experts' least likely to be asked . . . From the public arena sociology was by and large absent. Or rather it served as the outer limit of the relevant and the attention-worthy. . . . I was profoundly impressed by the intellectual ferment notable in numerous sociological gatherings (though in the small scattered chapels rather than in the opulent High Churches in places like Leicester, Durham, Warwick, or Goldsmiths' College), by students challenging and pressing their teachers to focus on the task to illuminate the fast changing social conditions and to make sense of unfamiliar life experience, by the ethical sensitivity of most even narrowly professional debates and sometimes an almost missionary zeal of their participants, by the (often excessive) openness and (on occasion unwarranted and gullible) curiosity for new ideas, and by the immense volume of self-reflection and self-scrutiny in developing a social knowledge fit for the changed social realities. There was a widespread – exciting – feeling of 'catching up' with lost time and of a new beginning – unpolluted by the long record of alleys proved to be blind, of frustrations and betrayed promises that cooled the fervour and held back the ambitions of continental sociologists.[14] (Bauman in Halsey, 2004: 206–8)

Surprisingly, Bauman omitted the presence of 'foreigner' academics – especially those who had escaped Nazi Germany and brought the 'continental' tradition to the UK.[15] He compared the British sociological milieu to what he already knew – Polish and Western European sociological environments. After the University of Warsaw, where sociology was a fashionable discipline, where major political opposition was born inside its departments and sociologists were important public intellectuals (even if they became scapegoats of an authoritarian regime and lost their jobs), Bauman came to the UK, where the discipline was relatively recent and not considered so important, and the status of the sociologist was low. Thus, he was interested in the second-rank institutions because of their innovative and open-minded, fresh dynamics. While his colleagues joined more prestigious places (Kołakowski and Brus – Oxford; Sendler – Chicago University; Baczko – Geneva University after Clermont-Ferrand), Bauman settled at the University of Leeds. 'When Zygmunt came here [to Leeds] nobody had faith that he would stay', says Keith Tester; 'Leeds . . . at the time was a very dumb, industrial city . . . at that time no one ended up in Leeds by choice'.[16] Once again, Bauman's choices were unconventional.

Soon after arriving, Bauman presented his proposal for the future development of the Department of Social Studies. He sought to reinforce the position of sociology by creating a school of social thought. This proposition awoke some worries among his future colleagues. The traces of their reactions could be read in a letter from Alan Dawe, dated 7 January 1971, to Bauman in Tel Aviv:

I am one of those who silently cheered when I listened to your conception of what the department should be like. The creation of a recognizable and distinctive school of sociology is something to which I should very much like to make whatever contribution I may be able to make. The second point follows from this, and echoes something that Dennis Warwick said during one of the meetings. He suggested that though it may have become less discernible of late, there is a Leeds tradition.[17]

According to Jack Palmer, the Leeds tradition was 'cosmopolitan', rather globalist and comparative-historical in its scope. At Leeds, John Rex had taught 'modules that focused on the sociology of "one world" in a sense that anticipates the notion of globalization – indeed, Roland Robertson who first defined the term as we know it today worked at Leeds during this time'.[18] As Dawe mentioned in the letter to Bauman, in the prolongation of Weber, and criticizing Marxist determinism, Rex proposed the more complex conflict theory. His students – Bob Towler and Dawe himself – followed their mentor on different paths, but their students were recognizable in the UK as 'Leeds-trained students'. While '[f]or various reasons . . . things have become somewhat moribund here in the last year or so', Dawe offered Bauman his help, suggesting that some of his colleagues 'are just waiting and eager to return to the job of creating a Leeds tradition again'.[19]

A professor from Eastern Europe was being charged with rebuilding and creating a sociological tradition at Leeds. This was a huge challenge: 'Upon Professor Bauman's arrival . . . , the sociology curriculum underwent significant revisions, but the importance of international (and indeed historical) comparison remained central to the sociological imagination fostered in the students of the day' (Bagguley, Campbell and Palmer, 2018: 38).

Max Farrar remembers those beginnings:

Zygmunt, for his part, was amazed to find that no one in his department taught phenomenological sociology. So he asked a young lecturer to read Alfred Shütz and tell the third years all about the new sociology that was emerging. I already liked Weber and Sartre so I read it up and enjoyed what little I could understand. This tells us that Zygmunt was never stuck in a particular sociological rut: he respected the broad field of sociology. Thus the bunch of us who became PhD students in his department in 1972 were from all the theoretical branches of the sociological tree. One was in the International Socialists. Another waved Althusser's flag. Another repeated the adage 'The Marxists have changed the world; the problem is to understand it.' This wit consigned himself to the library where he spent the rest of his career. Zygmunt, on the other hand, seemed to want the hundred flowers to bloom.[20]

With his ideas and tireless vitality, Bauman had some of the important features of a head of department.

Department head at Leeds

Early in May 1971, while still in Tel Aviv, Bauman received a letter from J. V. Loach:

Dear Professor Bauman, I am sorry to have to tell you that Professor Hanson collapsed and died in the House of Commons last week while

attending a Select Committee on Nationalized Industries. Although
he had been ill on earlier occasions with heath trouble, it came as a
great shock to all of us. The Vice-Chancellor asks me to say that we
would be grateful if you would act as Head of the Department of
Social Studies but he has meanwhile asked Mr. Kirk to undertake this
duty until your return to Leeds.[21]

Bauman frequently mentioned the impact of chance in biographies: the powerful role of the uncontrolled element that can
suddenly change a trajectory in a significant way. One example of
such a turning point in Bauman's life was this: the death of the
previous head of the department, which led to his appointment to
replace him. While Bauman was an excellent scientist, researcher
and teacher, he had never led the administration and management
of a large team of university teachers. Moreover, he was completely
ignorant of the context and culture of the department, which was
an entirely unknown political, scientific and economic environment.
The first years were not easy.

There are some significant differences between Janina's English
and Polish editions in regard to Zygmunt's wellbeing during the
first years of Leeds life. His British colleagues could read from
the English book that Bauman 'as a breadwinner, suffered most,
bearing the burden and heat of the day. Only slowly, very slowly, did
he come to terms with his new role and his new surroundings. But
at least he did belong to a certain place right from the start, being
anchored to the department and defined as its head' (J. Bauman,
1988: 142).

The Polish version is much less optimistic:

It was hard for all of us. Mostly for Zygmunt. Long-time faculty
employees looked reluctantly at the new boss, a foreigner, a stranger
from the East, from a world with a foreign ideology and culture.
He awakened in them a feeling of suspicion, perhaps even anxiety.
He spoke with a foreign accent, knew what they did not know, and
ignored everything about the everyday affairs of English life. He was
uncensored. He felt like a stranger. He was a stranger. And he never
ceased to be one, despite the fact that with the passage of years he
gained more and more respect, trust and sympathy. (J. Bauman, 2011:
115)

That Bauman 'felt like a stranger . . . and never ceased to be one'
might surprise some of his British colleagues, who had the impression that Zygmunt came to feel at home in Leeds. But ambivalence
is a common feeling for immigrants. The Baumans had spent forty
years in another culture and would have remained in Warsaw had
they had the choice. 'Being an outsider' means a constant play

between one's insider and outsider status, a permanent dynamic game. While he seemed at home, Bauman never hid his strangeness. As he told Włodek Goldkorn:

> after escaping from communism, I did not join the anti-communists, although they presented me numerous offers, abundant and tempting. I was not looking for compensation for being expelled by Polish nationalism in the hospitality of Israeli nationalism. In England, by mutual consent and to mutual satisfaction, I do not pretend to be an Englishman and they do not consider me to be such. Maybe that's why my strangeness bothers neither me nor them.[22]

Despite the differences and obstacles, in other words, there was mutual consent about the role the immigrant played and his place in society. As long as their hosts offered them similar living conditions to the natives, perhaps it was correct that they didn't have to become English. It is rare anywhere in continental Europe to meet a university head of department who originated in another country, let alone one invited to take this prestigious position when he or she was just off the boat (and not only due to the lack of mastery of the language). In this respect, Great Britain is highly unusual, and Leeds University in particular was an exceptional place in its diversity, cosmopolitanism and openness to scholars coming from cultures other than Western European ones. Notwithstanding, one can imagine the incredible challenge facing Bauman when he accepted the departmental leadership.

'When I came to Leeds', Bauman told me in 2013:

> it was not a bad university at all, although I was the first sociology professor there. Before it was different, the manager of the chair was a demographer and not a sociologist, but in general there were mixed social sciences. To my surprise, and I was astounded to find it, about 3/4 of what I brought in my head from Warsaw and what is related to sociology was absolutely *terra incognita* for the department's employees, and it was the first time they had heard about it. Their knowledge was very narrow. [Their fieldwork, research, reading was done] mainly in England and in English, because English people, as it is known, do not read much in foreign languages. Warsaw was completely unique. . . . [I]t was an atmosphere that was exceptionally favorable – so when someone had a talent, this talent took on colors and shapes because there were so many possible intellectual fertilizers that everyone found something. Our team was unique – the work organization was unique, it never happened again in my life . . . In Warsaw we were a team of people discussing and presenting each other's work; every project interested all the other team members. Nobody was actually lonely there, we did not work in

isolation. Nowhere else have I seen this . . . and not at Leeds, during the 20 years I was a head of the department there. The professor in the next room did not know what his neighbour was writing about, what he was thinking etc. Everyone worked in solitude. Of course, there were seminars and that was good because from time to time someone expressed something . . . but at these seminars the speaker was usually invited from outside. People from the inside met each other over coffee talking about girls and I do not know what else, but the least about their work. There was no team thinking. Wherever I was, it was like that.[23]

The solitary work and absence of team thinking – or 'talking science' moments, as scientists in the laboratory describe it[24] – is probably among the most frequent complaints of isolated researchers. Sharing fresh ideas and observations is something that helps a lot to advance cognitive work. This is why the managers of scientific activities in some institutions invite or even require researchers to take coffee together regularly, to have 'let's talk science' moments. Usually, Bauman said, he would be invited to research centres for some months, with the instruction 'go and stay, think, see, do whatever you want', but, although there were interesting people from around the world there, they had minimal contact. The exception was in Canberra, at the Australian National University, where he was a visiting scholar in 1970 and again in 1982: 'At this institute it was imposed – you had to meet at 10 in the morning for coffee. We met for half an hour and that was very good.'[25]

This was quite the opposite of his working life in Leeds: 'The first 10 years in England were very hard', he told me.

There is a system whereby they do not promote people from inside the university and if there is a professorship the opening is announced in the whole country . . . When I arrived, there was one professor in the department and until the end of his life he was the head of the department. He was like a convict [condemned to the administrative work]. This is stupid, because he may be a very good professor, thinker and teacher, but here he has to be an administrator. Why combine the two things? It was a mystery to me. I hate administration terribly and therefore I felt very bad. The arrival of a person from outside is always a shock – a traumatic shock. You know nothing about him. He's a stranger, completely unknown. What kind of human is he? Does he like beef or mutton? Does he like sitting on committees or would he prefer to talk to students? Is he wicked, or envious, or a helpful person? No one knows. And I was this stranger to the third power – not only did I come from another university, I was from another country, another culture with another language.

'And from another system of higher education', I said.

'Yes! . . . For the first 10 years here, I had to constantly assure people that when I said fork I did not mean spoon. . . . because they were constantly wondering, "What did he really mean by that? What are the hidden thoughts behind this?" But 10 years was enough for them to reach a consensus that I was a normal creature.'[26]

Ten years is typically the amount of time that emigrant researchers say is required for them to be accepted by the local environment as 'one of us' (Wagner, 2011). However, Bauman was not really a typical 'emigrant scholar' since he became head of department as soon as he got to Leeds. This role required a huge amount of administrative work that most people in academia dislike and often treat as 'dirty work'.[27] Bauman didn't care for administrative tasks and was unhappy he had to spend time on committees and meetings, yet he knew how to make those necessary duties a little bit more interesting than they usually were, some colleagues recall. There were the traditional tensions between the head of the department and administrative staff, though no one recalled anything specific. Perhaps Bauman was guilty of being a stickler for rules, that stereotypical rigidity attributed to people from Poznań. Or perhaps his lack of experience as a British student could have been the source of tensions. At Warsaw University, sociology had been in fashion, and his students came from the capital's elite. At a British public university that was not Oxford or Cambridge, study habits were different. Some collaborators remembered hearing gossip that he was not a docile boss. On the other hand, however, he was remembered for organizing very short meetings (as always, he tried to do everything fast). Above all, his managerial 'trick of the trade' was his humour. He mastered the art of 'riposte', defusing the most problematic situations and tension-heavy conflicts by telling 'funny stories'. The faculty grew to anticipate Bauman's 'Polish jokes', which were frequently repeated on campus.[28] They were part of his charisma and aura as a teacher. Some were recalled for years after the last meeting Bauman ran as a head of the department, in 1991.

The so-called 'Polish jokes' were actually Jewish jokes, treasures of Ashkenazi culture that were popular in postwar Poland. Bauman had some little books with collections of Jewish jokes and very often told one of them, frequently with the double goal of inspiring laughter and thought. Deep knowledge was hidden in those stories, such as the particular advice for those who were overloaded by work: 'get a goat. Take care of her each day. After two months, give back the goat. Then you'll have a lot of free time and you won't complain any more about overload.' This is a 'light version' of the Jewish classic about the rabbi's advice to the stressed-out father with a house packed with children.

Those short moments of relaxation were vital to release some of the accumulated stress of long days. His entire life, Bauman worked very hard, living up to the Polish stereotype of *Poznaniaks* as well-organized, responsible and serious people.[29] Bauman was the Weberian ideal-type of that stereotype.[30]

Bauman's office was on the central campus. During his years at Leeds, he always maintained the same schedule: 'I always drive in at 6 a.m. . . . for two reasons. First, when I come in at 6 a.m. it takes me ten minutes, while if I leave at 7 or 7.30 it takes me an hour. Secondly, it was the only time at the university when I could write something, think something before the clients, students and colleagues came in with such-and-such different matters etc.'[31]

As he had learned in the Army, waking early gave Bauman personal time, a measure of freedom and agency. At the university, the head of the department's time belongs to the institution. Bauman's early arrival added something to his personal work. One of Bauman's Ph.D. students, Terry Wassal, recalled that 'after a party in the department, Richard, Ian, Aidan, Steve Malloy and myself were having a last drink before clearing up at about 5.30 in the morning when ZB arrived to start his day's work'.[32] This habit set an excellent example for the students. Wassal remembered Bauman's 9 a.m. lectures:

> This seemed to be his preferred slot no doubt because of his habit of getting into the department in the early hours of the morning. . . . He used to walk in at 9 a.m. on the dot and start delivering his lecture immediately with no concessions to the hour or late comers. But the theatre was always packed. No one wanted to miss his lectures. Back in the late 70s and early 80s this was not normal student behaviour![33]

Bauman's lectures could seem a bit messy because he liked to connect them in some way with the big news of the day (leaving very early, he had time to read the headlines or listen to the radio during his travel to the university). Bauman would alternate between standing and sitting at his desk, a scrap of paper with some bullet points in his hand. The lectures were engaging – since his youth, Bauman had trained to speak to large groups of people who were not predisposed to be interested in what he said.[34] He taught without imposing his way of doing things, and tried to make people believe in themselves. Not everyone liked his style or the content of his lectures, but students agreed that he was a charismatic teacher.

Unfortunately, Bauman's assessment of his academic work at Leeds was sour, due to the overload of administrative work:

> Here in Leeds, when I was the head of the department . . . during 20 years I wasted my time. I had no time for thinking or writing. . . . [with] engagement in the administration and in the committees and all

those things after which nothing remains . . . This is really a time-killer and you are so exhausted. When I was back at home at 7 or at 8 in the evening, I was able to do nothing. Nothing.

Some scholars feel happy with the prestige and power of the head of the department's position. For Bauman it was a time-killer. After retiring, Bauman was openly critical of the system: 'it's a terrible waste of time for grants and all that. All those works are nothing. [Bauman was referring to time-consuming tasks such as grant applications and other administrative work.] Nothing results from this, except the homage paid to some powerful force, which is completely unnecessary. A force whose only purpose is to confirm its indispensability.' Yet Bauman had managed to find some time to pursue his sociology work despite the administrative overload. His publication activity decreased compared to the Polish period, but teaching enabled him to conduct sociological discussions and exchange ideas, especially with Ph.D. students.

Mentoring Ph.D. students – Bauman and Tester

In our 2013 interview, Bauman was harshly critical of the educational system for academia:[35]

The university system is full of internal contradictions, and this is not at all conducive to creativity. On the contrary! The system exists to further reproduction and cut off all possibilities of deviation. The universities are the last vestige of the Middle Ages' artisanal corporation. In this system, the student must pass through an examination in which he shows he will do nothing other than what his master taught him – the masters are part of the commission. This is why I had always had a dilemma when I directed the Ph.D. students. Because I have this stupid idea that science is there to break the canons and not to freeze them. I wanted to inspire some creative spirit in my Ph.D. students, but I knew very well that, if I did, it could put them in a dangerous situation. Because, after they get their examination Ph.D. commission and go before the jury – so-called peer review – the jurors will each have completely different expectations,[36] but one thing in common: they will give the candidate the lowest grade possible. So, in asking my Ph.D. student to be creative, I was acting against his interest. For this reason, I came up with a formula that went something like this: listen and do not think differently and do not invent too much. Show that you read everything you were supposed to read, cite the sources in a huge number and stay close to the methodology in fashion. Write your Ph.D. thesis and defend it and then . . . throw it away! And write a book about what you actually learned during your Ph.D. training.

These are two different things: a good Ph.D. thesis doesn't show a lot of creative ideas . . . a good book is different. You are reading it and you are amazed – Eureka! This is the internal contradiction of the university. And this system of peer review enables the editor to avoid making a decision and hide his responsibility behind the reviewers. The consensual[37] opinion? What is such a thing? . . . What we have called 'consensual opinion' is actually putting everything at the same mediocre level.[38]

Bauman's strategy in Leeds resembled Hochfeld's in Warsaw, in the sense that both compromised to adapt to their audience. The only difference was the field of compromise – in Poland, the issue was politics, while in British academia the problem was related to conventions in the Beckerian sense, In his book *Art Worlds* (1982), Howard Becker analysed the dynamic and changing process of the elaboration of conventions, which are never totally broken but only changed so as to prevent communication from becoming inefficient, leading to the rejection of the work of art. To make an 'innovation', the artist must respect most of the rules, changing only a few.[39] The exercise of adaptability in the narrow context of precise expectations is difficult for a lot of young adepts of scholarly work. Being stuck in a trap between the conservative, quasi-feudal system and the expectation to be creative (without any definition of this term) requires complex strategies. The mentor is a key person in this long-lasting challenge.

Bauman mentored numerous Ph.D. students, among them the sociologists Roy Boyne, Richard Kilminster and Alan Warde; Doug McEachern (politics professor); and sociologists Alex Gordon and Peter Green; Marc Davis, who founded the Bauman Institute; and Max Farrar, who left academia to engage in social work and politics. In the 1970s, Ph.D. students were supervised by one professor. Bauman taught a seminar to all his Ph.D. students. He supervised projects not directly related to his work, but his students were impressed by Bauman's erudition and extensive scholarship – they appreciated his eclecticism as well as the freedom he allowed them. Everyone could find a way to make their own project in an independent way. Some specialized in post-modernity, some did not. For some it was a three-year Ph.D. programme and diploma; for others, it meant embarking on a radical social science path.

The mentoring relationship is delicate, with high expectations on each side. While the majority of such professional relationships are determined by the institutional frame and evolved in this professional context, sometimes the mentor/mentee relationship exceeds the frame of the institutional collaboration, lasts longer than the time devoted to the Ph.D. project and is transformed into friendship. This type of mutation occurs rarely; however, if professional

projects are conducted after the Ph.D. study, this kind of relationship may influence the careers of both collaborators. I have defined
this process as a career coupling.[40] The Bauman–Tester relationship
is one example of it.

Keith Tester was one of the most brilliant of Bauman's Ph.D.
students. Originating from a working-class English family, he wrote
his thesis on the rights of animals and published his 'thesis book'
– *Animals and Society* – in 1992. Tester maintained a close relationship with his mentor after doctoral training, and became his friend
and collaborator. Tester was not Bauman's creation; he had strong
life engagements (animal rights) and a serious scholarly background
before meeting Bauman. However, their relationship does fit within
the three-stage model of career coupling: matching, fusion and symbolic collaboration.

'I first met Zygmunt in September 1985 when I went to Leeds to
do my Ph.D. as a doctoral student', Tester said:

> People often ask me – did I go to Leeds for Bauman? The answer is no
> . . . I could not go to Leeds for Bauman because I did not know who
> Bauman was at that time. So why did I want to go to Leeds? Because
> I'd never been there before. This is the sole reason. . . . I was his Ph.D.
> student from September 1985 to June 1989, and Jeff Marshal was my
> other supervisor.[41]

Tester did not choose Bauman – it was a chance event. During the
period of Ph.D. training, Bauman had a loose relationship with his
students, testing them for their potential:

> Being supervised by Zygmunt was a very different experience. . . .
> When I did my Ph.D., for most people doing a Ph.D. was about
> writing a thesis. With Zygmunt it was totally different. . . . The first
> time I met him: [Bauman asked] 'Have you got your library tickets?'
> Then: 'Do you often do your research there?' That was one little state-
> ment typical for him. Then, another – in the corridor: 'if you don't
> blow your trumpet, no one else will blow it for you!' And he just
> walked away . . . And, finally, the worst advice that you can give to
> the Ph.D. student: 'Don't network with anybody – if you are good,
> they will network with you!' If you want to be an academic, this is
> disastrous advice.

In this last sentence, we see an echo of what Bauman defined in
our 2013 interview as the internal contradiction of the university
world (as a social world in the Beckerian[42] sense). Bauman's advice
was general and related to the behaviours of the Ph.D. student:
intensive work in the library, actual work instead of networking. His
style of supervising was indirect and almost informal.

So, when I was supervised by him . . . I met Zygmunt far less frequently, and with him the conversations were always: 'What film you have been watching? What novel have you just read? Have you read Conrad? No???? You must! Go read Conrad!' He rarely asked me what I was doing, and the only sociology he ever required me to read was some essays by Simmel and Elias: *The Civilizing Process*. He never said: 'You must read others [sociology authors] . . . just those two: Simmel and Elias.' . . . I am not that sure that he was enthusiastic about Elias. . . . I think he was testing me – in retrospect . . . testing where you were going to go . . . I think that it was related with the project I was doing at that time on the nonism sensibility and Elias was one of the possible roads to go through and I think that he used it as a test: where are you going to go?[43]

Tester was right. Evaluation of the disciple's potential is the most important task at the first stage of the career coupling. Tester was also impressed by the controlling style of Bauman's mentoring, represented by the sentence 'You *must* read this!' – said with a tone that brooked no opposition and was the quintessence of Bauman's style. His advice went beyond the studied domain to culture in general, reading and film, while providing a huge degree of freedom – or even the absence of advice – on the sociological literature. The focus was not on the sociology discipline *per se*, but on the formation of a specific, creative and critical way of thinking: Mills' 'sociological imagination'. This was a much more difficult challenge than simply educating a good professional in sociology. Bauman loved challenges.

Relationships of teaching and mentoring are unique (the same professor maintains different ties with each student) and dynamic. Both parties need to live up to the other's expectations in a delicate interactive process, which both Bauman and Tester passed through with success. Bauman liked good listeners. Anyone who expected a 'classical dialogue' had to be patient, or the relationship with Bauman was not good.[44] Tester was an excellent listener who knew when to speak and not to speak. He attributed Bauman's style of mentoring (so different from other British professors) to Bauman's personality. In fact, though, Bauman had brought his model of the master–disciple relationship from Poland – Bauman himself had experienced it during his Ph.D. training (see chapter 8). In this model, the mentor enjoyed huge authority but the student had important freedom in choosing his or her Ph.D. topic.[45] The mentor's powers of control were shaped into a kind of responsibility for the wellbeing of the student, and sometimes they extended beyond the professional domain.[46] The student had a life outside of the university, and progress in a chosen speciality also depended on his or her life conditions. In postwar Poland (and other Eastern-European-bloc countries), the problem was living conditions and poor nutrition (students had stipends but the access to food was frequently difficult). Some mentors cared about those basic needs, trying to help their students in difficult times – Hochfeld was an example of this.[47] In the UK, a respect for privacy reigned in most mentor–student relationships, and such ties were distanced and strictly professional. Thus, Tester was surprised by the degree of attention that Bauman devoted to him when Tester had a family emergency:

> When I was doing my Ph.D. starting in late September 1985, our relationship was quite distant . . . that's how I experienced it. In late 1986 my father suffered a stroke – he didn't die but for two weeks he was in intensive care and we were expecting him to, but afterward he improved. When I returned to Leeds, Zygmunt came to see me and asked immediately: 'How is your father? How are you?'

Tester was touched by this attention, impressed that Bauman had even learned of his father's condition. This event showed Tester that Bauman cared about him, and after that moment their relationship changed. However, the major turning point was when he obtained his Ph.D. degree: 'His first words were not "congratulations", but "Now the real work begins."'

This began the next stage of career coupling, defined as fusion. When master and disciple had trust and mutual understanding, they could work at the highest level – 'fusion' reflecting synergic co-operation animated by passion and the satisfaction of being 'in phase', or simply being understood without further explanation. Bauman had this kind of relationship with Tester, though they did not meet daily and sometimes went months without meeting. Tester's intellectual interests (animals, moral panic, compassion) were not at all related to Bauman's work. He was an independent intellectual who, as a part of his work, dealt with Bauman's scholarship.

> After I got my Ph.D. our relationship changed. . . . [It] was: 'Come to my house! There is someone who I would like you to meet.' And it became quite a regular thing: 'Come over for dinner.' Spontaneously. . . . That would happen 4/5 times in a year. . . . Our relationship became closer once there was no formal relationship and that makes sense. We were in very close contact those years and those conversations really encouraged me.

When they decided to write a book together, 'Bauman floated the idea in 1999 and within two years it was done', Tester said. They knew each other well enough to work at a fast, efficient pace.

It is characteristic of the fusion period that professional and private lives become entwined. Despite their age difference and previously formal relationship, Bauman and Tester became friends and close collaborators. Their relationship was transformed from a mostly unidirectional transmission of knowledge to an exchange. For Bauman, Tester was the perfect listener, raising pertinent questions that the public would have about his work. It was a safe environment for Bauman to express his thoughts – in contrast to his many interviews with journalists, who had less time and space for him and lacked the specific vocabulary, sociological knowledge and humanities-cultivated imagination – elements Tester had in abundance. The conversations with Tester were pleasant, comforting and inspiring. He was Bauman's disciple, his spiritual son.

With time, the relationship passed to the third stage (symbolic co-operation), when Tester decided on his own to write about Bauman's work:

> I then started to work on a book about his work. That became one of my main things, and at that time our relationship remained very friendly; however, he never, ever discussed my book with me [*Social Thought of Zygmunt Bauman* was published in 2004]. The only question he ever asked me concerned the coverage of the book. . . . But – I don't know how – somehow, I knew that he liked it. He was quite content with that book.

In this third phase, the nature of their relationship changed. Tester left the classical track of academia. The values transmitted by Bauman and incorporated by Tester (they matched his personality and familial education) made it impossible for him to advance in a milieu where writing and intellectual activity could be pursued only as a second occupation after teaching and administration. Tester's conclusion about Bauman as a mentor leaves no doubt about the unconventionality of the standards Zygmunt transmitted to some of his students: 'This is a kind of character formation and a sort of view that the Ph.D. thesis is just a vehicle, unimportant in itself . . . he [Bauman] actually was not interested in it . . . and that was fine. What he was interested was incubating a sense of vocation. The question of career was unimportant.'

Bauman was nonconformist and focused on what was important to him – intellectual activity and general scholarly formation. Fast, focused and passionate, he drily rejected those who did not live up to his tests. 'This approach is very much "sink or swim"', Tester said:

> I would imagine that if you sank it would be quite ruthless . . . If you did not develop as an intellectual, he [Bauman] would lose interest in you – I would imagine. . . . The relationship developed into something deeper after the Ph.D., so the Ph.D. was kind of a validation for me:

'Yes, I can see myself as an intellectual.' And he saw it like that: 'Yes – you are intellectual . . . Start working . . . now we will talk about interesting things.'

They talked a lot about their favourite movies and film directors. The passion and deep knowledge that mixes serious leisure (Stebbins, 2007) and professional work transformed their friendly talks about 'must-see movies' into culture analysis and critical discussion. When Tester was in trouble with health problems, Bauman sent him a collection of all of Swedish director Ingmar Bergman's films. It was 'you must see these films', but more than that. Bauman showed emotions in two ways, according to his daughter Anna: by feeding people, or giving them presents. The movie boxes were a sign from Bauman: 'I'm worried about you.' There was another packet with Buñuel's works. Tester wrote a book about the French film director Eric Rohmer, and Bauman was passionate about Austrian director Michael Haneke. They discussed novelties and classics – films, books, politics and family. Tester's wife Linda and their daughter Maddy were invited over regularly, along with other guests – they were a part of Bauman's circle of trust.

Bauman designated Tester to be his biographer and they talked almost to the end, exchanging letters with questions and responses concerning Bauman's life. Tester asked very good questions and knew how to discuss even delicate issues. They agreed without any spoken words on topics to discuss and topics to omit – with the proximity that allows close collaborators to work with deep understanding without speaking.

Tester never told Bauman that he did not intend to write this biography. He made this decision, Tester told me, because he was not fluent in Polish. Polish history was too complex, too overlapping to learn and understand. The cultural messages were too heavy and inaccessible, the whole picture too fuzzy. Zygmunt was his friend, mentor and spiritual father. Despite this unique proximity, Keith confessed to me at the end of our interview, 'I don't think I knew Zygmunt – I don't think there was a "Zygmunt to know".'

Tester definitely knew Bauman better than most people who claimed they knew him. But he faced secrets and a certain inscrutability in Bauman, and respected this by declining to write his biography.

Zygmunt Bauman died in January 2017. Tester died unexpectedly two years later.

14

An Intellectual at Work

We all know that knowledge production is not a matter of immaculate conception, even if in everyday gossip we are suckers for the idea of romantic genius.

(Peter Beilharz, 2020 MS: 208)

Writing as a craft[1]

Learning the craft

Bauman started writing at the age of 11 (in 1936). Eighty years later, in a letter addressed to Tester, Bauman wrote:

there were things that I wished to share with others, and words were just servants, noticeable only when stood in my way and uncared for once the job of putting them on paper was over. The first letter to a youth supplement of the 'Nasz Przegląd' daily I sent (and got published) at the age of 11 – and it was solely because I had just read the story of the French orientalist Jean-François Champollion, managing after more than [a] hundred years to crack the mystery of Egyptian hieroglyphs lying unread for millennia – and was tremendously impressed and excited to share that story with the world.

In the following years, during the war, in the Army and as a political officer, Bauman was in charge of speeches and 'lectures' sharing revolutionary ideas and promises of a better and equal future. Similar tasks – writing political tracts and discourses – were assigned to him in the postwar years, when he led the KBW's officer training. The formation of their political 'consciousness' was Bauman's duty. At the intersection between his military career and university enrolment, Bauman published two fiction pieces under the name 'Julian Żurowicz' (see chapter 8). With the paper he wrote as an 11-year-old, these are probably the only texts he published before his sociological training.

In 2013, at the beginning of my meeting with Bauman,[2] he introduced his work with two basic statements: (1) 'I am not like the people you study, who work in a team – I am an old wolf and I work alone';[3] (2) 'I only run what is called recycling – secondary processing of other people's thoughts.'

Both sentences were his 'self-presentation' and contained two messages. The first was a coded message: 'I am not an interesting case for you'; if true, it meant I should exclude Bauman from my 'sample', since my work was about collaboration. The message was that I should stop at the entrance (to his house).

Nevertheless, I stepped in, because preliminary analysis of his career contained serious evidence that he was not only 'working alone'. He was also involved in several collaborations, visible and hidden, that I was to discover later.

The second sentence was an elegant way for Bauman to generate the sympathy of a visitor by reducing distance. He probably targeted me as a fieldworker/ethnographer, doing 'real' research,[4] while he was 'only' recycling ideas. It was a kind of intellectual seduction and conversational rhetoric that created a relaxed and pleasant ambiance and offered an immediate basis for friendly discussion. Definitely, Bauman was a charming host. However, it was not true that he never conducted first-hand research. In Poland, he had carried out surveys of Party youth, for example – and, moreover, he was an excellent observer, a quality that is perceptible in his texts and the photographs he took in a period of enthusiastic hobby photography in the 1980s. Those who walked with Bauman in the streets got a deep sense of his perceptive abilities. 'It was quite an experience to walk with him on the streets of Leeds because he had a different way of seeing things', said Irena, his daughter: 'He saw the poverty before he saw anything else.' His repertoire of skills included the capacity to observe the environment and to capture what most passers-by would never see. It is exactly what experimental researchers are looking for, and, since Ludwik Fleck's groundbreaking work (published in 1935),[5] sociologists have recognized this capacity as a core scientific 'talent' – the ability to detect what others ignore, and effectiveness in explaining not only that the phenomenon exists, but that it is important.

This is what Bauman's writing was about. This was his 'story to share with the world', as Bauman wrote. In one of his letters to Tester, Bauman referred to Orwell's approach to writing:

Orwell names the 'perception of beauty (. . .)[6] in words and their right arrangement' as one of the four main motives of his writings. I would be lying if I said it about myself. In fact I had already several academic publications behind me – when by a stroke of undeserved luck PWN (Polskie Wydawnictwo Naukowe, my publisher at the time) assigned Maria Ofierska as my editor. She literally opened my eyes to 'the beauty of words' and 'their right arrangement'. It did not come lightly to her – she encountered an originally resentful, later enthusiastic, but alas perpetually obtuse pupil; I remember, with a mixture of deep remorse and enormous gratitude, her heroic – simultaneously Herculean and Sisyphean – effort of drilling or knocking respect and a modicum of appreciation for the powerful charm and the charming power of words into a head furnished with the thoughts to be expressed while conspicuously lacking the knowledge, and above all the feeling, of how to do it properly. Whatever I know about the sublime art of writing, and of the writer's responsibility for the beauty of words on top of the correctness of the ideas, I owe to her, and I am still ashamed of not having been capable of rising to the sky-high standards she set for me but ultimately failed in her effort to lift me to their level. Most certainly, I am not (unlike Orwell) what the French call 'le littéraire' and the Germans 'der Dichter'; my craft is not 'les belles lettres' – a literature that is 'an end in itself'. Though I would not say that it wouldn't make me happy if I could master that craft.

It is interesting to note that Bauman would mention Ofierska half a century after their encounter. How many authors acknowledge the role of editors in the process of their professional training? His style was particular – at *Krytyka Polityczna*, where he published texts in the twenty-first century, the editors used the expression 'pisać Baumanem' (Baumanian writing). It was considered complicated and sophisticated, with a lot of elaborate metaphors and long imbricated sentences. This is not really a text that you will read on the bus – it requires focus and careful rereading.

Working languages

Bauman was able to write in Russian (his principal language in middle and high school), Hebrew and French (with some help from Janina), but he formulated his sociological ideas in two languages: Polish and English. The transfer from one language to another is not only a matter of mastering grammar and vocabulary. Initially, in Britain, 'I did not have the courage to write in English', Bauman said in our interview:

> I came with an English-language knowledge, but it was 'conference language'. When I went abroad [from Poland] and I spoke English, I delivered papers, people were enthusiastic about my English on the principle, 'looks like a monkey but scratches his head almost like a man'. However, [once in Leeds] I was a local professor – and the students . . . they did not care whether I was a foreigner or not. They had a professor and what could have been an element of charm turned into a cruel failure and huge disadvantage. So, during a long time, I did not have the courage to write in English.[7]

To people who have mastered complex and new ideas in their mother tongue, writing in another language at the same level of precision, sophistication and exactitude seems frequently like an inaccessible skill. 'These are two different things', as Bauman explained:

> passive knowledge of language is relatively sufficient for my needs, because I can read and use relatively few important languages [Bauman read in Polish, Russian, English, Hebrew, French, German and Czech; shorter texts in Italian and Spanish]. However, as far as active language knowledge is concerned, I am not a polyglot – no question. If you do not know the language perfectly, you cannot know what you will create – There is what comes into your mind, but you only say what you can say, and that is quite different. I don't like such situations . . . [because] then, we make shortcuts – take the easy way. You cannot be really creative in a language you have not mastered completely – you cannot – this is a problem.[8]

Some writers switched languages with great success; sometimes what seemed to be a handicap became a distinctive mark, and sometimes even an asset. This was the case with Bauman's two favourite writers – Joseph Conrad, the famous English-language novelist[9] whose mother tongue was Polish, and the Czech Milan Kundera, who wrote in French. These, and others, were encouraging examples to Bauman. After working very hard on his English for ten years, Bauman could write at a level that satisfied him.

Bauman said the sociological aspect of language immersion explained how long it took before he felt comfortable writing in English: 'Ten years were partly taken by administration and in general the process of entering into this environment. . . . I was accused before I proved I was innocent. [In other words, people assessed both his imperfections and his original propositions – Bauman loved neologisms – as linguistic mistakes.] It was the opposite of how the English judicial system functions. And then, [after ten years – around 1980] . . . I became part of the landscape, an element in it – a weed growing next to the road.'[10]

The 'weed . . . next to the road' wrote and published in English at an incredible pace as soon as he was freed from his institutional duties (in 1991). These final years before his retirement seem to have been more peaceful: 'I appreciated very much that my colleagues were supportive and liked each other, and we understood each other, and then there was liberation because after another 10 years [after mentioned period of 10 years of learning before writing directly in English], I retired and then the real life started.'

Bauman was used to say that his 'real life' started in Leeds in 1991 when he retired and was able to devote his working time to writing.

This was when he published the majority of his books. His English was by then excellent – though, like most authors (including those writing in their native languages), his texts were in need of a good editorial hand, especially when they were targeted at a larger public. Several very good copy-editors worked on Bauman's manuscripts for Polity Press, the major publisher of his work in the twenty-first century, and made them beautiful in English. Says the press's editor, John Thompson, about one of them: 'She just has a great sense of style, she helped to turn his work into really fluent text. Zygmunt writes very well in English. But it is clearly a second language . . . His style was a little awkward and it needed that fluency. He was always deeply appreciative of our work. He was a wonderful author because he obviously appreciated everything we did.'[11]

Bauman, of course, did not welcome all changes, Thompson adds:

> He didn't like text changes, so if you went back and said 'Why don't you develop this argument further, or, could you take this part off?', he didn't like it. He was kind of 'take it or leave it'. That was Zygmunt. He did what he wanted to do. . . . But when it came to this issue of style and fluency in English, he was always completely grateful and never objected to anything. For example, for the blurbs on the back of the book, I asked Zygmunt to provide drafts for me, but I basically rewrote them, turned them upside down to get at their different meanings. . . . and he would say, 'Thank you so much, this is wonderful what you've done.' . . . He didn't object to changes of this kind. . . . He wanted to focus on the development of ideas.[12]

This attitude made Bauman an 'easy' collaborator and an author that editors liked to work with. Bauman relied on them. In *Modernity and the Holocaust*, he wrote: 'To David Roberts goes my gratitude for all his editorial care and patience' (Bauman, 1989: xiv). Bauman knew he did not entirely belong to the language and culture in which he wrote, but to another universe that was unknown to his new co-citizens. As something of a stranger, he needed to trust his editors. Their job was to make his manuscripts into the best books possible. His job was writing.

Working space
When his daughters left home for university in 1974, Bauman moved from his tiny office to a slightly bigger room, although he never managed his working space the way Janina did. She wrote at a large and beautiful desk in a room with 'everything in its place'. Zygmunt's room contained a small desk, which had been put in backwards so the stabilizing bar, normally at the back, was in front, making it hard to get one's legs under the desk. Bauman was tall and had to squeeze to get his long legs under the bar. It was the

most unergonomic position imaginable. Not only that, the desk was broken; Bauman fixed it temporarily but it remained wobbly for years. His office chair was a very simple object, made from wood with a plastic seat; earlier he had used a stool covered with lambskin. Bauman always joked that, in his job, the most important thing was the quality of the *Sitzfleisch* (from German – literally, the 'meat of the bottom'). But this reference to a sturdy bottom may have contained a double-entendre. Bauman was often punished or criticized, by his peers, hierarchies and authorities. In Poland, children were usually punished with smacks on the rear end. Therefore, if you wrote certain things that were sure to draw attacks, it was important to have 'thick skin' in that area.

Bauman had good *Sitzfleisch*, apparently, but he also had an aching back. 'Dad was always sitting in an uncomfortable position, as if the suffering was indispensable to his writing. He never asked more from life than necessary', said Irena. Added Lydia: 'It was not beneficial to his back. But it was like an obligation for him, not to have any comfort.' She remembers the complete disorder on his desk, covered by tobacco, ashes, manuscript pages and reprints, journals and books – everything mixed together. 'He wrote like this, in a complete mess', Lydia continued: 'Firstly it was the typewriter with tobacco everywhere, then he used the computer and it was the same mess.'

Bauman's first computer was an Amstrad, to which he was very attached and over which he suffered severe remorse when he had to replace it, with a cheap but good-quality PC (Dell) with a big, old screen. Bauman was not a fan of technology. When he had a question or technical problem, he met with Tony Bryant, his friend and 'technology' expert. His indifference to the machinery was visible. The computer keyboard was full of tobacco. His tobacco and pipes were loyal companions of his workplace in Leeds. The pipe replaced the cigarettes the Baumans had consumed in abundance. When he was writing, he smoked intensively, and he would stop smoking only rarely and for a few moments when he spoke. After Bauman's death, Irena found thirteen pipes, more than twenty lighters and many packets of Clan Aromatic tobacco. The specific smell of it was omnipresent in the office and the whole house.

Behind the desk was a large and solid shelf with hundreds of books that Bauman employed for whatever book he was currently working on. The office also had a round coffee table with numerous books lying on it in disorderly fashion (or in a secret order known only to the owner of the space), with newspapers (Polish *Gazeta Wyborcza*, French *Le Monde*, American *New York Times* and British *Guardian*) and some manuscripts and letters. Two simple and functional armchairs were there for reading and meeting collaborators. The office had three windows, two on the western side and one facing east, which was important since Bauman saw the sun rise each working day.

Daily work routine

Bauman always wrote from the early morning, starting his day when it was dark outside (4.00 –4.30 a.m.). Before coming to the university, he often had two hours of writing under his belt. After he retired, Bauman spent the first half of his days at home writing. The Greeks didn't realize that Venus, which is brightest just before sunset and again in the morning, was a planet, and they referred to its two manifestations as the Morning Star and the Evening Star. 'I have a theory', Bauman told me half-seriously in 2013, that 'somehow, people are divided into these two stars. Clearly, Ola is an Evening Star, who writes the most wonderful things at midnight. I'm the Morning Star: what I haven't written before noon will not be written that day.'[13] 'Ola', the Polish diminutive for Aleksandra, was the sociology professor Aleksandra Jasińska-Kania, Bauman's partner in the last few years of his life. This was her account of the perfectly organized day of her 'Morning Star':

> He [Bauman] usually woke up around four in the morning and, after quickly browsing through the daily press, wrote until eight, when he woke me up for breakfast. He hardly could wait until I finished eating, saying: 'I have a lot of work to complete today.' Then he ran to continue his writing in his office in an upstairs room of the house. I stayed downstairs in another office inherited from Janina. Among my correspondence I usually found emails from Zygmunt, including attachments containing his writing from that morning for me to read. I could barely finish reading and answering letters before noon, when he was calling me to have drinks before a lunch that he had prepared and set to cook in the oven (he loved cooking). This was his favorite time of the day: when we were drinking and discussing our morning work – mainly his writing, because mine had not started yet. I could only begin to work seriously after lunch and a short siesta, but when I was finally finding some inspiration to write, Zygmunt would ask whether we could take a break and listen to music or watch a movie he had prepared for our evening entertainment. We had different cycles of our daytime activities. I called him a lark and myself an owl. . . . He was the Morning Star, and I was the evening one. I had a hard time keeping pace with him. He could write 4 or 5 books during one year, while I was glad to write 4 or 5 articles in the same time. (Jasińska-Kania, 2018)

This impressive vitality, which slowed only in the final months of Bauman's life, was one of the elements that contributed to his achievements. Equally important were his discipline and the processes he developed for writing his books.

Writing books

Bauman did not employ a single method for writing his books. Like many other scholars, he used his teaching as a basis for some of his titles. This strategy – 'a course first – a book after', is popular and practised in different disciplines. Bauman did it with huge success in Poland and continued the tactic in Leeds. 'This is normal; you cannot separate didactic work from writing', he said: 'They have to be intertwined because it is the same brain; and that's actually how it was basically [in my case] – first the course and then the book.'[14]

While one can imagine how a book emerges from teaching or conversations, the process of conceptualization that transforms vague and disordered thoughts into an original book seems more inaccessible. In his case, Bauman told me:

> There were themes that found no justification in the courses but created an outlet for other things I was thinking about. I had fantastic experiences, for example with a book . . . I did not think about this book at all. I did not plan it at all. I went to a concert at Harrogate [in Leeds Exhibition Centre] and Yoyo Ma was playing Beethoven sonatas on the cello. Yoyo Ma is a great virtuoso but what I thought [at that moment] had nothing to do with the sonatas he performed. I came out of this concert with a clear plan for a book about which I never thought deliberately. Of course, the elements were already in my head, but they connected at that concert.[15]

Scientists frequently describe similar 'Eureka' moments. Listening to classical music – in particular, live performances – seems to stimulate these moments, so sought after by all creative people.[16]

Writing his books was not always a joyful creative process for Bauman. For, while he enjoyed considerable esteem as a global thinker, he was touched by doubts about his work and had difficult moments that only the closest members of his entourage were aware of. Peter Beilharz, close friend and sociologist, wrote: 'Early in our relationship he would send me proofs in the post. The more he wrote, into the last years, the more dismissive he was of his own work, and the less inclined to share in these ways' (Beilharz, 2020 MS: 136).

This tendency could be the result of ageing and tiredness, but those who met Bauman would not be fully satisfied with this explanation. He was full of vitality, and such hesitation was more likely a by-product of his creative intellectual work. His self-criticism was evident in the sour humour and cynical ripostes he sometimes addressed to himself and his work, expressing a kind of fragility and hesitation about his writing. 'As he put it later, in dialogue with Alain Touraine at Asturias, he saw himself as a follower rather than a leader or pioneer', wrote Peter Beilharz (2020 MS: 199). This kind of self-doubt was also evident in Bauman's remark to me in our first interview, when he described himself as a recycler of 'other people's thoughts'.

Those doubts and feelings of insecurity appear in declarations he made to close friends predicting the end of his writing career. Beilharz wrote that Bauman announced each new work in this way: an average of one a year (Beilharz, 2020 MS). He said the same to his friend Antony Giddens in 1995: 'I am still smarting after the blow and trying to find my feet. As it happens, I do not think I'll produce another book ever.' Bauman knew how to ask for advice and to trust his friends: 'As you've surely noticed by now, the essays I sent you spill all over the place . . . Can you find one connecting idea (except for the old man's cantankerous grumblings)? Is there any "natural order" in which the essays might be arranged?'[17] Bauman's editor John Thompson comments: 'It was very characteristic with Zygmunt that when he finished a book he said: "That's it, I'm gonna take a break now."' Thompson was used to this. He recalls that he would tell Bauman to '"just take it easy for a while", and of course he never did... The next morning he would be starting a new text.'[18]

Bauman published dozens of books after declaring the end of his writing activity the first time. Beilharz explains: 'Bauman of course played games with me, and with himself. When I came to visit regularly he would each year give me the manuscript of the latest book, saying to me here it is, my last book. This was not only play. On 6 March 1999 he wrote to me that he was unsure as to whether he would be around long enough to finish *Liquid Modernity*' (Beilharz, 2020 MS: 84). That book, as it turned out, would mark the beginning of Bauman's global fame.

Liquid Modernity was the first in a long series of books about 'liquid' phenomena in various fields.[19] Liquidity was the basis of the construction of a post-modern theoretical world. It inspired changes of perspective in several people, as seen in the implementation of the term 'liquid' as a keyword labelling a new theoretical approach. Bauman alone wrote major books about post-modernity through this lens, but his theory also attracted authors and specialists from different branches of the social sciences. Some of them called on the Baumans, who welcomed guests to their home, where new people were constantly turning up for dinner and discussion. The content of these mostly informal meetings was in several cases transformed into 'conversational' books.[20]

Conversational collaborations

'Baumanian' hospitality and conviviality created perfect working conditions for making books organized from focused conversations. Different topics were discussed and analysed. Some pieces reinforced the extension of Bauman's approach into such areas as media, architecture and management. Others contributed to the spread of Bauman's approach to current world issues: consumption, inequality, migration and war. The partners in these conversations were social scientists, but also journalists, writers, literature specialists, philosophers, artists, cultural critics, management specialists and architects.

Bauman started this 'genre' with Polish scholars: the philosopher and cultural studies specialist Anna Zeidler-Janiszewska and the philosopher Roman Kubicki, who organized visits by Janina and Zygmunt to Poznań beginning in the late 1980s. Their first book, *Humanista w ponowoczesnym świecie – rozmowy o sztuce życia, nauce, życiu sztuki i innych sprawach* (A Humanist in the Postmodern World: Conversations on the Art of Life, Science, the Life of Art and Other Matters) published in 1997, contains several elements of Bauman's biography and was never translated into English. Zeidler-Janiszewska conceived of the book, Kubicki recalled in an interview.[21] The conversations started in Poland, and everything was recorded, and then the Polish hosts came to Leeds, stayed at the Bauman house for a week and continued the discussions:

> Then we did transcriptions, but the text was changed and completed by Zygmunt and had various versions. This is why, when we did the second, enlarged edition (published in 2010) – it was not recorded, we only communicated via e-mails. Which is not so good, because the dramaturgy is different, so it was not the same. The first stage was interesting but after all those e-mails – Zygmunt liked to add new things, sometimes we also added something, and finally he had a long monologue, which we cut after with our questions to make it more dynamic and 'conversational'. So very often it was response first, questions later.[22]

Bauman did not check the final proof; he trusted his collaborators. For illustrations in the 2010 edition of the book, Bauman provided photographs he had taken in earlier years. Zeidler-Janicka, Kubicki and Chrzanowski chose which pictures to use; Bauman let them. 'He sometimes "played" a super-modest person who doesn't care about himself', said Kubicki – 'I think that it was his strategy of reducing distance. It was important for him to put people at ease. And he was a wonderful storyteller.'

These anecdotes were obviously a distinctive treat that people with high career positions in Poland were frequently missing in their 'socially distant' relations. Bauman did not play the part of a star or an 'important intellectual'. Yet people felt that his self-ironic posture was a strategy. He had 'natural authority' and people respected him, were intimidated, and sometimes even feared him. During his years as department head, Bauman had used anecdotes and jokes to make departmental meetings 'digestible' and he employed the same technique during the working sessions that produced the 'conversational books'. He liked a nice, fun ambiance and was pleased when people liked him. Managing people who like their boss is much easier – Bauman had learned this as an 18-year-old officer leading soldiers twice his age.

Three years after the publication of the Polish conversational book, Bauman agreed to work with sociologist Peter Beilharz on *The Bauman Reader* (published in 2000), which became a milestone in the reception of Bauman's post-modernist work. It was an important sign of the recognition of Bauman's theories, confirming him as a 'classic' author.[23]

The English-language debut of the conversation-book, co-authored with Keith Tester in 2001, forged the path for further collaborative projects. From 2001 to 2017, he published fifteen books with twenty different co-authors. Of the twenty co-authors, three were women: the philosopher Anna Zeidler-Janiszewska, management professor Monika Kostera, and his daughter Irena Bauman – an architect. In 2019, during a symposium devoted to Bauman's legacy, Irena Bauman gave an interesting description of her father as a book collaborator, pointing out the pertinent issue of writerly loneliness:

> The device of writing through a conversation is worth reflecting on especially in the context of Zygmunt not being the greatest team worker. I think maybe we underestimate the intellectual and the sheer physical effort that is vested in writing a book and that no matter how brilliant the mind might be there is a loneliness that increases with age – the loneliness of being older than anyone else around you and a certain type of isolation that comes with it that maybe none of us can imagine until we are almost there ourselves. So maybe the shift to this style of writing was a . . . catalyst to sustain the habit of daily writing and partly a way of managing this growing isolation.[24]

This fine analysis helps us understand the energizing influence of Bauman's co-authors. But descriptions of the collaborative process indicate Bauman was not that impressed by the energy of his younger peers. Irena Bauman recalled:

> The method was for Jerzy [Kociatkiewicz] or Monika [Kostera], the two management specialists, to pose an idea regarding some aspect of management and pass this text to one of the other three authors in random sequence until all three completed the cycle at which the next idea would mark the next chapter. The system should have worked

were it not for the different levels of dexterity (and of other commitments) we each had in terms of the speed of our responses. In my
case I needed considerable time to absorb what others were saying
and to formulate and write down a response that would resonate and
advance the thinking. Four to six weeks was my ideal time for each
chapter and two to three weeks were needed by Monika and Jerzy. So
basically between us, we felt guilty throughout the process for slowing
Zygmunt down to an unacceptable pace since his turn-around was
about two or three days. I once suggested that surely if we were to
measure a society's success by the wellbeing of its weakest members,
we should also measure the correct speed of writing by its slowest.
This did not resonate.

One characteristic that Bauman maintained to the end of his life
was his timing. He did everything very fast, and it was difficult
for people to follow him. This particularity made collaborations
problematic, but an even more important difficulty was related to
his need to keep control of the group's process. 'These themes of
control, lack of teamwork and extreme generosity were also present
in the process of writing our book', Irena Bauman said. His 'extreme
generosity' in the collective writing project was evident in Bauman's
sharing of ideas, time and availability with his co-authors. He was
generous in a very efficient way. He mastered the art of compliments
and encouragement. He showed that he believed in his collaborators and, by his involvement in the project, made people exceed
their usual performances. Irena Bauman used the Belbin method[25]
– a human resources tool – to describe which of nine categories her
father fitted as a team member:

He was definitely a shaper – basically someone who provides the
necessary drive to insure that the team keeps moving and does not
lose focus in its momentum. [The shaper's] strengths are, they're
challenging, dynamic, they thrive on pressure and they have drive
and courage to overcome difficulties and challenges. And now
the allowable weaknesses: they can be prone to provocation and
may sometimes offend peoples' feelings . . . And we should not be
surprised that shapers run the risk of becoming aggressive and ill-
humoured in their attempts to get things done. I had experienced
such moments [as a team member with Zygmunt]. Now, the other
trait is a team worker, and I was very interested to see what kind of
team worker traits my father might have: a team worker helps the
team jell, using versatility to identify the work required and complete
it on behalf of the team. Their strengths are cooperativeness, percep-
tivity, diplomacy, good listening and the smoothing of friction. . . .
[W]eaknesses can be indecisiveness in crunch situations and the tendency to avoid confrontation – that was never the case. Team players

are said to be hesitant to make unpopular decisions – this was definitively not the case here.[26]

Such an analysis could only be performed by someone who knew
Bauman intimately, not only because of its accuracy, but foremost
because it bravely touched on difficult points, which are perceived
as negative character traits. Bauman was sometimes feared by his
friends and collaborators. He could be authoritarian and dry, cynical
and ironic, at times mischievous. Most of his close entourage spoke
about his 'controlling behaviour' – he wanted to control things that
were important to him . . . people included.

Aleksandra Jasińska-Kania moved into the Lawnwood Garden
house in the period during which these collaborative projects were
at their peak. In my 2013 interview with Bauman at their house,
Aleksandra described the projects in the following way: 'when
Zygmunt's work became known and began to have a big impact in
the world . . . younger people turned to Zygmunt with questions.
Most of the works that have been created over the past few years. . .'

'Four years', Bauman interjected.

'. . . with the intention of explaining and continuing his thoughts',
she continued: 'these are joint works and they rely – on a kind of
debate.'[27]

Bauman described the conversational process as 'a challenge and
a reaction, which is again a challenge for the other party. . . . It starts
by kind of formulating questions and then the answer and more
. . . None of these conversations [was] planned in advance – that is
. . . when we started them we did not know in which direction they
would go – that depended on the conversation.' Aleksandra concluded in a solemn way, typical for a university professor, 'usually
the younger people approach the master', but she was immediately
cut off by Bauman who nonchalantly put in: 'Usually??? There is no
older person than me today!'

This kind of sour, age-related humour, with many disagreeing,
clarifying interjections, was typical of how Bauman spoke at this
time. This exchange is a good illustration of the ambiance Bauman
created and that accompanied the process of conversational-book
creation. As Irena Bauman underlined, her father needed company
and the exchange of ideas to pursue his intellectual work. As
Jasińska-Kania noted, Bauman was eager to share what he had
written immediately after his morning work. He sought immediate reactions to freshly composed drafts. He needed a conversation
partner to push his ideas forward, to strengthen arguments and
complete his analysis, or simply for feedback. Intellectuals need
partners to forge new ideas (many today complain at the lack of
'milieu' and the absence of 'scientific talks' – Wagner, 2011). In the
final period of Bauman's life, this role of listener and discussant

was fulfilled mainly by Jasińska-Kania. Bauman dedicated his last book to her (*Retrotopia*, 2017). Before, during over sixty years, the most important and longest discussion partner and collaborator was Janina Bauman, though she remains partially in his shadow.

The main collaborator: Janina Bauman

From a sociological perspective, the relationship of Zygmunt and Janina is a most fascinating collaboration, in that it contributed to important creative work by both.[28] Zygmunt Bauman never co-authored a book with Janina. Each wrote separately. Yet the two discussed everything together, and Bauman's writings were inspired by their conversations. These exchanges began from the start of their life together. Both were students who wrote texts; Janina studied journalism and wrote daily in her secret journal. When they met as students, they probably reviewed the essays each was assigned as part of their admission procedure. Bauman was a brilliant student, but a careful reader's eye is always precious. When Bauman enrolled in the university and began his intensive writing, Janina was already working as a script overseer, checking the quality and political correctness of screenplays. She read a lot and corrected page after page; she was also for several months a translator of dialogues from French into Polish.

At home, in parallel, Janina read Bauman's drafts as an integral part of her spousal role. They were a fused couple, sharing passions for books, movies, theatre and . . . writing. After her long hours at the Polish Film office, she returned home to encounter Zygmunt talking about his current texts and all the issues that were important to him. Bauman always had a lot of important points to share, manuscripts to show, pages to correct. He worked fast and did a lot. Despite being overloaded with her own work, Janina gave Zygmunt her free time. The daughters remembered their mother coming back from her office and 'father jumping on Mum with the last written pages in his hand', even before she had taken her coat off. The Bauman house was a place where 'work–life balance' was an empty slogan. While woman's work is traditionally composed of cooking and cleaning, Janina's duty was listening, discussing and editing. She was not a sociologist, but could give her opinions on style and content. Like other wife-homemakers, Janina's work was invisible, the result of a tacit agreement. She was generally Zygmunt's first editor.

This situation changed after they moved to England. In Poland, Bauman had written in Polish, and the same was true in Israel, where Janina edited his texts before he sent them to translators. In Leeds, the situation changed. Janina was fluent in French but needed to

make an extreme effort to master English. She attended university
literature classes, read extensive English literature, noting down any
words or expressions that were new. She did so well that her friends
remember her English writing as excellent. Unfortunately, during
the first years, she was not confident enough to speak English freely.
This was not unusual, for many people who are accustomed to
having mastery of their vocabulary and speech are hesitant to speak
in a foreign language, no matter how well they have learned it. It
was painful for Janina not to be able to speak English at the level
she desired. This weakness was not helped by the fact that, in the
beginning of their residence in Leeds, for the first time in her life
she had become a housewife. When the children left the house for
college in 1974, she decided to become professionally active again,
enrolled in the library school and eventually became a librarian in a
Leeds middle school.

If Janina's previous contributions to Zygmunt's work remain
invisible, her translations of his books from English to Polish
gained important recognition. Comparing Bauman's 1986 autobiographical manuscript in English and in Polish translation reveals
an impressive mastery. The second part of this manuscript (written
probably around 2009) was translated by someone else, and the
style is recognizably different. Janina was an excellent translator,
and her craft as a writer was top-notch. She knew the value of each
word and could formulate a complex story with just a few of them.
Her titles were remarkable, as Bauman and their friends often noted
in correspondence (see letter from the philosopher Lena Eilstein).[29]

In addition to editing, translating, listening and discussing the
work of her husband, Janina was a recognized documentarist. At
Maariv (the biggest Israeli journal at the time), she excelled at preparing documents, as shown by the quality of her research files at the
Bauman collection in Leeds. She prepared collections of pieces from
newspapers with handwritten notes and other information necessary to transform these sources into scholarly references. Among
the pieces she wrote at the time are reviews of Holocaust books
published in 'Jewish studies' reviews; later, Janina was involved
in various research projects. One focus was the Roma and Sinti
people and their Holocaust tragedy and postwar stigmatization, and
the near absence of historical works about their Shoah – *Parajmos*
(J. Bauman, 1998). Another project concerned the oral history and
testimonies of Shoah survivors living in Leeds. She was fascinated
by the life stories of 'ordinary people'. The accumulation of work
on related topics suggests she was preparing an academic book (or
a thesis). However, Janina never got a degree and no book was ever
published from these notes. Perhaps she was preparing material for
Zygmunt, part of their intellectual cottage industry?

But Janina's childhood dream of becoming a published writer did come true. After her sister and mother died, Janina realized there was no one else who could tell their story of survival, which she viewed as her duty – to them and to pass along the story to her daughters and grandchildren. Her book, *Winter in the Morning: A Young Girl's Life in the Warsaw Ghetto and Beyond, 1939–1945*, was published in 1986. It was well received, considered among the best testimonies of the Holocaust, and rare because it presented the perspective of a teenage girl. While Janina worked on that book, she was mentally immersed in the painful past and partially absent from her present life. This was a new situation for Zygmunt, who during this time lost his partner for intellectual exchanges. In the introduction to her book, Janina thanked her 'husband, for putting up with her protracted absence during the two years of writing', when she 'dwelled again in that world "that was not his"' (J. Bauman, 1988: vii).

The crucial difference that would always separate the couple was that Janina was a Holocaust survivor. It was a liminal experience they could not share. Bauman, to be sure, had had limited experience of the German racist laws, having been forced to wear the yellow badge in late September 1939 in Włocławek before escaping to the Soviet Union. As a Polish officer, he had witnessed Nazi horror as part of a security unit that occupied Majdanek, the Nazi death camp. His group was the first Polish unit in that place after it was liberated by the Red Army. While the experience was shocking – one that he never spoke about in public – Bauman was a witness, rather than a survivor, of the Holocaust.

Janina did not discuss her wartime experiences before leaving Poland. The topic arose at times in Israel, where the Shoah became an important area of study in the late 1960s. When they moved to Leeds, Janina and Zygmunt had no time to dwell on their painful childhood. Their life was about the present – their twins finishing school, the family adaptation, caring for Janina's mother. When the girls went off to school and Alina, Janina's mother, died in 1980, she began work on her memoirs.[30] It was only after Janina finished her book, however, that her discussions with Zygmunt about this period began. He was shocked to read her book. He could not directly share her experience, but the transmission of her feelings, and her understanding of the Holocaust, affected him deeply and led him to write about his own understanding of this tragedy.

In 1989, Bauman published one of his major works, *Modernity and the Holocaust*. In the preface, he wrote:

Having read Janina's book, I began to think just how much I did not know – or rather, did not think about properly. It dawned on me that I did not really understand what had happened in that 'world which was not mine'. What did happen was far too complicated to be explained in that simple and intellectually comforting way I naively

imagined sufficient. I realized that the Holocaust was not only sinister
and horrifying, but also an event not at all easy to comprehend in
habitual, 'ordinary' terms. This event had been written down in its
own code which had to be broken first to make understanding possible. (Bauman, 1989: vii–viii)

The two Baumans' books can be read in parallel, constituting
together a perfect *chef d'oeuvre* that joins practice with theory. An
ethnographical account (by Janina) is crowned by theoretical analysis (by Zygmunt). The books reflect both authors' experience and
knowledge. Zygmunt dedicated his book to Janina. Janina devoted
hers to the memory of her mother and sister (she dedicated a subsequent work, about their life in postwar Poland, to Zygmunt). The
core message of Bauman's book is that modernity produced the
Holocaust not by accident or the folly of a leader, but as an effect
of rationalization. He demonstrated that modernity could result
in the detached, precisely planned and organized destruction of an
ethnic group, employing members of that very group in their own
'elimination'. The first condition for producing this deadly industry
was to dehumanize the victims. Hate speech, pogroms, racial laws
and construction of 'otherness' enabled its organization. Bauman
followed Hughes (1962) in the statement that this could be produced
by other societies, and was not a phenomenon limited to Germans.
Making clear the role of capitalism in a state-organized, massively
planned genocide was a groundbreaking discovery. This new interpretation of the Holocaust constituted a paradigm change (in the
Kuhnian sense) and occurred thanks to Janina's work.

The astonishing image of Janina as a young girl cleaning the
empty Ghetto apartments of murdered Jews, then organizing their
looted possessions (jewellery, silverware, furniture, etc.) for transport to Germany where they'd be used by other people – a 'hyena'
economy planned with the utmost efficiency, the only waste being
the millions of people designated for elimination ... made an
immense impression on Bauman. The unimaginable pain of this
situation takes on flesh when it emanates from the person one is
closest to in life. Zygmunt, of course, knew what had happened
in Nazi-occupied Poland. He also lost the major part of his Polish
family. However, Janina's thick description (Geertz, 1973) was a
revelation to Bauman, and enabled him to create an original analysis of the Holocaust.[31] Before Bauman – except by Hughes (1962)
– the Shoah was considered a unique, inexplicably tragic phenomenon that could never recur. *Modernity and the Holocaust* argues
quite the opposite: that it resulted from a devilishly perfected industrial genocide.

Bauman would not have found this analysis without Janina
Bauman's book; the two works represented a connection of field

data and theory. When such connections occur in the experimental life sciences, any prize attributed to the work would go to both authors. This is rarely the case in social sciences and humanities. The context for the publication of both works was favourable for broadcasting their message, notes Griselda Pollock, the art historian and critic, who was a close friend of the Baumans. 'This era witnessed a rapid expansion of Jewish studies and Holocaust cultural memory in Great Britain, in parallel with a reshaping of Jewish Americans' sense of identity. Jewish people stopped being black foxes and became white foxes', said Pollock.[32] The Baumans' books came out at the right place and time for a strong reception. The first conference on 'Jewish studies' was organized at Leeds University (previously, 'Semitic studies' included Arabic- and Hebrew-language works together). It was expected to draw 20 to 40 people but 200 registered for it, Pollock recalled. This interest was stimulating for the Baumans' work, although their collaboration extended beyond the field of Holocaust studies.

Their fused relationship was an essential factor in Bauman's key 21st-century theory – the idea of 'liquidity'. The term functions in the vernacular as well as in the scientific vocabulary; Bauman employed it to describe a social science phenomenon that is a typical feature of the present time.

In Polish, the term is *płynny*, an adjective that happens to describe the specific social context of the Warsaw Ghetto. In his book on the role of the Polish Catholic Church in the Holocaust, Jacek Leociak cites Ludwik Landau's *Chronicle of the Years of War and Occupation* from 23 August 1940: '*Everything is liquid, everything is uncertain.* The carefully tended conflicts between the Christian and Jewish population grow: the Christian inhabitants of Zielna and Sienna streets are petitioning to be left outside [the Ghetto] walls, saying their "eternally Polish" streets were only recently tainted by "Jewification"'[33] (Leociak, 2018: 71). Landau's *Chronicle*, published in 1962 in Warsaw, was a rare and supremely important source for scholars of the Holocaust, and one that one or both of the Baumans must have read, and probably spoken about. The term 'liquid' perfectly depicted the Ghetto reality, in which the New World was limited by a wall built inside the Old World. In this new 'liquid' space, the old rules disappeared and the new ones were incomprehensible. Chaos was everywhere.

In the late 1980s, 'liquidity' was not yet the powerful concept it would become. It was the editors at Polity Press who converted 'the liquid' into Bauman's essential theory.

Under the wings of Polity Press

Bauman's career success, in terms of his presence as an author and position in the space of intellectual exchange and global idea transfer, was certainly due in large part to the efforts of his editor over a thirty-year period. Polity Press was created in 1984 by Anthony Giddens, David Held and John Thompson. Bauman, his close friend Giddens and Urlich Beck were the 'fathers' of the new modernity. And it was Giddens who persuaded Bauman to publish his work with Polity. 'Polity helped make Bauman, and liquidity, a brand name, a trade icon. There would be no Bauman as we know him without Polity, and likely no Liquidity either', Beilharz notes (2020 MS: 206).

Thompson, then a Cambridge graduate student, met Bauman in 1979 or 1980 at a conference on critical theory in Leeds, where Bauman contributed to a project devoted to Habermas.[34] They began an intense collaboration when Polity republished three important Bauman books: *Legislators and Interpreters* (1989 for Polity), *Modernity and the Holocaust* (1989) and *Modernity and Ambivalence* (1993). His books were not always commercial jackpots. Bauman's 'favourite child', as Peter Beilharz called it – *Mortality, Immortality and Other Life Strategies* (1992) – was highly regarded by specialists, but the general public was not much interested in it (Beilharz, 2020 MS: 84). His biggest success came in 2000 with *Liquid Modernity*. It was a departure in style for Bauman – essays addressed to a larger public. The passage from academic texts to a more general audience was difficult: Bauman created a specific style of developing analyses and building arguments over forty years of writing practice. It would seem impossible to make a major stylistic change well into one's seventies. The role of editor was crucial in this shift and it depended heavily on the latter's relationship with Bauman.

'There was a lot of dialogue', Thompson recalled: 'I'd ask what he was working on, what he was interested in. He always asked for my views and I would suggest ways to shape his arguments. Sometimes he was happy to respond to my suggestion, other times not. . . . Zygmunt was enormously creative, he was unstoppably creative. He was just extraordinary.' Polity resonated with Bauman's style and metabolism, and helped shape the intellectual project, providing high-quality editing that made his texts broadly accessible to an English-language audience without damaging the complexity of the content. Bauman was under special care at Polity, explains Thompson: 'We produced a specific design for his books, a specific style and presented it in a nice way with a kind of stylish appearance. . . . We paid attention to the cover titles of the books. Sometimes Zygmunt had good titles and sometimes he didn't and we needed to work on them, and we came up with titles that made the difference.'

The most spectacular example was the decision to take the concept of 'liquidity' from Bauman's manuscript and make it the title of his book. Afterward, this became a key concept for several books with the 'liquid' in the title. Polity transformed his books *Liquid Modernity* and *Liquid Love* into bestsellers.

Polity had an excellent international department. Bauman's books were translated into thirty-six languages, and he was the most prolific Polity author. More than that, he became a brand in the market of trade books grounded in academic social science, a very unusual phenomenon in social sciences. Fruitful long-lasting collaborations among people involved in several of his book projects were key to the success of the books. It was all about stability, a relationship that lasted thirty years thanks to mutual understanding and the pleasure of working together. 'It was a really enjoyable and creative process and this is really unique', Thompson says: 'frankly, we rarely have this kind of good relationship with someone who is doing really creative and interesting things . . . and we enjoyed it'.

The quality of this relationship was partly due to Bauman's willingness to accept the corrections made by his editors, which went along with the *politesse* and sympathetic attitude he always showed people working on his projects. He transformed the handicap of not being a native speaker into an advantage in this context, for it kept Bauman from interfering with his editors' good judgement. This is an unusual attitude, as we know from the legions of quarrels among authors and their editors. Bauman was not like other authors. His choice of Polity as his major editorial house was also unconventional. Bauman had published with the biggest and most famous academic publishers (Cornell University Press, Columbia University Press, New York University Press, Basil Blackwell, Routledge, etc.) before switching to Polity. When Anthony Giddens proposed to him that he publish there, it was a risky step. Polity was a relatively new house. But all new enterprises, particularly publishing houses competing with older established names, must show a level of energy coming out of the gate to emerge with success, and that was also the case with Polity. It attracted a lot of passionate people who worked with great commitment in various segments of the company. This was beneficial for Bauman. This was his tempo and his environment: fast, passionate and different from established institutions. The collaboration was almost immediately a success, and he was their most important author.[35] Bauman had enough experience with other houses to know that the relationship was a good match, that he was in the right place at the right time.[36]

After his retirement from academia, Bauman wanted to make his writing and message more visible to the world at large. Griselda Pollock remarked that Bauman was 'a stranger' – his sociological thinking did not grow in the English language and culture. He needed a 'translator' – not a literal one, but a cultural translator – a team able delicately to transform his message into a clear understandable message. Polity was able to find the words perfectly adapted to the audience Bauman targeted, which included young readers. John Thompson was impressed to see how, despite being seventy years older than some of these readers, Zygmunt was able to keep his 'finger on the pulse'. He was in touch with the youth.

Success began with the publication in 1989 of *Legislators and Interpreters* and *Modernity and the Holocaust*, and never stopped. 'Bauman was sometimes given to repeating himself', according to Beilharz (2020 MS: 208)

> Though this is also a strategy, and a strength rather than a weakness. Little books, or long essays, become his forte. Behind these *essais* or instalments in the critique of liquid modernity, you can hear his spoken voice. It is not the perfect pitch of Anglo academic culture, but the elongated, shifting intonation of a conversation in pursuit of its objects, and subjects. (Beilharz, in the earlier version of his MS)[37]

After 1989, nearly all of Bauman's books were published by Polity. It was a fusional relationship and, as in all such intensive collaborations, there was probably a degree of pressure,[38] exerted by Bauman and Polity alike. Peter Beilharz reported:

> Bauman wrote to me occasionally that he was under pressure to deliver; though externalities alone cannot explain the incredible levels of output he achieved, four books each for 2013, 2015, and 2017 for example. Did he then write too much? Probably, though this was part of a strategy in which a steady, serial audience of academic readers was no longer to be taken for granted, and he had developed a serious need to write (Beilharz, 2020 MS: 208)

Did he then write too much? Bauman did everything too much. That was his *modus vivendi.*

Modus vivendi

Bauman did a lot. He read a lot and had a lot of books. He had a lot of friends. He had many passions and hobbies. He was what the French define as a *bon vivant*: he liked to cook, drink, watch TV, listen to music, drink, eat, smoke (too much), feed people (enormously), talk (all the time), entertain (as frequently as possible). He was a perfect host in a warm and welcoming home. When Peter Beilharz visited the Lawnswood Gardens house, he saw hundreds of books on the floor in the living room: 'Most of the titles were not in English, but were rather in Eastern European languages. I asked where they had come from, remembering that his library had been so thoroughly dispersed. . . . He looked up earnestly when quizzed about this cornucopia of books, and whence it came, and answered with barely a smile: "when I go to bed, they fornicate!"' (Beilharz, 2020 MS: 134–5).

The monkish style of Zygmunt's office contrasted strongly with the huge accumulation of books in his small working space, big shelves full of books in seven languages that supported his work in progress. There were also favourite volumes of poetry, mainly Polish poems, with anthologies of foreign poetry translated into Polish. Bauman wanted to have these treasures at hand during his morning working hours. In the living room were novels in different languages. Polish books were in another room, and these were the soul of the house. Janina explained in a 1994 interview with Joanna Janiak: 'My husband and I always underline who we are. We keep a Polish lifestyle, we make Polish dishes for our English guests; there are Polish books in our house, and of course English too – the Polish collection is in the other room' (Janiak, 2011 [1994]).[39]

The Baumans loved to host people in their home, but the process of rebuilding a life in Leeds was relatively slow. Their English acquaintances were few; they belonged to different worlds. Janina was the professor's wife, and their guests did not expect anything other than small talk from her:

> Nobody ever asked me what my profession was or what I had done in Poland. I was a wife, a professor's wife and my visitors seemed fully satisfied with that. The only questions they ever asked me were: 'How do you like it here?' or 'How old are your daughters?' Nobody ever asked me what my personal plans were or what I intended to do in this country. (J. Bauman, 1988: 146)

It must have been painful for Zygmunt to see his exceptionally witty, sparkling wife, the soul of their gatherings at home, become silent and withdrawn.

The distance between the Baumans and their new environment was also the consequence of social changes that England went through in the 1970s. As he recounted forty years later, in an interview with Tomasz Kwaśniewski:

> the vice chancellor of the University of Leeds was Lord Boyle. A truly English phenomenon: a leftist aristocrat, very critical of his own country. Careful and kind, he used to ask me how I felt in England, what I saw, and what I thought about it. So, I immediately responded that I liked English democracy. How surprised he was, and he protested! 'Is this supposed to be a democracy?!' What was a discovery for me, was for

him daily bread, which, when it's regularly on the table, goes unnoticed. But when I looked closer, I began to see what Lord Boyle meant.

'And what did you see?', asked the journalist.

First of all, greed was the main motive, a driving engine of the actions. And not because the English people are greedy, I do not think they are more greedy than other nations, but their lives are so arranged that greed is promoted. The second thing: superficiality in human interactions. It was striking, as in capitalism, the satisfaction of life's needs became independent from the hardening of interpersonal bonds. In a shopping mall you are a crowd, but you do not do things collectively. Everyone is looking for their own and follows their own.[40]

This superficiality, the Baumans found, was an obstacle to making new friends in Leeds.

In the Bauman house, the guest was the king. Zygmunt usually prepared the food and he plied his guests with drink – whisky, gin and tonic, a bloody Mary, vodka. Tony Bryant, a sociologist of science and technology, recalled that, before he came to lunch for the first time at Lawnswood Gardens, his colleagues from the university warned him: 'Be careful, you need to reserve the whole day. You will start at noon with a drink and finish drunk, at 5 p.m.' In fact, the visit ended at 7 p.m. and he was, indeed, drunk. He also had eaten quite a bit. Zygmunt loved cooking. He spent a lot of time in his tiny kitchen preparing dishes, and his speciality was hearty, meat-centric cuisine – steak, *escalopes flambées*, *kotlet schabowy*, goulash. Vegetables were not his specialty and he didn't really cater for vegetarians. His granddaughter remembered that, before a family reunion, Bauman spent hours preparing a meat dish; when his vegetarian grandson came in hungry after a long trip, there was nothing for him to eat. It didn't much bother Zygmunt. When Tester, who was also vegetarian, came to dine, Zygmunt prepared a menu with *frutti di mare*; he joked that all vegetarians ate fruit. Zygmunt was not really empathetic in such situations. He had survived wartime food restrictions, and was hungry for months on end in his youth. Excluding meat from the menu was, for him, as for the majority of his generation, a caprice of fashion – irrelevant and incomprehensible. A guest might be vegetarian on principle, because of a militant animal rights position (like Tester, whose Ph.D. thesis was on this issue), but that was of little importance.

A 'good guest' ate everything he or she was offered (it was impossible to eat everything Bauman offered). He enjoyed watching people eat his food even if he himself did not eat so much. Conversations were convivial and, in addition to cigarette or pipe smoke, which guests inhaled voluntarily or involuntarily, there was always red wine (usually Italian, but also French, Australian, Bulgarian, Chilean . . . so long as it was red[41]), or another alcohol chosen for that moment of the day, meal or mood. The kitchen was Zygmunt's kitchen and no guest was allowed to help out. A sign on the kitchen door read, 'Uwaga zły pies!' (Beware – savage dog!).[42] Actually, they never had a dog or a cat.

Bauman also served the food, bringing in new courses and changing plates and glasses the way it was done in grand restaurants. He cleaned alone and brooked no assistance. After lunch or dinner, it was time for a dessert, even if the guests had no room in their stomachs. Zygmunt loved desserts and never resisted a good cookie or cake. His granddaughter Zośka (the diminutive of Sofia) earned a place in the heart of her 'Dziadzia' (Granddad) by baking him cakes. Espresso – made in an Italian machine – followed dessert. The Baumans loved Italy and its *arte della vita*.

Bauman made his own beer, wine and Armagnac, which he called 'Baumaniac'. Tony Bryant explained that Baumaniac was only for special guests, and he enjoyed it each time Tony's father, Pawel Blumenzweig, came to visit. A Czech Jew who had escaped the Holocaust, Blumenzweig had changed his name to Paul Bryant in England and had a lot in common with Bauman. Bauman spoke Czech and liked its culture very much, so they had much to discuss. Zygmunt had probably learned home-brewing and distilling during or just after the war, when alcohol was scarce in Eastern Europe and became a kind of currency. As with all hobbies, once Bauman got started with something he learned fast and became deeply committed. The Canadian sociologist Robert Stebbins calls this kind of behaviour 'serious leisure'[43] (Stebbins, 2007). When Bauman got as far as he could with an activity, he stopped it completely and took up something else. This was the case with home-brewed alcohol and with photography.

It took him several years to learn to shoot pictures of city streets and people, Yorkshire panoramas and nature. He attended a photo club where he met other photo-passionate people and learned how to take portraits. Eventually he did a series of nudes as well, hiring models. He shot thousands of pictures and portraits of his guests and friends, and for a while he and his camera were inseparable. He set up his own darkroom (upstairs), and even mixed the chemicals for developing and printing, rather than buying ready-made ones. 'When you came to his home in those years, he offered you a drink and immediately took you upstairs to take your photo', recalled Tony Bryant: 'He took pictures of us, of my parents, of everybody. For years he was a keen and expert photographer and then he just stopped. Like, "OK, I've done enough of that."'[44]

Photography was a serious hobby that lasted over ten years. Then Bauman explained to his family that he had reached his limits and it interested him no more. Once he attempted to renew the activity, but the technology had advanced and Bauman was not interested in learning it.

Bauman's daughters defined those periods of fascination as 'Dad's phases'. Areas of secondary activity – photography, distilling – would for short periods become the principal focus of his time and effort. If such cycles seem unusual, they are not infrequent in the scientific world. Among life-science researchers using experimental methods in laboratories, I frequently observed people become fascinated with or 'crazy about' an activity or field that was different from their research projects (Wagner, 2011). Campuses of good research universities are full of passionate 'nerds' like Bauman, with their phases of bread-making, gardening, practising extreme sports, painting, drawing cartoons and learning exotic languages.

Many scientists love these challenges and may also be driven by the need to be the best and the first in everything. Tester recalled that, in 2013, Zygmunt was invited to give lectures in Girona, near Barcelona, for a month. Tester was his assistant: 'he was 88 [years old] and Girona is very hilly. . . . We stayed in the same hotel, and every morning he walked to the top of the mountain and he would make sure that he got there first. I had this general sense that if I had the arrogance to try to get there before him, he would trip me up or something. "I am like the young people – I can do anything!"'[45]

Like many scientists, Bauman wanted to control almost everything controllable. One of the last passions that Bauman dropped, just at the end of his life, was walking. He had developed a quasi-professional approach to hiking in Yorkshire, using maps, a compass and guides before such things became popular, and he and Janina regularly spent hours walking around Leeds for miles and miles. Over the years, the speed of their walking slowed and the distances shortened, but walking was always an important part of the day's schedule. One thing the Baumans had no interest in was small talk and superficial relationships. They had 'no will to conform', Janina wrote. And they organized their social life with people who shared a similar lifestyle, especially old friends from Warsaw.

The echo of Warsaw
The Baumans were lucky to have emigrated to England at a time when some of their best friends were within a few hours of Leeds by train. Maria Hirszowicz and her husband Łukasz, whom friends called Gidon, lived in London after emigrating during the 1968 state pogrom. He was a historian and polyglot, a specialist in contemporary Iran and the Arab world, known for his erudition and sense of humour (their London house was open to scholars and Polish opposition activists). Their relationship with the Baumans was like family; several times they spent Christmas and New Year's

Eve together. When Łukasz passed away, his wife Maria became very close to Janina, and offered her a great deal of support with her memoirs. The Hirszowiczes and Baumans discussed Polish politics and exchanged memories of their lost homeland. But, more than anything else, they shared a common passion – bridge. This card game, played by two couples, was very popular in Poland, which fielded some of the world's best competitive teams. It was a good sport for bright friends to share around a few drinks and an infinite number of cigarettes or pipes of tobacco.

When Leszek Kołakowski and his wife Tamara visited, the subject was not bridge but politics, endlessly – Polish matters, the New Left,[46] and other current events. They discussed books, films, philosophy and fiction, and exchanged gossip about former collaborators, Party *apparatchiks*, and all the faculty who remained and emigrated. Kołakowski was close to Polish underground organizations and their activity was the subject of long discussions about 'the conservative-liberal-socialist-international', as Kołakowski jokingly referred to the movement, large enough to contain both him and Bauman. Already in the late 1960s, their opinions had diverged about Marxism, left-wing parties and the future of Poland. Lasting several hours, political debates took place in the dense tobacco smog.

Both men were heavy smokers; they had the same gestures and smoked in a very theatrical way, Tester noted. Describing a TV debate between Foucault and Kołakowski, he said:

> Kołakowski does exactly the same thing with his pipe that Zygmunt does. Foucault is making a point that Kołakowski clearly disagrees with, and he's tapping his pipe, cleaning his pipe on the desk (making noise). He says nothing . . . just by gesture he shows everything . . . the body language is, 'you are saying something so stupid . . .' . . . Both 'revisionists' had mastered the art of non-verbal communication through pipe smoking.

Over the years, their friendship weakened and then died. Kołakowski grew increasingly distant from Marxism and progressively turned to Catholicism, while repenting for his communist past. Bauman was fascinated observing this change, and even had a short phase of curiosity about converting to Catholicism. He read extensively but the fascination passed after some weeks. Bauman always maintained a socialist, secular vision of the universe and politics. He and Kołakowski were in different camps, and not shy about saying so.

The first conflict occurred after the installation of martial law by General Wojciech Jaruzelski, on 13 December 1981. Opposition members were thrown in jail and the Army took over the streets of Polish cities and banned Solidarity as an enemy of the state. Kołakowski – the spiritual guru of Polish opposition – condemned Jaruzelski's decision, but Bauman's view was more nuanced. As a former soldier, he understood Jaruzelski's choice as the lesser of two evils – if he had not imposed martial law, the Soviet Army would have moved in in a repeat of the 1968 Czechoslovak disaster. Among all the group of exiled friends, only Bauman did not support protests against the action. Though he later recognized the military intervention as mistaken, Bauman would be remembered as a supporter of Jaruzelski's coup.

A final separation of Bauman and Kołakowski occurred in 2001, after the terrorist attacks of 9/11. The tragedy shocked the world, as Bauman wrote in a 23 September 2001 article in the weekly *Tygodnik Powszechny*, but he opposed declarations in which politicians and media announced a new war between 'our' civilization and 'their' barbarian world. Like some other left-oriented intellectuals, Bauman said capitalist exploitation and colonial relationships had fed the increase of terrorism. Kołakowski's daughter, the journalist Agnieszka Kołakowska, responded to Bauman with a lashing rebuke in *Rzeczpospolita* on 4 October 2001.[47] She wrote that Bauman 'thoughtlessly repeats opinions' in a text replete with 'insinuations, mystifications and falsifications'. Bauman's sentence about responsibility for the act was 'a postmodernist circus of subtle empty sentences', she wrote. Kołakowska noted that radicals such as Robert Fisk and Noam Chomsky had justified terrorism in a similar way but were less anti-American than Bauman: 'Our holy duty now is loyalty to America and our civilization', she concluded. Bauman considered the attack unjustified and aggressive.[48] He waited for Kołakowski's intervention – for discussion with him, at least. Nothing happened and their relationship ended.

Maria Hirszowicz would also fall out with the Baumans, apparently over divergences in political opinion. In her book *Winter in the Morning*, Janina warmly acknowledged Maria and her husband. By 2001, however, Maria's book *Traps of Engagement: Intellectuals in the Service of Communism* made no mention of the Baumans, although Bauman had studied young communists and their Party engagement in the 1960s, and Hirszowicz certainly knew about this. Her book is very critical of intellectuals who engaged in communism. It expresses a strong positivist conviction about truth and moral laws, a position that in 21st-century sociology is considered outdated. The book shows that Kołakowski gave the 'A' and Hirszowicz and other Polish intellectuals tuned on his note. Socialist values had fallen out of fashion, and the Baumans lost some of their best friends. This must have been painful, but Zygmunt never spoke about it publicly. In fact, he rarely spoke about any unpleasant personal issues.

In the 1970s, some of the Baumans' former colleagues and friends were able to leave Poland thanks to more relaxed travel restrictions, and came to visit the Baumans in Leeds. One of the first was Bauman's earliest co-author, Jerzy Wiatr. Another was Jerzy Szacki, who remembered the home-made wine Bauman greeted him with. Bauman remained *persona non grata* in Poland, his works banned, but some Polish friends came to Lawnswood Gardens anyway. Wiatr and Szacki might have had troubles upon their return, but they took the risk, and faced no repercussions: the regime in Poland was not as strict as in the USSR or East Germany.

Family and stepfamily
When Lydia and Irena went to university outside Leeds, Janina complained that their house was too big for only three people (Janina's mother, Alina Lewinson, spent her final years in Leeds with them). After 1980, the Baumans lived alone in their four-bedroomed house. But there were long periods when it filled with people again. When Irena finished her studies, she and her husband Maurice decided to settle down in Leeds and open their architecture studio there, and for several months they lived in her parents' house. Irena remembers that period as a particularly good time: 'We laughed a lot, we ate a lot, we drank a lot and we smoked enormously.' She was trying at the time to quit smoking, but instead her husband began to smoke. Despite all the information campaigns about the dangerous effects of smoking, the view at 1 Lawnswood Gardens was that no excess of food, alcohol or cigarettes was harmful. Enjoying life was the most important thing. Even in the 1940s, Bauman's Army superior observed that he liked alcohol but didn't abuse it. And that didn't change much. Zygmunt never drank enough to lose control. He was addicted only to smoking. He frequently joked that he was the living example that tobacco is not so dangerous, since he lived so long.

Over time, the circle of friends at the house increased beyond the Polish community. After Irena and Maurice left, Brian Cheyette moved to near Bauman's house.[49] He lived there from 1986 to 1996. He was young British scholar on a fellowship in Leeds studying anti-Semitism in British literature, a topic that interested the Baumans. This period in the mid-1980s was just the moment when modern Jewish studies were beginning, and the Holocaust and anti-Semitism were the most important topics in the Bauman home. In his introduction to *Modernity and the Holocaust*, Bauman acknowledged Cheyette for 'criticism and advice'. For a decade, the young scholar remained a close friend, coming by, Polish style, without a call or an appointment, for a coffee or drink, to discuss one of the thousand issues they cared about.

Another person who benefitted from close friendship with the Baumans was Janet Wolff, a specialist in the sociology of art and

culture who met Zygmunt in 1973 while working on her Ph.D. With
Bauman's recommendation, she began her academic career at Leeds
and was a frequent guest at their house for discussions on a variety
of topics, including the Holocaust. Janina acknowledges Janet
Wolff in *Winter in the Morning*; Wolff recalled that she was the first
to read drafts of many chapters (Wolff, 2011). Janina also acknowledged Griselda Pollock, the art historian who met the Baumans
in the first year of her appointment at Leeds in 1978. Pollock and
her husband, Antony Bryant – Tony – became very close friends.
Bryant worked briefly in the Sociology Department, with an interest
in Jewish familial heritage. The warm relationship with this group
seems to have been a kind of reconstruction of missing family for the
Baumans.[50] All had in common strong connections with Ashkenazi
culture and the Holocaust heritage. It was not a return to Judaism
as a religion – rather, finding wellbeing in a familiar, secular culture.

As happens in all families, there were non-shared areas of discussion. Bauman was completely closed to the recent scholarly tradition
of feminist studies. 'That knowledge in the sense of feminism as a
theoretical explanation and questioning – he did not get it', Pollock
says. However, 'he was very supportive of hiring and supporting
women in the department. . . . He was not at all the classical patriar-
chal figure. He was very nice to me, very respectful and recognized
something – without engaging in what I wrote or said.' Pollock, who
employed feminist critical theory, invited Bauman to seminars with
specialists in feminist criticism, but he showed no interest. Pollock
supposed this was because Bauman had no personal connection to
feminism, though she wondered why such a voracious reader found
it so hard to find her field interesting. 'His own experiences were
central', she said.

Pollock's critique undercuts Bauman's affirmation about the lack
of connection between personal experiences and the work of an
intellectual. We could ask why Bauman, always so sensitive to refugees and stateless, stigmatized and marginalized people, never took
an interest in feminism. 'Why was it so difficult to him to access
phenomena that were not directly linked to his experience?' asked
Pollock.[51]

It's a pertinent question.[52]

It was not unusual for intellectuals of Bauman's generation to
show little interest in feminism. It's worth considering that Bauman
grew up in a house run by a strong mother and a silent father.
Moreover, in the Soviet Union of his youth, healthy males were
absent because of the war, and women replaced them. It was a
country in which a young person could have the illusion of an equity
between men and women. Women's liberation and equality were
part of the official ideology (and, in several aspects, official reality)
in postwar Poland. Janina Bauman was a professionally active and

successful woman. For Bauman, discrimination against women was a problem of the past.

Bauman's methodology also put him at a disadvantage in understanding feminism. He was a 'natural observer', but did not practise ethnographic methods that enable sociologists to share the experience of another person and thereby expand the areas of their scrutiny. Working theoretically enables the author to access broad areas of human activity, but some dimensions remain inaccessible. Feelings and personal experience in intimate or hidden settings require a special, supplementary access – for example, to frequently inaccessible issues such as sexual abuse. Recognition of the limits of a social scientist's reflections is part of ethnographic craft – and of the critical feminist approach.

The third element to take into consideration is the gendered division of work. The vast majority of Bauman's co-authors were male. In his generation in Poland, there were examples of 'strong women who write theoretical texts', but they were exceptions (Maria Ossowska – Stanisław Ossowski's wife; Antonina Kłoskowska, the sociology of culture specialist). Other than Janina, Bauman's partners in discussion were mostly males. The Baumans were friends with Lena Eilstein, a philosopher, who reproached Zygmunt for his lack of understanding of communication and social organization in animals.[53] This was in the late 1980s and early 1990s. She pointed out some books and articles to him on the subject, writing in a letter to the Baumans that Zygmunt 'should get a dog', a sentence she also included in a review of one of his articles in the 1960s! Eilstein was convinced that personal experience (having a pet, in this case) would be more mind-opening to Bauman than attending a lecture (however, she also pointed him to the appropriate reading).[54] But Eilstein was considered in Warsaw's intellectual milieu as someone 'different', 'strange' and 'uncommon'. She left Poland with her elderly mother under pressure from anti-Semitism, but returned in the 1990s, finding she did not fit into American life. She remained the Baumans' close friend, while challenging his resistance to new approaches.

To complete this family picture, it is necessary to include two 'spiritual sons' of Bauman. The first was Keith Tester, the other Peter Beilharz, who lived in Australia and was a regular guest at Lawnswood Gardens. At least once a year, over almost thirty years, Beilharz visited the Baumans, and also kept closely in touch via e-mail. The first meeting of Beilharz and Tester demonstrates the way Bauman served as a matchmaker for people in his close entourage. Tester tells this story about meeting Beilharz for the first time, at Bauman's house in 2000:

Peter was already there when I arrived . . . I enter – we are going to the living room. Peter is just sitting there and what Zygmunt did then, he

makes Peter stand up, he puts one hand on my shoulder and another
on Peter's [shoulder] and said: 'I am going out of the room now, when
I am returning in 10 minutes you will be brothers . . . then he gave us
a shove and we fell back on the sofa, and he left the room and did
return after 10 minutes and asked: 'Are you brothers?' We were lucky
because we got on very well. . . . somehow it was about shaping his
world . . . he controlled us and we had no choice about it.

While for Tester this situation was, among other things, a sign
of Bauman's need for control, for Beilharz it was simply a familial
way of bringing friends together, a typical gesture of intellectuals
and strong personalities who try to manage their environment in a
friendly way. Beilharz, who was older than Tester and not Bauman's
student, was never concerned that Bauman could, or wanted to,
control him in any way. Even during their collaboration, Beilharz
felt free to write as he interpreted Bauman's work.

Controlling or not, Bauman was right – his wish that Peter and
Keith became 'brothers' was fulfilled, and at that moment they
began a long and deep friendship. As Beilharz concluded in his
book: 'So we were, in some sense, the sons. And he would often urge
us to the table; Children! My dears! Lunch is ready! You must eat!
There was a great deal of ritual clinking of glasses. *Na Zdrowie!*'[55]
(Beilharz, 2020 MS: 106).

15

Global Thinker

Non-liquid LOVE: janzygbau@

Janina and Zygmunt Bauman had a common email address, janzygbau@, created from the first syllables of their names, in keeping with their tightly coordinated existence. 'They worked on most things as a couple', as Tester said: 'actually . . . they were indivisible. . . . There wasn't a formal line between them. . . . Each had a separate identity but they were a single entity too.'[1] Bauman used to say that as soon as he was born (in November 1925), he 'ordered' himself a wife, who was born nine months later (August 1926). This can be read in two ways, with our current understanding of sexual politics. It's a message of love, framing the couple's romantic destiny; she was the Woman of his Life. At the same time, it expresses his position as the dominant male: he ordered the conception of his wife. The paternalistic vision and cynical sense of humour somehow describe their fusional relationship pretty well.

Bauman was a charmer and gallant who 'certainly wasn't embarrassed in showing that he loved Janina', Tester said.[2] In numerous interviews published in the Polish press, Bauman declared that he was in love, in a strong relationship, and with a discreet blink of an eye would let it be understood that he was under the control of his wife. Bauman once commented about his political engagement in Poland before 1968: 'Jasia also told me: "Give up, stop it, stop having illusions." Because we were discussing our life together. Yes, she was that voice [of reason]. But why didn't I listen to her? *After all, I was used to listening to Jasia.*'[3]

In Polish, the expression 'I was used to listening to . . .' *słuchałem się . . .* is a speech form (today a little old-fashioned) used by children to say, 'I am obedient to my parents.' The phrase contains a minor grammatical error: we can listen to someone (*słuchać kogoś*) or listen to ourself (*słuchać się*) – but not both.[4] Bauman's use of the quaint expression[5] illustrates something about their relationship, in the sense that he listened to himself (first) and Janina (also).

Bauman's Polish friends confirmed this self-presentation. Janina made the decisions, they said; she was a very strong personality. It was she, for example, who had refused to move to Australia,[6] and it was her preference – and not Zygmunt's – to go to Israel in 1968. To be sure, their relationship was more complex than one or the other being the dominant figure; sixty-two years of life together are rarely frozen in a single model of relationships. 'I will give you a picture', Tester recalled:

> Janina is sitting in the corner in a front room – smoking . . . and Zygmunt is going around making sure that everyone has food and drink. Janina was definitely the power . . . she kind of defined the situation and Zygmunt would facilitate her and enable her to flourish. Power means that she was in control, but it was not like that. They had different roles: she was the one who framed the event, he made it happen.

The term 'fusion' probably most adequately defines their relationship, which Janina described as a beautiful and romantic love story in her book *The Dream of Belonging*, published in 1988. They married on her birthday, 18 August 1948, forever linking her birthday to their marriage. But Janina was not prepared to be a spouse defined by her husband. Her family had determined she was to become a doctor; after the war, while living in the Ghetto and hiding places, she dreamed of becoming a writer. After her graduation, she kept her journal, which was difficult for a professionally active woman with three children. Despite political instability, she was able to manage an interesting career trajectory as the indispensable negotiator between censors and film artists. She also represented Polish film at international festivals, a highly prestigious position in the peak years of Polish cinematography.

When their financial situation improved in the late 1950s, the Baumans began the ritual of a marriage anniversary lunch, during which they summed up the past year and predicted the next. 'We have carried on our celebrations year in, year out, never missing a single one, not even at the sad time of crisis that in the sixties threatened to wreck our marriage', Janina wrote; 'It has always helped to talk and to listen' (J. Bauman, 1988: 58). They had a time of crisis and passed through it. Interestingly, this discreet but significant information appears only in the English version of Janina's book. For the Polish audience, there were no crises, only a perfect couple. In his discussions and writings, Bauman underlined the importance of constant care and permanent efforts to maintain the early passion: 'Love . . . declines to promise an easy road to happiness and meaning. . . . It is something that always still needs to be *made* anew and remade daily, hourly; constantly resuscitated, reaffirmed, attended to and cared for' (Bauman, 2008: 132).

It needs practice and training each day: discussions, explanations, fixing broken parts, apologies and forgiveness. This is how trust and understanding are built. Bauman presented this vision as a model of how love used to be in the time before 'liquid modernity' – as opposed to the current era in which the quick exchange of partners as a kind of consumption makes it impossible to improve relationships, which become insecure and unstable. His own experience was the former kind, however.

For Bauman, happiness was what was important in the love relationship, and happiness was a topic that fascinated him. Maintaining happiness in a *longue durée*[7] relationship was one of the greatest challenges. How, in a liquid world, was it possible to create non-liquid love? In a 2011 interview with Justyna Dąbrowska, he described the complexity of love relationships:

> 'I love you?' – What does that mean? It means, in fact, I wish you all that is good, I want you to be happy . . . To support my wish with an act, I have to create an ideal of your person; that other person, the one that is your happiness, is the image of what is good for you. At some point (out of love for you) I become convinced that I know better than you how to make you happy. I step on your liberty. In the name of your wellbeing, I want to force you to do something other than what you would like to do. What happens if, to the contrary, I put your freedom above all other considerations? Then another trap lurks: a Pontius Pilate gesture . . . in short, indifference and anesthesia, and in either case, this is the moment to look for your love on a tombstone and start composing the obituary. (Bauman in Dąbrowska, 2019: 158–9)

This is a sad picture of love, trapped between too much control and too much freedom, between possessiveness and indifference. A troubling perception of love as a feeling that's based on an ideal image of the partner. To what extent was this about Bauman's own experience? We get some insight into this question by reading Bauman's reaction to Janina's autobiographical books. In a letter to Tester, Bauman notes that the character 'Konrad' in *A Dream of Belonging* stood for 'Janina's image of me, and I carefully resisted any, whether direct or indirect, interference with her portraiture' (Bauman, e-mail to Tester, 2016). Interestingly, Konrad is only the 'Zygmunt' character in the English version of the book. In Polish translation, the character's name is Zygmunt. Why was this change made? Did it reflect the effects of British culture, where privacy is a core value? Or was it the result of negotiations, discussions that took place, perhaps, during the anniversary-of-marriage dinner?

In her book about their shared life, Janina gave some discreet insights from those special evenings that occurred once a year, providing snapshots of moments of pause between epochs of their life together. '[S]till in the bar, we talk. We talk about yet another year of our married life, and about our daughters. We try to sum up what has been good, what bad, and what should be better. We think about what must be done in the coming year, and about all the things we cannot prevent – missiles, rising unemployment, Israel's military ventures' (J. Bauman, 1988: 59).

Sitting in a Leeds restaurant (probably in 1986 or 1987), celebrating one more year together, Janina and Zygmunt were grateful that, after four decades together, they could 'still sit peacefully together and talk and look forward to the year which is just beginning'. They enjoyed their approaching retirement, which Zygmunt awaited with impatience. They could not have imagined Janina's success nor Zygmunt's spectacular fame and creative output – and the extraordinary political changes of the coming years were entirely beyond view. They worried about Israel's military situation and the safety of their families there, but did not imagine that two years later the whole Eastern bloc would collapse. Two years later, they would be back in Poland for the first time in two decades.

Unrequited love: Poland

The German philosopher Franz Rosenzweig wrote, 'to what extent a Jew participates in the life of nations does not depend on him but on those nations'.[8] Bauman's relationship with 'Poland' – as a society represented by authorities and institutions – is a complex story. In large part, it is a story of unrequited love, of an individual who showed, his entire life, that he saw himself as a Polish citizen like any other. Bauman was not alone in this situation. This is a fundamental problem for all Poles with Jewish culture. Many intellectuals made public their reflections (Prokop-Janiec, 2013).

Bauman never published his texts, as Polish intellectuals such as Brandys, Morawski, Tuwim, Sandauer and many others did. His private manuscript is entitled 'The Poles, The Jews, and I: An Investigation into Whatever Made Me What I Am'. It is largely in this unique piece that Bauman discusses the issue.

Zygmunt Bauman was in love with Poland. He had perfect command of his mother tongue, loved Polish literature and poetry, excelled at school and proudly joined the Polish Army at the age of 18. After the war, he was actively engaged in the construction of a better society, following a Polish model of social justice, and became a talented scholar who defined himself as a *Polish* sociologist. At each stage of his long life – and even afterwards – however, his claim of full rights to being a Pole was challenged. Regardless of which politicians are in place, or whether capitalism or socialism rules the roost, the legitimacy of his declaration 'I am a Pole' is still questioned.

The following story, told by Bauman in 2013, reflects the constancy of this love–hate relationship.

When the Baumans crossed the Polish border in 1968, they assumed it was for ever. Yet as soon as Zygmunt got British citizenship, he started corresponding with Polish institutions in pursuit of manuscripts requisitioned by customs authorities. 'I got the answers and have kept them until today', Bauman told me.[9] The customs office told him all manuscripts had been sent to the Polish Academy of Sciences (PAN). He wrote to the president of the PAN, who said nothing had ever arrived there. Then he sent the letters from the customs office and PAN to Professor Henryk Jabłoński, the prime minister. 'He never wrote me back. No answer came.' (Bauman knew Jabłoński personally from Party meetings.) Around 2006, a doctoral student of one of Bauman's former students was researching at the IPN and located Bauman's file, hoping that it was the confiscated work. '[L]ike an idiot . . . I wrote to the IPN in good faith', asking for the return of his manuscripts and those of Janina, Bauman said. A short time later, Piotr Gontarczyk[10] wrote a contentious article about Bauman's wartime and postwar activities:

> The IPN never responded to my questions. So this conspiracy between the customs office and Prime Minister Jabłoński continues – nothing has changed . . . regimes come and go, prime ministers and presidents are replaced, the system changes, but there is such a thing as continuity in the secret services. They don't really change – the changes are minor – personnel transfers but basically the system is always there.[11]

This continuity that Bauman describes, and which Polish historians have also noted,[12] is astounding in that it covers three dramatically different periods – the regimes of Gomułka in 1968, Gierek in 1972, and finally the post-communist period. We should notice that the exception to this rule occurred in 2010 when Bauman obtained from the Minister of Culture the highest Polish decoration, the Medal for Merit to Culture – Gloria Artis. This event, however, attracted a lot of criticism, especially from the right-wing parties' supporters – a surprising continuity between the former communist regime and present-day right-wing people, who share the same reaction towards Bauman – always hostile, and always with the echo of anti-Semitism.

For them, Bauman was always an 'enemy of Poland'. Leszek Kołakowski, meanwhile, the most important leader of the 1968 revisionists, was welcomed back after the regime change in 1989. Why is this? From the first, Kołakowski was considered 100 per cent a Pole. He was not a Polish Jew, originating instead from a Catholic family, and he had returned to his ancestral religion. He was forgiven for his communist engagement once he switched sides and supported capitalism. Bauman could fix his origins, but public opinion and most of the intellectuals expected him to abandon his leftist ideas . . . in vain. Bauman maintained his belief in socialism. This was also why he never agreed to become a Cold War sovietologist, and declined offers from excellent universities (for example, Yale).[13]

The culprit

Bauman remained under the spotlight of the secret services long after he left Poland. Writing his name without capital letters, and in the plural, was a subtle element of the stigmatization process – Bauman was presented as a duplicitous person (Kraśko, 2017: 66). He was a special target of Ryszard Gontarz, among the most aggressive and anti-Semitic journalists of 1968. Gontarz published a paper entitled 'The New Road of Zygmunt Bauman', in which, in an ironic and vicious style, he analysed the distorted profile of Bauman from *Maariv* (see ch. 12), which had been translated into Polish and read in its entirety on Radio Free Europe. Gontarz, as an employee of the *Bezpieka*, had access to the secret police copy of the article (Dąbrowski, 2008). He used it to characterize Bauman as a Zionist agent, and a ringleader of 'fledgling revisionists' who had posed as a revolutionary Marxist:

> In the intellectual circles of the capital [Warsaw] . . . he was a star of the first magnitude. Until recently, many participants in the March incidents regarded him as their idol. Many young and naive people believed that Zygmunt Bauman was one of the leading interpreters of Marxism . . . this 'militant Zionist' who, under the direction of power-hungry political swindlers, was one of the students' spiritual leaders and teachers.

The article goes on to state that Bauman was guilty of sponsoring provocations by the youthful protesters, concluding: 'He was one of the moral perpetrators of the March events. He is one of the main culprits.'[14] As we know, this is all far from the truth.

According to Bauman's file, on 8 September 1968 the Party organized a meeting at the PAN Institute of Philosophy and Sociology where Bauman's interview in *Maariv* (broadcast on Radio Free Europe two days earlier) was read and discussed. The time was right for forging an image of Bauman that would help to discredit the whole revolt of March 1968. A *Bezpieka* agent wrote:

Participants at the meeting expressed their total disapproval of
Z. Bauman as a person and the position taken by him, emphasizing his
duplicity and his desire to make a career under any conditions, regardless of the country and political system in which he lives. There was
particular indignation among the gathered over Z. Bauman's statement
about the full solidarity of the Warsaw philosophical and sociological
environment. Listeners mocked and laughed at Z. Bauman's response
about the declaration of workers given to Bauman . . . at the end of
the gathering, one of the young scholars, a non-Party member and a
Catholic, thanked me very much for inviting him to the meeting, which
allowed him to learn the truth about Z. Bauman.[15]

Similar denunciations of the 'Bauman case' took place in various
Party sections at the university.

Condemned to absence

In the spring of 1968, Bauman's publications, as well as those of
other 'revisionist authors', were withdrawn from the bookstores,
libraries and other places where they were publicly accessible. His
name was put on the most restrictive censorship list: not even negative citations were permitted.[16] Bauman's positions as editor and
chair were given to non-Jewish Poles, as were other jobs abandoned
by people who were jailed or emigrated. People who would never
have been accepted as Ph.D. candidates took the places of students
who had fled or been tossed out of the university. Many scholars saw
their careers advance rapidly. For some, the impossible became real.
As Bauman often mentioned, the ethnic purge made thousands of
people happy by transporting them to inaccessible positions.
    After the events of 1968, sociologists at Warsaw University
followed the orthodox line. Some developed quantitative, survey-
based research with methodology increasingly imported from US
sociology (especially Parsons, Lazarsfeld and Merton). The banning
of works and anathematizing of individuals loosened the connections between Bauman and the Warsaw milieu. Many people cut all
ties, though a few (Wiatr and Szacki) stayed in contact – despite the
fact that their mail was being carefully checked by censors. What
survived in the collective memory was the anecdote about his boots
and the gun he brought to school while still in the KBW – a narrow
depiction of Bauman as a fearful figure.
    Gradually, the Polish underground gained strength at the univer-
sity. Unlike Kołakowski, Bauman was not at the core of this new
social movement; he followed it from a distance, from time to time
writing a paper about the Polish situation (his colleagues regularly
published their texts in *Annex*, an opposition review). Like most

Polish émigré scientists (Wagner, 2011), Bauman did not participate in the life of the Polish diaspora, which was often linked with the Catholic Church. Instead of looking for friends inside *Polonia* (the diaspora), Bauman tried to fit into the expectations of the Leeds University community. He was busy as a head of department and not really available for taking part in Polish 'struggles'. Unlike Kołakowski, his sociological topics were not connected with sharp critique of Marxism or with Poland. He was a general sociologist, analysing universal problems and working in Great Britain. He refused to specialize in Eastern Europe.[17]

Bauman also did not openly condemn the introduction of martial law in 1981, which was viewed as discreet support for the Jaruzelski regime and led former colleagues and friends to distance themselves. Bauman's contact with Poland was private: some old colleagues visiting him in Leeds, and correspondence with Polish friends, most of them abroad. The authorities had banned contact with Bauman. Many colleagues who remained feared the consequences of maintaining the relationship, or simply were not interested. He had been ejected from the Polish intellectual world.

Bauman's situation started to change in 1980. With the rise of the Solidarity movement, previous government decisions were criticized and challenged, and this critique reached the universities. In July 1981, the Warsaw University Senate asked the Ministry of Higher Education to retract its 25 March 1968 decision to evict faculty members, and requested the reinstatement of the purged professors.[18] The ministry responded[19] by requesting case-by-case defences of the faculty, which opened the possibility of rehabilitating at least some of them. The rector started sending letters to the evicted professors asking for them to return. But, of the six fired professors, only four were invited back – excluding Bauman and Hirszowicz. Why this omission? Ostensibly, the questionable legal status of the two accounted for them being left out – both had 'voluntarily' resigned their Polish nationality before leaving. The other four had managed to avoid this categoric decision.[20]

This story is told in a letter written by Włodzimierz Brus, who was contacted by the rector and immediately responded, saying it offended him. Brus said any exclusion of 'persons who resigned their Polish citizenship' was unjust and duplicitous, because their deracination had not been made freely. In addition, Brus noted, there was no formal requirement to be a Polish citizen to be on the faculty at a Polish university. 'Neither Maria Hirszowicz nor Zygmunt Bauman got a letter from the University of Warsaw seeking pardon for the pain and injustice provoked by their eviction', Brus wrote, and this unjustified discrimination 'suggests painful similarities (with the past) and awakens worries (for the future)'.[21]

On 10 November 1981, Rector Samsonowicz responded with a

letter to Bauman saying the university senate wished to reverse the 1968 decision. The last sentence in the letter was the one the ousted professors had been waiting to hear: 'In informing you of the above, I express my regret about what happened in 1968.'

Visibly, in 1981 the situation was still unclear. The institutions discussed steps to repair past damage, but no one wanted to apologize officially or take responsibility for what had occurred. Samsonowicz obviously was not responsible for the 1968 decision. But those whom the ban had harmed expected more from the institution that participated in imposing it.

On 13 March 1990, Samsonowicz, now minister of higher education in the first post-communist government, wrote a long letter to Bauman seeking forgiveness for his unjust treatment. It is a sincere letter, full of respect, requesting Bauman's return to the faculty of Warsaw University. The wind of 1989 had cleared many obstacles. By the mid-1980s, Bauman began to correspond with colleagues more intensely. In 1986, Lydia Bauman sought a visa to return to Poland with a group of university artists, but was refused.[22] Two years later, in 1988, the University of Warsaw invited Bauman to give a lecture at the university. The Baumans applied for visas, got them, and came to Warsaw for a short visit after twenty years of absence.

Homecoming!?

'I returned to Warsaw "indoctrinated" by Alfred Schutz, the author of a beautiful essay about what in English is called *homecoming*,[23] a term that is difficult to translate faithfully into Polish', Bauman said in an interview conducted in 1988:

> It's about going home, coming to it a second time. The essay is extensive but it adds up to this trivial thought: that homecoming is the arrival of a man who no longer exists to a place that doesn't exist. There are, however, expectations: people expect to see someone they remember from years ago, and the arrival thinks similarly. Agreement on this situation is very difficult. I was afraid of this arrival' (Bauman in Mieszczanek (interview), 1989: 160).[24]

The Baumans were wary of those mutual expectations, but also feared the authorities' behaviour. The previous system still existed, and the future was not clear. After all, Janina Bauman, as of 1988, was still on the list of undesirable persons in Poland – an impassable blacklist, in theory. Zygmunt had been removed from the list a couple of days before his return thanks to the intervention of colleagues who organized it.[25]

[A]fter the first shock at Okęcie airport, when after passing the passport control they stopped us and in a not very polite manner told us
to wait, explaining the contradiction between the fact that we had
visas and the existence of our names on the list of undesirable people;
after the turmoil in my head [when authorities let us in] after I saw all
those faces [of friends] I have not seen for years . . . By the second day
it seemed I was picking up conversations that were interrupted twenty
years earlier and that nothing had happened in the interim – neither to
me nor the people here. (Bauman, 1989: 160)

To see the city of their past with all the friends that they had
been unable to see for two decades was an emotional experience
for the Baumans. Just as the final days before their departure had
been emotionally charged, feelings of joy accompanying their return
were mixed with a tone of sadness. They reflected on time, which
passes too fast, and all the years when they missed so many people
who were close to them in their Warsaw life. Some former friends
who in 1968 had said nothing and kept silent, now asked for forgiveness, expressing shame at their behaviour, at their weakness
and fear of repression.[26] One imagines that the Baumans did not
sleep a lot during their first return to Poland, or in other visits that
followed with regularity thereafter. Their old friends were happy
to see them again and always had time for those special meetings.
New friends, acquaintances and scholarly colleagues mobilized new
teaching, writing and discussion projects. Bauman rarely refused an
offer, and his calendar became more and more jammed. They were
happy to find their old places, restaurants, theatres, museums and
the National Philharmonic. They bought books and records. They
visited other cities: Poznań, as well as Kraków and Lublin. They
made new friends with philosophers and cultural studies experts, as
well as artists. Bauman was in his 'photography' period and there
were organized shows, in a friendly atmosphere with a growing
circle of young people.
   Zygmunt accepted an offer from the Polish Academy of Sciences
to become a part-time professor. In May 1991, he was appointed
to the Committee of the Social Sciences at the Polish Academy
of Sciences, one of the most prestigious academic institutions.[27]
Through this process, Bauman in some ways recovered the place he
would have had if he had stayed in Poland. His principal employer
before 1968 – the University of Warsaw – was not in such a rush to
restore him, however – the process took 6½ years. The Philosophy
and Sociology Department Council voted on 20 June 1989 to return
the evicted faculty members (Hirszowicz and Bauman), requesting
the rector to take the necessary steps. But nothing happened, so the
request was made again five years later, in November 1994, and in
June 1995 the rector invited Bauman to return as a professor. A 4

January 1996 letter shows Bauman's response: he had decided to become a professor emeritus.[28]

This period also saw Bauman's return to Polish scientific journals. His first post-1989 article, 'The Fall of Lawmakers', appeared in 1990 in *Philosophical Studies*. In 1992, *Modernity and the Holocaust* appeared in Polish, published by Cultural Foundation Masada. The Baumans were close with the publisher's creator, Julian Wojdowski, who was also an exceptional author. A childhood survivor of the Holocaust, he published important texts about anti-Semitism, the Holocaust and the Jewish fate. Bauman's book was the first and only book published by Masada; Wojdowski took his life in 1991.[29] His widow, Anna Wojdowska-Iwaszkiewiczowa responded to the Polish Nobelist Czesław Miłosz when he asked why her husband took his own life: 'Are you not aware that the Holocaust kills even the survivors? It is impossible to live with.' However, some did . . . One way of 'living with' the Holocaust was to write and speak about it. That was Janina Bauman's way.

The Holocaust became the major topic in the Baumans' life at that time. Janina translated and published *Winter in the Morning* in Polish in 1989, and the book was well received, though Zygmunt always felt it deserved more attention. Bauman always asked his colleagues and the organizers of his visits to prepare events for Janina's books. Their Poznań friend, the artist and art professor Tomasz Kowalski, who organized several meetings with the Baumans, together with the philosophy professor Roman Kubicki and philosopher Anna Zeidler-Janiszewska,[30] would invite all his friends, students and family members to Janina's presentations. Her audience remained small compared to Zygmunt's, but she enjoyed responding to the public's reaction to her work.

The enthusiasm that their visits aroused in Poland was part of growing interest in Zygmunt's work. His book *Modernity and the Holocaust* placed him at the pinnacle of the university world, bringing prizes, invitations to talks and other prestigious events, and doctorates of *honoris causa*. Retirement would not mean a rest for the Baumans, who still hardly had time to accept all the invitations that came from around the world. Celebrity came at a good moment.

World recognition

The recognition started to build up even before the 'liquid turn' in Bauman's work. In 1989, the Italian Association of Sociology awarded Bauman the prestigious European Amalfi Prize for *Modernity and the Holocaust*.[31] His Italian success began at that moment and never ended. He became a star in Italy. Even his friend and editor, John Thompson, was surprised by this phenomenon, noting that authors and university professors in the UK rarely reach the celebrity Bauman enjoyed in Italy, Spain, Portugal and South America. In these places Bauman was viewed as a guru, a role he always said he disliked and refused to play. Bauman enjoyed speaking before large audiences, but he was less enthusiastic about parties and receptions. After his talks, Janina and Zygmunt were usually invited to receptions, dinners and cocktails, but the Baumans often ducked out with a friend, the artist Tomasz Kowalski told me. 'If Bauman was to become a celebrity, he was to be an unwilling one', Beilharz said: 'In an academic world where self-promotion is now a standard requirement, this is a rare thing' (2020 MS: 80).

Monika Kostera, the co-author of one of Bauman's last books, *Management in Liquid Modernity*, gave a detailed account of one occasion:

> In 1995, Zygmunt came to Warsaw. His talk took place in the Institute of Culture and there were a lot of invited people. It was difficult to get in: media, cameras, well-known people, and us. Well, after the lecture, which was poignant – he was an amazing person who spoke so simply and so beautifully about complicated social processes . . . – after this lecture, Ania [Anna Zeidler-Janiszewska] introduced me to Zygmunt and we talked. At some point Zygmunt said, 'Let's go', and a quick action was executed. Ania grabbed us and somehow we got out of there quickly with all these journalists and cameras and important professors [waiting for Bauman] . . . we escaped along a corridor. Ania knew this place and knew how to get out by the back door – The three of us sat in the 'Literacka' cafe – and had an absolutely fantastic time.

Though Bauman liked to escape crowds, he did very well in official functions. He was an amazing keynote speaker, had a very elegant way of talking and a rare verbal grace, responding to questions with his sweet-and-sour sense of humour. All those features made him sympathetic, and despite his declarations to the contrary, Bauman played the role of 'sage' to perfection. His advancing age increased his aura as a grand public intellectual, and he clearly liked speaking about contemporary problems and the changing world, especially with younger audiences. This was impressive, since most people his age had stopped following technological change, social evolution and global phenomena.

Bauman's physical charisma was expressed in his talismanic pipe-smoking, his height and white hair and the agility – rare at his age – with which he passionately delivered a global vision grounded in sophisticated analysis. He was a bewitching figure for a consumerist culture in which there is such primacy given to youth. Young people saw him as a Yoda, a wizened ancient one with the secrets to understanding human action and relationships. In short, Bauman transformed his age from a handicap to an advantage, employing his sociological imagination to create attractive ideas and communicate them to large groups of people.

As the Baumans got older, it was harder for him to accept even short separations, and he always travelled with Janina. This was problematic but non-negotiable. Janina stopped her yearly visits to Israel, a difficult concession because she missed her daughter and grandchildren and the beauty of Jerusalem in the evening, described so well in *Dream of Belonging*. In Leeds they were always working on the next talk, project or book, and constantly preparing for the next trip. But Janina was not always 'the professor's wife'. Sometimes Zygmunt was 'Janina Bauman's husband'. She was invited to speak about *Winter in the Morning* in Holland, Germany, Scandinavia and other places, at universities (Jewish studies, Shoah history) or events for the public. Beginning in 1995, she was frequently invited to the Anne Frank House as an author and survivor for educational and historical projects. She also became involved in the construction of Holocaust memory projects and education for tolerance. She frequently shared her wartime experience with students in Poland and in Germany, an emotional challenge. Zygmunt accompanied her on those trips, frequently giving talks at nearby universities. They were always together. In 1998, the city of Frankfurt presented Bauman with the Theodor W. Adorno Award – an incredible honour. Two years later, the publication of *Liquid Modernity* created a new departure. Bauman was 75 years old.

Global Bauman

Between 2000 and 2010, Bauman published at least one book a year. He wrote about things that interested people: consumerism, globalization, modernity, post-modernity, fear, love, hate and anti-Semitism. His vast training and experience, erudition, attention to popular culture such as movies, and comfort in four or five languages – English, Polish, Hebrew, Russian and sometimes French and Italian – gave him a wide field of play. Bauman put all those resources together to create readable and compelling books and thoughts. 'I did not truly "belong" to any school, order, intellectual camaraderie or clique', Bauman said in 2011:

> I did not apply for admission to any of them, let alone did much to deserve an invitation; nor would I be listed by any of them – at least listed unqualifiedly as 'one of us'. I guess my claustrophobia is incurable – feeling, as I tend to, ill at ease in any closed room, and always tempted to find out what is on the other side of the door. I guess

I am doomed to remain an outsider to the end, lacking as I am the
indispensable qualities of an academic insider: school loyalty, conformity to the procedure, and readiness to obey by the school-endorsed
criteria of cohesion and consistency. And, frankly, I don't mind.[32]

Bauman broke with the conventions[33] of academic writing. Some
scholarly milieus have problems with this transgression, and some
professional sociologists, especially in the UK, harshly criticized
his turn to the popular touch (see Kilminster, 2016, or Rattansi,
2017, for example). Overall, academic sociologists were ambivalent
about his writing. Tester saw Bauman's 'transgression' as part of
'the Zygmunt of "Control Zygmunt" – the one who says, "Watch
this film! Read this novel!", the one who has a very strong sense of
vocation, an extreme sense of humour as well, always playing off
of being an outsider very skilfully. It was a joke for him.'[34] Being
an outsider had become a privilege; it enabled freedom from academic conventions. Bauman had shed the shackles of academia and
become a free writer (Bauman, 2012). There was no other way for
him to continue to think, Bauman said in later interviews; he needed
to maintain a special connection with his readers, who included
activists. His engaged work inspired important social movements
that were anti-globalist or sought alternatives to its current forms.
But his remarkable huge public success came under a shadow: the
old story of his unrequited love for Poland.

Global and famous and . . . the culprit again . . .

During their visits to Poland, Janina engaged mainly in discussions of the Holocaust and its lessons, while Zygmunt participated
in academic events and became a kind of leftist spiritual leader
(the group Krytyka Polityczna frequently published his texts and
organized talks) – and presented his photographs. In 2004, Poland
joined the European Union, an event that was a source of optimism
and hope for democratic stability. Bauman became rector of the
Jan Józef Lipski Open University in Teremiski near Białowieża, in
eastern Poland. This institution, created by Solidarity leader Jacek
Kuroń, represented the utopian idea that a university should open
its doors to everyone, including in the most isolated places in the
country, with the idea that knowledge transmission (and construction) should not be limited to national or private universities or
students with high levels of social capital. These popular universities
have existed in Poland for nearly a century, and it is an honour to
be invited to lecture in them. The idea of education for all continued
a socialist ideal, implementing Gramsci's ideas and transforming
Bauman's words into deeds. The lectures he gave in a wooden barn

in the tiny forest village 200 kilometres east of Warsaw attracted a lot of people – ranging from locals to Warsaw intelligentsia and Belorussian neighbours. Young and old squeezed together in the barn.

In April 2004, Bauman received an honorary Doctorate of Letters from the University of Leeds, 'a rare honour in this country and a profound satisfaction', Janina wrote to Beilharz (2020 MS: 159). In total, Bauman would win twenty *honoris causa* doctorates in different countries. These ceremonies were always pleasant – except in Poland. By chance – apparently – just as the University of Warsaw was launching the process of awarding Bauman with its highest distinction, in June 2006 a historian of the IPN published a paper denouncing Bauman's communist past.[35]

The IPN is a powerful institution of post-communist Poland. It is both an archive of records from the communist-era secret police and other sources, and an agency that compensates victims as well as prosecuting those allegedly guilty of crimes under communism. Since the election of the right-wing nationalist Law and Justice Party in 2005, the IPN has increasingly also been used as a politicized tool to attack and marginalize opponents of the government, including much of the leadership of the Solidarity movement that helped bring down the communist regime. The use of selective IPN files for the 'lustration' or cleansing of Polish society led Solidarity leader and publisher Adam Michnik to declare in 2008 that the IPN, rather than preserving the nation's memory, was destroying it.[36] IPN's founding paragraph has been revised to a focus solely on communist – and not Nazi – crimes, and recently was changed to protecting the 'good name' of Poland against accusations of complicity in the Holocaust. More to the point, IPN officials have selectively leaked files to journalists in order to smear enemies of the current government. The victims of these smear campaigns have included personalities such as Lech Wałęsa, Jacek Kuroń – and Zygmunt Bauman.

In the mid-2000s, Warsaw University faculty were instructed to declare whether they had collaborated with the secret services, a tricky question for many, since, in order to travel, scholars had to sign a 'collaborative declaration' with the *Bezpieka*, even if they never really worked for it. Discussions on the subject generated a lot of public controversy. The logic behind lustration was actually the same as in 1968 – to purge society and solidify the control of the ruling party through successive elections. Increasingly, the IPN was essentially geared to distributing pro-government, nationalist propaganda.

The article about Bauman published in 2006 on the IPN's website did not contain evidence of a crime. It presented two *Bezpieka* files, one from 1950 that gave a positive assessment of Bauman's activities by his superior, Colonel Bibrowski, as a justification for his

promotion. The second was a certificate testifying that Bauman collaborated with military intelligence. The author of the IPN report,
Gontarz, argued that Bibrowski's assessment showed that Bauman
had been a team leader in KBW activities against underground
fighters in winter 1946. Since the newly empowered neo-nationalists
had declared these underground anti-communist fighters to be
national heroes, the fact of having opposed them became a crime, if
not a prosecutable one. There was no other specific evidence against
Bauman.

In previous chapters, I have presented a detailed analysis of the
context in which Bauman entered the military services. There is
no denying that Bauman actively supported the communist system
in the postwar period, nor that he was a KBW officer who served
in military intelligence for three years. The hate attacks against
Bauman that arose as a result of Gontarz's IPN article probably
stemmed from other causes. Firstly, Bauman never apologized for
his involvement in the communist enterprise in postwar Poland. He
said repeatedly that he viewed it has having been the best option at
that time in those circumstances. In an interview with the *Guardian*
in 2007, he said that he bore full responsibility for his actions, but
did not apologize because he did not feel he had done wrong.

Secondly, unlike fellow former communists such as Kołakowski,
Bauman did not entirely change his political stripes, and remained
on the left side of the political arena. Thirdly, he became extremely
famous, which attracted jealousy and rage. Last, but probably not
least, he was a Jew. The IPN article unleashed a series of rabid
attacks on Bauman by the anti-Semitic media. Bauman became
a mythical enemy whose 'cosmopolitanism' was a danger to the
construction and maintenance of a strong national identity in a
new European sphere. Hatred was mobilized by fear – the fear that
Poland was losing its specific culture, language, independence and
way of life in the new, 'liquid' spheres of the world.

One could speculate that the selective release of seemingly incrim-
inating evidence against Bauman was part of an intentional process
to undermine Bauman and scuttle his *honoris causa* distinction.
Bauman was one of the perfect targets for the IPN – a handy scapegoat for a nationalist right-wing government. He was famous, and
continued to embrace a socialist ideal and to criticize the perversities
of capitalism at a time when capitalism was not just a new economic
system in Poland, but a new 'religion'.

On 5 July 2006, in the same month the IPN article was published, the director of the Institute of Applied Social Sciences
(ISNS) wrote an official letter to the rector of the University of
Warsaw noting the approaching fiftieth anniversary of Bauman's
doctorate award and requesting its 'solemn renewal'.[37] This initiative was supported by the university's other sociological institute,

the Institute of Sociology (IS).[38] The 'solemn renewal of doctorate degree' is equivalent to an *honoris causa* (which cannot be awarded to a graduate of the same university; as Bauman got his Ph.D. at the University of Warsaw, a solemn renewal was the only option for him). The decision of the sociological institutes required agreement from the university Senate and a Commission for Honorific Titles that included the current and previous rectors. They were to meet to discuss the award after the summer break. In early September, the rector received protests.

On 7 September, Professor Jerzy Kwaśniewski sent a letter by e-mail urging that the honour be reconsidered:

In the face of recently disclosed information that Prof. Zygmunt Bauman was an officer and an agent of the communist security services, I am opposed to the request of the Faculty of Philosophy and Sociology and the Department of Applied Social Sciences and Rehabilitation for a solemn renewal of the doctorate . . . At the same time, I request that these department councils resume voting on the matter after their members read the IPN materials on the activities of Z. Bauman in the communist special services.[39]

The second letter came from Canada. Professor Maria Łoś, a sociologist, had graduated in the early 1970s from Warsaw and taught at the University of Ottawa on Eastern Europe and communism. Her 24 September letter to the rector also called for withholding the honour to Bauman 'until he explains his former role in the apparatus of repression. There is no doubt to me, that Professor Bauman has significant scientific achievements and has significantly influenced the shaping of social and ethical thought in the last twenty years.' However, 'a calm investigation and explanation' were required because of the IPN disclosures of '*previously unknown information* that Zygmunt Bauman was an officer of the communist security authorities in 1945–1953, as well as a secret military information agent, and that he actively participated in eliminating the resistance of the underground guerrilla.'[40]

The backdrop to the story of those letters is important to understanding the context of Bauman's shunning by the university. First, Kwaśniewski led a third sociological institute at the University of Warsaw that was in competition with the two institutes that were urging the honouring of Bauman. No other discipline at this university is organized in this way, and it reflects the complex relationships among networks that have developed over several generations. Łoś, by contrast, was a longtime emigrant and thus a 'foreign expert' whose letter from abroad weighed more than one signed by a scholar working in Poland. As a peripheral post-Soviet country, Poland and many of its citizens looked with absolute idolatry towards 'the West'.

Both Kwaśniewski and Łoś were close collaborators of Adam
Podgórecki (1925–98), who left Poland in 1977 and went to Ottawa,
where Łoś followed two years later. Łoś was Podgórecki's wife. She
had received her master's degree in 1966, and a Ph.D. in 1971, at the
Institute of Sociology, and knew Bauman personally. Kwaśniewski
also graduated from the institute and attended lectures with
Bauman. Podgórecki and Bauman were university faculty of the
same age and knew each other, but represented different sociological
positions. Podgórecki was a specialist in deviation, socio-technics
and the sociology of morality, which Bauman criticized in his post-
Poland works. Their biographical features also were different,
though both had left Poland for political reasons. Podgórecki was a
well-regarded Catholic anti-communist who originated in the Polish
gentry. Kwaśniewski had taken his place at the university when
Podgórecki left. Born in 1942 in a rural area, Kwaśniewski was also
a non-Jewish Pole. He was hired at the university in 1969, when the
anti-Semitic purge had opened up new places.

The second common point in the two letters was their level of
ignorance, which is surprising, especially since communist security
institutions were Łoś's area of expertise. Both sociologists should have
known there was nothing new in the IPN documents. There had never
been any secret about Bauman being a KBW officer when he began
his master's at Warsaw University. He came to campus in his military
uniform, having had no time to change it (like many others in the same
situation), and continued to wear the uniform after leaving the KBW
because he had no money for other clothes. If Łoś and Kwaśniewski
didn't remember this detail personally, they would have known it from
their older colleagues and friends – especially Podgórecki. Anyone
at Warsaw University would have known that KBW was part of the
secret military services, and it was no secret that, in the two years
after the war ended, all KBW units were 'combatting Polish guerril-
las'. Indeed, any Polish Army officer from this period spent at least
short periods chasing partisans in the forests – and Bauman was far
from being the only person at Warsaw University who served in the
military at the time. Yet no one ever found evidence that Bauman
had fired a weapon, let alone mistreated or tortured a prisoner. Such
people had trouble returning to Poland after the fall of communism;
Bauman never did.[41] Specialists did the dirty work in the postwar era,
and the authorities kept this secret even inside their units. Bauman
was a propaganda officer, a teacher and a Party intellectual.

Adding to the intrigue, there had been a scholarly quarrel in the
late 1970s which opposed Bauman's friends to Podgórecki, during
a polemic that arose over a paper that the latter published in 1976
about Polish sociology and its paradigms, approaches and methodology (Szacki, 2011 [1976]). Podgórecki, a supporter of 'positivist
sociology', heavily criticized – among others – Jan Szczepański

and Aleksandra Jasińska-Kania, and Jerzy Szacki responded with a short text, defending his colleagues. It could be compared to a conflict of the 'schools' or 'coteries' – however, the tone of the discussion imposed by the first text by Podgórecki was particularly aggressive and abrasive.

Finally, Łoś's and Kwaśniewski's letters suggest that the authors were supporters of lustration. Like Podgórecki, they followed paradigms that were the opposite of Bauman's – Łoś using the concept of late modernity; and Kwaśniewski, 'deviation and social norms'. Both specialized in punitive institutions and re-socialization, which Bauman criticized. Moreover, perhaps they hoped that someone else would get the coveted 'renewal of doctorate degree' that was being offered to Bauman. Other names had been proposed from outside the Sociology Department.

The official process restarted after the summer break. On 9 October, the rector informed the institutes of the negative decision of the Commission for Honorific Titles, justifying it based on the '[c]haracter of the academic and teaching achievements of the candidate'.[42] This short sentence provoked strong reactions from both the sociological institutes that had put Bauman's name forward. Their leaders sent indignant letters to the rector seeking more explanation.[43] The president of the Institute of Applied Social Science's academic council concluded on 31 October, 'The verdict of the Commission and the form of communicating this verdict have been interpreted as disregarding and challenging the competence not only of the councils of two Institutes representing sociology and social sciences at our university, but also many prestigious, well-respected Western European scientific institutions.'[44] The letter mentions the nine European universities that had awarded Bauman with the *honoris causa* distinction. On 27 November, the rector asked members of the Commission for Honorific Titles to provide more detailed responses within three days.

The final letter from the rector states:

Professor Zygmunt Bauman is a world-class scholar whose sociological achievements are undisputed, widely recognized and valued in Europe and in the world. However, the postwar activity of the professor as a political officer of the KBW and his ideological engagement among others at the University of Warsaw and the Higher School of Social Sciences at the Central Committee of the PZPR raises serious reservations and may be the subject of intense controversy. The renewal of the doctoral thesis promotes not only scientific achievements but also patterns of civic attitude. It has important didactic and educational meaning. At the University of Warsaw, fortunately, we have no strong aspiration to hold an accounting of the past or publicly condemn members of our community who were involved in the communist regime. . . . But it is hardly surprising that this is an obstacle to the highest honours. This was reflected in the results of the vote of both faculty councils. In this situation, the Commission fully and unanimously upholds its previous position.[45]

The University of Warsaw's rector was Professor Katarzyna Macukow-Chałasińska, a physicist elected in 2005 and the daughter of Jozef Chałasiński, a sociologist who had not got along well with Hochfeld (Chałubiński, 2017: 33–4 and ch.8) or Bauman. In the 1960s, Chałasiński wrote of himself that, during the Stalinist period, he was 'an altar boy of the established rite – Stalin worship' (Piskała and Zysiak, 2013: 294). Before turning against orthodox Marxism, Chałasiński had been an aggressive young communist who fought with his mentor, Znaniecki. All of this suggests that the failure of Bauman's honorary degree had a long history, one that reached into the 1950s and before, and included resentment towards Bauman among some of those who worked with him, and their students. After 1989, true Marxists were in a minority and Hochfeld's circle had lost its strength. Anything that smelled of communism was frowned upon, with reinforcement from popular anti-Semitic opinions. There is no direct proof of any conspiracy against Bauman, but a climate of witch-hunting and resentment framed the event.

The result didn't surprise the Warsaw sociology community, though many opposed the decision. One anonymous observer blamed the institutes for failing to lay the groundwork before setting in motion the *honoris causa* for Bauman: 'We were so sure he would get it because of his achievements and fame. But at the top, opposition was strong, and we lost. And afterwards there was shame.'

Ostensibly, the thesis of anti-Semitism seems weak: Jews such as the Israeli Professor Shmul Eisenstadt received honorary degrees from the University of Warsaw. But Eisenstadt had strong institutional backing and was a practitioner of functionalism, the major approach in sociology at the university. And, though born in Warsaw, he had fled to Palestine before the war, was educated in Israel, and never pretended to be a Pole. Bauman always presented himself as a Pole, and, for a lot of Poles, that was the problem. Today, anti-Semitism is not typically directed at Israeli citizens, but rather at present or former Polish Jews.

Bauman did not like to speak about the 'sad thing', but he was very disappointed. The worst thing was to be rejected by his academic *alma mater*, which had been such an exceptional intellectual environment in the 1960s. The prodigal son had once more been rejected, a kind of *déjà vu* almost thirty years after the first rejection. Bauman again was being denounced on the front pages of the newspapers (with repercussions in other countries, such as the *Guardian* article published in April 2007 titled 'Professor with a Past').[46]

The worst thing was this incredible consistency, in the liquid world. Despite radical changes that occurred in Poland after 1989, exclusion processes maintained an astonishing continuity. Whatever the regime, he fitted the role of 'culprit' and 'enemy' – his master status was unchanging, whether it was assigned because he was a Jew, a 'Zionist' or a former communist. Although it didn't appear in the university documents, Bauman's activism in 21st-century anti-capitalist movements was also a punishable activity in the nationalist press. He was the perfect enemy.

In a 2019 article entitled 'Polish Deadlock: Between Liberal and Right-Wing Anti-Communism', Jakub Majmurek remarked:

> Right-wing anti-communism has no single figure that gathers its dis-courses, like *homo sovieticus*. The closest to this is probably the figure of 'Major Bauman' – as the right-wing press calls the outstanding sociologist, Zygmunt Bauman. 'Major Bauman' brings together the narrative of 'race war' and the Soviet conquest, the figure of the elite of the Third Polish Republic and the modern Western left, and as such is the ideal object for attacks from right-wing anti-communism.[47]

The Baumans continued to visit Poland after 2006, but less joyfully than in the past. Friends, collaborators and enthusiastic supporters of Bauman's work organized new events, and he gave lectures at the co-operative university Collegium Civitas, and the Institute of Applied Sciences created by Krytyka Polityczna. But these were outside the mainstream of Polish higher education. With the exception of the Polish Academy of Sciences, this world no longer welcomed Bauman. More Polish universities rejected *honoris causa* proposals (for example, Poznań's Mickiewicz University), and Bauman declined a decoration from Wrocław's private Lower Silesia University. After the hate action organized by fascist groups that had disturbed his lecture in Wrocław a few months earlier (June 2013 – see Introduction), Bauman wished to avoid similar prob-lems; he did not want to be a 'problem' for others. Already in 1988, Bauman said ironically:

> because whatever I did with the sincere conviction that it was for the good of Poland was considered an element of the Zionist world con-spiracy in which I wanted to give Krakow to Israel, it seemed to me that I became a King Midas in a way that if the touch of King Midas turned everything into gold, with me – everything I touch turned to shit. I apologize for the unpleasant word, but I felt that way. .... I felt that I could only disturb and not help my colleagues. And that maybe it would be better for them, if I leave, if they do not have to carry me on their backs with all the other weights. (Bauman, cited in Mieszczanek, 1989: 164)

The exclusion continued not only in academia but more generally. Bauman never recovered his citizenship, although President
Aleksander Kwaśniewski asked him at an event why he had not got
it back. It would be a small formality, Kwaśniewski said.[48] Bauman
never pursued it, and it is not clear whether he ever considered
doing so. After all, he did not resign from his Polish citizenship – he
was evicted from Poland with his family and resignation from the
citizenship was imposed. There was no other choice. Requesting
his citizenship back would certainly have been time-consuming. It
might have also seemed risky, since Bauman's life had been one of
multiple rejections from Polish society. 'If I did not become a Pole
and nobody let me do it, it is the fault of Poland, not mine', wrote
Bauman's Polish editor, Włodzimierz Wojdowski ('Judaism as
Fate' in Molisak, 2004: 318). Yet unlike Wojdowski, who remained
in Poland to give permanent testimony on the Holocaust, Bauman
remained a Pole, in spirit at least.

Legends: Jackboots and iron – deconstruction

Chapter 8 began with this anecdote, which concerns a story that cir-
culates at Warsaw University. Bauman frequented his department
as a student wearing a military uniform and with a gun in its holster,
which would sometimes clatter onto the floor during the seminar.
The hero of the story is Bauman – the professor's name varies.
Interestingly, when I interviewed Bronisław Baczko, a philosopher and colleague of Bauman, he gave a slightly different account:
'When I was at the university the first years, I was still in the Army
[Baczko was a political officer, at a higher rank than Bauman – he
benefitted from a military apartment in the beautiful buildings that
were just near the university campus]. It was not always possible to
take time to change into civilian clothes as I ran directly from the
office to the lectures. And it was me who dropped my gun on the
floor!' Another interviewee – Karol Modzelewski – recalled this
anecdote with Kołakowski in the principal role, not Bauman. That
version was confirmed by Jerzy and Barbara Szacki who, after some
hesitation, recognize Kołakowski as the gun's owner ('he always
had his the head in the clouds – it could only have happened to
him'), and the place was not Warsaw but Łódź.

All these reported versions could be true. All the heroes of the
story – Baczko, Kołakowski, Bauman – were in possession of guns
in their first years at the university. They were in active military
service (except Kołakowski, who was not in the Polish Army – but
he was a member of a radical communist group and, like all his colleagues, he had a gun for self-defence). What does this anecdote tell
us?

First, about the context – in the postwar period, not everyone had returned to civilian life after the Liberation. The university welcomed those who were still active soldiers. We should remember that Poland in these years was still at war – guns were like mobile phones today: every active person carried one with them, especially those who supported the new system. All three heroes of this same story had a gun and took it to the university. This story is simply an illustration of the unusual nature of those stormy times. Why does this anecdote mention mainly Bauman? Because Kołakowski washed his hands of his communist past, Baczko plunged into his scholarly work, completely disappearing from the Polish academic milieu, and Bauman . . . he stayed as always – leftist, and famous! In the twenty-first century, Bauman became a world celebrity, a Global Thinker.

He was also the only one to be the target of a hate campaign in Poland (even if the biographies of both Kołakowski and Baczko were entangled in communist engagement). The anecdote contained a hidden message: Bauman was dangerous; everyone should be afraid of him. This could justify the accusations made by the press, and the lack of enthusiasm by university authorities to attribute the highest award to him. Bauman never denied his previous communist engagements. He explained several times that, in that postwar period, the communist programme was the most attractive and egalitarian – he saw it as the best plan for Poland at that moment. Unlike the majority of people engaged in the construction of communist/socialist Poland after 1989, who became critical of the leftist approach, Bauman remained true to the values that had led him to support communism during that period.

Jasia . . .

The rejections and disillusions were difficult, but Bauman was used to them. But he was not prepared for the loss of Janina after almost sixty-two years of marriage. Bauman showed Janina his love, but if love was a constant tension between freedom and control, as Bauman described, his was much closer to the latter. He needed her, and she was always nearby, at his computer screen, travelling, walking hand in hand, discussing after he finished his daily writing, watching the latest 'must-see' film. She was always a bit in his shadow.

She had her own writing and her own passions, of course. Close friends and family remember the beautiful ceramic *garnki*, or pots, that she made for them – she was an artistic ceramicist who produced rare and beautiful work. 'My mother suddenly started making pots in Leeds', Irena recalled. She always gave them as presents, and Irena's daughter, a professional art expert who specialized in ceramics, said that Janina had invented a new adhesive method: 'It was very difficult work, and these pots are beautiful, and we did not understand what she was doing, or what an interesting artist she was. We failed to understand all those years.'

We can ask what accounts for this lack of recognition or struggle to impose her own will and desires – why she stopped her regular trips to Israel, why she did not push to write more books, why she never had a show of her ceramic work, or tried to sell it. Janina was enveloped in a kind of nostalgia or sorrow, some friends say – perhaps because she was living in Zygmunt's shadow, perhaps because of the incalculable losses of her childhood. Or for many reasons. Emigration caused many struggles. 'When you change your language you lose your capacity to be funny; you are deadly serious', her friend Griselda Pollock notes. While Janina wrote her books in English, 'she never had this ability to say what she wanted in English'. While others found Janina's spoken English very good, it certainly was not at a level with which she felt entire comfort. In her first book, Janina discussed her awkwardness with English as she learned to shop in Leeds. 'Learning a new language for everyday life involves making a fool of yourself, which may involve humiliation. Silence is an alternative strategy', said Peter Beilharz. English was Janina's fifth language, and she did not begin learning it until her late forties. In Polish, she was less reserved; she had a sense of humour and a kindness that, as some friends recall, made Zygmunt more 'accessible'. In addition to those linguistic limits, of course, her painful past never went away, for Janina's first identity was as a Holocaust survivor. She focused on sharing this unshareable experience, and it hurt. As Jan Gross noted in his autobiographical book (Gross and Pawlicka, 2018), Holocaust studies are a special field of activity. They strongly affect the author and never allow a moment's rest. The duty of transmission is stronger than the pain of recalling its horrors.

Towards the end of her life, Janina struggled with a heart ailment that resulted from the extreme conditions of her teenage years. Zygmunt was 'literally spoon-feeding her'[49] in her final years, yet the Baumans managed to spend their sixtieth wedding anniversary in Warsaw at the Hotel Bristol. It was the last time they came to Poland together. Back in Leeds, the Baumans spent many days in the clinics and hospitals of the National Health Service waiting for treatment. Bauman refused to pay for private care as a matter of principle. Why should he and his wife get better care than others who couldn't afford it? He hated to wait, but Bauman waited patiently. The Global Thinker sat in the corridors of public hospitals dealing with the shortages in care that resulted from the devastating reforms started by Margaret Thatcher. It was still a public trust, and Bauman stuck to his ideals – for his wife's treatment, and later for his own.

Janina died at age 83, on 29 December 2009. The man whom she had shadowed during her English life also began to disappear. Every living person has a shadow. If the shadow goes, it means that the person who cast it is there no more. Both die.

from the hip you shoot, my god,
untroubled by fluky strikes
and your people, your creators
you dispatch to kingless justice
hooded courts

chaos rules your blue beyond
sparks within you and without
your ways are unknown to us
and no doubt to you the most
heady fog

when a sage's ken you envy
into stones you turn his eyes
then you raise yourself above us
unencumbered by remorse
mortal's pain.
                    (Włodzimierz Holsztyński, 'Crossroads', trans. Barbara
                    Nykiel-Herbert)[50]

After Janina's death, Zygmunt Bauman remained home. He asked close friends not to call on him. Family and close friends were increasingly worried that he would follow Janina. For a year he mourned, losing his vital energy . . . for the first time in his life, he was not in a hurry.

A few months after her death, Keith Tester came to the house, and the meeting was very painful. All that Zygmunt wanted to do was to show him pictures of Janina. 'All of those around him thought we would lose him soon', recalled Monika Kostera. Bauman said his life was finished. He would never travel anymore, never go to those places he visited with Janina, never do anything now she was gone. There is a touching documentary entitled *Love, Europe, World* by Krzysztof Rzączyński, who followed Bauman with a camera during his first visit to Poland without Janina. Their daughters came with him. In one scene, Bauman is walking and he says, 'I am alone.' Lydia responds, 'No Dad, you have us.'

The daughters organized their time around being with their *tata* (dad). Bauman's clan was strong and they collaborated diligently to make sure Zygmunt was accompanied to all his professional events, which, despite his initial misgivings, continued. In 2010, he shared with Alain Touraine the Príncipe de Asturias Prize for communication and the humanities. The same year, in the UK, he attended the creation of the Bauman Institute within the School of Sociology and Social Policy at Leeds, a crowning achievement. Bauman participated in events at the Institute organized by its creator and director Mark Davis until the last months of his life.

Bauman's work began to move him from his morbid inertia. He was engaged in a new book of dialogues with his friend, the former Jesuit priest Stanisław Obirek. They discussed God and humankind, a very interesting project for two outsiders who had belonged to big organizations and actively constructed utopias that never worked out. In their book, they discussed the existence of God from two perspectives – those of a believer and of an atheist. Obirek believed that this work was therapeutic for Bauman, helping to ease his desperation as he passed through the mourning period.

Some months after Janina's death, Bauman said to his daughters: 'This is a matter of choice now: either I die, or I choose life.'

He chose life.

Back to life

For his eighty-fifth birthday, in 2010, Bauman received the 'Gloria Artis' gold medal, the most prestigious decoration for cultural achievement in Poland. The ceremony was led by the Polish Minister of Culture and National Treasure. Bauman was happy about the distinction, though in pain and depressed. He invited to his party a colleague whom he had met for the first time at Warsaw University in 1954 – Aleksandra Jasińska-Kania.[51] Starting in 1956, they worked in the division of political sociology under Hochfeld. Their career timing was different: Bauman quickly finished his doctorate degree and habilitation. Aleksandra Jasińska changed topics (partly for political reasons) and Ph.D. advisers. She finally finished her thesis in 1967, working under Bauman's supervision. Aleksanda Jasińska married her colleague from the department, Albion Kania, and the two Baumans and Kanias were friends who met from time to time before 1968. Aleksandra visited the Baumans in Leeds in 1988 while in Oxford as a visiting scholar. Zygmunt also had professional connections with Aleksandra; they published several times in contributory books, for example in a book about values and morality published in English.[52]

Meeting again at Bauman's party in 2010, they had the first in a series of long discussions about their lost life-partners (Aleksandra's husband had died sixteen years before), the process of becoming a widow or widower, the sorrow and mourning and stages of pain, suffering and recovery. Bauman realized that these discussions helped him bring out and identify his feelings, and to share them. This mixture of sociology and psychology from a friend was the best therapy he could get. Bauman's deep friendships with Jasińska-Kania and the former priest Obirek were very positive, and he progressively recovered his vitality. Jasińska-Kania was key – she knew how to transform a sad discussion into a positive and finally joyful exchange. The next year, when Bauman received an invitation to teach at the Collegium Civitas – the first non-public university in Poland, created by Polish Academy of Sciences professors – he got the rector to bring in Jasińska-Kania as his collaborator, and they conducted a seminar together. He came to Warsaw once a month, and Aleksandra ran the seminars in his absence.

'After one of his lectures he proposed to me', wrote Jasińska-Kania: 'It was hard to believe that the miracle of falling in love could happen to people who were 80 years old, but we both felt like we were 16 again' (Jasińska-Kania, 2018). It was a very fast process – 'that was very much like him', one of his daughters recalled: 'He just said that he had fallen in love.' At the time, Lydia and Irena thought their father would move to Warsaw permanently, or that the new couple would share their time between Leeds and Warsaw. Instead, Jasińska-Kania moved to Leeds. Zygmunt started to appreciate life again, and began new projects – four new dialogue books in 2013 alone. He resumed his intensive travel schedule, started entertaining guests and recovered a very similar life to the one he had spent with Janina: writing in the mornings, cooking for Aleksandra, spending the evening talking, singing, reading, watching TV, and discussing all the time. They shared an interest in sociology, in reminiscing about the Hochfeld circle, and their affinity for Russian culture and language, in which both had grown up. As a daughter of communist activists, during World War II Jasińska-Kania had grown up in a kind of Soviet nursery with children of communists from around the world. Younger than Bauman at the time, she absorbed many aspects of Russian culture, and this was a common ground for the two when they met as octogenarians. They would sing Russian childhood songs, read Russian literature and discuss Russian films. It was something new for Bauman to have a partner to recall the vast, beautiful Russian landscapes of his youth, the frigid Russian winters and the generosity of the Russians with whom they had shared those dark years.

They also communicated about their love with others, which surprised a lot of people. Again, Bauman was unconventional. In our societies, relationships that start this late tend to evoke suspicion and cynical comments. There was also gossip about their union, but Bauman did not care – as usual, he did what he wanted. Aleksandra – 'Ola', as her friends and Ph.D. students called her – shared Bauman's attitude. She understood well how someone who suffered from media attacks would feel, for she was the daughter of Bolesław Bierut (see chapters 8 and 9), the Stalinist president of postwar Poland who had died in 1956 when Stalinism collapsed. Jasińska-Kania's mother, Małgorzata Fornalska, was a communist who had died in 1943 at the hands of the Nazis as a martyr for Poland. During the communist years, her name was celebrated and taught to schoolchildren; after the regime change, her name disappeared.

Jasińska-Kania was writing a book about her parents and their concept of the struggle for freedom in Poland. Who could understand her better than Bauman? Their friends and family appreciated Aleksandra – 'she saved our Zygmunt', one of them said. She gave him five more years of productivity, through a strong friendship, professional collaboration and connection between two Slavic tempers – passionate and quarrelling. Friends observed that Zygmunt grew less preoccupied than he had been since Janina's final years. It was a relationship they both needed. After getting engaged at Bellagio in Italy on New Year's Eve 2012, they were married at Leeds City Hall in the presence of their daughters, including Aleksandra's only daughter, who came from the United States, where she is a professor of mathematics.

Over the next few years, the new couple toured regularly in Poland and other places, including Israel, which they visited together in 2013. This was Bauman's fourth return to the country, which he never ceased criticizing over its militarist policies and what he saw as mistreatment of the Palestinians. Still, his close family lived there, including grandson Michael Sfard, who would become one of the leading human rights lawyers in Israel – a living legacy of the ideas of his grandfather.[53]

The old/new couple's life attracted the interest of journalists – if only Oprah could have had them on her show. In newspaper articles, they discussed the difficulties of being an unmarried couple, even an old one, in our societies. Hosts were uncomfortable, not knowing whether to reserve one hotel room or two, or how to present Jasińska-Kania. 'Life-partner' did not run trippingly off the tongue. Bauman worried more about practical elements of elderly life: access to health care. Always well organized, he carefully arranged his retirement, pension and insurance coverage, and did what he could to manage such issues for Aleksandra as well. He liked having someone to look after.

Aleksandra left Warsaw and took her professor's pension from the university to spend the last years of Bauman's life with him in Leeds. Their life had two speeds, she would write: very active while on professional trips, and slower when they were home writing (see Jasińska-Kania, 2018). They travelled so intensively that each had a KLM Flying Blue Platinum Membership card – more than sixty trips a year, including to Brazil, where audiences loved him. They visited Boston and Washington, DC, at the end of 2013; Bauman even gave a lecture there. Jasińska-Kania regularly spent her

Christmas in the United States, where her daughter, granddaughter and other relatives lived.

Their youthful enthusiasm and endurance were surprising. After a lecture in Lublin in 2012, Bauman slipped on the stairs of the Brama Grodzka theatre and broke his left arm, but fate smiled on him. The father of the co-organizer of Bauman's talk was an orthopaedist, and the physicians in Accident and Emergency took care of him immediately, getting the break diagnosed and treated – no surgery was required – and getting him back to his hotel the next morning. The very next day, Aleksandra gave his lecture and they went on to the next city on his tour without missing a beat. Physicians were impressed by his good humour, tolerance of pain and excellent health. Ironically, the next stop on his tour was Kohlberg,[54] the city where he'd injured the same arm in battle in March 1945. 'Every time I visit Kohlberg I have problems with this left arm', he joked: 'I wonder what it is about this city?'

Increasingly, however, Bauman was confronted with hate speech and neo-Nazi groups. He was baffled and frightened by the resurgence of fascists, especially after the June 2013 episode in Wrocław. The groups that had stood up to hurl abuse at him there – organizations called ONR (Obóz Radykalno-Narodowy), and Młodzież Wszechpolska[55] – had the same ultra-nationalist ideologies as the anti-Semitic politicians that implemented the rules that had forced him onto the ghetto bench eighty years before (Cała, 2012). This was too much like déjà vu for Bauman, and he decided to stop travelling to Poland after the Wrocław brawl, though some of his friends and other observers saw it as a one-off occurrence of hooliganism spilling over that was directed at the city's mayor.

In 2015, Adam Michnik tried to organize a symposium for his ninetieth birthday, but Bauman's word was final: 'I will never return to Poland.' In a letter to his friend, Bauman wrote that he felt he had been evicted from Poland for the third time in his life.[56]

The young hotheads weren't the only ones to attack Bauman. In 2014, Andrzej Przyłębski, a professor of philosophy from Poznań University, wrote a letter to the German philosophical journal *Information Philosophie* disputing the character of the attacks on Bauman at Wrocław.[57] The students had no anti-Semitic intent, he argued – they were justified because the KBW unit Bauman led was equivalent to the SS. While other academics wrote in to denounce Przyłębski's letter, such opinions circulated among some faculty members, who attacked Bauman for failing to apologize for his engagement with communism and its security formations. While these critics speak only of Bauman's communist past, and not his Jewish origin, the stereotype of Judaeo-communism remains powerful in Poland, and hateful opinions are expressed even at the universities.[58]

After the German journal controversy ended, a new protest against Bauman arose. On 1 May 2016, a large photograph of Bauman was burned during a right-wing demonstration[59] promoting 'POLexit' – the idea that Poland should follow Great Britain in divorcing the EU (to avoid Islamization, the Right said). Supporters of the extreme-right groups said Bauman's image was being burned 'because of his opinions and his curriculum'.[60] But xenophobia was growing in Poland, where anti-Semitic and anti-immigrant opinions were increasingly acceptable. The following year, a mannequin representing a Jew was burned in the central square of Wrocław.

In 2014, some months after his talk in Wrocław, Bauman was having a smoke in Warsaw airport while changing planes for Tallinn, where he was giving a talk. There, in the middle of an international airport, a man attacked Bauman, shouting racial slurs and calling him a criminal and dirty communist. Such attacks could no longer be categorized as minor excesses. Bauman's past had suddenly returned to haunt him. Perhaps it was this moment that decided Bauman to write his last book, *Retrotopia*?

Following his Shadow . . .

The final year of Bauman's life – 2016 – was an Italian year. In June, Aleksandra and Zygmunt left for Cagliari – the capital city of Sardinia, where they were invited for a city festival in one of the 'happiest' places in the world, despite its high level of unemployment and low median income. Bauman was invited to give a key lecture, and happiness was one of his preferred topics. Bauman would ask friends whether they were happy and what made them happy. Was it possible to be happy? Had God not condemned us to permanent suffering? Listeners at Bauman's talk remembered it as a very emotional one. Sardinia is an exceptional place and all that Bauman loved was there: good wine, excellent food, astonishing landscapes with a unique quality of light so appreciated by artists. One of Bauman's favourite thinkers, Antonio Gramsci, was from Sardinia. Bauman had read *Letters from Prison* at the beginning of his sociological life, and he owed much to the book, which kept Marxism from being ruined for him. And so, although he had never been to Sardinia before, Bauman felt almost at home. It was also a part of Italy that he loved very much.

'In Europe he enjoyed going to Italy most of all', Jasińska-Kania said:

He loved Italian people, food, landscapes, cities, monuments, and museums. We both especially admired the massive attendance at the Festivals of Philosophy, and the large audiences at lectures, which is a specific and enchanting characteristic of Italian culture. Coming to Italy for such events was a very festive occasion for us. Zygmunt always was happy to meet his friends in Italy, and it was here that he found his most valued co-writers or collaborators in publishing his works.

Italian engagements gave Bauman some new energy, but his health was starting to decline. His heart was weak, his hearing limited, his vision getting poorer. Bauman complained of being more and more isolated from the world. He was writing *Retrotopia*, a work dedicated to Aleksandra. The world he observed and analysed for years was shifting its focus to the past. People were looking backward and plunging into dangerous extremes. The memory of our societies was shorter than the lifespan of a person. It was as if we needed another war to remember how deadly war was. Were we doomed to repeat the same tragedies that had killed so many people?

Finishing this project, Bauman wrote to his old friend Janet Wolff, asking her to collaborate on the next one:

> I wonder, dear Janet wise, beautiful, and excelling by all scores, what your response would be were you to receive a suggestion of engaging (or trying to) in a dialogue-book on culture(s) with an old man before the arthritis reaches his brains? A conversation addressed not to fellow academics, but to culture's practitioners and cultural practices' objects (and probably containing more questions than answers – those, in Maurice Blanchot's verdict, curses of the questions)? Think freely, respond frankly. I'd fully understand if your response were that you can think of more attractive enjoyments in one's life! Such would be probably my response to a similar suggestion . . .[61]

His brain never did give out, but the rest of his body did. His final months saw the cancellation of many trips and talks, which he excused with gracious letters (which always included the texts of the talks he had been unable to give). However, he had a last dream to fulfil and he wanted at any price to realize it. Bauman was singularly interested in the papacy of Jorge Mario Bergoglio, Pope Francis, who had broken the convention of an imperial, opulent Vatican, setting an example with his modest lifestyle and proximity to ordinary people. This was closer to the Christian message of charity and empathy, but also compatible with a socialist approach (focusing on the care of the weaker and less privileged in society). Bauman felt he had a lot in common with the Pope, despite the contrasts imposed by belonging to different spiritual systems. Bauman and Pope Francis were both public celebrities whose past was connected with dictatorial regimes and civil war. They both had slightly tarnished issues in their past (Bauman's KBW period, Bergoglio's

activity during Argentina's military Junta). Both were accused by
the press of having been active supporters of bad regimes. But,
most importantly, both Bergoglio and Bauman were focused on the
weakest parts of society and the future of the world. For Bauman,
Papa Francesco represented hope. And the Pope, apparently, had
some interest in Bauman.

'In Florence, there was a Monsignor Paglia, who had a very close
relationship to Francis', said Stanisław Obirek: 'Paglia wanted to
bring them closer [Bauman and the Pope]. He found that Francis
needed intellectuals because he had intuition but lacked the language required to translate the intuitions – related to openness
and dialogue – in an understandable way. Zygmunt was already
impressed by Francis. And it ended with the invitation for Bauman
to come to Assisi.'[62]

The Community of Sant'Egidio, known for charity work and dialogues for tolerance, organized a conference in Assisi in September
2016 and a meeting was set up with Pope Francis during the conference. Bauman's family and Aleksandra tried to persuade him to
cancel his trip, but Bauman would not be stopped. 'I would crawl
to meet him', he told Jasińska-Kania. They met, exchanging some
words of respect and hope: 'Bauman compared Pope Francis to a
light in the tunnel in the search for the survival and integration of
humanity, and the Pope laughed, jokingly saying that it was the first
time in his life that he heard the metaphor of a tunnel being applied
to him' (Jasińska-Kania, 2018).

Two months later, Bauman and Jasińska-Kania were back in
Italy for the last time together. This was a short stay – two nights
in Florence. The title of the talk was 'The End of the World' and
it was Bauman's last. The analysis of terms such as 'the end of
the world' and 'the end of time' was his adieu to an Italian public
that had always shown interest in Bauman's work. Back in Leeds,
Bauman felt worse than ever. The family kept all his plans to the
minimum – no more visitors or collaborators; focus on the family.[63]
The daughters and Aleksandra surrounded Zygmunt with love. The
priority was to improve his health, though it appeared increasingly
hopeless. He was under medical care at home – since Janina's illness,
he had hated hospitals, but despite this he always sought his care in
the NHS, whatever its imperfections. As he did in his life in other
situations, he maintained his life philosophy to the end. There was
no reason to take more from life than the minimum – no special
treatment.

There was a final Christmas celebration, and then, welcoming
the New Year 2017, Bauman said: 'It will be a short year.' Indeed.
Zygmunt Bauman died on 9 January 2017.

He followed his Shadow . . .

Conclusion

Legacy

It will continue . . .

Zygmunt Bauman (1992: 18)

On 19 November 2018, Bauman's friend Tomasz Kowalski created a singular monument in Poznań to celebrate what would have been his friend Zygmunt Bauman's ninety-third birthday. He sculpted Bauman's initials, ZB, in blocks of ice 93 centimetres in diameter and had them placed on Prusa Street, near the house where Bauman was born in 1925. What could be more appropriate than this ephemeral piece of art, which, from a solid, became liquid and disappeared with time. Bauman, who declared that he did not like official celebrations and monuments, would certainly have accepted this liquid homage from his artist friend.

Without a doubt, Zygmunt Bauman's work has particular relevance in capturing the most important changes of the twentieth and early twenty-first centuries. Bauman is a major scholarly figure in sociology, philosophy and cultural studies, and his work will be discussed and developed at conferences, symposiums and institutes for years. Bauman wrote during most of his life and his works contain a variety of content, styles and forms. They were written and published in a multitude of languages for a variety of audiences. Perhaps the best way to delineate his legacy is to consider the three major periods of his intellectual activity: Polish, British and global.[1]

In the first period, Bauman wrote in Polish for an academic audience in Poland, though his texts were translated into other languages (mainly English, but also French, Czech, Hebrew, etc.). Early in his career, Bauman openly supported a diversity of scientific traditions and opposed a dogmatic Marxist approach. 'Let all flowers bloom', he wrote: 'The optimal conditions for the development of scientific philosophy and sociology can only arise when in the centres educating philosophers and sociologists and at universities there are various kinds of philosophy and sociology representing a variety of scientific schools' (Bauman, 1956: 6). During his Polish period, which ended abruptly in 1968, Bauman also published some works addressed to a wider audience.

During the second period (1968–2000), Bauman's writing was mainly directed towards Anglophone scholars. His first book published in English, in 1972, *Between Class and Elite: The Evolution of the British Labour Movement. A Sociological Study*, was a translation of a book published in 1960 in Polish, so it can be considered as belonging to the Polish period of his career. Between 1968 and 1972, there was a transitional period, during which Bauman continued his previous works and wrote about Poland and Eastern Europe. The second English book, *Culture as Praxis* (1973), was a translation from Polish. He began writing his own work in English in the early 1980s, and acquired international academic recognition in 1987 with *Legislators and Interpreters: On Modernity, Post-Modernity, Intellectuals*. His academic masterpiece, *Modernity and the Holocaust*, was published in 1989, establishing Bauman as a 'classic' author in sociology and gaining him a firm place in the literature. Additional books devoted to modernity and post-modernity made his interpretation of social dynamics accessible to a growing circle of readers. *Thinking Sociologically: An Introduction for Everyone*, published in 1990, emphasized his wish to tell the stories of Western society to Western readers. *Mortality, Immortality and Other Life Strategies*, published in 1992, was not a bestseller but won wide recognition from specialists. A post-modern vision of our world had become the connective tissue of his 1990s writing, a vision that crystallized over the decade and is perceptible in his work on globalization processes and consumerism. This intellectual process of shaping the dynamics of reality is clearly represented in *The Bauman Reader*, compiled by Peter Beilharz, which reinforced Bauman's reputation as a classic twentieth-century intellectual. It was released in 2000, the same year that *Liquid Modernity* became a master synthesis of Bauman's previous analyses of social change and a starting point for other publications that reinforced and popularized his vision of a 'liquid world'. With the publication of this book, Bauman debuted the last period of his activity.

At this point, Bauman's work broke out of its academic framework and scholarly conventions to reach a wider audience. The multiple forms of expression Bauman mastered, however, were based on common philosophical and sociological references, similar more or less well-known intellectuals (philosophers, sociologists, anthropologists, political scientists, journalists) and artists – works of fiction, poetry and film. In this later period, even popular culture forms like television programmes became sources of reflection about changing contemporary societies. Bauman at this point also changed the focus of his expression to topics of more general interest: private relationships, love, happiness, consumption and loneliness, as well as the processes of individualization, globalization, inequality and poverty, discrimination and immigration.

Bauman's prolificacy attracted criticism – the most common being that his work was repetitive. While this is no doubt true, his repeated emphasis on certain themes led Bauman's books to reach a wider audience, establishing him as a teacher who invited society to look in the mirror and understand what it saw. Bauman's ability to reach and draw a large public to accept the 'liquid' metaphor established him as a leading global intellect. In his final period of activity, Bauman no longer pretended to publish for a scholarly audience. He himself mentioned that he was recycling his ideas and the ideas of others. He used second-hand data not because he did not know how to do empirical research, but rather out of a desire to reach a larger public.

Although Bauman's 'global' books should be read as the engaged writing of a public intellectual, they gained a scholarly following in some areas. The academic world gradually accepted his style of communication, and in several countries his legacy has found a home – for example, in Scandinavian universities and business schools.[2] There are Polish Baumanist philosophers, sociologists, anthropologists and cultural studies scholars, and his work is embraced by academics in South America and Southern Europe, particularly in Italy, Spain, Portugal and Brazil.

The approach Bauman took in his later work also has had an impact on pedagogy. University professors seeking to keep the attention of their young audience as they open new topics of discussion have found Bauman's approach to be very efficient. Academic teachers use Bauman as a link enabling them to communicate with students who are just starting their higher education in social sciences and the humanities. For many members of this audience, Bauman's are the only books they have read to learn about how our society works.[3] Knowing this, academic teachers employ Bauman as a backstage reference who can help build and frame an analysis for understanding society's dynamic (liquid) processes. These late-stage books enable a connection between non-academic and academic work, a passage between those two different publics.

Bauman's decision to change his audience after he retired paid off. In a period in which surveys announce the death of the book, many of Bauman's are bestsellers, translated into thirty-four languages, with record-breaking sales among people who, it is claimed, can't focus on a long newspaper article. Who would have imagined that so many young people, seemingly lost in a sea of electronic games, avatars, virtual love affairs, tweets, chats and the latest smartphone would buy and enjoy so many of his books? How did he manage this?

Bauman knew how to depict and interpret the social dynamics that shape Western civilization. He shed a light on consumerism, commodification, globalization, neocolonialism, migration and the liquidification of social relationships, processes and structures. Bauman knew how to address a 'difficult audience' – he'd been dealing with them since his youth. When he introduced semi-illiterate soldiers in the Soviet Union to the complex issues of social equality, justice, Marxism and socialism, Bauman did not use the vocabulary of the social sciences. He simply explained the future world those soldiers would have to live in. Bauman acquired these communication skills very young in a setting of immense pressures; no doubt, we could believe that he had a 'natural' ability in this area. His listeners followed him in the Army during World War II, in military schools after the war, and at universities in different countries. In the last period of his life, Bauman maintained this relationship as a storyteller and translator of the contemporary world, but this time with an audience that, by its enthusiastic size, confirmed the rightness of his interpretations. The public, through his work, gained an appreciation of what was new in their lives, a reality that had nothing in common with the experience of earlier generations. Thanks to Bauman, these phenomena became intelligible, if depressing. His vision of a liquid world convinced many people.

In an era in which Western societies seem to have abandoned the notion that wisdom is transmitted by wise old men and women, Bauman managed to reach children 'born in the time of liquidity', although he was old enough to be a great-grandfather to many of them. With so many bestsellers, Bauman may have become a victim of his own success, played out by calls to write about every topic under the sun. Public expectations grew proportionately to the number of his published books. He became a sort of guru against his will, celebrated for 'opening our eyes' to certain social phenomena, sensitizing the public to what it was failing to see – an antidote to consumerism, a lens through which to see and comprehend poverty, inequality and discrimination. Bauman's readers were an important part of anti-globalist movements such as Occupy. He also inspired some quantity of young people to follow scholarly pursuits in the social sciences – putting on their 'Bauman glasses' made them want to learn more.

Bauman gave no prescriptions for how to live – everyone had to find their own way; they could continue their liquid lives or engage in change. Bauman declined to predict the future. He spoke about the present in relation to a past he knew well. The secret of his success as a convincing translator and interpreter of contemporary times was certainly related to his long and rich biography, his *longue durée* perspective on the twentieth-century European experience, his own experience of repeated exile and estrangement. Bauman would disagree with this hypothesis linking the intellectual to his life story, saying that if it were so he could only write about his own experiences.

He avoided writing a memoir, though he was preparing a biography with Keith Tester in the final years of his life. In 2015, Bauman told me: 'nothing interesting happened in my life. Nothing specific – many people went through all those turbulences. I am just a typical product of my times.' This was true, to an extent, although of course the entire generation of Polish Jews born in the 1920s experienced dramatically 'interesting' times, and the sequence of his own life is nothing short of extraordinary. His was a life of struggle within a set of systems that were anything but homogeneous. In Poland, living under a system that exerted great pressure on all its citizens, he chose a path that wavered between compromise and independence. After 1968, he refused to become an exiled specialist on Eastern Europe: an anti-leftist Sovietologist firmly within the camp of capitalism, liberalism and neoliberalism.

His uniqueness appears most acutely in the final period of his life, when he stepped out of an academic background to interact with a new public as a synthesizer of all the 'common experiences' he went through, transforming them into expressions of general values, a warning message addressed to the next generations. Others besides Bauman followed the duty of *Zahor* (remembrance) and *Tikkun Olam* (improving the world). Bauman did it in a way that drew the public's interest as few others have.

I would argue that Bauman was most successful in a realm related to his personal experience, in the permanent struggle between his identity and the identity assigned him by society: his *master status*. His life was the perfect example of the contradiction of status (Hughes, 1945). This occurred at school in Poznań, in the Polish Army, as a Polish professional, in Israel – whose policies towards the Palestinians he disagreed with – and again in Poland. In twentieth-century Poland, you were a Jew or a Pole – you had to choose. Bauman did not want to choose, yet Polish society continually pushed him out.

The Poles did little to endear themselves to the people they refused to admit into their tribe. If I had embraced the Polish view of the world, culture, history, and the 'Polish identity', it was hardly by invitation. Most Poles I knew did everything to force me to change my mind, they tried really hard to make me feel unwelcomed, foreign and undeserving. Yet if I did what they wanted me to do, I would confirm the very principle of tribalism, the tribal right to reject and to persecute, the very reason for hatred and suffering. The cause of hatred rejoices when it evokes a mirror-image tribal hatred as its response. And who

is more obliged to challenge the principle of tribalism and hatred, than
I – a Jew and a Pole? (Bauman, 1986/7: 42)

Even in Israel, Bauman felt he was in a society that could not
dispense with tribalism, to his great regret. Like many Jewish intellectuals, he supported a cosmopolitan version of Jewish identity.
Jews did not need to live in their own state. Their culture could
enrich any land where they were citizens. Bauman believed the
Jewish diaspora had a cultural mission, and he believed in the power
of the outsider, who, by nature of his or her being, was sensitive to
the underprivileged and believed in a better world:

> Our [Jews'] history has been a never ending lesson in what happens
> once the human race crumbles into tribes. The meaning of our history
> is all in that lesson. Setting ourselves as a tribe – as one tribe among
> many – we can only forfeit that meaning. Being truly Jewish means to
> strive for a world without tribes. A world which does not divide into
> mine and foreign people. (Bauman, 1986/7: 44)

As he told *Haaretz* in 2013:

> It hurts me, hurts me tremendously, to watch the forgetting and aban-
> donment of our collective mission and duty, imposed upon us by our
> tragic history, to alert the world, to not let it forget, about the evil
> endemic to any and all nationalist hatreds, to be in the forefront of the
> ongoing fight against the breeding of hatred, to remember the ambi-
> tion of the founders of Israel to 'be a light unto the nations'.

Via his writing, Bauman followed both prescriptions: *Tikkun Olam*
and *Zahor*.

In Leeds, Bauman was a Pole, a welcomed immigrant. His
Jewishness was not a stigma, nor was it a special advantage. He was
seen as a Pole with the typical Polish culture of hospitality, opulence
in food and drink, vodka, talk and smoke. In Leeds, Bauman's identity did not contrast with his master status. He played the role he
had chosen: that of university professor and Polish émigré.

On the road (except in Poland), he was the famous old man with
a lot of grey hair and pipe smoke, an institution whose books sold in
thirty-four languages, a frequent flier with cachet and celebrity rare
among academics. In most parts of the world, people recognized his
work. They spoke in the terms Bauman had invented and saw the
world through his lens. Most of them disregarded or were ignorant
of his status issues: Pole or Jew, communist or socialist, philosopher
or sociologist.

He had achieved something almost impossible to attain – a unique,
singular master status, as none other than Zygmunt Bauman.

Appendix

Working on Bauman

The work on this book started in 2013 as a chapter project for a book with the provisional title 'Looking in the Mirrors – the Careers of Sociologists'. The idea, developed with a colleague – Christophe Brochier, a French sociologist – was to create sociological miniature studies devoted to selected aspects of an intellectual career, and illustrated by case studies of chosen sociologists. Bauman was an extreme case of a career determined by big politics and history; his case offered points of reflection about scholars' capacity to overcome the limits of their context, including forced changes in primary writing language. Bauman transformed into an asset a series of forced migrations that could have been disadvantageous, or even disastrous, in many lives. Moreover, his late fame challenges the common idea of early career development as a *sine qua non* of a successful scholarly career.

I should reveal that I was not a 'Baumanist' at the outset of this work, and our choice of Bauman for the initial book project was influenced by his biography and not at all by his work. As a sociologist educated in France, I never read him extensively (Bauman is present in the French academic universe mostly in the area of cultural studies). In our laboratory, focused on field research, Bauman was perceived as a kind of essayist and public intellectual. I had read only extracts from *Modernity and the Holocaust* and skimmed his biographical- conversational books (in Polish). Unlike most people who knew Zygmunt Bauman but were ignorant of the fact that his wife was also a writer, I had read two books published by Janina Bauman immediately after their Polish publication. I was an immediate fan of her work and recommended it to my colleagues and students. In short, before 2011, I knew Zygmunt Bauman primarily as 'the husband of Janina Bauman'.

I first heard Bauman speak in 2011 when he gave the opening address for the new academic year at Collegium Civitas in Warsaw, and was fully impressed by his talk; the beauty of language that nobody used, in an elegant and slightly outdated fashion, struck me deeply. I only began reading Bauman's texts several months before interviewing him in 2013. I had been lucky in gaining the support of sociology professor Aleksandra Jasińska-Kania, his second life-partner, who convinced Bauman that my text about his career would be useful to other scholars. He accepted my proposition of the interview at his home in Leeds. It was 1 November, some months after the events in Wrocław. The discussion lasted over two hours and the topics concerned his sociological career path. At the end of that interview, I asked him if I could consult his files in the IPN archives. He responded that I didn't need his permission, which was true, yet I preferred to have his agreement since the IPN collections include former secret service archives with personal and sensitive data, much of it of obscure origin and uncertain validity. Bauman was not at all against the idea. His only request was that, while at the IPN, I try to find some documents the customs services had seized from him in 1968. 'These were my manuscripts', he said, 'and most importantly, the diaries of my wife'.

Back in Warsaw, I visited the IPN archives, and my project of a chapter devoted to Bauman's career took a new form. I plunged into the many boxes, folders and electronic files, diving ever deeper into Bauman's past, which was the ostensible source of the 'scandal' that led to the Polish right-wing media's pursuit and harassment of him.

But, the deeper I went into the documents, a more nuanced picture emerged. And as that careful reading progressed, I became upset, as a person, and at the same time scientifically fascinated by what I found in the available sources and the image of Bauman that was projected and maintained by the majority of news media and part of the scholarly milieu in Poland. I was also surprised that Bauman had never tried to defend himself or share his personal story, but, after all, this was his right, and it was also a common story among his generation. And it is a complicated story, whose understanding requires a good knowledge of Polish history. It took me almost six years to write this account.

I felt a kind of 'scientific pressure' – I didn't pay a cent for my education in Poland and France, and my research positions were always funded by taxpayers. That gave me a feeling of being part of a social contract, which in turn impelled me to clarify Bauman's past and to defend him from misunderstanding and erroneous accusations, and to expose the impact of xenophobia, nationalism and anti-Semitism in the past to help liberate us from these old ghosts.

In late 2013, I began trying to find publications that explained Bauman's 'Polish life'. All the available texts were partial and contained erroneous information – and that wasn't counting the political propaganda and products of anti-Semitic hate speech. Even in the scientific literature or respectable news media, I found many misunderstandings. For example, one commonly reads the sentence, 'Bauman was born to a poor Jewish family.' The statement implies that, as a poor Jew growing up in Poland in the 1930s, Bauman must have spoken Yiddish and attended religious school, *yeshiva* – an observant Jew who helped his father out with his small business. Nothing is true in that picture. Bauman was born in an 'assimilated' household and his mother tongue was Polish. He attended synagogue – one attended by other assimilated Jews – only sporadically, and was enrolled in Polish public schools. Nor did he ever help his father, who was an accountant. The family did have financial problems. The crisis of the 1930s that hit the European middle class hit the Bauman family as well. The many CVs that Bauman filled out – they were very popular documents during the Polish People's Republic[1] – did refer to his family as poor, but for strategic purposes. The intent was to hide his father's 'bourgeois' origin, since, in the new Poland, connections to capital were a huge drawback. *Bauman: A Biography* presents and deconstructs many similar stories, legends and failures of comprehension.

During the writing of this book, I was disappointed by the huge gap between what I discovered in documents and the public image attached to Bauman's name (in Poland, but also abroad). Since there was no well-documented text about Bauman's life, I decided to write one. I conducted interviews with people who were his collaborators, friends, family members and students. Among them were people who remembered Bauman from his Polish years, including those who were engaged, as he was, in the implementation of communism *à la polonaise*. I tried to understand those times, when the new Poland was a real concrete project. I spoke to people who told me that engagement in building communism had meant a way of ending the anti-Semitism that determined the contours of their lives in prewar Poland. As Bauman's colleague, philosopher Stefan Morawski, wrote: 'Julian Stryjkowski[2] convincingly explained that by becoming a Communist he ceased to be a Jew' (Morawski, 1996: 111). For Bauman, as for this whole generation of Poles who were perceived only as Jews in prewar Poland – and as second-class citizens because of it – communism offered the real promise of a world without ethnic discrimination. To examine the phenomenon of communist engagement as a way of losing the stigma of being Jewish, I combined historical scholarship with sociological analysis.

I treat the documents I uncovered in various archives (Party, university, secret services) as products of people acting in particular circumstances, rather than as 'objective evidence'. For this reason, all the documents I use are cited extensively and analysed in detail, so the reader can understand their significance and read them in the language of their time to appreciate the context of Bauman's life. From this perspective, the simple contemporary reading of some chosen piece of documentation paled into insignificance. The story is much more complex than it seemed to be, which does not mean that Bauman was involved in some obscure activity for which he would be charged. Behind those documents lurk complex processes that might escape a contemporary reader. Extensive presentation of the historical frame is necessary for understanding of events. War, civil war and postwar, Stalinism and socialist dictatorship influenced the trajectory of everyone who lived through them. To judge people in those circumstances without knowing their situation and their particular knowledge at the moment is simply unscientific.

As a sociologist, following the interactionist paradigm and Hughes' 'understanding the participant's perspective', I cannot pursue any approach other than seeking deep comprehension of the events and processes in their context. So, presentation of the circumstances takes up a lot of space here. Through Bauman's life, we can understand the major historical and political changes that occurred in Poland and Europe during and after the war. He lived through major tragic events that occurred in this part of the world and experienced prewar discrimination, World War II and Nazi occupation, escape, a refugee's fate in the Soviet Union, enrolment in the Polish Army, incorporation in military intelligence, an academic role under Stalinism and the Thaw, the Cold War and international academic mobility, an anti-Semitic purge in 1968, student riots, expulsion, forced migration to Israel, and departure a short period later for Leeds, England, where he found finally, a stable work environment and, eventually, a degree of world celebrity. Were a Hollywood director to put his hand to Bauman's life he would be accused of 'overdoing it'.

Bauman was never really enthusiastic about sharing his story. He expressed reserve at our first meeting, and again during our second interview, in November 2015, when I told him I planned to write his biography. He opposed the idea of a biography ('there are so many interesting topics – my life was not really exceptional – someone is already working on it', he told me). Yet he did not refuse an interview. This was typical of Bauman; he rarely refused to meet people or to accede to their wishes. During the second interview, I recorded his recital of the war period – painful memories of escape, isolation, engagement and fighting. Some of the information was public already, some was new. It was an emotional exercise for Bauman – explanation made him tired and it moved him to be taken back to this difficult time. He was not enthusiastic about a discussion focused only on himself. Without the help of Aleksandra Jasińska-Kania, who, days before our meeting, discussed Bauman's younger years with him to stimulate his memory, my interview would not have succeeded.

While it was difficult to discuss his past with Bauman, two other people had done some of this work before me. The first was Tomasz

Kwaśniewski, a journalist with *Gazeta Wyborcza*, the leading Polish newspaper, which regularly published interviews with Bauman as well as some of his writing. While many Polish journalists wrote about Bauman, only Kwaśniewski was able to enter into the kind of close relationship that enables private confidences. In English, Bauman discussed his past with Keith Tester. His former Ph.D. student, disciple and close friend was designated by Bauman as his biographer. They started to work on this project and exchanged e-mails, but after several months of work Tester resigned. The major problem for him was the impossibility of dealing with the Polish side of the biography (historical complexity, cultural and linguistic specificity). When I arrived on the scene, Keith Tester offered me his huge, unlimited support and deep friendship. He followed my work, chapter by chapter, and shared all his material with me – a rare example of scientific exchange and generosity in the competitive scholarly world. This relationship was abruptly cut off by Keith's unexpected death in January 2019.

Access to the private Tester–Bauman correspondence that was a preparation for Tester's planned biography of Bauman was a great help to my book, though it did not influence the core narrative. Bauman's death in January 2017 was the turning point in my work. When I met him, he was in excellent form and I expected he would read my work one day. Bauman was neither my guru nor my friend, but I was happy to find the family documents stuck in the IPN archives – especially the precious Janina Bauman journal written in the Warsaw Ghetto and confiscated in 1968 by the Polish authorities.

My gut told me that one of the core issues in Bauman's life – if not the principal one – was the tension between his Polish and his Jewish identity. This was further confirmed at the end of 2017 when the Bauman family gave me an unpublished autobiographical essay that Bauman had written in the form of a seventy-page letter to his daughters and grandchildren, entitled: 'The Poles, The Jews, and I: An Investigation into Whatever Made Me What I Am'. The text, the first part written in 1986/7, the second twenty years later, contains his family story and the reconstruction of his feelings at the time. Bauman was perfectly aware of the risks and limits of such reconstructions. The text, written in English, contributed significantly to my assessment of documents, books and other material gathered to shape this biography.

Bauman's private archive, part of the Special Collection Archive of Leeds University, is another rich resource. Access to these private documents completed the complex picture that I sketched out for this book – the story of a life trapped by History, a single human swept up in the storms of his time who, like some others, managed to keep hold of the quasi-religious belief that his action could shift the winds. When Bauman realized that the storms were too strong and humans too weak to modify their deadly impacts, he started to reflect on the storms the way older, sage people do.

Bauman was not a prophet. He was a scholar – philosopher – public intellectual. *Bauman: A Biography* is about his trajectory, and transformation, from activist to global thinker. How did this happen?

Bauman: A Biography is my attempt to answer this question, a biography that chronologically traces the life of Zygmunt Bauman as a witness and active participant of his times. The approach employed in this work is ingrained in the sociological tradition of the University of Chicago, where, more than a century ago, amid a rapid influx of immigrants, a group of scholars developed the tools for analysing people's life trajectories. They studied life stories as dynamic paths resulting from interactions with others (and, to a lesser extent than today, as the results of individual decisions). The Chicago sociologists placed the face-to-face relationships of people in the larger context. In this regard, this book shows how politics, history and economics shaped Bauman's life, and the lives of others. The dynamics of these macro processes are related in the book from the micro perspective. Bauman's life is a story of a human fate and the limits of his agency – a topic frequently analysed by Bauman himself, though without reference to his own personal experiences. The feeling of identity (Who am I?) and *master status* (How do others perceive me?) are two axes that cross in this work.

Everett Hughes (one of Chicago's leading sociologists) created in 1945 the concept of *master status*. With this term, he defines the social identity imposed by others.[3] There are also less precise definitions of master status as the dominant role, whatever it may be (student, friend, son, Scottish male). I will stick to the Hughesian analysis. To explain his concept, Hughes (1945) employed an example from the medical world in the 1940s USA, where racial divisions were clearcut. Hughes' Ph.D. student Oswald Hall studied medical careers in the city, focusing on the role of race in careers.[4] Hall elaborated the list of expectations that a medical doctor had to fulfil. Master status converges exactly with this stereotypical image attached to a given profession, position or status. Contradiction of status occurs when someone tries to play a role while lacking the necessary features imposed by society. This situation occurs often when people from discriminated groups occupy prestigious positions, or try to.

Bauman's experience was a common one in Poland. Bauman had many other roles: student, soldier, officer, scholar, academic, father, emigrant and immigrant. But the status that dominated was his ethnic-cultural origin, which imposed perceptions and strongly influenced his interactions with others.

The agency of an individual living in permanent tension between identity and master status is highly limited. Here I have explored how Bauman dealt with those tensions, and whether he was able to resolve them. *Bauman: A Biography* focuses on the negotiations between roles that he wished to play and those which were imposed on him. Bauman implemented precise strategies which enabled him to manage his trajectory within a restricted range of possibilities.

This book describes the significant people in Bauman's life, and his activity and choices as a scholar and observer of society who wished to create a better world. Bauman's life is not presented as an exceptional path of a genius, but as a trajectory of an individual who, during most of his life, was in some sense emblematic of his generation. I base this view on my study of scientists who belonged to the same generation and shared similar biographies. Their vitality, engagement, work ethics and professional activity, combined with passions, made their life achievements outstanding. Most of them shared the important biographical component of familial cultural capital, and limits imposed by belonging to a discriminated population.

My perspective is also a consequence of sociological training on occupations, and especially the study of careers. The concept of the career is employed to depict Bauman's trajectory under various dynamics. I am following here the interactionist approach developed in the studies of creative professions by Howard Becker (1963, 1982). Putting social interaction in the foreground shows that an individual career is not a consequence of a solitary ascension to success, but rather a suite of collaborations and relationships that shape and push ahead the work of specific individuals. I am following Becker in his 'social worlds' approach. This concept was elaborated by interactionists and concerns a social universe, a social milieu of a given activity with its own discourse (culture).[5] Becker approached writing as a craft. For him, the craft is a basic element of the creative work. (Becker, 1982: ch. 13) Writing is a solitary activity, but an intellectual career results from many sources of inspiration, exchanges and discussions. In this book, I have sought to bring out from the shadows elements that usually remain hidden when someone becomes famous. This approach helps us to understand how Zygmunt Bauman became a Global Thinker – how he went from being a student facing racial discrimination in western Poland, to a teenage war refugee living deep in the Soviet Union, to becoming one the most read and famous intellectuals of the early twenty-first century.[6]

Notes

Introduction

1 The lecture had been organized by the Friedrich Ebert Stiftung, an intellectual branch of the German Social Democratic Party; the independent Ferdinand Lasalle Centre of Social Thought; and the Department of Social and Political Philosophy of the University of Wrocław (Chmielewski, 2015). It was described as a 'fusion' of Jewishness (Bauman and Ferdinand Lasalle were Jews – the latter buried in the Wrocław Jewish Cemetery) and Germanness – since the Ebert Stiftung is a German institution – and Leftness, since the speakers and organizers could be classified in that category. An analysis and detailed account of the event by its organizer, Professor Adam Chmielewski, can be read at https://adamjchmielewski. blogspot.com/2015/07/academies-of-hatred.html.
2 Ibid.
3 After Liberation, the NSZ units continued their anti-communist struggle and attacked groups tied to the new Soviet-style political system in Poland.
4 Narodowe Odrodzenie Polski (NOP: National Rebirth of Poland), Polish national radical and nationalist political party that uses the symbols of interwar fascist organizations. The National Radical Camp – ONR – was established in 1981, and in 1992 registered as a legal party (Cała, 2012; Rudnicki, 2018).
5 This Polish right-wing nationalist organization refers to the movement with a name that existed during the Second Polish Republic. Since 2012, the group has been registered as an association (see Rudnicki, 1985, 2018).
6 About the methodology employed in this book, see the Appendix.
7 For more, see the Appendix.
8 The content of Bauman's work is only briefly and very partially discussed in this book, which gives a very detailed account of his life and career but leaves a detailed examination of his arguments to others. Most of his work after he took up a position at the University of Leeds is in English, so I decided to focus my account more on the lesser-known aspects of Bauman's life.

1 A Happy Childhood 'Under Such Circumstances'

1 The article was published simultaneously in the newspaper *Gazeta Warszawska*.

2 Roman Dmowski was one of the most powerful politicians before, and in the first decades after, partition. He co-founded Narodowa Demokracja (the National Democracy Party), which was built on a nationalist ideology and powerful patriotic feelings. One of the core slogans in the multicultural country was the 'liberation' of Polish society from Jews. Strong anti-Semitism and open hostility to non-Christian Poles (in 1931, 75.2 per cent of the population were Roman Catholics) were the driving forces of this party. The party, known as ND or Endecja, from its acronym, was particularly popular in the Wielkopolska region, whose capital was Poznań. The ND's presence in local government in Wielkopolska was among the strongest in Poland, and the extreme-right newspapers (*Kurjer Poznański* prominent among them) that upheld its viewpoint sold briskly. Anti-Semitic texts were common. Młodzież Wszechpolska, the youth wing of ND, created in 1922, aimed to exclude Jewish students and professors from university positions, and lobbied Parliament to pass laws imposing an anti-Jewish ban. As Brykczyński reports, Roman Dmowski was 'co-author of the doctrine of national egoism. He managed the work of the Polish delegation in Versailles (1918), but he never managed to take power in the country. He believed that Poles are doomed to an eternal struggle for survival with other ethnic groups, especially Jews and Germans' (Brykczyński, 2017: 31).

3 Text entitled: 'The Poles, The Jews, and I: An Investigation into Whatever Made Me What I Am' (1986/7). I am deeply grateful to the Bauman family for the permission to cite this important document.

4 A large literature about Polish anti-Semitism has emerged in the past decades in Polish – Cała (2012), Tokarska-Bakir (2012, 2018), Keff (2013) and Michnik and Marczyk (2017) – as well as in English (Blobaum, 2005). This complex topic will be largely discussed in the last chapter.

5 *Longue durée* is a concept (elaborated in the late 1940s) of the French historian, and member of the Annales school, Fernand Braudel; it concerns the historical analysis of the particular phenomenon examined across several epochs.

6 Brykczyński (2017: n. 33).

7 'Marshal Józef Piłsudski, former socialist revolutionary and freedom fighter, was the first leader of the reborn Poland. He spoke about himself as a Lithuanian, and became a symbol of the state idea of Polishness, which accepted everyone who was ready to be part of the Polish nation, regardless of their ethnic origin or religion' (Brykczyński, 2017: 28).

8 Author of *Imagined Communities: Reflections on the Origin and Spread of Nationalism* (1983).

9 https://sztetl.org.pl/pl/miejscowosci/p/586-poznan/100-demografia/21585-demografia. About 2,000 people were counted in the statistics as 'Jews'.

10 An illustration of Endecja's support in Poznań was the massive reaction to the murder of the first Polish president, Gabriel Narutowicz, by a fanatical supporter of Dmowski's party, the artist Niewiadomski. People put altars in their windows, and Poznań's streets were full of the image of Niewiadomski, who was treated as a national hero since he had killed a 'mason' elected with the support of ethnic minorities. (I would like to thank Wojciech Grondys for this observation.) Poland in 1920 was divided into two political currents: socialist and open to the minorities, and extreme-right anti-Semitic. After the election of the first Polish president, demonstrations and battles between the supporters of the two currents created an environment of insecurity and instability (people believed to

be Jews were harassed on the streets). As Brykczyński showed, the hostility focused on the Jewish community resulted in the deadly attack on Narutowicz, although this was presented as the act of a mentally ill person (Brykczyński, 2017).

11 I would like to thank Leszek Kwiatkowski – a Hebrew specialist from Poznań University – for the suggestion of an English translation and the information about the term 'Jew-infested'; and Joanna Tokarska-Bakir – anthropologist and historian from Warsaw University – a specialist in Jewish studies, for the indication of another term: 'As for the word "zażydzenie" to mark the distance and to indicate the antisemitic genealogy, I would translate it in German: as verjudung, because in this language [it] appeared for the first time. You could of course give English term 'jewification', following the English translation of Heidegger's *Black Notebooks*, but then the word returns to the 'natural' anti-Semitism proper to the large masses lacking of memory' (quoted from private correspondence between IW and Joanna Tokarska-Bakir, June 2017).

12 https://sztetl.org.pl/en/towns/p/586-poznan/99-history/137881-history-of-community.

13 The change is well illustrated by the family of Polish-Israeli photographer Fira Mełamedzon-Salańska, Eastern Jews who had fled to Poznan. Mełamedzon-Salańska, ten years older than Zygmunt Bauman, was born in Russia but lived in Poznań from 1927 to 1939. '[T]he former Poznań Jews felt German, and after the creation of Polish state, most of them left the country' (Niziołek and Kosakowska, 2016:66).

14 Archiwum Panstwowe w Poznaniu - Karta meldunkowa Baumann (869). Here, Bauman's name has a double 'n', following German use.

15 All demographic data cited in this chapter – if without source – come from the website www.sztetl.org.pl.

16 Actually it was common practice to change such data even before World War II. In places where administration was not unified, or disrupted due to changes in regime or language, the archives were places of 'historical construction' more than a repertoire of facts.

17 In this part of Europe, the changes of language and alphabet and the co-existence of several languages spoken concurrently were not exceptional. This resulted from the multi-ethnic composition of territories, wars and occupations that took place over centuries. To this political instability we should add the irrelevance of family names, which only became widely used in the nineteenth century. Previously, only noble and aristocratic families employed their coats of arms and family name in a very ordered way (in relation to lands and properties, titles and positions).

18 Institute of National Remembrance (IPN) BU 0193/8207, p. 238.

19 By 'education', Bauman refers to general secular education.

20 I was unable to find his name.

21 IPN BU 0193/8207, p. 238.

22 One of the massive waves of emigration from Poland to Palestine took place in 1924–5 and is called Grabski's *Aliyah*. Grabski was prime minister at the head of a government that imposed high taxation on small peasants, artisans and shop owners, many of them Jews. (*Aliyah* is the term for Jewish immigration to Palestine, and later Israel, from the diaspora.)

23 *Melamed*: a teacher in Jewish religious schools.

24 Tomasz Kwaśniewski was at that time a journalist for *Gazeta Wyborcza*

(the most important Polish newspaper). He interviewed Zygmunt Bauman several times.

25 *GW* is *Gazeta Wyborcza*. The majority of interviews with Bauman were published in this newspaper.

26 *Kurjer Poznański*, 19 November 1925, R. 20 nr 313-31/49.

27 After Dmowski failed to obtain a mandate in 1912, the 'Endecs' organized a massive economic boycott of Jewish stores in Warsaw; this largely poisoned Polish–Jewish relations in the largest Polish city; Brykczyński (2017: 33). As Dmowski explained: 'The sons of great nations know how to go for bread or for a career, or to serve the interests of their people, [even] into the depths of wild Africa [if necessary] ... And here you will go among your compatriots, who will advise you, except the few, who fear the competition. And the competition will not be with Poles, but with the Jews – your fathers knew it and made it' (*Kurjer Poznański*, 18 November 1925, p. 2).

28 Bauman notes that his family was unable to afford a 'pianoforte' and instead had a smaller version of this instrument – an upright piano.

29 Author's interview with Zygmunt Bauman conducted in Leeds, 1 November 2015.

30 According to historian Natalia Aleksiun, 'Zionism – understood as the movement and ideology of the development of Jewish national consciousness through the establishment of its own state in Palestine and the Renaissance of the Hebrew language, was one of the most important phenomena in the recent history of Jews.' In the note on page 19: 'This term was used for the first time by Nathan Birnbaum in 1890 in the pages of the journal "Selbstemanzipation". He emphasized the necessity of creating a political party coordinating activities aimed at colonizing Palestine' (Aleksiun, 2002: 19).

31 Zygmunt's father settled in Israel after World War II.

32 See note 22.

33 In the English version of her book, Janina Bauman calls Zygmunt 'Konrad'. In the Polish version, she uses 'Zygmunt' (for further explanation, see final chapter).

2   A Pupil Like No Other

1 See chapter 1.

2 This is an old, as well as current, topic in sociology – from Thrasher's study of gangs in Chicago (1927) to Elijah Anderson's work, *Codes of the Streets* (2000). However, in Poznań's case, anti-Semitism plays a core role more than other urban teenage phenomena.

3 The concept 'democratic state' is a matter for discussion – interwar Poland's history was troubled, with many elements of a sterile democracy. Its prosperity also was relative, but interwar Poland never suffered the large-scale hunger crises experienced in other European countries.

4 Interview with Tomasz Kwaśniewski, *GW*, 21 November 2010.

5 I would like to thank Maciej Gdula for this story about the dog – he learned it from Aleksandra Jasińska-Kania, who was his Ph.D. mentor and the life-partner of Bauman in the last five years of his life.

6 CISZO schools (Tsentrale Shulorganizatsye), also absent in former Austrian territories.

7 Beginning in the 1920s, the BUND was a popular Jewish socialist party. Its official Yiddish name was Algemeyner Yidisher Arbeter Bund in Poyln. One of its leaders, Marek Edelman, a surgeon and hero of the Warsaw Ghetto Uprising, described its followers thus: 'The Bundists did not wait for the Messiah, nor did they plan to leave for Palestine. They believed that Poland was their country and they fought for a just, socialist Poland, in which each nationality would have its own cultural autonomy, and in which minorities' rights would be guaranteed' (quoted in the *Telegraph*, 4 October 2009: www.telegraph.co.uk/news/obituaries/politics-obituar ies/6259900/Marek-Edelman.html).

8 Włodzimierz Szer (1924–2013) was a scientist – in the last stage of his life, a professor in the New York University Medical School. Szer also produced a memoir (Szer, 2013); I interviewed him in 2011 in San Diego.

9 Marian Turski was born in Druskieniki, 26 June 1926. He survived the Łódź Ghetto, the Auschwitz-Birkenau camp, the Walk of the Dead. From 1945, he lived in Warsaw; he was a member of the youth section of the PPR (Polska Partia Robotnicza – the Polish Workers' Party) and worked for the PZPR (Polska Zjednoczona Partia Robotnicza – Polish United Workers' Party) press, in the historical department of the weekly *Polityka* from 1958. He is the vice president of the Jewish Historical Institute Association in Poland, and the head of the Council of the Museum of the History of Polish Jews; he is also a member of the International Auschwitz Council.

10 Kijek (citing Frost, 1998) says 80 per cent of Jewish children aged 7–14 were enrolled in public primary schools in Poland; he underlines the financial benefits (public schools were free, while the private religious schools popular in the Jewish community charged fees), and Polish government policy, which struggled with the private Jewish educational system – both its religious and non-religious schools (Kijek, 2010: 171).

11 According to Natalia Aleksiun, ORT was founded in 1880 under Czarist control. The organization supported occupational training – craftwork and artisanal education – among Jewish community members. From 1921, ORT became an international institution. For more, see www.jhi.pl/psj/ORT.

12 Hechaluc – not related to a particular party, a youth organization that aimed to educate young people in a Zionist-socialist way, and to prepare youth for *Aliyah*.

13 Zionist young pioneers, close to the Hitachduth Zionist-Socialist Party of Workers; Gordonia organized factories and kibbutzes and prepared people for emigration to Palestine.

14 The so-called Aryan paragraph was a racist restrictive regulation in place across Nazi Germany in various professions, corporations, associations, etc. A paragraph in these groups' guiding documents excluded people of 'non-Aryan race', and it was usually aimed at Jews. In interwar Poland, many institutions had an 'Aryan paragraph' that limited membership to Polish Catholics. See more in Natkowska (1999).

15 *Numerus nullus* – from Latin for 'number zero', refers to the total exclusion of certain groups of candidates for studies (Kopaliński, 1980: 679). The *Larousse* dictionary provides a fuller definition: 'discriminatory limitation of the number of persons admitted to the competition, a function, a grade – as conforming with the decision taken previously by an Authority'. In the context of academia, it was in practice an exclusion of a given group – in the case of interwar Poland (especially after 1935), Jews, but also Ukrainians and Belorussians.

16 In a paper devoted to the situation of Jewish university students, Aleksiun wrote: 'The Jewish Academic House served as a meeting place for students who gathered there for lectures and political discussions: Zionists, Bundists, folkists and Communists' (Aleksiun, 2014: 126).

17 'By 1937 Poland had five state-recognized universities, in Cracow, Warsaw, Lwow, Vilna and Poznan. There were also fifteen other major educational institutions. In the 1923–24 academic year, 8,325 Jews and 23,810 non-Jews were enrolled in the universities. By 1937–38, only 4,791 of the 48,168 students (10%) were Jewish' (Rabinowicz, 1964).

'Most of the students were enrolled in the faculties of law and philosophy. In 1932–33, Jewish students made up 8% of the medical school class, 2% in pharmacy ... There were 20 Jews among the 2,000 professors. Captain Peter Wright of the British Mission reported in 1919: "Jewish professors, however able, have been turned out of the university; Jewish doctors, however famous, have been turned out from the hospitals"' (Rabinowicz, 1964: 151). 'While the Government officially denounced and unofficially endorsed the Numerus Clausus, a number of Polish scholars raised protesting voices ... In the autumn of 1925 there were 400 Jewish candidates for the medical faculty in Cracow. Only 13 were admitted' (Rabinowicz, 1964: 154). More about the situation of Jewish students at Polish universities in the 1918–39 period can be read in Aleksiun (2014), Rudnicki (1987) and Natkowska (1999).

18 According to the fliers of the Liga Zielonej Wstążki, it was created for Polish academics (professors and students) to struggle through organized and planned actions against 'Jewish influence on Polish society'. The fliers contained three demands: (1) boycott of shops, services and professions; (2) breaking all contacts with Jewish colleagues and collaborators; and (3) supporting *numerus clausus* at each university (in Rabinowicz, 1964).

19 The protest letters were signed by scholars in the USA and in Europe, but without success, as the discriminatory practices were retained.

20 Including Tadeusz Kotarbinski, Rudolf Weigl, Ludwik Krzywicki, Mieczysław Michałowicz, Franciszek Venulet and Zygmunt Radliński. On Weigl, a professor of microbiology in Lwów, see Allen (2014); on Michałowicz, Venulet and Radliński – professors in the Medical School at Warsaw University – see Aleksiun (2014: 123); about Krzywicki and Kotarbiński – professors of philosophy at Warsaw University – see Markiewicz (2004: 110).

21 Aleksiun noted: 'Among the minority who voiced their protests were the Union of Polish Democratic Youth (Związek Polskiej Młodzieży Demokratycznej) and the Union of Independent Socialist Youth (Związek Niezależnej Młodzieży Socjalistycznej)' (Aleksiun, 2014: 129, n. 96).

22 In traditional Jewish communities, the matchmaker selects the marriage candidates and organizes the meetings of families and candidates.

23 Polish form of 'Mizrahi' – a group of Jews from North Africa and Asia, called also 'Arabic Jews'.

24 APW – KW PZPR – personal file – Bauman 16 421 (3183).

25 AIPN BU 0193/8207.

26 Gimnazjum Berger Archives, Archiwum Miasta Poznania, IVb-4-736, Katalog główny klasy Ia – I am grateful to Anna Kłódź for her help with access to these data.

27 From the interview I conducted in 2015 in Leeds.

28 This gradual process is depicted through the perspective of two

neighbouring families in the amazing French–Italian movie, directed by Ettore Scola, *Unfair Competition* (2001), about the rise of fascism in Italy).

29 Kristallnacht: 9–10 November 1938, in Germany – massive pogroms against the Jewish population with permission of the authorities.

30 For more, see Skórzyńska and Olejniczak (2012) and Tomaszewski (1998).

31 In this section, all citations of Zygmunt Bauman are from his letter to his daughters, written in 1986/7.

32 According to Niziołek, 'Poznanian Haszomer Hatzair was located on the first floor of the unused synagogue of the Bracia (Brudergemeinde) commune from the mid-nineteenth century, at ul. Szewska 5. It was a synagogue for Reform Jews, who after the formation of independent Poland mostly went to Germany' (Niziołek and Kosakowksa, 2016: ch. 1, n. 18).

33 Religious ceremony for boys entering into adulthood (around 14 years old). One of the basic rituals that Jewish families organize for their children.

34 About turning points, see Hughes (1971); Abbott (1997).

3 The Fate of a War Refugee (1939–1944)

1 All words in square brackets are added by the author.

2 During previous military conflicts (the 1794 Kościuszko Uprising or World War I), Polish Jews were part of Polish units. The rejection of Jews by the Army started with the Polish–Bolshevik War (1919–21).

3 Most probably, this took place on the night of 2–3 September.

4 From author's interview with Zygmunt Bauman conducted in Leeds, 1 November 2015.

5 These were concentration camps in Polish territories.

6 In Polish, a powerful idiom – *atmosferka nieprzyjemna*.

7 The bombers attacked not only military or strategic targets such as train stations, train tracks and military installations, but also civilian spaces: cities, towns and escaping people. The roads, filled with civilians, were also part of the 'strategic goal'. The 'Blitzkrieg' was based on this technique of terrorizing the civilian population. On 25 September 1939, the first carpet bombing took place, which killed 10,000 people in Warsaw. It was already clear at this point that Germany had military control of all Polish territory (except for the eastern areas temporarily ceded to the Soviets). The attacks on the civilian population, including hospitals, were not necessary for the victory of the Third Reich.

8 The German Army was in Włocławek by 14 September 1939. 'The persecution began as soon as the German Army entered Włocławek. ... Twenty-three Jews, who were praying ... were arrested on September 22, 1939. Upon arrest, a few (7–10) of the Jews were killed by shooting or stabbed with bayonets, and their bodies were buried in the backyard ... Individual murders, beatings of Jews moving around the streets by uniformed Germans and the so-called "plays" were all common. Contributions were a way of exploiting the Jews financially' (from the Museum of the History of Polish Jews website: www.sztetl.org.pl/en/article/wloclawek/5,h istory/?action=view&page=6).

9 A detailed description of Nazi terror towards the Jewish community in

Włocławek can be accessed on a website established by the Jewish Historical Institute Association: www.sztetl.org.pl/en/article/wloclawek/5,history.

10 All strong, healthy horses were seized by the Polish Army; civilians had only old animals.

11 Author's interview with Zygmunt Bauman conducted in Leeds, 1 November 2015.

12 Poles living in Prussian-occupied Poland typically spoke German, which the Bismarck regime had imposed as the official language. It was helpful in business and also an important marker of social status.

13 In the private manuscript, Bauman wrote: 'The captain must have been deeply impressed by my father's refined, literary German, as he asked him politely to act as the spokesman for the rest of the refugees, and promised whole-hearted cooperation' (Bauman, 1986/7: 29–30).

14 Author's interview with Zygmunt Bauman, Leeds, 1 November 2015. The bridge he refers to was on the Narew River. Bauman noted that the Soviet assault rifles hung on strings – a very specific image of the impoverished Red Army soldier that contrasted with the well-equipped and 'elegant' Wehrmacht officer.

15 In November 1939, after temporary control of the border by the Wehrmacht, German border control units (Grenzschutz) were sent from the former Polish–German border to these new demarcation lines. The Grenzschutz units had a reputation of being cruel and aggressive. Before November 1939, many refugees had escaped into the territories controlled by the Soviet Union.

16 This region is full of swamps and, especially in the autumn and spring, 'floating meadows' are common.

17 Russian and Polish are Slavonic languages – basic words in both languages could be understood even without previous exposure.

18 Author's interview with Zygmunt Bauman, Leeds, 1 November 2015. Because Polish and Russian are both Slavonic languages, Bauman could easily transform the Polish expression – 'Moja mama jest tutaj' – into 'Maja mat' tut,', which is not correct Russian, but perfectly understandable.

19 The Polish territories under German control had different statuses. The central part was *Generalgouvernement für die besetzten polnischen Gebiete*, while territories in Western Poland, including Poznań, were simply incorporated into the Third Reich. Eastern territories until 1941 were under Soviet control.

20 Because of the refugee influx, the number of inhabitants grew about 30 per cent from 1939 to 1941, when the population was almost 10,000.

21 There were familial, friendship and political party networks. For example, Włodzimierz Szer and his father were supported by a large and helpful network of contacts in the BUND. Throughout their travels, jobs, food and other necessities of life were provided by 'friends from the Bund'.

22 AIPN BU 0193/8207 p. 12. In another document – his CV dated from October 1949 for Party admission, Bauman mentioned his mother's workplace: Officer's canteen nr2, 'Wojengorodka' in APW – KW PZPR – personal file – Bauman 16 421 (3183).

23 Well-known term employed for 'creative accounting' in Poland.

24 Author's interview with Bauman conducted in Leeds in 2015.

25 The paragraph mentioned was the famous Paragraph 11 (see note 26).

26 A law (Paragraph 11) restricted the number of Poles permitted to live in

cities; in addition, former Polish state employees, teachers, professional soldiers and those originating from aristocratic families were all banished 'to Siberia' (deported). People judged to be opponents of communism were sent to labour camps. Historians enumerate four waves of deportations, the last one organized in June 1941, and all were made by the Soviet secret police, the NKVD. Deportees had a different status from prisoners or other forced labourers under the NKVD's control. In rare cases, Polish citizens who escaped the Nazi invasion and survived in the eastern USSR were not under NKVD control. This was visibly the case with the Bauman family.

27 Szer described this multicultural environment in the following way: 'the Russians [post-invasion] opened schools where teaching was done in four languages: Polish, Russian, Yiddish and Belorussian' (Szer, 2013: 93).

28 AIPN BU 0193/8207 p. 12. The discrepancy in grade numbers Bauman listed here are explained by the postwar change in Poland's educational system. When the war started, Bauman had finished Year 1 of gymnasium and was preparing for his second year. In Belarus, he jumped directly into the third-year class. The Soviet system was different – the first year of gymnasium was called the fifth year of school, so that, by jumping the second year of gymnasium, he was skipping the sixth year in the Soviet system. Bauman went through the seventh and eighth years of schooling while in Mołodeczno.

29 Bauman used the English word 'teenager' – a word that was not in use in Poland in his teen years, but was clearly easier for him to invoke in English.

30 Enhanced women's rights were a notable positive aspect of the Soviet system, opening the door to suffrage, education – including higher education – and many 'masculine' professions.

31 Author's interview with Bauman conducted in Leeds in 2015.

32 AIPN BU 0193/8207 p. 12.

33 APW – KW PZPR – personal file – Bauman 16 421 (3183).

34 Interview with Wacław Szybalski in May 2010. For more about Szybalski, see Wójcik (2015).

35 According to a personal questionnaire (*ankieta*) from 23 October 1949, Bauman was also a school librarian in Mołodeczno; most probably, this role was accorded to excellent students who assisted a professional – adult librarian – on a voluntary basis: APW – KW PZPR – personal file – Bauman 16 421 (3183).

36 See in scholarly texts (Tokarska-Bakir, 2012; Gross, 2001, 2006; Gross and Grudzinska-Gross, 2012) and memoirs by survivors and their descendants (Grynberg, 1994, 2002).

37 The most important and widely known book in English is *Neighbors: The Destruction of the Jewish Community* by Jan Tomasz Gross, published in 2001. It provoked a huge reaction, because understanding of Polish attitudes towards the Jewish community under Nazi occupation had been neglected and mostly reserved to the historian community.

38 The German name for the invasion of Soviet-held territories.

4 Russian Exodus, 1941–1943

1 Author's interview with Bauman conducted in Leeds in 2015.

2 As mentioned above, the Soviets condemned people to Siberia for hundreds of reasons (for more on this, see Hnatiuk (2016), Allen (2014); 'condemned

to Siberia' is a common expression for being sent to the Gulag, with punishment by hard labour and penurious living conditions in an isolated or distant place. The Gulag has no clear geographical definition. Usually it meant the Siberian region, but some prisoners ended up in Kazakhstan, the Caucasian Republics, or the Kamchatka Peninsula.

3 The name of the *kolkhoz* was mentioned by Bauman in his CV from 27 March 1947: APW – KW PZPR – personal file – Bauman 16 421 (3183).

4 All information from Bauman's CV written in 1949 is from APW – KW PZPR – personal file – Bauman 16 421 (3183). .

5 Warsaw University Archives – employee file: Zygmunt Bauman – akta osobowe (personal files).

6 'The golden frame was for only the highest grades for all subjects, and it gave you practically open access to the university. A silver frame meant a mix of good and excellent grades ... and the third came without a frame' (Szer, 2013: 122).

7 The grading culture in this part of the world encouraged high marks, probably more so than in other parts of the world. (For example, in France, there is a popular saying that 'Only God gets 20 out of 20; 18 for the teacher, and 16/20 is the best a student can hope for.')

8 The original in Cyrillic is in APW – KW PZPR – personal file – Bauman 16 421 (3183). 'J. D.' stands for 'railway college'.

9 I was unable to confirm how this document ended up in the archives of the Party; it may have been transferred from Bauman's military files and forwarded to the political organizations – first the PPR and then the PZPR – which would explain its location in the archives: APW – KW PZPR – personal file – Bauman 16 421 (3183).

10 AIPN BU 0193/8207 p. 12 – życiorys (CV).

11 Ibid.

12 AIPN BU 0 1224/1505.

13 It was October and November, but in this area we can use the term 'winter'.

14 Author's interview with Bauman conducted in Leeds in 2015.

15 AAN – Ministerstwo Szkolnictwa Wyższego 2860 – 61/72, pp. 50–1.

16 AIPN BU 0 1224/1505.

17 Archives APW, KW PZPR, akta osobowe działaczy (files of activists) in Bauman's file: Zygmunt Bauman sygnatura 16 421 (3183), CV from 1949, p. 2.

18 APW – KW PZPR – personal file – Bauman 16 421 (3183).

19 For depictions of such jobs, see famous Russian movies (*Siberiade* by Konchalovsky) and Polish literature (Hłasko's short stories). These jobs were iconic because of their isolation, wildness, extreme working conditions (bad climate), closeness to nature and difficulty. To some extent, this kind of work played an allegorical role in depicting oppression under the Soviet system.

20 Author's conversation with an ex-Bauman student who wished to stay anonymous.

21 After April 1943, *New Horizons* was published as a journal of the Union of Polish Patriots (ZPP) in Moscow; according to Marian Stępień, *New Horizons* played a significant ideological and political role among Polish intelligentsia living in the USSR during the war, by laying out a programme of socialist political changes for a future Poland bound by an alliance with the USSR (*Polish Literature, Encyclopedia Guide*, vol. II (*N–Ż*) (Warsaw, 1985), p. 45): http://1917.net.pl/node/21385?page=1.

22 Jędrychowski was one of the journalists who wrote in *New Horizons*; he
  presents its history in the *Quarterly of the History of the Polish Press*:
  http://bazhum.muzhp.pl/media//files/Kwartalnik_Historii_Prasy_Pols
  kiej/Kwartalnik_Historii_Prasy_Polskiej-r1980-t19-n4/Kwartalnik_His
  torii_Prasy_Polskiej-r1980-t19-n4-s45-61/Kwartalnik_Historii_Prasy_Pol
  skiej-r1980-t19-n4-s45-61.pdf.

23 For the political context of the creation of the ZPP, see Krystyna Kersten:
  'Wanda Wasilewska, summoned to Moscow in January [1943], was "to be
  put to good use in Polish affairs", because as Stalin said to her husband
  Aleksandr Korniejczuk, … "the situation looks like it will probably come
  to decisive conflict between the Polish government-in-exile and the Soviet
  Union" and "in this situation Wanda could do much"' (1991: 8).

24 J. Jałoszynski, 'Niektóre problemy dotyczące powstania i struktury organ-
  izacyjnej Związku Patriotów Polskich w ZSRR' [Some of the Problems
  Associated with the Creation and Organizational Structure of the ZPP
  in the USSR], *Najnowsze Dzieje Polski* [Warsaw] 9, 1962, p. 165, cited in
  Nussbaum (1991: 2009).

25 Ibid.

26 Numbers 1–5 were issued in Kuibyshev and were not widely distributed;
  information about the journals was diffused in the Soviet press only after
  the creation of the Polish Army allied with the Red Army.

27 There is no clear indication whether Bauman learned about the creation of
  the ZPP in February 1943, or after the party's official creation in June.

28 'Wanda Wasilewska (born 1905) was the daughter of Leon Wasilewski,
  one of the leading activists of the Polish Socialist Party–Revolutionary
  Faction … a historian and diplomat. From her early youth she was deeply
  involved in political action, at first in the Union of Independent Socialist
  Youth … and the Society of Workers' Universities …, and then in the
  Polish Socialist Party' (Kersten, 1991: 8–9).

29 Wasilewska speech published in *New Horizons*, 9, 5 May 1943, p. 7, from a
  radio speech on 28 April 1943.

30 The Katyń massacre was the mass execution of Polish military officers
  by the Soviet Union during World War II. The discovery of the massacre
  precipitated the severing of diplomatic ties between the Soviet Union and
  the Polish government-in-exile in London. For more on this, see: www.
  britannica.com/event/Katyn-Massacre.

31 'Curzon Line, the demarcation line between Poland and Soviet Russia
  that was proposed during the Soviet–Polish War of 1919–20 as a possible
  armistice line and became (with a few alterations) the Soviet–Polish border
  after WWII'; cited from: www.britannica.com/event/Curzon-Line.

32 In Nussbaum (1991: 20, n. 14): *Organizacja i Działania Bojowe Ludowego
  Wojska Polskiego w Latach 1943–1945* [*The Organization and Armed
  Action of the Polish People's Army 1942–1945*] a selection of source materi-
  als, vols. I–IV (Warsaw, 1958–65); vol. IV, pp. 8–9.

33 Speech by Wanda Wasilewska, 'We Are Going to the Front', *Nowe
  Widnokręgi* (*New Horizons*), 3, 18, 20 September 1943, pp. 8–9.

34 The popular song 'Holy War' was composed in 1941, just after the
  German invasion of the USSR, by Aleksander Aleksandrov (creator of the
  famous Aleksandrov Choir). The lyrics were written by Wasilij Lebiediew-
  Kumacz. See www.youtube.com/watch?v=JQPmwzMopJw.

5 'Holy War'

1 'Julian Żurowicz' was the pseudonym Bauman used in publishing two 1953 novels: the first concerning the battle for Kołobrzeg, the second about the activity of the KBW (Korpus Bezpieczeństwa Wewnętrznego (Internal Security Corps)) in postwar years. Both were published by the Polish Defence Ministry in a series of war stories.

2 In Russian – командировка – a certificate directing the person who received it to be sent to an indicated place.

3 AIPN BU 0 1224/1505 Odpis życiorysu; signature por. Paszkiowicz, Warszawa [Warsaw], 27.12.49.

4 APW – KW PZPR – personal file – Bauman 16 421 (3183), CV from 1949; 1949 PZPR party candidacy questionnaire.

5 Author's interview with Bauman conducted in Leeds in 2015.

6 Ibid.

7 AIPN BU 0 1224/1505 Odpis życiorysu; signature por. Pasakiewicz, Warsaw, 27.12. 49.

8 The ZPP created, in May 1943, a Polish division inside the Red Army. The 1st Infantry Division, called the Tadeusz Kosciuszko Division, was commanded by General Zygmunt Berling. For more, see Nussbaum (1991).

9 The story is corroborated by Bauman's CV (handwritten) dated 27 March 1947: 'In January 1944, I was directed by the *Wojekomat* to work in the war industry, but at the distribution point in Gorkij, I was directed to the militia of Moscow. There, I was assigned to the 7th officer's branch of traffic regulation for the post of inspector R.T.R. [Russian Traffic Regulation]. Being in Moscow, I had the opportunity to contact the head of the military ZPP capt. Naszkowski and with his help I got out of the militia directly to the First Polish Army in the USSR. I received a referral to Sumy, where I arrived in April 1944': APW – KW PZPR – personal file – Bauman 16 421 (3183).

10 Gulag was a specific form of confinement that existed under, first, Czarist jurisdiction, then Soviet. See, for example: Applebaum (2004).

11 On the 'Anders Army', see Redlich (1971); Redlich gives a different estimate of the number evacuated. Also see Davis (2015).

12 It was a common practice; see Redlich (1971).

13 This was the case of David Wieczner, whom the Anders Commission rejected with this explanation. I am grateful to Włodzimierz Holsztyński for this information.

14 Gutman was a leading specialist on the history of the Shoah and created the International School for Holocaust Studies.

15 Gutman, 'Jews in General Anders' Army in the Soviet Union', available on the Yad Vashem website: www.yadvashem.org/odot_pdf/Microsoft% 20Word%20-%206217.pdf, pp. 8–9.

16 Ibid., p. 8. There were exceptions: historian Stefan Patuszka put the number of Jewish soldiers in the Anders Army at 4,000 – see Pastuszka (2010). However, there is no consensus concerning this information.

17 Even there, there were cases of ethnic discrimination in the selection process; see Nussbaum (1991).

18 *Pod sztandarem 4 Pomorskiej Dywizji Piechoty im. Jana Kilińskiego* (Under the Flag of the 4th Pomeranian Infantry Division Jan Kilinski), published in 1978. It is important to keep in mind the limits of this kind of source. The books published in the period 1947–89 were under censorship. This

procedure obliged authors to adjust their narrative to the official line of history. The book has no hostile opinions or even light criticism of the Communist regime or Soviet wartime politics. Moreover, Zygmunt Bauman does not appear among the soldiers mentioned in the book. This is the result of the ban imposed from 1968 on mentioning Jewish emigrants (and also people who emigrated after 1945). Their names were erased from all books, historical accounts, etc. Taking into consideration those limits, the book is an imperfect source of data about the history of the 4th Division.

19 AIPN BU 0 1224/1505.
20 If he started in mid-May and finished 16 June, that would mean the training lasted about a month.
21 Author's interview with Bauman conducted in Leeds in 2015. Before World War II, officers were required to have a baccalaureate degree.
22 'Pop' is also a term designating an Orthodox priest – which has here a cynical note, as the clergy were excluded from the Red Army.
23 Two of the major attitude problems, both analysed later in this chapter, were anti-Soviet attitudes and anti-Semitic behaviour. Note the binary categorization that Nussbaum employs: Poles and Jews – both had been Polish citizens, and the first in fact signified mostly Polish Catholics; the second, Polish Jews. Yet this categorization was commonly employed by Polish researchers in the twentieth century – some still use it.
24 17 September 1939. Piłsudski was a national hero, general, politician and symbolic figure of Poland's interwar period, and a legend for the majority of Poles. This is why to present him in a negative light was perceived by regular soldiers as an anti-patriotic attitude
25 Putrament talked a lot about agricultural reform, key for the new regime, which seized property from large landowners (owners of 50 or 100 hectares, depending on the region) and gave it to the peasants. Part of the requisitioned land became state property; small owners got 2–3, and later 5, hectares. In the western territories, the limit was higher (7–15 hectares) (*Mała encyklopedia* rolnicza,1964: s. 660). For more, see Słabek (1972).
26 In the *wągrówka* (the outline of talking points composed by Wągrowski), a lot of space was devoted to the prewar economic situation of the working class. Mieczysław Wągrowski (1902–67) was one of the creators of the 1st Tadeusz Kosciuszko Division, and he was in charge of the models for the political talks performed by political officers in the whole Army. Using those models, the educators maintained consistency in the explanations and analysis of presented topics.
27 The inhabitants of Silesia and Łódź were Wehrmacht soldiers recruited among Polish citizens, who belonged to the ethnicities which were considered by Nazis as Germanic (Silesians, Pomeranians).
28 For more about the presence of Jewish Poles in the interwar Communist Party, see chapter 8.
29 'Ż' is the first letter of 'Żyd': 'Jew' in Polish.
30 AIPN BU 0 1069/788 7157. Finally, another file informs with details: 'April, 16th 1944, nomination for Master Corporal (MCpl); August, 26th 1944 – Warrant Officer (WO)' (AIPN BU 0193/8207 Personal Files – progress career on – https://katalog.bip.ipn.gov.pl/informacje/54260.
31 Author's interview with Bauman conducted in Leeds in 2015.
32 The 5th, and not the 6th, Light Artillery Regiment was actually called 6th

PAL – Pułk Artylerii Lekkiej. During our interview, Zygmunt warned that he didn't remember all the details and asked me to check and correct the information.

33 About 100,000 American trucks were sent to the Soviet Union during World War II (Wikipedia, https://en.wikipedia.org/wiki/Studebaker_US6_2%C2%BD-ton_6x6_truck).

34 See the Introduction.

35 According to Szer, each platoon or company had a designated soldier who sang or chanted songs during the march; sometimes he sang spontaneously, without a command (Szer, 2013: 135).

36 ['Whether the Warsaw Uprising Was Needed'], *Gazeta Wyborcza*, 178, 01/08/1997 OPINIE, p. 16.

37 Curzon Line: see chapter 4, n. 31.

38 I am grateful to Keith Tester for sharing with me his interviews and private correspondence with Bauman.

39 This day became, for many years, a national holiday commemorating the new Polish political regime.

40 Karski observed of the Polish government in exile: 'the London government was afraid of the reaction of the underground military forces [in the country] – they were afraid to be discredited because of their excessive submission to the allies [who agreed with Stalin about the future of Poland]. At the same time – and this was the tragedy of the entire war – the government in London, communicating with their delegates in the country, overestimated their political power in the international arena all the time. ... This assessment was completely unrealistic' (['Whether the Warsaw Uprising Was Needed'], *Gazeta Wyborcza*, 178, 01/08/1997 OPINIE, p. 16).

41 *Kolkhozniks*: workers in the *kolkhoz* – national Soviet farms.

42 In English, see Davis (2004).

43 The Uprising collapsed on 4 October and after that Nazi troops proceeded with the destruction of Warsaw – street by street.

44 See Czapigo and Białas (2015).

45 In Polish: 'Ja byłem jeszcze smarkaty a to zasychło jak na psie.'

46 In Polish, 'czyn pierwszomajowy'. In post-1945 Poland, the Party decreed 1 May was a day of collective voluntary work. Before World War II, the day was celebrated with large marches by unions and Left-oriented parties.

47 According to Nafalski: 'The victorious troops of the 4th division, not stopping at Klietz, came out on the banks of the Elbe River and settled along the river. Allied troops were stationed on the west side. The river carried joyful voices of mutual greeting and congratulations ... on both banks. Here, the 4th division completed its combat trail of 1.5 thousand kilometres' (Nafalski, 1978: 391).

6 Officer of the Internal Security Corps

1 People's Commissariat for Internal Affairs (Russian: 'Narodnyj Komisariat Vnutriennych Dyel').

2 Fejgin was born in 1909 in Warsaw; he was a prewar communist (KPP). In May 1945, he represented the General Board of the Politico-educational Unit of the Polish Army and was in charge of creating the Interior Security Unit.

3 AIPN BU_0_1224_1505 p. 67. Handwritten CV dated 15 August 1950.
4 Bauman probably would have been recruited to one of the many internal security groups regardless of which unit he fought with during the
   war; many division soldiers were recruited into the KBW in May 1945
   – especially political officers.
5 According to Jan Gross: 'In addition to an underground military organization, the Home Army (Armia Krajowa, AK) which at its peak boasted over
   300,000 sworn-in members, an elaborate network of institutions was set up
   in occupied Poland, which together came to be known as the Underground
   State (Państwo Podziemne). This "state" included clandestine versions
   of prewar political parties and a shadow government administration
   (Delegatura) headed by a representative of the legal Polish government-in-
   exile. ... The Underground State was founded by the government-in-exile
   from London' (Gross, 2006: 6–7).
6 Following the creation of the National Council for the Country (Krajowa
   Rada Narodowa: KRN) by the Polish Workers Party on 31 December
   1943, the Soviet-controlled Polish Committee of National Liberation
   (Polski Komitet Wyzwolenia Narodowego: PKWN) was created on 20
   July 1944, by members of the Union of Polish Patriots.
7 The KRN – National Council for the Country – was a temporary government that, as a result of Western pressure on Stalin, initially included
   various political groups. Pro-Stalin communist leaders were the largest
   and most powerful group. Mikołajczyk, sent by the London government-
   in-exile, became vice president of this 'unification' government. From the
   start, propaganda against Mikołajczyk's Polish Peasant Party made the
   idea of a reconciliation government impossible to implement. Mikołajczyk
   and his supporters were presented as counter-revolutionary reactionaries
   and enemies of the new system that 'won' the fixed 1946 referendum and
   1947 election. Mikołajczyk eventually fled Poland to escape jail.
8 The 'most politicized and feared branch of the Security Service, colloqui-
   ally called the *Bezpieka* or UB, deployed all over the country through a
   network of Public Security Offices (Urzędy Bezpieczeństwa Publicznego)',
   and part of the MBP (Ministerstwo Bezpieczeństwa Publicznego – Ministry
   of Public Security), writes Jan Gross: 'Twice as numerous as the UB was the
   ubiquitous regular police force or Citizens' Militia (Milicja Obywatelska,
   MO) also subsumed under the Ministry of Public Security. A uniformed
   quasi-military branch of the Security Service, the Internal Security Corps
   (KBW), and an auxiliary police force ... Voluntary Reserves of the Citizens
   Militia, were also available' (Gross, 2006: 14, n. *).
9 Here, the person registered as the apartment tenant was Maurycy Bauman.
10 AIPN BU 0 1224/1505. Document of the Provincial Office of Public
   Security in Poznań addressed to the Head of the Division of the 3rd
   Department of Personnel MBP in Warsaw – dated, Poznań, 30 December
   1951; 'Interview about a citizen. Bauman Mosze [Moshe], who resided
   recently until 1939 in Poznań at Prusa street No. 17/5. In the course of
   the interview, it was established that the citizen: Bauman Moshe (closer
   data was not established) Jewish nationality, Polish citizenship, social class
   – commercial, marital status – spoused; lived at this address until the outbreak of the September Campaign [1939]. According to citizen Przyworski,
   who is living now at the above-mentioned address – above-mentioned
   Bauman until 1939 ran the company 'Baumann and Rychwalski' at St.,
   Rynek [Old Market Place], a textile market with his partner. With the

outbreak of the September Campaign, he and his family fled to Włocławek and did not return to the area again. His son-in-law with a daughter escaped to Argentina in 1939. He had Argentinean citizenship.' Signature illegible – Chief of the 'A' Faculty of the WUBP in Poznań.

11 Maurycy's son-in-law actually had a British, not Argentinean, passport. Zygmunt's father was Maurycy, not Mosze (Yiddish version).

12 If Bauman was a captain, as stated in the testimony, this event would have happened after 20 December 1946 there, when the costume of the KBW (a navy ribbon on the cap) was widely known. The report would then have called him a 'KBW captain' instead of a 'Polish Army captain'.

13 Historian Lukasz Krzyzowski wrote a book *Ghost Citizens: Jewish Return to a Postwar City* (2020), devoted to the history of Jews from Radom (a city 100km south of Warsaw. Of the 20,000 who were registered in 1939 (a third of all inhabitants), only 959 remained in the summer of 1945, and by the end of October 1946 only 111 Jewish survivors remained in Radom. In 1950, there were 30 (Krzyzowski, 2017: 95). Only a few were able to get back their homes or businesses. Jewish life was not reborn in Radom or in the majority of Polish cities. They became ghost citizens; according to Dominika Michalak: 'this term shows that someone is building their economic and social position on someone else's life achievements. A "ghost writer" is denied the status of an author, a "ghost citizen" lacks the normative status of a community member. Just like a "ghost writer" has left an actual mark in a discourse (after all he or she writes the text), a "ghost citizen" has actually contributed to the community life. Nevertheless, they both are denied recognition. As social and economic actors, they are not only deprived of their property, but also treated as nonexistent by a community. The analogy is obviously far from complete. A ghost writer often gets paid for his or her job while no one thinks they owe anything to a ghost citizen. For instance, their property is taken yet the theft is not recognized. ... they are present physically but no longer legitimate' (from personal correspondence with Dominika Michalak, 7 May 2018). Only recently (and as the consequence of the book published by Krzyzowski, and the media discussions that occurred afterwards) have commemorative inscriptions been fixed in the places that are connected to events of the Holocaust. This example is not unique to Poland.

14 Alina Cała estimates that, in the years 1944–7, in Polish liberated territories, over 1,000 Jews were killed (Cała, 2014: 17). Various estimates have been published (Cała, 2014: 17, n. 3).

15 PRL is the acronym for the Polish Peoples' Republic, in use from 1952 to 1989. Previously it was known as People's Poland (from 1944), and after 1989 as the Republic of Poland.

16 The title of the book about those postwar years by Marcin Zaremba is *Wielka Trwoga* (Big Fear; 2012). The author is following the terminology of French historian George Lefebvre, who employed this term in his analysis of the events of the French Revolution (*La Grande Peur de 1789*, published in 1932).

17 Tadeusz Łebkowski spoke about two revolutions: (1) for democracy and independence; and (2) for communism: *Myśli o historii Polski i Polaków* (Thoughts on the History of Poland and the Poles) (1983).

18 J. Tokarska-Bakir, *Pogrom Cries: Essays on Historical Anthropology of Poland 1939–1946*, forthcoming from Peter Lang Gmbh (English translation of *Okrzyki pogromowe* (2012)).

19 Italics added.
20 Functionaries and supporters of the new state were the main victims of violence by underground forces. After the 1989 transition in Poland, the historical interpretation of their actions changed. The previous regime had characterized them as bandits; post-1989, these forces were described as mythical *Żołnierze Wyklęci* ('Cursed Soldiers'). Right-wing historians, with the support of the IPN, have contributed to the glorification of the participants, while remaining silent about the terror these groups inflicted upon the civilian population in the countryside, as well as the criminal acts (mostly killings) targeting Jewish survivors. The general enthusiastic tone and the lack of a critical approach make use of those historical texts very difficult.
21 A swell (in Polish, literally 'a dead wave') is a natural phenomenon of the sea following a storm; the same occurs in the earth or air following an earthquake or an atomic explosion. The apparent calm can be dangerous for big boats, especially for sailing vessels. In the context of Poland 1945, this metaphor was used by Polish intellectuals, who described the Jewish tragedy as 'Martwa Fala' (Skibińska, 2018: 856–7, n. 591).
22 We will probably never know the true number of Jewish victims of Poles but Polish-Canadian historian Jan Grabowski, in an interview with a *Haaretz* journalist, gave a rough figure of 200,000 – during World War II: 'Precise numbers are very hard to come by', he observes, but 'about 35,000 Polish Jews survived the war in Poland (excluding those who fled into the Soviet Union and returned after the war). We also know that close to 10 percent of Jews fled the liquidated ghettos in 1942 and 1943 – which would give you a number of about 250,000 Jews who tried to survive in hiding. Subtract the first number from the second and you will see the scale of the "dark" territory, in which the Poles, for the most part, decided who lived and who died.' '[My] count is very, very conservative', he notes, 'because I have not included here the human toll of the Polish "Blue" police, who were a deadly force not only after the liquidation of the ghettos but during these so-called liquidation actions.' To support his argument, he recruits Emmanuel Ringelblum, the historian of the Warsaw Ghetto, who said that the 'Blue' police alone were responsible for 'hundreds of thousands of Jewish deaths' (Grabowski, in *Haaretz*, 11 February 2017: www.haaretz. com/world-news/.premium.MAGAZINE-orgy-of-murder-the-poles-who-hunted-jews-and-turned-them-in-1.5430977; see also Engelking and Grabowski (2018).
23 As Skibińska remarks in the same article: 'People who were good, well meaning, and genuinely helped the Jews survive the nightmare of the war, usually shared their fate after the war. In order to avoid harassment and assault, they would conceal their noble deeds, since, according to the Catholic Nationalists' cultural code, helping Jews was a reprehensible, shameful, and criminal act, whereas "getting rid of them" was an act of patriotism' (Skibińska, 2014: 61).
24 Returnees: people who escaped the Holocaust in the USSR. Survivors: 50,000 in Polish-occupied territories – about half were liberated by the Red Army from concentration and death camps (Cała, 2014: 17).
25 Kazimierz Wyka created a concept of disabled economy ('gospodarka wyłączona'), which signifies the central psychosocial phenomenon of the years of occupation: 'It was not so much about trade, but about jumping on loot, with sated purring in the intervals' (Wyka, 1984: 295). Joanna

Tokarska-Bakir followed this idea and concluded: 'The Polish third state, the bourgeoisie, arose as a result of inertial entry to the place emptied by Jews. As Wyka said: "To the place of the unbaptized – the baptized." "For Germans – fault and crime, for us [Poles] – keys and the safe". [Wyka 1984: 292, 293]' (Tokarska-Bakir, 2018: 286).

26 Compare to Chęciński's estimations from 1984: 'As the Second World War drew to an end, the 1,000-year-old Jewish community in Poland was no more: some ninety percent of its three and a half million – nearly one-tenth of Poland's pre-war population – had succumbed to the Holocaust. ... Estimates of the number of Jewish survivors under Nazi rule have ranged from 25,000–50,000; while the number of Polish Jews who survived in the Soviet Union has been put at 250,000–300,000 [n. 1: Paul Lendvai, *Anti-Semitism in Eastern Europe* (London, 1971), p. 25; cf. Georg W. Strobel, *Das polnisch-jüdische Verhältnis: Der Bestand der jüdischen Minderheit in Polen* (Cologne, 1968), pp. 2–3]. According to a recent study in the postwar years, "altogether about 250,000 Jews remained in Poland for varying periods of time" [n. 2: Lucjan Dobroszycki, 'Restoring Jewish Life in Post-War Poland', *Soviet Jewish Affairs* 2, 1973: 59; see also Władysław Góra, *Polska Rzeczpospolita Ludowa, 1944–1974* [*The Polish People's Republic, 1944–1974*] (Warsaw, 1974), p. 147], though other sources put this figure as high as 400,000 (Chęciński, 1982: 7)'; Krzyzowski reports that almost 43,000 survivors were in Poland at the beginning of May 1945; at the beginning of 1946, after repatriation from the USSR, the number rose to 244,000 (Krzyzowski, 2020).

27 In the Soviet system, the family name appears first, followed by the given name.

28 According to the APW – KW PZPR – personal file – Bauman 16 421 (3183) – Personal Questionnaire – 30 points, signed by Bauman, dated from 31 August 1945.

29 A battalion could theoretically have 300 to 700 soldiers.

30 Interestingly, the PPR's leaders were sufficiently tolerant to accept the existence of the section of Roman Catholic Church military clergy (Depo, 2012: 132).

31 This term is used in the personal questionnaire from 31 August 1945.

32 PPR units in the KBW did not exist formally before 1947 (Depo, 2012: 132, n. 36).

33 APW – KW PZPR – personal file – Bauman 16 421 (3183) – Personal Questionnaire.

34 Interview *Gazeta Wyborcza*, 28 June 2013.

35 APW – KW PZPR – personal file – Bauman 16 421 – 'Podanie'.

36 After 1948, the PPR and PPS were unified in the creation of the PZPR, but at that point in Poland there was only one real party. The PSL was modest and weak – not a party but a faction (*stronnictwo*).

37 APW – KW PZPR – personal file – Bauman 16 421 (3183). In the Party Archives, conserved documents – among others his party ID – confirm this date.

38 The exact term in Polish, *świadomy*, means aware, well-informed and analytical, with an understanding of the power relationships in society.

39 APW – KW PZPR – personal file – Bauman 16 421 (3183) – Rekomendacja Kazimierz Faryna.

40 AIPN BU 0 1224/1505 – citation from 'Note about Z. Bauman' dated 24 April 1969. Opinion by Jan Szachoćko from 3 December 1945.

41 Andrzej Werblan, born in 1924; historian, communist functionary, author of books on Stalinism in Poland and a biography of Gomułka, his friend.

42 The Nuremberg Laws were three legal texts, adopted by the Reichstag and prepared by Hitler in September 1935. They provided the legal basis for the exclusion of Jews from German society.

In my interview, Andrzej Werblan gave a fuller explanation about this fascinating issue: 'This conflict was maintained to the end – to 1938 [when Stalin resolved the Party and imprisoned and killed several leaders] – and it was the big drama of that party. The problem was that this KPP faction refused to take into consideration that the lack of support from the population was not due to the Jewish origin of their leaders but to the Party opinion about independence. In the PPS (the Socialist Party), there were also a lot of leaders with Jewish roots but nobody called them *Żydokomuna* – so the problem was not in the national composition but the relationship with Soviet Union and to Polish independence.'

43 The anecdote was recounted by Werblan during the interview.

44 'Professor with a Past' by Aida Edemariam: www.theguardian.com/books/2007/apr/28/academicexperts.highereducation.

45 Actually someone completed this in the wrong order, as *Semion* is written above the printed word 'category', and 'inf.' is written above the printed word 'pseudonym'.

46 I would like to thank Regina Chernyszko-Epstein for her fast response concerning this and other questions related to the Russian-Jewish culture and language.

47 I would like to thank Bella Szwarcman and Piotr Paźnik for the confirmation that this kind of practice was noticed in the late 1930s. According to Natalia Aleksiun (private conversation), it was not formally inscribed in any official documents.

48 Some information that would usually be mentioned on the cover is missing. At the foot of the cover page, the IPN archive number, 00681/157, is written by hand, and on the bottom left is a small number (of the printing services?) with '1970' – probably the year of production of the cover-file. This indicates that the cover is not original and the folder was reorganized (in 1970?).

49 https://inwentarz.ipn.gov.pl/slownik?znak=I.

50 The Polish system was '[p]atterned after the NKVD and using its parent organization's wealth of experience ... the task [was that] of infiltrating every stratum of Polish society without exception. In every major administrative, economic, cultural, and scientific institution, at least one full-time Bezpieka functionary, with a network of informers and intermediary agents, was to be installed' (Chęciński, 1982: 62).

51 https://inwentarz.ipn.gov.pl/slownik?znak=R#172. UB – Security Office – became SB – Security Service ; the name changed in 1956 after some changes in the organization.

52 The pencil required wetting (with saliva) to work. Invented in 1857 by K. Puscgerm, and patented on 10 July 1866 by Educib Clark. Because of chemicals used in production, the pencil caused infections and burns of the oral mucosa. It was commonly used by the Czarist administration in the late nineteenth and twentieth centuries.

53 I would like to thank the persons who helped me decrypt this phrase, Ryszard Wójcik, as well as anonymous Russian–Polish translators.

54 AIPN BU 0 1069 788.

55 Ibid. Italics on English words have been added.
56 Ibid. The folder contains other, more neutral documents, such as: lists of friends and colleagues, family members (including the sister in Palestine), with addresses and military level (the majority of his friends and colleagues were soldiers).
57 Ibid.
58 In post-1989 Poland, a so-called 'lustration process' was performed – people who cooperated with internal secret services were excluded from some functions after the political changes.
59 Interview with Michał Komar, 18 November 2017, Warsaw.
60 'Seduction' is an ironic term.
61 Lipiński (2016).
62 Edemariam, 'Professor with a Past'.
63 Cited in Gmyr (2012: 167); journal no. 34, 1946, p. 1.
64 In *Gazeta Wyborcza*, 28 June 2013: Tomasz Kwaśniewski, 'Dałem się uwieść' [I Let Them Seduce Me], interview with Bauman: http://wyborcza. pl/magazyn/1,124059,14189361,Bauman__dalem_sie_uwiesc.html.
65 'Pro-independence' signifies here: anti-Soviet, anti-communist, anti-socialist. They were made up of two-thirds former Home Army troops, with the rest from branches of the NSZ and NZW.
66 Kazimierz Krajewski and Tomasz Łabuszewski (IPN), *Ziemia Ostrołęcka w walce z komunizmem 1944–1954*; Fundacja Pamiętamy OSTROŁĘKA, October 2008: www.solidarni.waw.pl/pobierz/FundacjaPamietamy/ostro leka.pdf, p. 25.
67 AIPN BU 0 1069/7887157.
68 *Gazeta Wyborcza*: Kwaśniewski, 'I Let Them Seduce Me'.
69 APW – KW PZPR – personal file – Bauman 16 421 (3183), Kwestionariusz osobowy z 25 10 1948 (nr doc. 50) [personal questionnaire dated 25 October 1948].
70 I wish to thank Beata Kowalczyk for her help and research conducted in the IPN archives in 2017–18. This section relies heavily on the material she prepared.
71 This is a popular term used by right-wing politicians as part of their historical policy strategy (re-writing twentieth-century Polish history). The term appeared in 1993, then was popularized by journalists and anti-communist historians; in 2011, the Polish government introduced the National Day of Commemoration of Cursed Soldiers – 1 March.
72 He died in September 2003.
73 There are several trial reports that included indications of Młot's role and activities (AIPN BU 1023515 – twenty-two volumes), including records of crimes, and notes about robberies, attacks and illegal actions. Nevertheless, one document – a testimony by his assistant – is cited extensively on the following pages. The use of the report of the interrogation of Kania – Młot's assistant – is motivated by his style in presenting the information as well as the number of details included in the narration. The actions described by Kania are also documented elsewhere (the security services have other documents proving the activity of Młot). In short, this is not the accusation of a single source.
74 Participants in the underground postwar activity are, in authoritarian Poland (post-2015), treated as national heroes.
75 For 'MO', in contemporary terminology, we could say: 'Special Commando Group'.

76 AIPN BU 1023/515 vol. 2.
77 Several political changes occurred this year. See chapter 9.
78 The examples that follow are contained in the file titled: 'Protocol of the interrogation of the suspect', dated 13 August 1948. The suspect is Czesław Kania: AIPN BU 1023515t_2.
79 District XVI was the area under the control of 'Młot'.
80 In his article, Kijowski provided more examples of the murder of civilians (Kijowski, 2010: 190).
81 AIPN BU 1023/515 vol. 2.
82 Ibid.
83 The pseudonym was taken from Felix Dzerzhinsky – a Polish and Russian revolutionary known for his cruelty.
84 AIPN BU 1023/515 vol. 2. The document is titled a 'notecard for a criminal act by: members of the band directed by "Las"'.
85 Gambetta (1993).
86 AIPN BU 1023/515 vol. 2.
87 AIPN BU 0189/62 vol. 1 digi arch., pp. 11–13.
88 AIPN BU 1023/515 vol. 2.
89 Jerzy Kijowski emphasizes that 'the Jewish kehilla in Ostrołęka ... constituted a serious group of the city's inhabitants up to 1939, reaching even 83% (1916)' (from a website devoted to the Ostrołęka Jewish community at http://rozmaitosci.com/okruchy-wspomnien-o-zydowskiej-ostrolece).
90 For more about the activity of underground organizations after 1945 in the killing and persecution of Jews, see Skibinska (2014); Cała (1988, 2014); Tokarska-Bakir (2018), Engelking and Grabowski (2018).
91 Skibińska n. 108, p. 53: 'Yisrael Gutman and Shmuel Krakowski, *Unequal Victims: Poles and Jews during World War II* (New York: Holocaust Library, 1986), pp. 120–134; Aleksandra Bieńkowska, 'Partyzantka polska lat 1942–1944 w relacjach żydowskich', *Zagłada Żydów. Studia i Materiały*, vol. 1 (2005), pp. 148–164; Alina Skibińska and Dariusz Libionka, '"Przysięgam walczyć o wolną i potężną Polskę, wykonywać rozkazy przełożonych, tak mi dopomóż Bóg." Żydzi w AK. Epizod z Ostrowca Świętokrzyskiego', *Zagłada Żydów. Studia i Materiały*, vol. 4 (2008), pp. 287–323.' 'Moreover we should remember that Independent Jewish units, usually numbering up to a few score members, faced severe scarcity of provisions because farmers would not voluntarily provide them with food' (Skibińska, 2014: 53). 'We should also remember that anti-Semitism and persecution of Jews also was carried out by the Polish Peasant Battalions (Bataliony Chłopskie – BCh) and People's Army (Armia Ludowa – AL). However, there were some extremely rare exceptions like the GL/AL units, which did accept Jews' (Skibińska, 2014: 53).
92 N. 41 by Żbikowski: 'Quoted from Kazimierz Krajewski and Tadeusz Łabuszewski, Białostocki Okręg AK– AKO, VII 1944–VIII 1945 r. (Warsaw: Volumen, 1997), pp. 795–797. Henryk "Gryf" Jastrzębski, acting regional delegate for the government (in exile in London), expressed a more moderate view on the situation in Białystok in his report dated 11 August 1944: "Thanks to the benevolent care of the Christian-Polish community, some 3,000 Jews remain in the region. They are all resigned to breaking their ties with their current home, i.e., Poland, and emigrating to America. They will not be drawn into the work of the Polish underground. Some of them work in PKWN offices." However, according to situational

report no. 11 by the Białystok Regional AK Command, written slightly later, on 5 January 1945: "Dispatch by commandant of the Bielsk district: the Jews are colluding with the NKVD and almost all of them possess short arms. They spy on local residents and newcomers. In Drohiczyn, the Soviets killed a Jew by accident. The Jews, believing the Poles to have been responsible, murdered nine Poles ... From a dispatch by commandant of the Wysokie Mazowieckie district: the Jews allegedly keep their distance from everything, but in fact are NKVD confidants. They denounce anyone who has anything previously owned by Jews, on occasion employing blackmail, demanding between 10 and 15 metres [1,000 to 1,5000 kg] of rye for allegedly worn-out things. They do not spare even those who sheltered them, but demand large payments from them" ("Białostocczyzna 1944–1945 w dokumentach podziemia i oficjalnych władz", in Jerzy Kułak, ed., *Dokumenty do dziejów PRL*, vol. X (Warsaw: Instytut Studiów Politycznych Polskiej Akademii Nauk, 1998), pp. 45, 98' (Żbikowski, 2014: 83–4).

93 Polish movie; in cinemas from January 1947; the story of a musician engaged in the underground activity in Warsaw during World War II.

94 *Socrealizm* (socialist realism) was an artistic, politically engaged current promoted by the winners of the October Soviet Revolution and implemented in several Eastern European countries through Stalinist influence. It was an important propaganda tool in the hands of the one-party state, and for a period, other artistic currents were forbidden. Artists were instructed to represent work activities, and workers and peasants in different contexts.

95 This feature is considered as a main characteristic of the literature in that genre – see Wojciech Tomasik, 'Aparat bezpieczeństwa w literaturze polskiej okresu socrealizmu', *Pamiętnik Literacki: czasopismo kwartalne poświęcone historii i krytyce literatury polskiej*, 85, 3, 1994, pp. 73–85.

96 It was a pillar of the political change that occurred after 1945.

97 This name has a doubly negative connotation. In Polish, Wrona means 'crow', and in folklore the crow is symbolically ignoble and connected to evil powers. In addition, the choice connotes the German coat of arms, with its black eagle, while the symbol of Poland is the white eagle. During the occupation, it was common to say that the Germans had 'a black crow' as their coat of arm. It was very contemptuous signification.

98 The name is derived from *dwór*, meaning 'mansion'. A free translation might be 'person who serves in a mansion'.

99 Since Poland after independence had difficulties with inflation, it was common to make transactions in US dollars. These practices were partially or totally illegal after 1945 – however, they were very common.

100 Agnieszka Gajewska, in her excellent book *Holocaust and the Stars: The Past in the Prose of Stanisław Lem* (Poznań, 2016), analysed the works by Stanisław Lem, the science fiction author, showing how his traumatic experience of the Holocaust, which he did not officially discuss, appears in his literature.

101 The military court or army police has the right to ask and receive this kind of strategic information.

102 From his handwritten CV, dated 27 March 1947.

103 The document does not mention the Cross of Valor that Bauman received, according to previous documents, after the Battle of Kolberg in 1945.

104 AIPN BU 0193/8207.

105 Faryna was the officer who sponsored Bauman's enrolment into the PPR some months before signing this document.
106 AIPN BU 635/9 60; 1581/75/9, p. 3. This document concerns over 850 soldiers.
107 AIPN BU 635/9 60; 1581/75/9, p. 4.
108 Joanna Tokarska-Bakir (2018: 736): note 2319/20 – Report of inspectors KBW, APIN BU 635 9, pp. 11–15.
109 AIPN BU 0 1069/788 7157.

7 'A Man in a Socialist Society'

1 AIPN BU 0 1224 1505: transcript of Bauman's lecture at a scientific session organized by the Regional Student Council of the Rural Youth Association in Łódź, 9–10 December 1967, titled 'Moral and Ethical Values of the October Revolution. A Man in a Socialist Society', pp. 3–4.
2 Edemariam, 'Professor with a Past'.
3 Administratively, only the left side of the Vistula River was included in Warsaw. After the liberation, districts on the right bank (Praga and others) were incorporated as well. The city had been subjected to three waves of destruction: (1) the September siege of 1939, when 15% of the total number of buildings was destroyed; (2) in April of 1943, when a further 12% fell during the Warsaw Ghetto uprising; (3) in the Warsaw Uprising of 1944, 'and especially after its fall, when the German occupier deliberately destroyed 58% of all buildings, which together meant a dramatic and difficult to imagine 85% of the city's buildings had been destroyed' (Mórawski, 2003: 360). The district of the Old City was the most damaged – fewer than 10% of buildings remained in January 1945.
4 *Gazeta Wyborcza*: Kwaśniewski, 'I Let Them Seduce Me'.
5 A popular bookstore chain.
6 *Gazeta Wyborcza*: Kwaśniewski, 'I Let Them Seduce Me'.
7 Under international agreements, citizens of the Second Polish Republic living in areas incorporated into the USSR could return to Poland. The largest wave took place in the first half of 1946. Jews made up fewer than 200,000 of that number, and the majority soon left Poland; in 1947, Jewish Committees registered 90,000 people in the country (Cała, 2014: 17).
8 The decision to build the Common House was taken on 3 April 1948; PPR and PPS members ended up donating over 1.5 billion zlotys to its construction. For more on this, see Witold Pronobis, 'Kongres Zjednoczeniowy – Powstanie PZPR', *Acta Universitatis Nicolai Copernici*, Historia XV – Nauki Humanistyczno-społeczne – zeszyt 102, 1978, pp. 21–37.
9 In 1948, PPR was unified with PPS and became PZPR.
10 Actually, the biggest institution in the district was a jail infamous for holding political prisoners.
11 Janina Bauman's 1988 book *A Dream of Belonging: My Years in Postwar Poland*, which she dedicated to her husband, is a good source of intimate details about the Bauman household in this period.
12 Modzelewski and Werblan (2017: 35–49). This excellent book about political life in postwar Poland is a series of discussions between two historians who were central postwar actors on opposite political sides. According to Werblan, Stalin preferred to organize the elections and to falsify them. He

opposed the 1946 referendum, but the PPR leaders decided against Stalin in order to gauge the mood of the people.

13 Edemariam, 'Professor with a Past'.

14 This is a common Party expression which means, effectively, trying to get more commitment to communist activity. In postwar Poland, depending on the year, regime and circumstances, both 'socialist' and 'communist' were employed as terms for the direction of change in the country. According to the usual official discourse, Poland was a socialist country on the way to communism. The common perception was that Poland maintained some elements of 'relative freedom', thus diverging from other countries in the Soviet bloc. This was true in that the leadership accepted the existence of small private firms, discreet church activity, and ownership of small plots of land and houses or apartments. This produced a feeling of a partial freedom, though the situation was dynamic and years of 'relative freedom' often alternated with periods of great rigidity.

15 See chapter 7. Bibrowski led the KBW Political and Educational Board.

16 Archives of KBW, 1950 – I am grateful to Joanna Tokarska-Bakir for this document.

17 *Gazeta Wyborcza*: Kwaśniewski, 'I Let Them Seduce Me'. See chapter 1 re Sanacja and Endecja. Sanacja was Piłsudski's prewar fraction, which took power in a military action aimed at creating a 'healthy' political life ('Sanacja' originated from the Latin word 'santos', meaning healing).

See chapters 1 and 2 about the material situation and the limited access of Jews to public secondary and higher education in prewar Poland.

18 Gazeta Wyborcza: Kwaśnieski, 'I Let Them Seduce Me'.

19 APW – KW PZPR – personal file – Bauman 16 421 (3183), Party questionnaire (Ankieta dla aktywu partyjnego – PZPR Komitet Centralny – 23 October 1949).

20 Bauman's career progress is visible on the IPN website: https://katalog.bip. ipn.gov.pl/informacje/54260.

21 AAN, file 2935 Ministerstwo Oświaty; Akademia Nauk Politycznych pismo – 3 June 1947.

22 Course information from 7 July 1947 is available at AAN, file 2935 Ministerstwo Oświaty.

23 www.britannica.com/biography/Manfred-Lachs.

24 During all three years, students were also supposed to take foreign-language classes, including Russian, French, English and German: AAN – 2935 – ANP.

25 E-book devoted to Manfred Lachs: https://issuu.com/ikmpsa/docs/ manfred_lachs_w_podrozy__ktora_nazy, p. 185.

26 Ibid., p. 320.

27 The difference between the two versions is not related to the quality of the translation. Janina Bauman translated her book into Polish. She may have thought the Polish audience would be more familiar with the postwar context and would understand the significance of Bauman's KBW responsibilities.

28 Under German occupation, Polish citizens had no right to a secondary education (only professional training was allowed). High-school and university courses were organized by the underground, but, due to the clandestine character of those conspiratorial institutions, their offerings were limited. For more about this, see Dławichowski (1983).

29 Janina's maternal grandfather was Aleksander Fryszman, a famous urologist who owned a clinic on Tłomackie Street in Warsaw, where he worked with his son, Janina's uncle, Jerzy Fryszman – also a well-known urologist and founder of the Polish Association of Urologists. Janina's father, Szymon, was also a urologist, while his brother Julian, who died in the Holocaust, was a physician. Another uncle, Leon Plocker, was a famous gastroenterologist and an engaged communist. The Fryszman-Lewinsons were a typical 'Warsaw doctors' family' – Jewish origins, educated in the best medical schools (mostly in Russia, Austria, Germany, Switzerland and France) and 'assimilated' – meaning that, at home, they spoke Polish, their children were educated in the best Polish schools (before the segregationist law), the men served in the Polish Army, and their religion, if practised at all, was more of a cultural expression than the result of strong beliefs.

30 In 1988, Janina Bauman published in the UK her first autobiographical book, *Winter in the Morning: A Young Girl's Life in the Warsaw Ghetto and Beyond, 1939–1945*. This account is a reconstruction of war experiences based partially on the author's journal written as a teenager.

31 Eva's birth name was Rundstein.

32 In a luxurious building at 5 Sienna Street.

33 https://sztetl.org.pl/pl/miejscowosci/w/18-warszawa/100-demografia/220 81-demografia.

34 As described in chapter 2, racial segregation was institutionally imposed and an anti-Semitic ambiance was generalized in Poland.

35 Janina Bauman kept a journal starting in her teenage years and maintained the habit all her life. These extremely precious and unique notes, most of which were preserved through the war, constituted the basis for her two autobiographical books published in the late 1980s. The book about her war experience is one of the most important and rare child testimonies from the Warsaw Ghetto and the 'Aryan' side published after the war. The second book narrates her life in postwar Poland. The story outlined in this chapter is based on these two publications.

36 See chapter 5.

37 People who lived outside Germany, but were culturally and ethnically considered German.

38 AIPN BU 0 1224/1505, p. 131. Bułat gave a declaration on the war history of Alina Lewinson and her daughters. The 26 June 1957 date suggests that it was taken on the occasion of Alina Lewinson's emigration to Israel.

39 During the German occupation, Warsaw Jews were forced to live in the Ghetto. On the Polish 'Aryan' side, buildings, public spaces and public transportation were divided between Poles and Germans.

40 Being hidden on the Aryan side offered Jews a chance to survive. There is an extensive literature about life in hiding: Bikont (2017); Nalewajko-Kulikov (2004); compare with Paulsson (2003).

41 The best-known network that placed Jewish children in Aryan homes was the Sendler activity (see Bikont, 2017). On Jewish children hidden on the Aryan side, see www.yadvashem.org/odot_pdf/Microsoft%20Word% 20-%204874.pdf.

42 This sounds 'noble' in Polish.

43 Stanislaw Likiernik provides one exceptional account of spending the war hiding his Jewish origins (Likiernik, 2001: ch. 6).

44 This issue is highly controversial in Poland and has been the subject of various publications. See Grabowski (2013) and, in Polish, the biography of nurse Irena Sendler by Anna Bikont (2017).
45 At the start of World War II, 359,827 Jews were registered in Warsaw. In 1940, an additional 90,000 came from German-annexed territories; at its peak in April 1941, the Ghetto population was 450,000. The evacuation 'actions' from 22 July through 21 September 1942 resulted in the expulsion and death of 275,000 Jews. Only a tiny number survived the Ghetto Uprising and its liquidation. In 1946, there were 18,000 Jews in Warsaw. See the historical website of the Polin Museum: https://sztetl. org.pl/pl/miejscowosci/w/18-warszawa/99-historia-spolecznosci/138212-historia-spolecznosci.
46 It was impossible to nourish three people on one modest salary.
47 According to Natalia Aleksiun (*YIVO Encyclopedia*), Berihah is a 'clandestine, Zionist-organized mass movement of about 250,000 Jews from Eastern and Central Europe following the Holocaust. The goal of Berihah (Heb., flight or escape) was to bring the Jews to Palestine. The term refers to both the migration itself and the organization that assisted it. The immigrants were mainly Polish, though Slovak, Romanian, and other Jews participated. Austria and Czechoslovakia served as transit countries from which Jews moved first either to Germany or Italy' (www.yivoencyclopedia.org/printarticle.aspx?id=219).
48 Joanna Tokarska-Bakir provides a step-by-step account of the carnage and its participants in *Coursed: A Social Portrait of the Kielce Pogrom* (2018), She masterfully destroys the thesis of communist provocation, revealing the background of various participants in the massacre and the dynamics of the situation.
49 Natalia Aleksiun, 'Berihah', *YIVO Encyclopedia*: www.yivoencyclopedia. org/printarticle.aspx?id=219.
50 Janina Bauman's autobiographical account was clearly written from the perspective of a woman in love, but some of her praise for Zygmunt resonates with the personality described by co-workers and friends interviewed by me. One trait that Janina quickly noted was Zygmunt's capacity to do what seemed to him to be right without first seeking the approval of any of those around him. For example, despite being a communist officer, Bauman kissed Janina's hand after their first encounter – a popular behaviour that, by the late 1940s, would have been perceived as bourgeois. It could be deconstructed also as a sign of independence or lack of conformity with the reigning signifiers in a socialist country.
51 Without proper treatment and good hygiene, TB was often a fatal infectious disease.
52 AIPN BU 0 1224/1505 – Bauman questionnaire from 1950, reproduced in the note from 24 April 1969.
53 Leon Plocker (1888–1968), educated in university clinics in Berlin, Paris and Basel, was also a military physician. After receiving his doctorate in Basel, he returned to Poland and took part in the Polish–Soviet war (1920) as a soldier-physician. He worked as a voluntary physician in the Warsaw Ghetto and during the Warsaw Uprising, and following Liberation led the central clinic of the Ministry of Public Security. He was the private doctor to the leaders of the ministry, the most powerful institution in postwar Poland.

54 Colonel Henryk Toruńczyk, born in 1909, son of a socialist BUND activist, was a prewar communist and textile engineer (educated in Belgium); he engaged in Spain in the International Brigade (1937–9); and was the last commander of the Botwin Company, and chief of staff in the Polish Dabrowski Brigade (in Polish, 'Dąbrowszczacy').

55 Colonel Leon Rubinsztein (also spelt 'Rubinsztajn') (1912–61), company chief in the International Brigade in Spain; postwar department chief in the Ministry of Public Security.

56 AIPN BU 0 1224/1505 – Information from the note from 24 April 1969, based on the Bauman KBW personal files (pp. 2–3). The document contains an error in Janina's family name – 'Lewinzon' instead of 'Lewinson'.

57 I wish to thank to Professor Katarzyna Sierakowska for information concerning interwar marriages of Polish officers.

58 The main source about Bauman's life in this period comes from the Polish version of Janina Bauman's book (2011), which contains many more details than the English edition.

59 Several interviewees noted this was the case in the postwar period, when a climate of suspicion was ever-present.

60 In the first pages of this chapter, I included more details about this important event.

61 About his career progress, see the second section of this chapter.

62 Zygmunt was a supporter of Legia Warszawa.

63 Famous chocolate factory, created by Karol Wedel in 1851 in Warsaw, nationalized in 1949.

64 Chaim's son Lejb Fogelman is a Polish-American lawyer, a key actor in the privatizations that took place after the fall of communism in 1989. He told this story to Komar.

65 'The greatest difficulty when trying to describe the awareness of Poles in the years of Stalinism is a characteristically conflicted mixture of fear, falsehood and pretentious explosions of enthusiasm with genuine, sometimes even fanatical support for the dictatorship and its actions. It is impossible to untangle this knot because almost everyone was saying the same words and sentences, chanting the same slogans and if they did not believe them completely, they did not betray their lack of belief even to their own children' (Modzelewski, 2013: 60).

66 See Lipiński (2016).

67 I conducted this interview in November 2017 in Warsaw. About Turski's childhood, see chapter 2.

68 About engagement of this generation, see Hirszowicz (2001). Hirszowicz was one of Bauman's university colleagues.

69 See, for example, Nesterowicz (2017).

70 The term originated in 1936 during the Spanish Civil War and designated Republicans who secretly supported Franco's Nationalists. For Poland in World War II, it referred to ethnic Germans living in Polish territories before 1939 who backed the German invasion. In the postwar context, Fifth Columnist referred to anyone who, while ostensibly backing the new regime, secretly opposed it and supported enemies, especially foreign ones.

71 The whole story is in J. Bauman (1988: 92–7).

72 Polish version of J. Bauman's book (2011: 75).

73 AIPN BU 0 1224/1505 p. 129 ('Secret').

74 Andrzej Wajda (1926–2016) was a prominent Polish film and theatre director, winner of an honorary Oscar, Palme d'Or, Golden Lion, Golden Bear, BAFTA and César awards. The story of his script's censorship is at J. Bauman (1988: 114).
75 Interview with the author in December 2015.
76 APW – KW PZPR – personal file – Bauman 16 421 (3183).
77 It is worth noting that this event occurred before Stalin launched the 'Doctors' Trial' (December 1952).
78 Adam Schaff (1913–2006), a Marxist philosopher.
79 APW – KW PZPR – personal file – Bauman 16 421 (3183).
80 AIPN, personal file Zygmunt Bauman, part III, file 7–7v.
81 APW – KW PZPR – personal file – Bauman 16 421 (3183).
82 https://katalog.bip.ipn.gov.pl/informacje/69545.
83 Archives UW, student files Zygmunt Bauman WFS – 23.496.
84 Ibid.
85 Ibid.
86 APW – KW PZPR – personal file – Bauman 16 421 (3183).

8 A Young Scholar

1 This story continues to circulate within the Faculty of Philosophy and Sociology at Warsaw University. For a short analysis of this anecdote, see the final chapter.
2 This historical section is based mainly on Antonii Sułek's presentation of the Institute of Sociology, University of Warsaw – including the list of MAs (statistical analysis by author), available on the official website of the Institute of Sociology at www.is.uw.edu.pl/wp-content/uploads/mgrisuw1933-2004.pdf.
3 About the changes after 1945, see Kraśko (1996).
4 Leon Petrażycki (1867–1931): lawyer, sociologist of law and philosopher, educated in Kiev, Berlin, Heidelberg, Paris and London. Taught law in Czarist Russia, and supported the vote for women. In Poland from 1919, where he took the Chair of Sociology. Opposed discrimination against Jews.
5 Ludwik Krzywicki (1859–1941): Marxist intellectual, sociologist, economist, politician. One of the first Polish Marxists (he translated the first part of Das Kapital into Polish, and also some of Engels' works), and he was a member of the positivist movement. Krzywicki studied mathematics in Warsaw, and ethnology, archaeology and anthropology in Zurich and Paris.
6 Stefan Czarnowski (1879–1937): sociologist, folklorist and historian of culture. Educated in Leipzig (philosophy, psychology and economy), Berlin (theory of sociology and history of art) and Paris (painting, sociology and religious studies). He was a socialist who later supported the revolutionary workers' movement.
7 Stanisław Bystroń (1892–1964): ethnographer and sociologist, educated in Kraków and Paris (ethnography). Taught ethnography, ethnology and sociology in Poznań, Warsaw and Kraków (Jagiellonian University).
8 Florian Znaniecki (1882–1958): Polish-American sociologist whose theoretical and methodological work helped make sociology a distinct academic discipline. Educated in Warsaw, Paris and Switzerland (Ph.D.

in philosophy), he was co-author of *The Polish Peasant in Europe and America* (1918–20), a methodological bible for qualitative sociologists for two decades. He was a father of humanism in sociology.

9 The founding of sociology is often attributed to the University of Chicago, which in 1892–3 opened the Department of Social Science and Anthropology, later renamed Sociology and Anthropology – see Chapoulie (2001: 36).

10 See Kłoskowska (1989), and Bartoszewski (2007). Kłoskowska focused on the intellectual work of Ossowski and Chałasiński, and Bartoszewski analysed the underground university activity (in 1944, he estimates there were 3,500 clandestine students). Bartoszewski recounts the story of a sociology lecturer and his students who were captured by the Gestapo in Poznań, and killed: www.is.uw.edu.pl/wp-content/uploads/Socjologia-na-UW.-Wyd.2-2012.pdf, pp. 119–24.

11 Information in this section is based on A. Sułek, *The History of the Institute of Sociology*, on the official website of the Institute of Sociology, University of Warsaw: www.is.uw.edu.pl/pl/instytut/historia-instytutu-socjologii.

12 Stanisław Ossowski (1897–1963) was a sociologist educated in Warsaw (philosophy with Kotarbiński and Tatarkiewicz, among others) and in Paris, Rome and London. A supporter of humanistic sociology (beliefs as a basis for social bonds and relationships) and co-creator, with his wife, of 'the science of science' – an opponent of positivism.
   Maria Ossowska (1896–1974), educated in Warsaw (philosophy), was a specialist in ethics.

13 Nina Assorodobraj (1908–1999): specialist in historical sociology (she introduced the study of memory and historical consciousness); educated in Warsaw and in Paris, worked after habilitation in Lwów. She was professor at Łódź University postwar, then Warsaw. Marxist and activist (PPR then PZPR).

14 This intellectual current was created in 1895 by Kazimierz Twardowski (1866–1938), the philosopher and psychologist. Educated in Vienna, he worked at Lwów University, where he was a famous teacher. The Lwów–Warsaw School of Philosophy contains elements of mathematics, psychology, logic and semantics.

15 Tadeusz Kotarbiński (1886–1981), philosopher, specialist in logic and ethics. Member of the Lwów–Warsaw School. Educated in Lwów (philosophy) and Darmstadt (architecture). Professor from 1919 at Warsaw University. He was strongly opposed to the anti-Semitic laws imposed at the university in the 1930s. From 1945, he organized the system of higher education in Poland and was the first rector of Łódź University.

16 Władysław Tatarkiewicz (1886–1980), philosopher, historian of philosophy, historian of art, specialized in aesthetics. Member of Lwów–Warsaw Philosophical School.

17 In Poland, it was not rare to accumulate two or even three parallel positions.

18 Julian Hochfeld (1911–66).

19 See chapter 7.

20 This process is illustrated through the number of master's students and their advisers. In 1952, of sixty-three people who graduated with a thesis in social sciences, twenty-six were advised by Ossowski, twenty-two by Assorodobraj; in 1953, there were only five master's students, of whom Ossowski supervised two and Assorodobraj three; in 1954, the year of

Bauman's thesis exam, there were twenty-two master's candidates, and Marxist faculty supervised the majority: Hochfeld (seven), Assorodobraj (four), Schaff (three) and Wojnar (three). Ossowski had been banned from teaching.

21 This information is from a student *carnet* – with a grade transcript (*index*) preserved in the Bauman student archives at Warsaw University.

22 Interviews conducted in 2016.

23 for more about the master–students relationship, see Wagner (2011, 2015).

24 Barbara Szacka said: 'I was not at the Ossowski seminar for a very simple reason. Ossowski had a very special style of practising science – a unique style. He was a man of unprecedented knowledge. He mastered the history of European culture and he moved very freely and at the same time with a logical accuracy – he jumped from one topic to another very freely. ... because of my previous education, I couldn't follow him'.

25 In this same interview, Jerzy Szacki remarked, 'there were people who completed his seminar but it was hard to say they were his students in the sense of continuing his thought ... for example Nowak. From this point of view, Bauman and I are more students of Ossowski than was Stefan Nowak.' As suggested by the letters sent by Ossowski (in the last years of his life), he had a very good relationship with Bauman.

26 Jerzy Wiatr (born 1931), sociologist, political scientist, communist activist. He was a Member of Parliament (1991–7) and minister of higher education (1996–7). Friend of Bauman at Warsaw University from 1952. They co-authored texts. He belongs to Hochfeld's School of 'Open Marxism'.

27 Bi-monthly, then weekly, socio-literary journal (1947–57), published first by the Academic Union of Youth Struggle, then the Academic Union of Polish Youth, then the Union of Polish Youth.

28 Wiatr said also: 'later our children would call us "uncle". We were more than friends, we were almost family, and so it remained until the end.'

29 Actually, Schaff, in his letter to Walicki in 1982, described Bauman as 'this Stalinist', suggesting he thought Bauman was a sincere supporter of Stalin.

30 Interview conducted on 3 April 2017 at the Institute of Sociology, Warsaw University.

31 See Nalewajko-Kulikov (2004).

32 Here Wiatr refers to the Suez Crisis (also called Operation Kadesh, or the Sinai War), a military conflict among Israel, the UK, France and Egypt that started on 29 October 1956.

33 Kołakowski became an orphan at the age of 15; his mother died in the first days of his life; his father, a military socialist and journalist, was killed by the Nazis in 1943. Kołakowski came under the care of other members of his family and friends of his father (members of a socialist group). He grew up in the houses of the Warsaw intelligentsia and, despite wartime conditions, obtained an excellent education through underground classes and foreign-language training.

34 From 1946, he was enrolled in PPR (Merda, 2017: 138).

35 Tomasz Potkaj, 'Rozmawiaj ze mną na poważniejsze tematy' [Discuss with Me about More Serious Issues], *Tygodnik Powszechny*; www.tygodnik.com.pl/apokryf/18/potkaj.html.

36 Ibid.

37 *Kuźnica* was the Marxist weekly literature journal, edited in Łódź from 1945 to 1950.

38 Tomasz Potkaj, article in *Tygodnik Powszechny*; www.tygodnik.com.pl/apokryf/18/potkaj.html.
39 Kołakowski ostensibly followed Kotarbiński to Warsaw, but Schaff was the key figure in his life – institutionally, politically and philosophically.
40 The expression refers to elite schools, usually military ones, and originates in Turkey, where the Janissaries were ruthless soldiers expertly trained to protect the leader.
41 Tadeusz Kroński (1907–58), philosopher and historian of philosophy. Educated in Warsaw (by Tatarkiewicz and Kotarbiński) and Prague. One of the strongest supporters of Stalinism in Poland. He is considered to be a spiritual father of the Warsaw School of ideas headed by Kołakowski, Baczko and Pomian.
42 AUW – Personal file of employee: Bauman – Certificate ending active military service, dated 27 March 1953 – to present the new employee.
43 AUW – Personal file of employee: Bauman – Request for employment, dated 21 January 1953.
44 Marek Fritzhand was twelve years older than Bauman. A Marxist philosopher and ethics specialist, during World War II Fritzhand was a political officer in the Kościuszko Division.
45 'At many universities, classes in sociology at law and economic faculties could not take place due to the lack of lecturers' (Kraśko, 1996: 126).
46 AUW, employee file – Bauman – letter to PAN from HR UW – L.Dz. I29/K/54 (dated 15.IV.1954).
47 AUW, employee file – Bauman; CV dated 23 January 1953.
48 Schaff wrote about anti-Semitism in Poland in chapter 7 of his book *Próba podsumowania* (An Attempt at a Conclusion) (1999).
49 AUW, employee personal file – Bauman – Życiorys naukowy 1965 (Scientific CV).
50 Kołakowski had some trouble with the procedure but defended his Ph.D. on Spinoza. Tadeusz Kroński and Maria Ossowska were the reporters.
51 This title was mentioned in his academic CV from 1965. On the website of the Institute of Sociology another title is mentioned: 'The Science of Nature and Social Science by Rickert and Windelband'. A question mark after the title suggests this information is not confirmed. However, the area of study reminds the same.
52 Jan Legowicz (1909–92), philosopher and historian of philosophy; specialist in medieval and ancient philosophy. Educated in Lwów and Freiburg.
53 AUW, employee file – Bauman; Protokół Komisji Egzaminu Dyplomowego (Protocol of the Commission of the Exam for Diploma), dated 25 June 1954.
54 AUW, employee file – Bauman – letter to PAN from HR UW – L.Dz. I29/K/54 (dated 15.IV.1954).
55 According to a document from Party files: 'In 1953/54 he was a member of the executive department of P.OP. [Podstawowa Organizacja Partyjna – the basic Party organization]. In this year [1955] he served as the organizer of the Party group in the Chair of Dialectical and Historical Materialism' (APW – KW PZPR – personal file – Bauman 16 421 (3183)).
56 Author's interview with Barbara Szacka and Jerzy Szacki, Warsaw, 2016.
57 Bauman, in his preface to Bauman (1964b: 19), in Saltherwhite (1992: 197, n. 10).
58 Chałubiński (2017) /

59 Friedman (1966).
60 See chapter 2.
61 Friedman (1966).
62 This view was held in certain circles. Before World War II, Poland was an independent country; after 1944, the state was under Soviet control, the economy was devastated by war and the country did not benefit from the Marshall Plan. As Western Germany's economic health and industrial development moved forward, Poles shared a huge feeling of historical injustice.
63 It was extremely brave to say this publicly, since the official discourse was victorious and friendly to the USSR.
64 For the detailed story, see Gdula (2017).
65 'Referring to his favorite author, Kazimierz Kelles-Krauz, Hochfeld used the concept of "open Marxism". It consisted of three basic elements, in my opinion' (Wiatr, 2017a: 18–19): 'First of all: treating all claims of Marxism as verifiable scientific theses, not quasi-religious dogmas adopted on the basis of institutional authority, which was characteristic of Marxism–Leninism at the time, and even earlier in the official Marxism of the Second International (see contemporary criticism of Edward Bernstein's revisionism). Second, readiness to accommodate the discoveries and claims that were beyond the reach of Marxist thought that would withstand scientific scrutiny – which was tantamount to rejecting a rigid division into "Marxist" and "bourgeois" sociology. And finally, the readiness to enrich and revise Marxist theory based on new facts, which, among other things, justified the need to conduct empirical sociological research. Such research was neither "Marxist" nor "non-Marxist." ... [T]he programme of open Marxism formulated by Hochfeld logically resulted from a recognition of the need to enrich theory with knowledge from new social phenomena.'
66 On Kelles-Krauz and Open Marxism, see Snyder (1997).
67 J. Hochfeld, 'Rewizje i tradycje', *Przegląd Kulturalny* 15, 1957; Hochfeld, 'Kelles-Krauza marksizm otwarty', *Nowa Kultura* 48 1957.
68 See the last part of the previous chapter.
69 Maverick: a person with unconventional behaviour, named after Samuel A. Maverick (1803–70), Texas rancher, who did not brand his cattle (*Collins Dictionary*: www.collinsdictionary.com/dictionary/english/maverick). For the category of the maverick in sociology, see Becker (1982: 233–46).
70 Strzelecki passed himself off as a street cleaner to enter and exit the Ghetto on rescue missions (see governmental website, CVs of Polish scientists: http://ipsb.nina.gov.pl/a/biografia/jan-strzelecki-socjolog).
71 www.is.uw.edu.pl/wp-content/uploads/mgrisuw1933-2004.pdf.
72 See chapter 4 in Grochowska (2014). This biography of Strzelecki, a secretive and modest person, also gives a broader picture of Polish intellectuals working under restrictions on freedom. Andrzej Walicki, historian of ideas and younger colleague of Strzelecki in Łódź, remembered that in the organization Życie (Life) to which Strzelecki and Kołakowski belonged, Strzelecki was trusted as a 'human over organization man', while Kołakowski awakened fear; those close to him believed he would 'denounce in a just cause' because of his blind devotion to the Party (Walicki, cited in Grochowska, 2014: 170). For the text in Polish: http://lewicowo.pl/o-socjalistycznym-humanizmie.
73 As explained in previous chapters, the KBW did not always support Moscow policy unconditionally (as did the UB). But by 1952/3, when

Bauman was fired, the organization was Stalinist, and a Polish road to socialism was no longer an option.

74 Aleksandra Jasińska-Kania – Bauman's second wife.

75 www.is.uw.edu.pl/wp-content/uploads/mgrisuw1933-2004.pdf.

76 According to the official website of the Institute of Sociology, the following scholars defended master's theses in 1954: Aleksandra Jasińska (Kania): 'The Objectivity of Nature and Society' (Schaff); Albin Kania: 'The Present Stage of the Class Struggle and Party Politics in the Countryside'; Włodzimierz Wesołowski: 'The Role of the Party and of Marxist–Leninist Ideology in the Creation of the Consciousness of the Polish Workers in the Light of "Workers' Memories"' (Hochfeld); Jerzy Wiatr: 'The Bankruptcy of the Moral Authority of Capitalism in Interwar Poland in the Light of "Workers' Memories"' (Hochfeld).

77 Franz Borkenau (1900–57), Austrian scholar and writer. In his work, he linked Marxism with psychoanalysis. Worked in Frankfurt (Social Research Institute), then in 1933 escaped Nazi anti-Semitic repressions and lived in Paris, Panama and London. After the war, he was back to Germany (Marburg) and became openly anti-communist. Including his writing in the reading list was exceptionally courageous in postwar Poland.

78 Grochowska uses 'In the Muzzle' as a chapter title in her biography of Jan Strzelecki (Grochowska 2014: 325).

79 Bauman and Wiatr, for example, co-authored two articles.

80 Author's interview, Leeds, 2013.

81 For an artistic portrait of the Stalinist period in Warsaw, see the movie *Rewers* (2009) by Borys Lankosz.

82 Polish Stalinism was lighter on campus than in other Soviet-bloc countries. Marxist science was introduced in the 1950s, but, for example, Lysenkoist genetics was only taught for a single year in Warsaw, and even that year students could also take underground lessons in 'bourgeois' genetics. See William Dejong-Lambert (2012).

83 The first text published in a philosophical journal was 'Marksa "Przyczynek do krytyki ekonomii politycznej". W związku z nowym polskim wydaniem', *Myśl Filozoficzna*, 2, 1954, pp. 157–87. A new Polish edition of Marx's book *A Contribution to the Critique of Political Economy*, it appeared in *Philosophical Thought* in 1954.

84 Other chairs and institutions were managed by individuals deeply involved in Stalinist implementation, whether because of fear, opportunism or true belief.

85 Even after 1989, salaries were still usually modest and state-paid – and without job security.

86 AUW, employee personal file – Bauman – document from 15 February 1953. No. A/II/463/52.

87 AUW, employee personal file – Bauman – document from 24 February 1953. No. N/II/593/513. This kind of document is a regular paper signed by all teaching staff (professors usually have fewer teaching hours).

88 AUW, employee personal file – Bauman – document from 20 April 1953. No. N/II/1177?19/52.

89 See chapter 6.

90 The document was signed by the head of human relations at the university, Irena Kurowa: AUW, employee file.

91 Letter dated 26 October 1954, from the University of Warsaw pro-rector

to the Ministry of Higher Education requesting permission to create a second full-time position in higher education: AUW, employee file.

92 Document of the School of Party PZPR; APW – KW PZPR – personal file – Bauman 16 421 (3183). See also Puławski (2009, 2018).

93 This was an apartment owned or managed by the university. It was very difficult to get an administrative allocation of an apartment; the number of children in the family could play a decisive role in the process.

94 Janina wrote that she forgot Zygmunt's birthday that year, and that it made him sad. They spent 19 November like any ordinary day (J. Bauman, 1988: 121).

95 Janina Bauman suffered from post-pregnancy complications worsened by former tuberculosis (J. Bauman, 1988).

96 There was always a struggle between the Stalinist and pro-Polish versions of socialism. The first won after the fusion of PPR with PPS, and was led by Bierut. The second option was at first represented by Gomułka, who lost power after the creation of PZPR and was jailed in 1951 and tortured by the infamous Department X.

97 Most of the information in the following section was completed with the help of the analysis by Modzelewski and Werblan from their excellent book of discussions moderated by Robert Walenciak (Modzelewski and Werblan, 2017).

98 Barbara Szacka recalled, 'Zygmunt complained that the situation with baby-twins was difficult' (author's interview with Barbara Szacka and Jerzy Szacki, Warsaw, 2016).

99 The Party's new policy shifted towards lifting some state and Party controls, and also punishment and marginalization of Stalin's supporters. Divisions over the new direction produced instability throughout the communist-led countries, except in places such as Albania, which did not recognize Stalin's crimes. For that reason, the presence of foreign visitors on the day of the speech was forbidden – it was an 'internal' meeting.

100 The reparation process started immediately, with amnesty for political prisoners and the liberation of people serving sentences in the Gulag. Several victims were 'rehabilitated' – including post-mortem actions to 'rehabilitate the memory of the victims of Stalinism'. These included abusively liquidated organizations such as the Polish KPP (Communist Party), dissolved in 1938 by Stalin's order.

101 The perception of a sudden death was probably compounded by the secrecy that had surrounded his poor health.

102 All interviewees underlined that Aleksandra Jasińska-Kania was a modest and helpful person. She did not employ her father's name, and many students, and even Party members, were unaware she was the daughter of the president.

103 Kemp-Welch, with humour, concluded that Western intelligence services paid around $1 million for the speech – and could have had it much cheaper if they'd shopped in Warsaw (Kemp-Welch, 1996: 189).

104 According to his obituary, published in the *Independent* on 17 November 2007, Victor Spielman (Victor Abranovich Grayevsky), a Kraków-born journalist and spy, transmitted the speech to the CIA via the Israeli secret services. In April 1956, while visiting his girlfriend in a Communist Party office, he saw the published version and convinced her to borrow it. Spielman then took it to Yaakov Barmor, who worked for Shin Bet,

which transmitted it to the CIA (www.independent.co.uk/news/obituar ies/viktor-grayevsky-400700.html#r3z-addoor). However, Werblan has cast doubt on this version. He compared the Polish translation with the 'official transcript' translated by the CIA and found differences indicating that the CIA had worked from the Russian text. Werblan explained that Khrushchev wanted the speech to reach the West, and knew that, with its vast resources, the CIA would make this happen (in Modzelewski and Werblan, 2017: 102–3).

105 Bauman is speaking about the intentional famine of the 1930s that killed about 5 million people and was organized and implemented by Stalin – for more, see Applebaum, 2018).

106 Anti-communist radio that broadcast in Eastern Europe. However, the most popular anti-communist radio transmitted in Poland was Radio Free Europe – Radio Wolna Europa. Both were forbidden.

107 *Gazeta Wyborcza*: Kwaśniewski, 'I Let Them Seduce Me'.

108 Janina Bauman also read about the Katyń massacre in German journals, where she discovered the name of her father on the list of the victims. But she believed the attribution of the massacre to Soviet soldiers was propaganda, and that the Nazis had killed the Polish officers. This version was maintained by the communists after World War II.

109 For more, see Jedlicki (1963).

110 The weekly journal was very popular. Considered by the authorities to be a revisionist medium, they were closed in October 1957 (see Modzelewski, 2013: 86).

111 This last point was erased in one of the numerous reforms of higher education in the twenty-first century. The model described in this chapter concerned people doing their Ph.D. in the late 1950s.

112 AAN, Ministerstwo Szkolnictwa Wyższego, 2860. Personal folder, Zygmunt Bauman. The opinion by Hochfeld for the opening of the Ph.D. title process. All information and cited documents concerning Bauman's Ph.D. thesis are in this folder.

113 Ibid.

114 On the official website of the Institute of Sociology, Warsaw University, the title of the Ph.D. thesis is slightly different: 'Program polityczny Brytyjskiej Partii Pracy' ('Political Program of the British Labour Party'). See www. is.uw.edu.pl/pl/instytut/dorobek-instytutu/doktoraty.

115 AAN, Ministerstwo Szkolnictwa Wyższego, 2860 – opinia – handwritten document signed 'Marek Fritzhand'.

116 AAN, Ministerstwo Szkolnictwa Wyższego, 2860. Report of vote – 20 June 1956. The report on the whole defence ceremony (which was composed of the introduction, presentation of the dissertation by Bauman, presentation of the reviews by reviewers, public discussion, secret elaboration and vote, promotion) was signed two days later, 22 June 1956.

117 AAN, Ministerstwo Szkolnictwa Wyższego, 2860, CK-I-3a/135/56/7.

118 AAN, Ministerstwo Szkolnictwa Wyższego, 2860, CK-I-3a/135/56.

119 AAN, Ministerstwo Szkolnictwa Wyższego, 2860 – opinia – handwritten document signed 'Marek Fritzhand'.

120 'Those active in the struggle for change had been warned to stay away from home at night lest they be arrested' (J. Bauman, 1988: 127).

121 According to Werblan, Chinese opposition convinced the Soviets to call off intervention in Poland (Modzelewski and Werblan, 2017).

122 The emigration wave saw about 51,000 people obtain Israeli visas (about 8,000 of them ended up in other countries) from 1955 to 1960. This number included 14,000 people repatriated from the Soviet Union (see Stola, 2017: 117).

123 The same year, Maria Hirszowicz – Bauman's friend – also defended her Ph.D., prepared under Hochfeld's supervision. Her thesis was titled 'Studium o sprzecznościach międzymocarstwowych we współczesnym kapitaliźmie' ('Study on the Contradictions between the Superpowers in Modern Capitalism'). The team became really strong, not only intellectually but also institutionally.

124 On the rehabilitation of Polish sociology after October 1956, see Łabędź (1959).

125 'Other decisions concerned agrarian policy (against collectivization), focusing industry on [food] products, and relationships with the Church. All these points made the situation in Poland much different from in other communist countries' (Łabędź, 1959).

126 Socjologia na Uniwersytecie Warszawskim, 2007: 210–17: www.is.uw.edu. pl/wp-content/uploads/Socjologia-na-UW.-Wyd.2-2012.pdf.

127 Author's interview with Bauman about his academic career, Leeds, 31 October 2013.

128 A. Schaff, 'Polska na III Międzynarodowym Kongresie Socjologicznym', Nauka Polska, 4, 1956, pp. 217–23.

129 A. Schaff, Aktualne zagadnienia polityki kulturalnej w dziedzinie filozofii i socjologii (Państwowe Wydawnictwo Naukowe (PWN) Warszawa), 1956), pp. 41, 44–5.

130 Janina Bauman certainly had this publication in mind when she spoke about critical texts (1988: 115).

131 Z. Bauman, M. Hirszowicz, W. Wesołowski and J. Wiatr, 'Wczoraj i jutro naszej socjologii', Nowa Kultura, 46, 1956.

132 Bauman (1956: 6).

133 In 1957, a critical article by Bauman was also published in Twórczość (Creativity, a literary monthly) entitled: 'Treaty on Bureaucracy'.

134 Saltherwhite mentions: 'Bauman wrote of Stalinism that, even without examining the causes, it was possible to see that Stalinism had destroyed the very essence of Marxism: It sold out social man as the starting point for philosophy and the relationship of that man to his social–natural environment as the subject of philosophy; by the same token it strangled the deeply rooted revolutionary humanist content of Marxist philosophy [n. 20, p. 134 – from Bauman, 'O przezwyciężenie dezintegracji filozofii marksistowskiej,' Myśl filozodiczna 6, 26, 1956] ... of the context of Marxist philosophy was continued in an essay Bauman wrote in conjunction with another sociologist, Jerzy Wiatr, in which they specifically discussed the relationship of contemporary sociology to Marxism [n. 21 – Jerzy K. Wiatr and Zygmunt Bauman, 'Marksizm i socjologia współczesna', Myśl filozoficzna 1, 1957]. They began by discussing the category of "ideology" as a "class-based, deformed reflection of social reality" [n. 22, p. 3, n. 1]. The conclusions they drew from this, however, were the opposite of those reached by the traditional Marxist approach. Rather than saying that something is true because the proletariat holds it to be so, the position of the proletariat was to be held up to scrutiny as well, in accordance with the criteria of verification and falsification. Just because the proletariat is in the ideal social position to discern the true nature of reality does not mean

that it cannot also succumb to ideology, in the sense given above [n. 23, p. 6]. When Wiatr and Bauman speak of the ideal where the "ideology" of the proletariat becomes "science", they depart from their definition of ideology as a "deformed reflection of reality; even though they qualify the term in the new context, they seem to be shifting definitions. The "ideology" of the proletariat is conceived of here in two mutually conflicting senses': Saltherwhite (1992: 20–2).

135 In Polish, 'if you cannot not-think': 'jeśli nie możesz nie-myśleć'.
136 'Ignoranci i impotenci', interview with Bauman by Tomasz Kwaśniewski, *GW*, 21 November 2010.

9 Years of Hope

1 This term was not employed as a noun in 1957, but 'post-doctoral' was used as an adjective.
2 www.fordfoundation.org/media/2418/1957-annual-report.pdf, p. 42.
3 For more, see Czernecki (2013).
4 This was the practice even in the late 1980s. In 1985 and 1986, when I took summer classes in France, West Berlin and Italy, the procedure was less strict, but visits to the intelligence office were still required. After 1989, the rules changed and Polish citizens kept their passports at home.
5 In the immediate postwar era, English was not as popular as it became later in the century. Poles generally learned Russian (compulsory until the 1990s), German and French.
6 Mills' letters to Bauman were transferred by the Bauman family to the Bauman Archive, Leeds.
7 According to *Encyclopaedia Britannica*, 'Hungarian Revolution, popular uprising in Hungary in 1956 … Encouraged by the new freedom of debate and criticism, a rising tide of unrest and discontent in Hungary broke out into active fighting in October 1956. Rebels won the first phase of the revolution and Imre Nagy became premier, agreeing to establish a multiparty system. On November 1, 1956, he declared Hungarian neutrality … This revolt was bloodily stopped by Soviet military intervention': www.britannica.com/event/Hungarian-Revolution-1956.
8 Ralph Miliband, 'C. Wright Mills', *New Left Review*, 1, 15, May–June 1962: https://newleftreview.org/I/15/ralph-miliband-c-wright-mills. Whereas Miliband mentioned Schaff and Kołakowski, he said nothing about Hochfeld or Bauman.
9 Born in 1916 in Texas, Mills got his bachelor's degree in sociology and a master's in philosophy at the University of Texas at Austin. For his Ph.D., he went back to sociology, finishing his dissertation at the University of Wisconsin–Madison in 1942. After teaching at the University of Maryland (and writing intensively for Left journals such as the *New Republic* and the *New Leader*), in 1945 Mills moved to New York City, where eventually he became a full professor at Columbia. He visited the USSR and other European countries during his sabbaticals, dying in 1962 of a heart attack.
10 www.theguardian.com/politics/2015/feb/22/tariq-ali-fierce-socialist-ralph-miliband-music-delivery.
11 The biography of Ralph Miliband is based on Lipman's text: www.lipman-miliband.org.uk/pdfs/RalphMilibandfullbiog.pdf.

12　See first chapters of the book.

13　Bauman said ten months in a 2010 interview; in some files, his return date is given as July; in others, August.

14　According to a 1957 Ford Foundation report, the British Council managed $25,000 for an exchange between the United Kingdom and Poland (see www.fordfoundation.org/media/2418/1957-annual-report.pdf, p. 42).

15　Janina Bauman gave the figure £38.50; the difference may be explained by the twenty-two years between publication of Janina's book and the interview with Zygmunt Bauman, as well as the Polish habit of rounding numbers.

16　'Ignoranci i impotenci', interview with Bauman by Tomasz Kwaśniewski, *GW*, 21 November 2010: http://wyborcza.pl/duzyformat/1,127290,868354 2,Ignoranci_i_impotenci.html.

17　Conclusion from the study of Polish post-doc scientists' experience in the late twentieth and twenty-first centuries: Wagner (2011).

18　In Polish, 'pasta' was the word *kluski*. 'Ignoranci i impotenci', interview of Bauman by Tomasz Kwaśniewski, *GW*, 21 November 2010.

19　AAN – document from personal files, Zygmunt Bauman, Uniwersytet Warszawski, Ministerstwo Szkolnictwa Wyższego 81/5.

20　At Harvard in 2010, there was a popular saying among post-docs: 'eat/ sleep/post-doc', an apt description of their focus on work (the collection of small, expensive flats around research institutes in the Boston area reflects this lifestyle).

21　This was not simply the opinion of a loving spouse. The productivity of Bauman's stay is confirmed by the quality of his book *Klasa. Ruch. Elita. Studium socjologiczne dziejów angielskiego Ruchu Robotniczego* (1960, PWN); published later in English as *Between Class and Elite: The Evolution of the British Labour Movement. A Sociological Study* (Bauman, 1972).

22　'Ignoranci i impotenci', interview with Bauman by Tomasz Kwaśniewski, *GW*, 21 November 2010.

23　Cited in Czernecki (2013: 299), from 'Report on Ford Foundation Scholars', FFA, R530, G57-321.

24　The process of habilitation varies. In France, for example, publication occurs after habilitation; the manuscript is presented as a basis for habilitation, and after reviews and an exam, the corrected manuscript is published.

25　In Poland, due to the internationalization of scientific careers, and progress of the British model of higher education (which is without habilitation), some call for making academia 'more democratic' by abolishing the feudal, complex hierarchical system. In the late 1950s, there was also a call to eliminate an earlier reform that copied the Soviet academic model. The frequent changes arising from these discussions meant that scholars in the early 1960s rarely had any idea how changes might affect their career progress in a given year.

26　All the cited documents concerning Bauman's habilitation are from the AAN – Ministry of Higher Education – University of Warsaw 46 – folder Personal Files – Zygmunt Bauman.

27　AAN – Ministry of Higher Education – University of Warsaw 46 – folder Personal Files – Zygmunt Bauman. This is a two-page draft manuscript of an official letter to the minister of higher education.

28　The letter is dated 28 September 1960.

29 AAN – Ministry of Higher Education – University of Warsaw 46 – two-page document, dated 5 December 1960, titled: 'Wykaz publikacji'.
30 I would like to thank Dariusz Brzeziński for this information.
31 By contemporary academic standards, this book could be considered a didactic book for sociologists, and people working in human relations and business schools, etc. The categories mentioned in the text were imposed by the ministry, while attribution of the works in those categories was performed by Bauman himself.
32 Bauman had a slightly higher teaching load than his colleagues. According to the official document signed by Hochfeld, Hochfeld had 150 hours each year, while Bauman taught 120. His colleague Maria Hirszowicz had 90 hours, while Szymon Chodak had 60. Three other Ph.D. students (Jankowska, Jasińska-Kania and Wesołowski) each taught 120 hours in the academic year.
33 AAN – Ministry of Higher Education – University of Warsaw 46 – two-page document, dated 30 June 1965, entitled: 'Życiorys naukowy' (Scientific Curriculum), p. 2.
34 Information obtained from interviews with Bauman's friends.
35 This is probably also related to the complex story of the *honoris causa* – which is a renewal of a doctorate at Warsaw University, a ceremony that was refused. Bauman has a lot of opponents inside of his former institution – see chapter 13.
36 Toruńczyk studied at the Institute of Sociology (1964–8) and was a leading opposition figure, beginning in 1963. In 1968, she was condemned to two years in jail for 'anti-state activity'. In 1980, she emigrated to France where she created the monthly *Literary Notebooks*. Her father, Colonel Henryk Toruńczyk, was a friend of Janina Bauman's uncle and signed Janina's certificate of 'good moral behaviour' before their marriage in 1947 (see chapter 5). (I am grateful to Barbara Toruńczyk for her testimony and permission to use it in this book.)
37 AIPN BU 0 1224/1505 'Doniesienie dot. dr Zygmunta Baumana – 'Henryk'.
38 Jan Tomasz Gross, interview conducted in New York City, April 2016.
39 A 3+ was an average grade; the grades were: 2 – insufficient, 3 – sufficient, 4 – good, 5 – very good. Gross was a former physics student who transferred into sociology. Physics 'was too difficult for me, so I moved to sociology'; Gross did not pass an entrance exam, but was transferred thanks to family relationships – sociology was very popular at that time, and it was only thanks to informal support that this kind of manoeuvre was possible.
40 See in the next pages.
41 After leaving an institution, the Ph.D. mentor usually continues to supervise the thesis. This is why after leaving the Party Higher School for Social Research Bauman kept his Ph.D. students.
42 AAN – Ministry of Higher Education – University of Warsaw 46 – document dated 30 June 1965, titled: 'Wykaz kierowanych prac doktorskich' (List of Mentored Ph.D. Theses').
43 Ibid.
44 AAN – Ministry of Higher Education – University of Warsaw 46 – two-page document, 'Życiorys naukowy' (Scientific Curriculum), p. 2.
45 Oskar Lange, a famous Polish economist.
46 Szacki is referring to Oskar Lange, *Calosc i rozwoj w swietle cybernetyki* (Totality and Development in the Light of Cybernetics), published in 1963.

Bauman probably read Norbert Wiener's book *Cybernetics: Or Control and Communication in the Animal and the Machine* (1948) and/or his *The Human Use of Human Being* from the 1950s. The Russian-born American writer Wassily Leontief's book on economic cybernetics was published in Poland in 1963 (*Studia nad strukturą gospodarki amerykańskiej* (Warsaw: PWN, 1963). In the late 1950s and early 1960s, this field attracted some social scientists and was a 'hot topic' in international meetings.

47 Interview with Barbara Szacki and Jerzy Szacki in their home in Warsaw, August 2015.

48 In the first group, the most important piece was the manual titled *An Outline of the Marxist Theory of Society* (1964), a 577-page book, the first of its genre (systematization of the Marxist theory of society) ever published. In the second category (especially sociology of sociology), the most important work is the *Visions of a Human World* – which saw repeated editions and numerous translations: AAN – Ministry of Higher Education – University of Warsaw 46 – document dated 30 June 1965, pp. 5–6.

49 AAN – Ministry of Higher Education – University of Warsaw 46 – document, dated 30 June 1965, twelve pages, pp. 4–7.

50 Ibid., quote from p. 6.

51 According to his scientific CV dated 30 June 1965, Bauman was also an editor of other social science journals. Ibid.

52 The most detailed list of travels, dated 1 April 1968, was elaborated by the secret services: AIPN BU 0 1224/1505 – 'Notatka służbowa' z dnia 1 kwietnia 1968'. This document contains some errors in the dates.

53 AIPN BU 0 1224/1505 – 'Notatka służbowa' – Note of service from 1 April 1968. The document contains an error regarding the 1959 World Congress trip – it took place in Stresa in September, not Venice in April. However, the note may refer to a passport request rather than the travel period.

54 AIPN BU 0 1224/1505. Some sources offer different versions; I was unable to confirm all dates in the official documents.

55 AIPN BU 0 1224/1505 – 'Notatka, Tajne', dated 15 March 1968. This document has many errors: it claims Bauman was in London in 1957 for fifteen, rather than nine, months, and mistakenly reports he gave summer classes at Syracuse University twice – in 1964 and 1966, while in fact he was there only in 1966. The period given for his visiting professor position in Manchester is also wrong.

56 AIPN BU 0 1224/1505 – 'Notatka służbowa' z dnia 1 kwietnia 1968'.

57 Bauman Archive, Leeds: a letter dated 25 January 1966, from Peter M. Worsley, professor at Manchester University. Worsley was surprised by those difficulties, while previous visiting professors (Ossowski and a Soviet scholar) did not have any problems with getting a working visa.

58 AIPN BU 0 1224/1505 – 'Dokumenty Biuro – 'C' Naczelnik wydziału IV departamentu III. – wyjazd służbowy do USA od 3 08 – 1966 do 10 09 1966 delegacja Ministerstwa Szkolnictwa Wyższego; wyjazd do Francji – 4-IX 1966 na 8 dni – służbowy delegacja Min Szkolnictwa'.

59 His passport files (number of passport 35846 and professional no. E043405) note that, on 6 June 1967, Bauman applied for a passport to travel to the UK.

60 The correspondence is deposited in the Leeds University Archives. Jack Palmer and Dariusz Brzeziński are doing the first analysis of Bauman's

correspondence. Future historians of sociology will have plenty of work with the careful reading and analysis of Bauman's international activity.

61 The institutions mentioned here are those the scholars were affiliated with at the time they sent the letter(s).

62 Bauman's correspondence with Polish scholars abroad after he had left the country and was not restricted by censorship will be discussed later.

63 Julia Kristeva (b. 1941), famous philologist, psychoanalyst and writer; professor at Paris Diderot University.

64 This chapter does not refer to letters Bauman received after 1968 from his Polish friends and colleagues.

65 This is a conference centre (Syracuse University, New York State) in the middle of a forest, near a lake and far from a city – probably why Bauman also employed the stereotype of a boring place.

66 'My father lived, on the contrary in the world of spirit, in life-long exile from practice: What he gained in sophistication he lost in religious orthodoxy. He visited a synagogue once a year on the Day of Atonement, on which he observed the fast (but most of his life he half-fasted without observance) ... He became early and for the rest of his life remained a secular Zionist; or, rather, Zionism was his religion': Bauman to Keith Tester, 2016.

67 Janina visited her mother in 1963.

68 AIPN BU 0 1224/1505 – 'Nota służbowa' – mistakes in this document suggest that the writer used the Baumans' requested dates of departure rather than the dates of their actual travel.

69 Zygmunt Bauman, 'Essay on a Marxist Theory of Society': http://clas siques.uqac.ca/contemporains/Bauman_zygmunt/essai_theorie_marxiste_ de_la_societe.html. This text is the first chapter of Zygmunt Bauman's book with the same title, from Ed. Anthropos.

70 Julian Hochfeld's letter to Zygmunt Bauman (in Manchester), from March 1966: Bauman Archive, Leeds.

71 The term 'servant' is a prewar word, and sounds 'politically incorrect', especially when employed by a socialist sociologist. But in 1966, more respectful terms were not in common use.

72 Interviews with Bauman's daughters, 2019.

73 Janina Bauman's book *A Dream of Belonging* relates in detail each stage of her career – a fascinating account of the backstage of the state film industry in postwar Poland.

10 Bad Romance with the Security Police

1 The term 'national memory' is the topic of several texts and scholarly discussions. The recent book by Konrad Matyjaszek (2019) offers a useful introduction to the subject.

2 For extensive books devoted to the processes that culminated in the events of 1968, which rely mainly on *Bezpieka* documents, see Friszke (2010) and Eisler (2006).

3 For example, Department III, Section IV, Ministry of Interior Security (in charge of travel abroad). The notes were produced in several copies, which were placed with different services.

4 Bauman Archive, Leeds.

5 https://inwentarz.ipn.gov.pl/archivalCollection?id_a=2033&id_pz=9808& id_s=10366&id_ps=17872.
6 The IPN archives are not complete – some documents of SB are missing. This is also possible that I was not able to get access to all documents.
7 *Kultura* was a monthly published by the Literary Institute, created in 1946 in Rome by Jerzy Giedroyc. After Giedroyc moved to France, the journal was published from Maison Laffite in the western Parisian suburbs. *Kultura* and another publication, *Zeszyty Literackie*, were platforms for independent Polish intellectual life abroad. Thanks to illegal transfer and underground circulation of the texts, they were an important resource for intellectual freedom within Poland.
8 AIPN BU 0 1224/1505, 'Notatka służbowa tajne' – 23 – XI 1962.
9 International Press and Book Club, at the corner of Nowy Świat and Jerozolimskie. Bauman was probably invited to discuss his latest book, *The Society in Which We Live* (*Społeczeństwo w którym żyjemy*, 1962).
10 AIPN BU 0 1224/1505, 'Notatka służbowa'.
11 For detailed analysis of the activity of these clubs, see Andrzej Friszke (2010), *Anatomia Buntu: Kuroń, Modzelewski i Komandosi* (Anatomy of the Revolt: Kuroń, Modzelewski and Commando).
12 There were other circles opposed to the government and Party, but the ones mentioned in this chapter played the most important role in campus political activity.
13 Adam Michnik (born in 1946), became a political journalist, writer and editor-in-chief of the leading Polish newspaper *Gazeta Wyborcza*. Jan T. Gross (born in 1947), teaches history at Princeton University and is a major specialist in Polish anti-Semitism and twentieth-century Eastern European history; Włodzimierz Kofman is a world-renowned researcher in planetology in France (CNRS); and Aleksander Perski is a professor of psychology in Sweden, creator of the Center for Stress Studies at Uppsala University. All except Michnik were expelled from Poland in the anti-Semitic purge of 1968. The authorities incited Michnik to emigrate, but he refused.
14 Eisler (2006: 62).
15 Manturzewski studied this group in particular (see Gross and Pawlicka, 2018: 231–2) and, as an amateur filmmaker, made a TV programme about the youth and their aspirations. The press praised them as a most interesting group of young people (Friszke, 2010: 365); they were prodigies, a group of celebrities. Gross was heralded in *Polityka* magazine as a rising star (for more, see testimony of Nina Smolar in Gross and Pawlicka, 2018: 255).
16 Interview conducted with Adam Michnik in Warsaw, 24 April 2017. All citations of Michnik are excerpts from that interview.
17 When the authorities analysed the names of students who signed the petition supporting Michnik (January/February 1967), they saw that these included: Joanna Szyr, daughter of the vice prime minister; Irena Grudzińska, daughter of a senior forestry official; Ewa Zarzycka, daughter of the head of the Warsaw City Council; Jerzy Paweł Sztachelski, son of the minister of health and social care; Jacek Kochanowicz, son of the vice president of the Committee of Employment and Pensions; Ryszard Kole, son of the vice Minister of finance; and Janina Radkiewicz, whose father led the Office of the State Reserve (Rutkowski, 2016: 493).
18 The parents' culture was transmitted symbolically. Sometimes the younger

activists sang the Internationale in Yiddish (part of the BUND tradition); they also sang Russian protest songs.

19 Jan Józef Lipski, six months younger than Bauman; writer, critic, historian of literature, and dissident.

20 Interview with Adam Michnik conducted in Warsaw, 24 April 2017.

21 The context of the times was more complex than is usually presented: 'In journalism, political science and historiography, there are occasional disputes over whether the Polish People's Republic after 1956 was a totalitarian or authoritarian state. I do not want to disavow these disputes, because something important is still in them. It seems to me, however, that we are dealing here with the confusion of two different orders, which does not serve either theory or empiricism. Totalitarianism and authoritarianism are theoretical concepts created by political scientists. On the basis of theory, it is easy to distinguish them, it is a matter of precise definitions. But theory is gray and stiff while knowledge, like the tree of life, is green, its branches rustling and moving in the wind. It is difficult to arrange them in precisely defined categories. The historian draws attention to this shimmering tree rather than the labels' (Modzelewski, 2013: 90).

22 See, for *Komandosi*, Friszke (2010); also Eisler (2006: ch. 2).

23 The ambiance of the period is portrayed in the French movie *Tricheurs* (1958) by Marcel Carne, and in Hass' Polish films *Wspólny pokój* (1959: Shared Room) and *Jak być kochaną* (1961: How to Be Loved). Regarding the French 'jeunesse' in the social sciences, see Sohn (2005: 123–34).

24 Michnik, 17 at the time, was mentioned by name by Gomułka.

25 Friszke showed that a complex power struggle among various networks within the Warsaw Party lay behind the decision (Friszke, 2010: 370–1).

26 This group began with summer camps for the ZMP (Union of Polish Youth, 1954–6) through the creation of the Walter Fellowship Team in 1956, and eventually became a scouting troop (*hufiec*) in 1958 (Bikont and Łuczywo, 2018: ch. 8, n. 3). Over 800 people were 'educated' by Kuroń in the ZHP (Związek Harcerstwa Polskiego (Union of Polish Scouts)) (see also Friszke, 2010). Interestingly, Bauman's daughter Anna attended Kuroń's summer camp as a teenager. This is why Bauman was aware of Kuroń's activities from the late 1950s and early 1960s.

27 There were controversies surrounding his death. He was a popular figure in Poland in the 1950s.

28 Kuroń worked with youth from the early 1950s, a period of unrelenting Stalinism.

29 Janusz Korczak, born in 1878, devoted his life to the struggle for children's rights. He was raised in a family of progressive Jews (his lawyer father was a member of Haskala, a Jewish intellectual movement strongly influenced by the Enlightenment, which spread between the mid eighteenth and mid nineteenth centuries, starting in Germany and popular in the various part of the Jewish Diaspora; for more, see Feiner, 2004). He received a Russian general education (Warsaw at the time was under Czarist rule). In the orphanage under his direction, children created their own republic with its own parliament, court system and newspaper. During the German occupation, he refused offers to help him escape and remained in the Warsaw Ghetto with his children until they were deported to Treblinka. See Berger (1989). The Polish film director Andrzej Wajda made a biographical movie, *Korczak*, in 1990.

30 About Modzelewski's Italian experience, see Modzelewski (2013: 98–101).

31 They corresponded to Orinn Klapp's definition of symbolic leaders (Klapp, 1964). Kuroń and Modzelewski paved the way for the struggle for Polish democracy. Each spent long periods in jail (Modzelewski wrote his Ph.D. thesis behind bars), with years of underground activity. Kuroń was the creator of KOR (the Committee for the Protection of Workers). Modzelewski and Kuroń were the first brains of the Solidarity movement (Modzelewski came up with the name 'Solidarity' and was its first spokesperson). Both belonged to the nucleus of opposition that enabled Polish society to end the period of the one-party state and state-directed economy, and after 1989 both held state positions. Kuroń was minister of labour and social policy while Modzelewski was a senator. While Kuroń remained active in politics until his death in 2004, Modzelewski became a full professor of history at Warsaw University, specializing in the Middle Ages.

32 Modzelewski spoke with the head of ZMS, Smolar, and, from the Party side, Brus gave his permission to organize the meetings. Aleksander Smolar (economist, sociologist, political scientist and journalist) and economist Włodzimierz Brus (in Modzelewski, 2013: 101) were both expelled from Poland after the 1968 anti-Semitic purge. A detailed description of the club can be found in Bikont and Łuczywo's (2018) biography of Kuroń.

33 Bogdan Jankowski was a friend of Kuroń and Michnik, a specialist in electronics and a well-known Polish alpinist.

34 Włodzimierz Brus born in 1921 in Płock, and died at Oxford in 2007 after emigrating to the UK in 1972. Tyler Cowen of George Mason University considers him one of the two most important economists of the twentieth century. See Gewirtz (2017).

35 AIPN BU 0 1224/1505. The document, 'Doniesienie', is dated '14 XII 1962', but it actually covers a meeting the day before, on 13 December.

36 Interview conducted 27 July 2015 in Warsaw.

37 Hostile to the state and Party.

38 AIPN BU 0 1224/1505 – the three-paged typewritten document contains inscriptions: 'source: "Amatorka"' (suggesting a female amateur: Friszke says IPN historians identified her as Barbara Dziwiszek-Kowalik) (Friszke, 2010: 83, n. 7).

39 Another milieu that cradled the opposition was the Catholic Church and its Club of Catholic Intelligentsia (KIK).

40 Bauman (1962b).

41 Reviewers did not include Stalin as a reference but the impact of the Stalinist style remained for years after 1956.

42 AIPN BU 0 1224/1505, Report No. 330/63 from 1963, 6 September.

43 AIPN BU 0 1224/1505, 'Wyciąg z notatki o aktualnym stanie polskiej filozofii i socjologii dot. Zygmunta Baumana', pp. 8–13.

44 AIPN BU 0 1224/1505, notes concerning the manual *Outline of Sociology: Issues and Concepts*, p. 7.

45 This article was published in the journal *Kultura i społeczeństwo*, with subheadings amazingly describing the content using musical vocabulary (in Italian). This kind of borrowing at that time was rare and shows Bauman's originality and unconventional writing style. To be sure, it contained many common tropes – their use was obligatory – but we must be mindful that all publications had to pass the control of the censor.

46 International exchanges (mainly through the Ford Foundation in the late 1950s and 1960s) also had an impact. Polish scholars went to Columbia University where they learned the new quantitative methodology that

came into fashion: opinion polls were considered 'objective', which confirmed the positivist approach in social science, which was far from the interpretative approach practised by Bauman. See Pleskot (2010).

47 AIPN BU 0 1224_1505, denunciation about the Bauman assistants. Dated 8 December1964. Signed 'Henryk'. Information – a report on the reaction of university people regarding detention in jail of Modzelewski and others.

48 AIPN BU 0 1224/1505, 'Wyciąg z notatki', p. 35 of 224.

49 *Po Prostu* was a literary journal closed by the authorities in 1957 because of oppositional content. Bauman published there.

50 Polish sociologists, and especially Bauman, were very important for the development of sociology in Czechoslovakia. The Polish scholars introduced Western works there. For more, see Kilias (2016).

51 The term employed was 'kaszanka' – which is filled with cereal and animal blood: a 'poor man's' sausage.

52 Melchior Wańkowicz (1892–1974), famous Polish writer, journalist and reporter; he was arrested in October 1964, officially because of a speech of his that was sent to be read on Free Europe Radio. He spent five weeks in jail before trial and was condemned to three years in prison, but authorities never carried out the sentence because of his celebrity (outside Poland) and his US citizenship.

53 The authors were inspired by the work of Yugoslav dissident Milovan Djilas and Stanisław Ossowski. The influence of this Open Letter abroad was very important. It was translated by radical leftist groups into several languages and became, along with Djilas' book, a classical work for Trotskyist, Maoist and anarchist movements in Western Europe. In Paris in 1968, movement leader Daniel Cohn-Bendit called himself 'Kuroń-Michnik'. The text was also celebrated in anti-Franco Spain, and in Cuba (Bikont and Łuczywo, 2018: 447–8).

54 The divergences of political opinions (Krajewski was a Maoist, Tekjowski a national communist) slowed the editorial process. Group member Andrzej Mazur, meanwhile, worked for the *Bezpieka* (Modzelewski, 2013:103–4). From the point of view of the authorities, Bauman was also associated with the letter via his assistant, Bernard Tejkowski, who belonged to the group.

55 Modzelewski said this was due to the compatibility of their sections, as well as their great mutual trust (Modzelewski, 2013: 104).

56 For a detailed examination, see Friszke (2010), Modzelewski (2013); Bikont and Łuczywo (2018).

57 AIPN BU 0 1224/1505, Notatka służbowa z dn.: 21/04/1965, p. 3. Document dated 21 June 1965.

58 AAN 14/136, file 121–2, in Friszke (2010: 195).

59 Rutkowski wrote about Bauman's defence of Tejkowski after a Party meeting in January 1965, noting that Schaff was a delegate to the Party unit at the Philosophy Department (2016: 468). We should remember that Schaff was two levels above Bauman in the university hierarchy, and the decisive voice.

60 AIPN BU 0 1224/1505, Wyciąg z informacji z dnia: 21 April 1965.

61 Modzelewski used a shorter term that defines the skinheads – an ultra-nationalist group.

62 AIPN BU 0 1224/1505, Wyciąg z doniesienia z dnia: 05/06/1965 (extract from spying of TWC pseudonym 'Kazik' from 5 June 1965) (handwritten).

63 AIPN BU 0 1224/1505, memo note about doc. Dr Zygmunt Bauman from 21 April 1965, p. 2. In Polish universities, students organize 'circles' to improve their knowledge in a specific area. A professor (usually chosen by students) heads the group, helping them organize meetings and other activities.

'Consciousness' is the term used in the Marxist approach – class consciousness is a 'historical phenomenon, born out of collective struggle. ... conscious human practices [are] ... conjunction of subjectivity and objectivity in history' (brittanica.com; www.britannica.com/topic/class-consciousness).

64 AIPN BU 0 1224/1505, Doniesienie z dnia 11 czerwca 1968, odtworzone z taśmy mikrofonu- przez Winter. str 2. Source TW Winter W-wa April 11, 1968; Secret – denunciation (reproduced from a mini-phone tape), p. 2 (according to IPN records, 'Winter' was Janina Koblewska (1918–97), lecturer at the National Film School in Łódź, and specialist in children's movies).

This fundraising action was organized in March 1965. For more, see Rutkowski (2016). Being kicked out of one university made it nearly impossible to find another university job. In socialist Poland, it was very difficult to pass the necessary exams to get a job in higher education, and being fired signified the loss of place – and, for males, two years of military service.

65 AIPN BU 0 1224/1505, Doniesienie z dnia 11 czerwca 1968, odtworzone z taśmy mikrofonu- przez Winter. str 3. Source TW Winter W-wa April 11, 1968; Secret – Denunciation (reproduced from a mini-phone tape), p. 3.

66 AAN, Ministerstwo Szkolnictwa Wyższego, Uniwersytet Warszawski, Personal Folder Zygmunt Bauman 46 Letter of Prodziekan doc. dr Adam Podgórecki to the Rector of UW requesting the return of a supplement because of resignation from the Party's Institute of Social Sciences (formerly the WSNS). 22 October 1964.

67 In the interview, Modzelewski told me that he read this book in the jail and it was for him very important lecture.

68 Among them, Aleksandra Jasińska-Kania, who was previously Hochfeld's student. It might seem unusual for colleagues from the same MA seminar to become Ph.D. student and Ph.D. adviser – however, Aleksandra was younger than Zygmunt and spent much longer on her Ph.D. thesis than he did. She actually changed the topic (because of political reasons) and practically wrote a second thesis under Bauman's supervision (she got it in 1967).

69 AAN, Ministerstwo Szkolnictwa Wyższego, Uniwersytet Warszawski, Personal Folder Zygmunt Bauman 46. Opinion of prof. Maria Ossowska concerning promotion for 'extraordinary professor'. 7 September 1965.

70 Ossowska's opinion was not negative, simply not as effusive or lengthy as the others.

71 My interview with Werblan took place in Warsaw, 9 October 2015.

72 In Poland, Christmas Eve is already a day of festivity – however, it was a Catholic celebration and Party members were supposed to be atheists.

73 AAN, Ministerstwo Szkolnictwa Wyższego, Uniwersytet Warszawski, Personal Folder Zygmunt Bauman 46, handwritten note, p. 147.

74 I am grateful to Natalia Aleksiun for identifying the writer as Jerzy Tomaszewski, her Ph.D. mentor. Tomaszewski is a common Polish name, and in 1960 there were several Warsaw University professors by that name.

75 In 1961, the Chair of the Sociology of Political Relations was renamed the Chair of Sociology II, and in 1964 as the Chair of General Sociology.
76 Letter from Szymon Chodak to Bauman dated 29 March – Bauman Archive, Leeds.
77 The reaction of the university authorities was immediate, but focused initially on Kołakowski and Michnik.
78 The Mathematics, Physics and Astronomy Faculty was well known and respected for its excellence and long tradition in Poland. Several of the professors were internationally known. It is important to note that the department was practically free from Party influence – a 'world apart'. In fact, the Party worried about the lack of political engagement in the department (Rutkowski, 2016: 492).
79 Lityński was a member of dissident groups, while Holsztyński emigrated in 1968 during the anti-Semitic purge, although he was not connected with the opposition movement. See other accounts: Friszke (2010); Rutkowski (2016).
80 Unfortunately, Lityński's erroneous account of events is the basis for the official version of them, and the action of mathematicians is rarely evoked.
81 Excerpt from a private letter in January 2018. I am grateful to Włodzimierz Holsztyński for our extensive correspondence.
82 It was mainly Egypt, Syria and Jordan that were engaged in this conflict.
83 AIPN BU 0 1224/1505, Notatka dot doc. dr Baumana Zygmunta, 14/06/1967.
84 AIPN BU 0 1224/1505, Notatka informacyjna, 17 July 1967.
85 AIPN BU 0 1224/1505, Notatka informacyjna, 17 July 1967. Italics added.
86 In 1953, he was officially evicted from KBW not as a Jew but as the son of a Zionist.
87 AIPN BU 0 1224/1505, 28 July 1967, letter from municipal command of Warsaw's militia to chief of Department III Office 'C'. MSW requests all documents about Bauman, who since the end of July has come under strict observation. This category concerns people suspected of being active enemies of the state, who were previously viewed by the secret services as people who did not support the socialist system or were critical of the Party and government. For more, see the IPN website: https://inwentarz.ipn. gov.pl/slownik?znak=K#84.
88 See Friszke (2010: 451–2).
89 Friszke wrote that the first salon was organized in the apartment of Jadwiga Staniszkis on 12 or 13 October 1967, devoted to the question of 'the nation' – the key speaker was Modzelewski.
90 AIPN BU 0 1069/788 7157, Notatka, 22 April 1969, p. 3. Translation by Netrepko-Herbst.

11 The Year 1968

1 AIPN BU 0 204/7/5 44680/II, Note on Bauman, dated 5 January 1968 – information on the bottom that the copy was sent to Department I, Section 3.
2 AIPN BU 0 11224/1505, Note about university situation, dated 21.2.68, p. 2.
3 AIPN BU 0 11224/1505, Wyciąg z doniesienia 'M-5' z dnia 15 marca 1968 – Inspector of Department III, Captain J. Cioczek, wrote in a note dated 21 February 1968 that secret informant 'Kazik' (probably a member of faculty)

had reported he was unaware of Bauman's action: 'He promises that next week he will try to learn the motivation for such a drastic decision. He will speak with Pomian who should know the causes. If [Kazik] has the opportunity, he will speak about it with Bauman. He will report back on this.'

4 This information is not corroborated by historians. Eisler reports that Morawski and Baczko opposed resignation and wanted to be kicked out of the Party, which happened on the eve of their ejection from the university (25 March 1968). Morawski compared it to 'the Middle Age ritual of rape with the goal of seizing the virginity of women who had been condemned to death' (Eisler, 2006: 441). In other words, they were expelled from the Party before being kicked out of the university.

5 AIPN BU 0 1224/1550, 'Doniesienie' źródło 'Winter', 11 April 1968.

6 Actually, Brus turned in his card earlier and with no explanation. His wife, Helena Wolińska-Brus, was expelled from the Party when she disagreed with a Gomułka speech on 19 June 1967. Her husband resigned in an act of protest against her expulsion (Rutkowski, 2016: 498).

7 Bauman is mistaken here – the date was 3 January, according to a *Bezpieka* document. Janina Bauman, in the Polish version of her autobiography, mentions the 4th (Bauman quit the day before the Party meeting).

8 Author's interview with Zygmunt Bauman conducted in Leeds, 1 November 2015.

9 About the analysis of the event, see Friszke (2010: 515–22).

10 Gustaw is the hero of *Forefathers*; he passes through a transformation into a national hero named Konrad. In Janina Bauman's autobiographical *roman à clef*, she gives her husband the name Konrad.

11 Janina Bauman had privileged access to every cultural event in Poland.

12 According to the translation of the article found in *Bezpieka* files, there is information about the expulsion of Brus and Bauman. Actually, this is wrong, as both gave back their ID cards – and left the Party: Friszke (2010: 526, n. 160) AIPN 0330/327, vol. 19, files 218–19; original of the document, AIPN 443/16.

13 See chapters 1 and 2 about Endecja's anti-Semitism in interwar Poland.

14 French: 'vagabond'.

15 This is an allusion to Gomułka's expression about a Fifth Column, made in his 19 June speech, in describing a 'Zionist group' acting clandestinely in Poland.

16 Wieszcz narodu zszedł na *Dziady*,
   Czy już o tym wiecie?
   Gdy go Michnik i Szlajfery
   Okrzykują w świecie. Rzekł tak mądrze ktoś niedawno
   O piątej kolumnie,
   A Polacy w Żydów ślepią,
   Bo jak zwykle-durnie.
   Dalej bracie, karabele
   Każdy w dłonie chwyta.
   Żyda za pejs i za morze
   Rada znakomita.
   Im ta Polska, w którą plują, Daje nadal łaski.
   Ty studencie piwko ciągniesz,
   Czekasz na oklaski.

This text was published in various versions; see in Friszke (2010: 544–5)

17 The same day, a bomb exploded in the bathroom of the building where the censors worked. In 2006, Eisler reported that those responsible were never discovered. It was never clear whether the bombing was a provocation, an act aimed at preventing a meeting of writers, or a bona fide act of opposition (Eisler, 2006: 196).

18 Out of 365 voters, 221 supported the petition; more in Eisler (2006: 199–203).

19 Michnik and Szlajfer were arrested on 6 March but freed two days later.

20 Author's interview with Barbara Szacka and Jerzy Szacki, 14 August 2015, in Warsaw. Unless otherwise stated, all quotations from the Szackis in this chapter are from this interview

21 This section (chronology, data and description of events) is mainly based on Friszke (2010: 556–81) and Eisler (2006: ch. 5). A map of the campus from that day is in Eisler (2006: 236, 246, 249).

22 '[I]n March 1968 at the Warsaw Mechanical Factory ... metal rods 50–60 cm in size were prepared, then filled with rubber' (Eisler, 2006: 248).

23 The official version was: honest workers had come in to protect the 'people's power' from the bad students.

24 The security services had planned everything in advance: although the Faculty Council cancelled its meeting that day, the *People's Tribune* (the main Party journal) published an article the following day that condemned the council for its incorrect vote. 'The script was ready regardless of what we did', Jerzy Szacki commented.

25 Interestingly, these opinions were published also by the Catholic journal *Słowo Powszechne* (Eisler, 2006: 282–3).

26 The Polish version of Janina's book from 2009 contains more details about that afternoon. I include in my description elements that are missing from the English version published in 1988.

27 www.youtube.com/watch?v=UuRWvmHRlKk shows the entire speech by Gomułka from 19 March 1968; the analysed fragment is at 1″; official record archived by Karta, an educational/research institution.

28 Gomułka presented the March events and what led to them as a conspiracy, focusing in part on the writer Paweł Jasienica, whom he described as a supporter of the prewar system, an anti-communist fighter after the war, and a reactionary.

29 www.youtube.com/watch?v=UuRWvmHRlKk; analysed fragment is from 49′28″.

30 Ibid.; analysed fragment started at 1h25′55″.

31 *Gazeta Wyborcza*: Kwaśniewski, 'I Let Them Seduce Me'.

32 There were five names, but Brus was an economist, the others from the Philosophy Department.

33 www.youtube.com/watch?v=UuRWvmHRlKk; analysed fragment is from 1h36′3″. It is interesting to recall that Gomułka's wife was a Polish Jew.

34 Ibid., 1h38′.

35 www.mpolska24.pl/post/4240/przemowienie-na-spotkaniu-z-warszaw skim-aktywem-partyjnym-wygloszone-19-marca-1968, from 1h38′28″.

36 Ibid., 1h44′.

37 In the Polish version of her book, Janina Bauman wrote that, while there were no more Jewish shops, it would be easy enough to find the addresses of the people named by Gomułka, since every phone booth had an address book that contained phone numbers and addresses (J. Bauman, 2011: 156).

38 Eisler wrote that, in his first publication about this horrific time, he had learned 'about the wardrobe where Edda Perska was hidden in the spring [1968]'. But, to avoid 'irrelevant associations with the Holocaust', Eisler wrote, 'I omitted this drastic episode' (Eisler, 2006: 222).

39 *Bezpieka* agents showed one student arrested during the protests a Nazi anthropological album and some photos of Professor Bronisław Baczko for comparison, asking if she recognized her professor in one of the pictures of a typical Jewish type (in this case, a *clochard*) (see Eisler, 2006: 88). Similar associations were made by the far-right press in 2019, which put a picture of Jan Gross on the front page with a huge headline, 'How to Recognize a Jew' (see www.publicseminar.org/2019/04/how-media-political-and-religious-elites-shape-plebian-resistance/?fbclid=IwAR1 Xat1TS2sVxCK5sNzXSRE9OIXfMi4J9mCwSJYzHPmg5kuV0kXIn PuC7Kg).

40 'The Jews would have to raise the funds for their transport ... [and should pay] the money for their exit permits. Thus, with savage cunning, Eichmann had evolved a scheme whereby his victims had to organize their own forced departure. The deported Jews were allowed to take only personal belongings with them, and Eichmann and his Nazi bullies watched with gloating satisfaction as tearful families left the homes they had been born in ... Who was to take these homeless, stateless waifs? Eichmann did not care. There was controlled emigration to some countries, Eichmann gave hundreds of them false passports with their exit permits and packed them off' (Clarke, 1960: 41). I would like to thank Aleksander Perski for his explanations, article and exchange of letters about his text and Clarke's book.

41 For the analysis of the language of 1968, see Głowiński (1991).

42 Meng indicates the position of groups close to the Catholic Church in March 1968: (A) 'A mere three days after the first riots, PAX's newspaper published an article that explained the outburst of student unrest as the result of a "Zionist" conspiracy that had corrupted the Polish youth and the intelligentsia, making them turn away from their "patriotic responsibility for the People's Republic" in "Do studentów Uniwersytetu Warszawskiego", *Słowo Powszechne*, March 11, 1968' (Meng, 2008: 248); (B) for the Catholic intellectual group ZNAK, 'the students protesting on the streets were hardly part of the lay Catholic intellectual milieu. Most of them identified themselves with the secular Left that at this point wanted little to do with the Church. Znak bravely stood up for them at a dire moment, but its intervention throughout the spring of 1968 was limited in one crucial respect. The parliamentary group remained completely silent about the anti-Zionist campaign. ... By now the anti-Zionist campaign was at its peak and even Znak was being attacked for its "Zionist" leanings. ... The Znak group remained entirely silent about these absurd charges and the hundreds of Jews now fleeing from Poland' (Meng, 2008: 256–7). (PAX was a Catholic organization that collaborated with the government, in some ways like an anti-Semitic intellectual club.)

43 *Gazeta Wyborcza*: Kwaśniewski, 'I Let Them Seduce Me'.

44 Under Eichmann both types of pogrom – state- and mob-led – occurred.

45 Some have theorized that earlier pogroms also resulted from state manipulations. However, Tokarska-Bakir's excellent study (2018) of the Kielce Pogrom proved that it emanated from the local society – all social classes included.

46 Or under partial control. Moreover, in street fighting there was also a

third actor – the security forces and/or army, which protected one group or another group depending on the context (see Tokarska-Bakir, 2018).

47 E. C. Hughes wrote about Nazi Germany and its 'Jewish problem' using the term 'dirty work'. Hughes' lecture at McGill University was given in 1938/9; his article wasn't published until 1962.

48 The existence of such lists and their use for firing people recalled some of the worst periods of Nazi occupation, such as the firing of French functionaries by the Vichy regime. See Baruch (1997).

49 Gomułka's speech also included the line, 'Due to their cosmopolitan feelings, however, such people should avoid fields of work where national affirmation is indispensable.'

50 Eisler wrote: 'A depressing impression is left by the multi-page, detailed list of who went to work, at what time, who called whom and when, with whom and for how long they talked. The report is extremely meticulous, even including the addresses of people with whom those under surveillance have been in contact. From this documentation you can learn, for example, that Zygmunt Bauman was with his wife at dinner at "Teatralna" ... The greatest impression comes from the lists of well-known people from the world of culture with annotations appearing next to their names: "At home" ... On March 22, not only Kołakowski, Bauman and Staszewski did not leave their houses (understandable in the circumstances) but also Ficowski, Karst, Kijowski, Leopold, Pollak, Słonimski, Szechter, and Woroszylski' (AIPN 0296/99, vol. III, in Eisler (2006: 2012)).

51 From the interview conducted in 2013; also cited in several books following the interview published by the Israeli newspaper *Maariv* in August 1968 (Eisler, 2006) – the translation of the article as well as the extract from it from Radio Free Europe in Bauman's file, AIPN BU 0 1069/788.

52 The news swept all of Poland in fact, with constant repetition on the radio and TV and in the press.

53 AIPN BU 0 204/7/4460/II; extract (Wyciąg) from the note from discussion with Captain 'Janusz' conducted 2 April 1968 – Warsaw, 24 April 68, Secret.

54 Eisler supports Friszke and Zaremba, who underlined that students were one of the important categories, but the feature unifying all those who were active in March 1968 was their age (Eisler, 2006: 396).

55 I am grateful to Arthur Allen for this precious information.

56 Author's interview with Bauman conducted in Leeds, 31 October 2013.

57 Estimates range from 13,000 to 22,000, depending on the definition of 'March 68 emigration'; not everyone who left in 1968 was obviously part of the group forced out as a result of the riots and government crackdown. Some left by marrying foreigners, or took tourist trips abroad and remained, or found professional reasons for departure.

58 Michael Meng remarks: 'The issue remained dominant across the forty-year history of the communist state as the often-entangled stereotypes of the "Jewish-Communist", "Zionist", "non-Pole", and "cosmopolitan" emerged with varying degrees of intensity in 1945–46, 1956, 1968, and 1981. One reason is the geographically and historically specific intensity of the *żydokomuna* anti-Semitic stereotype in Poland, but another is the history of the Holocaust in that country. The verbal hate of 1968 ... intensely attacked the idea of the Holocaust and shaped afterwards the mode of discussing it. It is probably true that communist officials were particularly well suited to pen this linguistic hate. ... The virulence of 1968 and the attack on the Holocaust occurred in Poland because the

communist regime, unlike its East German counterpart, had almost no limitations on the intensity of the anti-Jewish hatred it could embrace. Its predecessor never produced the "Final Solution" or a Quisling supporter of it. As Kazimierz Wyka noted in 1945: "If Polish anti-Semitism had comprised itself as collaborationist, it would later have been destroyed or at least unmasked. But since it never had a Quisling character, it retained its position and is still considered a mark of patriotism." [Wyka, 1945, quoted in Huener, 2003: 41] Although anti-Semitism certainly never entirely disappeared in postwar, divided Germany, Wyka points to an at least partial explanation for postwar Poland's particularly uneasy, contested relationship with the Holocaust … in 1968' (Meng, 2008: 339–40).

59 In Polish, nicknames are frequently applied to children and close relations. Anka was one of Anna's pet names.

60 In interviews I conducted with scientists who left Poland because of the anti-Semitic campaign, I learned of some abuses by teachers. In one school, two daughters from a family were verbally attacked, and after leaving received a hate-filled letter from their teacher and fellow students.

61 See Simon Goldschalk's psycho-sociological work on trauma in second- and third-generation Holocaust survivors, and also the work of psychiatrist Tobie Nathan on refugee children's trauma. There are also studies of the epigenetic impact of trauma.

62 The train for Vienna departed from this station. In 1968–9, it became infamous because of the number of people who left Poland for ever through it. There were many dramatic farewells involving elderly parents who could not leave and might never see their children and grandchildren again. Adding to the dread of the place, it was the departure station for the death camp Treblinka during World War II. Marcel Łodziński made a movie about the emigration titled *Dworzec Gdański* (*Gdansk's Train-station*).

63 'Goj/Goyim': in Yiddish – 'non-Jew'.

64 AIPN BU 0 204/7/4460/II Donos, źródło 'Stolarski', dated 24 May 1968: 'Secret'.

65 In some families, when children asked their parents what language they were speaking, the parents responded 'French'. During World War II, use of Yiddish meant a death sentence, and many Jewish families had been careful about its use in the prewar era. Zygmunt's grandparents were both Yiddish speakers.

66 Many of these families spoke or employed Yiddish at home rarely. Yiddish writers, poets and teachers would have been an exception, or those who kept the language alive out of concern about its extinction. During World War II, those who spoke Yiddish as their first language, and Polish with a Yiddish accent, had very little chance of survival.

67 Bauman's emigration folder (AIPN BU 0 204/7/4460/II) contains a bill for 5,000 złoty for the procedure – more than a month's salary for Bauman.

68 AIPN BU 1268/13779 Podanie do Rady Państwa PRL from 13 May 1968, signed 'Z. Bauman'.

69 There were some who resisted and refused to leave Poland, the most famous being Adam Michnik, who repeatedly refused to emigrate. He told one *Bezpieka* officer who asked him to emigrate that he would do it when the officer agreed to emigrate to Moscow. One of the best books about this era was written by anthropologist Joanna Wiszniewicz, *Życie przecięte. Opowieści pokolenia marca* (*Life Cut Short: Stories of the March Generation*) based on interviews with emigrants (Wiszniewicz, 2008).

About the difficult decision to emigrate or not, see the interesting book by writer and psychologist Michał Grynberg, *Księga wyjścia* (*The Book of the Exit*), published in 2018.

70 In such situations, the embassies of Denmark and Holland helped to borrow money, though this was usually arranged by Jewish organizations.

71 Bauman also provided a certificate from the Union of Authors, indicating his financial situation in relation to author's rights.

72 AIPN BU 1268/13779 Wniosek, 17/05/1968.

73 According to Polish law, children become Poles automatically if their mothers are citizens.

74 The same info. (same handwriting) on another document, on 30 May 1968, Vice Minister Świtała gave permission for the departure of Bauman's family. See AIPN BU 1268/13779 Notatka służbowa dot. Bauman Zygmunta – wyjazd na pobyt stały do Izraela, 28 May 1968.

75 Świtała was not a *Bezpieka* officer, and did not have real power of decision in the Ministry of Interior Affairs (suggestion of Wikipedia).

76 http://ohistorie.eu/tag/marzec-68/?print=pdf-search&fbclid=IwAR026 eV_0PeYtw49r9tBX33DdM9nnOrqkQw3ySNr8tLZIgPWodM1_vFV YWI.

77 Author's interview with Bauman conducted in Leeds, 31 October 2013.

78 Eisler citing testiony of Szapiro (Eisler, 2006: 125).

79 This expression is the title of the book by Joanna Wiszniewicz, *Życie przecięte. Opowieści Pokolenia Marca* (2008).

80 Author's interview with Bauman conducted in Leeds, 31 October 2013. Leon was a member of the student protest committee. Bauman believed that, even under the *Bezpieka* system, Poland's legal system was legitimate and would be respected. He was quite right to believe so. The first judgments respected fully the law and, under the defence of the best (prewar) attorney, a lot of opponents were not condemned. However, from spring 1968 the situation changed. The attorneys who defended dissidents were dismissed, and the court passed under political control. Nevertheless, Leon Sfard, like most participants in the March 1968 events, was freed after a few months and, like Anna, became stateless and left for Israel. For more about Leon Sfard, see: https://marzec68.sztetl.org.pl/en/osoba/leon-sfard.

81 AIPN BU 1638/5/4 108/55/4. The letter was sent to: Dyrektor Kontroli Ruchu Granicznego MSW, 4 June 1968.

82 All would return for short stays, but in 1968 they were convinced they were leaving for ever. Twenty years before the free election and 'the end of communism' in Poland, no one could imagine such a thing would be possible.

83 This sentence is borrowed from Janina Bauman's book, the penultimate sentence: 'Now, I belong to nowhere' (1988: 202).

12 Holy Land

1 This citation from Janina's journal comes from IPN files: AIPN BU 0 1069/788 7157 – Note – April, 22, 1969, p. 3. I would like to thank to Barbara Nykiel-Herbert for the translation.

2 I am deeply grateful to Lydia Bauman and her sisters Anna Sfard and Irena Bauman for their trust and access to this unique document, as well as for the interviews and discussions that were the basis of most of this chapter concerning family matters.

3 The term 'thick description' was also employed in private correspondence by Anna Sfard.

4 Janina Bauman's diary was confiscated by customs in 1968. Her books *Winter in the Morning* and *The Dream of Belonging* were reconstructions of that diary, mainly thanks to the copies made by Janina's mother after the war.

5 It is interesting to compare Lydia's account of travel with Janina Bauman's book *A Dream of Belonging* (1989).

6 That term was employed by Lydia Bauman.

7 This was a spectacular act of solidarity and protest against the Polish authorities, which was possible thanks to the ephemeral liberalization of Czechoslovakia, which the Soviet invasion bloodily suppressed in August 1968.

8 Ha-Sochnut ha-Yehudit L'Eretz Yisra'el, organization created pursuant to Art. 4 of the British mandate over Palestine (approved by the Council of the League of Nations in 1922) to organize the immigration of Jews to Palestine, and their settlement. See https://sztetl.org.pl/en/glossary/jewish-agency-sochnut.

9 According to Stola, of about 13,000 people who left in the state pogrom, 28 per cent went to Israel. In 1968, 1,349 Polish Jews went to Israel; and in 1969, 1,735. The other emigrants chose to go to Western Europe, North America and Scandinavia (Stola, 2010: 222). At the Jewish agency in Vienna, stateless persons could learn their options. For those who chose Israel, the situation was simple and the process went quickly. Those who wished to emigrate elsewhere had to wait for a visa. The United States required the immigrant to have a sponsor, which could take several months to find and process. The waiting was often done in Italy, mainly in Rome.

10 Schönau was open from 1968 to 1973, when a terrorist attack led the Austrian government to close it. About 200,000 people, mostly Russian Jews, stayed there en route to Israel.

11 The university communities in France, Czechoslovakia and Yugoslavia protested at his dismissal.

12 Jewish organizations (HIAS, JOINT and Sochnut) financed the émigrés during the waiting period, paying for their housing, food, health care and sometimes education, but they were expected to repay the sums once their situation in the new country allowed it.

13 AIPN BU 1093/8207 – report signed by the inspector, Department IV, Section 3 – Lieutenant Wacław M. Król; dated 18 July 1968.

14 Manuscript by Lydia Bauman, p. 8.

15 Six months later, he published in *Kultura* a celebrated article titled: 'On Frustration and Jugglers' (Bauman, 1968).

16 I use the term 'double presence' here following Abdelmalek Sayad's work on Algerian immigrants and his concept of double absence (contrary to the transnational vision of double presence) (Sayad, 2004).

17 See, for example, Wiszniewicz (2008).

18 Interview with Anna Sfard conducted 20 April 2019.

19 Available on YouTube: www.youtube.com/watch?v=kJytV7s-aUU&list=RDkJytV7s-aUU&start_radio=1&t=21&pbjreload=10.

20 The film was based on the famous book by Russian writer Boris Pasternak, who won the Nobel Prize for Literature in 1958. Pasternak was unable to receive the prize personally, and his book, which did not fit into Soviet

aesthetics, was never published in the Soviet Union. Eventually translated and published in Italy, the book became a tool of the anti-communist struggle, employed by the CIA – itself a remarkable spy story that was revealed by Finn and Couvée recently (2014).

21 'Jerusalem of Gold; and of Copper, and of Light; Behold I Am a Violin for All Your Songs') (translation from the site www.hebrewsongs.com).

22 'Obcy wśród Obcych' (Strangers amongst Strangers) is the metaphor employed by Kossewska to describe the March 1968 *Aliyah* (Kossewska, 2015).

23 The 1956 events produced the so-called 'Gomułka *Aliyah*'. The 1967 war and breaking-off of relations between Israel and Poland provoked several departures of Polish Jews.

24 Obviously, the 1968 immigrants had a choice of their destination, but Israelis tended to view them all as exiles rather than convinced Zionists.

25 Elżbieta Kossewska is the author of a book on the Polish press in Israel from 1945 to 1970 (Kossewska, 2015).

26 Goldkorn, born in 1952, left Poland in 1968 for Israel, and after some years left Israel and settled in Italy. He became a journalist and writer, working for several years as the head of the culture department at *Esspresso* – a major Italian magazine. He was a friend of Bauman and published several interviews with him.

27 This term refers to the fruit of a native cactus. As Goldkorn described it: 'Sabra – a sweet and delicate inside seemingly somewhat rough and arrogant; the stereotype of a Jew born in freedom, speaking Hebrew from birth, uninfected by the evil of the Diaspora and the shameful Yiddish slang – a brave Jew and at the same time a good farmer and a beautiful male, preferably blonde with blue eyes' (Goldkorn, 2018).

28 Common historical knowledge of the Holocaust was incomplete at that time; particularly absent was knowledge about the many revolts and uprisings among those condemned to death in the concentration camps and ghettos.

29 Goldkorn (2018). 'This is Asia' was a common reaction from Poles – especially those who were familiar with Asian republics in the Soviet Union from time they spent there during World War II (see testimonies in Wiszniewicz, 2008).

30 Anna's friend Małgorzata Tal mentions her in a story about her first days of settlement, saying Anna welcomed her and her mother at the Ben Gurion airport. Both women were lost in this environment, and Anna helped them to organize their new life (Wiszniewicz, 2008: 579).

31 The Israeli press in the Polish language from the 1960s underlined the privileged reception that Israel provided for the Jews who arrived in waves from Poland in 1956 and 1968, in comparison to the Sephardic *olim* (Kossewska, 2015: ch. 4). The treatment accorded to Polish emigrants was due to their level of education. The requests for emigration were submitted to the Polish passport office mainly by intellectuals, including at least 500 academics and researchers; 200 journalists and editors; 60 radio and TV employees; 100 musicians, visual artists and actors (Stola, 2010: 223).

32 Stanisław Obirek, co-author and friend of Bauman, said that Sandler mentioned that Bauman was very active politically in Israel after 1968.

33 Elżbieta Kossewska told me that *Kultura*'s editor, Jerzy Giedroyć, solicited Bauman's texts many times.

34 Bauman continued his focus on Poland, writing about it in Polish, for years into his Leeds stay. It was only after he'd been in the UK for ten years that he began to write sociological texts directly in English.
35 Roman Karst (1911–88) literary critic, translator, writer and Professor of Literature at Stony Brook University.
36 University professor, specialist in theatre theory, critic of literature, Marxist, emigrated in 1966 to the USA.
37 The strong attachment to their previous fatherland, and their 'October 1956 values', were elements that distinguished the '68 *Aliyah* from previous Polish émigrés.
38 While there were no doubt some true 'Zionists' in the group, most of the 1968 emigrants seem to have had good professional standing in Poland before 1967, and no plans to leave the country. See Stola (2010).
39 About the identity problem due to forced emigration in 1968, see Wiszniewicz (2008), Grynberg (2018).
40 Uri Ram is a sociology professor at Tel Aviv University, and the author of a historical book on the Israeli state's relationship with the development of Israeli sociology (Ram, 1995). I conducted the interview with him in Tel Aviv on 20 May 2017, in English.
41 Interview conducted in Tel Aviv, 20 May 2017.
42 Private correspondence, 4 June 2019.
43 Information about the article is provided in the file AIPN BU 0 1069/788 7157 note from 22 April 1969: 'Secret'. Translation of the article from *Maariv*, August 1968 – from Hebrew into Polish, by *Bezpieka* translators; from Polish into English by myself, p. 2.
44 Ibid., p. 3.
45 Ibid.
46 I am grateful to Anna Sfard for this story of the *Maariv* publication. She noted that a similar situation arose later with David Sfard, Leon's father, a specialist in Yiddish literature. He gave an interview to the same journalist and the effect was similar: fabrications (interview with Anna Sfard, conducted 20 April 2019).
47 Saying attributed to Tuaregs (according to French Wikipedia), but in France commonly attributed to King Louis XIV ('the Sun King').
48 Functionalism is a theoretical framework for constructing a theory of society as a complex system. In the context of Israel, the most important is Parsonian functionalism, as Uri Ram explained: ' Eisenstadt was to Israel's sociology in both substance and function what his colleague and mentor Talcott Parsons was to American sociology. He was the first to institutionalize in the discipline a truly dominant "paradigm" and used the same theoretical framework, functionalism, and for a comparable purpose: to confer scientific legitimacy upon the ruling elite and the social order it constructed. ... Parsons's functionalism was specifically congruent with American corporate capitalism, so was Eisenstadt's functionalism congruent with the Israeli variant of bureaucratic capitalism' (Ram, 1995: 44). In this paradigm, Israel is presented as a '[h]armonious and homogeneous society' in the process of social evolution. This vision of the process of Israeli nation-building is insufficient as it lacks historical specificity and an empirical approach (Ram, 1995: 48.) There were three phases of functionalism – see Ram (1995).
49 This interview was conducted in Tel Aviv, May 2017.
50 AAN, Ministerstwo Szkolnictwa Wyższego 2860; letter from the Ministry

of Higher Education to the rector of Warsaw University – dated 11 December 1968 (DU-4-198-2/68).

51 This term is commonly employed in French academia. Leading intellectuals were called 'Mandarins' to describe the nature of their relationships with students and collaborators. They had 'courts' of students, collaborators and fans, which they were known to exploit in exchange for rewards such as support in career development.

52 Eisenstadt in an interview conducted by Shalva Weil in Leeds, February 2010; extracts published in 2011 on the European Sociological Association website, in its official journal, *European Sociologist*: www.europeansoci ologist.org/sites/default/files/public/ES_issue31.pdf.

53 One of Bauman's most important texts on Israeli–Palestinian relations was published in *Haaretz*: 'Israel Must Prepare for Peace', 8 August 1970. He also wrote a paper in 2013: www.haaretz.com/.premium-israel-derelict-in-duty-to-warn-the-world-1.5229873.

54 Stavit Sinai mentioned that Eisenstadt was involved in the Haganah and was implicated in the military campaigns of 1948 (Sinai, 2019: ch. 1). I am grateful to Jack Palmer for this information.

55 Moreover, they were engaged in different educational systems. The Ph.D. track in continental Europe lasts about eight years (three for a bachelor's + two for an MA + three for a Ph.D.), while in Israel's UK-based model, the system is three years for a bachelor's + three to four years for a Ph.D. Unlike in continental Europe, the MA is not compulsory.

56 Uri Ram remarked: 'Eisenstadt's eminent status in Israeli sociology was promoted by his worldwide standing. He was a frequent keynote speaker at international sociological events, a winner of many prestigious professional awards and prizes, and a much sought-after visiting professor by foreign universities (a partial list includes: 1956 consultant to the UNESCO Conference on Cultural Integration of Immigrants in Havana; 1955–1956, Fellow in the Center for Advanced Studies in the Behavioral Sciences at Stanford, California; teaching at different times at the universities of Oslo, Chicago, the Massachusetts Institute of Technology, and Harvard University)' (Ram, 1995: 25).

57 Interview conducted by Shalva Weil in Leeds, February 2010.

58 Ram remarked: 'Edward Shils places Eisenstadt's intellectual stature on a par with Weber, Durkheim, and Parsons (in mainstream sociology at the time it was usual to omit any mention of Marx as one of the ancestors of the field; E. Shils, 1985:4–6)' (Ram, 1995: 25).

59 Interview conducted in 2017; the subject wanted to remain anonymous.

60 Interview with Uri Ram conducted 24 May 2017 in Tel Aviv.

61 Interview conducted by Shalva Weil in Leeds, February 2010.

62 Interview conducted with Emanuel Marx in Tel Aviv, 23 May 2017.

63 Interview with Anna Sfard, 20 April 2019.

64 Bar mitzvah is a religious ceremony during which teenage boys (and girls, in a bar mitzvah) lead chosen prayers in the synagogue as a ~~sign~~ of religious maturity. This is an important event in Jewish families.

65 Excerpt from a letter to the current author sent May 2017. Hazan also mentioned his post-Israeli-period relationship with Bauman and his work: 'I continued to pursue occasional contact with Bauman and had the privilege of having his endorsements for two books that I published *Serendipity in Anthropological Research* (edited by myself and Esther Hertzog in honour of Emanuel Marx) and *Against Hybridity: Social Impasses in a*

Globalizing World. Bauman's work and vision have been a constant source of inspiration for me, especially in my research on aging and death, such as his wonderful book: *Mortality, Immortality and Other Life Strategies* where he offers a theory of the status of terminality in modern and postmodern settings.'

66 Excerpt from ibid.

67 Emanuel Marx, interview conducted on 23 May 2017 in Tel Aviv.

68 George Simmel (1858–1918), German philosopher and sociologist, an interdisciplinary thinker who published about different problems of his contemporary society. He was the father of interactionists and also influenced several twentieth-century thinkers, among them Zygmunt Bauman.

69 AIPN BU 0 204/7/1.

70 See Kossewska (2015).

71 Writer and musician Viola Wiman 'left Poland 50 years ago and still has not arrived in Israel' (in Grynberg, 2018: 128); this situation, known as 'Lot's wife syndrome', is a recognized phenomenon among the *olim* (see Kossewska, 2015).

72 *Yeridim* (Hebr.): 'those who descend (from Jerusalem / the mountain)' – in short, 'failing'; this term contrasts with the *Aliyah* who settled permanently in Israel.

73 See more on the impact of the departure of March *Aliyah* members in the press in Kossewska (2015: chs. 4, 6, 7).

74 The ceremony took place in Stockholm, during a holiday visit. They wanted to have a secular ceremony, which was not possible in Israel at that time. In Sweden, they also saw Warsaw friends similarly evicted in 1968 (Grynberg, 2018).

75 The book was published in 2017 in Polish and in 2018 in English after being recovered by Dariusz Brzeziński. The story of this discovery is told by Brzeziński in Bauman (2018).

76 AIPN BU 0 204/7/1 44680/1.

77 The process of recovering them took more than a year; however, the original documents are still at the IPN in Warsaw. Unfortunately, this occurred after Janina Bauman died in 2009, well after she published her two autobiographical works. For these, she was forced to recover the information from the copies made by her mother and from her memory.

78 I am referring here to the increase in anti-Semitism in Poland (see EU survey, 2018: https://fra.europa.eu/en/publication/2018/2nd-survey-discri mination-hate-crime-against-jews) and the scandalous events that followed the historical conference at EHESS in Paris at the end of February 2019; see www.publicseminar.org/2019/04/the-subtext-of-a-recent-international-scandal-part-one-2.

79 Bauman prepared his raw notes in Polish which he then translated to English, followed by another translation into Hebrew for the delivery of his lectures, as is visible in the Bauman Archive, Leeds. There is, for example, a handwritten list in English that is probably a syllabus outline for a course on social class.

80 A letter on the French translations, dated 16 January 1969, includes a memorandum of agreement and three contracts. I am grateful to Jack Palmer for his help with documents from the Special Collection.

81 'Those who got any sort of offer from the US or Western Europe left Israel immediately', said Stanisław Obirek (interview conducted in Warsaw, 24 September 2018).

82 *Gazeta Wyborcza*: Kwaśniewski, 'I Let Them Seduce Me'.
83 'With Israel's dramatic victory in the 1967 Six Day War, Jewish progressives faced their greatest challenge. The New Left, splintering along racial and ideological lines, grew critical of the Jewish State, equating its occupation of the West Bank and Gaza Strip to the imperialist impulses of the United States in the Cold War. Many in the New Left rejected Zionism, labeling it a chauvinistic, even racist, manifestation of nationalism.' See www.jewishvirtuallibrary.org/new-left.
84 In Poland, as in Israel, some interviewed persons wished to remain anonymous.
85 According to Kossewska: 'In Israel, it was not easy to be a communist or even a Marxist. Zionism contained religious elements … [Zionism] was associated with prosperous philanthropy from wealthy people ([Zionism] lived in symbiosis with capitalism). It also caused conflicts with the Arabs, who until the 1950s could not be members of Israeli Zionist parties. That's why Mapam could be not communist, but Maki could be anti-Zionist and Arab-Jewish. Communist agitation often was attracted to the boycott of the Jewish state. In contrast to the Zionist groups, the communists' aggressive criticism of the ruling apparatus and state institutions mobilized the Jewish emigration movement in the opposite direction – away from the state (Yerida)' (Kossewska, 2015: 433).
86 The Labour Party was created on the base of Mapai, the party supported by Tova, Bauman's sister.
87 'Many other Israelis spoke critically of what they considered a lost opportunity, no matter how flimsy the circumstances. … Dr. Goldmann said he was disappointed over the Cabinet's rejection. "It might have been the beginning of some way to avoid another war or escalation of the Middle East conflict", he said.' See James Feron, 'Cabinet Veto of a Goldmann–Nasser Meeting Decried in Israel', *New York Times*, 7 April 1970: www. nytimes.com/1970/04/07/archives/cabinet-veto-of-a-goldmannnasser-meeting-decried-in-israel.html.
88 According to a witness, who remains anonymous. In Polish: 'Trzeba stwierdzić, że Izrael nie chce pokoju.'
89 *Haaretz*, 8 August 1970.
90 Bauman in an interview with Domosławski, 'Gaszenie pożaru benzyną' (Extinguishing a Fire with Gasoline)', *Polityka*, 16 August 2011: www. polityka.pl/tygodnikpolityka/swiat/1518590,1,rozmowa-artura-domoslaw skiego-z-prof-zygmuntem-baumanem.read.
91 This metaphor was mentioned by a family member of Zofia Braun, who moved to Israel in 1968 (in Grynberg, 2018: 183).
92 Interview conducted in Israel, May 2017.

13 A British Professor

1 Kołakowski, after being a visiting professor in the USA, settled in the UK in 1970 as a professor of philosophy.
2 A company that loans money for real estate acquisitions.
3 Letters from Kołakowski (1970/1) in personal correspondence of the Baumans: Bauman Archive, Leeds.
4 Before moving in, Bauman ordered work on the windows to seal them

tighter. Accustomed to Poland's cold winter, the Baumans paid attention to such details.

5 See Anne-Catherine Wagner's work on families of expatriates (diplomats and highly skilled professionals) and the impact of regular change of countries on their children's emotional stability.

6 Janina Bauman, in one of her autobiographical books, provided more details on the subject (J. Bauman, 1988).

7 Document from Bauman Archive, Leeds.

8 The note contains also a minor error: the year of his Ph.D. thesis was 1954 instead of 1956 – perhaps introduced inadvertently.

9 Jack Palmer is a sociologist, deputy director of the Bauman Institute, who was one of the co-authors of the study devoted to the history of the Leeds Department of Social Studies. I am grateful to Jack for our extensive correspondence and his help related to the Leeds period of Bauman's life and the Leeds context.

10 Max Farrar's personal website – obituary notice written a year after Bauman's death, at www.maxfarrar.org.uk.

11 Keith Tester, in an interview in London on 2 November 2018, said: 'It is Miliband who got the job for Bauman at Leeds, or he made it happen.' See also the biography of Miliband by Newman (2002).

12 His research interests switched from colonial issues to problems in British society (he published several articles in the *New Reasoner*, the New Left journal), and he became a sociology teacher and sociologist.

13 Max Farrar's personal website: www.maxfarrar.org.uk.

14 By 'history man', Bauman probably refers to *The History Man* (1975), a campus novel by Malcolm Bradbury. I wish to thank John Gaunt for the indication of this connection.

15 I am grateful for this remark to Jean-Michel Chapoulie, who also is critical about Bauman's description of French sociology and its position in French society (private correspondence of author, July 2019).

16 Interview with Keith Tester conducted 2 November 2018 in London.

17 Letter of Alan M. Dawe to Zygmunt Bauman, dated 7 January 1971: Bauman Archive, Leeds.

18 Correspondence with Jack Palmer, 16 August 2019.

19 Letter of Alan M. Dawe to Zygmunt Bauman, dated 7 January 1971.

20 Max Farrar's personal website, obituary written a year after Bauman's death.

21 Airmail letter from Dr J. V. Loach, dated 3 May 1971: Bauman Archive, Leeds.

22 Włodzimierz Goldkorn, discussion with Zygmunt Bauman entitled 'Ludzie w ciemnych czasach' ('People in the Dark Times') (in Polish), *Odra* (2013/10).

23 From author's interview with Bauman about his academic career, Leeds, 31 October 2013.

24 Wagner (2011) – mostly people doing experimental work in the life sciences area.

25 From author's interview with Bauman about his academic career, Leeds, 1 November 2013.

26 Ibid.

27 This is evident in studies I conducted between 2003 and 2015 in the EU and in the USA, focusing on scientific and scholarly careers (see, for example, Wagner, 2011, 2014, 2016).

28 I am grateful to Alan Warde, Bauman's Ph.D. student and, later, colleague from the department (interview conducted 23 August 2019 in Manchester), as well as Antony Bryant for their account about Bauman as a department colleague and as a friend (interview conducted in Leeds, 31 October 2018).

29 The other characteristics attributed to *Poznaniaks* are: love of the city; use of the local language; a specific accent; being disciplined, reliable and frugal – or even stingy. Being down to earth and balanced contrasts with the stereotypically romantic eastern Polish character, and is no doubt due in part to the contrasting influences of Russian and Prussian occupation under partition.

30 German sociologist Max Weber elaborated the scientific approach, using ideal-types created a priori.

31 From author's interview with Bauman, Leeds, 1 November 2013.

32 https://baumaninstitute.leeds.ac.uk/this-is-not-an-obituary; testimony of Terry Wassall.

33 Ibid.

34 See more at https://baumaninstitute.leeds.ac.uk/this-is-not-an-obituary.

35 In this section, I assess the Bauman–Tester relationship of master–disciple using a theoretical tool I developed in ethnographic research (in the artistic world of virtuoso musicians and in scientific laboratories). The extracts are from interviews conducted in 2013 (with Bauman) and 2018 (with Tester).

36 This opinion matches the assessment in Michele Lamont's excellent book about academic judgement, *How Professors Think* (2010).

37 In Polish, the term was *wspólna*; it means 'common', but also 'shared by people in common' – here translated as 'consensual'.

38 From author's interview conducted in Bauman's house, Leeds, 31 October 2013.

39 See Becker (1982: ch. 2).

40 About the process of the career-coupling phenomenon for scholars, see Wagner (2006, 2011); for music virtuosi, Wagner (2015).

41 I conducted the interview in London Public Library on 2 November 2018, a few months before Keith Tester died.

42 See Appendix.

43 Additional excerpt: 'At that time in the middle 1980s there was a split in the Leeds department – Bauman's group and Elias' group. It was not hostile but there was not actually greatly supportive conversation between the two. My best friend at that time was doing his Ph.D. with Richard Kilminster, a major follower of Elias ... my friend and I, we never had a conversation about it, but we watched ... Why had Zygmunt and Elias' relationship broke down? Something happened. ... someone said something happened at a dinner party. Elias said something that Zygmunt objected to – everything collapsed after that. Again – is that true? – I have no idea.' About the Elias–Bauman conflict, see laudatio discourse on Richard Kilminster by Stephen Mennell from 5–6 April 2018: www.academia.edu/36377493/Laudatio_Richard_Kilminster?auto=download.

44 Max Farrar said this at a symposium devoted to Bauman at Leeds University in January 2019.

45 The student could choose his or her literature and tools of investigation. In other academic settings, the mentorship can be a feudal type of relationship in which the student decides nothing and is simply a low-priced worker.

46 I wrote about this phenomenon in analysing the mentoring of classi-

cal musicians (Wagner, 2015), as well as Ph.D. students in life science (Wagner, 2011).

47 Hochfeld paid a scholarship for his assistant, Strzelecki, out of his own pocket (see Grochowska, 2014).

14 An Intellectual at Work

1 This section is written from the perspective of the sociology of work and is not taking into consideration such elements as style of writing or its content.

2 When I met Bauman for the first time in 2013, I did not have the idea of writing his biography, but was interested in his work – not in the content, but in the craft. This is the typical approach of sociologists of work – specialists in academic careers and creative occupations.

3 This sentence I recall from my memory; it was made before I turned on my recorder.

4 First-hand research means that a scholar is collecting raw data him-/herself and is not exclusively using existing publications for his own writing.

5 Kuhn later popularized and developed Fleck's approach in his book *The Structure of Scientific Revolutions*. Fleck was a physician and microbiologist, but after his death in 1961 was better known in sociology and history of science for his revolutionary ideas, published twenty-six years before Kuhn's work, in *Genesis and Development of a Scientific Fact* (1935).

6 Brackets are original to Bauman's letter – probably the place for the reference details.

7 Author's interview with Bauman conducted in Leeds, 31 October 2013.

8 Ibid.

9 About Conrad and his style of writing, in relation to the native language difference, see biography of Korzeniowski (Conrad's family name), entitled *Joseph Conrad: A Life*, by Zdzisław Najder (2007).

10 Author's interview with Bauman conducted in Leeds, 31 October 2013.

11 Interview conducted in Cambridge, 2 November 2018.

12 Ibid.

13 Author's interview with Bauman conducted in Leeds, 31 October 2013.

14 Ibid.

15 Ibid.

16 Data collected by the current author between 2003 and 2015.

17 Letter dated 13 September 1995; conserved in the Bauman Archive, Leeds.

18 Interview with John Thompson, conducted 2 November 2018 in Cambridge.

19 'In the first decade of the new millennium Bauman was producing a book a year, including the little books – on identity, community, individualization, Liquid Life, Liquid Fear, Liquid Times, works on consumption and consumer ethics' (Beilharz, 2020 (MS): 83). A complete list of publications can be found on the Bauman Institute website, and in a special issue of the journal *Thesis Eleven*, devoted to Bauman: 11 (2020).

20 Peter Beilharz noted: 'In 2013 there were four books, three in the form of conversations, which became the new preferred mode of discourse, representing the conversational model taken to its logical conclusion' (Beilharz, 2020 (MS): 82).

21 Zeidler Janiszewska, Kubicki and Chrzanowski organized several events

related to the Baumans, including lectures, conferences, photographic exhibitions, and meetings with the authors.

22 Interview conducted 27 November 2018 in Poznań.

23 For more about this, see Beilharz (2020).

24 Talk by Irena Bauman, 17 January 2019, Leeds University, at symposium 'Bauman's Legacy – Thinking in Dark Times'. I am grateful to Irena Bauman for sharing the manuscript and giving permission to use the recorded version of the speech.

25 Meredith Belbin (born 1926) created a model of nine team roles for identifying people's strong points and weak points in the workplace. For more, see www.belbin.com.

26 This excerpt was type-recorded during the symposium 'Bauman's Legacy'.

27 From 2009 to 2013, ZB published eleven books, of which six were not conversational.

28 Other texts will explore this issue further; the topic requires a separate book.

29 The letters from Lena Eilstein are in the Bauman Archive, Leeds.

30 More about Janina Bauman and her writing can be found in Wolff (2011).

31 Interestingly, when Bauman worked on his book, he exchanged some letters with Eisenstadt. The main topic of that correspondence was the Holocaust and modernity. Suddenly, the correspondence stopped. (Jack Palmer is working on this intellectual relationship, analysing the letters deposited in the Bauman Archive, Leeds.)

32 Interview with Griselda Pollock, Leeds University, 31 October 2018.

33 Emphasis added. Literally 'infested by Jews' – for more about the term, see chapter 1.

34 All citations of John Thompson are from the interview conducted on 2 November 2018 in Cambridge.

35 Polity's publishing successes before Bauman included translations of Bourdieu and Habermas (see more in Robbins, 2012: 158–9).

36 In the study of scientists' careers, most interviewees use this expression. The role of chance and 'being in the right place at the right moment' often refers to their collaborators (more in Wagner, 2011).

37 Citations from the first version of Beilharz (2020 MS). Bauman was accused of self-plagiarism, a frequent phenomenon with authors, particularly those who publish extensively. With over seventy books, it would be impossible not to repeat oneself.

38 Bauman was also accused of overusing Wikipedia, a frequent time-saving practice in contemporary academia, resulting from pressure and short deadlines requiring exact and precise citations. Bauman worked alone. He had no research assistant (Janina worked for him sporadically). And he only used Wikipedia at the last stage of his activity, when he wrote essays. He did not use it for his academic publications.

39 Joanna Janiak filmed in 1994 a documentary for Polish TV about Janina Bauman, and did an interview with her, published in the journal *Little Town Poznań*.

40 'Ignoranci i impotenci', interview with Bauman by Tomasz Kwaśniewski, *GW*, 21 November 2010.

41 I wish to thank Peter Beilharz for his remark on red wine.

42 While some guests interpreted this sign as Bauman's warning, Janina had put up the sign. The kitchen was definitely her husband's space.

43 By serious leisure, Stebbins meant hobbies executed at a professional level.

44 Interview in Leeds with Tony Bryant, 31 October 2018.
45 Interview with Keith Tester, London, public library, 2 November 2018.
46 In 1973, British New Left supporter E. P. Thompson published a 100-page letter to Kołakowski (see *Socialist Register*, 1973); see also Tester (2006).
47 http://niniwa22.cba.pl/wina.htm?fbclid=IwAR1iGD6U7vOH47sxo40zV7 I1z1FbWwkd_NblU46fpPEuFtC5jw-FiaB3mU4.
48 Keith Tester told me in the interview that Bauman was really pained by this situation.
49 'In 1986, the year in which I moved to Leeds, Janina Bauman published *Winter in the Morning: A Young Girl's Life in the Warsaw Ghetto and Beyond* (Virago, 1986). I had just completed my doctoral thesis at the University of Sheffield via the Hebrew University, Jerusalem. My thesis was on racial representations of "the Jew" in British culture and my head was full of new approaches to the historiography of European antisemitism. After an exploratory visit to test out my suitability, I quickly became a neighbour of Zygmunt and Janina. There began a conversation – focusing on Zygmunt Bauman's largely ignored Jewish turn (1986–1996) – that lasted for nearly a decade' (Cheyette, 2020).
50 This circle was composed mainly of people who were related to (worked and studied in) the Department of Arts and Humanities.
51 For example, sexual abuse or masculine domination.
52 See Griselda Pollock, *Thesis Eleven*, 2020 (Special Issue devoted to the Legacy of Bauman's work).
53 There is an extensive correspondence from Eilstein in the Bauman Archive, Leeds.
54 Letter to Janina and Zygmunt Bauman, by Lena Eilstein, 1990. Bauman Archive, Leeds.
55 In Polish, 'Cheers'.

15 Global Thinker

1 Interview with Keith Tester, London, public library, 2 November 2018.
2 Ibid.
3 *Gazeta Wyborcza*: Kwaśniewski, 'I Let Them Seduce Me'; emphasis added.
4 There is also a popular expression 'I am listening (myself) to my wife' – with the same error.
5 This is vernacular language. 'Brałem pod uwagę jej zdanie' (I considered her opinion) would be a more typical way of putting it.
6 Bauman had been offered a job in Canberra after a three-month visiting professorship (see chapter 12).
7 Term borrowed from French historian Bredel, who analysed the phenomenon using a broad historical perspective.
8 Levinas (1976).
9 All those documents are in the Bauman Archive, Leeds.
10 P. Gontarczyk, published an article in the IPN journal entitled 'Towarzysz "Semjon", nieznany życiorys Zygmunta Baumana' (Comrade 'Semjon', unknown CV of Zygmunt Bauman), *Biuletyn IPN*, 6, 2006. Based on two documents, he presented Bauman's activity out of context, ignoring other documents in Bauman's folder and making no critique of his sources. It was a politically oriented paper aimed at discrediting Bauman,

an authority for all Polish left-oriented groups and much of the young intelligentsia.

11 Author's interview with Bauman, Leeds, 1 November 2013. All the documents that Bauman sent to the prime minister, customs office and the president of PAN were deposited in the secret-service archives and reside today in the IPN archives.

12 The same conclusion was formulated by Andrzej Werblan, who opposed revisionism in 1968 but became a historian in 1989, writing an excellent book about Stalinism in Poland and a biography of his friend Gomułka.

13 See interview with Simon Tabet (2017).

14 Ryszard Gontarz, 'Nowa Droga Zygmunta Baumana', *Kurier Polski*, transcript in AIPN BU 0 1224 1505.

15 AIPN BU 0 204/7/1/4468 / II, 'Note from a conversation with Captain "K.O."', Warsaw – document dated: 20 September 1968 – 'Secret'.

16 One sociologist, in a letter to Bauman in 1989, explained that her first recollection of him was when she was ordered to redo her master's thesis to delete all references to Bauman's work.

17 He rejected a professorship offer from Yale University because it required a focus on Soviet-bloc countries.

18 Letter of 8 July 1981 from Samsonowicz to the minister of higher education. I am grateful to Anna Sfard for this document, as well as others concerning her father's relationship with Polish higher education institutions. The documents were part of an exhibition devoted to the fiftieth anniversary of the March 1968 events, organized in 2018 by Museum Polin in Warsaw. The documents are held at the Bauman Archive, Leeds.

19 The letter is dated 10 August 1981, and signed by the undersecretary of state.

20 Kołakowski, who began his exile as a visiting professor in Canada and then the USA, kept his Polish passport. Baczko (visiting professor in Clermont-Ferrand) and Brus also kept their citizenship. Morawski stayed in Poland.

21 Letter of 1 November 1981 from Włodzimierz Brus to the rector of Warsaw University, Henryk Samsonowicz (Bauman Archive, Leeds).

22 The story is told by Bauman in his 1988 interview with Anna Mieszczanek, which was published in the collective book *Landscape After the Shock* (1989).

23 He used this English term.

24 Mieszczanek's book was first published by an underground press, and later, after Bauman's banishment ended, in an official edition. I would like to thank Dariusz Brzozowski for leading me to this interview and providing the history of its publication.

25 According to the documents of the *Bezpieka*, Bauman was deleted from that list on 14 June 1988, but Janina only in January 1989.

26 There were also written apologies – for example, a short letter from Wesołowski, Bauman's close colleague from Hochfeld's circle. See Bauman Archive, Leeds.

27 Letter signed by Marek Ziółkowski, the president of the Committee of Sociology, PAN; Bauman Archive, Leeds.

28 In this document, Bauman also declares that he does not intend to ask for damages related to his exile. Document in the personal folder for Zygmunt Bauman (no. 4982) in the Archives of the University of Warsaw.

29 Anna Wojdowska-Iwaszkiewiczowa, in a Polish Radio 2 broadcast on 4

April 2013: www.polskieradio.pl/8/380/Artykul/822897,Holokaust-zabija-nawet-ocalonych.

30 Anna Zeidler-Janiszewska died in 2017 before I could interview her. She was one of the Baumans' closest friends in Poland.

31 https://web.uniroma1.it/disp/en/events/european-amalfi-prize.

32 Dawes (2011: 131).

33 Conventions in the Beckerian sense (Becker, 1982).

34 Interview with Keith Tester, London, public library, 2 November 2018.

35 Gontarczyk, 'Towarzysz "Semjon"'.

36 Adam Michnik, 'On the Side of Geremek', *New York Review of Books*, 25 September 2008.

37 According to this document, the vote of council members was held on 21 June with these results: of the 43 votes counted, 34 were in favour, 6 against, with 3 abstentions.

38 The IS voted on 18 July with 28 in favour, 8 against and 3 abstentions.

39 AUW, personal file – Bauman, copy of the 'Letter sent by e-mail' by Professor Jerzy Kwaśniewski, on 7 September 2006 at 21.26.

40 AUW, personal file – Bauman, letter from Professor Maria Łoś, 24 September 2006. Emphasis added.

41 His colleague Helena Wolińska, the first and third wife of Włodzimierz Brus, had been a prosecutor in the Stalinist era and signed death warrants. In the post-communist era, Poland made extradition requests for her. She remained until her death in the UK.

42 AUW, personal file – Bauman. Sentence copied from two letters from the presidents of the Councils of the ISNS and IS.

43 AUW, personal file – Bauman. Letter from the president of the IS Scientific Council, dated 27 October 2006.

44 AUW, personal file – Bauman. Letter from the president of the IS Scientific Council, dated 31 October 2006.

45 AUW, personal file – Bauman. Printed e-mail – version undated, from rector to ISNS and IS Council presidents.

46 www.theguardian.com/books/2007/apr/28/academicexperts.highereducation.

47 Majmurek (2019): http://serwer1745813.home.pl/numery/PT_nr31_2019_Anticommunisms_Discourses_of_Exclusion/PT_31_2019_Anti-Communisms_Discourses_of_Exclusion.pdf, ISSN 2081-8130, DOI: 10.14746/prt.2019.1.10.

48 This story was told by Aleksandra Jasińska-Kania in the interview conducted in December 2017 in Warsaw.

49 I would like to thank Peter Beilharz for this information.

50 I am grateful to the poet Włodzimierz Holsztyński and translator Barbara Nykiel-Herbert for their talents.

51 This section is based on two interviews with Aleksandra Jasińska-Kania conducted in her Warsaw apartment in 2017 and 2018. The complete story of their relationship is published in a paper by Jasińska-Kania (2018) in *Thesis Eleven.*

52 *Morality in the Age of Contingency*, ed. P. Heelas, S. Lash and P. Morris (Oxford: Blackwell, 1996).

53 Their relationship was so close that secret services (most probably Israeli), researching some sensitive documents that concerned Michael Sfard's activity (bringing peace between two separate communities), came to Leeds, broke into Bauman's house when its inhabitants were absent and

made their investigation. In order to put some pressure on Sfard, the secret services left signs that they had been there.

54 Aleksandra decided to visit this city.

55 There were also members of other organizations: NOP (Narodowe Odrodzenie Polski) and Solidarni 2010.

56 This information was mentioned in his obituary, written by his friends and collaborators from Poznań. I am grateful to Professor Roman Kubicki for bringing this to my attention.

57 *Information Philosophie*, 2, 2014, p. 82.

58 See my article about anti-Semitic actions that took place during the Holocaust history conference in Paris: Wagner (2019).

59 http://wroclaw.wyborcza.pl/wroclaw/1,35771,20006221,marsz-przeciw-ue-dutkiewicz-to-konfident-krzycza.html.

60 http://wroclaw.eska.pl/newsy/policja-ma-nagrania-ze-spalenia-przez-naro dowcow-zdjecia-dutkiewicza-i-baumana-pojda-do-analizy/165142.

61 I am grateful to Janet Woolf for the permission to cite this letter.

62 Interview with Stanisław Obirek, conducted in Warsaw, 25 September 2018.

63 Aleksandra Jasińska-Kania wrote in a letter addressed to the author (27 January 2020): 'the last text [Zygmunt] wrote before his death, leaving me to finish it, was ordered by Carlo Bordoni for the *Prometeo* magazine. [This is] our joint article 'That West Meant to be Declining', published in 2017 in Italian, in Polish in 2018 in *Odra*, and in 2019 in English in *Thesis Eleven*'.

Conclusion

1 This categorization was employed by Wiatr (2017b).

2 Arne Johan Vetlesen at Oslo University, Tommy Jensen and Nick Butler in Stockholm, Mats Alvesson and Karin Jonnergård from Lund, Lena Olaison and Michał Zawadski from Jönköping, and Daniel Hjorth from Copenhagen.

3 This assumption is based on discussions with university teachers in various EU countries, Brazil and the USA, informally conducted over five years at academic meetings.

Appendix

1 PRL is the acronym for the Polish Peoples' Republic, in use from 1952 to 1989. Previously it was known as People's Poland (from 1944), and after 1989 as the Republic of Poland.

2 Stryjkowski was a writer and journalist, specializing in Polish–Jewish relations.

3 Example given by Hughes (1945): a young African American's master status did not enable him to be a physician. Hughes gave the following two situations as examples: (1) if there is a car accident at night, an Afro-American doctor will be able to act as a physician in case of emergency and danger to life, if he is the only medical doctor in the place. The second example: an elderly lady sick with the flu calls for a doctor and, when she opens her door, realizing that the doctor is an African American, cancels

the visit, pretending that she is much better now. Hughes concluded that, if the situation does not represent a high risk (an elderly not-Afro-American women suffering with flu), the patient will cancel the medical visit, waiting for another physician who will be not a person of colour. The Afro-American doctor did not meet the expectations of the elderly woman – she imagined that he would be white. The master status of a medical doctor is anything but a person of colour (this was in the 1940s).

4 Oswald Hall defended his Ph.D. thesis 'The Informal Organization of Medical Practice' in 1944.

5 The concept was first employed by Shibutani (1955) and discussed by Strauss (1959). In the 1980s, it was popularized by Howard Becker through his book *Art Worlds* (1982). Adele E. Clarke and Susan Leigh Star concluded that Strauss and Becker 'defined social worlds as groups with shared commitments to certain activities, sharing resources of many kinds to achieve their goals and building shared ideologies about how to go about their business', in *The Social Worlds Framework: A Theory/ Methods Package*: www.researchgate.net/publication/261948477_The_ Social_Worlds_Framework_A_TheoryMethods_Package.

6 A separate sociological article about the precise methodology I have employed in this book will be forthcoming in the academic press.

Bibliography

Zygmunt Bauman – cited works

1956. 'Przeciw monopolowi w nauce' [Against Monopoly in Science], *Po Prostu*.

1959. *Socjalizm brytyjski: Źródła, filozofia, doktryna polityczna* [*British Socialism: Origins, Philosophy, Political Doctrine*]. Warsaw: Państwowe.

1962a. *Socjologia na co dzień* [*Everyday Sociology*]. Warsaw: Iskry.

1962b. *Zarys socjologii. Zagadnienia i pojęcia* [*Outline of Sociology: Issues and Concepts*]. Warsaw: Państwowe Wydawnictwo Naukowe.

1963. *Idee, ideały, ideologie* [*Ideas, Ideals, Ideologies*]. Warsaw: Iskry.

1964a. *Zarys marksistowskiej teorii społeczeństwa* [*An Outline of the Marxist Theory of Society*]. Warsaw: Państwowe Wydawnictwo Naukowe.

1964b. *Wizje ludzkiego świata. Studia nad społeczną genezą i funkcją socjologii* [*Visions of a Human World: Studies on the Genesis of Society and the Function of Sociology*]. Warsaw: Książka i Wiedza.

1966. *Kultura i społeczeństwo. Preliminaria* [*Culture and Society: Preliminaries*]. Warsaw: Państwowe Wydawnictwo Naukowe.

1967. 'Moral and Ethical Values of the October Revolution: A Man in a Socialist Society'. Transcript of Bauman's lecture at a scientific session organized by the Regional Student Council of the Rural Youth Association in Łódź, 9–10 December.

1968. 'O frustracji i kuglarzach' [On Frustration and the Conjurers], *Kultura*, 12, 5–21.

1972. *Between Class and Élite: The Evolution of the British Labour Movement. A Sociological Study*. Manchester University Press [Polish original 1960].

1973. *Culture as Praxis*. London: Routledge & Kegan Paul [republished in 1999 with new foreword].

1989. *Modernity and the Holocaust*. Ithaca, NY: Cornell University Press.

1992. *Mortality, Immortality and Other Life Strategies*. Cambridge: Polity.

1997. *Humanista w ponowoczesnym świecie – rozmowy o sztuce życia, nauce, życiu sztuki i innych sprawach* [*A Humanist in the Post-modern World: Conversations on the Art of Life, Science, the Life of Art and Other Matters*], with R. Kubicki and A. Zeidler-Janiszewska. Poznań: Zyski i S-ka.

2001. *Thinking Sociologically*, 2nd edn, with Tim May. Oxford: Blackwell Publishers.

2008. *The Art of Life*. Cambridge: Polity.

2012. *This Is Not a Diary*. Cambridge: Polity.

2013a. *Moral Blindness*, with L. Donskis. Cambridge: Polity.
2013b. *What Use Is Sociology?* with K. Tester and M. H. Jacobsen. Cambridge: Polity.
2014. *State of Crisis*, with C. Bordoni. Cambridge: Polity.
2015a. *Management in a Liquid Modern World*, with I. Bauman, J. Kociatkiewicz and M. Kostera. Cambridge: Polity.
2015b. *Of God and Man*, with S. Obirek. Cambridge: Polity.
2015c. *On the World and Ourselves*, with S. Obirek. Cambridge: Polity.
2016a. *Liquid Evil*, with L. Donskis. Cambridge: Polity.
2016b. *In Praise of Literature*, with R. Mazzeo. Cambridge: Polity.
2017. *Retrotopia*. Cambridge: Polity.
2018. *Sketches in the Theory of Culture*. Cambridge: Polity [originally intended for publication in 1968, and first published in Polish in 2017].

General bibliography

Abbott, A. 1997. 'On the Concept of Turning Point'. *Comparative Social Research* 16: 85–105.
Aleksiun, N. 2002. *Dokąd dalej? Ruch syjonistyczny w Polsce (1944–1950)*. Warsaw: Trio.
Aleksiun, N. 2014. 'Together but Apart: University Experience of Jewish Students in the Second Polish Republic'. *Acta Poloniae Historica* 109: 109–37.
Aleksiun, N. 2017. 'Intimate Violence: Jewish Testimonies on Victims and Perpetrators in Eastern Galicia'. *Holocaust Studies* 23, 1–2 (special issue: 'Jews and Gentiles in Central and Eastern Europe during the Holocaust in History and Memory').
Allen, A. 2014. *The Fantastic Laboratory of Dr. Weigl: How Two Brave Scientists Battled Typhus and Sabotaged the Nazis*. New York: W. W. Norton & Co.
Anderson, E. 2000. *Code of the Street*. New York: W. W. Norton & Co.
Applebaum, A. 2004. *Gulag: A History*. New York: Anchor Books.
Applebaum, A. 2018. *Red Famine: Stalin's War on Ukraine*. New York: Anchor Books.
Bagguley, Campbell and Palmer, J. 2018. 'Public Service and Jippi-Jappa – 100 Years of Leeds History'. *Network Magazine of the British Sociological Association*, Spring.
Bartniczak, M. 1972. 'Ze starych i nowych dziejów Ostrowi Mazowieckiej. Nazwa, Herb i geneza miasta'. *Ziemia*: 52–74: http://ziemia.pttk.pl/Ziemia/Artykul_1972_006.pdf.
Bartoszewski, W. 2007. 'Tajny komplet na Żoliborzu. Tragiczna karta z dziejów nauki podziemnej'. In *Socjologia na Uniwersytecie Warszawskim*, ed. Sułek A. Warsaw: IFiS PAN.
Baruch, M. 1997. *Servir l'État français*. Paris: Fayard.
Bauman, J. 1986/7. *Winter in the Morning: A Young Girl's Life in the Warsaw Ghetto and Beyond, 1939–1945*. Bath: Chivers Press.
Bauman, J. 1988. *A Dream of Belonging: My Years in Postwar Poland*. London: Virago.
Bauman, J. 1998. 'People's Fear: The Plight of the Gypsies'. *Thesis Eleven* 54, August: 51–62.
Bauman, J. 2011. *Nigdzie na ziemi. Powroty. Opowiadania*. Łódź: Wydawnictwo Oficyna.

Becker, H. 1963. *Outsiders: Studies in the Sociology of Deviance.* New York: The Free Press of Glencoe

Becker, H. 1982. *Art Worlds.* Berkeley: University of California Press.

Beilharz, P. 2020. *Intimacy in Postmodern Times: A Friendship with Zygmunt Bauman.* Manchester University Press [pages indicated from the MS].

Berger, L. 1989. *Korczak, un homme, un symbole.* Paris: Magnard.

Bikont, A. 2004. *My z Jedwabnego.* Warsaw: Wydawn. Prószyński i S-ka.

Bikont, A. 2017. *Sendlerowa.* Wołowiec: W ukryciu. Wyd. Czarne.

Bikont, A. and Łuczywo, H. 2018. *Jacek.* Warsaw: Agora, and Wołowiec: Czarne

Blobaum, R., ed. 2005. *Antisemitism and Its Opponents in Modern Poland.* Ithaca, NY: Cornell University Press.

Brykczyński, P. 2017. *Gotowi na przemoc. Mord, antysemityzm i demokracja w międzywojennej Polsce* [original title: *Primed for Violence: Murder, Antisemitism, and Democratic Politics in Interwar Poland*]. Warsaw: Wyd. Krytyki Politycznej.

Cała, A. 2012. *Żyd – wróg odwieczny?* Warsaw: Wydawnictwo Nisza.

Cała, A. 2014. *Ochrona bezpieczeństwa fizycznego Żydów w Polsce powojennej: Komisje Specjalne przy Centralnym Komitecie Żydów w Polsce.* Warsaw: Żydowski Instytut Historyczny.

Chałubiński, M. 2017. 'Powroty do Juliana Hochfelda'. *Studia Socjologiczno-Polityczne* 1, 6: 27–41.

Chapoulie, J.-M. 2001. *La Tradition sociologique de Chicago.* Paris: Seuil. [English version: Columbia University Press, 2020].

Chęciński, S. 1982. *Poland, Communism, Nationalism, Anti-Semitism.* New York: Karz-Cohl Publishers.

Cheyette, B. 2020. 'Zygmunt Bauman's Window: From Jews to Strangers and Back Again'. *Thesis Eleven* 1–19, February, 67–85.

Chmielewski, A. 2015. 'Academies of Hatred' (blog): https://adamjchmielewski. blogspot.com/2015/07/academies-of-hatred.html.

Chmielewski, A. 2020. *Politics and Recognition: Toward a New Political Aesthetics.* London: Routledge.

Clarke, C. 1960. *Eichmann: The Man and His Crimes.* New York: Ballantine Books.

Czapigo, D. and Białas, M. 2015. *Berlingowcy. Żołnierze tragiczni.* Warsaw: RM.

Czapliński, P. 2015. Katastrofa wsteczna. *Poznańskie Studia Polonistyczne – Seria Literacka* 25, 45.

Czarny, B. 2015. 'Wpływ aspirantów Katedry Ekonomii Politycznej w Instytucie Kształcenia Kadr Naukowych w Warszawie na polską ekonomię po II wojnie światowej'. *Ekonomia* 41: http://ekonomia.wne.uw.edu.pl/eko nomia/getFile/760.

Czernecki, I. 2013. 'An Intellectual Offensive: The Ford Foundation and the Destalinization of the Polish Social Sciences'. *Cold War History* 13, 3: 289–319: http://dx.doi.org/10.1080/14682745.2012.756473.

Dąbrowska J. 2019. *Miłość jest warta starania. Rozmowy z Mistrzami* [*Love is Worth Trying: Conversations with Masters*]. Warsaw: Agora.

Dąbrowski, F. 2008. 'Ryszard Gontarz. Funkcjonariusz UB i SB, Dziennikarz PRL'. 'Komentarze Historyczne', *Biuletyn IPN.*

Davis, N. 2004. *Rising '44: The Battle for Warsaw.* New York: Macmillan Publishers.

Davis, N. 2015. *Trail of Hope: The Anders Army, an Odyssey across Three Continents*. Oxford: Osprey Publishing.

Dawes, S. 2011. 'The Role of the Intellectual in Liquid Modernity: An Interview with Zygmunt Bauman'. *Theory, Culture & Society* 28, 3, 130–48.

DeJong-Lambert, W. 2012. 'Lysenkoism in Poland'. *Journal of the History of Biology* 45, 3, August: 499–524.

Depo, J. 2012. 'Korpus Bezpieczeństwa'. *Bezpieczeństwo. Teoria i Praktyka* 1, 6: 125–39.

Dławichowski, K. A. 1983. 'Szkoły jakich nie było' [The Schools Which Did Not Exist]. *Koszalińskie Towarzystwo Społeczno-Kulturalne*; Koszalin 1983, tom 1–4.

Eisler, J. 2006. *Polski Rok 1968*. Warsaw: Instytut Pamięci Narodowej.

Engelking, B. and Grabowski, J., eds. 2018. *Dalej jest noc. Losy Żysów w wybranych powiatach okupowanej Polski*. Warsaw: Centrum Badań nad Zagładą Żydów.

Feduszka, J. 2001. *Gdzie słońce wschodzi i kędy zapada. ... Granice przez czasy, religie, krainy, miasta, wioski, podwórka, rodziny. Katalog wystawy w Muzeum Zamojskim*: www.roztocze.horyniec.net/Roztocze_Poludniowe/ Granice.html.

Feiner, S. 2004. *Hadkalah and History: The Emergence of a Modern Jewish Historical Consciousness*, trans. Naor Ch. Silberston. Littman Library of Jewish Civilization. Liverpool University Press.

Fijuth-Dudek, A. 2018. 'Marzec 68 Leopolda Ungera': http://ohistorie.eu/tag/ marzec-68/?print=pdf-search&fbclid=IwAR026eV_0PeYtw49r9tBX33DdM 9nnOrqkQw3ySNr8tLZIgPWodM1_vFVYWI.

Finn, P. and Couvée, P. 2014. *The Zhivago Affair: The Kremlin, the CIA, and the Battle Over a Forbidden Book*. New York: Pantheon Books

Fleck, Ludwik. 1935. *Style myślowe i fakty*. Warsaw: IFiS PAN.

Friedman, S. 1966. 'Julian Hochfeld (1911–1966)', *Revue française de sociologie*, 7, 4.

Friszke, A. 2010. *Anatomia Buntu*. Kuroń: Modzelewski i Komandosi. Wyd Znak.

Friszke, A. and Karski, J. 1997. 'Czy Powstanie Warszawskie było potrzebne'. *Gazeta Wyborcza* 178: 16.

Frost, S. 1998. *Schooling as a Socio-political Expression: Jewish Education in Interwar Poland*. Jerusalem: Magnes Press.

Gambetta, Diego. 1993. *The Sicilian Mafia: The Business of Private Protection*. Cambridge, MA: Harvard University Press.

Gdula, M. 2017. 'The Warsaw School of Marxism', *State of Affairs* [Warsaw: Instytut Socjologii Uniwersytet Warszawski] 13, 197–226.

Geertz, C. 1973. 'Thick Description: Toward an Interpretive Theory of Culture'. In *The Interpretation of Cultures: Selected Essays*. New York: Basic Books.

Gewirtz, J. 2017. *Unlikely Partners: Chinese Reformers, Western Economists, and the Making of Global China*. Cambridge, MA: Harvard University Press.

Głowiński, M. 1991. *Marcowe gadanie: Komentarze do słów, 1966–1971*. Warsaw: Wydawn. Pomost

Gmyr, M. 2012 'Represyjne działania Wojsk Bezpieczeństwa Wewnętrznego województwa łódzkiego w pierwszym półroczu 1946r'. *Aparat Represji w Polsce Ludowej 1944–1989* 1, 10: 167–83: http://bazhum.muzhp.pl.

Goffman, A. 1959. *The Presentation of Self in Everyday Life*. New York: Anchor Books.

Goldkorn, W. 2013. '"Ludzie w ciemnych czasach" – rozmowa z Zygmuntem Baumanem'. *Odra* 10, 14–19.
Goldkorn, W. 2018. *Dziecko w śniegu*. Wołowiec: Czarne.
Grabowski, J. 2013. *Hunt for the Jews: Betrayal and Murder in German-Occupied Poland*. Bloomington: Indiana University Press.
Gray LeMaster, C. 1994. *A Corner of the Tapestry: A History of the Jewish Experience in Arkansas 1820s–1990s*. Fayetteville: University of Arkansas Press.
Greeted, C. 1973. *The Interpretation of Cultures*. New York: Basic Books.
Grochowska, M. 2014. *Strzelecki. Śladem nadziei*. Warsaw: Świat Książki.
Gross, J. T. 1998. *Upiorna dekada. Trzy eseje o stereotypach na temat Żydów, Polaków, Niemców i komunistów 1939–1948*. Kraków: Towarzystwo autorów i Wydawców Prac Naukowych Universitas.
Gross, J. T. 2001. *Neighbors: The Destruction of the Jewish Community in Jedwabne, Poland*. Princeton University Press.
Gross, J. T. 2006. *Strach. Antysemityzm w Polce tuż po wojnie. Historia moralnej zapaści*. Znak: Krak.w.
Gross, J. T. 2010. 'Niepamięć zbiorowa'. In *Przeciw Antysemityzmowi 1936–2009*, ed. A. Michnik. Kraków: Universitas.
Gross, J. and Grudzinska-Gross, I. 2012. *Golden Harvest: Events at the Periphery of the Holocaust*. New York: Oxford University Press.
Gross, J. T. and Pawlicka, A. 2018. *Bardzo dawno temu, mniej więcej w zeszły piątek...* Warsaw: WydAB.
Grynberg, H. 1994. 'Ludzie Żydom zgotowali ten los'. *Prawda nieartystyczna* [Warsaw: PIW].
Grynberg, H. 2002. *Drohobycz, Drohobycz and Other Stories: True Tales from the Holocaust and Life After*. London: Penguin.
Grynberg, M. 2018. *Księga wyjścia [The Book of the Exit]*. Wołowiec: Wyd. Czarne.
Halsey, A. H. 2004. *A History of Sociology in Britain*. Science, Literature, and Society. Oxford University Press.
Hardy, J. 2009. *Poland's New Capitalism*. London: Pluto Press.
Hirszowicz, M. 2001. *Pułapki Zaangażowania. Intelektualiści w służbie komunizmu [Traps of Engagement: The Intellectuals in the Service of Communism]*. Warsaw: Scholar.
Hnatiuk, Aleksandra. 2016. *Odwaga i strach*. Wrocław: KEW.
Hochfeld, J. 1982. 'Marksizm-socjologia-socjalizm. Wybór pism'. *Studia Socjologiczne* [4, 7, 1962], ed. Jerzy J. Wiatr. Warsaw: PWN.
Huener, J. 2003. *Auschwitz, Poland, and the Politics of Commemoration, 1945–1979*. Polish and Polish American Studies. Athens: Ohio University Press.
Hughes, E. 1962. 'Good People and Dirty Work', *Social Problems*, 10, 1, 3–11.
Hughes, E. Ch. 1945. 'Dilemmas and Contradictions of Status'. *The American Journal of Sociology* 50, 5, 353–9.
Hughes, E. Ch. 1971. *Sociological Eye*. Chicago: Aldine-Atherton.
Janiak, J. 2011 [1994]. The interview with Janina Bauman 'Polski styl'. *Miasteczko Poznań – Żydowskie Pismo o Małych Ojczyznach* 1, 8.
Jasińska-Kania, A. 2018. 'Living with Zygmunt Bauman, Before and After'. *Thesis Eleven*, 86–90.
Jastrząb, Ł. 2015. 'Raporty o antysemickich wystąpieniach w Polsce po I wojnie światowej'. *Pamiętnik Biblioteki Kórnickiej*. 0551-3790. Z. 32.
Jaworski, M. 1984. *Powstanie i działalność Korpusu Bezpieczeństwa Wewnętrznego*. Warsaw: Akademia Spraw Wewnętrznych, Katedra Historii i Archiwistyki.

Jedlicki, J. 1993. *Źle urodzeni czyli o doświadczeniu historycznym. Scripta i poscripta.* London: Annex.
Jedlicki, W. 1963. *Klub Krzywego Koła,* Paris: Wyd. Instytut Literacki.
Jędrychowski, S. 1980. 'Nowe Widnokręgi: ze wspomnień (część III)'. *Kwartalnik Historii Prasy Polskiej* 19, 4: 45–61.
Keff, B. 2013. *Antysemityzm. Niezamknięta historia.* Warsaw: Wydawnictwo Czarna Owca.
Kemp-Welch, T. 1996. 'Khrushchev's "Secret Speech" and Polish Politics: The Spring of 1956'. *Europe-Asia Studies* 48, 2, 181–206.
Kersten, K. 1991.*The Establishment of Communist Rule in Poland, 1943–1948,* trans. J. Micgiel and M. H. Bernhard. Berkeley and Los Angeles: University of California Press.
Kijek, K. 2010. 'Między integracją w wykluczeniem. Doświadczenia szkolne jako czynnik politycznej socjalizacji młodzieży żydowskiej w Polsce okresu międzywojennego'. In *Jednostka zakorzeniona? Wykorzeniona?* ed. Aleksandra Lompart, University of Warsaw Press.
Kijowski, J. 2010. 'Powiat Ostrołęka w pierwszej dekadzie rządów komunistycznych, Mazowsze i Podlasie w ogniu 1944-1956'. In *Powiat Ostrołęka w pierwszej dekadzie rządów komunistycznych*: http://mazowsze.hist.pl/17/Rocznik_Mazowiecki/395/2010/13021.
Kijowski, J. 2014. 'Okruchy wspomnień o żydowskiej Ostrołęce', *Żydzi w Ostrołęce*: http://rozmaitosci.com/okruchy-wspomnien-o-zydowskiej-ostrolece.
Kilias, J. 2016. 'Socjologia polska i czeska: wzajemne stosunki , ich charakter i konteksty' [Polish and Czech Sociologies: Mutual Relations and Contexts]. *Stan Rzeczy* [Warsaw: WUW] 10: 283–315.
Kilias, J. 2017. *Goście ze Wschodu. Socjologia polska lat sześćdziesiątych XX wieku a nauka światowa.* Kraków: Nomos.
Kilminster, R. 2016. 'Overcritique and Ambiguity in Zygmunt Bauman's Sociology: A Long-term Perspective'. In *Beyond Bauman: Critical Engagements and Creative Excursions.* ed. M. H. Jacobsen. London: Taylor Francis.
Klapp, O. 1964. *Symbolic Leaders: Public Dramas and Public Men.* London: Taylor and Francis Group.
Kłódź, A. 2015. *Tajemnica Pana Cukra.* Warsaw: Wielka Litera.
Kłoskowska, A. 1989. 'Wojna i socjologia', *Kultura i Społeczeństwo,* 33, 2.
Komar, M. 2015. *Zaraz wybuchnie.* Warsaw: Czuły Barbarzyńca Press.
Kopaliński, W. 1980. *Słownik wyrazów obcych i zwrotów obcojęzycznych.* Warsaw: Wiedza Powszechna.
Kossewska E. 2015. *Ona jeszcze mówi po polsku, ale śmieje się po hebrajsku Partyjna prasa polskojęzyczna i integracja kulturowa polskich Żydów w Izraelu (1948–1970).* University of Warsaw Press.
Kozińska-Witt, H. 2014. 'Reakcja samorządu krakowskiego na akty gwałtu dokonywane na ludności żydowskiej w okresie Drugiej Rzeczypospolitej (według sprawozdań prasowych)'. *Kwartalnik Historii Żydów* 251, 559–82.
Koźmińska-Frejlak, E. 2014. 'The Adaptation of Survivors to the Post-war Reality from 1944 to 1949'. In *Jewish Presence in Absence: The Aftermath of the Holocaust in Poland, 1944–2010,* ed. Feliks Tych and Monika Adamczyk-Grabowska. Yad Vashem Jerusalem: The International Institute for Holocaust Research.
Krajewski, K. and Łabuszewski T. 2008. 'Ziemia ostrołęcka w walce z komunizmem 1944-1954'. *Fundacja Pamiętamy*: www.solidarni.waw.pl/pobierz/FundacjaPamietamy/ostroleka.pdf.

Kraśko, N. 1996. *Instytucjonalizacja socjologii w Polsce 1920–1970*. Warsaw: WN PWN.

Kraśko, N. 2017. 'Zygmunt Bauman: Człowiek – Uczony – Profeta'. *Zdanie* 1–2, 172–3.

Kuhn, T. S. 1960. *The Structure of Scientific Revolutions*. Cambridge, MA: Harvard University Press.

Kzyzowski, L. 2020. *Ghost Citizens: Jewish Return to a Postwar City*. Cambridge, MA: Harvard University Press.

Łabędź, L. 1959. 'The Destinies of Sociology in Poland'. *Soviet Survey* 29.

Łabędź, L. 2012. 'Odmiany losu socjologii w Polsce'. In *Socjologia na Uniwersytecie Warszawskim. Fragmenty historii*, ed. Antonii Sułek. Warsaw: Wydawnictwo IDiS PAN, 2007, 208–17, trans. from English (M. Bucholc, 'Vicissitudes of Sociology in Poland').

Lamont, M. 2010. *How Professors Think: Inside the Curious World of Academic Judgment*. Cambridge, MA: Harvard University Press.

Landau, L. 1962. *Kronika lat wojny i okupacji*, vol. I: *Wrzesień 1939 – listopad 1940*. Warsaw: PWN.

Landau-Czajka, A. 2006. *Syn będzie Lech. Asymilacja Żydów w Polsce międzywojennej*. Warsaw: Neriton.

Łepkowski, T. 1983. *Myśli o historii Polski i Polaków*. Warsaw: CDN.

Leociak, J. 2018. *Młyny Boże. Zapiski o Kościele i Zagładzie*. Wołowiec: Wyd. Czarne.

Levinas, E. 1976. 'Entre deux mondes (la voie de Franz Rosenweig)'. *In Difficile Liberté*. Paris: Albin Michel.

Likiernik, S. 2001. *By Devil's Luck: A Tale of Resistance in Wartime Warsaw*. Edinburgh: Mainstream Publishing Company Ltd.

Lipiński, P. 2016. *Bicia nie trzeba było ich uczyć. Proces Humera i oficerów śledczych Urzędu Bezpieczeństwa*. Wołowiec: Wyd. Czarne.

Majmurek, J. 2019. 'Polish Deadlock: Between Liberal and Right-Wing Anti-Communism'. *Praktyka Teoretyczna* 1, 31, 174–7.

Mała encyklopedia rolnicza. 1964. Warsaw: Państwowe Wydawnictwo Rolnicze i Leśne.

Maramorosch, K. 2015. *The Thorny Road to Success: A Memoir*. Bloomington: iUniverse.

Markiewicz, H. 2004. Przeciw nienawiści i pogardzie. *Teksty Drugie* [Instytut Badań Literackich Warszawa] 6: http://rcin.org.pl/Content/53490/WA248_69054_P-I-2524_markiew-przeciw.pdf.

Matyjaszek, K. 2019. 'Produkcja Przestrzeni Żydowskiej w dawnej i współczesnej Polsce'. Kraków University. https://universitas.com.pl/produkt/3878/Produkcja-przestrzeni-zydowskiej-w-dawnej-i-wspolczesnej-Polsce.

Meng, M. 2008. 'Shattered Spaces: Jewish Sites in Germany and Poland after 1945'. Ph.D. dissertation, University of North Carolina at Chapel Hill.

Merda, R. 2017. 'Adam Schaff wobec ewolucji poglądów filozoficznych Leszka Kołakowskiego. O sporach programowych w polskim marksizmie'. *Folia Philosophica* (Katowice) 38, 137–46.

Michnik, A. and Marczyk, A. 2017. *Against Anti-Semitism: An Anthology of Twentieth-Century Polish Writings*. Oxford University Press [Polish original 2010].

Mieszczanek, A. 1989. 'Homecoming' [interview with Bauman]. In *Krajobraz po Szoku* [*Landscape After the Shock*]. Warsaw: Przedświt.

Miłosz, Cz. 1953. *The Captive Mind*, trans. J. Zielonko. London: Secker & Warburg.

Miłosz, Cz. 1999. *Wyprawa w dwudziestolecie* [*An Excursion through the Twenties and Thirties*]. Kraków: Wydawnictwo Literackie.

Modzelewski, K. 2013. *Zajeździmy kobyłę historii. Wyznania poobijanego jeźdźca.* Warsaw: Iskry.

Modzelewski, K. and Werblan, A. 2017. *Modzelewski–Werblan. Polska Ludowa*, ed. R. Walenciak. Warsaw: Iskry.

Molisak, A. 2004. *Judaizm jako los. Rzecz o Bogdanie Wojdowskim.* Warsaw: Wydawnictwo Warszawa.

Morawski, S. 1996. 'Kto-m zacz?' In *Losy żydowskie, Świadectwo żywych*, ed. M. Turski. Warsaw: Stowarzyszenie Żydów Kombatantów i Poszkodowanych w II Wojnie Światowe, 80–118.

Mórawski, K. 2003. *Dzieje miasta*, Warsaw: Książka i Wiedza.

Nafalski, J. 1978. *Pod sztandarem 4 Pomorskiej Dywizji Piechoty im. Jana Kilińskiego* [*Under the Flag of the 4th Pomeranian Infantry Division Jan Kilinski*]. Warsaw: Wydawnictwo Ministerstwa Obrony Narodowej.

Najder, Z. 2007. *Joseph Conrad: A Life*. Rochester, NY: Camden House.

Nalewajko-Kulikov, J. 2004. *Strategie przetrwania. Żydzi po aryjskiej stronie Warszawy* Warsaw: IH PAN.

Nathan, T. 1994. *L'Influence qui guérit*. Paris: Odile Jacob.

Natkowska, M. 1999. *Numerus Clausus, Getto Ławkowe, Numerus Nullus, Paragraf Aryjski, Antysemityzm na Uniwersytecie Warszawskim 1931–1939.* Warsaw: ŻIH.

Nesterowicz, P. 2017. *Każdy został człowiekiem* [*Everyone Became a Human*]. Wołowiec: Czarne.

Newman, M. 2002. *Ralph Miliband and the Politics of the New Left*. London: The Merlin Press.

Niziołek A. and Kosakowska, K. 2016. *Fira. Poznańscy Żydzi. Opowieść o życiu. Albumy i wspomnienia Firy Małamedzon-Salańskiej.* Poznań: Wyd. Exemplum.

Nussbaum, K. 1991. 'Jews in the Kościuszko Division and First Polish Army'. In *Jews in Eastern Poland and the USSR, 1939–46*, ed. N. Davies and A. Polonsky. Studies in Russia and East Europe. London: Palgrave Macmillan.

Pastuszka, S. J. 2010. *Życie kulturalne w Polskich Siłach Zbrojnych na Zachodzie w czasie II wojny światowej.* Warsaw: Kielce.

Paulsson, G. S. 2003. *Secret City: The Hidden Jews of Warsaw*. New Haven, CT: Yale University Press.

Perski, A. 2013. 'Polenrevoltens antisemitiska vändning'. *Dagens Nyheter*, 29 April, 16–17.

Piskała, K. and Zysiak, A. 2013. 'Świątynia nauki, fundament demokracji czy fabryka specjalistów?' *Praktyka Teoretyczna* 3, 9: www.praktykateoretyc zna.pl/PT_nr9_2013_Po_kapitalizmie/11.Piskala,Zysiak.pdf.

Pleskot, P. 2010. 'Jak wyjechać na Zachód? Procedury wyjazdów polskich uczonych do państw kapitalistycznych z ramienia uczelni wyższych i PAN w latach 1955-1989'. In *Naukowcy Władzy, władza naukowcom. Studia*, ed. P. Franaszek, Warsaw: Instytut Pamięci Narodowe.

Prokop-Janiec, E. 2013. 'Jew, Pole, Artist: Constructing Identity after the Holocaust'. In *Holocaust in Literary and Cultural Studies*. Warsaw: Teksty Drugie / IBL PAN: http://tekstydrugie.pl/wp-content/uploads/2016/06/Teksty_Drugie_2013_s.e.vol_.2_Holocaust_in_Literary_and_Cultural_Studies.pdf.

Przyłębski, A. 2013. 'Rectification'. Information Philosophie 3: 130

Puławski, A. 2009. *W obliczu Zagłady. Rząd RP na Uchodźstwie, Delegatura Rządu RP na Kraj, ZWZ-AK wobec deportacji Żydów do obozów zagłady (1941–1942)*. Lublin: IPN.
Puławski, A. 2018. *Wobec 'niespotykanego w dziejach mordu'. Rząd RP na uchodźstwie, Delegatura Rządu RP na kraj, AK a eksterminacja ludności żydowskiej od 'wielkiej akcji' do powstania w getcie warszawskim*. Chełm: Stowarzyszenie Rocznik Chełmski.
Rabinowicz, H. 1964. 'The Battle of the Ghetto Benches'. *The Jewish Quarterly Review* 55, 2, 151–9.
Ram, U. 1995. *The Changing Agenda of Israeli Sociology: Theory, Ideology, and Identity*. Albany: State University of New York Press.
Rapoport, Y. 1991. *The Doctor's Plot of 1953*. Cambridge, MA: Harvard University Press.
Rattansi, A, 2017. *Bauman and Contemporary Sociology: A Critical Analysis*. Manchester University Press.
Redlich, S. 1971. 'Jews in General Anders' Army in the Soviet Union, 1941–1942'. *Soviet Jewish Affairs* 2, 90–8.
Robbins, D. 2012. *French Post-War Social Theory: International Knowledge Transfer*. Thousands Oaks, CA: Sage.
Rocznik Statystyczny miasta Poznania – Rok gospodarczy. 1921. (1. kwietnia [April] do 31. grudnia [December]).
Roland, P. 2017. *The Jewish Resistance: Uprisings against the Nazis in World War II*. London: Arcturus.
Roth, W. and Jal, M. 2002. 'The Rashomon Effect': www.researchgate.net/publication/242742606_The_Rashomon_Effect.
Rudnicki, S. 1987. 'From "Numerus Clausus" to "Numerus Nullus"'. *Polin. A Journal of Polish–Jewish Studies* 2, 246–68.
Rutkowski, T. P. 2016. 'Na styku nauki i polityki. Uniwersytet Warszawski w PRL 1944–1989'. In *Dzieje Uniwersytetu Warszawskiego po 1945*. Warsaw: Wydawnictwo Uniwersytetu Warszawskiego.
Saltherwhite, J. H. 1992. *Varieties of Marxist Humanism: Philosophical Revision in Postwar Eastern Europe*. University of Pittsburg Press.
Sayad, A. 2004. *The Suffering of the Immigrant*. Cambridge: Polity.
Schaff, A. 1999. *Próba podsumowania*. Warsaw: wyd. Scholar.
Shibutani, T. 1955. 'Reference Groups as Perspectives'. *The American Journal of Sociology* 60, 6, 562–9.
Sinai, S. 2019. *Sociological Knowledge and Collective Identity: S. N. Eisenstadt and Israeli Society*. London: Routledge.
Skibińska, R. 2014. 'The Return of Jewish Holocaust Survivors and the Reaction of the Polish Population'. In *Jewish Presence in Absence: The Aftermath of the Holocaust in Poland, 1944–2010*, ed. F. Tych and M. Adamczyk-Grabowska. Yad Vashem and Jerusalem: The International Institute for Holocaust Research.
Skibińska, A. 2018. *'Martwa Fala'. Zbiór artykułów o antysemityzmie [The Swell: A Collection of Articles on Anti-Semitism]*, preface by S. R. Dobrowolski. Warsaw: Spółdzielnia Wydawnicza Wiedza.
Skórzynska, J., and W. Olejniczak. 2012. *Do zobaczenia za rok w Jerozolimie – deportacje Polskich Zydow w 1938 roku z Niemiec do Zbąszynia*. Posnań: Fundacja TRES.
Słabek, H. 1972. *Dzieje polskiej reformy rolnej 1944–48*. Warsaw: Wiedza Powszechna.
Słonimski, A. 1938. 'Dwie ojczyzny'. *Wiadomości Literackie* 3.

Smolar, A. 1983. 'The Rich and the Powerful'. In *Poland: Genesis of a Revolution*, ed. A. Brumberg. New York: Vintage Books: 42–53.

Snyder, Timothy. 1997. *Nationalism, Marxism and Modern Central Europe: A Biography of Kazimierz Kelles-Krauz (1872–1905)*. Cambridge, MA: Harvard University Press, 1997.

Sobiecka, M. and Ślężak, M. e-book devoted to Manfred Lachs: https://issuu. com/ikmpsa/docs/manfred_lachs_w_podrozy__ktora_nazy.

Sohn, A.-M. 2005. 'Les "jeunes", la "jeunesse" et les sciences sociales (1950–1970)'. In *Sociologues et sociologies. La France des années 60*, ed. J.-M. Chapoulie, O. Kourchid, J.-L. Robert and A.-M. Sohn. Logiques sociales. Paris: l'Harmattan.

Stebbins, R. 2007. *Serious Leisure: A Perspective for Our Time*. Piscataway, NJ: Transaction Publishers

Stola, D. 2010. *Kraj bez wyjścia? Migracje z Polski 1949–1989*. Warsaw: IPN.

Stola, D. 2017. 'Jewish Emigration from Communist Poland: The Decline of Polish Jewry in the Aftermath of the Holocaust'. *East European Jewish Affairs*, 47, 2–3.

Strauss, A. 1959. *Mirrors and Masks: The Search for Identity*. Glencoe, IL: Free Press.

Strauss, A. 1978. 'A Social World Perspective'. In *Studies in Symbolic Interaction*, vol. I, ed. N. Denzin. Greenwich, CT: JAI Press.

Sułek, A. 2002. *Ogród metodologii socjologicznej*. Warsaw: Scholar.

Sułek, A. 2011. *Obrazy z życia socjologii w Polsce*. Warsaw: Oficyna Naukowa.

Szacki, J. 2011 [1976]. 'Kilka uwag o artykule prof. A. Podgóreckiego'. *Studia Socjologiczne* 1, 60, 226–9

Szer, W. 2013. *Do naszych dzieci. Wspomnienia*. Warsaw: Żydowski Instytut Historyczny im. Emanuela Ringenbluma.

Sznajderman, M. 2016. *Fałszerze pieprzu. Historie rodzinne*. Wołowiec: Wyd. Czarne.

Sztompka, P. 2004. *Recenzja dot. dorobku prof. Shmuela Noaha Eisenstadta in Uchwała nr 262 Senatu Uniwersytetu Warszawskiego z dnia 17 listopada 2004*: www.uw.edu.pl/wp-content/uploads/2014/05/Eisenstadt.pdf.

Tabet, S. 2017, 'Interview with Zygmunt Bauman: From the Modern Project to the Liquid World'. *Theory, Culture & Society* 34, 7–8: 131–46.

Tester, K. 2001. *Conversations with Zygmunt Bauman*. Cambridge, Oxford, Boston and New York: Polity.

Tester, K. 2006. 'Intellectual Immigration and the English Idiom (Or, a Tale of Bustards and Eagles)'. *Polish Sociological Review* 155, 275–91

Tester, K., Jacobsen, M. and Bauman, Z. 2006. 'Bauman Before Exile – A Conversation with Zygmunt Bauman'. *Polish Sociological Review* 155.

Thompson, E. P. 1973. 'An Open Letter to Leszek Kołakowski'. *Socialist Register* 10.

Thrasher, F. M. 1927. *The Gang: A Study of 1,313 Gangs in Chicago*. University of Chicago Press.

Tokarska-Bakir, J. 2008. *Legendy o krwi. Antropologia przesądu*. Wołowiec: Wyd. Czarne.

Tokarska-Bakir, J. 2012. *Okrzyki Pogromowe. Szkice z antropologii historycznej Polski lat 1939–1946*. Wołowiec: Wyd Czarne

Tokarska-Bakir, J. 2018. *Pod Klątwą. Społeczny Portret Pogromu Kieleckiego*. Wołowiec: Wyd. Czarna Owca.

Tomaszewski, J. 1998. *Preludium zagłady. Wygnanie Żydów Polskich z Niemiec w 1938r*. Warsaw: PWN zawa.

Tuwim, J. 1968. 'Polish Flowers'. In *The Dancing Socrates and Other Poems*, trans. Adam Gillon. New York: Twayne.

Wagner, I. 2006. 'Career Coupling: Career Making in the Elite Worlds of Musicians and Scientists', *Qualitiative Sociology Review*, 2, 3: www.qualitativesociologyreview.org/ENG/archive.eng.php.

Wagner, I. 2011. *Becoming a Transnational Professional. Kariery i mobilność polskich elit naukowych*. Warsaw: Wyd. Naukowe Scholar.

Wagner, I. 2014. 'Works and Career Aspects of Ghetto Laboratories'. In *Re-searching Scientific Careers*, ed. Katarina Pripic, Inge van der Weijden and Nadia Ashuelova, special issue of *Social Studies of Science* (Russian Academy of Science and ESA RN STS).

Wagner, I. 2015. *Producing Excellence: Making of a Virtuoso*. New Brunswick, NY: Rutgers University Press.

Wagner, I. 2016. 'Discovering the Secret of Excellence: Everett Hughes as a Source of Inspiration in Researching Creative Careers'. In *The Anthem Companion to Everett Hughes*, ed. M. Santoro and R. Helmes-Hayes. London: Anthem Editions, pp. 193–210.

Wagner, I. 2019. 'Confronting Polish Responsibility for the Shoah in Paris', The New School for Social Research, *Public Seminar* website: www.publicseminar.org/2019/04/the-subtext-of-a-recent-international-scandal-part-one-2.

Weil, S. 2010. 'On Multiple Modernities, Civilizations and Ancient Judaism'. An interview with Shmuel Eisenstadt. *European Societies*, 12, 4.

Wiatr, Jerzy. 2010. 'Julian Hochfeld – ideolog PPS wybitny polski socjolog. Działanie polityczne a refleksja naukowa.' In *Polscy socjaliści w XX wieku: ich rodowody oraz uwarunkowania ich działalności*, ed. Skrabalak Maria Witold. Warsaw: Philip Wilson.

Wiatr, Jerzy. 2017a. 'Otwarty Marksizm i odrodzenie socjologii: rola Juliana Hochfelda i Zygmunta Baumana'. *Studia Socjologiczno-Polityczne*, n.s. 1, 6 (wyd. Instytut Socjologii Uniwersytet Warszawski): 13–25.

Wiatr, Jerzy. 2017b. 'Zygmunt Bauman – wielki uczony polskiej i światowej lewicy'. *Myśl Socjaldemokratyczna* 1–2: http://fae.pl/tozsamosc-lewicymysl2017.pdf.

Wincławski, Włodzimierz, 2006. 'Wyimki z kalendarza socjologii polskiej', ISSN 0033-2356: http://cejsh.icm.edu.pl/cejsh/element/bwmeta1.element. desklight-56c53d29-c20e-4acc-bdff-2524c2f004fd/c/KRONIKA.pdf.

Wiszniewicz, J. 2008. *Życie przecięte. Opowieści pokolenia Marca*. Wołowiec: Wyd. Czarne, Sękowa.

Witkowski, R. 2012. *The Jews of Poznań: A Brief Guide to Jewish History and Cultural Sights*. Poznań: Wydawnictwo Miejskie Posnania.

Wójcik, Ryszard, 2015. *Kapryśna gwiazda Rudolfa Weigla*. Gdańsk University Press.

Wolff J. 2011. 'A 'Small, Limited World': Janina Bauman's Personal and Historical Stories'. *Thesis Eleven* 107, 1, 29 November.

Worsley, P. 2008. *An Academic Skating on Thin Ice*. New York and Oxford: Bergahn Books.

Wyka, K. 1945. 'Potę ga ciemnoty potwierdzona'. *Odrodzenie* 23 September.

Wyka, K. 1984. *Gospodarka wyłączona, w tegoż, Życie na niby. Pamiętnik po klęsce*. Kraków: Wyd. Literackie.

Zaremba, M. 2012. *Wielka Trwoga. Polska 1944–1947 Ludowa Reakcja na Kryzys*. Kraków: Znak.

Żbikowski, A. 2014. 'The Post-War Wave of Pogroms and Killings'. In *Jewish Presence in Absence: The Aftermath of the Holocaust in Poland, 1944–2010*, ed. F. Tych and M. Adamczyk-Grabowska. Yad Vashem and Jerusalem: The International Institute for Holocaust Research.

Żurowicz, J. [Bauman, Z.] 1953a. *Na Kołobrzeg!* Warsaw: Wydawnictwo Ministerstwa Obrony Narodowej.

Żurowicz, J. [Bauman, Z.] 1953b. *W Krzeczuchach znów spokój. Opowieść o żołnierzach KBW.* Warsaw: Wydawnictwo Ministerstwa Obrony Narodowej.

Archives

AAN	Archiwum Akt Nowych (New Acts Archives), Warsaw.
AIPN	Archiwum Instytut Pamięci Narodowej (Archives of the Institute of National Remembrance), Warsaw.
AMP	Archiwa Miasta Poznania (Municipal Archives of Poznań).
APAN	Archiwum Polskiej Akademii Nauk (Archives of the Polish Academy of Sciences).
APZPR	Archiwum Państwowe w Warszawie, Komitet Warszawski PZPR.
AUW	Archiwum Uniwersytetu Warszawskiego (Archives of the University of Warsaw).
Bauman Archive, Leeds	Janina and Zygmunt Bauman Archive, Leeds University Special Collection.

Index